D1232755

Applied SOA

Applied SOA

Service-Oriented Architecture and Design Strategies

Mike Rosen
Boris Lublinsky
Kevin T. Smith
Marc J. Balcer

WILEY

Wiley Publishing, Inc.

Applied SOA: Service-Oriented Architecture and Design Strategies

Published by
Wiley Publishing, Inc.
10475 Crosspoint Boulevard
Indianapolis, IN 46256
www.wiley.com

Copyright © 2008 by Wiley Publishing, Inc., Indianapolis, Indiana

Published simultaneously in Canada

ISBN: 978-0-470-22365-9

Manufactured in the United States of America

10 9 8 7 6 5 4 3 2 1

No part of this publication may be reproduced, stored in a retrieval system or transmitted in any form or by any means, electronic, mechanical, photocopying, recording, scanning or otherwise, except as permitted under Sections 107 or 108 of the 1976 United States Copyright Act, without either the prior written permission of the Publisher, or authorization through payment of the appropriate per-copy fee to the Copyright Clearance Center, 222 Rosewood Drive, Danvers, MA 01923, (978) 750-8400, fax (978) 646-8600. Requests to the Publisher for permission should be addressed to the Legal Department, Wiley Publishing, Inc., 10475 Crosspoint Blvd., Indianapolis, IN 46256, (317) 572-3447, fax (317) 572-4355, or online at http://www.wiley.com/go/permissions.

Limit of Liability/Disclaimer of Warranty: The publisher and the author make no representations or warranties with respect to the accuracy or completeness of the contents of this work and specifically disclaim all warranties, including without limitation warranties of fitness for a particular purpose. No warranty may be created or extended by sales or promotional materials. The advice and strategies contained herein may not be suitable for every situation. This work is sold with the understanding that the publisher is not engaged in rendering legal, accounting, or other professional services. If professional assistance is required, the services of a competent professional person should be sought. Neither the publisher nor the author shall be liable for damages arising herefrom. The fact that an organization or Website is referred to in this work as a citation and/or a potential source of further information does not mean that the author or the publisher endorses the information the organization or Website may provide or recommendations it may make. Further, readers should be aware that Internet Websites listed in this work may have changed or disappeared between when this work was written and when it is read.

For general information on our other products and services or to obtain technical support, please contact our Customer Care Department within the U.S. at (800) 762-2974, outside the U.S. at (317) 572-3993 or fax (317) 572-4002.

Library of Congress Cataloging-in-Publication Data:

Applied SOA : service-oriented architecture and design strategies / Mike Rosen . . . [et al.].
  p. cm.
 Includes index.
 ISBN 978-0-470-22365-9 (paper/website)
 1. Web services. 2. Software architecture. 3. Computer network architecture. 4. Information resources management. I. Rosen, Michael, 1956-
 TK5105.88813.A69 2008
 006.7'8 — dc22

             2008015109

Trademarks: Wiley, the Wiley logo, and related trade dress are trademarks or registered trademarks of John Wiley & Sons, Inc. and/or its affiliates, in the United States and other countries, and may not be used without written permission. All other trademarks are the property of their respective owners. Wiley Publishing, Inc., is not associated with any product or vendor mentioned in this book.

Wiley also publishes its books in a variety of electronic formats. Some content that appears in print may not be available in electronic books.

About the Authors

Mike Rosen is chief scientist at Wilton Consulting Group, which provides expert consulting on software architecture, SOA, and enterprise architecture. He is also director of enterprise architecture for the Cutter Consortium and editorial director of the SOA Institute. He frequently speaks at industry symposia and contributes to industry journals.

Boris Lublinsky is lead architect at Navteq, where he is responsible for SOA and BPM implementations. He is a frequent contributor to technology magazines and a speaker at industry conferences. Boris is also an SOA news editor for InfoQ.

Kevin T. Smith is a technical director at ManTech MBI (formally McDonald Bradley, Inc.), where he builds highly secure and data-driven SOA solutions for the U.S. government. He is the author of many SOA technology articles in industry magazines, such as the SOA/Web Services Journal, and has coauthored several technology books, including *The Semantic Web* (Wiley, 2003), *Professional Portal Development with Open Source Tools* (Wrox, 2004), *More Java Pitfalls* (Wiley, 2003), and *Essential XUL Programming* (Wiley, 2001), in addition to the books where he has written chapters as a contributing author. Kevin has led SOA workshops and has presented at numerous industry conferences, such as the RSA Security Conference, JavaOne, the Semantic Technology Conference, the Apache Open Source Conference, Net-Centric Warfare, the Object Management Group, and the Association for Enterprise Integration.

Marc J. Balcer is the founder of ModelCompilers.com, a provider of tools and services for realizing the power of model-based development, and the coauthor of *Executable UML: A Foundation for Model-Driven Architecture* (Addison-Wesley, 2002). He has over 15 years of experience in developing, deploying, and managing projects based upon executable models and model-driven development techniques.

As a party to many enterprise development projects, Marc has witnessed firsthand how the precision of application and architecture models can make the difference between spectacular success and miserable failure. He has applied Executable UML to projects in such diverse areas as medical instrumentation, transportation logistics, telecommunications, and financial services.

Credits

Executive Editor
Robert Elliott

Development Editor
Sydney Jones

Technical Editor
Jim Amsden

Production Editor
Laurel Ibey

Copy Editor
Foxxe Editorial Services

Editorial Manager
Mary Beth Wakefield

Production Manager
Tim Tate

**Vice President and Executive
Group Publisher**
Richard Swadley

**Vice President and Executive
Publisher**
Joseph B. Wikert

Project Coordinator, Cover
Lynsey Stanford

Proofreaders
Nancy Carrasco, Kathryn Duggan

Indexer
Jack Lewis

Cover Image
Paul Cooklin/Jupiterimages
Corporation

Acknowledgments

Well, who to thank for all the help? First, thanks to all the people who supported me throughout this process. There were many, but a few stand out for special mention: all my friends and clients who cut me a little slack when I might have been slightly unresponsive during the final push to finish everything; my friends in the travel industry who inspired the case study; everyone at Cutter Consortium for constant encouragement; SOAInstitute for providing a forum to teach and discuss all things SOA; Robert Elliott at Wiley, who had the uncanny timing to call me during a lull in my consulting practice and ask if I wanted to be involved in an SOA book; and Sydney Jones, our project editor, for putting up with our changes and delays. I hope she wasn't just being nice when she said we weren't the worst group of authors ever. Thanks to Jim Amsden, a friend and colleague, who also turned out to be the best technical editor you could imagine; Jeroen van Tyn and Laura O'Brian for the great Business Use Cases in Chapters 6 and 7 and Appendix A; my good friend Ken Orr for teaching me about business architecture, processes, and semantics over the years; my coauthors, for contributing to a collaborative project where we all learned from each other and everyone's chapters, and the book, benefited; and most importantly, to my awesome wife, Tamar Krichevsky, who not only put up with it all, but who also read every single chapter of the book and compiled and wrote the fantastic Evaluating SOA Services appendix. Thanks.

— Mike Rosen

I would like to thank Mike for calling me out of the blue and asking whether I would like to participate in this exciting project. I really enjoyed collaborating with Mike, Kevin, and Marc. It allowed me to learn more about SOA and significantly improved the quality of my chapters. Many thanks to the people whom I used to work with over the years, especially Didier Le Tien, Dmitry

Tyomkin, and Deborah Shaddon, for always challenging me with tough architecture questions and pointing at deficiencies in my solutions; Jay Davidson and Edward Kuffert for explaining to me the importance of business architecture and the way the insurance industry works; and Jerry Daus, Matt O'Neal, and Maria Mernandez for helping me to understand how IBM software works and the best ways to use it. I am also thankful for all of the failed and successful projects that I worked on, which taught me what is important and what is not, and why things fail or succeed. Most importantly, to my wonderful wife, Lilia, for patiently putting up with me spending more time with my computer than with her. Thanks.

— Boris Lublinsky

I would like to thank my three talented coauthors, Mike, Boris, and Marc — it has been a pleasure working with you on this exciting and challenging project. Mike, you did a great job of guiding us in this process, and I would especially like to thank Boris for his additions to the chapters on Composing Services (Chapter 8) and SOA Governance (Chapter 12). I would like to thank Vaughn Bullard for his suggestions on Chapter 12 and Layer7's Toufic Boubez for his support of my discussion on dynamic policy adaptation ("Policy Application Points") in Chapters 11 and 12. Special thanks to Ken and Myrtle Ruth Stockman for allowing me to use their nicknames in one of my examples, and thanks to my "readability editors," Helen G. Smith and Lois G. Schermerhorn.

I would like to thank my company, ManTech MBI (formerly McDonald Bradley, Inc.) in Herndon, VA, with special and sincere thanks to those who encouraged my writing of this book on my own time — specifically, thanks to Danny Proko, Bill Pulsipher, Waymond Edwards, John Sutton, Gail Rissler, Mark Day, and Ken Bartee. I would like to give my thanks (and apologies) to my wonderful wife, Gwen, and my sweet daughters, Isabella and Emma! Thank you for putting up with me as I went into isolation for countless nights and weekends while writing this book. I would like to thank Ashland Coffee and Tea, who once again didn't kick me out when I camped out there for days at a time for writing, research, and of course, caffeine.

Thanks to the Washington Redskins, who thoughtfully did not have a good enough football season that it would distract me from writing on Sundays. Thanks to other people, places, and things that most likely affected my writing in a positive way (in no particular order): Gavin Sutcliffe; Eric Monk; Nick Duan; Sue Lee; Joanie Barr; John Medlock; Kyle Hendrickson; Tom Diepenbrock; Scooby-Doo; Jeff Phelps; Ruben Wise; Kim Gumabay; Mike Hoops, the AMC Pacer, Ralph Perko, Kathleen Ferris, Brad Giaccio, Kevin Moran; Mike Daconta; Leo Obrst; Fox; my community group (Russ and Debi Garber, Ed and Lori Buchanan, Steve and Ani Tetrault, Ed Hoppe); Kyle Rice; Thai Gourmet in Kings Charter; the Apostle Paul; Sean, Jen, Garrett, and Parker Cullinan; Daniel Buckley; Ken Pratt; Adam Dean; Mike Rohan; Carl and

Sharon Smith, Emma when she sleeps past 4:00 A.M., Bill, Farron, Casey, and Will Smith, New Hanover Church, Grace Community Presbyterian Church, Mungo, and T3. Finally, all glory, laud, and honor to the one who was, who is, and who is to come.

— Kevin T. Smith

Many ideas emerge from the everyday work of developing real solutions. In addition to my coauthors, I would like to acknowledge the contributions, criticism, and insights from current and former colleagues, including Steve Dowse of International Asset Systems, and Brian Itow, Gary Marcos, Julio Roque, and Matt Samsonoff of AZORA Technologies. Most importantly, I would like to thank my partner, Canares ("Chicho") Aban, for his dedication and support during this project.

— Marc J. Balcer

Contents at a Glance

Contents

Service Specification   534
Implementation Layers   535
Operation Procedure   536
Summary   538

Chapter 14   Case Study — Service-Based Integration in Insurance   541
ACME Insurance   542
High-Level Integration Design   547
Establishing Policy Submission   548
Rate Insurance Policy   551
Assess Insured Location   552
Get Driver's Information   553
Generate Policy Notice Documents   554
Collect Policy Financials   555
Work with Documents   556
Integration Requirements for the ACME Implementation   556
Integration with Existing CICS Transactions   557
Integration Approaches   558
ACME's Implementation of a CICS-Based Integration   562
Integration with the Existing COM Components   565
ACME's Implementation of Integration with COM
   Components   567
Integration Based on the Existing Java APIs   568
ACME's Implementation of Integration Based on Java APIs   569
Integration with the Existing J2EE Applications   570
ACME's Implementation of Integration for J2EE-Based
   Applications   572
Integration with Existing Databases   573
ACME's Implementation of Database Integrations   575
Integration Based on the Vendor's Web Services   576
ACME's Implementation of Integration Using the Vendor's
   Web Services   577
Summary   578

Appendix A   Business Use Cases   579
Business Use Case BU01 — Quote Insurance   579
Basic Workflow   580
Alternative Workflow: Unacceptable Risk   582
Performance Goals   582
Business Use Case BU02 — Process Application   582
Basic Workflow   583
Alternative Workflow: Unacceptable Risk   585
Performance Goals   585

Introduction

Welcome to *Applied SOA: Service-Oriented Architecture and Design Strategies*. This book is designed to fill a gap that we see in available SOA information. The current collection of SOA books and articles is rich on high-level theory but light on practical advice. At the other end of the spectrum are the Web Services books that concentrate on APIs and programming, but gloss over the architecture. This book focuses on an area that most other books ignore, offering the reader a practical guide for applying design strategies to service-oriented solutions. It targets the practical application of SOA and appeals to architects, analysts, designers, and CTO/CIOs, as they roll out concrete strategies and designs for their organizations and projects.

The book starts by discussing the expected benefits of SOA and the architectural principles needed to realize them, which lead to successful solutions. Then, it provides an overview of the process for designing services and service-oriented solutions. Each major step of the process is followed by a chapter that describes the detailed practices and principles for that step, with handy tips and techniques for applying them. Of course, no SOA solution would be complete without integrating legacy systems and applications, providing security, or having appropriate governance, so these topics are also covered in depth. Throughout the book, the principles are demonstrated with relevant examples. Finally, the book concludes with two different extensive case studies that illustrate the architecture and design strategies.

Why This Book Was Written

Service-Oriented Architecture (SOA) is the current state of the art in IT application architecture. As a result, platforms and tools that support SOA are hitting the market every week. Every major software vendor, including IBM, Microsoft, Oracle, and SAP has embraced SOA and is investing billions of dollars to service-enable their product sets. SOA is here to stay, and it is likely to be the predominant architectural style for the next decade.

Most SOA implementations are based on Web Service technologies, which have matured to the point where there are many mission-critical implementations in production. In addition, the training industry has ramped up to provide considerable variety and opportunity for education in SOA and Web Services. Yet, real service-oriented applications have not followed suit and the promised benefits of SOA have not been realized for most organizations. Generally, the available literature and education fall short of providing what companies really need to be successful.

As we work with companies that are starting with SOA, or struggling with their current approach, we see several common areas of confusion:

- First, what is SOA? In particular, what are the architectural aspects of SOA compared to just Web Services or other distributed technologies? And beyond that, how should the architecture influence design?

- Second, what is the relationship between business and SOA? What is hype and what is real? How does functional decomposition at the business process level translate into requirements and design for business services?

- Third, how do you design a good service? This seems to be the most misunderstood aspect of SOA. A meeting rarely goes by where someone doesn't ask, "How big should a service be?"

- Fourth, how do you effectively integrate existing applications and resources into a service-oriented solution? How can this be done while avoiding the pitfalls of traditional EAI approaches? What does a good integration service look like?

- And finally, how do services fit into overall enterprise solutions? What is the layered and tiered structure of an SOA application architecture? Where do security, transactions, naming, and the other aspects of distributed enterprise solutions fit in?

Anybody can build a service; that's not the challenge facing IT professionals today. In fact, the tools make it incredibly easy (often too easy) to build services, especially poorly designed ones. The first challenge is to build a good service, based on solid design principles. But still this is not enough. The services must also fit into an overall architecture that results in services that can be combined into larger business processes within the enterprise. In other words, the architecture and the design process must provide an enterprise context that influences the design and implementation of services.

The next decade will be filled with winners and also-rans. Those companies on top will have learned how to use IT as a strategic differentiator that provides them with a sustainable competitive advantage. This will be built on a foundation of SOA that exposes the fundamental business capabilities and information as flexible, reusable services. These services will support a layer of business processes that can be easily changed to provide new products and services to keep ahead of the competition. But this is easier to show in a Visio diagram than to actually achieve. The good news is that this book starts to show you how. The bad news is that it's still hard.

The goal of *Applied SOA: Service-Oriented Architecture and Design Strategies* is to provide the architecture and design principles and methodology that address these challenges and empower the reader to develop successful implementations that deliver the expected benefits of SOA.

Who This Book Is For

This is primarily a technical book, focused on architects, designers, business analysts, IT managers, and executives. It is not a book about writing code; in fact, there is no code in the book. It is about architecture and design, what the important principles of SOA are, and how they should be applied. It delves into each of the important aspects of architecture, including business, information, application, and technology, as they relate to service-oriented solutions:

- **Architects** will learn the relationships between architectural concerns, enterprise context, and the SOA design process. This is particularly important in making architecture actionable. As architects, you should always remember that creating architecture itself provides little value. The value comes from using the architecture to help projects meet immediate needs, but in a way that also meets the needs and longer-term goals of the overall enterprise. This is critical to realizing the promise of SOA.

- **Designers** will learn a step-by-step process for the analysis and design of services, and what the different types and styles of services are. They will come to understand what information is required from the business for complete service design, how that relates to process and information models, and how it shows up in the different design artifacts. But most importantly, they will learn how to start thinking in terms of SOA; in other words, how to shift their design paradigm.

- **Business analysts** will learn the relationship between business strategies, goals, and objectives, and the capabilities and information that are used to achieve them. The direct link between capabilities, business services, and business processes will be illustrated. Analysts will learn how to use business process models as the link between business architecture and IT design, specifically SOA.

- **Managers and executives** will get an understanding of the SOA architecture and design process that will enable them to understand, govern, plan, and manage SOA projects that deliver value to both their immediate project and to the enterprise.

What This Book Covers

This book provides architects, designers, and analysts with the principles and techniques necessary to create superior-quality service-oriented architectures and solutions. It enables them to go beyond building services to actually deliver on SOA's promises of agility and flexibility by providing practical and actionable advice that leads directly to better architecture and design.

Thus, the book is about the architecture and design of service-oriented solutions and systems. It is not a high-level overview of the benefits of SOA, nor is it a user's manual for the technologies and standards of SOA implementation (i.e., Web Services). Instead, it focuses on the difficult area in between, to provide a methodology for designing not only simple services but also service-oriented solutions that incorporate legacy integration and security.

The book is technical in that it provides detailed, step-by-step procedures and examples of architecture and design. However, it generally does not delve into APIs and code, except to illustrate the design implications of certain technologies and standards. In addition, this book contains two detailed case studies that illustrate the concepts and techniques presented throughout.

How This Book Is Structured

This book is structured in three sections: an overview of the architecture, service and solution design, and case studies:

Part I: Understanding SOA — This section provides the motivation for SOA and the architectural requirements needed to meet them, then describes SOA architecture structure and principles, and finally describes the process for getting started with SOA in the enterprise.

- **Chapter 1**: **"Realizing the Promise of SOA"** describes the primary motivations for SOA in the industry, such as improved flexibility, reduced costs, and competitive advantage. Given these motivations and expectations, what is really required from IT to deliver on that promise? This question is explored in depth and the answer presented as the requirements that SOA architecture must meet to achieve the promise.

- **Chapter 2: "SOA — Architecture Fundamentals"** describes the SOA reference architecture and how that meets the challenges and requirements laid out in Chapter 1. It describes the overall enterprise context, the architectural layers and tiers, the domain-specific concepts and abstractions, and specifically what a service is and the important architectural characteristics of a service.

- **Chapter 3: "Getting Started with SOA"** describes the overall process for initiation of SOA activities, aligning SOA with the business, identifying and specifying services, designing service interfaces and implementations, and creating solutions

Part II: Designing SOA — This section explores the details of each step in the design process. It is roughly divided into two main areas: Chapters 4–7 cover the design of services and Chapters 8–12 focus on building enterprise SOA solutions.

- **Chapter 4: "Starting with the Business"** describes a business architecture approach for SOA and how to use business architecture and business process modeling to define services.

- **Chapter 5: "Service Context and Common Semantics"** focuses on the overall enterprise context for SOA, specifically the common semantic model and the service inventory. It describes how to discover the common semantic model, tips and techniques for developing it, how to create and use a service inventory, and how it fits with the semantic model.

- **Chapter 6: "Designing Service Interfaces"** digs into the details of service interface design. It shows how to use the business and enterprise contexts established in Chapters 4 and 5 in the service interface design and discusses issues of interaction and usage style in terms of design. Then, it presents an in-depth example of the design of an interface for an automobile insurance solution.

- **Chapter 7: "Designing Service Implementations"** continues with details on the design of the service implementation. It describes the techniques for defining the technology independent design of service operations and the specification of schema for the documents that are the inputs and outputs for those operations. It extends the example from Chapter 6 to illustrate the design of the service operations.

- **Chapter 8: "Composing Services"** goes into detail about the important techniques of service composition. It describes the tradeoffs and advantages of a variety of different approaches, addresses the role of Business

Process Execution Languages (BPEL) and Service Component Architecture (SCA) in composition, provides some useful do's and don'ts, and finishes with an example of a service composition using BPEL.

- **Chapter 9: "Using Services to Build Enterprise Solutions"** describes the role services play in an overall enterprise solution. It describes how services fit into the classical *n*-tier architecture, discusses issues of service location and discovery, exception handling, management and monitoring, service evolution, and the use of Enterprise Service Buses (ESBs) to implement SOA solutions.

- **Chapter 10: "Designing and Using Integration in SOA Solutions"** focuses on the difficult problem of creating services that integrate existing applications and data. It starts with the architectural issues of service-based integration and then goes into details about the design and implementation of integration services, providing a toolbag of techniques and tradeoffs for different integration scenarios.

- **Chapter 11: "SOA Security"** addresses the thorny questions of security. Again, it starts with an architectural overview of the different types of security and the type of threats and challenges they address. Then, it provides an overview of the most common security standards in SOA. Next, it presents a set of "security blueprints" or guidelines for determining the right security solution, and the patterns for applying them. The chapter finishes with suggestions and a game plan for the security architect.

- **Chapter 12: "SOA Governance"** takes up the issues of keeping your SOA solutions and architecture running and on track. It describes the life cycle of services, and the issues of management and governance throughout the different phases of the life cycle. This includes tips and techniques for practical SOA governance.

Part III: Case Studies — This section illustrates architecture and design principles and strategies by exploring two different case studies in depth. The first focuses on designing business services to support business processes. The second focuses on integrating existing applications into a service-oriented solution.

- **Chapter 13: "Case Study — Travel Insurance"** provides a case study of an SOA implementation from the travel industry. The case study starts with the business architecture and works through to the design of the service interface and implementation, highlighting the architectural concerns and design strategies presented in Part II.

- **Chapter 14: "Case Study — Service-Based Integration in Insurance"** provides a case study of the implementation of integration services in the insurance industry. The example illustrates the design and implementation of multiple different integration services based on existing customer information control (CICS), commercial off-the-shelf (COTS), Java, database, and other systems and shows how they can be used in an enterprise solution.

- **Appendix A**: **"Business Use Cases"** provides the detailed use cases for the example used in Chapters 6 and 7.
- **Appendix B**: **"Evaluating SOA Services"** provides a handy list for evaluating services against the important architectural and design criteria presented in this book.
- **Appendix C**: **"Additional Reading"** provides a list of resources on SOA and all of the references used while researching the book.

What You Need to Use This Book

Beyond a basic desire to learn about architecture and design, there are no other requirements for the book. Many of the design and implementation examples use UML models, so a basic ability to read these models will help, but it is not necessary. We have tried to steer clear of complex models.

Final Thoughts

This book is meant to lay out the important aspects and strategies of architecture and design for SOA solutions. Our challenge was not deciding what to put into the book but deciding what to cut out. As it is, we went way over our original estimate for length. It is not possible to cover every possible aspect of design and architecture for SOA solutions in a single text. We have provided a lengthy list of references and other readings in Appendix C to supplement the material here.

But we do think that we've covered material that is not well served by most other SOA books, and that is critical to SOA success. We sincerely hope that you find it useful and are able to incorporate it into your SOA solutions.

Understanding SOA

In This Part

Realizing the Promise of SOA

Those who do not remember the past are condemned to repeat it.
— **George Santayana**

Everyone has heard the many promises and benefits of Service-Oriented Architecture (SOA), and you've all probably heard a dozen different definitions of what SOA is or isn't. We're going to take a different approach. We want to paint a picture of what SOA can deliver and the promise of SOA, and then describe the challenges that organizations face in realizing that promise. Together, the vision and the challenges provide a set of requirements that the architecture must meet to make your implementation of SOA successful at delivering the promised benefits. Throughout the book, we'll describe the detailed architecture, design principles, and techniques that meet those architectural requirements, make the architecture actionable, and deliver results. In this chapter, you look at:

- What did and didn't work in the past
- The promise of SOA to the enterprise
- The challenges of delivering on that promise
- How to meet the challenge (the subject of this book)

But first, let's start with a little story. The scenario is true although the names have been changed.

Once Upon a Time ...

Back in 1994, a major U.S. bank was trying to resolve a problem with customer service. Like pretty much every bank at that time, all of the different products (i.e., different types of accounts) were implemented on different mainframe systems. When you telephoned the customer service representative, you spoke to a beleaguered person with numerous green screen terminals on his or her desktop.

If you wanted information about your checking account, the customer service representative went to one terminal and entered your account number. If you wanted information about your savings account, the representative had to get a different account number from you and enter that in a different terminal. Each account system had a different interface. Together, they provided a confusing mix of commands and interaction that necessitated expensive training and was error prone. Customer satisfaction with problem resolution was low, employee satisfaction was low, and retention of both was problematic.

So what's a bank to do? First, they set about rationalizing the interface to all of the systems into a consistent interface, on a single terminal. Solutions such as 3270 emulators and PCs were tossed around but discarded because they only reduced the number of terminals, not the complexity of multiple interfaces. Instead, the bank took a gamble on a relatively new, distributed technology, Common Object Request Broker Architecture (CORBA).

The specific technology they chose is less important than the approach. The first thing they did was to create distributed objects to represent the different types of accounts. These objects provided an abstraction layer between the user interface and the mainframe systems that actually implemented the accounts. Next, they wrote a new user interface, using Visual Basic (VB), that provided account information to the customer service representatives by accessing the different systems via the CORBA objects.

It took about 6 months to get the basic functions in place — a new user interface, VB/CORBA bridging, and simple account objects — and then they were able to start replacing some of the green screen terminals. At this point, they began to understand the potential of the approach. They had essentially implemented the beginnings of a 3-tiered application architecture by separating the presentation, business logic, and operational systems. Figure 1-1 shows a simplified view of their solutions.

The next enhancement was to implement a customer relationship object in the logic tier. What this did was to take any account number or customer name, find all of the accounts that belonged to that customer, and provide that information to the customer service representative. Now, the customers didn't need to keep track of all their different account numbers in order to do business with the bank. The next incremental improvement was to automatically look up

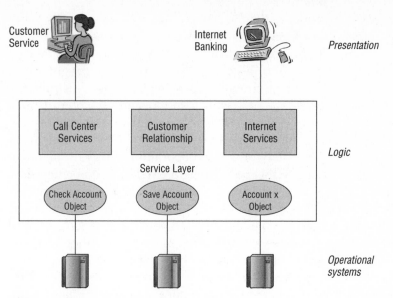

Figure 1-1 Bank customer service solution

information about each account and display a summary on the customer service representative's terminal. Now, without any additional effort on their part, the representatives had a broader view of the customers and a better understanding of their relationship to the bank. This allowed them to better serve the customers requests and at the same time offer additional value or services (i.e., turn a customer support scenario into a sales opportunity). Customer and employee satisfaction started to go up as the new approach started to pay off.

Over the next 2 years, the bank continued to provide more business objects in the logic tier and better features in the interface. The bank built up a library of about 250 objects (services) that served the needs of multiple channels, including the initial customer service representatives as well as ATMs and touch-tone dial-in systems. Things were going along smoothly in 1997 until a disruptive technology had a huge impact on banking, and everything else for that matter. All of a sudden, everybody wanted to do Internet banking.

Again, what's a bank to do? Well, while most of their competitors pondered the problem and scrambled to look at solutions like screen scraping, this bank didn't have to. They had invested in building up an architectural approach to the problem, namely separation of presentation from logic and logic from operational systems, and they had invested in building up an effective library of services in the logic layer. Therefore, all they had to do was implement a new Internet presentation. Of course, some minor changes to services were required as well as some new services to support security and other Internet specifics, but the bank's challenges were comparatively simple and they were up on the Internet in less than 6 months. This was a full 6–12 months faster than their competitors, who struggled to catch up. And it was a real implementation that built toward the future, not a quick-and-dirty hack that needed to be replaced later. Many of the bank's competitors have never caught up.

Two years later, the bank merged with another major bank. This time the problem was how to integrate the new bank's systems into the other bank's Internet operations. Imagine the challenges involved, and imagine the surprise when 100% of the combined customers were able to access their accounts via the Internet on the first official day of merged operations! Okay, in reality, a few months were spent making this possible before the official opening day, but again the architectural investment paid off. Instead of adding a new presentation, the bank added new systems to the operational layer and enhanced the logic layer so that it was possible to access the new types of accounts and systems. Only very minor changes were required in the presentation layer.

Since the initial introduction of their Internet banking capability, the implementation and infrastructure has been enhanced to support tens of millions of transactions per day. And, since the merger, hundreds of other banks have been acquired and merged into the architecture. They were the competitors that never caught up, that never invested in architecturally sound IT solutions.

But of course, all of this didn't just happen by accident. The bank was fortunate to have a perceptive, skilled, and forward-thinking architect involved in the project. The architect quickly realized both the potential and the challenges and set about making changes to address them. First and foremost was the adoption of an architecture that distributed responsibilities across layers and tiers.

Second, the bank understood the challenge of creating the right kind of services in the logic tier and of having developers reuse them. To accomplish this, the bank created a new position, a reuse manager, for fostering and managing reuse. This person was responsible for helping developers create the right services with the right interfaces, helping presentation applications find and reuse services, and setting out an overall vision and roadmap of what services would be needed over time.

Finally, the bank realized that the existing organizational structure was not conducive to creating or using services. Instead of having monolithic application groups, they divided IT into groups that built the business services, and into other groups that used the services in their presentations and applications. After some obvious learning curves and attitude adjustments, the bank was able to drop the time to enhance or develop new user applications from 6 months under the monolithic model to 4–6 weeks under the service model. And, the more services that were added to the service library, under the careful direction of the reuse manager, the shorter this timeframe became.

So, with a successful implementation of SOA, the bank was able to improve customer retention and satisfaction, reduce costs and time to market, take advantage of disruptive technologies, quickly absorb acquisitions, and keep ahead of their competitors. No wonder businesses are interested in SOA. From a more technical point of view, the bank was able to integrate multiple systems, support multiple channels and devices, scale horizontally to support very large-scale and highly reliable requirements, incrementally add new functionality, manage reuse, and converge on a common service infrastructure.

The moral of the story is this: SOA isn't about technology, and SOA doesn't just happen. SOA is an architectural approach to building systems that requires an investment in architecture and IT, a strategic and business vision, engineering discipline and governance, and a supporting organizational structure. Ignore these things and you end up with another broken promise. Put them together well, and you can deliver the promise and potential of agility, flexibility, and competitive advantage.

Learning from History

As can be seen from this story, SOA is not new. It has been around for years, well before the term was coined, by most accounts, in 1996. Forward-thinking companies like the bank whose story was told earlier, and many other finance and telecom companies were able to implement service layers using a variety of distributed technologies, including CORBA and the Distributed Common Object Model (DCOM). Other technologies, like Tuxedo, were inherently service-oriented and stateless, and formed the basis of some of the largest, high-performance, distributed applications of their day.

So while it is not difficult to find companies that were successful in implementing SOA, it's much easier to find companies that failed in their SOA. IT graveyards are filled with failed projects and sometimes the vendors of the technologies that promised the elusive, and ultimately ineffective, silver bullet. Figure 1-2 shows a brief timeline of SOA activity.

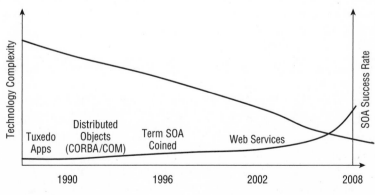

Figure 1-2 SOA timeline

What Went Wrong?

You might ask why some projects succeeded while others failed. Luckily, you have the opportunity to look back and examine both the successes and failures to discover patterns, and to then plan a path forward that avoids the failed behavior and embraces the successful activities.

Looking at the failures uncovers two main patterns. First, the technologies that we mentioned were too difficult for the average programmer to master. Distributed computing with CORBA or DCOM was just too difficult for the masses. Sophisticated IT departments had the system programmers and architects to manage these technologies, but most organizations did not. Visual Basic (VB) programmers and other client/server Rapid Application Development (RAD) application programmers didn't cut it, and the underlying platforms did not have enough of the complexities of distributed applications built into them.

The other problem was that, as an industry, we had not yet figured out what a good service was. No one knew what the right characteristics of a service or its interface or interaction style were. And if you could figure these things out, you then had to describe them in a service abstraction, and finally implement the service abstraction on top of the object abstraction naturally provided by the distributed technology. Again, some sophisticated people figured all this out, but most didn't. The hurdles to create any service were so great that most attempts failed well before the developers had to worry about whether they were building good services or what SOA meant, how to build it, or how to use it.

The situation today is much better. Web Services are much easier to use than previous technologies. This is not because the technologies are really any simpler (see the sidebar "It's Not So Simple"), but mostly because the tools and environments have advanced greatly. It is now possible to develop services without really knowing what a service is or anything much about distributed technologies (we can debate whether this is good or bad later . . .).

Instead, the implicit knowledge of distribution and services is built into the platform, whether it is based on Java, .NET, or something else. And the service abstraction layer is built into the Web Service technologies.

IT'S NOT SO SIMPLE

Distributed technologies have had a long history, a history that tends to repeat itself. In the early days, we came up with the Distributed Computing Environment (DCE). Originally, this was a Remote Procedure Call (RPC) mechanism aimed at allowing different UNIX systems to communicate. Once the basics were worked out, people tried to use it for real enterprise applications and realized that it needed more capabilities such as security, transactions, reliability, and so on.

> Next was CORBA, a mechanism for distributing objects. Initially, it was pretty simple, until people tried to use it to create real enterprise applications. Soon they realized that it needed security, transactions, reliable delivery, and so on, and it became complicated.
>
> So a simpler technology was invented, Java. And all was well and good until people tried to use it to build real enterprise applications. All of a sudden it needed to have security, transactions, messaging, and so on.
>
> Finally, Web Services came along, invented by developers so ignorant of history that they actually had the audacity to call the protocol SOAP, Simple Object Access Protocol. And all was fine until people tried to build real applications with it and discovered that they needed security, transactions, reliable messaging, and so on. You know the rest.
>
> Hmm. What will be next?

What Went Right?

If you look at what worked, you get a broader picture. Not every company that mastered the technology managed to succeed with SOA. As has always been true with IT, technology alone is not enough to solve business problems.

The first thing that successful companies had was an understanding of not only how to use the technology but also what to do with it. These companies had an architectural vision that described the construction of applications in terms of a logical distribution of responsibility across tiers. The architecture went on to describe how services fit into that mix, what services were, how to build them, and how to use them.

The next, and equally important, aspect shared by successful companies was a business vision that described what business the company was in, what information and processes were necessary to run the business, what capabilities were needed to support those processes, and what services were needed to provide those capabilities. In addition, the vision included a roadmap that allowed for a prioritization and ordering of service implementations.

The vision and roadmap were combined with processes that helped the organization implement them. Two major aspects of this were: first, to help applications use existing services and, second, to help service providers create the right services, ones that didn't overlap with existing services or leave gaps in the roadmap.

Another aspect of successful SOA implementations was a structure that supported the consumer-and-provider nature of services. In addition to an organizational structure that separated these roles, the underlying architecture and infrastructure supported the discovery and publishing functions of consumers and providers.

Finally, the architecture and process were tied into an implementation methodology that supported the use and creation of services within applications and was informed by the overall enterprise context, business vision, and roadmap.

What Can You Learn?

So, what can you learn from this? First, success is not based on the technology. Technology can cause you to fail, but it doesn't make you succeed. Although previous technologies were too hard for most organizations, and the current technologies and tools are much better, there is more to it. You need to know how to use the technologies to build enterprise applications, not just isolated services. This requires architecture, vision, reuse, process, and organization, as illustrated in Figure 1-3.

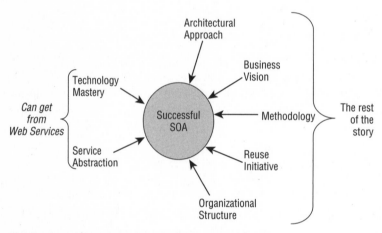

Figure 1-3 Ingredients of historically successful SOA

The Promise of SOA

Another way to assess the promise of SOA is to look at the motivations and expectations of the people who are engaged in SOA activities. In a 2006 survey conducted by the Cutter Consortium, the motivations for SOA included a range of technical and business reasons. The most common motivations were: agility, flexibility, reuse, data rationalization, integration, and reduced costs. Some of the more telling specific responses included:

- "Strategic reuse of assets across multiple department's applications"
- "Need to provide more agile support to business processes, and to handle change management impacts more efficiently and effectively"

- "Master Data Management"
- "Speed and ease of project deployment, concerns with duplication of work between projects"
- "Support external collaborators"
- "Efficiency in terms of time to market and development cost"
- "Bring together diverse lines of business across many geographies with faster speed to market"
- "Integrate legacy systems"

Not surprisingly, the motivations for adopting SOA echo the concerns that most enterprise IT organizations are struggling with.

The Challenges of SOA

If we examine the history and look at the goals or motivations for SOA, we can determine the challenges that organizations face in delivering on its promise. Let's restate the expectations, history, and goals in terms of four questions and then look at the issues they raise and the corresponding architectural requirements.

- What is required to provide agility, flexibility, and the strategic reuse of assets across multiple departments?
- What is required to bring more efficiency in terms of time to market and development costs, while delivering new capabilities to the organization?
- How will the integration of existing applications or enterprise data help to bring together diverse lines of business across geographies with faster time to market?
- How will SOA's agility and flexibility improve relationships and provide better alignment of business and IT?

Figure 1-4 illustrates the four major challenges facing SOA adoption today.

Reuse

Reuse seems to have been the holy grail of software for decades. But the objects and components failed to live up to the promise of the marketeers. Now, services are the next great hope for reuse. If we're smart enough to learn from the past, we can be more successful with services. SOA will march on either way (see the sidebar "Does SOA Need Reuse?").

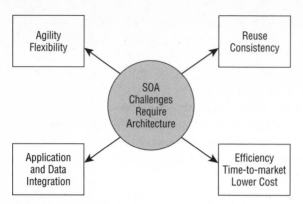

Figure 1-4 SOA challenges

DOES SOA NEED REUSE?

The object revolution of the late 1980s promised great increases in productivity and reductions in cost based on reuse. However, the reuse didn't really happen, except in some limited situations. But, it turns out that object orientation provides a better paradigm for development of complex software systems and that it is the prominent model supported by development tools. Every time you use a web page, you see object reuse. Thus, it has been widely adopted in spite of not attaining the promise of custom object reuse.

Components came along in the 1990s, promising to solve the reuse problem that objects hadn't. The advantage of components was that they provided a way to package functionality that matched the distributed, web-based systems that were being built. Once again, reuse was not achieved on a large scale. Yet, components are entrenched in modern systems because they bring with them all of the advantages of application servers such as distribution, scalability, and redundancy.

Now, the 2000s bring back the promise of reuse with services. Services provide a larger-granularity, run-time unit of functionality and reuse. Will enterprises be any more successful in achieving reuse with services than with previous technologies? At one level, services may not make that much difference. The march toward service orientation is well underway. Product vendors are structuring everything from infrastructure to software applications to development tools to support a service-oriented approach. Similar to objects, the advantages of services as a construction paradigm for enterprise applications will make SOA a reality regardless of how much the independently developed services actually get reused. So, services will probably be the future architectural and development paradigm, if for no other reason than because they are better for the software providers that provide infrastructure, tools, applications, Independent Software Vendors (ISVs), and so on.

However, many of the benefits that organizations hope to achieve with SOA require that services be reused within their environment. Those enterprises that achieve reuse will reap more of the benefits, be more agile, and be more competitive. Therefore, it behooves us to look at what did and didn't work in terms of reuse, and apply those lessons to services. Guess what? In every instance, technology was not the issue when it came to reuse. It's true that services have some technical features that make them better for reuse than components, just as components had technical features that were superior to those of objects. But the main roadblocks to reuse have, and will continue to be, organizational, methodological, and political.

Let's look at these issues from the perspective of the service consumer. When an application or process wants to use a service, it first needs a way to find and evaluate candidate services. Then, once it decides to use the service, it has dependencies on that service. Therefore, the service consumer needs to be guaranteed that the service will operate reliably, that bugs will be fixed in a timely manner, that requests for enhancements will be considered, that it will continue to operate and be supported for a reasonable amount of time, and, most importantly, that new versions of a service won't cause existing consumer applications to stop working. To make things more complicated, in an enterprise, the service consumer often needs to rely on another organization for that guarantee.

The following list discusses the architectural requirements for effective reuse:

- The ability to publish, search for, evaluate, and register as a consumer of a service
- Sufficient variability in service function to meet consumers' needs
- Capabilities for managing and maintaining a service life cycle across organizational boundaries
- The ability to guarantee the availability and lifetime of a service version
- Mechanisms for decoupling the consumer's life cycle from the provider's

CONSISTENCY, CONSISTENCY, CONSISTENCY

We often promote reuse as a way to reduce development costs or time to market. Although you can achieve improvements in both these areas, often it is consistency that is the most important value of reuse. SOA allows you to separate access to functions or data such that every application that needs to make use of the function or data can use the same service to get it.

(continued)

CONSISTENCY, CONSISTENCY, CONSISTENCY *(continued)*

How many enterprises suffer from redundant data or applications? (All of them, probably.) What is the result? Users get different results depending on how they go about doing something. When the users are customers, this results in dissatisfaction and lost customers. You've all heard of problems such as a customer having to call multiple different departments to correctly change his or her address, or an item being available through one system, but not another.

Imagine an enterprise-wide customer service that manages the shared customer information (such as addresses) for all systems and only needs to be changed once. Or, a single inventory service used by all order-management processes where they get consistent results about availability. SOA provides an approach for consistency of processes and data for both internal and external customers. This is something that the business sponsors understand and are often more willing to pay for than the promise of reduced costs and reuse.

Efficiency in Development

Making development more efficient means building more functionality, in less time, at less cost. Doing so depends on a variety of factors, including the reuse of services and the ability to quickly compose applications from those services. This in turn requires a different approach to service and solution development than the approach that was used in the past.

Developers of services can no longer create services in isolation, but rather, the services must fit into the overall architecture and conform to the enterprise business and information models. However, the initial version of a service cannot be expected to meet the requirements of all possible, future users. There has to be a managed process for deciding on, funding, and implementing enhancements to accommodate those additional users. But at the same time, enhancements to services need to be done in a controlled fashion that maintains the integrity of the service architecture and design, and conforms to versioning and compatibility requirements.

Developers of solutions that will consume services need to be able to easily find existing services and to evaluate them, determine what they do, and request enhancements. Furthermore, methods and tools for modeling and composing business processes from existing services need to be established. When projects are implementing business processes, a system design methodology is needed that focuses on composing business processes from the existing services. And, there has to be a variety of different kinds of services available, at different levels of organizational scope and granularity, to fully support the composition of business processes.

There also has to be an analysis and design methodology for the services themselves that describes the characteristics of the different types of services and explains the interaction, interface, and implementation design decisions.

Finally, there have to be organizational changes to support service development and use across the enterprise that match the consumer and provider nature of services.

The following architectural requirements are necessary for effective development productivity:

- Have a reference architecture that guides the development of services.

- Use Business Process Management (BPM) to define business processes, based on service composition and a layered set of services. Use BPM to drive the discovery and design of required services.

- Have efficient processes that manage the integrity of the total set of services for both providers and consumers in accordance with the overall vision and the business and information models.

Integration of Applications and Data

The integration of existing applications and data is perhaps the most perplexing challenge facing enterprise IT organizations. Billions have been spent over the past decades on enterprise application integration (EAI) to implement application integration, but results are mixed. Too often, fragile and unmaintainable solutions have been put in place that created a rat's nest of point-to-point connections over a variety of different technologies and protocols.

SOA, based on Web Services, promises to simplify integration by providing universal connectivity to existing systems and data. But, as with everything else, technology is only a small part of the solution. Again, you can look at what did and didn't work with EAI to craft a strategy for moving forward. And when you do, you see that an overall, enterprise-wide, architectural solution is required. You should no longer be connecting individual applications directly with point-to-point connections, but rather, providing services that connect individual applications into the overall enterprise.

The really hard part, however, is getting the new interfaces to the existing system right. Here, the tools are often our own worst enemy. The vendors trumpet their wiz-bang Web Services Description Language (WSDL) generators that can take an existing schema or application programming interface (API) and generate a service interface. Although this is seductive, it is wrong. You should not be exposing the data models or APIs of 20-year-old applications directly as services. The chances that these old APIs represent what your enterprise needs today are slim at best. Instead, you should transform them into new interfaces that meet the strategy, goals, and requirements of the enterprise today and in the future.

A similar situation exists for data integration. How many millions were spent on failed projects to implement a global enterprise data model? Too often, applications could not be retrofitted to the model, the cost of change was too high, or business units wouldn't go along with the changes. Yet, for services to fit together into a business process or to be composed together in a meaningful way, they have to share a common data model and semantics. Here's the difference, however: They do not have to agree on every single item and field of data. They have to agree only on what the shared, enterprise-wide data should be. Then, each application can translate between its own, internal version of the data and the shared, enterprise (external) representation of the data.

The following architectural requirements are necessary for integration:

- Have an enterprise, common semantic model for the shared information.
- Have a reference architecture that differentiates between business services and integration services.
- Have a reference architecture that describes common patterns for integration.
- Have infrastructure capabilities that enable semantic transformation between existing systems and the enterprise model.

Agility, Flexibility, and Alignment

Agility and flexibility occur when new processes can quickly and efficiently be created from the existing set of services. Achieving agility and flexibility requires an easily searchable catalog that lists the functions and data provided by the available services. In addition, an efficient way to assemble the business processes from the services needs to be available.

The services that compose the catalog must support a variety of different processes, at a variety of different levels, and have minimal gaps or overlaps in functionality. At the same time, the services must share and conform to a common enterprise semantic model. This doesn't just happen by itself, or by accident. The SOA architectural approach needs:

- A business architecture that lays out a roadmap for the processes and services of the enterprise now and over time, and identifies the functional and application capabilities to support those services. In addition, the business architecture needs to specify the desired outcomes so that business processes can be measured against achieving them.

- An information architecture that lays out a roadmap for the shared enterprise semantics and data model.

- An application architecture that defines a hierarchy of service types, how to compose processes from services, how to produce and consume services, and how to measure services contributions toward business outcomes.

- A technology architecture that defines what the technologies are and how they are used to support processes, services, integration, data access and transformations, and so on.

Obviously, business needs to be involved in the development of the enterprise business and information architecture and roadmaps. But, that alone does not achieve alignment of business intentions with implemented IT systems. There has to be a process that directly integrates the enterprise architecture (business, information, application, and technology) into the development process. In addition, there needs to be an organizational and governance structure in place to support and enforce it.

The following list defines requirements of SOA for alignment:

- Have a reference architecture that defines the business and information aspects of SOA and their relationship to the enterprise.

- Have an enterprise, common semantic model that is used to inform the service interface design.

- Use model-based development techniques to ensure traceability between the business models and the implemented systems.

- Have processes that enable and validate conformance.

Table 1-1 summarizes the overall architectural requirements needed. Obviously, there is some overlap between the architectural requirements for the different challenges. This is a good thing. It indicates that a holistic architectural approach can not only meet the different challenges but also integrate the solutions.

Table 1-1 Summary of architectural requirements

CHALLENGE	ARCHITECTURAL REQUIREMENT
Reuse	Ability to publish, search for, evaluate, and register as a consumer of a service.
	Capabilities for managing and maintaining a service life cycle across organizational boundaries.
	Ability to guarantee availability and lifetime of a service version.
	Mechanisms for decoupling the consumer's life cycle from the provider's.
Efficient Development	Have a reference architecture that guides the development of services.
	Use BPM to define business processes, based on service composition and a layered set of services.
	Have efficient processes that manage the integrity of the total set of services for both providers and consumers in accordance with the overall vision and business and information models.
Integration of Applications and Data	Have an enterprise, common semantic model for the shared information.
	Have a reference architecture that differentiates between business services and integration services.
	Have a reference architecture that describes common patterns for integration.
	Have infrastructure capabilities that enable semantic transformation between existing systems and the enterprise model.
Agility, Flexibility, and Alignment	Have a reference architecture that defines the business and information aspects of SOA and their relationship to the enterprise.
	Have an enterprise, common semantic model that is used to inform the service interface design.
	Use model-based development techniques to ensure the traceability between the business models and the implemented systems.
	Have processes that enable and validate conformance.

Meeting the Challenge

Examining the promise of SOA and the goals of the organizations that adopt it leads to a set of requirements for meeting the challenges laid out in this chapter. Let's summarize the requirements for SOA.

Reference Architecture

Creating and maintaining a reference architecture is one of the more important but difficult best practices for SOA and is an important critical success factor in achieving SOA goals. Yet, often, organizations will have only an informal architecture, or none at all. Figure 1-5 shows the major components of an SOA reference architecture. The reference architecture represents a more formal architectural definition, one that can be used for objective validation of services and applications. For SOA, the reference architecture should:

- Support enterprise concepts, particularly the subarchitectures of business, information, application, and technology
- Specify a hierarchy and taxonomy of services and service types
- Define how services fit into an overall enterprise application, such as a portal
- Provide a separation between business, application, and technology concepts
- Be integrated into the development process

Chapter 2 covers the reference architecture in detail.

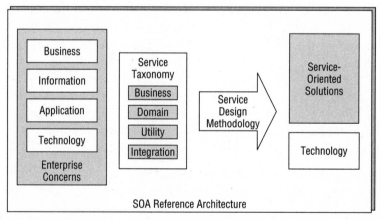

Figure 1-5 Aspects of an enterprise SOA reference architecture

Common Semantics

Defining a common, enterprise semantic and information model is key to achieving agility and flexibility. Without it services cannot be easily combined to form meaningful business processes. For example, imagine a process that combines different travel activities, such as air, hotel, and rental car into a trip based on a customer and their companions. The customer wants to see all of the related activities and only wants to provide the information once. The airlines require the names of all passengers; the rental car agency needs to know if additional travelers are over age 25 and their relationship to the primary traveler; and the hotel needs a different set of information. If the services don't have some common understanding of what a customer is, and what a travel companion is, it won't be very easy to automate the combined processes or provide a single view or interface to the customer. Without common understanding, rather than agility and flexibility, each process requires special case code to combine the data. The common semantics should:

- Identify information that must be shared across the enterprise and between services
- Define the meaning and context of that information
- Identify techniques for mapping enterprise semantics to existing application data models

Chapter 5 describes the development of the common semantic model, and Chapter 6 shows how it is used in the design of service interfaces.

Governance

Governance has been defined as the art and discipline of managing outcomes through structured relationships, procedures, and policies. Governance enforces compliance with the architecture and common semantics and facilitates managing the enterprise-wide development, use, and evolution of services. Governance consists of a set of policies that service providers and consumers (and their developers) must conform to, a set of practices for implementing those policies, and a set of processes for ensuring that the policies are implemented correctly. There is typically an organizational structure in place to define and implement governance policies and often a repository to automate and enforce them. Governance of SOA should include:

- Policies regulating service definition and enhancements, including ownership, roles, criteria, review guidelines, and so on.
- Identification of roles, responsibilities, and owners.
- Policy enforcement that is integrated directly into the service repository (where appropriate).
- Guidelines, templates, checklists, and examples that make it easy to conform to governance requirements.
- Review of service interface definitions for new services and enhancements to existing services. The review ensures that the service definition conforms to standards and aligns with the business and information

models. The review is typically done by a service review board or the unit responsible for the service.

- Architectural review of solutions and services to ensure that they conform to the SOA and enterprise architecture. This review is typically done by an architecture review board.

Warning! Governance should not be primarily a review activity. If architecture is nothing more than extra steps in the process or a burden to developers, they will just ignore it. Effective governance follows a carrot-and-stick approach with an emphasis on enabling developers to build conforming applications (the carrot) and automating governance activities and policies. Reviews (the stick) should be a final check where process is minimal and exceptions are actually the exception.

We've seen countless articles and presentations (surprisingly by vendors) that talk about governance as a required activity from day 1. But we don't agree. There are enough challenges and barriers to get over for SOA to work, that you don't need another one to start with. When you have only a few services, you don't need a lot of processes to govern them. Figure out how to build and use services first, and then add governance. If you have to go back and correct things, fine. Certainly make sure that you have governance before you have 100 services, but don't put it in place when you have only one service. Chapter 12 discusses governance.

TYPES OF GOVERNANCE

We often discuss governance in terms of four different aspects of a service's life cycle:

- ◆ **Design-time governance** — Policies and procedures to ensure that the right services are built and used

- ◆ **Deploy-time governance** — Policies that affect the deployment of services into production

- ◆ **Run-time governance** — Policies that affect the binding of consumers and providers

- ◆ **Change-time governance** — Policies and procedures that affect the design, versioning, and provisioning of service enhancements

We have primarily discussed design-time and change-time governance as architectural requirements. Obviously, deploy-time governance is important for operational quality. Although automated run-time governance functions can provide benefits and sophistication to a SOA implementation, we don't think that it is a critical factor in achieving overall SOA success and value. Of course, it is important to specify policies regarding security and the authorization of

(continued)

TYPES OF GOVERNANCE *(continued)*

service consumers and providers. However, many successful SOA
implementations today use very simple mechanisms to implement this rather
than a sophisticated registry to automatically apply the policies during binding.
On the other hand, governance of service interface design is necessary to
achieve a consistent overall set of services, which is critical to achieving SOA
success.

Business Process Modeling

Business processes need to change relatively frequently yet be based on stable
underlying capabilities. The flexibility to do this comes from being able to
quickly construct new business processes from business services, which are
relatively stable. Business processes should:

- Be specified using Business Process Models and executed in a business
  process management system

- Be composed of activities that are implemented by business services
  (provided by the SOA)

- Pass information into, out of, and within the processes in the form of
  documents, which are built on top of the common information model

Chapter 4 describes the use of BPM in addressing business requirements
and influencing service design.

Design-Time Service Discovery

To reuse services, you have to be able to find the services that exist, and
you have to be able to examine them to see if they perform the functions
required, provide the appropriate qualities of service, are reliable, and so on.
It is important to understand the distinction between a run-time registry and
a design-time repository, even though both functions may be implemented by
the same software. A registry is used at run time to identify a service endpoint
for a requested service interface. This is where run-time governance policies
may be enforced. A repository is used at design time to find existing services
for inclusion in processes during the design of that process. This is critical to
enabling service reuse. Service discovery does not necessarily have to be based
on a repository (although repositories do a good job of it) but should provide
the following functions:

- A catalog of available services.
- Sophisticated search capabilities for identifying potential services.
- Capabilities for examining a service, its interface and implementation, and design and testing to determine if it is appropriate for the desired usage. This will often be through links to documents, models, code, reports, and the like that are stored in other systems.
- Metrics on service usage.
- Notification to interested parties about upgrades to services or other events.
- Automation of certain governance policies.
- Direct integration into the development environment.

In subsequent chapters, we provide methods for describing and categorizing services to assist you in locating them during development. Chapter 5 describes the creation and use of the service inventory in the discovery and design of service interfaces.

Model-Based Development

Model-based development is a best practice in software engineering in general and in SOA as well. Models provide a way to conceptualize and describe a system without getting bogged down in details, and to describe the major parts of a system and their relationships. A model-based development approach for SOA should incorporate the following:

- A higher level of abstraction for software development and the ability to visualize software and service designs
- Support for a domain-specific language (DSL) for the implementation of SOA
- Automatic integration of SOA reference architecture into the design environment and DSL
- Separation of business, services, and technology concerns

The design methodologies throughout this book use a model-based approach to SOA design, based on a set of SOA domain concepts and abstractions that make up a domain-specific language for SOA. Although it is helpful to be able to generate development artifacts directly from design models, and in fact many tools do exactly that, it is not strictly required. The proper design of services is critical to achieving SOA goals, and models are the lingua franca of design. What is required is the design of service interfaces and implementations, and a way to pass those design models to development as specifications for construction. Of course, the more you can generate, the easier and less error prone that hand-off will be. Chapter 7 focuses on the technology-independent design of service implementations that lead to a model-based approach.

Best Practices in SOA Analysis and Design

There's a clever saying that goes "In theory, there's no difference between theory and practice, but in practice there is." This difference is most often seen in the clash between architecture and development.

The architecture team is responsible for understanding the big picture. They must answer questions such as: How will SOA support the overall enterprise goals? How will it fit with other initiatives such as Single Sign-On (SSO)? What standards and technologies are important? How do they fit in with the enterprise technology roadmap? What strategy and tactics should be employed to introduce and phase in SOA? How will it be sold to management and the business? All of these are important and difficult questions that must be answered, and the architecture team or steering committee is the right place for this. We often call this a top-down approach.

The development team is responsible for implementing and deploying individual services. They have a different set of questions to answer: How will an individual service be implemented? How will the master data definition be translated to the individual systems of record that contain the data? How will the service be deployed? How will the service be managed? How will new versions be implemented and deployed? How will services be registered and discovered at run time? How will services be discovered and reused at design time? How will dependencies be minimized and managed? Again, these are very important and difficult questions that must be answered. We might call this a bottom-up approach.

With these questions and concerns, the architecture team is trying to maximize the value that SOA can provide in the delivery of enterprise solutions. Value comes from enabling and creating an enterprise service layer that supports the flexible creation of business processes. Value comes from being able to quickly modify these business processes without having to make difficult and expensive modifications to existing operational systems. Value comes from having consistent behavior across the enterprise for the same business function (i.e., having the business function implemented in a single service). Value comes from having modular business capabilities that can be outsourced or sold as a service. To support this, the SOA has to describe how the different organizations in the enterprise can contribute to the overall SOA, and at the same time, meet their immediate business requirements.

Meanwhile, the technical team is trying to provide value by implementing specific business functionality in the best, most efficient, and most cost-effective manner — not just in the short term, but with an eye toward the total cost of ownership of IT systems. The manager of a technical team we worked with put it best. He sees SOA as a way to minimize and manage the collateral damage caused by changes. We've all heard the horror stories, such as the case of adding two digits to a part number that required $25 million and 1 year to implement (but added no business value), because it touched on almost every system in the enterprise. By applying a separation of concerns, having a Master Data Schema, and a set of services to manage the fundamental business entities, the required changes could have been isolated and minimized.

The theory naturally leads toward a top-down approach in which processes and services are driven by an overall enterprise model. These projects are often started with a high-level business process model or an overall enterprise system analysis activity. The practice leads us to a bottom-up approach in which services are implemented to meet a specific, immediate business requirement or project. These projects often start by service-enabling legacy systems or incorporating simple external services. Yet neither of these approaches is very effective. In order to meet both the enterprise goals and the immediate project goals, these organizations and concerns have to meet in the middle. Chapter 3 describes the overall process of initiating SOA and designing services based on a middle-out approach.

Summary

Effective SOA (and architecture in general) is the careful balance and blending of the big picture and the immediate requirements. It is the practical application of theory to meet a set of goals, now and in the future. In this middle-out approach, the architecture team provides an overall SOA that offers the guidance and context necessary to support the implementation and reuse of services. This is provided as a set of guidelines, patterns, frameworks, examples, and reference implementations. The technical teams use these to incorporate the requirements (business and information context) into their designs so that the services they implement provide the necessary business functions that are needed immediately, but can easily be extended to support other processes and services in the future. These are the roles of the reference architecture, the architecture-driven design process, and the domain-specific modeling approach.

Chapter 2 describes the SOA reference architecture and how it meets the challenges and requirements introduced in this chapter. It describes the overall enterprise context, the architectural layers and tiers, the domain-specific concepts and abstractions, and specifically what a service is and the important architectural characteristics of a service.

SOA — Architecture Fundamentals

Any problem in computer science can be solved by another layer of abstraction.
— **Butler Lampson**

Chapter 1 discussed the expectations for Service-Oriented Architecture (SOA) and the requirements for delivering on those expectations. At one level, the extent to which expectations are met will depend on how successful an organization is at creating and reusing services. To be more specific, success will not depend on any individual service, but on the overall collection of services and how well they support the ability to modify existing solutions and build new ones faster to meet changing requirements. We went on to describe the SOA reference architecture as the foundation that allows reusable and composable services to be created with a scope that is larger than any single project. So, just what is architecture, and what are the components of the SOA reference architecture? This chapter describes:

- The general principles of architecture

- The basics of SOA

- Business-driven SOA

- The relationship of SOA to other architectures

- What a service is and the characteristics of a service

- Service types and purposes

- The SOA reference architecture

What Is Architecture?

Software architecture is a description of a software system in terms of its major components, their relationships, and the information that passes among them. In essence, architecture is a plan for building systems that meet well-defined requirements and, by extension, systems that possess the characteristics needed to meet those requirements now and in the future.

A fundamental purpose of software architecture is to help manage the complexity of software systems and the modifications that systems inevitably undergo in response to external changes in the business, organizational, and technical environments.

There is no single, industry-wide definition of software architecture. The Software Engineering Institute (SEI) web site includes a long list of definitions for the term "software architecture" at www.sei.cmu.edu/architecture/definitions.html. Some definitions provide details and context to the abstract definition given above, and expand on the notions of a system description, requirement specification, and planning. Others are just as abstract but provide a different viewpoint for thinking about architecture. It is instructive to read them all, if only on the chance that one of them will make you think "Aha!"

Here is a definition of software architecture from *The Rational Unified Process — An Introduction* by Booch and Kruchten (1999).

Software Architecture encompasses the significant decisions about:

- *The organization of a software system,*
- *the selection of the structural elements and their interfaces by which the system is composed, together with their behavior as specified in the collaboration among those elements,*
- *the composition of these elements into progressively larger subsystems,*
- *the architectural style that guides this organization, these elements and their interfaces, their collaborations, and their composition.*

Software architecture is not only concerned with structure and behavior but also with usage, functionality, performance, resilience, reuse, comprehensibility, economic and technological constraints and tradeoffs, and aesthetics.

Most definitions agree that software architecture describes the composition of systems, but differ in the perspective of what a system is and what composition implies. We like this definition because it is detailed but broad enough to cover many perspectives and scopes.

While traditional software architecture is focused on the construction of software applications, SOA is focused on the construction of solutions with an enterprise or cross-organizational scope, based on the interactions between consumers with needs (often business processes) and providers with capabilities (services).

We like to describe architecture as having to answer three main questions:

1. What are the important concepts?

2. What are the relationships among them? How do these relationships describe the behavior of the system?

3. How do the concepts and relationships provide value higher up? How do they serve the purpose of the overall system rather than the purpose of the individual parts?

So, a typical software architecture might describe the structure of classes (a key concept) or components, their relationships, and their value in the software product. Similarly, SOA describes the structure of services (a key concept), their relationships, and the value they bring to enterprise-wide processes and solutions.

Architectural Styles

Most products, applications, and enterprises have unique architectures, although many of them may be very similar. For example, the architecture for an e-commerce application at one company probably resembles that of an e-commerce application at another company of like size and business function. This implies that there is a difference between a specific architecture and the type of solution it defines. The common industry term for the latter is *architectural style*.

In terms of the architectural questions presented previously, the architectural style is the vocabulary of concepts and relationships, and a set of constraints on how they can be combined to meet the higher-level goals and to form a particular architecture. An architectural style is a family of architectures related by common principles and attributes. In other words, an architectural style contains a well-defined set of patterns that constitute a common way for enterprise solution components to interact with one another. For example, we consider client/server, 3-tier, *n*-tier, and enterprise application integration (EAI) approaches all to be architectural styles.

A useful metaphor to describe styles is the construction of a cathedral. All cathedrals have certain underlying construction principles. For example, the basic floor plan is that of a cross. And while there is also wide variation among cathedrals, a few common characteristics emerge such as Romanesque and Gothic. These two architectural styles define a specific set of patterns that transform the basic cathedral into an easily identifiable style.

The choice of an architectural style for enterprise solutions is typically made as a result of engineering tradeoffs in response to a specific set of requirements. For example, an *n*-tier architectural style is designed to meet requirements of distribution, scalability, interface flexibility, device independence, business service reuse, application integration, and so on. Specifically, the *n*-tier architecture is designed to provide web-based and other types of client access to information and services that reside within the enterprise, which might in fact be implemented in a legacy application.

SOA can be defined as an architectural style promoting the concept of a business-aligned enterprise service as the fundamental unit of designing, building, and composing enterprise business solutions. Multiple patterns describing definitions, implementations, and deployment of the SOA solutions complete this style. Throughout this chapter, we define the concepts, relationships, constraints, and patterns that make up the SOA architectural style.

Architectural Principles and Practices

Before diving into the specifics of SOA, let's review some important architectural principles and practices that we apply throughout the chapter:

- Separation of concerns
- Architectural views
- Accommodation of change
- Abstraction
- Consistency
- Business derivation
- Patterns
- Facilitation
- Communications

The *separation of concerns* is the most fundamental principle of architecture. Concerns are kept separate so that independent elements remain independent. The benefit is that a change in one part of the system does not adversely affect other parts. In other words, they can change independently. A familiar example of this principle is the separation of interface from implementation.

Architectural views provide another important separation of concerns by the inclusion or exclusion of specific details and the presentation of information to different stakeholders. Architectural views or perspectives are designed to address specific concerns of software development or the important enterprise groups and organizations that play a part in the full life cycle of enterprise solutions. Typical software views are logical, deployment, process, and network. Typical enterprise architectural views (concerns) are business, information, application, technology, and implementation. Coincidentally, SOA implementation and design map well to these sets of architectural concerns.

Accommodation of change refers to the fact that the architecture should provide flexibility, so that future application requirements can be more easily satisfied. A flexible architecture identifies both future application requirements and areas that are likely to change. Tracking industry trends helps identify some areas of potential change. These areas must be addressed explicitly in architecture. If the specifics of flexibility and independence are not included in the original design it is very likely that the architecture will contain implicit couplings, which are much more difficult to deal with when change inevitably occurs.

Abstraction is a key architectural tool used in decoupling, accommodating change, and separating concerns. There is a saying in the industry that "any problem in computer science can be solved by adding a layer of abstraction." An abstraction layer provides indirection between two layers, allowing for increased flexibility. Typically, the abstraction also provides a higher level of interaction. For example, rather than writing directly to a database, you write SQL, which provides a higher-level interaction model, as well as an abstraction and indirection layer above the lower-level database interfaces. The abstraction provides higher productivity (in the sense that one SQL statement corresponds to many invocations of the lower-level database interfaces) and also supports multiple different datastores.

One of the main goals of architecture is the promotion of *consistency* and reuse. Thus, one difference between software architecture and Service-Oriented Architecture is that of scope. SOA is concerned with providing consistent services throughout the entire enterprise, so that they can be used by many different families of solutions. SOA must promote the development of business capabilities in such a way that they are easily reused by the different business processes.

Business derivation is perhaps the most important architectural principle, which acknowledges that an architecture's raison d'etre (and that of IT itself) is to support the enterprise's business — that is, the strategies and goals of the organization.

A *pattern* is a template for a solution to a specific set of requirements, and as such it is a tool for describing architecture. The father of the pattern movement is generally acknowledged to be Christopher Alexander, a professor of architecture (as in buildings, not software) at Berkeley. He put it this way "Each pattern describes a problem which occurs over and over again in our environment, and then describes the core of the solution to that problem, in such a way that you can use the same solution a million times over, without ever doing it the same way twice."

Facilitation means that an architecture should make it easy to build solutions that conform to the architecture. Thus architecture is not only about describing what the system does; it must also provide the means to construct the system and its components.

Communications has to do with the fact that an architecture provides the mechanism for people to communicate about, and reach a common understanding of, IT systems. These architectural principles allow you to describe architecture unambiguously, at different levels of abstraction, and in a context understandable to each stakeholder.

DEATH BY ARCHITECTURE

Perhaps nothing is more drawn out and aggravating for an IT organization than what we call *death by architecture*. This classic story happens all too often. The high priests and architects depart for the ivory tower and return some months or years later with "The Revealed Truth" in the form of 1000 pages of architecture documents. In the meantime, new applications have been developed and requirements have changed, and the architecture is out of date on delivery. Other reasons may contribute to its being dead on arrival. It may be irrelevant to the development organization or might not have enough buy-in to be accepted. It may be hard to understand its value or how it achieves business goals, or dozens of other reasons.

Obviously, we believe in the value and importance of architecture, and we hope to convince you as well. But don't confuse belief in the importance of architecture with support for ivory-tower architecture projects. There are right ways and wrong ways to do everything, and SOA architecture has more than its share of wrong ways. So don't give up on the idea of architecture, even if your experience with architecture thus far has been painful. We have seen very successful architecture projects, and they are a joy to behold. The world's most successful applications are based on solid architectures and solid implementations.

However, architecture is hard to do well. It fails most frequently because IT does not have the will to implement the associated organizational changes required to make it work. Other common reasons are poor project management, changes in leadership or sponsorship, and changes in priorities. Sometimes, the architecture group itself is to blame. But there is no doubt that it is a primary responsibility of the chief architect to avoid death by architecture. Here are some suggestions:

◆ Quickly create an architectural vision and strategy. It should take about 1 month to develop this "high-level architecture." Use this to prioritize and guide the implementation of the architecture.

◆ **Pick an appropriate project** to start implementing the first pieces of architecture, one that is important enough to get noticed, but not so critical that outside pressures will make it impossible to do the right thing.

◆ **Implement a small portion of the architecture at one time,** as part of a project that is delivering real business value to the organization. Use your architectural vision to help pick areas that demonstrate architectural values, such as reuse and consistency. Services and frameworks are often good candidates. Continue to incrementally implement more of the architecture as part of subsequent projects.

◆ **After every project, integrate the lessons learned into the next iteration of the architecture.** Keep it current. Constantly solicit feedback from development. Get their buy-in by demonstrating that architecture makes their job easier.

◆ **Implement, collect, and report metrics** to prove the value in terms of cost, time, and quality.

◆ **Know the difference between great and good enough.** It will never be perfect. A good-enough project delivered on time beats a late-but-great one every time.

◆ **Don't try a big bang approach.** It never works. SOA should be business driven and based on a vision of what processes, capabilities, and services you'll need over time. However, you don't have to have the entire enterprise business model complete before you can get started on the first few services.

What Is Service-Oriented Architecture?

SOA is an architectural style for building enterprise solutions based on services. More specifically, SOA is concerned with the independent construction of business-aligned services that can be combined into meaningful, higher-level business processes and solutions within the context of the enterprise. Anybody can create a service; that is not the challenge of SOA. The real value of SOA comes when reusable services are combined to create agile, flexible, business processes. Unfortunately, that does not just happen by itself. Achieving it might be easier to manage if a single organization is creating all of the services, but that is not the case at most large organizations. So, part of the architecture of SOA is responsible for creating the environment necessary to create and use composable services across the enterprise.

In other words, architecture enables different organizations to independently implement services that meet their immediate needs, yet can also be combined into higher-level business processes and enterprise solutions. This requires that services:

- Have similar size, shape, form, function, and other characteristics
- Conform to enterprise standards
- Communicate at a technical level
- Communicate at a semantic level
- Don't have gaps and overlaps in responsibilities

As mentioned earlier, architecture has to answer these three questions: What are the important parts? What is the relationship among the parts? How do they combine to provide value to the level above them?

In terms of SOA, the important parts are:

- **Processes** — High-level business functions, often spanning applications or LOBs
- **Services** — Modular units of business functionality
- **Integration** — Connection to and exposure of existing applications and/or data as services
- **Existing systems** — Existing legacy systems, commercial off-the-shelf (COTS) applications, and data that the enterprise wants to leverage
- **Documents** — High-level units of business information, such as a purchase order, or an EDI document
- **Semantics** — The underlying meaning of information that is exchanged in processes
- **Transformation** — The conversion of information from one format or semantic to another
- **Communications** — The ability of services to communicate with each other

Figure 2-1 illustrates a layered SOA architecture, including two important concepts for each layer. On the left are the functional concepts that you use to construct systems and processes. On the right are the informational concepts that you use to pass, describe, or manipulate data at those different functional levels. In other words, you are explicitly recognizing the fact that enterprises are a combination of process and information. Each layer needs both abstractions. Yet, too often, SOA only focuses on the functional aspects, ignoring the important data concepts. Instead, you should present the functional and data abstractions together. The connections between layers represent the relationships between the functions.

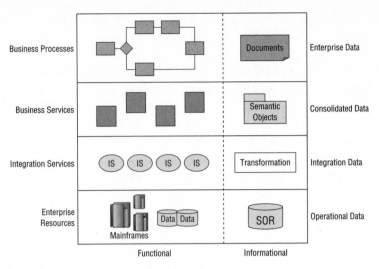

Figure 2-1 Architectural elements of SOA

From bottom to top, the layers are:

- **Enterprise resources and operational systems** — This layer consists of existing applications, legacy, and COTS systems, including Customer Relationship Management (CRM) and Enterprise Resource Planning (ERP) packaged applications, and older object-oriented implementations. These applications provide business operations — transactions that represent single logical units of work in the enterprise's operational systems. The execution of an operation will typically cause one or more persistent data records to be read, written, or modified in a System of Record (SOR). Operations have a specific, structured interface, and return structured responses. Data at this layer resides in existing applications or databases.

- **Integration services** — Integration services provide integration between and access to existing applications. The separation between the integration services and the business services is critical to maintaining a flexible enterprise environment. This often involves the transformation of data and functions from what's desired at the business service level to what is actually possible in the existing systems.

- **Business services** — Business services provide high-level business functionality throughout the enterprise. This layer provides a service interface abstraction and integration of the layer below, breaking the direct dependence between processes and existing systems. Services are managed, governed sets of enterprise assets responsible for ensuring conformance to service level agreements (SLAs). Business services provide business capabilities through logical groupings of operations. For example, if you view CustomerProfiling as a service, then the logical group of operations it contains might be: Lookup Customer by Telephone Number, List Customers by Name, and Save New Customer Data. Note that all operations will not necessarily come from the same operational systems, or in some cases, the operations will be replicated across multiple similar systems. Thus, the business services provide a virtual implementation of related business operations. Business services operate on semantic data objects, virtual data that describes the information that must be shared or passed between services. It is often aggregated from multiple existing systems. Note that the business service layer will be composed of many different types of services, discussed later in the chapter.

▪ **Business processes** — A business process consists of a series of operations that are executed in an ordered sequence according to a set of business rules. Often, the business process is described in a Business Process Model, such as those conforming to Business Process Modeling Notation (BPMN), and executed by a specialized business process management system (BPMS). The sequencing, selection, and execution of operations is termed *orchestration*. Business processes provide long-running sets of actions or activities. They are composed of business services and typically encompass multiple service invocations. Business processes operate on business documents. The processes and documents are composed from the services and objects of the layer below, according to a Business Process Model and a common semantic data model. The scope of these processes is often the entire enterprise. Examples of business processes are: Initiate New Employee, Sell Products or Services, and Fulfill Order.

Completing the answer to the third architectural question, these concepts and relationships provide value to the enterprise by:

▪ Providing a single, consistent place to access data or perform business functions

▪ Isolating and exposing existing application data and functions

▪ Creating reusable, combinable building blocks for the construction of business processes

Figure 2-1 shows a typical layered perspective of SOA that addresses the composition and integration requirements of SOA and business processes, but not so much the run-time, governance, organizational, or enterprise requirements. We will expand on these layers in Chapters 9 and 10 when we discuss implementing enterprise solutions. Figure 2-2 illustrates a different perspective on SOA.

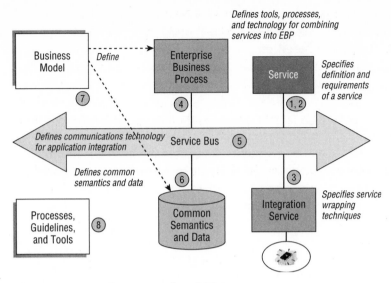

Figure 2-2 Enterprise perspective of SOA

SOA needs to describe the following aspects of services within an enterprise:

1. A definition of services, the granularity, and types of services
2. How services are constructed and used
3. How existing packaged and legacy systems are integrated into the service environment
4. How services are combined into processes
5. How services communicate at a technical level (i.e., how they connect to each other and pass information)
6. How services interoperate at a semantic level (i.e., how they share common meanings for that information)
7. How services align with the businesses strategy and goals
8. How to use the architecture

The numbered circles in the figure correspond to the numbered list. Let's look at these in more detail.

1. Defining a Service

First, you have to determine what a service is and means. An SOA should define the different types and granularities of services, such as domain services, business services, and enterprise business processes. The characteristics (and differences) of each should be clearly specified. At the same time, not everything should be a service. The SOA should also specify what kinds of software constructs should not be services. For example, the logic that displays data on a web page based on a user's profile should not be a service, whereas the logic that retrieves the user's profile and authorization information should be.

2. Defining How Services Are Built and Used

Services are intended to operate within the larger enterprise context (semantic and behavioral environment). The SOA must be clear about how services should be used in an enterprise solution (e.g., what standard features they have, what required interactions there are, how they support management capabilities, etc.).

The architecture must define the structure of a service and how to build one. We will discuss the details of different types of services in the next section. For each type of service, the architecture should specify:

- **Granularity** — The appropriate size of the service.

- **Type or style of interface** — Guidelines for interface design. For example, business services should be large-grained services that pass data through documents, whereas utility services provide discrete common functions where the input is often a single simple parameter.

- **Configuration mechanisms** — Standard mechanisms for configuring services should be defined. This allows for the use of a common configuration service, and more importantly, for common configuration data to be shared between services. For example, several different services may require the specification of a customer authorization file. Rather than repeating that information for each service, a better approach would be to allow the services to share the information. SOA enables the mechanisms required for sharing.

- **Other artifacts** — The set of artifacts that are required to support a service, such as design models and specifications, documentation, test plans, and so on.

- **Associated information** — Additional information that should be part of a service to support run-time and design-time inspection, such as the version, author, date, keywords, and so on. Note the two different and important types of service information: design time and run time. Although these have some overlap, they are largely different. Design-time information is used to search for and locate services, to determine if they are appropriate for the desired usage, and to describe what they do and how they are used. Run-time information is used more for management operations to track what is running at any give time.

- **Dependency management and other patterns** — Specific design patterns that should be followed to keep services independent and reusable.

In addition, the architecture must describe the complete life cycle of services, including maintenance, evolution, versioning, and backward-compatibility requirements.

3. Integrating Packaged and Legacy Systems into the Service Environment

The reality is that much of the business functionality in an enterprise today is not in the form of a service. An essential part of an SOA is how this functionality can be exposed as services and connected to the service bus. The SOA must specify the general mechanism for defining these services, wrapping them, and connecting them to the bus, with specific implementations for the most common type of system.

4. Combining Services into Enterprise Processes

An important goal of an SOA is to enable the reuse of services throughout the enterprise to support a variety of different applications. The SOA must describe the methods, tools, and infrastructure for combining services into larger business processes.

5. Specifying the Technology Infrastructure

A technical infrastructure must be in place to enable integration, service composition, and communication among services. However, there are many different types of infrastructures, and even within the same type, there are many different options. For example, if the infrastructure is Web Services, then the architecture might specify that WS-I Basic Profile v1.1 and Security Profile v1.0 be used. All aspects of interaction with the technical infrastructure such as protocol versions, security, and application utilities must be addressed to ensure integration at the business process level.

Specifying the Technology Infrastructure

The technical infrastructure to enable services to communicate must be completely specified, along with the guidelines for using that infrastructure. This includes:

- **The communications mechanism** — How messages, requests, and data are transported

- **Failover mechanisms** — How communication failures are handled, including failover and recovery
- **Discovery and location transparency** — How services are advertised and discovered in a location-transparent manner

Note that the architecture does not imply any specific technology for this bus. It could be implemented by Web Services, an Enterprise Service Bus, an application server platform, or other middleware. However, it is important that the architecture specifies a solution for communications issues, and that the chosen solution addresses these issues.

Specifying the Application Infrastructure Required to Support Services

A service is less valuable in isolation. Rather, its value lies in its ability to be combined with other services to create an agile enterprise. To do this, it must be designed to fit into a specific environment. In addition to the communications infrastructure, this solution environment (infrastructure) and the services it provides must be described by the architecture. For example, how do services cooperate in a Single Sign-On (SSO) security framework? What are the defined security policies required between consumers and producers (security messaging, access control policies, etc.)? In addition, if all services support specific management interfaces, logging, or configuration, the infrastructure should define services to utilize and manipulate the information provided through them.

6. Defining Common Semantics and Data

The SOA must define the common semantic environment in which the services operate. For example: What data schema must be common throughout the enterprise for consistency and interoperability? What must be common to achieve enterprise goals and enable consistent business processes?

Note that the common enterprise information model is *not* trying to define every detail of every piece of data in the enterprise. Rather, it is trying to define the subset of information that is passed between services, and that must have a common meaning within an enterprise process.

7. Aligning Services with the Business

A business model is key to understanding the requirements for a common environment and creating information and services to support it. The business model should answer certain basic questions: What business is the enterprise in? What outcomes are required to meet the enterprise goals? What processes and services are necessary to achieve those outcomes? What capabilities are needed to implement the processes, and what services will be used to expose those capabilities? The SOA does not necessarily define the business model, but it must define how the business model is used to design domain, business, and enterprise business processes, and how it drives SOA requirements.

8. Determining How to Use the Architecture

Finally, the cleverest architecture in the world will not be successful if it can't be used. An architecture is not complete until it defines how it will be used to support the development of solutions that conform to it. The following sections discuss the elements of this process.

Determining the Development Environment, Frameworks, Infrastructure, and Tools

These are all required to support the SOA program. It is not enough to describe what services are; the architecture must enable the easy and efficient creation of those services. Even more, it must specify how the architecture fits with and supports the development process to add value rather than overhead. We are not proposing that SOA should mandate any particular development environment at an enterprise level. Our experience is that that kind of centralization is not effective. What is important, however, is that the architecture understands the aspects of services that must be consistent across the range of development environments, and creates standards, guidelines, examples, frameworks, plug-ins, or the like that support these development environments and processes. This ensures that architecture becomes a normal consideration during design and development, rather than an additional step in the process.

Defining Metrics for Measuring Success

An SOA is only effective if it meets the business goals that drive the SOA program. The architecture must choose metrics to demonstrate those goals and a method for collecting and reporting the metrics.

Business-Driven SOA

SOA is not new. There are prominent examples of enterprises that have successfully implemented them and have realized numerous advantages, including reduced costs and improved competitiveness. Unfortunately, these examples are few and far between because implementing a successful SOA is hard. In the past, few organizations had the skill to overcome the architectural, technical, business, and organizational challenges required for successful implementations. And while many of those challenges still exist, several technologies are converging to make SOA more obtainable to enterprises staffed by mere mortals.

Web Services provide a convenient technology for the infrastructure of services. However, the nature of distributed systems dictates that those services be defined at a higher level. Business services designed to exchange business documents written in Extensible Markup Language (XML) take this into account, but present new challenges in terms of creating business compositions and processing business documents. Business Process Management (BPM) provides a perfect solution and complement to the implementation of services and SOA. BPM provides the development and execution environment for combining services into larger enterprise processes. Business Process Execution Language (BPEL) is designed to work explicitly with Web Services and provide coordination and integration of Web Services into higher-level business services.

Of course, if we have learned anything from the IT industry, we should have learned that technology alone doesn't solve business problems; at best it can act as an enabler. Some combination of technology, business, and organization is always required to meet business goals. This is even truer with SOA. An SOA can enable an agile enterprise, where higher-level processes are quickly and inexpensively composed from an inventory of more fundamental business services. But alone, it is not enough. It must be accompanied by business design (i.e., a business model). The business model is critical to creating a set of services that can actually work together to provide higher-level value. You can implement an SOA without an overall business model, but you will end up with only a pile of incompatible services, rather than an inventory of services that lead to an agile, flexible enterprise.

The business principle behind SOA is to build up a collection of independent services that can be quickly and easily combined in a variety of ways into different, higher-level business services and business processes. Chapter 8 addresses service composition. This is what gives an enterprise the agility to offer new capabilities and respond to competitive pressures. Businesses want to use SOA to create value and help achieve a business strategy. Doing this, however, requires an understanding of what the strategy is and making sure that the right processes and services (building blocks) are being created to achieve that strategy.

The "LEGO" analogy is often used to describe the service-oriented enterprise. Imagine that the LEGO blocks represent different services. You can even think of the different sized and shaped blocks as different types of services in the enterprise. Using a combination of blocks, you can assemble many different things like houses, hotels, and garages. This is fine if you want to create buildings, but what if you want to assemble a car or a plane? Then, you need a set of LEGOs that includes wheels, nose cones, and so on. In other words, you need to plan ahead and know what kind of things you're trying to construct in order to have the necessary building blocks on hand. In business terms, you need to know what business you're in and where you're headed in order to have the right services in the inventory to meet business needs. The more you know about your strategy and requirements, the more capable you are of creating the right services to get you where you want to go.

Furthermore, it is not enough to simply have services; you need the right kind of service to meet your needs now and in the future. For example, a security service that provides authentication may be enough for a simple application, but it wouldn't suffice enterprise-wide. However, enterprise security services that provide authentication, authorization, security policy retrieval, security policy enforcement, security credential discovery, and auditing would work for all applications in the enterprise, including the small ones. In other words, you need to know enough about where your business is headed, and how services might be used in multiple environments, to accommodate present and future scenarios. Without this knowledge, many of the services that are built will be headed in the wrong direction, causing either unnecessary rework, or worse yet, replication of services and inconsistencies in business processing.

A business model is the place where you define these things. At a high level, the business architecture describes the goals and value chain of the enterprise and the processes required to support them. At a more detailed level, it describes the business services, workers, policies, rules, activities, and information necessary to implement the business processes. Enterprises that have taken the steps to create a business model will vouch for its value, and you won't find a really successful example of an SOA that doesn't include some form of business-driven planning. In summary, the business architecture defines the business processes that drive what capabilities and services are needed, and then BPM can be used to exploit these capabilities to create agile business solutions. The key is to not forget architecture and go directly from business processes to BPM solutions. Although this is not a book on business architecture, Chapter 4 addresses some of the important aspects of the business domain with respect to services.

EASY DOES IT

We've discussed the necessity of having a vision of the future enterprise needs, and creating the right kind of services. But don't confuse that for a waterfall approach. For SOA to work, you need to balance two different forces simultaneously. One is the need to think ahead, and the other is the need to

(continued)

EASY DOES IT *(continued)*

deliver things. Luckily, SOA supports both goals with an incremental approach. Let's look at the security service example again. Do you provide a simple service that only does authentication, or do you provide a more enterprise-strength service that supports authentication, policy, authorization, and auditing? The answer is yes. You do both. You plan for a service that will support the enterprise, but you implement only the authentication part first. However, because you have planned ahead, the structure of the service will enable it to be easily extended, and the authentication capabilities will naturally integrate with the policy, authorization, and auditing functions when you implement those features in future versions of the service.

SOA and Other Architectures

To put SOA into perspective, let's see how it compares to two other important and related architectural disciplines: Enterprise Architecture and software architecture.

Enterprise Architecture

Enterprise Architecture (EA) is another area of IT that is experiencing rapid adoption and development. EA is supported by a conceptual framework that subdivides the overall subject of Enterprise Architecture into manageable, digestible pieces. These divisions are called architectural perspectives, views, domains, or subarchitectures. Common approaches break EA into business architecture, information architecture, application architecture, and technology architecture. Let's use these same perspectives to look at SOA.

To achieve reuse of services by multiple business processes, the SOA must also describe how the different services fit together within the context of business processes. This requires a *business architecture* that defines the overall service landscape. The business model is often divided into service groups, and perhaps individual services within those groups. For each group, it defines the roles and responsibilities of the services or groups, their relationships to each other, and their place in the overall enterprise. Chapter 4 describes business architecture in more detail.

Services must also share a common set of semantics. This requires an enterprise *information architecture* that defines what information must be common and shared among services in order to use them together in a meaningful way. Chapter 5 describes the common information model in more detail.

In order to be able to use different services in different processes in a plug-and-play manner, the services need to have a similar structure, and the services must play relatively equivalent roles within the overall structure of solutions. This requires an *application architecture* that describes the structure of enterprise solutions, the architectural elements that make up that structure, the rules for using elements and the relationships among them, and the roles and responsibilities of the individual elements. This is covered in Chapter 9.

Finally, the *technical architecture* provides a detailed definition of the infrastructure for supporting services and SOA. In addition, the architecture defines what a service is and exactly how the service uses the SOA infrastructure.

Similar Structure Is No Coincidence

Both EA and SOA are concerned with an enterprise scope (or at least a scope beyond a single application) and with aligning IT systems to support business requirements, strategies, and processes. It's no coincidence that the architectural structure of SOA is similar to that of EA. Of course, EA includes all of the different architectures and application styles in an enterprise, not just SOA. But a successful SOA requires that the same set of EA concepts be incorporated into the architecture. Figure 2-3 extends the earlier version of SOA to illustrate this relationship.

On the right side of Figure 2-3 is a simplified version of Figure 2-2, providing a representation of the major components of SOA. On the left side of Figure 2-3 is a representation of the main perspectives of EA. The arrows show the following relationships between EA and SOA:

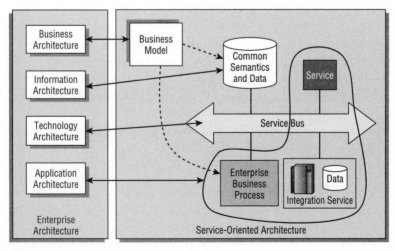

Figure 2-3 EA and SOA

- The business architecture includes the SOA business model and describes how the services and service groups defined by that model relate to and support business processes and the outcomes that tie them to business goals and strategy.

- The information architecture includes the SOA common semantics and describes what the common semantics are, how they are defined, and how they relate to other operational and analytic data.

- The technology architecture includes the SOA service bus and describes how the service infrastructure supports services, distribution, binding, security, performance, and so on, and how it integrates with the rest of the enterprise infrastructure.

- The application architecture includes all SOA-related solutions and describes how services are constructed, how existing applications are exposed as services, how business processes are composed from services, and how services support and relate to other applications styles such as portals, business-to-business (B2B) applications, and so on.

The similarities in composition suggest that SOA should be structured along the lines of EA. This does not mean that an organization has to have EA in order to be successful with SOA. But it does mean that if an organization does have EA, that EA should be integrated with and help formulate the SOA.

Software Architecture

Earlier, we defined software architecture as encompassing the significant decisions about the organization of a system, the structural elements that make up the system, the system composition from those elements, and how the systems are deployed to provide run-time capabilities. There are many different aspects to building software, and once again, architectural perspectives provide a mechanism for dividing the problem into individual concerns. The most common approach to software perspectives comes from the "4+1 Views," originally developed in 1987 by Phillipe Kruchen of Rational Software and now part of the Unified Process. Figure 2-4 shows an illustration of the views.

Each view represents a different set of important and related concepts that can be understood separately and that often have their own sets of expertise. This means that each view can be modeled (i.e., each view can be represented by a distinct set of models) and that these models can be assembled to create a complete system.

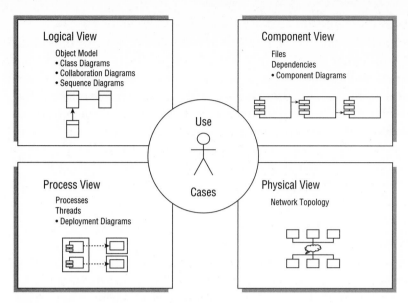

Figure 2-4 4 + 1 Software architectural views

Logical View

The logical view describes the problem from an abstract, platform, and technology-independent perspective. It is the one that most often comes to mind when you think of the ideas of "analysis," "design," or "modeling." The concepts in the logical view are expressed as a set of structural, behavioral, and information models. The logical view describes the software elements that meet the system's functional requirements. In SOA, you use the logical view to describe the design of individual services, their interfaces, and their operations.

Component View

Once the structural elements have been identified, you need to decide how to group or package them, and how different packages interact. This is the concern of the component view. In SOA, packages are often organized around services or service groups. Services are organized in a variety of ways, such as by their subject matter. For example, business and domain services deal with issues of the business, whereas foundation services deal with generic and reusable supporting subject matter such as authentication, authorization, and logging. The service inventory, introduced in Chapter 4, divides a system into its distinct subject areas. The component view also describes how different subject areas interact.

Process View

The process view describes the kinds of components — code and other executable artifacts — that need to be built in order to realize a system, and how those artifacts are assigned to executable processes. While the logical view is about the problem, the process view is about the implementation. But it is not an elaboration of the logical view; it is a completely independent (but related) view that describes a specific implementation. There can be more than one process view to support a given logical view. In SOA, the process view describes the executable artifacts needed to support services and how they are organized into processes. These implementation-specific aspects are not covered in this book.

Physical View

The physical view defines the different real and logical systems (machines, programs, network nodes, hosts, etc.) that compose and are necessary to realize a solution. In a very simple system, there may be only one machine containing the services, their logic, and their data.

More complex solutions will generally contain separate and redundant machines and nodes for the services, databases, existing systems, and so on. Additionally, the different services may be supported by different systems, and these systems may exist inside and outside corporate and divisional boundaries. In SOA, the physical view describes the configuration and systems that host the consumers and providers of services to meet specific nonfunctional and quality of service (QoS) requirements. Again, these implementation specific aspects are not covered in this book.

Use Case View

The use case (or scenario view) presents the system as the capabilities are envisioned by the end consumer. It models a system in terms of business scenarios, organized by use cases. This view is shown as overlapping the others, because the contents of these models generally incorporate elements of each other's views. For example, a use case contains not only the functional requirements (the logical view) but may also include utility-level issues such as authorization and logging, and nonfunctional requirements that lead to platform design decisions and system organization decisions. In addition, the use case view is what ties all of the other views together to provide traceability across the views in relation to specific use cases.

In SOA, the use case view describes use cases and scenarios. A single use case will often involve several different services, and a single service will often be used by many different use cases. Chapter 6 shows you how to look across multiple use cases to provide a broader perspective during service design.

A WORD ABOUT TECHNOLOGY INDEPENDENCE

Another important separation of concern (yes, there are many) is the difference between the logical design and the technology implementation. The concept of technology independence means that you want to completely design the logic of your system without introducing technology-specific details. Then, you make an explicit mapping step to translate the technology-independent logic to a technology-specific implementation.

For example, Web Services are a popular technology for the implementation of SOA solutions. But, Web Services are not required to implement SOA. So, at the analysis and design level (the logical view), you work with generic, technology-independent concepts such as services, interfaces, and documents rather than specific concepts such as WSDL and SOAP. Then, when you implement a service interface, you map it to WSDL (hopefully, with a nice tool).

But perhaps you say: "I've already selected Web Services, so why do I care?" A perfectly good question, with a perfectly good answer. Web Services are a rapidly evolving technology. Suppose that you design your service interfaces explicitly with WSDL v1.1. What happens when you need to upgrade to WSDL 2.0? You will have to change both your design and your implementation. The changes will be more or less extensive depending on the extent that you assumed WSDL v1.1 specifics in your design. If, however, your design follows good SOA architecture and design principles, independent of WSDL, and then your implementation process does a mapping to WSDL, the upgrade to WSDL 2.0 (or SOAP or UDDI or XSD) will not require any design changes. Experience has shown that platform-independent designs provide more flexibility, better extensibility, and better longevity, and can reduce the cost of upgrading by as much as 90%. We follow a platform-independent approach in this book.

EA, 4+1, and Services

Both EA and software architecture use the concepts of views. And, in fact the views have reasonable overlap. Primarily, the difference is a matter of scope and intent. EA is intended to span all the solutions and applications in an enterprise, and to tie business and IT concerns together. Software architecture is intended to describe the implementation of a single solution and to tie design to implementation to deployment.

The primary areas of overlap are in the application and technology views of EA. The EA application view describes how solutions are constructed of services and the types of services that exist. The 4+1 logical view describes the design of individual services, and the 4+1 component view describes the interaction between them. The EA technology view describes how solutions are implemented on specific technologies to provide commonality across technologies, implementations, and infrastructures. The 4+1 process and physical views show how service designs are implemented on specific technologies and deployed on specific infrastructures.

Conveniently, all of these different architectural concepts and techniques are consistent and complementary. Architecture uses a variety of approaches, concepts, techniques, and tools to solve any given problem. Good architecture ties all of these together according to fundamental principles and common underlying concepts and abstractions. So, let's get back to the important concepts of SOA.

What Is a Service?

The fundamental concept in SOA is a service, so what exactly is a service? We define a service as a discrete unit of business functionality that is made available through a service contract.

The service contract specifies all interactions between the service consumer and service provider. This includes:

- Service interface
- Interface documents
- Service policies
- Quality of service (QoS)
- Performance

One of the main differences between a service and other software constructs (such as components or objects) is that a service is explicitly managed. The QoS and performance are managed through a service level agreement (SLA). In addition, the entire service life cycle is managed — from design, to deployment, to enhancements, to maintenance.

Figure 2-5 shows the major parts of a service.

There are two main aspects to the service itself. In the diagram, the top part of the service is the service interface, and the bottom of the service is the service implementation. A service specifically separates the interface from the implementation.

The service interface specifies the service operations, that is, what the service does, the parameters that are passed into and out of the operation, and the protocols for how those capabilities are used and provided. A service typically contains several different, but related, operations. The service implementation is how the service provides the capabilities of its interface. The implementation may be based on existing applications, on orchestrating other services to combine their capabilities, on code written specifically for the service, or all of the above. What is important here is that consumers of the service should see only what the service does, not how it's implemented. The producer of a service is free to change the implementation of a service, as long as he or she doesn't change the interface or the behavior. For example, a new service might be completely based on existing functionality in a legacy application. Once the interface contract is finalized, consumers can start to use the service. In the meantime, the producer may create a new, modern implementation, and retire the old legacy application, which runs on a platform that is no longer supported. Users (consumers) of the service may never notice the difference as long as the behavior and contract do not change.

In other words, you can think of the service interface as the point through which consumers (with needs) interact with providers (with capabilities). The interface defines the style and details of the interactions. The implementation defines how a particular provider offers its capabilities. This concept of a *connection point* allows you to better factor decoupling into the design of your solutions.

There are also two different aspects to both the interface and the implementation. These are the functions that are performed and the information that they are performed on. In other words, a service is a combination of a set of functional service operations and the corresponding virtual business data that is passed into and out of the operations. Virtual business data is an abstraction of business entities (tied to an enterprise schema) that are independent of data storage or implementation. The service operation signature describes the parameters that are passed in and out of an operation. The information model (or enterprise schema) describes the structure and meaning of the virtual business data passed in and out.

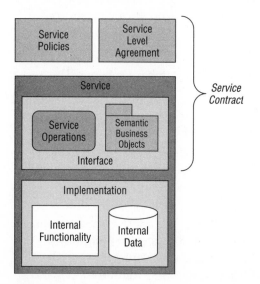

Figure 2-5 Components of a service

The distinction between the virtual information in the service interface and the logical and physical data in the service implementation is critical. At the service interface level, what is important is the information that must be passed between services to enable and complete the business process. This is information that must be agreed to and must be common to all the services that participate in the process. However, internally, many of these services have a different superset of the information, potentially in a different format. Luckily, you do not have to know or agree on all of the different details of the internal data models of all the services involved (which would be impractical if not impossible). Instead, the separation of the interface from the implementation (with regard to the information model) allows you to easily translate between the common (virtual) definition and the internal (physical) implementation.

A Word about Information Architecture

Now is a good time to clarify an important aspect of information architecture as it relates to services. You can describe the different types of information in terms of three layers: physical data (sources), domain (service) data, and semantic data. Physical data is the persistent enterprise data, usually preexisting. Domain data is the classes that encapsulate information needed to implement services. This uses the classic object/relational mapping. Semantic data is the information exchanged between service consumers and providers and is often a non-normalized view on domain data or data sources. The mappings between these three represent the mining of data for different purposes. The separation of concerns isolates the service consumers, service providers, and persistent sources to provide more reusable, maintainable, agile solutions.

Figure 2-6 shows these relationships among the various types of data.

- **Physical data** — This is the data that is actually stored on disk. The details of how it is stored are described in a database schema. The schema is optimized for the performance characteristics and requirements of the particular datastore.

- **Domain data** — This is the data that is used in the service implementation. It is described in a standard data model and describes all of the information that is used in the implementation of a service. It represents the private knowledge of the data. A subset of the data is the service's view of the common information. Service data is a view of the physical data and may come from one or more physical datastores.

- **Semantic data** — This is the data that describes the common understanding of business entities and information that must be shared between services. It is described in the shared information model and is closely aligned to the business model. It is used to describe information that is exchanged through service interfaces. Semantic data is a normalized view of the common data from all the different services.

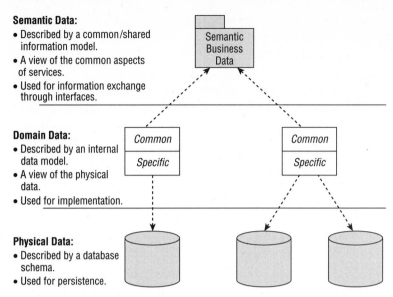

Semantic Data:
- Described by a common/shared information model.
- A view of the common aspects of services.
- Used for information exchange through interfaces.

Domain Data:
- Described by an internal data model.
- A view of the physical data.
- Used for implementation.

Physical Data:
- Described by a database schema.
- Used for persistence.

Figure 2-6 Types of information

The last important aspect of the service interface is the service level agreement. This specifies two important performance criteria about the service: the technical performance in terms of response time, throughput, availability, and reliability, and the business performance in terms of business units of work performed within a certain timeframe and to a specific quality level.

Chapter 5 deals with the design of the common semantics, and Chapter 6 addresses the design of the service interface.

Service Characteristics

In addition to the specific structure of a service shown in Figure 2-5, good services have the following specific characteristics:

- **Modularity and granularity** — In SOA, business processes are decomposed into modular services that are self-contained. Services themselves can be composed from other modular services, and can be mixed and matched as needed to create new composite services.

  Granularity is a quality of functional richness for a service — the more coarse-grained a service is, the richer or larger the function offered by the service. Coarse-grained services provide a greater level of functionality within a single service operation. This helps to reduce complexity and network overhead by reducing the steps necessary to fulfill a given business activity. Often this is accomplished by composing smaller tasks into a single coarse-grained operation. Fine-grained service operations provide the exchange of small amounts of information to complete a specific discrete task. An example of a coarse-grained service is one used to price an insurance quote. A fine-grained service (which would be used by the pricing service, among others) might return risk information based on the zip code of the applicant.

■ **Encapsulation** — Services exhibit a strict separation of the service interface (*what* a service does) from the service implementation (*how* it is done). Encapsulation hides the service's internal implementation details and data structures from the published interface operations and semantic model.

■ **Loose coupling** — Coupling describes the number of dependencies between a service consumer and provider. Loosely coupled services have few, well-known and -managed dependencies. Tightly coupled services have many known and, more importantly, unknown dependencies. The degree of coupling directly affects the flexibility and extensibility of a system. We discuss coupling in detail later in the chapter.

■ **Isolation of responsibilities** — Services are responsible for discrete tasks or the management of specific resources. A key characteristic of service design is the isolation of responsibility for specific functions or information into a single service. This provides one (and only one) place for each function to be performed, providing consistency and reducing redundancy.

■ **Autonomy** — Autonomy is the characteristic that allows services to be deployed, modified, and maintained independently from each other and the solutions that use them. An autonomous service's life cycle is independent of other services.

■ **Reuse** — Together, modularity, encapsulation, loose coupling, isolation of responsibilities, and autonomy enable services to be combined into multiple business processes or accessed by multiple service consumers from multiple locations and in multiple contexts. In other words, services are shared and reused as building blocks in the construction of processes or composite services.

■ **Dynamic discovery and binding** — Services can be discovered at design time through the use of a design-time service repository. Although it is theoretically possible to dynamically discover services at run time, we have yet to see this work in practice. See the sidebar "Dynamic Discovery and Binding."

However, service consumers can be dynamically bound to providers during run time. In this scenario, the consumer asks the registry for a specific service and is routed and bound dynamically to the appropriate service provider. The dynamic binding of a service consumer to the service provider enhances loose coupling and enables additional capabilities such as mediation.

- **Stateless** — Service operations are stateless. This means that they neither remember the last thing they were asked to do nor care what the next is. Services are not dependent on the context or state of other services — only on their functionality. Stateless services provide better flexibility, scalability, and reliability.

  Note that this is typically a design goal, but it isn't always practical (for long-running service interactions, for example).

- **Self-describing** — The service contract provides a complete description of the service interface, its operations, the input and output parameters, and schema. The contract may also contain pre- and postconditions and constraints about the operations.

- **Composable** — Services can be composed from other services and, in turn, can be combined with other services to compose new services or business processes.

- **Governed by policy** — Relationships between service consumers and providers (and between services and service domains) are governed by policies and service level agreements (SLAs). Policies describe how different consumers are allowed to interact with the service — in other words, what they are allowed to do.

- **Independent of location, language, and protocol** — Services are designed to be location-transparent and protocol/platform-independent. In other words, they are accessible to any authorized user, on any platform, from any location (within reason).

DYNAMIC DISCOVERY AND BINDING

One of the overpromised characteristics of services is the concept of dynamic discovery and binding. Let's take a look at each of these.

Dynamic discovery means that a consumer of a service can go to some central location to discover that a service exists and get all the information necessary to start using the service. This is a useful concept at development time. The story goes like this: You know that you need a service that does such and such, so you go some place and look for services that might do what you need. Once you find one, then you can figure out how to use it. In most enterprises, this is done through some combination of a service repository and word of mouth.

Now think of the way a computer program is structured. You know that you have to accomplish specific goals by doing certain things with certain information. So, your program goes about collecting the information and then applying the algorithms to it to achieve the desired result. But you don't write programs that don't know what they're trying to accomplish and that go out

(continued)

DYNAMIC DISCOVERY AND BINDING *(continued)*

looking for random functionality that they can somehow utilize to accomplish unknown goals. The idea that a program would dynamically discover services at run time, figure out how to use them, and reconstruct itself flies in the face of how you build, test, or deploy systems. Although it might be theoretically possible (only after the semantic web is a reality), we don't see it affecting enterprise SOA for a while.

Let's look at another touted aspect — *dynamic binding*. Here, the idea is that a program is going to read the description of a service interface and dynamically construct the request and response handling in order to use the service. If the user of the service is going to be a person interacting though a user interface, it would be possible to write a program that dynamically constructs a form to ask the user for the service's inputs, constructs and sends the requests, and then displays the results. However, if the user of a service is another program, which is often the case with SOA, then this doesn't make sense. If you're writing a program to use a service, then you need to know what parameters to pass to the service request and how to process the service response. Generally, you do not want or need this to be dynamic, nor can you justify the cost of writing a program smart enough to do it. So, while it is theoretically possible, and there may be a few examples where dynamic interface discovery makes sense, in our experience it is not practical. However, the other aspects of dynamic binding, and the dynamic connection of the consumer to the provider endpoint, are useful.

Service Granularity

Granularity describes the size of a service. This doesn't mean size in terms of kilobytes of code. It means the amount of business function that is performed in a single request/response exchange of messages.

One of the most common questions asked about SOA is: "How big should a service be?" We're often told that services should be coarse-grained, but of course it's not that simple. There is no, single, correct granularity for a service. Rather, the right granularity depends on a variety of factors such as: Who are the intended users of the service (partners, business processes, other services)? What are the topology and performance requirements (LAN, WAN, etc.)? What is the intended scope of the service?

In any complex system or environment, you should expect to see a wide range of service granularities. Figure 2-7 shows a hierarchy of the following service types and granularity:

- **Enterprise business processes** — These business processes span the entire enterprise and can make use of the underlying services.

- **Business services** — Business services are the most coarse-grained services. Business services expose high-level, composite business functions to the enterprise. The functions and information match closely to the semantics and syntax required of business processes. Data integration services at this level support the consolidated data required by enterprise processes. Business services can be either of the following:

  - **Line-of-business services** — Specific LOB functionality that is exposed externally to the rest of the enterprise

  - **Common business services** — Allow all applications to share basic business functionality and exhibit common behavior (e.g., Structured Information Management)

- **Domain services** — Domain services are medium-grained. They provide business-related services that are specific to a business domain and are used by many different business services in that domain (e.g., membership validation) but may not be exposed outside of the domain.

- **Utility services** — Utility services are the least coarse-grained. They provide lower-level services that provide common functionality across the enterprise (e.g., address book or part number validation).

- **Integration services** — These expose existing applications as services for use by the rest of the enterprise, and provide consistent consolidated access to enterprise data that is spread across many different data sources. The granularity of integration services will be partially dependent on the existing systems that they expose. Integration services typically involve a transformation between the enterprise model and application model, both at a functional and informational level.

- **External services** — These provide access to systems and applications provided by suppliers or partners external to the enterprise (e.g., credit card validation or shipment tracking). The granularity of external services will depend on the particular service provider. Although traditionally these were relatively fine-grained, new software-as-a-service providers are creating a wide variety of services in all areas.

- **Foundation services** — These provide fine-grained capabilities that are used in the construction of higher-level services, independent of any business domain (e.g., security, logging, and orchestration). These are the capabilities traditionally called services that supported infrastructures such as CORBA or COM. Unfortunately, we can't just stop calling them services, but we do need to distinguish between them and the business-related services listed here. These are sometimes also called technical or infrastructure services.

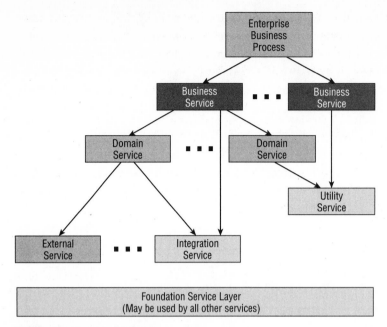

Figure 2-7 Service hierarchy

Let's look at an example. Suppose that you want to create a new business process to provide quotes for automobile insurance policies. The steps involved in the quoting process are to collect information, validate the request, underwrite the request, price the policy, create the quote, and send it to the customer. These major steps, or tasks of the business process, are implemented by business services. Figure 2-8 shows a modified service hierarchy specifically to illustrate this business process.

In order to establish a price, the insurance company needs to:

- Determine the driver's history with the state motor vehicle department
- Determine the driver's history with the independent insurance bureau
- Determine the risk associated with the driver's residence location
- Determine the make and model of the vehicle
- Use the existing pricing application that is running on the company's mainframe

The company has implemented a "driver history" service within the automobile LOB. This domain service uses two external services: one from the department of motor vehicles to get the driver license record and one from the insurance bureau to get a driver claim history. The company has also implemented a VIN (vehicle identification number) domain service to get make and model information. Both of these services are medium-sized and generally useful within the Auto line-of-business (LOB). A Location utility service is used to get information related to the driver's residence. This service takes the postal code as input and returns risk information. This is a small, discrete function that is useful across the entire enterprise. Finally, the company has written a Pricing integration service as a wrapper around its existing mainframe pricing transaction.

The Pricing business service acts as a coordinator for all the rest of the services. When its pricing operation is called by the business process, the pricing operation in turn calls operations on each of the other services (namely Driver History, VIN, and Location), collates the returned information, calls the Pricing integration service, formats the response, and passes it back to the business process, which moves on to next step in the process, the Quoting Service.

One of the ways to determine how big a service should be is to say that a service's modularity should correspond to the expectations of the service's user. For example, we described the relationship between business processes and business services by saying that a process is decomposed into tasks, and the tasks are implemented by operations of business services. So, the correct granularity of a business service corresponds to the size of a task within a business process. Likewise, you build larger services by assembling smaller ones together. Similar to how a business process can be thought of as an assembly of business services, a business service can be constructed by combining other small and medium-sized services. So, the correct granularity of a domain service is the normal decomposition of a business service, and so on. Obviously, this is not a specific measurement, but a rough guideline.

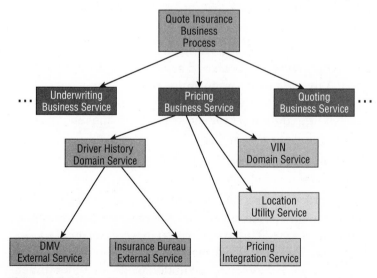

Figure 2-8 Service hierarchy example

Service Dimensions

As the previous discussion suggests, size is not the only important and distinguishing characteristic that determines how a service is used. Figure 2-9 shows four dimensions of a service: Scope, Ownership, Granularity, and Construction. Every service has some aspect of each dimension.

- **Scope** — Scope defines the organizational boundaries that a service is expected to operate in. For example, a service with an enterprise scope is expected to be used by processes or other services across the entire enterprise (i.e., other LOBs). At the opposite end of the scale is a service that is used by only a single application or organizational group. "So, who cares?" you might ask. Shouldn't all services be available across the entire enterprise? It turns out that there is a direct correlation between the scope of a service and the responsibilities and costs of managing, maintaining, and enhancing it. On a simple level, this seems fairly obvious. The larger the user base, the more the support costs. So, for practical reasons, you may want to limit the scope of services in order to limit the liability of particular service providers and encourage participation in the overall enterprise SOA.

- **Ownership** — Ownership defines the organizational unit that is responsible for support of a service. In an SOA, this extends well beyond simple maintenance and operations to the overall life cycle of the service. Some of the thorny ownership questions are: How are the different requests for new enhancements managed and prioritized across the many different users? How many versions of the service will be supported simultaneously? What kind of backward compatibility will be required? How long will previous versions be supported?

  A common organizational approach is to have a central service group that is responsible for ownership of shared services across the enterprise. In addition, each LOB (or smaller organizational unit) may have some services that they individually own. Any of the possible combinations of ownership and scope could exist for services within a given organization.

  Note that services are often used to cross ownership boundaries and establish value exchange across corporations.

- **Granularity** — Granularity describes the size of a service in terms of the amount of business function that is performed in a single request/response exchange of messages. This was covered extensively in the previous section. Note that a service designer runs into the issue of granularity very quickly (well before he or she understands the other dimensions), which is why it is usually the first question asked about services.

■ **Construction** — Construction refers to how the service has been implemented. For example, it may be implemented directly as code such as a small granularity service or it may be composed of other services such as a business service. But there are also some other very different options that warrant careful consideration. The service may essentially be a service wrapper around some existing function or data in a legacy or COTS application. We call this an integration service. Or, the service may be provided (as is) by a business partner, such as the ability to locate a shipment with FedEx based on its tracking number. We call this an external service.

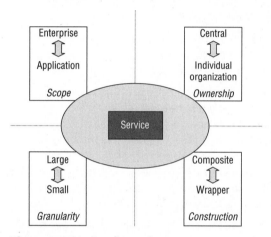

Figure 2-9 Service dimensions

It turns out to be important to differentiate integration and external services from other services. The tools and techniques that you use to construct integration services are sufficiently different that you need to treat their creation differently. External services require a different mechanism for discovery. Once you find them, however, you have no control or influence over them. Another important distinction occurs in the use of the service. Both integration and external services generally require translation between the semantics and syntax of their interfaces and that of the enterprise business processes they will support.

SERVICE DEFINITIONS

Keep the following service definitions in mind:

◆ **Service** — A specific style used to provide functionality based on a service contract. The interaction of the services is specified in the service

(continued)

SERVICE DEFINITIONS *(continued)*

interface. The service acts as a connection for consumers who need to inter-act with providers with specific capabilities. Normally, a service is further characterized by loose coupling and offers a process-centric rather than data-centric interaction style.

◆ **Interface** — An interface defines the interaction with a service. It groups related capabilities via a set of related operations. The interface defines the inputs and outputs of the service operations and any preconditions, postconditions, and constraints of those operations. The interface may be specified in terms of an interface definition language (such as WSDL or COM IDL), or as an interface class (as in Java).

◆ **Process** — A business process is a set of coordinated tasks and activities that lead to accomplishing a specific organizational goal. In terms of SOA, a process can be used to coordinate business services.

◆ **Granularity** — Refers to the size or amount of functionality in a given inter-action. For example, a very fine-grained interaction would be to set or get a single attribute value of an object. A very coarse-grained interaction would be to get all of the values of a collection of objects in a single interaction. These are examples of interface granularity. Granularity also refers to the value of a given interaction. For example, Add Member is a higher-grained service than Validate Address. The appropriate granularity of a service and interface is based on the intended usage and applies to the type of service.

◆ **Composite service** — A service with an implementation that is a composite of other services.

◆ **Atomic service** — A service with an implementation that does not require or use any other services. This is the lowest level of service composition.

◆ **Foundation service** — A foundation service is a utility that aids in the con-struction of other services, such as a business rules engine, data-routing service, or workflow system. These services do not provide any specific business functionality but instead provide higher-level technical capabil-ities for the construction of services. (The terms infrastructure service and foundation service are used synonymously.)

◆ **Business service** — A business service is a specific kind of service that offers a higher granularity of business value (such as Evaluate Escrow, or Recalculate Payments). It is typically composed of several lower-level or finer-grained services.

◆ **Domain service** — A domain service is a lower-level service that provides business functionality within a specific business domain. It provides impor-tant, shared capabilities within a domain, but it is not intended to be exposed outside of the domain. For example, validating the correctness of payee data is a function (service) that is shared by several different aspects of claims processing but is not intended to be used by other domains. Domain services provide common functionality that is used in the composition of business services.

◆ **Utility service** — Utility services are the smallest, or least coarse-grained. They provide lower-level services that provide common functionality across the enterprise (e.g., address book functionality or part number validation).

◆ **Integration service** — An integration service exposes existing applications as services for use by the rest of the enterprise, and provides consistent consolidated access to enterprise data that is spread across many different data sources. The granularity of integration services will be partially dependent on the existing systems that they expose. Integration services typically involve transformation between the enterprise model and application model.

◆ **External service** — An external service provides access to systems and applications provided by suppliers or partners external to the enterprise (e.g., credit card validation or shipment tracking). The granularity of external services will depend on the particular service provider. Although traditionally these were relatively fine-grained, new software-as-a-service providers are creating a wide variety of services in all areas.

◆ **Enterprise business process** — An enterprise business process is a specific kind of business process that spans business domains within (or outside) the enterprise.

◆ **Workflow** — Workflow is a style of computing in which a process is decomposed into a series of steps, activities, conditions, and the like. Work activities flow from one step to the next based on conditional evaluation. Workflow is typically executed by a workflow management system that supports developing workflows, dispatching work to queues, process management, and so on. Frequently, workflow systems include activities that are carried out by humans, where the work items are placed in a person's inbox and completed items are placed in his or her outbox.

◆ **Orchestration** — Orchestration is a specific type of workflow that is generally applied to the construction of business processes from business services or of composite services from smaller services, and does not include human-performed activities. Orchestration often includes a conductor or controller that is managing, controlling, or directing the interaction between other parts so that they do not have direct dependencies on each other.

(continued)

SERVICE DEFINITIONS *(continued)*

◆ **Business Process Management (BPM)** — Wikipedia defines this as "an emerging field of knowledge and research at the intersection between management and information technology, encompassing methods, techniques and tools to design, enact, control, and analyze operational business processes involving humans, organizations, applications, documents and other sources of information." You can think of it as a type of process construction that emphasizes the management of business processes in addition to the technology of orchestration. A key function of BPM systems is monitoring to ensure processes are meeting the intended business objectives. In addition, they may include auditing, reporting, and other functions.

◆ **Business Process Model** — A model used to define the execution and composition of higher-level processes from lower-level services. Process models are executed by orchestration or BPM tools. Both business services and enterprise business processes can be defined by Business Process Models.

Loose Coupling Is King

A principle characteristic of a service is *loose coupling*. Coupling refers to the extent of dependency between modules, components, or services consumers and providers. Loosely coupled services (it's actually the consumer and provider that are loosely coupled) have few well-known dependencies, whereas tightly coupled services have many known and, more importantly, unknown dependencies. A system's degree of coupling directly affects its overall flexibility. The more tightly coupled a system, the more a change in one service will require changes in other services or service consumers.

There are many dimensions to coupling. In distributed systems, traditionally coupling was thought of with respect to time, and discussion about it was framed in terms of synchronous versus asynchronous communications mechanisms. However, in service-based systems, the more important dimension of coupling is the ≪used≫ and ≪used by≫ relationship between consumers (those with needs, who use capabilities) and providers (those with capabilities that are used by consumers).

SOA is about organizing functional capabilities into services and limiting the coupling between consumers and providers to specific service interfaces. That way, changes to a function only effect the consumers connected to the service providing that function. All other consumers who are interacting with the same provider, but through different service interfaces, are unaffected.

Object-based analysis and design are concerned with low coupling and high cohesion. In other words, you want to design the responsibility of a class or subsystem so that it's as independent as possible from other classes (low coupling), giving it the highest potential for reuse in multiple scenarios. At the same time, however, you want to group related responsibilities in the same class (high cohesion) to centralize related business rules and access to common data, and to minimize unnecessary messaging or interactions.

These principles of coupling and cohesion apply to services, but a service-oriented architecture takes loose coupling much further. This is important for several reasons. In an enterprise, the producer and consumer of services are frequently decoupled in terms of organization, schedules, and priorities. In other words, the application that is consuming a service has a different life cycle than the service itself. What happens when the group that develops and maintains the service decides to upgrade? One option is to demand that consumers of the service upgrade at the same time. Although that may sound reasonable to some (producers mostly), it is not reasonable to service consumers. The ultimate result of such a policy is that other groups will not use the service and instead will develop something themselves that they have control over. If service providers want to promote use of their services, they must understand that the users of the service will be different organizational units, with different schedules, priorities, and business drivers. Given this, it is important to enable the independent evolution of both the service consumer and provider (for example, loose coupling). This is done through a variety of techniques, technologies, and policies.

In an SOA, you want to achieve loose coupling in terms of the following:

- Location transparency
- Interface and implementation
- Data
- Versioning
- Interoperability and platform independence
- Usage, assumptions, and knowledge

These are discussed in the following sections.

Location Transparency

Location transparency relieves the service consumer of the need to know anything about the location of the service. Instead, the consumer goes to a well-known service registry to dynamically look up location information. The service registry (as an intermediary) can provide many other important system attributes in terms of availability and performance. For example, a load-balancing mechanism can be used to distribute requests across multiple service instances for increased availability. New service instances can be added to increase throughput without any change (or knowledge) to the client. Service locations can be moved as systems are migrated, or for redundancy and failover purposes.

Location transparency is not new. It has been used since the early implementations of DCE (Distributed Computing Environment, from the Open Software Foundation) in the mid-1980s. However, SOA extends the service directory (the fundamental building block of location transparency) to a service registry, where not only the location of the service is determined, but also the service interface contract. A service consumer can locate an appropriate service at run time by providing a set of selection criteria to the registry. The registry will then return a pointer to the most appropriate service based on both the consumer's and system's criteria. The use of the registry in enterprise solutions is discussed in Chapter 9.

Interface and Implementation

Another fundamental concept of distributed applications is the decoupling of the interface from the implementation (also known as encapsulation in object-based systems, or information hiding in data systems). This allows a service implementation to change (such as changing internal data representation, or migrating from a legacy system to a new implementation) without requiring changes of the service consumers. SOA reduces coupling and dependency between service providers and consumers by ensuring that the interface contract is their only means of interaction. Chapter 6 describes loose coupling in service interface design.

Data

You can also think of decoupling in terms of the definition of data. The concept of information hiding directs you to define a public view of the data (the semantic data) and then map it to the internal view (the domain data) or implementation. A service should never expose its internal data structures. Even the smallest amount of internal information that is exposed outside the service will result in unnecessary dependencies. Only the information available in the semantic model is exposed through the interface. In the service implementation, that information is transformed between the semantic information model and the internal schema to isolate the two. In other words, the internal data definitions are mapped into the semantics of the external contract. The contract depends only on the service's problem domain, not on the internal implementation details.

This allows the internal view to evolve without affecting clients, and prevents clients from making assumptions about the implementation. Chapter 7 describes the transformation between semantic and domain data in the service implementation.

Versioning

Services will inevitably evolve to meet new requirements. However, as services are used beyond organizational or enterprise boundaries, the producer of a service cannot control when the consumer of a service will update his or her implementation. Additionally, as more and more consumers come to depend on a specific service, it becomes more difficult logistically to manage a forced version migration. At a business level, if the service consumers cannot maintain control of their own application life cycle and release schedules, they are unlikely to make use of that service. An SOA must take these issues into account through a combination of infrastructure, interface design, data definition, dynamic binding, and versioning policy. For example, the infrastructure for the service definition, lookup, and invocation must support version numbers and multiple simultaneous versions.

Service providers must conform to a versioning policy. A typical policy would describe two classes of upgrade: minor enhancements and major enhancements. Minor enhancements are bug fixes and other small changes that do not change behavior or interfaces (although they may enhance capabilities in simple ways). Major enhancements change interfaces and/or behavior. A typical policy would require backward compatibility between minor version updates. In addition, it would require two major versions to be supported continuously, or a minimum period (1 to 2 years) for a previous version to be supported. Versioning is discussed in more detail in Chapter 9.

Interoperability and Platform Independence

The requirement for services to support multiple consumers has implications in terms of communications, interoperability, and platform independence. You cannot assume that all of the consumers of a service will be using the same platform. This is especially true for large enterprises or consumers that are outside the enterprise boundaries. Therefore, you need a communications mechanism that is compatible across platforms. This allows any client to be able to access a service, and gives service providers flexibility in terms of platform implementation. (For example, because of acquisition, they may need to implement services now on an existing platform, while planning to migrate to the different, enterprise-standard platform over time.)

Web Services can help provide this interoperability, but it is not so simple. As mentioned earlier, Web Services are rapidly evolving. Consumers and providers should maintain as much independence from specific mechanisms as possible (see the sidebar "A Word about Technology Independence"). As an alternative, interface compatibility can be defined based on conforming operation signatures rather than type compatibility.

Usage, Assumptions, and Knowledge

SOA is a loosely coupled system of services and service consumers. At design time, loose coupling requires that services be designed with little or no assumptions or knowledge of any particular service consumer. The service implementation should make no assumptions as to the purpose, or technical or business characteristics, of the service consumer. A fundamental quality of a service is its ability to be reused in new or different contexts.

Common Service Patterns

They say "Parts is parts," but not all parts are the same and not all services are created equal. Given the wide range of values across the different dimensions mentioned so far, there could be a staggeringly complex variety of services. But it turns out that we can simplify things considerably by describing a set of common service types to be used in service design and then mapping those types to their specific values across the service dimensions at implementation. It also turns out that these common service types correspond to patterns of services commonly seen in successful SOA applications. A hierarchy of common service types was previously shown in Figure 2-7. Let's take a further look at the business service and business process.

Figure 2-10, which represents a business service, illustrates these concepts. The higher-level business service is constructed of lower-level, domain, utility, and foundation services. Orchestration is used to define how these different services are combined to form the business service. The business service is exposed by the service interface.

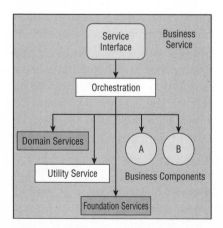

Figure 2-10 Construction of business services

As an example, a business service to determine insurance claim eligibility would first use foundation services to verify that the consumer has the authority to execute the service. Next, it would use domain services to perform claim format validation and utility services to validate addresses. Finally, it would use custom business logic (business components) or rules to determine whether the claim is within the coverage of the member's policy.

Of course, SOA frequently has a larger scope than a single business service. It may also have an LOB or enterprise scope that defines how business processes can be constructed at the enterprise level, combining capabilities from multiple LOBs. Figure 2-11 illustrates how an enterprise business process is constructed from business services, as well as from services offered by packaged applications, legacy systems, or COTS applications. In the latter two cases, the systems do not already conveniently provide their functionality as services, so they are wrapped by an integration service. But notice that the business process accesses the integration service through a business service. This is an important constraint of the architecture. The architecture, design, and implementation of integration services is covered in Chapter 10. A business process management system is used to define the sequence and interaction (orchestration) of the composed services.

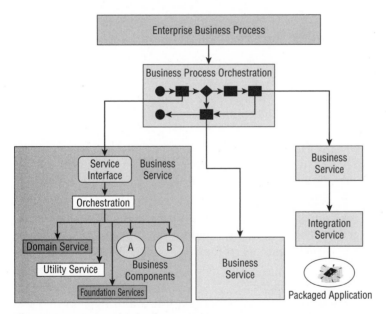

Figure 2-11 Enterprise business process

So let's look at the business service in more detail in the context of business processes and service dimensions.

- The scope of the business service must be sufficient to support the scope of the business process, which is typically at an LOB or enterprise level.

- The ownership of the business service must support the business process and the required cooperation among organizations or units. The right model for ownership will depend on the organization, politics, funding, trust, and so on of a particular enterprise. What is important here is that for the business process to use and depend on a business service, some trusted organization must own the service and must provide a level of guarantee to the business process owner.

- The granularity of the business service should match well to the granularity of function that is performed in a typical activity within the business process. This is generally a large or medium service.

- The construction of a business service is based on the composition of other services. Some benefits of this approach are that it allows the large granularity of business services to be created by combining smaller units; it allows business functions of limited scope to be exposed beyond that scope in an indirect, limited, and controlled fashion; and it allows the semantic and functional mismatch of business processes and existing systems to be bridged.

Service Types and Purpose

Another important consideration is separate from the size, scope, ownership, or construction of a service. That is the intended purpose of the service. To understand these different service types, you can apply the architectural principle of separation of concern. Designers have long applied the separation of data from logic as an important concept in constructing applications. This not only provides the opportunity for decoupling the different concerns but also allows for specialized environments in which to implement them.

BPM is an example of separating the workflow or schema of a business process from the rest of the logic so that the workflow can be executed and managed in a specialized environment, and so that the business can rapidly respond to changes by quickly modeling new processes. SOA facilitates this by providing business services as the basic building block of business processes.

Similarly, Business Rules Management (BRM) is an example of separating business rules or decisions from the rest of the application logic so that the rules can be executed and managed in a specialized environment and can easily be changed to support new business requirements. Again, SOA facilitates this by providing services that expose business rules and decisions (see Figure 2-12).

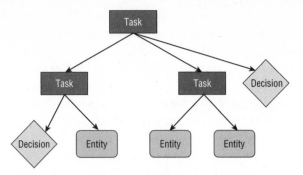

Figure 2-12 Service usage and dependency pattern

Typically, you construct the service layers with three broad categories of service:

- **Task services** — Services that implement a business function, such as a service that calculates the price of an insurance quote or validates the format of an address. Task services come in all different sizes, ranging from discrete utility services to large business services. Smaller services tend to be more general in purpose and provide a higher potential for reuse. Business services are often large compositions of smaller services and may be designed to support one or more specific process. As such, they have less potential for broad reuse across processes (but this is okay, because they have been composed from other reusable parts).

- **Entity services** — Services that primarily manage access to business entities. Examples of business entities are customers, policies, claims, and so on. They correspond to major business information concepts. Entities are usually medium to large in size. Entities tend to be independent of any particular business process and instead are part of multiple different business processes. Entity services provide a high level of potential for reuse. Note that we are talking about business entities here, not low-level data schema elements.

   In general, task services are active and do something to deliver value. Entity services support task services by adapting and providing information needed to implement the tasks. Care must be taken when designing entity services to avoid exposing internal data rather than business semantics.

- **Decision services** — Services that execute business rules to provide business decisions. An example of a decision service is Approve Creditworthiness. Decision services generally provide yes/no answers to complex questions, or support frequently changing externalized rules such as tax regulations. Decision services are usually composed into other services and are small to medium in size.

You combine these different service types to provide flexible business capabilities that support the activities of a business process. Best practices provide a variety of patterns, techniques, and tools for service composition that help you reduce dependencies, limit coupling, and maximize flexibility. Figure 2-12 provides a high-level illustration of a typical pattern designed to reduce dependency and increase reuse of entity services. The pattern shows a task-level process service orchestrating the combination of multiple processes. Each lower process provides access to one or more entity services. A process service might also make use of a decision service as part of its composition. However, an entity service is prohibited from directly invoking another entity service.

Figure 2-13 expands the service layer of Figure 2-1 to include these additional concepts. As before, the tasks of the business processes are implemented by services (most often task-focused services). High-level, task-focused business services are composed of other, smaller services. Now, you can create new and different compositions of services using the richer set of process, entity, and decision service types. In this way, you can combine the benefits of flexible, changeable rules with the benefits of modularity, flexibility, and reuse promised by SOA.

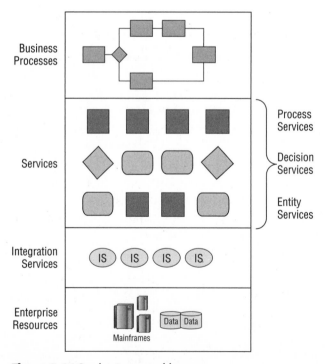

Figure 2-13 Service types and layers

SOA Reference Architecture

In Chapter 1, we described the requirements of SOA and introduced its reference architecture. Throughout this chapter, we have described the overall architecture of SOA. The reference architecture is the formal representation of these concepts.

The term reference architecture has as many different meanings as it has uses and thus can be a great source of confusion. Wikipedia says, "A reference architecture provides a proven template solution for an architecture for a particular domain. It also provides a common vocabulary with which to discuss implementations, often with the aim to stress commonality."

SOA reference architecture goes beyond this definition to support the following goals:

- Provide a common language for services and SOA
- Provide consistency of implementation, business purpose, and semantics across services
- Provide an architectural-based design methodology
- Support SOA governance
- Support EA
- Define how the reference architecture is used

Figure 2-14 illustrates the conceptual contents of the SOA reference architecture, including:

- **Service Metamodel** — This defines the concepts, characteristics, and details of a service and how services relate to other parts of the architecture. Specifically, this defines the service types (business, domain, utility, integration, external, and foundation), the service dimensions, and how these concepts are represented and manifest themselves in a service definition.
- **EA Perspectives** — Comprise the following standard EA domains:
  - **Business Metamodel** — This defines the concepts used to describe the business architecture. Defines the relationship of traditional business architecture concepts (strategy, goals, outcomes, organization, value chain, contexts, and processes) to service-oriented systems.
  - **Information Metamodel** — This defines the concepts used to characterize the information architecture such as semantic, domain, and physical data. It defines the relationship between traditional information architecture concepts and service-oriented systems.

- **Application Metamodel** — This defines the concepts used to characterize the application architecture. It defines the relationship between traditional application architecture concepts and service-oriented systems. For example, it describes how services are used in an *n*-tier architecture.

- **Technology Metamodel** — This defines the concepts used to characterize the technical architecture. It defines the relationship between technical architecture concepts and service-oriented systems. For example, how specific platforms and networks support service SLAs for quality of service.

- **MBD Perspectives** — These support model-based development approaches with specific profiles. MBD profiles are related to architectural metamodels, but provide a mechanism to embed the metamodel into a standard modeling and generation tool.

  - **Business Profile** — This defines the concepts used to describe the business problem in nontechnical terms. Furthermore, it defines the relationships among concepts, rules, and constraints.

  - **Application Profile** — This defines the logical structure of applications, typically in terms of layers, tiers, and architectural elements. It defines where and how services fit into the overall application structure.

  - **Platform Profiles** — A platform profile defines the details of the technology platform that will be used for implementation. There will typically be multiple different platform metamodels to support different technologies, such as .NET, Java, ESB, and so on.

  - **Transformations** — This defines how concepts in one model are transformed into concepts in another model and the traceability between model elements.

- **Process Metamodel** — This defines a process for the design and implementation of services, starting at the business level, moving through service design, to platform-specific implementation. It defines the overall workflow, the goals and concerns of each step in the process, the inputs, the metamodel elements involved in each step, the work products produced, and the metrics.

- **Governance Metamodel** — This defines the fundamental concepts of governance, what metamodel elements they apply to, relationships and constraints, and the interaction of governance with the rest of the reference architecture at design and run time.

- **Architectural Relationships Model** — This defines the relationships among all the different aspects of the reference architecture, and the relationships with other common architectural frameworks such as EA and software architecture.

- **Architectural Usage Model** — This describes how to use the reference architecture.

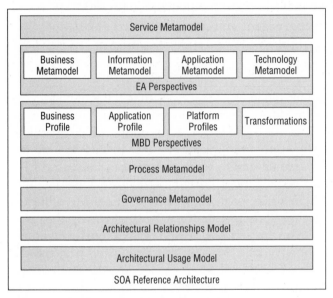

Figure 2-14 Reference architecture for SOA

This may seem like a lot, but all of these issues need to be addressed at one time or another in the development of enterprise SOA solutions. The reference architecture provides a mechanism for making sure that they all work together and support the overall goals of the organization, rather than working at cross-purposes. In addition, the architecture optimizes the relationships among the different aspects so that the right questions are answered at the appropriate times in the development cycle, by the appropriate roles.

Summary

Service-Oriented Architecture (SOA) is an approach to building systems that focuses on constructing applications from a combination of business and other services. This approach provides the potential to create agile enterprises that have maximum flexibility and minimum reaction time. In order to build up the inventory of services necessary to reach this level of flexibility, the SOA must enable the independent construction of services. However, although the services need to be developed independently in response to specific business requirements, they cannot be developed in a vacuum. They must be developed within the context and shared semantics of the enterprise.

In addition, care must be taken to limit the coupling between services or even well-designed, business-driven services will not provide the expected flexibility. Thus, you can think about SOA as defining:

- The capabilities necessary to meet business needs
- How those capabilities are organized (into interfaces)
- What participants provide and consume the capabilities
- How the consumers and providers connect via interfaces

As more and more solutions make use of services, managing dependencies between consumers and providers becomes a major concern. Therefore, one of the fundamental principles of SOA is loose coupling, which manifests itself in many forms, including the communications mechanism, separation of implementation and interface, data design, and versioning.

Achieving these difficult goals cannot be left to chance. A well-defined architecture provides the guidance, principles, and practices for achieving enterprise, business, and technical requirements. At the enterprise level, SOA corresponds to the principles and practices of EA. At the design level, understanding the relationship of BPM and SOA and applying the principles of cohesion and coupling lead to reusable, flexible services. At the implementation level, software architecture allows you to provide technology-independent designs and then to map them to specific technologies and configurations.

The remainder of the book is about applying the architecture to the analysis, design, and implementation of services and service-based solutions. In the next chapter, we provide an overview of the process that is elaborated on throughout the book.

CHAPTER 3

Getting Started with SOA

The secret of getting ahead is getting started. The secret of getting started is breaking your complex overwhelming tasks into small manageable tasks, and then starting on the first one.

— Mark Twain

We defined SOA as an architectural style promoting the concept of business-aligned enterprise services as the fundamental unit of designing, building, and composing enterprise business solutions. So how do you go about designing and building solutions and the services that support them? This chapter covers the role of the SOA methodology in the creation of enterprise SOA solutions and the methodology's major steps. For each step, a high level overview of its goals, requirements, and activities is provided.

The details of these steps are the topic of the rest of the book. In general, each major step in service design is covered in a chapter later on. Specifically, in this chapter, we cover:

- An overview of SOA methodology
- Defining the reference architecture
- Defining the business architecture
- Information design
- Identifying services
- Specifying services

- Implementing services
- Service design process

Finally, we end with some practical suggestions for getting started.

Overview of SOA Implementation Methodology

Enterprise SOA defines a set of business-aligned IT services (available to participants throughout the enterprise across multiple lines of business or even outside of the enterprise) that collectively address an organization's business processes and goals. These services can be combined in a variety of different ways to support enterprise business processes and business solutions. By ensuring that there is a business focus of its main constituents (business services and business processes), the SOA architectural style promotes alignment of business requirements and technology solutions. Both processes and services are driven by the business architecture and can be traced back to the business outcomes that they help to realize. The major forces shaping the SOA architecture and its major elements are shown in Figure 3-1 and discussed in the following list:

- The forces that drive the business and SOA — the enterprise business drivers — are at the top. These are things like strategy, competition, market forces, regulatory forces, and so on. They all combine to drive the business architecture (model) and to shape the measurement and feedback for enterprise-wide performance management.

- The business model is the representation of the business resources and processes that are required to meet enterprise operational, tactical, and strategic business goals. Having a business model is critical to the successful alignment of services with business goals and objectives, and consequently to the overall SOA implementation's success.

- The semantic information model defines the common business information for a given enterprise (such as customer, agreement, etc.). These objects effectively create an ontology of the enterprise data by defining common concepts (and their content) that describe the operations of the enterprise. Using the semantic information model to define business service interfaces leads to the creation of semantically interoperable services — a semantic SOA.

- Other aspects that enable SOA to provide value are: key performance indicators (KPIs) and portfolio rationalization. The KPIs enable quantitative assessment of the impact of SOA and allow business processes and services to be measured and optimized. Portfolio rationalization enables

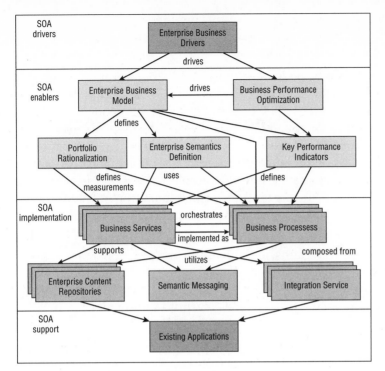

Figure 3-1 Major elements of enterprise SOA

the enterprise to simplify and consolidate infrastructure, applications, and data, where SOA plays a leading role in the implementation of the consolidation activities.

■ In terms of implementation, the primary aspects are business processes and services. The business processes orchestrate the execution of business services to implement enterprise capabilities as specified in the business model — for example, order processing or claims processing. Business processes are usually associated with operational objectives and business goals (such as insurance claims processing or engineering development processing) in the form of specific outcomes that can be measured against KPIs. These KPIs are collected as part of the process implementation and are usually used to evaluate organizational performance.

■ The services implement specific enterprise business functions and access the business data and resources. Well-defined, business-aligned services are a critical ingredient of a flexible, extensible enterprise SOA implementation. The structure of services allows them to be independently developed and deployed. Correctly defining and aligning services with the business and semantic models results in plug-and-play implementations that can effectively be combined into different enterprise-wide business processes and/or solutions.

▪ Information represents the data resources of the organization. Data resides in a variety of different stores, applications, and formats. Different levels of data are used by different levels of SOA constructs. The semantic information model defines the data for business processes and services. The information passed in business processes in the form of documents is based on the semantic information model. The documents provide a form of semantic message between processes and services. The SOA defines the mechanisms for transforming data from its native operational format to the semantic data required for the business processes.

▪ Documents can represent legal entities (such as financial documents, insurance policies and claims, and government regulations) that define the obligations of the enterprise and its partners. Documents are a vital part of modern enterprises and have to be included in the SOA implementations (along with the rest of the enterprise information) as first-class citizens.

▪ Information from existing systems and applications is made available to processes and services through a data virtualization layer.

▪ Functions from existing systems and applications are made available to services through integration services that expose the existing functionality through new service interfaces.

The effective implementation of service-oriented solutions is a complex undertaking that must take all of these different aspects into account. This requires cooperation among many groups within an enterprise, including management, business leaders, architecture, development organization, operations, and so forth. At an enterprise level, this would not be possible without a well-defined methodology, describing the major steps and work products, and the roles and responsibilities of each participating group. In the remainder of this chapter, we lay out a high-level methodology for enterprise SOA solutions. This methodology is shown in Figure 3-2.

The methodology consists of the following major activities:

▪ **SOA reference architecture** — Define the important aspects of the SOA reference architecture, in particular what a service is, the types of services and their relationships, design and implementation concepts and processes, and relationships to other architectures and communications.

▪ **Business architecture definition** — The first step is to define the enterprise business architecture. This influences the processes, services, information, and enterprise solutions that will be built.

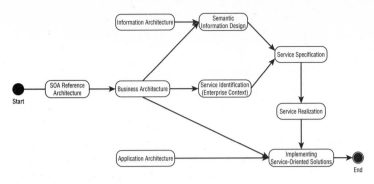

Figure 3-2 SOA methodology

- **Service identification** — Define a set of services within the enterprise context that supports the business architecture. The overall set of services makes up the service inventory.

- **Semantic information model definition** — Create an enterprise information model that defines the shared semantics of processes and services. This activity is often done in parallel with service identification. Note that the semantic model is influenced both by the business architecture and by the information architecture.

- **Service specification** — Create service contracts that can be used at design time for the selection of appropriate services in solutions. The service specification includes the service interface as well as other usage and dependency information.

- **Service realization** — Design and implement services.

- **Implementation of service-oriented solutions** — Build enterprise solutions from services. Also notice that the service-oriented solutions are influenced by the application architecture. It is important to note that this is not a linear, waterfall process. You do not need to have a complete business architecture or a completely specified service inventory before you can start designing and implementing services. The process is iterative and incremental. You start by creating a high-level business architecture and service inventory. Then you go about implementing the first set of services to support specific business goals. As you learn from this process, you update your SOA architecture, business architecture, service inventory, standards, governance, and the like. Then, you start building your next set of services.

Also notice that the structure of this book mirrors this process:

- The SOA reference architecture is covered in Chapter 2.

- Business architecture is covered in Chapter 4.

- Service identification is covered in Chapters 4 and 5.
- The semantic information model is covered in Chapter 5.
- Service specification and interface design are covered in Chapter 6.
- Service realization is covered in Chapters 7 and 8. Chapter 7 describes service implementation design, and Chapter 8 covers service composition.
- Service-oriented solutions are covered in chapters 9–12. Chapter 9 covers the overall issues and architecture related to enterprise solutions. Chapter 10 covers integration. Chapter 11 is on security, and Chapter 12 is on governance.

SOA Reference Architecture

One of the first things that needs to be done before embarking on enterprise SOA solutions is to initiate the SOA reference architecture as described in Chapter 2 and detailed in Figure 2-14. In reality, it takes some time to complete the reference architecture (if architecture is ever really finished). That is to be expected. It is not important to have everything worked out before you start or to have complete models, documentations, standards, and governance in place before allowing the first service to be designed and built. But, it is important to have an idea of what you're doing. It is important to have a high-level vision of the architecture and the context that the architecture provides in terms of the service hierarchy, service inventory, and semantic information model, before you create very many services.

We recommend creating what we call a minimum architecture. The minimum architecture determines the few things that absolutely must be standardized in order to meet the enterprise goals and clearly specifies them. Then, it puts an architectural vision in place for how the rest of the architecture might be defined, and a process for continual, incremental enhancement and improvement of the architecture. For enterprise SOA, those crucial things are the service definitions, service inventory, and semantic information model. We provided our vision of the SOA reference architecture in the previous chapter. It is based on our extensive experience with proven implementations, and we encourage you to adopt it. It is up to you to define the inventory and information models for your particular business, but we do explain the techniques for creating them.

In the next few sections, we describe a sample architectural roadmap. Your particular roadmap depends on your own requirements and circumstances, but this example illustrates the basic concepts and contents of a roadmap for an SOA architecture.

Minimum Architecture

The minimum architecture should specify:

- **What a service is** — The types and granularities of services. For example, business, domain, utility, integration, external, and foundation services.

- **Required interfaces and functions** — Interfaces or other functions that services are required to use or support. For example, all services must support the management interface and use the logging service.

- **Technical infrastructure** — What technology services use to communicate. For example, Web Services conforming to the WS-I Basic Profile v1.1 and Security Profile v1.0.

- **High-level semantic information model** — Identify the major enterprise business entities and documents. What information do they need in common to meet enterprise goals? What information needs to be shared between services? For example, a consolidated customer entity supports the business goal of having a single customer view. The high-level model should identify 20–40 business entities and documents.

- **Initial service inventory** — Identify the major service groups and services needed to support enterprise goals and processes. Determine an organizational structure (such as line-of-business or functional domain). Integrate appropriate industry standards or patterns. The initial inventory should identify 30–50 services and service groups.

- **High-level business model** — Identify the major enterprise business processes and the common processes that occur across enterprise domains. Identify the underlying capabilities needed to support those processes. The high-level business model should identify 10–20 major processes and 20–40 capabilities.

- **Service identification, specification, and design process** — This describes how the architecture and enterprise context fit into and support the development process.

- **Architecture life cycle process** — This is a feedback mechanism for the constant updating and enhancement of the architecture.

- **Roadmap** — The roadmap addresses at least two areas. The first is a rough priority order of service implementation based on dependencies, commonality, and usefulness. This doesn't specify a timeline, nor take into account other business drivers, but it provides an initial vision for building out the service inventory. The second is a high-level plan for building out the architecture.

The minimum architecture should take between 4 and 8 weeks to produce, depending on the size and complexity of the enterprise, and the experience, capability and number of architects.

9-Month Checkpoint

Once the architectural vision (minimum architecture) is in place, you can start to implement services and use them in enterprise solutions. Often, this begins with a small-scale or pilot project to really figure out how to do it, and then expand from there. The architecture and process needs to be updated based on the knowledge gained from this process. After 6–9 months, the following additional architecture aspects should have been developed:

- **Governance** — Processes for design-time and deploy-time governance are put in place.
- **Metrics** — Measurements to demonstrate the usage and value of SOA are defined. Implementation of metrics is started.
- **Services metamodel** — A formalized service definition is created in the form of a metamodel.
- **Integration services** — Patterns and techniques for how to implement integration services are in place.
- **Updated business and information models** — The models are updated to include prior implementations.
- **Updated service inventory and roadmap** — The service inventory and roadmap are updated to include existing services and to factor in new business models and other forces.

18-Month Checkpoint

Typically around the next checkpoint, the architecture and the organization are ready for a larger-scale rollout of SOA. For this to be effective, the architecture and processes need to be complete and clear enough for a broader audience of developers. At this point, the following aspects should have been introduced:

- **Updated architecture** — The architecture is updated based on past experience and projects. It is also documented more completely.
- **Formalized process** — Governance and development processes are enhanced, formalized, documented, and measured.
- **Design-time repository** — A design-time repository is introduced and integrated with the service inventory.
- **Versioning** — Versioning policies, procedures, and infrastructure are in place.

- **BPM** — Business processes are constructed using services to implement process tasks. The rules and constraints are clearly defined.

- **SaaS** — Services provided by external vendors or software-as-a-service providers make up a portion of the overall service inventory. Integration techniques, rules, and constraints are clearly defined.

- **Reporting** — Information from metrics is collected and reported on. Process and architectural improvements can be identified and measured. The SOA's value can be measured and demonstrated.

- **Integration with enterprise architecture** — SOA and EA activities are well coordinated.

- **Updated business and information models** — The models are updated to include prior implementations.

- **Updated service inventory and roadmap** — The service inventory and roadmap are updated to include existing services and to factor in new business models and other forces.

Long Term

Long term, there are many things you can do to continue to enhance the value of the architecture and improve organizational effectiveness and business agility. These are the more advanced aspects of the reference architecture. The ability to implement them and benefit from them depends on the maturity and capability of business and IT. Many organizations do not get as far as this with their architecture program, but we have seen the benefits of these activities when they are implemented and believe it is important to at least mention the possibilities:

- **Model-based development (MBD)** — Integrate the architecture into a model-based development process and tool.

- **Formal metamodels and perspectives** — Formalize the architecture in terms of metamodels and perspectives that support both MBD and EA.

- **Tool and framework integration** — Create tools and frameworks to automate compliance and implementation.

Business Architecture

The foundation of a business-aligned SOA implementation is an enterprise business model, containing the primary representation of the resources (business, IT, data, etc.) and processes involved in meeting the enterprise's operational, tactical, and strategic business goals. Business architecture (BA) is an essential component of a successful service-oriented implementation, providing consistency and flexibility of services across the enterprise.

We go into some length to define business architecture in the next chapter, so we're not going to try to define it here. Instead, we'll describe what aspects of BA we're concerned with when implementing an SOA or enterprise solution. BA must answer the following questions:

- What business are you in?
- What are the goals and objectives of this particular business?
- What outcomes are needed to achieve those goals?
- What is the strategy for achieving them?
- How will they be measured?
- What capabilities and information are needed to achieve those outcomes?
- What processes, services, entities, and rules are needed to implement those capabilities?
- What existing applications provide basic capabilities and information?
- How are the applications, processes, and so on, aligned with the business strategies and goals?

All very good questions. Business architecture helps you to understand and answer these questions, and it describes how to provide traceability, from the operational concepts of processes and services, through to the concepts of tactics and objectives, all the way up to business goals and strategy.

Business Processes

Business tactics and objectives are typically defined for particular business processes. A *business process* is a group of logically related (and typically sequenced) activities that use the resources of the organization to provide defined results. Business processes deliver value in the form of products or services, often to an external party such as a customer or partner.

In order to accommodate the needs of both executive management and business process owners, business processes are typically defined at two levels of detail: "One model, for the executives, contains a set of high-level business scenarios that show the intent and purpose of the organization. The other model, for the business process owners, contains a detailed set of use cases that define how the organization needs to function internally. For each high-level business scenario, you could define one, or several, detailed business use cases representing the same activities in the organization. . . ."

(IBM's Rational Unified Process [RUP] for SOMA). This kind of analysis can be thought of as a type of process decomposition.

The high-level scenarios are the high-level descriptions of what business systems do. This level of processes defines only the highest-level enterprise scenarios and is rarely detailed beyond the narrative. Processes, such as Order to Payment, fit this level. These descriptions typically serve as the input (starting point) for process decomposition. Such decomposition defines business processes (sometimes called level 2 processes), which are the foundation of the enterprise business model. Receive Purchase Order is an example of a process that supports the order to payment scenario. Level 2 processes are also a foundation for the definition of the process activities (steps that make up the processes), which are used for definition of the high-level business services. For example, the Receive Purchase Order process might be composed of Purchase Order, Customer, Inventory, Credit Checking, and other business services. In other words, business process decomposition provides three levels of hierarchy — top-level scenarios, made up of (level 2) processes, composed from business services.

The goal of SOA is to expose an organization's computing assets as reusable business services, implementing basic business capabilities, which can be (re)used and integrated more readily using business processes. The relationship between business services and business processes (shown in Figure 3-3) paves the way to a truly flexible enterprise:

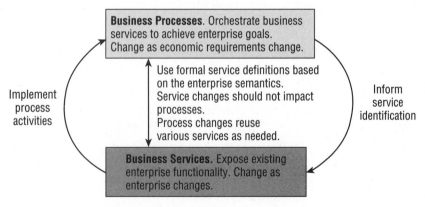

Figure 3-3 Relationship between business services and processes in SOA

- Business services support stable business artifacts, incorporating processing and rules whose interfaces change fairly rarely. (Note though that the service implementations can and typically do change frequently.)
- Business processes support fairly fluid business procedures and rules, which can change every few months or even weeks.

- The interaction between business processes and business services is based on the enterprise semantics, which minimizes the impact of service changes on the business processes and simplifies building processes from business services.

This separation of responsibilities enables business analysts and IT architects to reuse IT capabilities, encapsulated in business services, through the composition of business processes. This simplifies the creation of new processes and optimization of the existing ones. More importantly, once designed, processes can be quickly modified in response to market conditions. All this translates into increased business flexibility and competitiveness, while reducing the incremental costs of making frequent process changes.

Information Design

The next step in the process definition is creation of the enterprise semantics (semantic information model) — a definition of the standard business entities for the enterprise; for example, insurance policy, claim, and so on. A common semantic definition ensures that:

- Each term throughout the enterprise has a clear and concise definition.
- All enterprise terms are used consistently (mean the same thing and use the same definitions) throughout the enterprise.
- Each term is used in at least one process/activity definition.
- Only terms defined in the enterprise semantic information model are used by process/activity definitions.

The semantic information model is influenced by both the business architecture and the information architecture. The business architecture identifies the processes required to support the business goals and objectives. The semantic information model defines the information, concepts, and meanings that must be common throughout those processes to effectively pass information between the process steps. This corresponds to the information architecture concepts of semantic data as illustrated in Figure 2-6.

The semantic data is not the same as the domain data. It does not define all of the details of the information needed within each step of a process. Rather, it defines the information that must be common between then. Each individual process's step (implemented by a business service) provides any transformation required between the semantic information model and its own internal domain model.

NOTE In this context, objects and entities refer to business "things." We are using these terms without the connotations associated with object-oriented or entity-relationship modeling. In other words, business semantics described here are used only as a foundation for service interactions (messaging model), not for service implementation.

Although the semantic information model seems similar to a standardized enterprise data model, the two are radically different and should not be confused with each other. The semantic information model defines the messages exchanged by services. The messages implement interservice communication. Thus, they are transient and do not reside in a data store (at least not explicitly). In contrast, the enterprise data model defines the data structure and the relationships between data in the database. Because in practice implementation of the SOA involves service enabling of existing enterprise applications, changing the underlying data model is an extremely expensive proposition that often requires the complete rewriting of applications. In other words, it's probably not happening, so a system that provides interoperability without changing existing models is going to be better.

An SOA implemented, based on the semantic information model, provides a semantically interoperable SOA. Such an implementation offers enhanced interoperability between services. At the interface level, all of them work with the same objects. In effect, this eliminates the need for message transformations between services. Because service interfaces are created according to the standard enterprise semantic information model, it is guaranteed that every service can understand and correctly interpret any message, regardless of who the service consumer is.

THE FUTURE OF THE SEMANTIC INTERFACES

The introduction of semantic data for service contracts also allows for rethinking the design of service interfaces. It is no longer necessary to send specific request/response message pairs between the consumer and provider for each service operation. Because the interface data models for all services are driven by the same semantics, it is possible to introduce the notion of passing the service execution context around as part of the service invocation "thread." In this case, the service interface operations are massively polymorphic and expressed as:

```
Service.method (XML context in, XML context out)
```

The context in this case is a service execution context, expressed as an XML document supporting enterprise semantics. In this implementation, any particular service can extract data that it is interested in from the context.

This solution reverses responsibilities: Instead of the service consumer building a specific interface for a participating service, the service itself is

(continued)

THE FUTURE OF THE SEMANTIC INTERFACES *(continued)*

responsible for accessing the required information from the execution context and updating the context with the results of its execution. Such an approach minimizes the impact of service interface changes, as long as the required puts data is available in the execution context. This approach, of course, puts an additional burden on the service implementations, but it may be negligible compared to the expenses of realigning of the service consumers with the services interface changes.

This approach, however, can lead to significant control and data coupling between consumers and providers where the semantics of the service are hidden in the interpretation of data. This can make services more difficult to reuse, compromises encapsulation, and can make change management more difficult. (A provider interprets the data differently, changing the service, and consumers don't see this as a change in the service interface.)

There are plenty of industry (and cross-industry) consortiums today, defining data semantics for a particular industry, such as ACORD for insurance, or HL7 for healthcare. Their semantic dictionaries (if they exist) should be considered a starting point for the creation of enterprise semantic information models.

Service Identification

One of the most important tasks during implementation of a solution based on service-oriented principles is the proper definition of business services, based on the decomposition of the problem domain (see the sidebar "SOA and Decomposition").

SOA AND DECOMPOSITION

Decomposition is a well-known (and widely adopted) technique for dealing with complexity. The first software decomposition approach (introduced in the early 1960s) was splitting applications into separate jobs, each implemented by a separate program. Later, as more insight into program internals was gained, each program itself was split into modules or subroutines, according to its various functions.

The object-oriented (OO) paradigm introduced by Simula and Smalltalk in the 1970s strengthened the adoption of decomposition by introducing objects: modules of code, each of which implemented a model of a real thing. The idea was to represent in software the "things of the problem domain," for example customer, order, or trade. However the abstractions provided by objects turned out to be too fine-grained and intertwined with technical concepts to have a meaning on the business level. For various reasons, many object-oriented developers wound up spending most of their time dealing with technical constructs such as collections, graphical widgets, and so on. As a result, in most cases the objects of the problem domain disappeared inside amorphous modules, which no longer represented anything recognizable by domain experts. An additional problem with OO was the fact that although objects are an important decomposition approach during design and implementation time, they are not visible at either deployment or run times and consequently do not directly support either deployment- or run-time decomposition.

In the continued search for a better design paradigm, a different approach to decomposition was introduced in the late 1990s — components. The idea was to fix the problems of object orientation by raising the level of abstraction, increasing granularity, and creating a tighter linkage with the business "things."

Introduction of software components improved the creation of flexible, better structured, and more manageable software applications. Part of the improvement came from removing the object-reference-based coupling that was common in distributed object systems (there's that loose coupling thing again). However it did not solve the main enterprise IT problem: its application-centric nature. Both objects and components provide better design and development approaches for individual applications.

SOA brings decomposition to a higher level, as shown in the following figure. Instead of attempting to decompose applications, it decomposes the entire enterprise IT functionality.

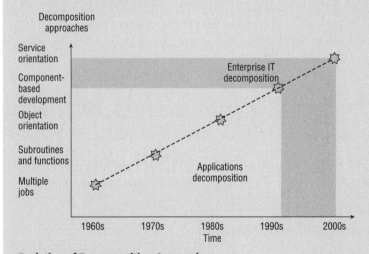

Evolution of Decomposition Approaches

It seems like the simplest approach to decomposition (and consequently service definition), is to directly expose the existing application's functionality as a set of services (decomposition based on the existing application portfolio) — similar to the traditional enterprise application integration (EAI) practice. Unfortunately, such an approach rarely works. It "is in essence technology first approach and is a recipe for disaster and/or serious over-engineering" (Gary Booch, "SOA Best Practices," Software architecture, software engineering, and Renaissance Jazz blog [March 11, 2006]). A better decomposition approach is based on the decomposition of the enterprise-wide business model: designing a set of services that define the enterprise architecture blueprint supporting the current business goals of the enterprise and providing capabilities for future changes. It requires you "to start with the scenarios/business needs, play those out against the existing/new systems, zero in on the points of tangency, and there plant a flag for harvesting a meaningful service" (ibid.).

Such an approach leads to the creation of a set of business-aligned IT services (available to participants throughout the enterprise across multiple lines-of-business or even outside of the enterprise) that collectively fulfill an organization's business processes and goals. The resulting business services are independent from the current enterprise application portfolio and support the "ideal" enterprise architecture.

Hierarchical decomposition, based on the enterprise business model is typically not sufficient for proper service identification. Although it provides an alignment between business and IT, it does not guarantee that resulting services will adhere to the basic service tenets. The service characteristics defined in Chapter 2 need to be considered in the design process.

But still this is not enough. The services need to be defined within the context of the overall enterprise. To do this, you need two things. First, you need to think about the way you design systems and decomposition differently. To overuse a phrase, you need a paradigm shift in design practice. Then, to support the new paradigm, you need an easy way to find the existing services.

For example, a typical approach to SOA design might incorporate this sequence:

- For each business domain, identify and analyze the processes.
- Break the processes down into tasks that are implemented by services.
- Look for existing services that perform the specified tasks.
- Use existing services when possible.
- Design and implement new services.

This probably seems like a pretty reasonable approach, but let's look at an SOA-focused sequence and compare:

- For each business domain, identify and analyze the processes.
- Understand what services currently exist (or are planned) and their responsibilities.
- Use existing services to frame the design, and break the process down into tasks that are implemented by services.
- Use existing services when possible.
- Design and implement new services where necessary.

The difference comes at the breakdown of processes into tasks and services. The difference may seem subtle, but the effect is huge. In the first approach, you are free to come up with almost any reasonable sequence of tasks to implement your process. There could be dozens of possibilities. Then, you look for existing services that do things your way, but probably don't find very many. Instead, you implement new services, but ones that overlap with existing services. In the SOA approach, you factor in the existing services first and then design around them. They provide a design constraint that limits the possible solutions to a few, instead of dozens. Now, when you use existing services, they've already been designed in, and they work with your new solutions and support your enterprise. Instead of promoting new services, you facilitated reusing existing ones.

The crux is this. You are not designing a solution or process from scratch. Instead, you are starting with an existing base and building your solution on top of it. You are extending and reusing, adding value to what exists, not duplicating responsibilities and adding inconsistencies. But to make this work, you need to be able to find the existing services. This requires an easy way to search for and find services at design time, and an organization of services that makes it easy to understand the overall set of services. We call the overall set of services the *service inventory*.

The service inventory lays out the overall set of services and their relationships to each other and the overall enterprise goals. You can think of the service inventory as a *responsibility map* of service interfaces. It should clearly describe the overall set of services, and what responsibilities the different service groups perform, and don't perform. The service inventory helps you in two important service design activities.

First, the inventory allows you to quickly scan the overall set of services at a high level and then to dig deeper into groups of services within a given area. This helps you to locate the services to support your look-first, design-later approach.

But at least as important, the inventory helps you to make decisions about what functions to include within your service implementations, and what functions you should expect to be performed by another service. If you need to implement a new service, you have to make sure that it doesn't duplicate functions that are already (or plan to be) implemented by other services. This is where the responsibility map aspect of the inventory is important. It must clearly define the boundaries of responsibility for services and service groups.

Service Specification

Once services and their corresponding semantic models are identified, they need to be described (specified) correctly. The complexity of proper service specification stems from the fact that there are two very distinct groups of service users that require information about services: business users (business analysts), who need to decide whether a particular service can be used in the solution that they are designing, and technical users (developers), who need to know how to write the code, invoking a particular service.

Business users need to understand what a service does in business terms, which requires answers to the following questions:

- What does the service provide for prospective clients? This includes a description of what is accomplished by the service, limitations on service applicability and quality of service (QoS), and requirements that the service requester must satisfy to use the service successfully.

- How is the service used? This includes a detailed definition of the content of service requests and responses, the conditions under which particular outcomes occur, and, when necessary, a step-by-step description of processes leading to those outcomes.

Technical users need to know how to implement service operations that require answering the following questions:

- How to interact with services? This specifies a communication protocol, message formats, including serialization techniques and service locations, for example, the service endpoint URL.

- What are the service invocation policies? This defines specific requirements for service invocation, for example, security requirements, required SOAP headers, and so on.

- What are service QoS guarantees? This specifies the quality-of-service characteristics that the service provides, including response time, throughput, availability, planned maintenance, and the like.

CURRENT PRACTICES FOR SERVICE SPECIFICATIONS

The notion of the service specification is widely recognized as one of the prerequisites for successful service usage. The problem is usually not the fact that a specification does not exist, but rather what the specification contains. Based on experience with object-oriented and component-based development, many architects and developers consider the service interface to be equivalent to the service contract. In the best cases, the service interface is supplemented by a free-form text document that captures some additional service information. Although this approach can significantly help, free-form documents are imprecise, hard to validate for completeness, and virtually impossible to process automatically.

For example, the popular web site `www.webservicex.net` provides a LloydsRiskCodeService service1 with the following contract:

Textual description of the functionality — "This service returns Lloyds risk code details for a given risk code or description."

Textual definition — "The following operations are supported:

- `GetLloydsRiskCodeDetailsByRiskCode` — This method returns Lloyds Risk Code details for a given risk code.

- `GetLloydsRiskCodeDetailByRiskCodeDescription` — This method returns Lloyds Risk Code details for a given risk code description."

The formal definition is in the form of the service WSDL and sample XML payloads (not shown here for brevity).

At first glance, the information seems sufficient to successfully use the service. However, let's take a closer look at how this contract can be used by different people.

On the business side, in order to decide whether the service is appropriate for solving a problem, the following questions must be answered:

◆ **What functionality does the service provide?** In our example, the information is supposed to be provided by the textual description of the functionality, but unless the user is acquainted with risk codes' definitions (`www.lloyds.com/Lloyds_Market/Tools_and_reference/Risk_codes.htm`) and can figure out which ones are really supported by the service, he or she can't decide whether it is appropriate.

◆ **What are the limitations of the service?** The textual definition does not provide any information about this. Examination of the service WSDL answers this question to some degree, but it's rare that business users ever look at it.

◆ **Which SLAs does the service support?** This is not specified in the service definition.

(continued)

CURRENT PRACTICES FOR SERVICE SPECIFICATIONS (continued)

♦ What are the requirements that the service requester must satisfy to invoke the service successfully? The service definition does not specify any requirements on the input parameters.

♦ What are the detailed definitions of the content of service requests and responses? Some of this information is provided by the formal definition in the form of WSDL and XML samples. This definition assumes that the business analyst can understand XML, and that WSDL correctly represents the data semantics.

Similarly, on the technical side, the following questions must be answered:

♦ What are the communication protocols, message formats, including serialization techniques, and service location? This information is provided by the formal definition in the WSDL.

♦ What are the errors that service invocation can produce? This information is provided by the formal definition in the WSDL.

♦ What are the service invocation policies such as security requirements, required SOAP headers, and so on? Some of this information (SOAP headers) is provided by the formal definition in the WSDL. Other characteristics such as invocation policies theoretically could be added to WSDL, but they rarely are.

♦ Which SLAs does the service support? This is not specified in the definition above.

So, you can see from this example (which is comparatively good) that much information needs to be provided in security specifications.

The service specification should define all of the relevant aspects of a service required by potential service consumers, including the *service expectations*, *interaction model*, *service constraints*, and the *service location*.

Service Expectations

The expectations define the result desired by the consumer who is using the service. This is also known as the real-world effect of using a service. For example, invoking the claims-processing service allows customers to get insurance payments. When potential customers invoke the service, they are not interested in a response indicating that their insurance company has merely recorded an application. Rather, they are interested in whether it will reimburse their losses.

Of course, the service provides encapsulation: The insurance company's internal systems record the claim without exposing this fact to the consumer. However, minimizing the client's assumptions about how the insurance company processes their claim increases the potential for smooth interaction.

Expectations associated with a service interaction are usually described in terms of the message traffic exchanged with the service. In some sense, similar to a service interface, it is possible to define expectations in terms of the kind of information that is provided by a service, as opposed to the information that is required for a current interaction.

Interaction Model

The interaction model defines the interaction between service consumer and provider through the service interface. Three key concepts are important in understanding what it is involved in interacting with services: information model, process model, and execution context.

- The information model defines the information that is exchanged with service consumers. This model should conform to the enterprise semantic information model. The scope of the information model includes the message semantics and their format (encoding). The message format defines the structure of the messages used for service invocation and response.

- The process (behavioral) model of the service defines the actions that consumers can execute on a service, the responses to these actions, and temporal dependencies between them. Temporal dependencies are mostly applicable to a conversational composite service, where interactions between the service consumer and provider can involve multiple service invocations.

- The service execution model defines the behavior resulting from interactions with the service. Some of this behavior can be private, and some public. The publicly visible portion of the service behavior is defined by the service execution model. The private behavior should never be made visible to service consumers.

Service Constraints

Service constraints describe rules, limitations, and facts about a service and its operations. Service constraints are usually expressed as policies. A policy is a statement of the obligations, constraints, or other conditions that either define service characteristics or have to be fulfilled by service consumers when invoking the service. There are two major types of policies that can be defined for a service:

- **Business-oriented policies such as hours of operation, return policies, and so on** — Business-oriented policies usually apply to the service operations, regardless of where and how these operations are deployed. For example, in order to invoke the claim processing service, a consumer must have a valid insurance policy.

■ **Infrastructure-oriented policies such as security, privacy, manageability, performance, and the like** — These policies are defined for a particular service endpoint address. This means that there can be multiple service deployments, adhering to different infrastructure policies. For example, an appraisal service can be exposed through two different URIs. One guarantees a two-business-day appraisal response time, while the second guarantees fulfillment in five business days. Typically, the service provider charges differently for using these different endpoints.

Service Location

Invocation of a service requires its location, that is, the endpoint address. The same service can have several endpoint addresses. Multiple endpoint addresses may be employed for several reasons. As in the dual-URI appraisal service example, each endpoint address could support different policies. Often, multiple endpoint addresses are also required for different service methods. For example, withdrawal and inquiry methods on a bank account service expose completely different QoS requirements. On the one hand, the withdrawal operation requires guaranteed (once and only once) service delivery, reliability, and transactionality. These involve fairly expensive infrastructure support. On the other hand, the inquiry operation has less strict requirements. In case of failure, its execution can be retried. Since the frequency of inquiry is, on average, 5–10 times higher than that of withdrawal, it is not cost-effective to use the same expensive infrastructure for both methods. Such situations require that the service specification support different endpoint addresses for different service methods. Additionally multiple endpoint addresses can be used to support multiple versions and different infrastructure constraints that a given service can have.

To summarize, a service specification should provide information about the service's behavior, interface, and policies. This information covers service expectations, the interaction model, service constraints, and the service location. It provides the basis for implementing service consumers, as well as for dynamically binding consumers to the service provider(s).

Services Realization

Once services are identified and their specifications are created, it is necessary to decide on the service realization. SOA solutions provide several options for realizing (implementing) services.

■ **Buy** — Purchase a complete implementation of a service that may be deployed and hosted internally.

- **Outsource (rent)** — Use a service provided by an external vendor. As Web Services and business-to-business integration become more prevalent, this option will be considered by more enterprises.

- **Build** — Provide an internal implementation of a service. With a build decision, there are multiple options:

  - **New implementation** — An implementation of a service is created from scratch. Of course, the new service can be a composition of other existing services. Not all of it is necessarily from scratch.

  - **Integrate or wrap legacy applications (systems) to expose the required service functionality** — This approach uses the existing capabilities directly but exposes them through new service interfaces.

  - **Modernization** — the repurposing of existing applications. This uses a combination of techniques. One common technique for services is business rules/processes extraction to pull out a segment of capability so that it can be used independently and exposed as a service.

Buying Services

Buying services might seem very similar to traditional buying decisions for software, but there is a big difference. Unlike a stand-alone application, a service has to fit seamlessly into the enterprise service infrastructure, which means that it has to support the following:

- Functional alignment with the overall business model, service decomposition, and service inventory.

- Usage of the enterprise semantic information model for service interface definitions.

- Support for the enterprise service infrastructure, including security, logging, exception handling, and so on.

These requirements are rarely met unless a service is custom designed and built for a given enterprise. As a result, services themselves are rarely bought. A more common scenario is buying packaged applications that provide the required capabilities and then doing an in-house service-wrapping implementation, exposing it as an integration service.

Outsourcing Services

Outsourcing assumes that an enterprise wants to concentrate only on the core business capabilities, while outsourcing (partially) other business functions. Such an approach allows the enterprise to focus its energy, money, and people on only the areas that are critical for a particular business or provide competitive advantage.

Outsourced services, or on-demand services, also called software as a service (SaaS), is an application delivery model in which a service provider hosts and operates a software application for use by its customers over the Internet. Customers use the application through an API accessible over the web. On-demand services provide a low-cost way for businesses to obtain the same benefits of commercially licensed software without the associated complexity and costs of development, ownership, or operations. The key characteristics of on-demand services include:

- Designed for use by customers through the Internet
- Hosted off-premises, not on the customer's premises
- Governed by a service contract

The service contract consists of a publicly availably interface, API, and a run-time service policy, which may include an SLA. At a basic level, the on-demand service is a software construct that happens to be hosted off-premise and that encapsulates a unit of work, which is made available through a service contract. Like any business contract, there is someone who provides the service and someone who consumes the service, only here, the provider and consumer are computer systems accessible over the Internet. The service has a public view, which is available to the consumer of the service via the contract, and a private implementation view, which is available only to the service provider.

When it comes to incorporating outsourced services, the range of issues is very similar to the issues an enterprise has to deal with when buying a service — the service has to seamlessly fit into the enterprise service infrastructure, which means it has to support functional alignment with the overall business model and support enterprise semantics. However, since the service is hosted off-site, there are a different set of issue concerning the enterprise service infrastructure, including security, logging, exception handling, and the like. Figure 3-4 shows two common approaches to incorporating SaaS into an overall SOA.

The first approach (left) uses the on-demand service directly. In this case, the interface API and semantic model defined by the service provider are used directly by the enterprise. The ability of an enterprise to use this approach depends on a variety of factors, including the flexibility and customization of the service (particularly its data model), the need and complexity of integration with other services, and the extent and flexibility of the existing SOA infrastructure.

The second approach delegates only the implementation to the on-demand service. In this case, the interface and semantics are defined by the enterprise, and the service implementation does whatever translation is necessary before invoking the on-demand service through its standard API. This approach

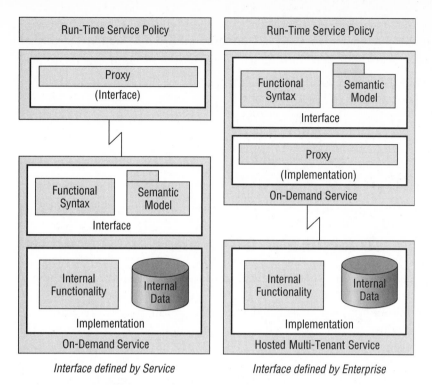

Figure 3-4 Integration of on-demand services

provides for better integration at the enterprise, especially of the semantic model, but it is more complex and obscures some of the benefits of service hosting.

Both models work well, but the issues of service operations can be a challenge for SOA, and a potential benefit of service hosting. The issues are twofold: the availability, reliability, scalability, and security of the operational infrastructure itself, and the versioning, maintenance, enhancements, and business performance of the service.

Many large enterprises have the experience and capacity in their data centers to support the required scalability and reliability, but in general, this capability has been out of reach of small and medium-sized businesses. However, when the service is hosted by the on-demand provider, the operational challenges are passed on to them. Of course, this means that it is important to choose a service provider who can meet these requirements. However, significant cost savings can be realized by doing so. Perhaps more important than the cost savings, are the scalability and reliability that can be obtained through the on-demand model. The same can be said for the service life cycle and SLA management. Maintenance, versioning, service enhancements, and monitoring of business performance can also be passed on to the on-demand service provider.

Because the service implementation (and maintenance, including modifications) is conducted by an external vendor, additional factors should be considered:

- The ability to swap service providers because of financial, technical, organizational, or any other issues
- The ability to shield an enterprise's business processes from inevitable changes in services that are out of the enterprise's control

Building Services

Earlier in this chapter we outlined three major approaches to in-house building of services. In reality, service implementation is virtually always a combination of all three approaches. It is rare that required service functionality does not exist in some shape or form in the present enterprise systems. It is also rare that existing functionality completely implements the required capabilities and interfaces.

One common approach to service implementation is component-based, where some components are new implementations, some are "wrappers" around existing enterprise systems, and some are created using a transformation of the existing applications. A component-based implementation of services requires defining two things: a way to create components and a mechanism for describing how those components work together.

Service Component Architecture (SCA) defines a general approach to doing both of these things. SCA specifies how to create components, combine them, and expose the component assembly as a service. Based on the SCA-defined programming models, components can be built with Java or other programming languages, or technologies. Whatever component technology is used, SCA defines a common assembly mechanism to specify how those components are combined and exposed as a set of services.

Each component implements some business logic that is effectively exposed as an interface by the component. A component can also indicate the services it relies on. In addition, a component can define properties that allow customization of the component's behavior. All of these aspects simplify the reuse and assembly of components into services.

Summary of Service Identification and Realization Concerns

Service concerns range from the ones exposed to the service designer (such as business alignment and reuse of existing IT functionality) to the ones that are visible to the service consumer (such as service specification, service interface, and access policies). Figure 3-5 illustrates these elements and the relationships between them.

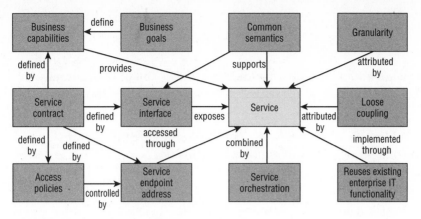

Figure 3-5 Service implementation concerns

■ A service business capability is defined by the enterprise business model, which includes the enterprise's business goals, business capabilities, and semantic information.

■ The service specification defines the business capability of the service, how to interact with it, and its interface, constraints, and service endpoint addresses.

■ The semantic information model defines the shared information that is passed into and out of service interfaces.

■ The service interface describes (in the technical terms) the capabilities of the service provided to potential consumers. The interface is defined as a service name and a set of operations supported by the service. The description of every operation includes definitions of the set of parameters required for service invocation (request) and, if applicable, the result returned by the service (reply). The description also covers the operation's functionality and it's pre- and postconditions.

■ Each service operation can be accessed through an endpoint address — usually defined as an address's network location. Every endpoint address is governed by a set of access policies. These policies define the communication protocol used for data transfer, actual service invocation, and QoS.

■ Granularity and loose coupling represent important service design attributes.

■ The service implementation strives for reuse of the existing enterprise IT functionality.

■ Service orchestration represents the prevalent mechanism for composing services into larger ones and building enterprise solutions out of services.

Service Life Cycle

Of course, a service is just beginning its life after it has been implemented. Then, it must go into production, be updated, and so on, until eventually it is retired (like that ever happens). Figure 3-6 illustrates the high-level service life cycle.

1. **Service identification** — Service identification is the first major step in the life of a service. It is driven off of the business model, process definition, and semantic information model. This results in the proposal for a new service.

2. **Service design and specification** — These are the steps where the service proposal is designed and specified, again in accordance with the functional business model and the semantic information model. Other nonfunctional requirements are also taken into account. After both the identification and specification phases, the functional and semantic models should be updated.

3. **Service implementation** — Next, the service is implemented using one of the techniques described earlier. Again, the implementation is in accordance with enterprise standards, security requirements, operational requirements, and so on.

4. **Service deployment** — After validation and testing of the implemented service, it is ready to be deployed — again, in accordance with policy and procedure for putting software into production.

5. **Service usage and enhancement** — Once the service is in use, it will inevitably requires enhancements and modifications. New users may require a more generalized or flexible implementation. New and existing users will have requests for new features. All of this has to be managed. A new version of the service has to go through the design and implementation phase again, with all that entails.

6. **Service retirement** — Eventually, the service will be retired. Perhaps this will only be the retirement of older versions of the service, or it could eventually be the entire service. Again, processes and procedures should be in place to manage this.

All of these steps of the service life cycle have constraints, processes, and procedures that need to be followed. It is the role of SOA governance to ensure that they are followed. Governance has been defined as: "the art and discipline of managing outcomes through structured relationships, procedures and policies." Infravio, "The Definitive Guide to SOA Governance and Lifecycle Management" (2006). Governance enforces compliance with the architecture and common semantics, and facilitates managing the

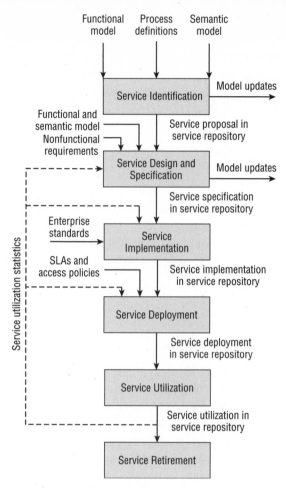

Figure 3-6 Service life cycle

enterprise-wide development, use, and evolution of services. Governance consists of a set of policies that service providers and consumers (and their developers) must conform to, a set of practices for implementing those policies, and a set of processes for ensuring that the policies are implemented correctly. There is typically an organizational structure in place to define and implement governance policies and often a repository to automate and enforce them. Governance of SOA should include:

- Policies regulating service definition and enhancements, including ownership, roles, criteria, review guidelines, and the like.
- Identification of roles, responsibilities, and owners.
- Policy enforcement that is integrated directly into the service repository (where appropriate).

- Guidelines, templates, checklists, and examples that make it easy to conform to governance requirements.

- Review of service interface definitions for new services and enhancements to existing services. The review ensures that the service definition conforms to standards and aligns with the business and information models. The review is typically done by a service review board or the unit responsible for the service.

- Architectural review of applications and services to ensure that they conform to the SOA and EA. This review is typically done by an architecture review board.

Governance should not be primarily a review activity, however. It is most effective if it follows a carrot-and-stick approach with an emphasis on enabling developers to build conforming applications and automating governance activities and policies. Governance is covered in detail in Chapter 12.

The Service Design Process

A friend says that homonyms are the root of most misunderstandings. In other words, you say the same thing, but actually mean something different. More than a few heated discussions about what SOA is or what's important have been caused by the participants having a different perspective of SOA or an SOA project. One of the most common clashes of perspective occurs between those looking to SOA as an enabler for BPM and those trying to kick off SOA from a grassroots effort. If we can clear up the confusion about what we're trying to say, we might not necessarily agree about everything, but at least we'll be arguing about the right things. Figure 3-7 shows five common perspectives for initiating SOA projects.

Top-Down Approaches

You've heard of top-down and bottom-up approaches to SOA, but what do these really mean? It is often as much a difference in scope and timeframe as anything else. A top-down approach takes a broader, more enterprise-based perspective and a more strategic point of view. This means that the top-down approach considers enterprise issues. It is concerned with the overall set of enterprise requirements, now and over time. It is as concerned with how the specific solution fits into the overall enterprise, its strategy, and its roadmap as it is with a particular project and its tactical requirements. Figure 3-7 shows two common top-down approaches:

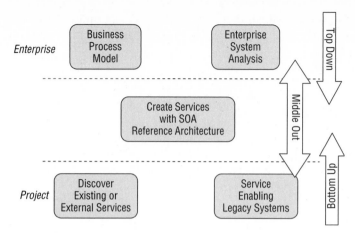

Figure 3-7 SOA project approaches

Enterprise System Analysis

Enterprise System Analysis strives to understand and account for the overall enterprise requirements. Typically starting with business goals and drivers, the analysis looks at the overall business architecture and information model. This sets the context for a service inventory and roadmap that identify the major entities, services, and service groups that are necessary to support the business goals over the next few years. The roadmap should also prioritize an order for implementing services so that the most important or widely usable ones are addressed first. The enterprise analysis should take into account a standard SOA platform, technologies, and standards. It should create a roadmap for their introduction concurrently with the business service roadmap, while maintaining the separation of concerns between the business design and technology.

Business Process Model

Another starting point for SOA is to develop business process models as a set of detailed business requirements (top-right box of Figure 3-7). In this approach, the tasks of the business process model are implemented by business services. The business process model may be an extension of the overall Enterprise System Analysis approach, providing the next level of detail (level 2) of the business architecture (which is, of course, better from an architectural perspective). But often, it is done on a project basis that is being driven by BPM-oriented project sponsors. To the extent that the enterprise context is ignored, the project misses opportunities to improve reuse, integration, and flexibility. In this case, it behooves the SOA team to understand the enterprise context on behalf of the business sponsor.

The crux of the top-down approach is an understanding of the enterprise context and roadmap, and integration of that into a project-based service design. This is often in contrast to the pressure to create immediate deliverables felt by project teams and their lack of understanding of enterprise requirements. The result is a conflict between enterprise architects or designers, who are concerned with understanding common semantics and creating extensible services; and technicians, who just want to do the most expedient thing. It should be pointed out that many times, architects are their own worst enemy in these discussions because they get hung up on the long term and fail to demonstrate how it can be achieved with minimal impact to immediate deliverables.

Bottom-Up Approaches

Bottom-up SOA starts from a perspective of existing systems, technology, or common services. The scope of bottom-up approaches is typically a specific project with immediate requirements. Generally, the project team doesn't feel that it has the luxury to consider a broader enterprise scope or longer-term timeframe, or it doesn't understand the value of that approach. Again, Figure 3-7 shows two common bottom-up approaches to SOA:

Utility Services

SOA is often introduced into an organization as a grassroots effort by a technology team that thinks it is the right technology and/or wants to be on the leading edge. When this occurs, there is no real business driver motivating SOA, only the ethereal benefits of reuse, lower cost, better quality, and faster time-to-market (all of which are achievable with SOA, if done right, but which are technology drivers, not business drivers). The team struggles to look for things that make sense as services and comes up with a set of common enterprise utilities (such as address checking or part number validation, etc.). These indeed make good utility services, but without projects identified to use them, and without business sponsors to fund them, they can go awry. And, because there is no organizational infrastructure to support them, they are undiscovered and underutilized.

Service Enabling

SOA has been touted as a replacement for EAI and the next best way to do integration. As such, SOA is often embarked on as a way to integrate data or functions from legacy systems. Here, the technology vendors are actually the worst enemy of the enterprise because they promote (and provide tools for) a simple-minded approach to service wrapping that exposes the existing data or function directly as a service interface. In fact, this is almost never the right interface to meet enterprise requirements, be flexible, or be extensible, but it is the easiest and fastest. Even when the designers are not taking short cuts, they are often thinking in a limited, point-to-point integration view of services, instead of exposing the existing system in the granularity, syntax, and semantics to meet the needs of the current and future enterprise.

The problem with a bottom-up approach is the narrow scope and lack of consideration of a broader context. History has repeatedly shown that projects done this way create long-term costs rather than provide long-term value. This is often not a conscience tradeoff, but rather a failure to understand the complete requirements. As often as not, it takes no more time and effort to design and implement good services than it does to design bad ones. But, convincing team members of this under a time pressure is a challenge. Conflicts arise when an architect tries to discuss enterprise processes, business models, semantics, and so on, with a developer, who has never even considered these aspects of services, can't understand their importance, and only sees them as a distraction.

Middle-Out: The Best of Both

There is general acceptance that a compromise approach is needed. The top-down approach is perceived as impractical, unnecessary, or not providing value. The bottom-up approach creates isolated services that aren't reused across the enterprise and don't deliver the benefits of SOA. A middle-out approach is frequently cited as being better, but what does it mean, and what is the key ingredient that actually makes it work?

What it means is that when a project team is engaged in an SOA design, it has to both push up into the enterprise scope and, at the same time, push down into immediate deliverables. In other words, the approach produces both a higher-level business and information architecture and design artifacts, and working and deployed services. And the secret sauce that makes this actually work is the SOA reference architecture. The reference architecture ensures that the enterprise context is present in the concerns, activities, and artifacts of everyday project development.

Process Summary

Figure 3-8 shows an overall middle-out process and its constituent parts for designing and implementing services. The process is structured around the activities, artifacts, roles, and repository required for each major area. Although the drawing is divided into discrete rows, in practice, they are all tightly related to each other. Note that this is only a representative drawing. The specific process and artifacts that you need for your organization may vary. First, let's look at what the different parts of the drawing indicate, then we will look at each individual process area.

Activities

Each activity focuses on a specific goal, such as modeling the business context or enabling services for use in solutions. The activities are constrained by the concerns appropriate to that goal. For example, the goals of the business analysis activity concentrate on understanding the business context and requirements from a business perspective. The business analysis activity should not address or be influenced by technical or infrastructure concerns. The activities describe how to meet the goal of the activity, including:

- The inputs to the activity — what artifacts to use
- The outputs from the activity — what artifacts are produced
- The architecture(s) that defines the framework and standards

Despite the implication of Figure 3-8, service analysis, design, and implementation is not a linear process. Iterations take place within and between each activity. The number of iterations and the path they take depend on whether you are creating new business capabilities or enabling the use of existing capabilities.

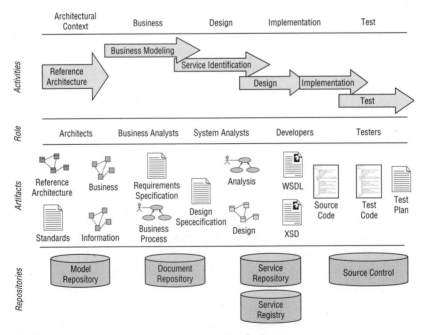

Figure 3-8 Processes and artifacts in service design

Artifacts

Every activity has inputs and outputs, whether it is a manufacturing process, a business process, or a software development activity. The general term for inputs to and outputs from the activity is *artifacts*. Artifacts may take many forms from specifications to models to executable code or test plans. The architecture, guidelines, and governance specify which artifact to use as input for a particular step of the process, and what artifact is produced or modified as an output from the step.

Repositories

The *repositories* indicate where specific artifacts are stored and managed. Notice that the overall process requires a variety of different repository technologies. Integration of these repositories represents a challenge to most tools and organizations.

Governance

Governance is an important aspect of the management of the overall process. The governance policies and procedures determine what artifacts are required at what point in the process. Governance also provides mechanisms to compare specific artifacts against standards to determine if a project is ready to enter the next phase. In each phase, the governance consists of a set of guidelines, examples, and standards to encourage compliance, and a review process to validate it.

Process Phases

The top of Figure 3-8 lists the high-level process phases involved in the overall development of services and SOA solutions.

Architectural Context

This is the early stage of SOA, where the organization is developing the reference architecture. Typically, this is done by the architecture team, who is responsible for producing a variety of architectural artifacts, including: the reference architecture, standards, business model, and semantic information model. The artifacts produced during this phase are at an enterprise scope and not limited to a specific project. Typically, this phase is done once for the enterprise, while subsequent phases of the process are done once for each project. There is however a feedback loop that continually updates the architecture and keeps it current. A model repository may be used to store and coordinate all the models.

Business

This is where you do the bulk of the business analysis and business process design. Typically, the activities of this phase are performed by a business analyst. The design phase overlaps with the architecture phase around the development of the business and information models. Often the architects create the initial, high-level models, and the business analysts fill them out with the next level of detail while working on a specific project. The primary artifact of this phase is business process models. In addition, some organizations may produce requirement specifications. The business phase provides the initial input for service identification.

Design

During design, you complete the service identification and service specification. These activities are usually carried out by a system analyst, who creates analysis and design models that describe the details of the service interface and implementation design, including the documents that are part of their interfaces. A design document or service specification document may optionally be produced. Service interfaces may be described in WSDL, and interface document schemas may be described in XSDs. A design-time service repository may be used to support searching for services according to information from their specifications.

Implementation

This is where the actual service implementation is done. Developers write source code to implement the service. This may include business components, integration access, SCA, and BPEL. A source code repository should be used to manage the source code. The run-time registry may also begin to be used to register the executable instance of the services.

Test

You should not forget testing and other preparations before a service can be put into production. This stage is usually carried out by test developers or all developers (depending on the testing strategy). Often, a test plan is written to guide the testing activities, or an agile approach may be followed. Artifacts produced are tests that are managed from a testing framework and stored in a source code repository.

No lines have been drawn between phases because the boundary between activities, and what role produces what artifacts, is naturally fuzzy. The important thing is to come up with a process that works for your organization and meets your goals. Experience has shown that the process at more mature organizations contains most of the elements of Figure 3-8.

Practical steps

As we have described in this chapter, there are a lot things that need to be considered for practical SOA implementations, including business, organizational, and technical changes. So when you decide to embark on an SOA implementation, the typical question is where to start. On the one hand, the linkage of SOA to the enterprise business model implies that an enterprise-wide SOA implementation is the most beneficial, providing the majority of SOA benefits. On the other hand, the sheer complexity of such an approach typically makes it impractical; it requires a lot of things to be in place and creates too much risk.

A common approach, advocated by many authors, is to start small and then organically grow SOA. Although it seems very attractive from the point of view of containing the risks and providing a good learning experience for the enterprise, such an undertaking too often provides very few benefits. The issue here is not that the choice is always wrong, but the fact that the projects are more concerned with the delivery speed than with setting up a foundation for future SOA growth. In fact, many of these projects are more concerned with creating Web Services, than SOA experience. They are often treated as technology, not the first steps in establishing SOA. Typical mistakes that occur in technology-driven implementations are:

- No attempt is made to align the implementation to the enterprise business model. This usually manifests itself where analysis is only concerned with the scope of the project, not the broader enterprise. (This is exactly the same as the good old application-centric approach, using a new technology: Web Services.) As a result, service definitions and implementation are application-specific, and their use (and reuse) on the enterprise level is extremely limited.

- As a result of skipping the business-model-based design, and the limited scope of analysis, business semantics are rarely introduced.

- Service definitions become significantly less important. Implementation involves a limited set of developers and business analysts, who deal with ambiguities through day-to-day discussions. Moreover, because services are limited in scope to a particular application, precise service contract definitions are not considered important. The absence of precise service definitions often leads to the absence of service registries. On this smaller scale, a repository is often considered as a waste of money and resources.

- Buy versus build versus outsource issues are rarely discussed. Because they are often not based on the enterprise business strategy, they typically come as predetermined requirements to the project implementation.

- Because of the limited scope of the project, which is often run by one or two project managers, the role of service governance is often viewed as an unnecessary overhead — a smaller scope requires significantly less coordination.

This does not necessarily mean that an approach that starts enterprise SOA implementations from small contained projects is wrong. In fact, we think it can be a practical approach. But, it only works when an enterprise SOA context and vision (the minimum architecture described earlier) is established first. In addition, common pitfalls just described should be avoided, and common factors in the following list considered, when choosing and planning a project:

- SOA is an architecture. It is a set of best practices, not a technology.

- SOA is not a panacea. It's especially useful for increasing asset reuse, providing better business visibility, and most importantly, increasing business agility in an environment of heterogeneity. But if your problem isn't one of these, SOA may not be the right approach.

- The biggest challenges with SOA are organizational, cultural, and political. People are resistant to change, to sharing assets, and to funding each other's projects. Compared to these challenges, technology is the easy part.

- The core SOA challenges are governance, quality, and management. Without governance, SOA is limited to project scope. Enterprise SOA efforts are doomed to failure. Quality in the SOA context becomes an ongoing, full life-cycle battle.

- The business side of the house doesn't want SOA. They want solutions to business problems. The most successful SOA initiatives aren't called SOA, but are closely tied to the problem they are looking to solve. SOA is more of the secret weapon IT brings to bear to solve business problems.

Based on these lists and the methodology presented in this chapter, we recommend that the initial SOA project decision and implementation consider the following:

- SOA implementations are not optimal for organizations with an ill-defined business architecture. Make sure that business architecture is defined, at least on the level of enterprise business processes and business semantics.

- Do not try to sell SOA to business leaders, but make sure that you choose a project that is sufficiently important to them. The project's success can ensure traction for SOA's adoption and business leaders' support.

- Ensure proper SOA organizational support. Ensure that governance includes both the organizational structure and technical support, and includes a service repository.
- Continue enhancing the enterprise business model. Make sure that:
  - Service identification directly supports (traceable to) the business model and is not derived directly from existing applications' functionality.
  - Service interfaces are based on the enterprise semantics information model.
  - Business processes allow for direct support and measurements of outcomes and KPIs.
- Set up standards and practices for the definition and description of service contracts.
- Ensure that attention is paid to the SOA infrastructure and appropriate foundation services are designed and put in place to support implementation and operations.
- Use existing application capabilities in your service implementation through proper componentization and integration services.
- Read the rest of the book for more details.

Summary

This chapter has defined the basic activities that an enterprise must engage in to create SOA solutions. First, the SOA reference architecture is the formal specification of services, their types and characteristics, how they support business processes, and how they relate to architecture and development processes. Put a minimum architecture in place to establish the SOA vision before doing anything else, then continue to build it out over time.

Business architecture is key to creating flexible, reusable services, and to aligning processes and services with enterprise strategy and goals. Common semantics are key to enabling services to work together. Both of these need to be created and continually updated.

Service identification uses the business and information models to drive service design. In addition, the overall enterprise context, as described in the service inventory, helps in identification of existing services, and in the allocation of responsibilities to new services. Service specifications describe what a service does and how to use it. They support discovery of services during service identification and business process design, and the specification of service details for implementation.

Service realization provides the implementation of services. We described three major approaches to implementing services: buy, outsource, and build. When building services, we described a middle-out approach to service design that has been proven to be more practical and effective than the traditional top-down and bottom-up approaches.

All of these aspects are part of an overall SOA life cycle. The life cycle is supported by the SOA methodology and enforced by SOA governance.

Part

II

Designing SOA

In This Part

Starting with the Business

The measure of success is not whether you have a tough problem to deal with, but whether it's the same problem you had last year.

— **John Foster Dulles**

The ever-elusive goal of corporations, large or small, East or West, is to align the business with IT. The burden often falls on IT to demonstrate how technology and systems provide value and help move the business forward. But what is it that IT is supposed to align with? How is it determined and specified? And who is responsible for it? All too often, business strategy and goals are too high-level, vague, or not well articulated. So, how can IT demonstrate alignment?

Business architecture (BA) is the key to achieving alignment. First, it provides a way to clearly determine and specify a business strategy, goals, and objectives. Then, it provides a way to measure outcomes against those objectives, and finally, it provides a way to specify business processes that achieve those outcomes. An effective architecture also provides traceability from the processes to the outcomes to the objectives to the strategy. It is this traceability that demonstrates alignment.

There are two different, but important, sets of questions that must be answered by business architecture. One set of questions applies at the enterprise level. What are the goals and strategies of the business? How will they be measured? This is the domain of enterprise business architecture. A different set of questions applies to individual projects. What are the processes, activities, services, and information needed for a specific project or solution? This is the domain of project business architecture.

In this chapter, we introduce both areas of business architecture. The enterprise business architecture determines the overall context that individual projects must work within, so this is addressed first. The project business architecture determines the business details of individual projects, in particular, the design of business processes, and this is addressed second.

Business processes need to change relatively frequently, yet be based on stable underlying capabilities. The flexibility to do this comes from being able to quickly construct business processes from stable and precise business building blocks. These building blocks need to be expressed in business terms, be usable without detailed knowledge of their implementation, and be sufficiently interoperable and variable so that they can be combined and recombined as the needs of the business change.

The promise of SOA to the businessperson is this very ability to create and modify business processes from *business services* — software components that are realizations of the basic business building blocks. It is essentially a manufacturing paradigm in which you create new systems by assembling existing components.

SOA may be a relatively recent phenomenon, but the concept of building new systems using existing components is as old as engineering itself. The challenge in successful component-based engineering (and SOA) is twofold: creating the right components (services) and having a foundation for reliably using those components. Unfortunately, too many IT efforts focus on the foundation, without paying adequate attention to the former, the business aspects of SOA. Without the right building blocks, even the best foundation is not that useful.

So, to effectively deliver business agility with SOA, you need to find and create the right business services. To do that, you need to find the business capabilities (operations and data) that form the basis for the services. You can approach this by business process modeling, a classic way of identifying business activities and the role of the project business architecture. But, for those services to be flexible and reusable across processes, to deliver on the promise of SOA, they also have to be identified within the context of the enterprise. This is the role of enterprise business architecture in SOA design.

This chapter introduces the basics of business architecture and business process modeling — not a detailed course, just enough to show how to understand the business motivation and to derive good business services from real-world business processes. It provides techniques for getting started with the models, explains the individual elements, and relates them to their realization as services. Finally, we introduce techniques for organizing these services by business organization, structure, and subject matter. We call this approach starting from the business, including:

- Business architecture
- Value chains and context diagrams
- Business Motivation Model (BMM)

- Business Process Models (BPMs)
- BPM and SOA
- Organizing services

Business Architecture

What is business architecture? Although there are many available definitions, here are a few that we found useful:

A rather wordy, but descriptive definition comes from the USDA:

The business architecture represents the functions and processes that support the business, the organizations that perform the business, the locations where the business is performed, and the factors that could cause the business to change. In other words, the business architecture addresses how the mission-critical functions of the organization are accomplished. It is a portrayal of how the organization actually accomplishes its mission rather than how it is organizationally structured to manage its mission. The business architecture also encompasses a strategic direction that an organization strives to attain. Major influences on the business architecture are laws and regulations, external and internal policies, organizational structures, organizational culture, business change, people, budgets, and technology drivers. This layer ignores any physical constraints and contains no element of system design.

The Open Group describes the business architecture view as:

Addressing the concerns of the users including consideration of the following:

- *People — the human resource aspects of the system. It examines the human actors involved in the system.*
- *Process — deals with the user processes involved in the system.*
- *Function — deals with the functions required to support the processes.*
- *Business Information — deals with the information required to flow in support of the processes.*
- *Usability — considers the usability aspects of the system and its environment.*
- *Performance — considers the performance aspects of the system and its environment.*

The business architecture view is derived from business scenarios, where each scenario is defined by describing the problem, environment, objective, human actors, system actors, and roles and responsibilities.

Finally, for a more succinct definition, you can turn to the recent article "Business Architecture: Aligning Strategy and Deployment" by William Ulrich

(BPMInstitute, June 2, 2006), which describes business architecture as "Conceptual views & physical instantiations of business strategy, governance structures, and processes — across the extended value chain."

What all of these definitions have in common are the concepts of strategy, organization, and business processes. In other words, the business architecture translates the business strategy into actionable processes. When you look into some details of this, you see that it involves people and systems (the actors and their organizations), information and information flow, and business processes and activities.

Not surprisingly, you see these same elements if you examine some of the standard ways of representing business architecture. For example, a business context diagram (see Figure 4-3) illustrates users, organizations, boundaries and information flows between them. A value chain diagram (see Figure 4-2) shows organizations and the chain of processes and information that provide business value. A business process diagram (see Figure 4-6) shows the sequence of processes executed by different organizational units, and the information flow between them.

Business architecture allows an organization to envision and articulate the essence of their organization while creating tangible ways to align business architecture with IT architecture. Business architecture enables a business to visualize, analyze, redefine, and reengineer the way it functions and communicates internally, with business partners, and with IT.

In other words, business architecture focuses on aligning business strategy with IT implementation, by:

- Identifying goals and strategy
- Identifying organizational structures and governance and their impact on strategy
- Applying the strategy across the entire enterprise
- Aligning with external entities
- Identifying quantifiable outcomes to measure the strategy
- Identifying the processes, rules, and information necessary to support the outcomes
- Managing and synchronizing the process model, business rules model, and information models:
  - Applying business architecture context to individual projects
  - Acting as a bridge between enterprise context and individual project requirements

- Working with business analysts and project teams in the design of business models to ensure that enterprise requirements and concerns are correctly incorporated

When we tie these definitions together, we come up with Figure 4-1, which illustrates the important concepts of business architecture and the relationships between them. It also shows that the overall business architecture can be divided into two main parts based on the scope of the architectural concerns. The top part of the drawing shows the *enterprise business architecture*. This is the part of business architecture at the enterprise level and that deals with the goals, strategies, outcomes, and common information, rules, and processes. The enterprise business architecture sets the overall context for individual projects.

The bottom part of the drawing shows the *project business architecture*. This is the part of business architecture that deals with individual applications, processes, and systems. Typically, an enterprise has one enterprise business architecture, and many (one for each major project) project business architectures. Ideally, there is an area of overlap where the enterprise business architecture drives common processes, rules, and information and affects the project business architecture and the solutions themselves. Unfortunately, in many (perhaps most) enterprises, there is a distinct gap between enterprise concerns and IT systems, rather than an overlap. It is this gap that effective business architecture addresses in order to align strategy with implementations, align processes with services, and enable an agile enterprise IT environment.

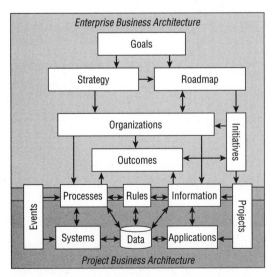

Figure 4-1 Aspects of business architecture

In addition to differences in scope, there are some other important differences between enterprise and project architectures, including levels of abstraction, types of models, and roles. At the enterprise level, business architecture is more abstract, dealing with the big picture and broad concepts. (Note that abstract does not mean that it is imprecise. See the "BMM" section later in this chapter.) A set of models that target these big picture concepts are used to express the details for the enterprise. In general, this work is done by an enterprise business architect.

At the project level, business architecture is more specific, dealing with concepts such as business processes, rules, services, and information. Different types of models, such as a Business Process Model are used to express these details for the project. In general, this work is done by a project architect or business analyst.

Although these two architectures are often handled by different people, they are not unrelated. Both are necessary, and both are complementary. It is the traceability between these two architectures that tie them together and provide the alignment between the business and IT. If you apply these architectures to the enterprise and project concerns of SOA, you can use the same traceability mechanisms to establish the alignment of SOA with the business.

Enterprise Business Architecture

The enterprise business architecture applies to the enterprise scope. Its area of concern spans individual applications, often identifying commonalities. The enterprise business architecture is concerned with:

- Formalizing business strategy into goals and outcomes
- Identifying common enterprise business semantics
- Identifying common enterprise processes and rules
- Identifying enterprise opportunities and value
- Developing strategic roadmaps
- Providing alignment and innovation
- Considering competitive forces and competitive strategies
- Aligning with external organizations (the virtual enterprise)

Project Business Architecture

The project business architecture acts as a bridge between the enterprise context (as expressed in the enterprise business architecture) and the project specific business model. The project architecture typically includes:

- Context diagrams
- Process models
- Information models
- Integration of enterprise semantics into project models
- Integration of enterprise semantics, common processes, and services into the project design

Value Chain

One way to get started with the business is to create a business value chain. The value chain was first developed by Michael Porter and described in his 1985 book *Competitive Advantage*. Figure 4-2 illustrates a sample extended value chain. (Note that this format of the value chain has evolved from Porter's original. The format we use is called an extended value chain.)

The value chain is divided into two main sets of activities. The activities on the bottom are called supporting activities. These are things like HR and finance that must be in place to keep the company operating, but that do not add value to the products or services. (Note that in Porter's version of the value chain, he lists the supporting activities on the top. We have moved them to the bottom because they are not the focus of the corporation.)

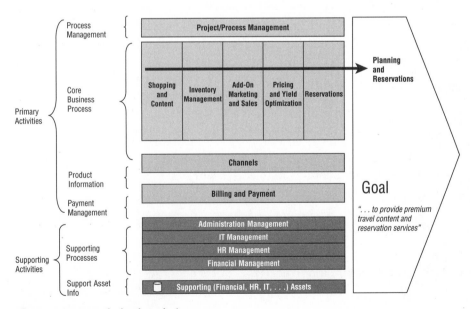

Figure 4-2 Extended value chain

The top part of the diagram describes the primary activities. The main business that our example company is involved in is Trip Planning and Reservations. This is composed of five main value adding activities: Shopping and Content, Inventory Management, Add-on Marketing and Sales, Price and Yield Optimization, and Reservations. These make up the primary activity, as identified by the arrow which connects the steps and ties them to the goals. (This is the traditional value chain.)

In addition, the primary activities consist of management functions such as Process/Project Management, Channel Management, Billing and Payments, and Information Management. These are all necessary to keep the primary value chain going, but do not provide specific value added services to the product.

We find that the value chain is useful for identifying the different functional areas of the company and focusing attention on the most important of them. It is a good mechanism for bringing out the goals and objectives. As well, it starts to identify areas of services. For example, each different step or primary activity in the value chain is likely to have one or more service groups associated with it. This provides a first step in creating a service inventory.

Business Context

The value chain provides one enterprise-level perspective on the operations of the business. You also know that business operations inside and outside of the enterprise are made up of interactions and exchanges of information between parties. To describe the overall set of interactions, you use a business context diagram, as illustrated in Figure 4-3. The context diagram includes the major parties, represented by the rounded rectangles, and the messages that they exchange, represented by the arrows. You create the context diagram by talking with the business analysts and walking through all of the different interactions required for end-to-end capabilities.

The context diagram is made up of the following semantic elements:

- **Actors** — The main parties of the interactions, (the rounded rectangles). Typical actors are people, organizations, or systems.

- **Messages** — Information exchanged between actors (the arrows). Messages are typically documents, packages, electronic communications, and the like.

- **Subjects** — The business matters that the messages are about. The subjects are not explicit in the drawing, but are implied by the interactions and messages. Subjects are typically things like products and services.

You can think of a shipping package (such as a box from a bookseller) as a metaphor for these elements of the context model. The package has a shipping label with From and To addresses. These are the actors. The package box itself (to which the labels are attached) is like the message. It moves between the

From actor and the To actor. The contexts of the box are the subject. It is what the message is about.

For example, in Figure 4-3 the customer and bookshop storefront are actors. The customer places an order, which is a message. The subject of the message (and hence the order) is books that the customer wishes to purchase.

Notice what a business context diagram provides:

- **Overall interaction** — The context model represents the overall interaction of all aspects of the system. It is purposely kept at a high level and includes only business concepts, no technology. It is a combination of all the different business scenarios and transactions. Any single scenario represents one path through the overall diagram (a subset of functional areas and messages). The context diagram is the first place that you can start to identify commonality in function and information.

- **Shared information** — The messages describe the information that must be shared and exchanged between parties to complete the different transactions. It does not describe the details of any information within the different functional areas, but only the information exchanged, that is, shared. Remember that this is exactly the information that you need for the semantic information model and to design the service interfaces.

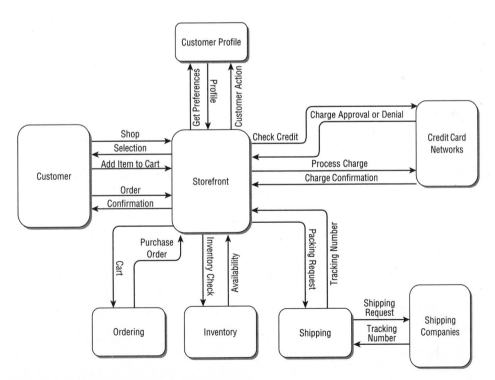

Figure 4-3 Sample business context diagram

You use business context diagrams because they provide an excellent communication mechanism with the business. They are intuitively understandable
and nontechnical. They focus on business concepts. The process of creating
them helps to bring a common understanding to the different parts of the
business. And, they provide the first step in identifying common functions
and data that are required for service design.

So, how does this relate to SOA? The business model and the semantic
information model have been identified as key components of SOA. These
two aspects are critical to moving an enterprise from simply building services
(which at best may incidentally work together), to having an architectural
approach that systematically leads to an organized collection (inventory) of
related, non-overlapping and composable services.

The SOA service and information models are directly related to the business
architecture. They intersect at the business process, as defined in the business
architecture, and are translated into service concepts in the service model,
where they are extended to the next level of detail. The information flow of
the business processes becomes the basis of the semantic information model
and the document definitions of the service interfaces. These relationships are
illustrated in Figure 4-4.

The left side of Figure 4-4 shows the business architecture aspects. Here, you
start with business strategy and goals as input to the business value chain.

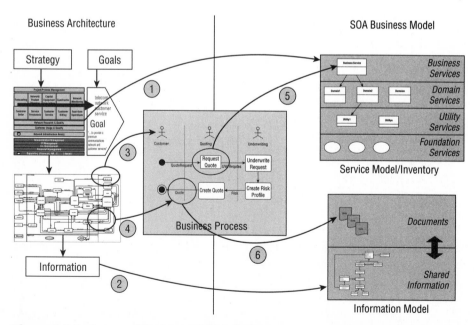

Figure 4-4 Business architecture and SOA design

The value chain helps you to identify the major areas of business activities, and to prioritize them in terms of importance and value creation. For each of these major areas, you need to specify the next level of details.

You use the business context model to identify the major parties, major areas of business capability, and the interactions between them. The context model leads directly to identification of the information model and specific Business Process Models.

The steps are fairly straightforward. (The numbers in the following list correspond to the numbers in Figure 4-4.) First, you establish the overall context:

1. The overall set of processes, as identified by the value chain, and the set of all context models provides the enterprise SOA context that is represented in the service inventory.

2. The enterprise information model describes the superset of information that is needed to be shared between services. This becomes the basis for the more detailed semantic information model.

Next, you refine context models into process models or scenarios:

3. Parties or functional areas in the context model become actors in the Business Process Models.

4. Messages in the context model become data that is passed into and out of the business processes.

Finally, you focus on the specific business processes:

5. Activities in the business processes are implemented by operations on services. The services fit within an overall service hierarchy, but at this level you are primarily identifying business services.

6. Inputs and outputs of the business processes become documents that are passed through service interfaces. The documents are derived from the semantic information model.

Note that the business architecture is purposely devoid of IT specifics, and that the business services are the realization of those business requirements in IT terms. Clearly, these are related (they better be), but they are not exactly the same.

We have described the relationship for a single process, but of course the business architecture and the service model are concerned with the totality of processes, services and information. They are concerned with the present, the near term, and the long term. Thus, the business model must identify all of the processes and information that exist today, those that are currently planned or being implemented, and the processes and information that are needed over time to realize the business strategy and goals.

Likewise, the SOA business model must describe today's services, documents, and information (those currently being implemented) and future services and information (those that provide the business capabilities required of the future business processes). In other words, the SOA service model is directly influenced by the business strategy and must identify services to provide all the capabilities required of that strategy. And, the SOA information model is directly influenced by the business information and must identify all of the information required for the future processes.

Of course, the level of detail, in which current processes, services, and information are described, is much greater than for the future. In your models, you do not need to (nor can you) identify every detail of the future. But, you must identify enough about your future needs to set the right direction now.

The SOA business model has some other important goals. It has to manage the sharing of services and information across processes. In other words, it needs to eliminate redundancy, overlap, and gaps between services. That ensures that each business capability is implemented once, by the organizational unit that is responsible for that capability, and that those services are used by all the different processes needing those capabilities. In addition, all of the information shared between services must be identified in the semantic information model. In other words, all services that are related to the same business concepts must use the same information to describe the same concepts. Finally, the SOA business model must ensure that all of the information passed into and out of the business services (mostly in the form of documents) is defined in the semantic information model.

You have looked at several different definitions of business architecture and identified some common components of strategy, processes, and information. Then, you looked at how these aspects of the business architecture are related to SOA. At the business architecture level, you need to ensure that your business architecture is internally consistent. That strategy, goals, organization, and so on are realized as processes and information. Then, you need to make sure that the business architecture is consistent externally with the SOA model, that it drives the long-term vision, and that you have complete and consistent traceability from strategy to process to task to implementation as a business service. For this, you use a Business Motivation Model.

THE TECHNOLOGY OF BUSINESS ARCHITECTURE

Okay . . . hold on . . . what the heck are they talking about now, you ask? Well, it's not exactly technology, but we want to talk about the formal architectural underpinnings of BA.

We say that service design should be driven by the business, or to be more precise, we say that BA must answer the following questions: What business are you in? What are the goals and objectives of this particular business? What outcomes are needed to achieve those goals? What is the strategy for achieving them? How will they be measured? What capabilities and information are needed to achieve those outcomes? What processes, services, entities, and rules are needed to implement those capabilities? What existing applications provide basic capabilities and information? Although this is where we usually stop, others might add: What organizational structure do you need to support them? What initiative, programs, and projects do you need to create, enhance and maintain them?

All good questions, so, how do you describe all of these things? Architecture should have two complementary views: a conceptual view, usually as a Visio diagram, designed to communicate concepts to a particular audience; and a formal view, usually as a formal model, designed to be a precise specification of the architecture that can be implemented and validated. If you use a standard notation, the formal model will use standard definitions and nomenclature that allow for common/shared understanding among architects who are conversant in the notation. For example, if the modeling notation formally defines what strategy means, then you have removed ambiguity about the meaning of strategy. Rather than debate what strategy means, you can instead focus on the contents of a particular strategy.

The Business Motivation Model (BMM) specification, published by the Object Management Group (OMG) provides the underlying architectural metamodel for describing much of the concepts mentioned previously. Tying it to our example, the BMM explicitly defines the following concepts: goals, objectives, strategy, tactics, policies, rules, and assessments.

You might ask why bother with the value chain at all? Can't you do everything it does in the BMM? Well yes, but there's a catch. Business people and executives are familiar with the value chain. It is easily recognizable and intuitive to the business. And who is the audience for this part of the business architecture? Although the BMM is more precise, often, it is considered too technical by the intended audience and simply dismissed. Is it fair? No. Is it reality? Yes. Anyone who has tried to show a UML model to a businessperson knows what I'm talking about.

The next question is how do you define the business processes? There are lots of proprietary versions of Business Process Models, and you could use one of them if you've already invested in a tool set, or you could use the emerging standard, Business Process Modeling Notation (BPMN). The notation itself is a standard way to represent and diagram business processes in visual models. It is based on an underlying metamodel called the Business Process

(continued)

THE TECHNOLOGY OF BUSINESS ARCHITECTURE *(continued)*

Definition Metamodel (BPDM). (Both BPMN and BPDM are described on the OMG page listed previously.) So, why have two separate specifications? To quote the OMG:

> *BPDM provides the capability to represent and model business processes independent of notation or methodology, thus bringing these different approaches together into a cohesive capability. This is done using a meta model — a model of how to describe business processes — a kind of shared vocabulary of process with well defined connections between terms and concepts. This meta model captures the meaning behind the notations and technologies in a way that can help integrate them and leverage existing assets and new designs.*

Earlier, it was stated that architecture must answer three important questions: 1) What are the important concepts? 2) What are the relationships between them, and how do those relationships describe the behavior of the system? 3) How does the system provide value (beyond the value of any single part)? This is essentially what these modeling specifications do. They define the important concepts, and they define the relationships between them. But, they do it in a standard way, so that people don't have to reinvent those concepts. Thus, the meaning is clear to everyone who knows the notation, and tools can implement and exchange standard models.

Just one word of advice, when talking to the business about business architecture, it's probably best to leave all these metamodel details out of the conversation.

Understanding the Business Motivation Model

The Business Motivation Model (BMM), published by the Business Rules Group and the Object Management Group (OMG) provides the underlying architectural metamodel for describing many of the concepts mentioned earlier. Version 1.3, the current version of the specification, was released in September 2007 (www.omg.org/technology/documents/br_pm_spec_catalog .htm). (Note: Some of the description of the model's concepts in this section are paraphrased from the specification.)

There are two major areas of the BMM:

- **The Ends and Means of business plans** — Among the Ends are things that the enterprise wishes to achieve — for example, Goals and Objectives. Among the Means are things the enterprise uses to achieve those Ends — for example, Strategies and Tactics.

- **The Influencers** — These are the things that shape the elements of the business plans, and the Directives and Assessments made about the impacts of Influencers on the Ends and Means.

Together, the Ends, Means, and Influencers answer the following fundamental business questions:

- What is necessary to achieve what the enterprise wishes to achieve? This is answered by describing the Means needed to achieve the desired Ends.
- Why does each aspect of the business plan exist? This is answered by identifying the Ends that each of the Means serves. This is what is meant by business motivation.

Notice that the Ends, Means, Directives, and Assessments correspond to the age-old questions of who?, what?, how?, and why?

A key to addressing business motivation is understanding the enterprise's aspirations — its Vision — and its plans for achieving that vision — its Mission. Refining these concepts to the next level of detail yields additional important concepts. Vision is amplified by Goals and quantified by Objectives. Mission is defined by Strategies (for approaching Goals) and carried out by Tactics (for achieving Objectives). The BMM uses the general terms *Ends* to refer to the aspiration concepts (Vision, Goal, Objective) and the term *Means* to refer to the action plan concepts (Mission, Strategy, Tactic). Figure 4-5 shows the main concepts and relationships of the BMM.

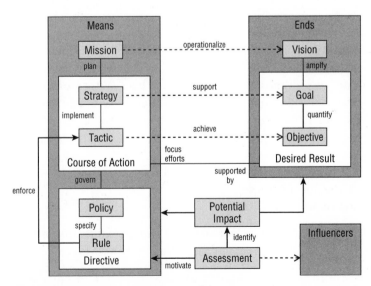

Figure 4-5 Business Motivation Model

Ends

An *End* is something the enterprise desires to accomplish. Note that an End describes what will be accomplished, but not how. A *Means* is any device, capability, technique, restriction, agency, or method that may be called upon, activated, or enforced to achieve the Ends.

Vision

Vision is an overall image of what the organization wants to be or become. It usually encompasses the entire organization and is long term in perspective. A Vision describes the future state of the enterprise, without regard to how it is to be achieved. A Vision is *amplified* by Goals. A Vision is supported or *operationalized* by Missions.

Desired Results

There are two types of Desired Results that the enterprise intends to achieve in order to meet its Vision: Goals and Objectives.

A *Goal* is a statement about a state or condition of the enterprise to be brought about or sustained through appropriate Means. A Goal *amplifies* a Vision — that is, it indicates what must be satisfied on a continuing basis to effectively attain the Vision.

An *Objective* is a statement of an attainable, time-specific, and measurable target that the enterprise seeks to achieve its Goals. An Objective *quantifies* a Goal. Objectives should be SMART — specific, measurable, achievable, realistic, and time-bound.

Goals and Objectives are somewhat fuzzy concepts, but you can generally say that a Goal tends to be longer term, qualitative (rather than quantitative), general (rather than specific), and ongoing. An Objective tends to be short term, quantitative, and specific, and does not continue beyond its timeframe.

Desired Results (the specific Ends) are supported by Courses of Action (specific Means), which can be either Strategies or Tactics. Generally, Goals are supported by Strategies, and Objectives are achieved by Tactics.

Means

The Means are the operational part of the BMM. They provide a mechanism to specify how the Vision is realized in terms of operational concepts.

Mission

A *Mission* indicates the ongoing operational activity of the enterprise. The Mission describes what the business is or will be doing on a day-to-day basis. A Mission is *planned* by Strategies.

Course of Action

A *Course of Action* is an approach or plan for configuring some aspect of the enterprise involving things, processes, locations, people, timing, or motivation, undertaken to achieve Desired Results. In other words, a Course of Action *focuses efforts towards* Desired Results. There are two types of Courses of Action: Strategies and Tactics.

A *Strategy* is one major aspect of the plan for the Mission. A Strategy represents the essential courses of action to achieve Ends — Goals in particular. A Strategy usually *focuses efforts* toward those Goals. A Strategy is more than a resource, skill, or competency that the enterprise can use. A Strategy is accepted by the enterprise as the right approach to achieve its Goals given the constraints and risks that the enterprise operates with. A *Tactic* represents the detailing of Strategies. In other words, Tactics *implement* Strategies.

Again, Strategies and Tactics are somewhat fuzzy, but generally you can say that Strategies tend to be longer term and broader than Tactics. Strategies are *implemented by* Tactics. Strategies usually *support Goals and focus efforts on* Objectives. Compared to a Strategy, a Tactic tends to be shorter term and narrower; they are Courses of Action that generally *achieve* Objectives.

In and of themselves, however, Courses of Action tend to be limited. They require Directives to be successfully applied in the business.

Directives

Directives describe the Policies and Rules for applying the Strategies and Objectives. In other words, Directives *govern* Courses of Action. Specifically, a Directive defines or constrains some aspect of an enterprise. It is intended to assert business structure or to control or influence the behavior of the business.

A Directive always has to do with constraints, governance or guidance. A Course of Action, in contrast, identifies an active approach in moving toward the Ends.

A *Business Policy* is a non-actionable Directive whose purpose is to govern or guide the enterprise. Policies sharpen Tactics because they make Courses of Action concrete at the operational level. In general, Business Policies exist to govern — that is, control, guide, and shape — Strategies and Tactics. A Business Policy provides the basis for Business Rules.

A *Business Rule* is a Directive, intended to guide or influence business behavior, in support of Business Policy. In other words, Rules *specify* the Policies. Business Rules sharpen the Business Tactics because they make Courses of Action concrete at the operational level. Business Rules *enforce* Tactics.

To compare the two Directives, a Business Policy tends to be less structured, less discrete, and usually not atomic — that is, not focused on a single aspect of governance or guidance. Also, a Business Policy tends to be less compliant with standard business vocabulary, and less formally articulated. In contrast, a Business Rule is highly structured and is carefully expressed in terms of standard vocabulary. A Business Rule should be discrete and atomic (that is, represent only a single aspect of governance or guidance).

Influencers

Of course, the enterprise does not exist in a vacuum. You can go merrily on your way toward implementing your objectives, but if you ignore the other forces (Influencers), you're in for a disappointment. An *Influencer* can be anything that has the ability to affect the business, often without direct exercise of command, deliberate effort, or intent. Influencers can be external or internal to the enterprise. Typical examples of Influencers are: a competitor, a customer, a supplier, a regulation, technology, corporate infrastructure, and management initiatives. Specifically, the business is concerned with the Influencers that can impact the employment of Means or achievement of Ends.

So, what are you to do about these Influencers? How do you differentiate between important ones and trivial ones? This impact of an Influencer *is judged in* an *Assessment*. Influencers, the "who" in business requirements, are neutral — they are more or less just there until someone makes an assessment of them as they relate to Ends and/or Means. An assessment indicates which Influencers are relevant to which Ends and/or Means and identifies the *Potential Impact* that they can have. Potential impact can be either a risk or a reward; it provides the "why" of business requirements — quantifying the value proposition. Assessments often take the form of a SWOT analysis: strength, weakness, opportunity, and threat.

Armed with this information, the enterprise can take action to address the potential impact. Often, a Directive is specifically motivated by the potential impact of an Influencer.

Alignment and Traceability

One of the key expectations of business architecture is that it helps to align IT with the business. You've all heard this statement so much that it is often treated as little more than a cliché. But, it need not be. The BMM provides a formal way to trace the tactics back to goals and objectives. Now, you need to take it one step further and tie IT systems to the tactics that they implement. For example, in SOA, business processes and services are the IT constructs that should implement tactics. So, you can create formal traceability between the services (IT) and the business by modeling a formal relationship between a service and the tactic it is intended to implement.

But why go to all of this trouble? Isn't it the business's job? Well yes, but it is our job as well. The business should have an idea of their strategy, goals, objectives, and tactics, but in general they will not be clear or precise enough to trace back to. As architects, you are equipped to help the business express the enterprise context in terms of a formal model, which will then enable IT to both achieve and demonstrate alignment.

NOTE There are many different ways to create and represent a business architecture. What we have (very) briefly described here is only one of many possible approaches. We find it works particularly well for determining the business information necessary for SOA. Hopefully, this glimpse into business architecture illustrates the value it can bring and encourages you to learn more about it from one of the books in our references section.

So far we have looked at the enterprise business architecture as a way to establish and specify the overall enterprise context. Now, we turn to the project business architecture, and specifically business processes, which use the enterprise context and other requirements to drive to the next level of detail.

Business Process Management and Modeling

Business Process Management (BPM) empowers a business analyst to align IT systems with strategic goals by creating well-defined enterprise business processes, monitoring their performance, and optimizing them for greater operational efficiencies. Each business process is modeled as a set of individual processing tasks. These tasks are typically implemented as business services within the enterprise. The BPM system provides a tool set that allows the business analyst to create process models using a notation system, such as BPMN, and then performs the business process automation, or execution of the model, by invoking the services.

BPM provides a wonderful abstraction for building business systems. But all too often in the past, it was used to build higher-level, more efficient, but nonetheless siloed applications, rather than contributing to an overall flexible, agile enterprise. This is where SOA comes in. SOA provides the platform of underlying capabilities that bridge between the business processes and the operational resources (as shown in Chapter 2, Figure 2-1). At the business process level, SOA provides interfaces that directly support executing process tasks. But it defines those interfaces within an enterprise context to support consistency and reuse. At the operational resource level, SOA exposes existing capabilities as integration services.

Together, BPM and SOA provide a perfect combination for enterprise computing. BPM provides the higher-level abstraction for defining business processes, as well as other important capabilities for monitoring and managing those processes. Services provide the functions that support those processes. SOA provides the capabilities for services to be combined and to support and create an agile, flexible enterprise. BPM without SOA is useful for building applications, but it is difficult to extend to the enterprise. SOA without BPM is useful for creating reusable and consistent services, but it lacks the ability to turn those services into an agile, competitive enterprise.

BUSINESS PROCESS MANAGEMENT OR BUSINESS PROCESS MODELING?

Wikipedia defines BPM as:

an emerging field of knowledge and research at the intersection between management and information technology, encompassing methods, techniques and tools to design, enact, control, and analyze operational business processes involving humans, organizations, applications, documents and other sources of information.

You can think of it as a type of process construction that emphasizes the management of business processes in addition to their execution. In other words, the focus of BPM is twofold: design and execute business processes, and manage and monitor those processes. A key benefit of BPM systems is monitoring to ensure processes are meeting the intended business objectives and performing auditing, reporting, and other functions.

First, a BPM system must provide for the creation of business processes. This is typically done through the use of a graphical tool that enables the drawing of the process. In other words, to create a Business Process Model. To complete the story, BPM provides a means to execute the process, as described by the model.

Sometimes the acronym BPM is confused with that for Business Process Model or modeling (the act of creating the model). We have tried to consistently mean management when we use the BPM acronym, and to spell out modeling.

Business process modeling is a technique for formalizing the steps of a business process, the people, organizations, or systems responsible for those steps, and the data associated with each step. BPM is particularly interesting in the context of SOA because it provides a language for utilizing reusable business services. This section of the chapter focuses on business process modeling.

Figure 4-6 shows a simple Business Process Model (using Business Process Modeling Notation (BPMN)) of the process by which a customer orders books from an online bookstore.

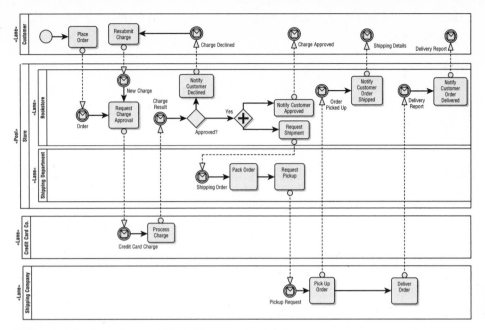

Figure 4-6 Business Process Model for ordering books

The process goes like this: Once a customer places an order, the customer's payment is processed by the credit card company. After the charge is approved, a shipping clerk packs the order and requests a shipment pickup from the shipping company. The shipping company picks up the order and then delivers it to the customer.

Basic Business Process Model Components

A basic Business Process Model consists of a few main components:

- *Process steps* are the rounded rectangles that define what is done. The names of the process steps should represent what is being done from the perspective of the business itself.
- *Gateways* divide and combine process flows, either by combining parallel flows or by dividing flows based upon some decision criteria.
- *Documents* represent cohesive sets of business data such as an Order or a Payment.
- *Process Flows* connect process steps and gateways, showing and enforcing specific ordering to the processes.
- *Data Flows* show how processes produce and/or consume specific data.

- *Lanes*, labeled with the names of *actors*, organize the steps by who does what. For example, the customer places the order. Lanes also provide points for the origin and destination of data flows, for example, showing how the shipping company is notified of the request to ship a package.

Executable Models

A Business Process Model is not just a way to graphically represent business processes. The model is a formal specification of that process. With the proper tooling and automation in place, these models can themselves be programs. When the models are expressed in a formal modeling language, such as BPMN (which we use in this book), the models can be interpreted by the BPM system and executed. Often, there is an intermediate step in the process. First, the BPMN model (which is a visual representation) is compiled into an executable language, such as BPEL (the Business Process Execution Language). BPEL is a standard execution language supported by many BPM and SOA systems and is a complementary technology that adds execution semantics to Business Process Models. BPMN, BPEL, and composition are covered extensively in Chapter 8. Skipping the details here, the point is that Business Process Models are not just pretty pictures. They are also the input to the BPM system that directs the execution of the business process.

A consequence of this is a scenario like the one illustrated in Figure 4-7. A business analyst is responsible for designing a business process in response to business objectives and other requirements. She goes to her BPM environment and draws a Business Process Model. To build the model, she chooses from palettes of existing process steps, documents, gateway conditions, and actors available in her business. The items in the palettes are realized by existing business service capabilities.

When all the capabilities that she needs already exist, she is able to completely specify and execute the new process without needing IT to build something for her. This concept is one of the great appeals of BPM. But sometimes the analyst cannot find the capability that she needs. In this case, she can define a new one to support one or more tasks in the business process. This then becomes the specification of requirements for a new business service. The system analyst in the development team uses that specification to create new business services or to modify existing services to meet the specified needs. In many cases, these services do not need to be built from scratch but instead can be composed from other services or can integrate capabilities already found in existing legacy systems.

Once all the services are in place, a BPM tool can then execute the new business process by running each of the individual business services in accordance with the flows defined in the model.

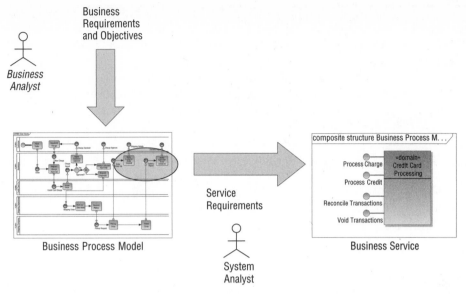

Figure 4-7 BPM and SOA

HYPE OR REALITY?

Clearly, the marketing hype around BPM is related to the ability of the business to create and execute Business Process Models without the need to interact with the evil IT department.

In reality, this rarely works. To start with, what business allows a new system to be put into production without testing, qualification, operational procedures, and so on? So, even if the business could create new business processes completely independently, there would still be some annoying IT details, such as quality, reliability, and security to deal with.

More often than not, pure business analysts are not enamored of modeling tools. It often takes an IT person, working with the business analyst, to create the detailed, formal, and executable versions of the process models. Then, there is the question of finding and using existing services. Perhaps if tools were better integrated, and development processes better defined and followed, it would be easy for business analysts to just drag and drop business services into their models. But it rarely is. Again, IT intervention is often required to make the right business services available to the business analyst.

Finally, there is the task of identifying and specifying new services. Because you want to insulate the process designers from the details of services, designers often don't understand what makes a good service and how to encapsulate those characteristics into the service design and interface (actually, many IT designers don't understand this either). So, all too often, the

(continued)

HYPE OR REALITY? *(continued)*

services specified by business analysts are the wrong granularity, too tightly coupled, have too many dependencies, and you name it, to be good services.

So, is all this BPM stuff a pile of bunk? Absolutely not! The benefits of BPM in the design of flexible business processes, and the ability to provide a business focused execution environment that complements SOA, are real. But, it's not quite as simple as drag and drop. There still needs to be a partnership between the business and IT. And, that partnership is enabled by Business Process Models, which provide a good common vocabulary for both sides to use.

Want to know what we think (in case you couldn't tell already)? It's not that simple, as explained in this chapter. . . . Read on.

Business Process Models in an SOA World

Plain business process modeling does not define where the processes, or documents, or gateway criteria come from; it just assumes that the business analyst will create these elements as necessary in order to properly define the business processes. Following a traditional software development paradigm, each of these elements becomes the specification of some component that will be built and then woven together following the structure of the Business Process Model.

But when used in an SOA context, the steps that make up the model should be implemented by well-designed business services. New business processes should use existing services as much as possible, balanced with the opportunities for identifying new services, as needed, to create the new processes. Here, governance plays an important role by setting up procedures to help find the appropriate services and to verify that new services are identified in accordance with enterprise goals and policies. Approaches to governance are explored in Chapter 12.

Furthermore, the Business Process Models should uniformly represent the problem and not a specific implementation of that problem. This ensures that the models, and the definitions of the business services that emerge from these models, are independent of particular technology and software architecture choices.

There are other concerns as well. The functional decomposition of processes into services can lead to tight coupling between processes and business services. This is often the case when processes are designed in isolation. Many business processes are quite goal-oriented; they are the steps to get a specific thing done. They are often more observed or anticipated scenarios, rather than reusable solutions made of reusable parts. Services come from looking across many processes to find commonality variability, reuse, separation of concerns, overlapping capabilities, and common information. Business analysts don't often do this, and many BPM tools don't have the capability to easily support it. This is where business architecture comes in for SOA and where the system analyst has the responsibility to understand the enterprise context when designing services to meet business process requirements.

How to Create Business Process Models

SOA presents several interesting challenges in creating Business Process Models and the business services that result from those models. How do you get the right level of processes? How do you avoid repeating the same thing over and over again while exploiting opportunities for reuse? How do you define steps that will ultimately lead to good business service design?

Business Process Models are formalizations of the required function, control, and data in a set of business processes. Properly designed, a business's set of activities can be completely described in Business Process Models. However, as with any design activity, you need criteria for grouping related Business Process Models, and criteria for ensuring uniformity among models created by different people at different times within the same organization.

This section introduces Business Process Models and the Business Process Modeling Notation in only enough detail to show how Business Process Models are a useful foundation for identifying business services. It is not intended as a detailed tutorial; there are lots of other resources available for that.

Use Cases

Many software design efforts begin by identifying use cases — the different capabilities to be provided to users of a system.

A use case diagram, such as that shown in Figure 4-8, can be thought of as a table of contents that says, "here's who is going to be doing what in our problem." The stick figures represent actors — the entities that can initiate and participate in the use cases. The ovals represent the use cases that the actors can participate in.

In some practice, the term *use case* is little more than modern software-speak for "informal requirements document." But they should be more than that. The techniques presented in this section help to create use cases and scenarios that are conducive to producing good and useful models, and that lead to good service design.

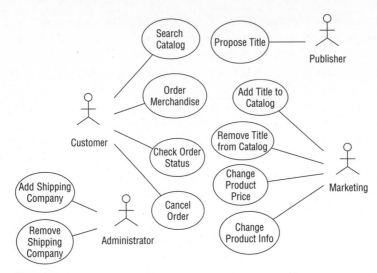

Figure 4-8 Use Cases for the online bookstore

Use Cases and Business Process Models

For each use case, create a Business Process Model that defines the sequence of steps that takes place in that particular use case, also called a use case scenario. For example, the model in Figure 4-6 represents the sequence of processing for the "Customer Orders Merchandise" use case. These Business Process Models effectively replace the dense textual form of the "Flow of Events" section in the typical use case document. If you insist on writing a textual "Flow of Events" section, treat it as a descriptive narration of the Business Process Models. Remember a picture can be worth a thousand words! And, remember that the Business Process Model should provide a complete, correct, and precise specification of the use case.

Defining the right level for use cases is a challenge for many modelers. A useful guideline is: Use cases should not be so small that their scenarios are only a single step. However, use cases should not be so grand that their process models are so large and complex that their purpose is no longer clear. A happy medium of a dozen or so steps is pretty typical.

One Use Case, Multiple Scenarios

Use cases define both a main flow and a set of alternate flows. The alternate flows describe processing differences that arise from different, less common, or unusual situations encountered during the flow of the use case.

For example, Figure 4-6 shows a customer ordering books in a best-case scenario when the customer's first credit card is charged and all books are in stock. However, if the customer's credit card is declined, he may provide a second account number, cancel the order, or place the order on hold. Likewise, if some books are not in stock, some of the order is shipped immediately, but the rest of the items are left back-ordered and shipped only when they are available.

Traditionally, these alternate flows are written as text in separate sections of a use case document. How can you represent these options on your Business Process Models? One option is to create individual models for each of the alternate flows. Although initially easy to do, the many combinations of outcomes (credit card approved or declined, sufficient stock present or not present, shipment deliverable or undeliverable) make it difficult to create and to maintain a set of coordinated diagrams.

A different approach is to draw a single BPM that uses gateways (decision points) to illustrate all possible situations and then to illustrate one scenario by coloring its path atop the model. Figure 4-9 shows this coloring technique applied to the process model in Figure 4-6. The highlighted path illustrates the ''customer charge rejected'' flow.

The coloring approach has the advantage of consolidating all options onto a single diagram so that changes to the flow caused by changes to the design of one scenario (or the addition of other scenarios) can be addressed by other scenarios. The problem with the approach is that it isn't supported by most tools, so in essence you have to print the diagram on paper and mark it with a highlighter. This can be a useful approach for thinking about the design because it keeps all of the related steps together, but it can be difficult to maintain and keep current.

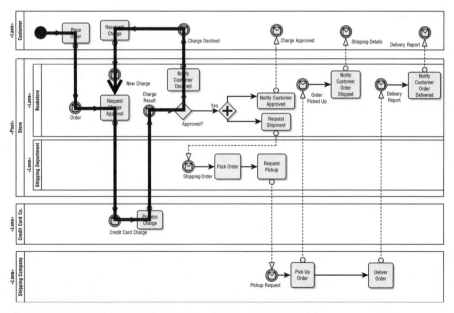

Figure 4-9 Scenario marked atop a Business Process Model

Regardless of how you address creating the model, it is important to understand that a given use case can have many scenarios, that those scenarios share common steps, and that they can affect each other.

Step Reuse

Scenario coloring consolidates a number of distinct use case flows onto a single diagram, thus ensuring greater consistency and reuse of steps across the different flows. Additionally, several models may share common processing steps, gateways, states, and documents. For example, the step of canceling an order is both part of a Cancel Order use case and the Order Merchandise use case.

The modeling environment used to create Business Process Models should provide palettes of existing process elements, preferably tied directly to repositories of existing business services, in order to facilitate this reuse. If this is not possible, manual processes should be implemented to facilitate discovery of reusable processing elements.

If not done properly, reuse can have a dark side: If a service is not sufficiently flexible, it will be largely reinvented in a slightly different form each time the capability is needed. When a business process modeler finds a service that's similar to what he needs, but it does not match it exactly, there is an opportunity to either extend the existing service or to create a new service. The default mindset should be to reuse and extend first, and to create new as a last resort. Service governance policies should address how extensions to a service are requested, designed, implemented, and deployed.

Documents

Documents are the means by which information is passed between steps in a process. They represent cohesive sets of business data, such as an Order or a Payment. This is the data that has to be shared (and have a common semantic definition) across multiple steps of the process. Documents are used as the inputs and outputs of business process steps. For example, in Figure 4-6, Request Charge Approval accepts an Order document. Often, the same document is used in multiple steps of the process. For example, the Request Shipment step produces a Shipping Order. This same shipment document is then the input to and the output of the Process Shipping Order and Pack Order steps, as illustrated in the model segment in Figure 4-10.

Identification of documents is an important aspect of tying BPM to SOA. The documents identified in the process model are used to specify the documents passed in service interfaces. In business processes, the documents should relate to real-world documents whenever they exist (things like purchase order, shipping manifest, binder, etc.). In services, the document schema must

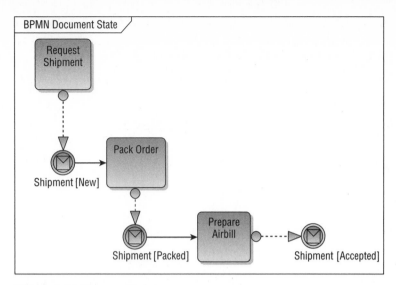

Figure 4-10 Document state

be based on the semantic information model. So, identification of documents during business process design needs to be coordinated with the information model.

Documents are often passed through several steps in a process. Referring back to Figure 4-10, Pack Order doesn't just look at the Shipment; it transforms it by adding the contents of the order to the shipment. The Pack Order *transforms the state* of the Shipment document. In the diagram, the state of the document is shown in brackets next to the document name. So in our example, Shipment is transformed from the [New] state to the [Packed] state. This is a common design practice for documents within business processes, and is most appropriate where it mirrors what is going on with real-world documents.

Let's put this into the perspective of the different types of data. The document specifies the information passed between process steps. It is at the semantic information level, conforming to the enterprise semantic information model. Each step of the process is implemented by a service, which receives the document in its interface, and transforms the semantic information into the internal domain data of that service. The service implementation is responsible for changing the state of the business entity and reflecting the new state in the output document. It is a subtle, but important, distinction. The document is a representation of state change. Services implement the state change.

Note that the use cases, and the Business Process Models and documents that realize them use only the vocabulary of the business problem and do not assume any particular implementation choices. For example, the processes in Figure 4-6 are "process charge" and "request pickup", not "transmit charge record to First National Bank" and "FTP an EDI 9090 to the post office."

The steps in a Business Process Model should represent single business activities. This is more than mere style; good Business Process Models should define elements that are independent of any particular implementation or technology.

Conditional Business Process Models

Let's look at some of the other important elements of Business Process Models.

Conditional Flows

Business processes often need to do different things based on the outcome of a particular step, evaluation of information, or execution of a business rule. Flows between steps can be labeled with conditions that route execution along one path or another depending upon an outcome, evaluation, or rule. The simplest pattern is a gateway with data input and one of several conditional outputs, as shown in Figure 4-11.

Gateways vary in complexity ranging from simple comparisons (that is, was the previous step successful?) to more involved comparisons of data or evaluations (that is, was the charge request over the credit limit?). Still others are complicated decisions that may ultimately be executed in a business rules' system.

Not surprisingly, the implementation of gateways also varies with the complexity. Simple comparisons are typically done within the business process execution itself. Complex decisions should be implemented by a decision service (which may call a rules engine) in the service layer. Evaluations will fall somewhere in between, depending on how often the criteria are likely to change, how reusable the evaluation is in other processes, and how complicated it is. Again, notice that we are always looking for commonality across processes that can be implemented as services and used to help realize multiple use cases. In this particular discussion, we're looking for common decisions. Chapter 8 covers the relationships of business processes and rules in more detail.

Conditional Operation Outputs

Some activities themselves may have conditional outputs. For example, after the Process Charge activity submits the charge to the credit card company, it returns a result indicating whether the charge has been approved or declined, as illustrated in Figure 4-12.

In this case, the decision function is implicit in the implementation of the step itself. Again, the actual implementation varies, depending on the business

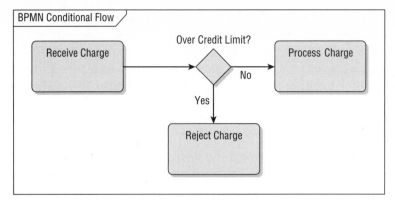

Figure 4-11 Gateway with multiple conditional outputs

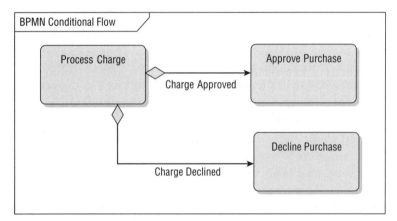

Figure 4-12 Activity with conditional outputs

service that implements the step. One common approach is to compose the business service from other services, including a decision service.

Care must be taken if choosing to model process steps with conditional outputs. Most service implementation technologies will not allow conditional outputs from a service operation, so this can make the implementation of the step more complex.

Recap: Processes and Services

Business process models provide the business analyst with a powerful tool for meeting business requirements and objectives. The models take a functional decomposition based approach to breaking down processes into steps, decisions, and documents. This is often the first step in the identification of business services.

However, in the design process, you will likely encounter situations in which the processes are rather trivial and the use cases are little more than "manage X," "create Y," or "edit Z." Such data management problems — sometimes referred to as CRUD (create, read, update, delete) systems — can and do have interesting and useful business services. Finding them, however, requires examining the information model itself and defining services to manage instances of the enterprise information. Chapter 6 covers this approach to finding services in more detail.

In the analysis of the business, during the business architecture activities, you generally can identify what are called fundamental business entities. These are things like customer, product, payment, and so on that represent an important business concept. Or, they may correspond to physical or legal documents such as application, binder, and policy. In general, they should be common across the enterprise and be part of the semantic information model. We typically define entity services to manage the CRUD behavior of these business entities.

But care must be taken to define appropriate services. Process steps that perform data management (as implemented by entity services in the service layer) should only act on semantic data, not on internal domain data.

Whereas the business process identifies the steps, decisions, and information, the implementation of these steps, decisions, and information is left to the service layer. Table 4-1 shows the relationship between Business Process Model elements and services. For each model element (left), the corresponding implementation in terms of services is identified (right).

Services are implemented with the goal of supporting business processes, but not just a single process, multiple processes. So, the design of the business process and the design of the services also have to take the big picture into account. Processes should be designed starting from the assumption that a service already exists that can implement a given step. Then, the process should be designed around using the existing service. If no service does exist, the process designer should think about how the step or decision could apply to other potential processes.

Table 4-1 How Business Process Model elements are realized by services

PROCESS ELEMENT	SERVICE CONCEPT
Step	Operation on a Business Service (Task)
Gateway	Operation on a Decision Service
Document	Input or Output Document
Entity	Entity Service

The Business Process Model provides the specification of requirements for the service. Then, it is the responsibility of the service designer to put the specific requirements of the requesting process into context with the rest of the enterprise and to create a reusable service with minimum coupling and dependencies and maximum flexibility. Let's look at some techniques for organizing the overall service space.

Organizing Services

Looking back to the example, how should the service operations for the bookstore be organized? Obviously, a single Bookstore service with dozens of documents and operations is a bit unwieldy. Not only is it rather large, but you may not want to expose all of the services to all potential users. Different divisions of the business should have responsibility for different services and be able to control the services that provide their divisions' capabilities. This helps isolate responsibilities and makes the services more usable across a set of processes.

Business process models are written in terms of the business. In an online bookseller, for example, the Business Process Models deal with steps involved with shopping, ordering, and shipping books. In other domains, the vocabulary is different; it is about different things.

This idea of "keep the models focused on the business" is intuitively easy to appreciate. Real systems are layered. An online bookstore is built using more generic concepts (subject matters) such as inventory, shipping, and credit card processing. These generic capabilities can also be found in other businesses: For example, both insurance and telecommunications need to make use of credit card capabilities.

Services can therefore be organized, or partitioned, along a variety of dimensions, for example, according to who is responsible for the service (organizations or providers).

Whenever the business is organized into multiple divisions, you can use a Business Organization Model such as the one shown in Figure 4-13 to structure the organization of services.

This model shows how the online bookseller is divided into distinct organizational units that support shipping, ordering, inventory, and customer support. The Business Process Models, their steps, decisions, and the documents can be assigned to different divisions based on which division should be responsible.

Yet another way to organize services is by business competencies and responsibilities (which does not always map to organizations). This helps organize the services around functional cohesion, which can yield more flexible and reusable services.

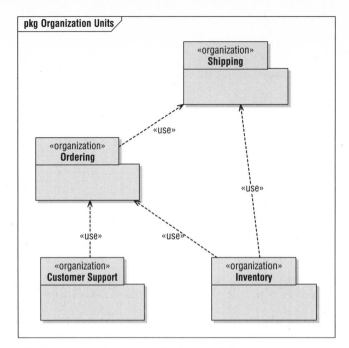

Figure 4-13 Business Organization Model

Or, perhaps the most common approach is to organize services along subject matter domains.

Domains

A *domain* is a separate real or hypothetical world inhabited by a distinct set of objects and subject to its own set or rules and policies (Shlaer and Mellor, *Object-Oriented Systems Analysis* [1988]; Mellor and Balcer, *Executable UML* [2002]). Figure 4-14 is a *domain chart* showing the different subject matters used to conduct an online bookselling business.

Each of the folder-like shapes is a *domain* represented by a UML package with the <<domain>> stereotype. Domain partitioning is sometimes referred to as *aspect partitioning*, whereby each of the different concerns, or aspects, in a system is separately identified and modeled.

The arrows between domains represent how one domain makes use of the capabilities provided by another. The Bookstore requires capabilities of Authentication (to make sure that participants are who they say they are), Logging (to record transactions), Inventory (to keep track of stock and reorder as necessary, Credit Card Processing (to get paid), and Package Shipping (to send orders to customers). The direction of the arrows represents the "uses" relationship.

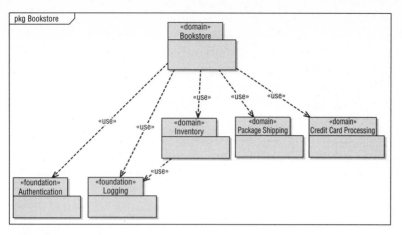

Figure 4-14 Bookstore business domain chart

WHAT IS A DOMAIN?

Like many things, the term domain is used in different ways in different places. In general, a domain is an area of focus around a single subject matter. The confusion comes in understanding the scope and context of that focus.

For example, if we look at insurance as an example, we might refer to an "insurance domain model" that defines overall insurance concepts across the industry. Such models might include ObjX available from the ACORD industry consortium, or the widely used IAA (Insurance Application Architecture from IBM). Here, the scope of domain is industry wide.

For a particular insurance company, such as ACME, their business domain is auto and property insurance. It is related (hopefully) to the industry domain models, but it is smaller and different. So, the domain can be described from an enterprise point of view. We call this the primary domain in our domain chart.

ACME is made up of many different functions, such as billing, underwriting, and claims processing. Each of these can be thought of as a domain, where each is focused on a specific subject area within the business. But each is also part of the larger insurance domain. So, domain can also be described from a functional or line-of-business point of view. When a particular service is limited to this scope, we call it a domain service.

In all cases, domain means a focused and related subject matter area. But sometimes, you need to understand the scope that this is being applied to.

The structure of the domain chart shows how one domain is based upon capabilities provided by other domains. Credit Card Processing, for example, provides services required to realize the Bookstore. This is more than merely a statement of software structure and who does what (Bookstore services call Credit Card Processing services), it is also a statement of who does not do something, that the Bookstore services do not directly process payments and instead assume that some other domain will carry out the payment processing.

Such organization provides two distinct advantages: First, higher-level services can be constructed without regard for the details of how more generic business and utility capabilities are provided. Second, the capabilities required of the lower-level domains can be discerned from the requirements placed on them by the higher-level domains.

Note that the domain chart is different from the business organization diagram. The packages in the domain chart are not divisions of the business; they are distinct subject matters that can be understood independently of one other. For example, the problem of maintaining and tracking inventory is generic and, by implication, reusable in contexts other than the online bookstore.

Many businesses also share common industry standards. The domain chart can be extended to show how two different booksellers make use of some common industry standard items, such as ISBN numbering. Each company can start with a common base and then specialize it to meet its own particular needs.

Types of Domains

A domain chart is drawn with respect to the business being modeled. The package at the top of the chart — and there is always only one — is the *principal domain* representing the subject matter of the business itself. Other domains provide capabilities that are used to realize the principal domain. *Generic* domains are generic business subject matters, such as Billing, Inventory, and Shipping. *Foundation* domains, in contrast, provide computer-technology-related capabilities such as Authentication and Messaging.

A domain's capabilities are abstracted as service interfaces. Consider the Credit Card Processing domain. It provides a capability to process a charge that accepts a credit card number, expiration date, the account holder's name, and the amount of the charge. This capability returns a code either approving or declining the charge. The capability is made available as an operation on a service interface. In other words, domains interact with each other through services. The interface provides the connection points between the capabilities offered by the domain (the provider) and the needs of the consumer. Sound familiar?

The complete definition of the domain's capabilities is expressed in the service specifications. These define the provided and required capabilities and the rules or protocol for using them. However, they do not specify (or even provide the least little clue to) the implementation of the service. The service specification does tell providers what they must do to implement the service.

More than coincidentally, there is a relationship between domain types and service types. Principle domains are implemented by business and domain services. Generic domains may be implemented by business, domain or utility services. Foundation domains are implemented by foundation services.

The Service Inventory

The service inventory provides a mechanism for organizing all of the services across the enterprise. It lays out the overall set of services and their relationships to each other. The service inventory provides the next level of detail of the capabilities of the business domains.

You can think of the service inventory as a "responsibility map" of domain capabilities and service interfaces. It should clearly describe the overall set of services, and what responsibilities the different service groups within a domain perform, and don't perform.

The service inventory provides a two-dimensional way of organizing services. One dimension relates to the type of service, specifically business, domain, utility, or foundation. The other dimension relates to the business domain partitioning described in the previous section.

Figure 4-15 shows a sample service inventory. At the bottom are the foundation services, the non-business-focused services that are used to construct applications. The middle layers are the different types of business related services. The top layer is the enterprise business processes. Notice how these layers correspond exactly to the service hierarchy presented in Chapter 2 Figure 2-7.

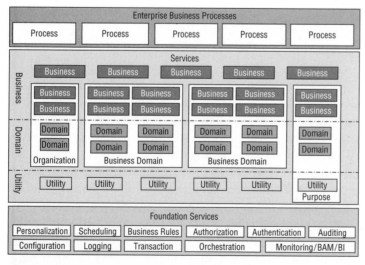

Figure 4-15 Service inventory

The middle layers are really the main focus of the service inventory. They are made up (from bottom to top) of utility services, domain services, and business services. Going from bottom to top of the drawing describes the service type dimension.

Going from left to right is the business domain dimension. Services, particularly the business and domain services, are organized according to different domains. As we mentioned earlier, there are a variety of approaches to domain partitioning, and any or all of them can be used to organize the service inventory.

Notice that some services are enterprise-wide, both at the business service and utility service layers. These apply to the principle domain and are not included in an individual subdomain.

The inventory helps answer two important questions:

- **What services exist?**   At design time, you need to know what services exist, what they do, and how they relate to other services. The inventory provides a convenient structure and visualization for taking the first step in locating and qualifying services.

- **What should a new service do?**   This is perhaps the more important function. When a requirement for a service has been identified, you need to determine how that service fits into the overall set of services. Specifically, what capabilities are the responsibility of the new service, and what capabilities should you expect to be performed by another service. The answers to this question are crucial in eliminating gaps and overlaps in service functions.

Of course, there are many ways to organize the service inventory. The best way for any given enterprise is related to its own goals, structure, organization, maturity, and so on. The specific structure of the inventory is not important as long as it provides a mechanism to easily answer the two questions above. Ideally, the service inventory is integrated directly with the service repository and the overall governance approach.

Summary

A fundamental requirement for technology is to align the business with IT. This is perhaps even truer for SOA-based solutions, but just wishing it doesn't make it so. Business architecture is the key to the alignment.

First, you must define what "the business" means. What are the goals and objectives of the business? What are its primary value adding activities? How do they relate and interact with each other, the customers, and partners. You use a variety of techniques including value chains and business context diagrams to answer these questions. In addition, you can use a formal Business Motivation Model to precisely define the goals, objectives, and strategies and tactics for meeting them. This is business architecture at the enterprise level.

Next, you turn to business architecture at the project level. Here, the primary activity is the creation of Business Process Models. Business process modeling is a useful analysis technique enabling you to find and create business services by enumerating business capabilities and information. Business Process Models describe the steps, decisions, information, and flow of the business processes. The steps and decisions are implemented by business services provided by SOA. The information is passed in documents.

But process design done in isolation does not lead to good services. You also need a way to understand and organize the big picture. Domain partitioning organizes a problem space by subject matter in order to break the problem into manageable chunks and to identify cohesive sets of responsibilities and minimize coupling. The service inventory provides another important way of organizing and categorizing the overall set of services to aid in service identification and implementation. Ultimately, the capabilities of each domain will be implemented by services, well organized in the inventory, and that can be traced back to specific tactics in the business model and provide the link to aligning business objectives with IT systems.

CHAPTER

5

Service Context and Common Semantics

SOA is useless without good data.
— Joe McIndrick

Chapter 4 showed how to use techniques of business process modeling and subject matter partitioning to identify business services that conform to a uniform business architecture. In this architecture, individual services do not exist in isolation — they should be usable in multiple contexts. In other words, these services should be interoperable. Uniform messaging semantics is one of the most important requirements for service interoperability. This ensures that service consumers and providers exchange data in a consistent way that enables their mutual understanding of the information they are intended to process.

This chapter starts by revisiting the importance of uniform messaging semantics and a semantic information model, and then introduces modeling techniques for creating that model based upon information modeling and object-oriented analysis principles. You learn how to synthesize a model by exposing details about a problem based upon the things in the domain. This technique has been shown, in practice, to provide a cohesive foundation for ensuring common semantics.

In constructing an information model, you learn how to model the world of a domain in terms of objects, attributes, and associations and extend these basics by using techniques of specialization and constraint modeling to achieve better model accuracy. We also show you how to partition large models, both to manage the modeling problem and to reflect the real complexities in large enterprises. Finally, the chapter covers usage of XML for representing these models.

In this chapter, you learn:

- The importance of semantics in SOA
- Components of core information modeling
- Information-modeling techniques beyond simple data modeling
- How to structure information models to fit and to reveal a service organization
- How to define documents based on the information model
- How to apply the common information model to define XML and to map data into existing services
- Best practices and pitfalls to avoid

The Importance of Semantics in SOA

Achieving real service interoperability can be harder than some SOA evangelists would have you believe. This is because a majority of SOA publications focus almost exclusively on the mechanics of constructing and combining services. Such *syntactic coupling* certainly achieves much, but it solves just one part of the problem. Many Web Service standards revolve around rules for addressing and binding to services, and they focus on the clear definition of syntactic contracts for service interfaces. Minimizing coupling at the syntactic level is critical, and SOA (especially with the help of the OASIS and W3C standards bodies and the WS-I organization) has made enormous progress.

Unfortunately, syntactic interoperability alone is not sufficient. For a real-world example, consider telephone systems; they are *syntactically interoperable* worldwide. Someone in the United States can use a phone to call someone in Mexico, and the other person can pick up the phone, hear the caller, and begin talking. However, just because they are connected does not necessarily mean that the two parties can successfully communicate or understand each other. If the caller only speaks and understands English, and the person on the other end of the phone only speaks and understands Spanish, the fact that they are connected does not help them communicate. In the same way, service consumers and service providers need to be able to "speak the same language" in order to effectively communicate.

There is more to semantic interoperability than just speaking the same language, however. In Web Services, Extensible Markup Language (XML) is used for carrying the payload of messages because it is an agreed-upon format and therefore an interoperability mechanism, but just knowing that data is marked up in XML isn't enough to have an understanding of what the XML-marked data means. Continuing the same telephone analogy, even if the two parties on the phone speak the same language, they still need a common understanding of the words of the language they are speaking. If an astronomer and a Hollywood socialite are talking, the phrase "star sighting" has a different meaning for both of them; both have a different understanding of the word "star." So their conversation is going to be confused at best. Semantic interoperability, therefore, involves having a common understanding of what the data actually *means*.

Semantic interoperability is an essential aspect of SOA because service consumers and service providers need to exchange information that both understand and that can be used to achieve a specific capability. Data that is not understandable is obviously not useful, and without semantics, data would simply consist of garbage strings of zeroes and ones that have no meaning. Without understanding the meaning of the data, service consumers and providers could misinterpret the data and ultimately bring undesirable effects to the business. Semantic interoperability between services and for your particular business domain increases your chances for success.

There are many levels of maturity for semantic interoperability, from the very simple to the very complex. Michael C. Daconta, Leo Obrst, and Kevin T. Smith, in their book *The Semantic Web*, (2003), refer to levels of data interoperability as the "smart data continuum," where data at the lowest level of interoperability has relevance to only certain applications, and where data at the highest level of interoperability can be discoverable and understandable between applications in different business domains. You can apply this concept to SOA by looking at three levels of interoperability maturity:

- **Project-specific interoperability** — The lowest level of interoperability involves creating data formats specific to a particular SOA project. In this case, schemas are typically created by looking at the functionality of specific services. Because the data in these projects is only relevant to the specific services in the project, interoperability with other projects is usually only achieved by transformations between similar messages from services and consumers in different projects (once other projects understand the meaning of your data formats). This interoperability approach is therefore doable, but is often short-sighted if existing data standards are not used.

- **Business domain-specific interoperability** — A higher level of interoperability revolves around the reuse of data standards within a business domain. By using accepted standard schemas for such a domain, data used in SOA projects can reuse message formats and can, therefore, interoperate with other services and consumers within that business domain. An example is services that utilize XML standards within the healthcare, insurance, or the military industries. As businesses have grasped the importance of semantic interoperability, many consortiums and industries have collaborated to build standard data formats, data models, and taxonomies related to their domains. Therefore, using such standards is good practice, as similar projects may need to interoperate with other systems in the same domain.

▪ **Business domain-independent interoperability** — In the highest level of interoperability, data formats use standards from multiple business domains. In this approach, service messages may include elements from schemas from several business domains, they may reference taxonomic classifications from different domains, and elements of the data may refer to elements in an ontology. By using semantic web technologies, services and clients from different domains can consume the data, and in many cases, they can use rule-based systems to infer new knowledge by the analysis of data. The bottom line is that the highest level of interoperability includes the maximum reuse of data standards and data definitions.

As you can see, semantics are important and dictate how interoperable your SOA will be. Without semantics, the network connectivity between consumers and services mean nothing. The more mature your project is on the maturity scale, the more flexible and interoperable your services are. For example, if your SOA revolves around data formats that you explicitly defined only for your project, then future interoperability between other applications may be difficult because you would have to explain to someone what "your" data standard means, and you have to understand the data standards of the other application. Therefore, the more you reuse accepted semantic data standards, the better off you are.

At the same time, if you are new to data standards, we're not advising you to jump into the highest level of interoperability maturity, focusing on ontology design and expert systems. A little semantics can go a long way. Your SOA governance should define guidance, policies, best practices, and procedures related to how you define your data formats for SOA. We talk more about this in Chapter 12.

HOW DOES THE SEMANTIC WEB RELATE TO SOA?

Tim Berners-Lee, James Hendler, and Ora Lassila, in their May 2001 *Scientific American* article "The Semantic Web," which coined the phrase with the same name, unveiled a vision of the future web. "The Semantic Web", they wrote, "is an extension of the current Web in which information is given well-defined meaning, better enabling computers and people to work in cooperation".
The Semantic Web is a vision, and much progress has been made in semantic technologies since that initial vision was proposed. The Semantic Web, like Web Services, builds on XML as a foundation. Languages such as XML Schema, the Web Ontology Language (OWL), and the Resource Description Framework (RDF) have come a long way in making the vision of the Semantic Web seem attainable.

SOA relates to the Semantic Web in that it needs to be data-centric in its messaging. The use of XML as an interchange format, the use of schemas to define and reference common vocabularies, the use of ontologies, and the use of registries for associating services with taxonomic classification is probably just putting us on the cusp of the Semantic Web vision.

So, is the Semantic Web "there yet" for SOA? Not quite — there is "Semantic Web" the utopian vision that we strive for, and there are useful semantic technologies that are currently reaching for the vision. Much progress is being made in academia, government, and the commercial space in semantic technologies. We expect that further developments in these semantic technologies will have a positive impact on SOA. For more information about the vision and how it relates to SOA, we recommend the book *The Semantic Web: A Guide to the Future of XML, Web Services, and Knowledge Management* (2003) by Daconta, Obrst, and Smith.

Core Information Modeling

The foundation of semantic interoperability is core information modeling. The information model defines the data and domain concepts that must be shared between services. Similar to domain partitioning (see Chapter 4) for identifying business services, core information modeling partitions the information domain to define information objects used for service communications.

To understand a domain, you need to understand the things in the domain (the objects) and their semantics (their meaning, rules, and policies). Information modeling provides the foundations for this understanding. In constructing an information model, you learn how to model the world of a domain in terms of objects, attributes, and associations.

Objects and Attributes

In order to understand a world — a domain — you begin by characterizing the things in it. This process is called *abstraction*. It involves sorting the unimportant things from the important things (e.g., fire hydrants are part of a dog's world, but they're not relevant to the problem of issuing and tracking dog licenses) and categorizing those important things according to concepts and perceptions of "likeness" and "difference."

Our notion of an object is based upon this notion of likeness. An *object* is defined as an abstraction of a set of things in a domain such that:

- All the things in the set — the instances — have the same characteristics

▪ All the instances are subject to and conform to the same behavior, rules, and policies.

The common characteristics are abstracted as the attributes of an object. The common behavior is abstracted as operations and events.

WHAT'S OOA DOING IN SOA?

Just because we're using techniques of object-oriented analysis (OOA) does not mean that object-oriented and service-oriented techniques are the same.

Object-oriented techniques — primarily those of object-oriented programming — have very different treatments of issues like granularity and association than those of SOA. They also have significant life cycle differences, and their usage adheres to two very different programming models.

Our use of OOA is purely for the purpose of defining the information in a domain in order to arrive at a uniform semantic model.

Classes, Attributes, and Instances

Figure 5-1 shows a simple information model for an online store expressed as a UML class diagram. Each of the boxes represents a *class* — one of the things with common characteristics and common behavior. Each of the names below the class name (such as the SKU, UnitPrice, Name, and so on for the

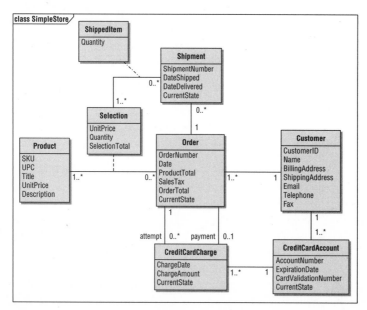

Figure 5-1 This simple information model is shown as a UML class diagram

Product) represents an attribute — one of the common characteristics of the class (compare to the data model definition). The lines between the classes represent the associations between the classes.

DOMAINS AS A POINT OF VIEW

The things that you see depend upon the domain that you are modeling. For example, consider this object:

Is it a Flying Aircraft? Or is it a Shipping Vehicle? That depends upon the domain you are modeling. If your domain is Air Traffic Control, you see the thing as a Flying Aircraft with an altitude, an airspeed, a heading, pilots, and so forth. On the other hand, if your domain is Freight Shipping, then that very same thing is a Shipping Vehicle with a pallet capacity, a tare weight, and onboard shipments.

Services need to represent cohesive capabilities, while at the same time being decoupled from ideas that are not relevant. Cohesion means that objects do not exist in isolation: An Aircraft in an Air Traffic Control domain makes little sense without control towers and flight plans; a Shipping Vehicle does not make sense without shipments and pallets.

However, good services are also loosely coupled from that which is not relevant to the domain. Altitude and airspeed are not as relevant to package shipping as they are to air traffic control. A single service that mixes the concepts of shipping and air traffic control is going to be far less useful than services that separate the two concepts.

When modeling, it's important to understand the context or point of view of the domain you're modeling in order to determine which characteristics of the airplane to model and which ones to ignore. This idea is important to developing a consistent semantic model because the model needs to incorporate all of the perspectives relevant to the domain, while excluding that which is not relevant.

Attributes and Instances

Attributes abstract the common characteristics of a class. Each attribute is intended to be relevant for every *instance* of the class, and each attribute is expected to have at most one value per instance. These rules are not just an academic nicety; they are important to ensuring a solid abstraction.

In Figure 5-1, a Customer can have multiple credit card accounts. Consequently, the account number and expiration date are attributes of a separate related object.

Each attribute also has a type that defines the legal values for that attribute. Techniques for defining types are covered in a later section.

Associations

The world is also full of relationships between things. In fact, these relationships are often more interesting than the things themselves! These meaningful relationships are formalized as *associations*.

REFERENTIAL ATTRIBUTES

Associations can be thought of as data. In traditional relational data modeling, attributes are added to one of the objects to answer the "which one" question. Although they may be present in implementations, such as relational databases, foreign keys or referential attributes are unnecessary (and, in fact, redundant) in an information model.

Pairs of classes may have more than one association between them. The different associations may have very different meaning, such as the separate owner, driver, and passenger of an automobile, as shown in Figure 5-2.

Multiple associations may be related in meaning, such as the attempted and payment charges in Figure 5-1. Role names (attempted, and payment) are used to distinguish between the related instances.

Association Multiplicities

Whenever two classes are related, you need to know for a given instance of one class how many related instances of the other class can exist. This is called the *association multiplicity*. In modeling different forms of relationships, you are concerned with only three numbers: zero, one, and many. Of course, although there's nothing to prevent you from using multiplicities such as 2 or

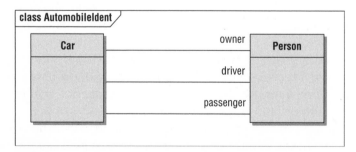

Figure 5-2 Multiple associations between classes

1.8, in practice, such fixed multiplicities can either hide real abstractions, such as the difference between the owner and driver of a car, or they can represent less-relevant implementation limitations.

The multiplicity of an association carries substantial meaning. Consider the relationship between the Order and the Customer in Figure 5-1. The fact that an Order requires one Customer, and a Customer has one or more Orders, means that a Customer does not exist until there is a corresponding Order.

Finding Classes

Classes do not represent just tangible things such as cars, airplanes, and books. Although these kinds of things provide a good starting point for information modeling, they are not the only classes that can be modeled. Classes can also represent roles played by people or things, interactions between things, incidents that happen at a point in time, and specifications.

Defining Types

Every value produced or consumed by a service — whether as an operation parameter or as part of a document — has a set of legal values. These sets of legal values are formalized as data types (and sometimes values valid for a particular data type). By formally defining data types, you ensure the overall accuracy and consistency of the information model. Data types typically represent core concepts of a particular domain and as such are often called *domain-specific* data types. Their names, their semantics, and their implementations are meaningful to the problem domain. Two data types defined for two different domains might have the same name, but they are different data types. For example, in a shipping domain, a customer definition has to include its shipping address and can omit any other attributes, while in the billing domain, a customer's billing information is the most important characteristic of the customer.

Domain-specific types are generally representable across several different technologies. Their value may be represented as an XML document (messaging), Java or C# class (processing), and/or a relational database (persistence).

Using domain-specific types helps you to be able to define one name for a type and then to have as many different implementations as necessary for the different technologies. Many kinds of subtle errors can be detected if your implementation technologies support strong typing (enforcement of rules defining which kinds of values are acceptable function inputs and outputs).

The domain-specific types provide a coordinated, platform-agnostic way to name each of the different kinds of data that will be input to, processed by, and output from each service.

Domain-specific types fall into three basic categories: *simple* types that represent only a single value, *composite* types that represent a single value that can be meaningfully subdivided into component values, and *document* types that represent sophisticated business data, built by combining simple and composite types, typically into a hierarchical organization.

Simple Types

Simple data types that represent single atomic values can be classified as either numeric, symbolic, or enumeration, depending upon the kind of information represented by the type.

Numeric Types

Numeric types represent quantities and measurements. Generally, these can be expressed in terms of a range and a precision. Some examples are:

```
Type A is 10..20 by 1
Type B is 0..max by 1
Type C is 32..212 by 0.01
Type D is -100..100 by 10
```

Numeric types may also be defined in terms of a unit of measure. Such *dimensioned numbers* are not just for physical quantities (feet, inches, meters) but can be used for money/currency values as well. Dimensioned numbers consist of both the dimension (length, money) and the unit in which the number is represented.

A numeric type does not only have to be represented as a traditional numeric value. Times and dates are also instances of numeric values, even though their display representations (10:35 P.M.) are more complex than simple integer numbers.

All numeric types share one basic characteristic: Arithmetic operations make sense. Two measurements can be added to form another measurement; a clock time can be subtracted from another clock time to yield a duration, and so forth.

The definition of a type includes both the structure of the type and the sets of operations that are permitted between values of that type and other types. As an example, consider services for managing intermodal shipping containers. Weight, linear dimensions, and volume dimensions are key properties of a shipping container. Weights can be added and subtracted; linear measurements can be added and subtracted, but a weight cannot be added to a linear measurement. Dimensioning also allows you to deal with both imperial (feet, pounds) and metric measurements: You know that your service needs to support operations to convert between different units.

Symbolic Types

While numeric types represent physical quantities and counts and support a wide variety of arithmetic operations, symbolic types represent labels, monikers, and other similar kinds of descriptive text. Like numeric types, they are defined in terms of their sets of legal values. But in the case of symbolic types, these values are described in terms of patterns of legal values.

These patterns can be very simple, specified in terms of a length, or specified in terms of a pattern (shown here as a regular expression):

```
// Very simple type
NameString is any text

// Symbolic types specified as a length
ZipCode is exactly 5 characters
PostalCode is between 3 and 12 characters
Password is at least 10 characters
ContainerCode is up to 6 characters
CommentString is up to 200 characters and can be null

// Symbolic type as a pattern
["+" digit+] ["(" digit+ ")"] digit+ [space digit+]*
```

Typical operations supported for symbolic types include combining (concatenation), splitting (substring), and parsing (splitting according to patterns or grammars).

Enumeration Types

Enumerations represent discrete values taken from some defined set. Some examples are:

```
ContainerCondition is (Clean, Dirty, Damaged)
OrderState is (New, Unpaid, Paid, Packed, Shipped, Delivered)
```

Enumerations are a third kind of type because they are not really numbers (even though they may be represented by discrete integer values behind the scenes) and are not really symbolic types either. A `ContainerCondition` cannot be concatenated to an `OrderState`.

Not every programming language and few database technologies support strongly typed enumerations. (XML, the .NET languages, and Java do support them.) However, enumerations provide a much more accurate and satisfying way to represent discrete values where the value is truly distinct from its implementation representations.

Composite Types

Many values encountered in real business problems have a dual personality: In some contexts, they are single atomic values. At the same time, they contain several individual components that can be meaningful on their own. The ubiquitous "Address" is an outstanding example of such a composite type:

```
Type Address is
     Street: string
     City: string
     State: UNSubdivisionCode
     PostalCode: PostalCode
     Country: ISOCountryCode
End Type
```

Composite types may themselves consist of other composite types.

Implementing Types

In reading this rather detailed definition of types, you're likely to be thinking, "but my language or database or middleware doesn't support this concept." And that's exactly the purpose of this extensive section. SOA generally requires you to represent the same real-world values in several different technologies; therefore, it is important that you start with a complete but platform-agnostic definition.

Beyond the Basics

The last section presented a basic introduction to information modeling. In order to create models that expose detail and help you to create a complete semantic model of a domain, you need to apply several more sophisticated techniques.

Identifiers and Uniqueness Constraints

To use the objects defined in the information model, you need to be able to refer to individual and collective instances of those objects. An *identifier* is a collection of attributes that by themselves, or in the context of some association, uniquely identifies an instance of an object (similar to the primary keys, defined in the entity/relational modeling).

The real world is full of identifiers. This book, for example, has an ISBN (International Standard Book Number) and a UPC (Universal Product Code). It is likely that the store from which you bought it gave it an SKU (Stock Keeping

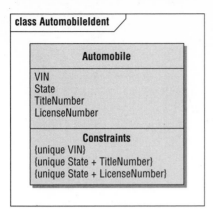

Figure 5-3 Identifiers of an automobile

Unit) code. Your car has a VIN (vehicle identification number). Your insurance policies and bank accounts have numbers. Business problems are full of such *natural* identifiers — ones that are designated by and used by the business.

Identifiers are modeled as uniqueness constraints. Figure 5-3 shows the three different identifiers of an automobile, listed as distinct uniqueness constraints.

Identifier and Identity

A class is not required to have an identifier in the information model. This distinguishes the concept of an identifier from the data-modeling concepts of keys or the programming concepts of pointers and handles. In this sense, the concept of identifier is distinct from the concept of object identity. While it is not necessary for a class to have an identifier in all cases, identifiers serve the purpose of providing a means to refer to an object.

Contrived Identifiers

Other objects do not have natural identifiers, but it is still important to be able to identify instances. In those cases, add a *contrived identifier* to the object. An attribute such as the `ChargeID` (on the `CreditCardCharge`) is an example of a contrived identifier.

Sometimes the business itself invents identifiers. Attributes such as an `OrderNumber` (on the `Order`) and the `ShipmentNumber` (on the `Shipment`) are needed by the business in order to uniquely identify instances of `Order`s and `Shipment`s.

Multiple Population Identifiers

When unifying data across parallel systems, such as the unification of accounts across multiple banks, some techniques may be needed in order to create one

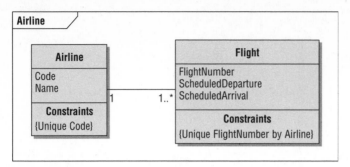

Figure 5-4 Subpopulation identifier

single population of `Accounts`. Solutions range from creating all new account numbers to creating compound identifiers by combining a unique code for each of the original banks with the original account numbers.

Subpopulation Identifiers

Finally, some attributes are unique but only in the context of an association to another class. A `Flight` number is only unique within the context of its related `Airline`. Figure 5-4 shows how the identifier of a `Flight` — the `Flight Number` — is marked as being relative to the association with the `Airline`.

Specializations

The basic definition of an object requires that all instances have the same attributes and that all instances conform to the same rules and policies. However, in the real world, there are many situations in which some attributes are meaningful in some cases but not in all cases. In the store, for example, some products are kept in stock, but others are only ordered when a customer requests them, as shown in Figure 5-5.

Specialization allows you to model the common attributes, associations, and behaviors in a superclass and then to model the different attributes, associations, and behaviors in separate subclasses. In Figure 5-5, a `Product` may be either `Stocked` or `Special Order`, each with attributes that are appropriate to the subclass.

Specializations may be quite complex. The following example in Figure 5-6 models the many complexities of bank deposit accounts.

Specializations may be complete or incomplete. A complete specialization, denoted by the `{complete}` tag, means that every instance of the superclass is an instance of one of the subclasses. In the bank example, every deposit account must be either a `Checking`, `Savings`, or `Retirement` account. There are no instances of deposit accounts that are neither `Checking`, `Savings`, nor `Retirement` accounts.

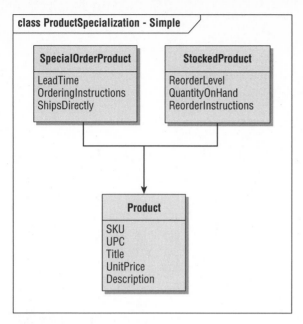

Figure 5-5 Simple specialization

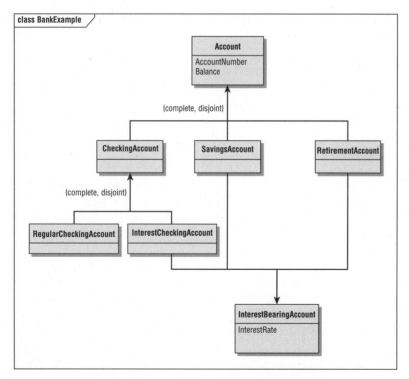

Figure 5-6 Illustration of complex specialization/generalization

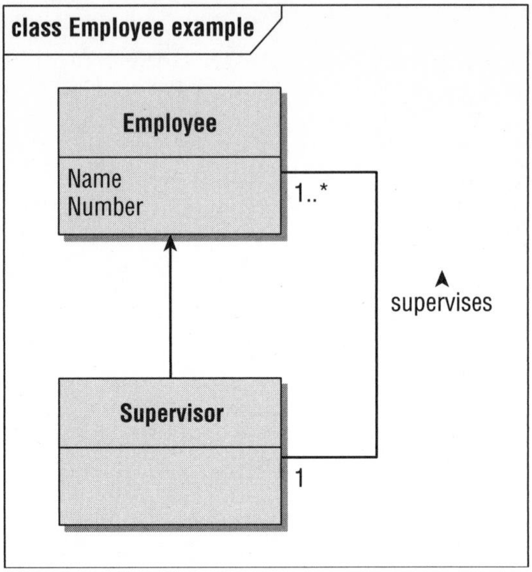

Figure 5-7 Simple Employee-Supervisor model

Incomplete specializations are useful for defining roles. In Figure 5-7, some `Employees` are `Supervisors`; every `Supervisor` is an `Employee`, but not every `Employee` is a `Supervisor`.

A superclass may be specialized in multiple dimensions. In Figure 5-8, a `Product` is not only a `Book`, `Recording`, or `Software`; it is also either `Stocked` or `Special Order`.

Derived Attributes

Each attribute represents an individual fact about an object. Some facts are basic information, but others can be computed from other facts about that object or related objects. Attributes of this sort are called *derived attributes* because their values are derived from the values of other attributes in the model.

A single-object derived attribute represents a fact that can be computed solely from attributes of that same object. (See Figure 5-9.)

Figure 5-9 shows a class with derived attributes. The volume of the container can be calculated from its height and depth. Gross weight is more complicated requiring the `TareWeight` and the `ContentNetWeight` of the associated `Shipment`. The derivation formulas may make use of computations provided

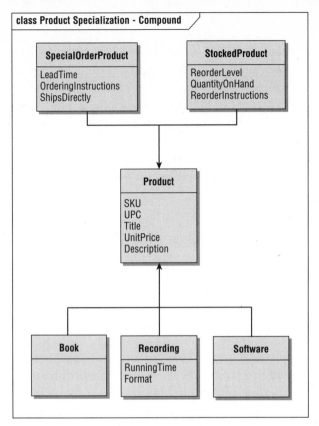

Figure 5-8 Specialization in multiple dimensions

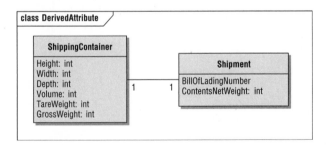

Figure 5-9 Illustration of derived attributes

by services inside or outside of the domain. For example, the total cost of an `Order` may include sales tax computed on that order using a Taxation Service. Note that in the semantic information model, we are defining the information, including derived attributes, but not the rules or formulas that calculate them.

Value Constraints

The information model defines the concepts of a domain in terms of data. Identifiers, derived attributes, and association multiplicities all formalize specific domain rules. An identifier states which attribute values must be unique for all instances or for subsets of instances defined by associations and other attribute values. Derived attribute formulas express the rules by which other values relate to one another. Association multiplicities express whether objects can have related instances and if so, how many. All of these are examples of constraints that formalize the rules of the domain information.

Structuring Information Models

When you have a domain whose model consists of several hundred objects, the model can become too big to be manageable, maintainable, or understandable. At this point, you need to partition the model. Not only is it very difficult to print such a class diagram on a single sheet of paper, but it is also difficult to comprehend all those objects at once. Moreover, different parts of the model may correspond to different lines of business, different areas of responsibility, or different areas of expertise within the enterprise. These reasons match very closely the kinds of criteria used for identifying distinct domain services.

A simple approach to dividing a large information model is to split it into clusters of closely related objects. Intuitively, think of cutting the model apart in places where the cuts would divide the fewest association lines, as shown in Figure 5-10.

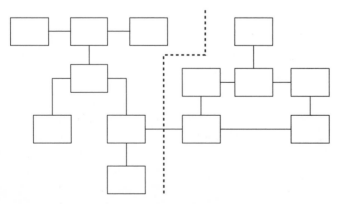

Figure 5-10 A model divided into clusters

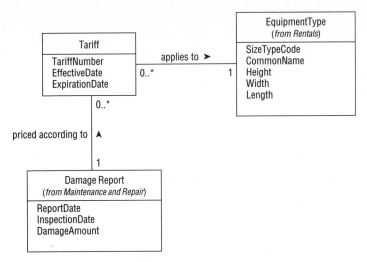

Figure 5-11 Referenced classes

Such a scheme organizes an information model into distinct packages. When a model is divided into packages, the cut-through associations still need to be shown in one of the clusters. Because every class belongs to one and only one cluster, the cut-through associations must be assigned to one of the clusters. The class that belongs to the other cluster is shown as a *referenced class* where the "from nnn" notation indicates the cluster to which the class actually belongs. (See Figure 5-11.)

Documents

A fundamental difference between service operations and object methods is that service operations are much larger granularity. Rather than many simple operations with simple parameters, services produce and consume big chunks of information known as *documents* (domain object containers). The concept of a document (things like a customer order, a shipping manifest, an invoice, and so forth) should be familiar from the analysis of the business problem. Business process models such as those in Chapter 4 show activities consuming and producing documents.

Documents can be thought of as hierarchical data structures with a main part and several, often nested, repeating parts. They often contain references to other business objects not contained directly within that document. A sample Order might contain the following data:

```
Order
    OrderNumber 2217843
    Date 12/15/2007
```

```
ProductTotal   $ 684.85
SalesTax       $  56.50
OrderTotal     $ 741.35
Selection
     UPC 0785357834163
     UnitPrice $45.99
     Quantity  2
Selection
     UPC 9780201748048
     UnitPrice $44.99
     Quantity  5
Customer
     Name       Samuel L. Clemens
     BillingAddress 1234 Tom Sawyer Drive, Hannibal, MO, 63401
     CreditCardAccount
         AccountNumber 9823-2132-7983
         ExpirationDate 2/2004
         CardValidationNumber 999
```

Defining Documents

Although domain objects (data types) define basic things within a given domain and are fairly stable, documents are typically containers of information, specific for a given service (or group of services). They are created by bringing together multiple domain objects to provide input/output for a given service operation. The other usage of documents is combining multiple domain objects that are typically used together; for example, header/detail information on the purchase order. Documents can be combined further to define a higher-level document.

Service consumers and providers exchange information — service data — when they interact. A document is a view of the semantic information model representing the part of that model needed for a particular service interaction. In order to maintain the relationship of the documents to the semantic information model, you use a document marking technique, as illustrated in Figure 5-12. To define a document, draw the structure of the document on top of the information model. Figure 5-12 shows how a Purchase Order is defined for a Store.

Start by selecting a root class, in this case the Order. The root class is shown with a double line. Then draw arrows along the association lines to other classes related as subelements. (Yes, that term is borrowed from XML.) Finally, draw dotted arrows to other classes that are not to be included in the document but instead are merely to be referenced by the content of the document. A useful technique is to try traversing the loop in different directions and seeing if the same objects can be reached. If so, it's a dependent loop, and one of the associations should be derived.

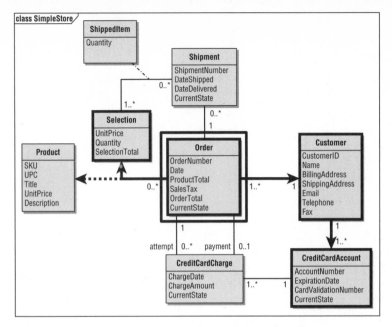

Figure 5-12 Purchase Order document definition

The result of this example is an `Order` document with multiple selections, each of which references a `Product`. The `Order` also includes the details of the `Customer` and the customer's credit card account.

Adapting the Information Model

The sample `Order` listed in the previous section has sections that match the classes in the document marking. However, you may notice that some of the attributes are missing. There is no `CurrentState` on the `Order`; several of the attributes on the `Customer`, such as the `ShippingAddress`, are not present. If your intent is for these attributes to be optional, then the information model needs to be modified so that the attributes are declared to be optional, as shown in Figure 5-13.

When building documents, you may also discover that you are missing some associations in the information model. The model in Figure 5-12 looks correct — but suppose that you want to have a variation of the `Order` that only refers to an existing customer and account. You do not want to have to respecify all of the `Customer` and `Account` data. Although you can have the `Order` reference the `Customer` (rather than include as a subelement), because the association between the `CreditCardAccount` and the `Customer` is one-to-many, there is no way to specify a single `CreditCardAccount`.

To solve this problem, modify the information model by adding an association between the `Order` and the `CreditCardAccount`. This now enables

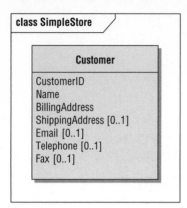

Figure 5-13 A class with optional attributes

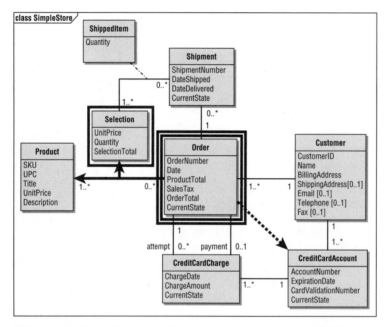

Figure 5-14 Order that refers (by reference) to an existing CreditCardAccount

you to specify a different form of the `Order` that refers to an existing `CreditCardAccount` and, by implication, to an existing `Customer`, as shown in Figure 5-14.

Multiple Documents

As we defined earlier, a document is a container of the multiple domain objects, designed to combine them in order to increase granularity of service operations. As a result, because of the requirements of the different

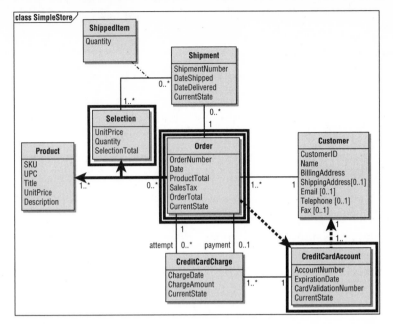

Figure 5-15 Order that contains a new CreditCardAccount for an existing Customer

service operations, there can be many versions of the same document. The two versions of the Order might be used for different scenarios: one in which a new customer places an order, and another in which an existing customer places an order with the same account. A third variation, shown in Figure 5-15, has a CreditCardAccount subelement that refers to an existing Customer.

The different forms of the Order document represent different order creation semantics: new customer, existing customer and new account, and existing customer and account. An Order Service can have one operation that accepts all three forms of the Order document where the specific behavior of the operation is determined by the different forms of the document.

Documents and XML

Domain data objects and documents represent a very useful design technique. However, in a majority of SOA implementations, these objects and documents are passed around in XML, the de facto standard for data messaging in service implementations. Because it is an agreed-upon standard, it is the building block of data interoperability. Jon Bosak, who led the effort to create XML in the W3C, was once quoted as saying "XML just clears away some of the syntactical distractions so that we can get down to the big problem: how we arrive at common understandings about knowledge representation." That says it all. XML is the agreed-upon low-level format with which you can define vocabularies.

The main reasons for the use of XML are:

- It has a standard syntax for metadata and a standard structure for documents.

- It is independent of programming languages and operating environment and can be effectively used to pass information between them.

- Virtually any programming language/operating environment provides good support for marshaling/unmarshaling XML payloads.

- It is, by its very definition, extensible, and its extensibility makes it easier to support changes, which are inevitable in SOA implementations.

- Because it is an open standard, and more importantly, because it is accepted by the industry and the major vendors as the standard, it is the key to low-level interoperability. (When Microsoft, IBM, Sun, and Oracle actually agree on something, you can usually count on its longevity.) The following shows the `Order` data from Figure 5-12 as an XML document:

```
<Order>
     <OrderNumber>2217843</OrderNumber>
     <Date>12/15/2007</Date>
     <ProductTotal>684.85</ProductTotal>
     <SalesTax>56.50</SalesTax>
     <OrderTotal>741.35</OrderTotal>
     <Selection>
          <UPC>0785357834163</UPC>
          <UnitPrice>45.99</UnitPrice>
          <Quantity>2</Quantity>
     </Selection>
     <Selection>
          <UPC>9780201748048</UPC>
          <UnitPrice>44.99</UnitPrice>
          <Quantity>5</Quantity>
     </Selection>
     <Customer>
          <Name>
                <FirstName>Samuel</FirstName>
                <MiddleInitial>L</MiddleInitial>
                <LastName>Clemens</LastName>
          </Name>
          <BillingAddress>
                <Street>1234 Tom Sawyer Drive</Street>
                <City>Hannibal</City>
```

```
            <State>MO</State>
            <Zip>63401</Zip>
      </BillingAddress>
      <CreditCardAccount>
            <AccountNumber>9823-2132-7983</AccountNumber>
            <ExpirationDate>2/2004</ExpirationDate>
            <CardValidationNumber>999</CardValidationNumber>
      </CreditCardAccount>
    </Customer>
  </Order>
```

Note how the structure of the order is immediately evident in the text of the document. The tags follow the structure of the document: elements, subelements, references, and attributes. However, there are some significant issues in the relationship of the model and the XML document that describes it. When designing XML documents, the following should be considered:

- XML uses a hierarchical data model. The hierarchical model differs significantly from OO representations and data models used in traditional databases, like the normalized relational data model, which aims for fast updates and retrievals; or the dimensional data model which aims to slice information in various dimensions; or pointers, which provide fast data traversal. As a result, common database design techniques (e.g., normalization, joins, foreign keys, etc.) or OO design (described in the preceding sections on classes, attributes, etc.) are rarely applicable to XML. They usually lead to an overly complex XML implementation. XML design typically requires significant denormalization of data to minimize cross-references between XML objects.

- As XML payloads are subject to marshaling/unmarshaling when crossing each service boundary, the use of "small" types in XML incurs significant serialization overhead, which in turn has a negative impact on performance. Every XML type is marshaled/unmarshaled into a separate object. This means that usage of "small" XML types leads to the creation and deletion of a large number of objects during execution. Therefore, it is recommended that you increase the size of XML objects during semantic information model design.

- Excessive nesting of XML types can lead to a significantly more complex XML processing of the payloads. It usually leads to creation of additional language objects during marshaling/unmarshaling and requires a more complex notation to access the data. Therefore, it is advantageous to minimize the amount of nesting in the XML payload's definition.

We talk more about best practices later in this chapter.

XML Schema

XML schema is a definition language that enables you to constrain XML documents to a specific vocabulary and hierarchical structure. XML documents can be validated against a schema, and this validation process can catch many structural and semantic errors in the document. The following code shows the XML schema for the Order XML document:

```xml
<xs:schema xmlns:xs="http://www.w3.org/2001/XMLSchema">
  <xs:element name="Order">
    <xs:complexType>
      <xs:sequence>
        <xs:element name="OrderNumber" type="xs:int"/>
        <xs:element name="Date" type="xs:date"/>
        <xs:element name="ProductTotal" type="xs:decimal"/>
        <xs:element name="SalesTax" type="xs:decimal"/>
        <xs:element name="OrderTotal" type="xs:decimal"/>
        <xs:element name="Selection" maxOccurs="unbounded">
          <xs:complexType>
            <xs:sequence>
              <xs:element name="UPC" type="xs:long"/>
              <xs:element name="UnitPrice" type="xs:decimal"/>
              <xs:element name="Quantity" type="xs:positiveInteger"/>
            </xs:sequence>
          </xs:complexType>
        </xs:element>
        <xs:element name="Customer">
          <xs:complexType>
            <xs:sequence>
              <xs:element name="Name">
                <xs:complexType>
                  <xs:sequence>
                    <xs:element name="FirstName" type="xs:string"/>
                    <xs:element name="MiddleInitial" type="xs:string"/>
                    <xs:element name="LastName" type="xs:string"/>
                  </xs:sequence>
                </xs:complexType>
              </xs:element>
              <xs:element name="BillingAddress">
                <xs:complexType>
                  <xs:sequence>
                    <xs:element name="Street" type="xs:string"/>
                    <xs:element name="City" type="xs:string"/>
                    <xs:element name="State" type="xs:string"/>
                    <xs:element name="Zip" type="xs:int"/>
                  </xs:sequence>
                </xs:complexType>
              </xs:element>
```

```
            <xs:element name="CreditCardAccount">
               <xs:complexType>
                  <xs:sequence>
                     <xs:element name="AccountNumber" type="xs:string"/>
                     <xs:element name="ExpirationDate"
type="xs:gYearMonth"/>
                     <xs:element name="CardValidationNumber"
type="xs:short"/>
                  </xs:sequence>
               </xs:complexType>
            </xs:element>
         </xs:sequence>
      </xs:complexType>
   </xs:element>
</xs:schema>
```

Service designs and specifications often include XML schemas in order to provide validation of the service input (and output) documents. The schemas are also useful for tools that help to design and implement services. However, as you can see by looking at the schema in the previous code, a schema isn't the sort of thing that you would really want to edit directly. Rather, you would like to model the schema and have it generated. Fortunately, there are a number of tools that provide simpler, often graphical, representations of XML schemas. Figure 5-16 shows the Order schema in graphical form.

Types in Schemas

Each element in a schema has a type. In the Order schema shown in Figure 5-17 the elements use standard XML schema types (denoted by the xs: namespace). However, the real power comes in defining the domain-specific types in the schema such that the schema can actually validate the values in the document.

For example, a legal U.S. zip code (postal code) consists of either five digits or nine digits in a pattern of five digits, hyphen, four digits. This can be defined in XML schema as a simple type as follows:

```
<xs:simpleType name="ZipCode">
  <xs:restriction base="xs:string">
    <xs:pattern value="[0-9]{5}"/>
    <xs:pattern value="[0-9]{5}-[0-9]{4}"/>
  </xs:restriction>
</xs:simpleType>
```

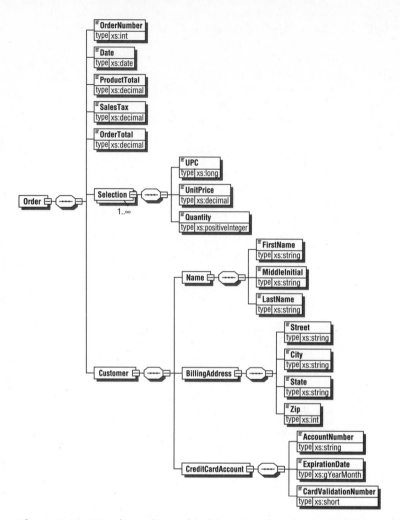

Figure 5-16 XML schema in graphical form (produced using XML Spy by Altova)

Then the `ZipCode` type can be used to define the `Zip` attribute in the schema. Complex types can be defined to represent structured data, such as the components of a `Mailing Address`:

```
<xs:complexType name="MailingAddress">
  <xs:sequence>
    <xs:element name="Street" type="xs:string"/>
    <xs:element name="City" type="xs:string"/>
    <xs:element name="State" type="xs:string"/>
    <xs:element name="Zip" type="ZipCode"/>
  </xs:sequence>
</xs:complexType>
```

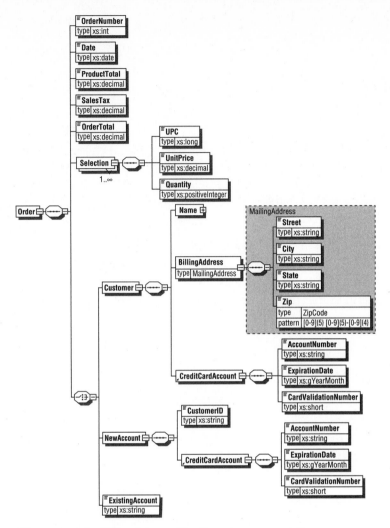

Figure 5-17 An XML schema with alternate representations

The value in defining domain-specific types in the information model and then using these to create schema types should be apparent: Documents can be validated before being delivered for processing, greatly reducing the amount of development work needed in order to implement document-processing service operations.

Document Variations in Schemas

A schema can also capture the different variations in the design of a document. Using these graphical forms, it is relatively straightforward to design documents with variations such as the several forms of the Order mentioned earlier and shown in Figure 5-17.

Designing for Change

One of the important requirements for designing an XML document for service interfaces is support for versioning (see Chapter 9 for more on the service versioning). Using XML schemas to define potential document changes allows an alignment with XML schema-versioning techniques (see the "Versioning Support in XML Schemas" sidebar), thus allowing for direct representation of versioning in the documents. Changes in schemas can be broadly divided into three major categories:

- Revisions represent document changes with no semantic meaning. For example, a change in white space, formatting, non-normative documentation, comments, and so on. A revision of an already published version must not affect the functionality of either service implementations or consumers.

  Additionally, the initial incremental revisions during development of a semantic schema, before it is published for production, can also be treated as revisions of the same version.

- Minor changes are backward-compatible changes to the document schema. Examples of minor changes to the schema include:
  - Changing the optionality of a local element or element reference from required to optional.
  - Adding a global element or type.
  - Adding optional elements to the existing type.
  - Changing the type of a global or local element to the type derived from the original type, by adding/restricting optional elements.

- Major changes are non-backward-compatible changes to the document schema.

  Examples of major changes to the schema include:
  - Changing the type of a local or global element by adding required elements or attributes.
  - Changing the optionality of a local element or element reference from optional to required.
  - Adding or removing an enumeration value.
  - Removing or renaming a global type or element.

VERSIONING SUPPORT IN XML SCHEMAS

The simplest way to denote versions in XML Schema is to use an (optional) attribute at the `xs:schema element — version`. The content model permits Dewey notation of `major.minor` version numbers.

Bacause XML parsers are not required to validate instances using version, it is possible to implement a custom representation of version, enabling the parser to include it in the validation process. Using this technique typically requires introduction of a versioning attribute as a fixed, required value for identifying a specific schema version. Although theoretically this is a good approach for schema versioning, it is not very practical. There are several disadvantages to this approach:

◆ An XML instance is unable to use multiple versions of a schema representation because versioning occurs at the schema's root.

◆ XML schema validation tools are not required to validate instances using the version attribute. The attribute is provided purely for documentation purposes and is not enforceable by XML parsers.

◆ Because XML parsers are not required to validate the use of the version attribute, additional custom processing (over and above parsing and validation) is required to ensure that the expected schema version(s) is being referenced by the instance.

◆ Marshaling/unmarshaling of XML documents is very rarely done using direct manipulation of the Document Object Model (DOM) tree. The most prevalent approach to marshaling is the generation of classes that support "automatic" marshaling, using tools like WSDL2Java, Castor, Eclipse Modeling Framework (EMF), Service Data Objects (SDO), XML Schema Definition (XSD), XSDObjectGenerator, and the like. In this case, classes are generated in the packages in Java or namespaces in C#, based on the schema namespaces, not the schema version.

Another option for denoting the schema version is XML namespaces. In this approach a new XML namespace is used for all major version releases. This approach is well aligned with the generation of marshaling/unmarshaling code. It allows code to be generated in different packages (namespaces), thus enabling a single-service consumer to work with several major releases of schema simultaneously.

The final option is to keep XML namespace values constant and add a special element for grouping custom extensions. This approach wraps extensions to the underlying vocabulary within a special extension element. This technique is favored by several industry-standard schemas. For example, the Open Application Group's Business Object Documents (OAG BODs) include a `<userarea>` element defining custom information that may not be part of the base vocabulary. This approach provides maximum extensibility of the schema

(continued)

> ### VERSIONING SUPPORT IN XML SCHEMAS *(continued)*
>
> constructs (schemas can be both forward and backward compatible) without the introduction of new namespaces. There are two disadvantages to this approach:
>
> ◆ It introduces significantly higher levels of complexity into the schema.
>
> ◆ It does not allow the implementation of multiple extensions across different portions of the XML instance, because all extensions must be grouped within the extension "wrapper."
>
> ◆ The most scalable approach to versioning of schemas is:
>
> ▪ Componentization of the overall schema into logical partitions, using multiple namespaces, thus allowing each to contain changes.
>
> ▪ Defining a new namespace (reflecting the major version information) for every major version of each schema.
>
> ▪ Denoting every minor version as a schema version in a major version namespace. Because minor versions are backward-compatible, generated marshaling/unmarshaling code is backward-compatible as well.

XML Patterns

With the multiplicity of tools that allow for the generation of XML documents, creation of documents might seem very straightforward. Once a UML model of semantic information is created, the appropriate tooling can be used to generate both the schema and XML instances. This approach does not require knowledge or a good understanding of XML and seems so simple that a lot of people have rushed into using it without thinking about the consequences. As a result, many implementations are stuck with "bad," hard-to-maintain XML schemas. We have seen a lot of cases where this approach leads to significant performance degradation, requirements for massive implementation changes, and so on. Here, we discuss some approaches that allow you to produce better, more maintainable XML documents. Some of the recommendations described here can be achieved through modification of the models, whereas others may require tweaking an XML schema produced as a result of the generation.

One of the things to keep in mind is that XML uses a hierarchical data model, which differs significantly from OO representations. This model is very well suited for implementing containment relationships, but the implementation of references (although possible through usage of IDs/IDREFs XML support) can lead to significant performance degradation during XML processing. The usage of direct references also often leads to hard-to-read XML documents. Let's take, for example, a multicustomer invoice. When modeling this document, we know that there are three types of relationships: customers to invoice, line items to invoice, and line items to customers. A straightforward implementation of a document like this looks like the following document:

```
<invoice>
<customer> ...
     <Item IDREF=1>
     <Item IDREF=3>
</customer>.
<customer> ...
     <Item IDREF=2>
     <Item IDREF=3>
</customer>.
<lineitem ID=1> ... </lineitem>
<lineitem ID=2> ... </lineitem>
<lineitem ID=3> ... </lineitem>
</invoice>
```

Here, both `Customers` and `Invoices` are direct children of the Invoice document, and relationships between them are defined using line items IDs. Although this XML document is perfectly valid, as the number of customers and line items grows, it becomes less readable and harder to process. A different implementation is shown in the following document:

```
<invoice>
<customer> ...
<lineitem> ... </lineitem>
<lineitem> ... </lineitem>
</customer>.
<customer> ...
<lineitem> ... </lineitem>
<lineitem> ... </lineitem>
</customer>.
</invoice>
```

Here, we changed relationships between customers and line items from references to containment. The resulting document contains more information (some line items can be repeated multiple times for different customers), but the overall document is cleaner and more readable. Based on these examples, we recommend using containment references as much as possible in the common semantic information design.

XML provides a very powerful mechanism for optional elements. Using these elements provides a simple extensibility approach to XML document design. This approach is not easily mapped to OO modeling, but we strongly recommend using it as much as possible. Typically, this is done by introducing additional attributes into the designed classes and then marking them as optional in a resulting document.

XML documents are used as the technical format for passing information between services. When these documents enter the service implementation, they have to be converted (marshaled) into language classes. If a document creates many small language classes, the marshaling becomes very expensive, because of the massive memory allocation required. A typical side effect of using small classes in XML is excessive nesting. In addition to entailing expensive marshaling, highly nested XML documents are typically hard to read and understand. This means that when you create the semantic information model, we recommend that you try to increase the granularity of semantic objects.

Inheritance is a very powerful mechanism for defining semantic data types. Whereas UML modeling supports only derivation by extension, XML provides a significantly richer set of derivation mechanisms, including the examples discussed in the following sections.

Derivation Using Abstract Classes

Abstract classes cannot be used in instance documents; they simply provide a placeholder for their derived types. In the following example, Magazine is an abstract type that has a Title and an Editor. A sports magazine (SportsMagazine) is derived from an abstract Magazine type, and therefore inherits both Title and Editor. This can be achieved by using the code extension base="Magazine" under a definition of SportsMagazine. In addition, the sports magazine will also have car advertisements, so you can add CarsAdvertizement to the inherited base type:

```
<xs:complexType name="Magazine" abstract="true">
<xs:sequence>
<xs:element name="Title" type="xs:string"/>
<xs:element name="Editor" type="xs:string"/>
</xs:sequence>
</xs:complexType>
<xs:complexType name="SportsMagazine">
<xs:complexContent>
<xs:extension base="Magazine">
<xs:sequence maxOccurs="unbounded">
<xs:element name="CarsAdvertizement"
type="xs:string"/>
</xs:sequence>
```

```
</xs:extension>
</xs:complexContent>
</xs:complexType>
```

As shown in the next listing, the instance document built using the schema above contains all the base class characteristics and the added `CarsAdvertizement` component:

```
<?xml version="1.0" encoding="UTF-8"?>
<Product xmlns="http://www.cna.com"
xmlns:xsi="http://www.w3.org/2001/XMLSchema-instance"
xsi:schemaLocation="http://www.Bond.com Product.xsd">
<Magazines>
<SportsMagazine>
<Title>Around NFL</Title>
<Editor>John Strong</Editor>
<CarsAdvertizement>Buick</CarsAdvertizement>
<CarsAdvertizement>Audi</CarsAdvertizement>
</SportsMagazine>
</Magazines>
</Product>
```

Derivation by Extension

Another approach to derivation is to use an extension without an abstract type. A `BookSales` type contains information about a book, and includes the number of books sold and the price at which they were sold. It is possible to extend the `Book` type to create a `BookSales` type using the extension base keyword. The following snippet of the `DataTypes` schema shows how this is done:

```
<xs:complexType name="Book">
<xs:sequence>
<xs:element name="Author" type="xs:string"/>
<xs:element name="Title" type="xs:string"/>
<xs:element name="ISBN" type="xs:string"/>
</xs:sequence>
</xs:complexType>
<xs:complexType name="BookSales">
<xs:complexContent>
<xs:extension base="Book">
<xs:sequence>
<xs:element name="Number" type="xs:integer"/>
<xs:element name="Price" type="xs:double"/>
```

```
</xs:sequence>
</xs:extension>
</xs:complexContent>
</xs:complexType>
```

This means that whenever the element BookSales is referenced, the XML instance document will include number and price information with the title, the author, and the ISBN as shown here:

```
<Sales xmlns="http://www.Bond.com"
xmlns:xsi="http://www.w3.org/2001/XMLSchema-instance"
xsi:schemaLocation="http://www.Bond.com Sales.xsd">>
<Books>
<BookSales>
<Author>Shakespeare</Author>
<Title>Complete Works</Title>
<ISBN>0517053616</ISBN>
<Number>234</Number>
<Price>14.50</Price>
</BookSales>
</Books>
</Sales>
```

Derivation by Restriction

Derivation by restriction is useful in cases where it is necessary to create a subset of the base type. One example is restricting the range of values in the initial definition. For example, a Pamphlet is similar to a Book in every way, except that it has no author. Instead of creating a base definition of Pamphlet and then extending it with the author (as we did in the derivation by restriction above), it is possible to use the code restriction base="Book" when creating the pamphlet, as shown here:

```
<xs:complexType name= "Pamphlet">
<xs:complexContent>
<xs:restriction base="Book">
<xs:sequence>
<xs:element name="Title" type="xs:string"/>
<xs:element name="ISBN" type="xs:integer"/>
</xs:sequence>
</xs:restriction>
</xs:complexContent>
</xs:complexType>
```

Disallowing Derivations

In programming, it is possible to declare some interfaces and classes *final* so that they are never subclassed. The same goal can be achieved in schemas by making some components final, as follows:

```
<xsd:complexType name="BondDefinition" final="#all">
<xsd:complexType name="BondDefinition" final="extension">
<xsd:complexType name="BondDefinition" final="restriction">
```

When the keyword, #all is used, the component can be neither extended nor restricted. In the other two cases, the final blocks either extension or restriction.

Unfortunately, using these inheritance mechanisms requires direct design of the XML documents.

There are also well-defined XML design patterns addressing decoupling and cohesion in XML schemas. They mainly address different levels of granularity of data types. These design patterns allow for simplification of refactoring in cases of semantic models changes. There are three design patterns that represent three levels of granularity when creating components:

- Russian Doll
- Salami Slice
- Venetian Blind

Russian Doll

When using this design pattern, components contain all the relevant components within themselves (like a Russian doll). In the following example the type Book is composed of the components Title, Author, and ISBN. These components are defined locally within the Book component:

```
<xs:element name="Book">
<xs:complexType>
<xs:sequence>
<xs:element name="Title" type="xs:string"/>
<xs:element name="Author" type="xs:string"/>
<xs:element name="ISBN" type="xs:integer"/>
</xs:sequence>
</xs:complexType>
</xs:element>
```

Characteristics of this design pattern include:

- **Opaque content** — The content of `Book` is opaque to other schemas and to other parts of the same schema. The impact of this is that none of the types or elements within `Book` are reusable.

- **Localized scope** — The region of the schema where the `Title` and `Author` element declarations are applicable is localized to within the `Book` element. The impact of this is such, that, if the schema has set `elementFormDefault="unqualified"`, then the namespaces of `Title` and `Author` are hidden (localized) within the schema.

- **Compact** — Everything is bundled together into a tidy, single unit.

- **Decoupled** — With this design approach, each component is self-contained (i.e., they don't interact with other components). Consequently, changes to the components have limited impact. For example, if the components are within `Book` change, it will have a limited impact because they are not coupled to components outside of `Book`.

- **Cohesive** — With this design approach, all the related data is grouped together into self-contained components, that is, the components are cohesive.

This design pattern provides the best encapsulation (all of the internal data types are defined inside the schema itself) but has the most limited reuse capabilities.

Salami Slice

In this approach, components are put together or aggregated by referencing different types. Thus, `Book`, `Title`, `Author`, and `ISBN` are all global elements. The `Book` type then references the other three as part of its definition as shown here:

```
<xs:element name="Title" type="string"/>
<xs:element name="Author" type="string"/>
<xs:element name="ISBN" type="integer"/>
<xs:element name="Book">
<xs:complexType>
<xs:sequence>
<xs:element ref="Title"/>
<xs:element ref="Author"/>
<xs:element ref="ISBN"/>
</xs:sequence>
</xs:complexType>
</xs:element>
```

This design pattern is referred to as Salami Slice because each component or type represents one slice. Characteristics of this design pattern are:

- **Transparent content** — The components that make up `Book` are visible to other schemas and to other parts of the same schema. The impact of this is that the types and elements within `Book` are reusable.

- **Global scope** — All components have global scope. The impact of this is that, regardless of the value of `elementFormDefault`, the namespaces of `Title` and `Author` are exposed in instance documents.

- **Verbose** — Everything is laid out and clearly visible.

- **Coupled** — In the example, you saw that the `Book` element depends on the `Title` and `Author` elements. If those elements were to change, it would have an impact on the `Book` element. Thus, this design produces a set of interconnected (coupled) components.

- **Cohesive** — In this design approach, all the related data is also grouped together into self-contained components. Thus, the components are cohesive.

The two design approaches differ in a couple of important ways:

- The Russian Doll design facilitates hiding (localizing) namespace complexities. The Salami Slice design does not.

- The Salami Slice design facilitates component reuse. The Russian Doll design does not.

Venetian Blind

In this pattern, all elements and components are defined as types. This means that when the component called `Title` is defined, it has to be referenced by the type `Title`, even though it is a simple type defined as a string. This illustrates the highest level of factoring components into their most atomic stage.

Because each component is a type, each can be qualified by a namespace if `elementFormDefault="qualified"`. The ability to show or hide namespaces like opening or closing a Venetian blind lends this design pattern its name:

```
<xs:simpleType name="Title">
<xs:restriction base="xs:string"/>
</xs:simpleType>
<xs:simpleType name="Name">
<xs:restriction base="xs:string">
<xs:minLength value="1"/>
</xs:restriction>
</xs:simpleType>
<xs:complexType name="Book">
```

```
<xs:sequence>
<xs:element name="Title" type="Title"/>
<xs:element name="Author" type="Name"/>
</xs:sequence>
</xs:complexType>
```

This design has:

- **Maximum reuse** — The primary components of reuse are type definitions.

- **Maximum namespace hiding** — Element declarations are nested within types, thus maximizing the potential for namespace hiding.

- **Easy exposure switching** — Whether namespaces are hidden (localized) in the schema or exposed in instance documents is controlled by the `elementFormDefault` switch.

- **Coupled** — This design generates a set of components that are interconnected (i.e., dependent).

- **Cohesive** — As with the other designs, the components group together related data. Thus, the components are cohesive.

The choice of a particular design patterns is driven by your requirements:

- The Venetian Blind design is the one to choose when your schemas require the flexibility to turn namespace exposure on or off with a simple switch, and when component reuse is important.

- When your task requires that you use element substitution, which is available to instance document authors, then use the Salami Slice pattern.

- When minimizing size and coupling of components is of utmost concern, then use the Russian Doll design.

Consistent use of these XML design patterns typically requires manual refactoring of the generated XML schemas. When deciding whether to use a particular pattern, it is necessary to weigh the amount of manual XML refactoring against the quality of resulting XML.

Best Practices for the SOA Architect

We have covered a lot of ground in this chapter, but it is also important to understand the "big picture," the common pitfalls and best practices related to semantic interoperability. This section provides information on the pitfalls to avoid and guidance on how to avoid them.

Using Abstraction to Avoid "SOA Stovepipes"

Earlier in this chapter, we talked about the basic level of semantic interoperability, which is developing data definitions and schemas that are specific to your project. Unfortunately, adopting such a methodology is sometimes short-sighted. When you do this, the data is tightly coupled to each service or application. This short-sighted technique is commonly referred to as building an "SOA stovepipe!" A service that communicates using messages that are only understood by the people who built it is not very interoperable at all. Unfortunately, this is a trap that is very easy to fall into, because of the following:

- **Point-and-click object–to–WSDL generation** — Many enterprise development tools allow automatic Web Service Description Language (WSDL) generation, where objects from previously developed programs can turn into services with the click of a button. Certainly, this is tempting when time is a factor in the development schedule (as it usually is), but have you ever looked at the WSDL results? The parameter objects that are passed into each service do not translate to intuitive messages, and the result is that understanding the XML payloads is dependent on understanding the initial application API. The resulting data is very tightly coupled to the application, and therefore, changes in the application result in having to change the WSDL, leading to chaos in operational deployments.

- **Database-to-schema conversion** — Sometimes developers create a one-to-one translation of database tables to XML schemas, either because there are "database-to-ML" tools that easily allow this to happen or because they are very familiar with the database. What happens is that the understanding of the resulting XML revolves around understanding the implementation of the underlying database, which means that your messages are tightly coupled to your database. If you ever change your database schema, you most likely have to change your XML messages, resulting in chaos.

- **Direct API–to–service bindings** — Similar to point-and-click WSDL generation, this pitfall happens when a developer creates a one-to-one relationship to the original API (whether it be new or legacy) to the service interface, disregarding the definition of data standards for the payloads being passed in service messages. Once again, the one-to-one relationship leads to tight coupling and chaos.

It is important to avoid these traps at all costs. All of these roads lead to semantic chaos. Mergers and acquisitions, regulation, market competition, and customer demands bring constant changes that are difficult enough without worrying about the constant changes that you have to make to keep up with services that are tightly coupled and inflexible. If you start with services that are too tightly coupled to your applications, you have no chance of keeping up.

The key to avoiding this trap is abstraction. Your SOA governance (see Chapter 12) should define processes and procedures for service design, and you should spend time on abstracting the underlying details of legacy applications and your databases.

TIP FOR THE "TOO LATE" SOA FIREFIGHTER

If you are brought in to try to solve the chaos related to SOA stovepipes, you can use a centralized, or hub-and-spoke, approach to data transformation with message brokers, where each service's proprietary semantic meaning is mapped to a logical data model. Semantic interoperability is achieved via a hub-and-spoke topology, which reduces the redundancy and maintenance cost of point-to-point integration. For more information, see the article, "Achieve semantic interoperability in a SOA" by Mei Selvage, Dan Wolfson, Bob Zurek, and Ed Kahan (June 2006).

Reuse Standards to Avoid Reinventing the Wheel

It is easy to invent your own data standards. You are in a time crunch; you need to develop something fast, and so you do, at the cost of reinventing what already exists. The result is that your shortcut is a barrier to future interoperability. Imagine, for example, that each doctor's office and hospital in the United States have a different schema for "Patient Record." Imagine how difficult it could be when a patient transfers from doctor's office to doctor's office, or from hospital to hospital. In the same way, even if you are not planning on initially integrating with other organizations, such situations always happen.

Make sure to look for standards that your SOA governance recommends. Certain approaches may include all or some of the following:

▪ **Using enterprise semantics** — In many successful SOA implementations, all of the services communicate based on the enterprise semantics. These semantics usually include a common vocabulary, a semantic information model, and common schemas. What is helpful is that such an approach does not require data transformations throughout the enterprise. Rather it is the responsibility of service consumers and providers to implement the abstractions from their internal data models to enterprise semantics.

■ **Using business-domain semantics** — Look for industry standards that you can reuse that are relevant to your business domain. In order to encourage interoperability within industries, many vertical industry standardization groups develop industry-specific information models, which often include XML messages and message schemas. For instance, the Association of Retail Technology Standards (ARTS) develops such standards for the retail industry, and the Agency Company Organization for Research and Development (ACORD) develops standards for the insurance industry. These models provide a greater level of semantic interoperability and encourage asset reuse. Some organizations even adopt the industry standard models as their internal enterprise logical models and semantic message models.

Typically, SOA governance initially looks for standards that apply to the business domain. Where those standards are not relevant, a team can focus on creating enterprise data standards. In many cases, a successful solution consists of the combination of the above.

Develop Information Models Based on Use Cases

A common pitfall involves "analysis paralysis" for data modeling. Here's a tip: Don't model the universe down to the level of DNA when you already have an idea of what your messages will be, and what your use cases are for your services. The last thing you need is for another data-modeling team to spend a year developing another schema or ontology starting with "person," "place," and "thing." Use cases are driven by your project's requirements and, therefore, must have a good requirements analysis phase. Based on that phase, look only at the entities required in the messaging of your SOA. Start from there. If no other enterprise standards or industry standards for those entities exist, start modeling for those entities and those entities only.

With Change, Crawl, Walk, Then Run

Many overzealous architects attempt to take on too much of the data problem at once. Especially when services are already deployed, they try to change semantics in all enterprise applications simultaneously. This requires too many changes in too many applications, it is unrealistically complex, it is expensive, and it becomes chaotic. An SOA team needs to provide initial guidance. Once you have that guidance (or if you don't have that team), take a look at the big picture, and see what changes will be the most important. Take an iterative approach with such changes. For more information on what a mature governance life cycle looks like that accommodates change, see Chapter 12.

Summary

Good service design should yield cohesive, interoperable services that are loosely coupled in their implementation and use. The process needs to be precise and detailed — after all, the goal is real working services — but must be agile enough to accommodate changes as the business and understanding of the business evolves over time.

A common semantic information model is a key tool for ensuring consistent shared information across services. Rather than approaching a domain from the perspective of business processes, it uses the business data to define semantics. Information models can be structured along the lines of the business in order to partition concepts specific to certain parts of the business, while capturing common elements, such as the concept of a Customer, for consistent use across the entire enterprise.

The common information model also provides the foundation for defining all of the documents that make up the inputs and outputs of services. Document definition using an information model can expose multiple reasonable variations on the business data, while ensuring consistency with a common model. These practices also make the process of designing documents, using technologies such as XML, far more straightforward and consistent than merely creating isolated schemas.

However, simple approaches to XML generation can result in overly simplistic schemas that result in tightly coupled data, maintenance issues, and performance problems. Understanding the issues related to creating XML schemas from information models is important to developing successful SOA solutions. Common design patterns help to address the issue and create better schemas and solutions.

Designing Service Interfaces

Parts Is Parts
— Wendy's

In previous chapters, we discussed the architectural implications of SOA, the issues related to composing larger services from a collection of smaller ones, and the issues involved in designing common information and semantics to span many different service interfaces. In this chapter, we tie these concepts together around the design of service interfaces. First, we review some of the important service concepts and look at the important characteristics of service interfaces. Then, we introduce a process for interface design and illustrate it with a detailed example. In this chapter, we cover:

- The service characteristics of granularity, scope, and visibility
- Service interaction styles, including parameter passing, document passing, and data passing
- Service invocation styles, including request/response, events, and mixed
- Service design guidelines
- The interface design process
- Sample problem space models
- Sample solution models

Services Revisited

Let's review the important aspects of services. A service provides capabilities that are accessed through its interface. The interface describes how those capabilities are presented and the rules and protocols for using them. The service is implemented through a variety of mechanisms, such as components, composition, and integration. So, we think of a service as a combination of its interface — the public view of the service, and its implementation — the private view of the service. In addition, both the interface and the implementation are a combination of functional and informational aspects. Figure 6-1 highlights these aspects of a service.

In terms of service interface design, this means:

- The service interface hides the details of the implementation.
- The service interface expresses the service's functions. This is done through the operations that the service interface provides.
- The service operates on information. The schema of the information is described in the parameters of the service operations. The schema is derived from a common semantic model.

This last observation leads to a very important point about services in an SOA. There is a difference between building services and having an SOA. It is not enough to simply build random services. Instead, an SOA demands that the services be part of an overall collection (or inventory) of services that are designed to work together and to be composed into business processes. For this to happen, you need to understand two critical aspects of the overall SOA context in order to design an effective service interface. These are:

- The specific responsibilities of the service operations and how these responsibilities relate to other services, that is, the relationship of the service to others
- The information that must be common and shared between this service and other services to enable those relationships and service composition

We cover these two points more extensively later in this chapter. In addition to the anatomy of the service, there are several different sizes, types, and other aspects that are important to interface design. We review these as well.

Service Characteristics

Three characteristics of services are particularly important in the design of service interfaces. These are: granularity, scope, and visibility.

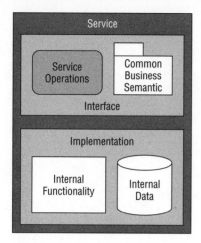

Figure 6-1 The anatomy of a service

Granularity

Service *granularity* describes the amount of business functionality performed by a single interaction (message exchange) with a service operation. We are often told that services should be coarse-grained. This is because larger granularity services are expected to be invoked less frequently, and the frequency of invocation is critical in distributed environments. There are also implications about the amount of data interchanged in service granularity. Fine-grained services are often called a lot and don't exchange a lot of data. Although all of this is true in most cases, it's not that simple. Rather than give strict definitions of granularity, it is better to describe a range from small utility services to large business services. There is not a single correct size for all services. Often, larger services are created by combining multiple smaller services. In addition to distribution and data, it is important that the granularity of a service interface match the functional modularity of the expected service consumers. For example, a business process expects to call services with granularity that corresponds to that of a process activity. Figure 6-2 illustrates the granularity of services.

Scope

Scope describes the intended range of users of a service. The largest scope is enterprise-wide, meaning that the service is intended to be used across the enterprise or across organizational boundaries. A smaller scope, such as a single solution, means that the service is intended to support only a specific solution. The importance of scope is that it provides the context within which the service interface must be defined, specifically regarding the scope of responsibilities and information.

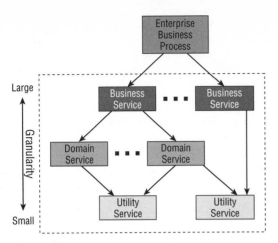

Figure 6-2 Service granularity varies according to intended usage

---

INTERNET SCOPE

Of course, there is a larger scope than the enterprise, that of extra-enterprise or Internet. For example, here are two different scenarios:

◆ **B2B exchange between business partners (such as a supply chain)** — In this case, the interface may be dictated by an industry standard organization or by a cooperative agreement. Semantics conform to industry standards where they exist. Sometimes a new interface is developed specifically for this service when no external context exists. General SOA principles should be followed, but there may be few requirements to compose these services into broader business processes.

◆ **Generally available services** — In this case, the service offers a function to the general public or customer base (such as package tracking or book information lookup). Again, the question of scope becomes one of what context must be applied to the service interface design. Sometimes, the interface must be designed to conform to a real or de facto standard (such as GIS coordinates). In other cases, the interface can be dictated by the service provider (such as Amazon book information). In either case, the individual service should be designed to fit within the overall set of services. (For example, all Amazon services should use the same definition of a book.)

Visibility

Visibility describes the range of users that are allowed to see the existence of a service, and subsequently to use it. Visibility is often described as either public or private. Public visibility means that all users within the intended scope are able to see the service. Private means that the service is not discoverable, but rather must be known about a priori.

Note that there is a difference between visibility and entitlement. Not everyone who is able to see that a service exists is necessarily allowed to use the service. Visibility provides a very broad approach that impacts how a service is (or is not) discovered, and affects the relationship between consumer and provider at design time. Entitlement provides a fine-grained approach based on the consumer's individual identity or role.

Table 6-1 shows how these different characteristics relate to the various types of service.

Interaction Styles

Another important concern in the design of service interfaces is the style of interaction between the service consumer and provider. The *interaction style* describes the pattern of the service's operation signatures, specifically how information is passed into and out of the service. The interaction style also describes the type and synchronization of request messages and response messages.

Table 6-1 Service types and characteristics

TYPE	VISIBILITY	SCOPE	GRANULARITY	RESPONSIBILITY
Business Service	Public	Enterprise	Medium to Large	Implements discrete business function across lines of business.
	Public	Line-of-Business (LOB)	Medium to Large	Implements discrete business function. Represents a logical group of related functions.
Domain Service	Private	Domain	Small to Medium	A domain-specific subunit of processing. General purpose, reusable.
Utility Service	Public	Enterprise	Small to Medium	A common subunit of processing. Supports semantic business objects. Applicable across multiple LOBs.
Integration Service	Private	Solution	Small to Large	Exposes business operations. Groups related transactions. Provides a single point of contact.

Sometimes, the interaction style is described in what is also called a Message Exchange Pattern (MEP). For example, the W3 C SOAP V1.2 specification describes two different patterns: the Request/Response MEP and the Request/SOAP Response MEP. The Request/Response MEP describes the details of how a SOAP request is sent to a service and how a SOAP response is returned. The other pattern describes how a non-SOAP request is sent and a SOAP response returned.

There are two separate concerns for MEPs. One is how the information is passed, and the second is the type of message and synchronization. Let's look at the information first.

Parameter Passing

In this style, the operation signature contains one or more individual parameters. An example service signature might something look like:

```
Response = service_operation (parameter1, parameter2, ...);
```

In this operation, the inputs are passed as parameters, which are typed by standard or custom data types. The response might be a single value or a complex type (such as a document). Figure 6-3 illustrates the simple parameter-passing style:

This is the simplest of the different interaction styles and works well where the operation has well-defined and constrained inputs. This interaction style works well with small granularity services and is most often the interface style seen on utility services.

Document Passing

In this style, the operation signature contains one request (input) document and one response (output) document. An example of a service signature is:

```
Response_document = service_operation (request_document);
```

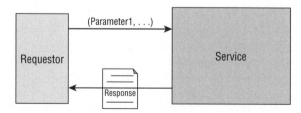

Figure 6-3 Parameter-passing style

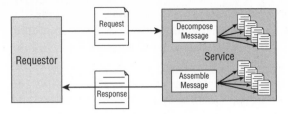

Figure 6-4 Document-passing style

In this operation, the inputs and outputs are passed as documents, which are typed by schema. Both the request and reply may be simple or compound documents. Figure 6-4 illustrates the document-passing style.

This interaction styles and works well with larger granularity services where the input and output may contain a lot of data. This is the interface style most often used with business services.

Where the service is more complex, the request and response may be compound documents. In other words, the document itself is composed of subdocuments. Figure 6-4 also illustrates how the business service might decompose the request into individual documents that are passed separately to the services that make up the business service. Likewise, the business service might need to reassemble the individual responses into the final response document.

Note that the document passing pattern is actually a special case of parameter passing, where the parameters are documents rather than some other data type. But in this case, the documents are based on the semantic information model and act as a type of Data Transfer Object or value object (a common pattern used in distributed systems, and that eliminates the use of reference passing).

Data Passing

This style of interaction supports services that are primarily designed to provide data access. In this style, the operation signature contains one or more request parameters and one response (output) document or dataset. An example of a service signature is:

```
Response_data = get_operation (entityID);
```

To avoid "chatty" interfaces, it is important to discourage access to single attributes. Therefore, the service signature may be optimized to support one or more specific (sub)sets of information, such as the following:

```
Response_dataset_Y = getY (entityID);
Response_dataset_Z = getZ (entityID);
Response_dataset_All = getAll (entityID);
```

In addition to specific subsets, the service usually supports an operation that returns the entire data set about a specific entity ID. For example, if the service provides Customer data, the `getY_operation` might return name, address, contact info, and the like. The `getZ_operation` might return account information about the customer, and the `getAll_operation` might return all of the information about the customer that the requestor is authorized to see, including address and contact. Figure 6-5 illustrates the data passing style.

Another common variation on the data-passing interface allows the requestor to pass in a specific query or to ask for a customized subset of information. There is one caution however with the use of customized subsets. Extreme care must be exercised to ensure that the separation of interface and implementation (e.g., data hiding) is not broken by exposing the internal structure of data to the requestor.

Finally, this interface style often supports getting information for a set of entities, rather than for a single ID; for example, it might be used to return dataset Y for all customers in New Hampshire. Again, caution must be exercised so that an unduly large result set is not returned, at least in a single message. (See the Megadata Pattern in *Building Business Objects* by Peter Eeles and Oliver Sims [1998] for a solution to this scenario, if it is to be supported.)

This interaction style is most often used with entity type domain and business services.

The previous styles describe how the information exchange between a service consumer and provider is formatted. Now, let's look at some of the ways that messages can be passed between them.

Request/Reply

This is the most common service invocation style. In the simplest, synchronous case, the requestor sends a request to a service and waits. When the service has processed the request, it sends a reply. The requestor receives the reply and resumes processing. Figure 6-6 illustrates the request/reply style.

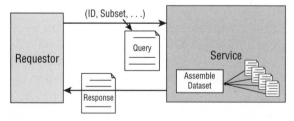

Figure 6-5 Data-passing style

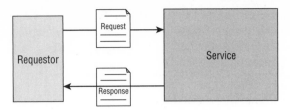

Figure 6-6 Request/reply invocation style

There are asynchronous variations on the request/reply style sometimes called store-and-forward. Often, the requestor does not want to block progress waiting for a reply. Instead, an asynchronous request is sent to the service and the requestor continues processing other tasks. Sometime later, the requestor looks for and processes the reply. This is essentially the model used when exchanging email. I can send you a message and then go about my other business. Later, I can check my inbox for your response and continue with that particular task. Obviously, this works great for a lot of things. Of course, there are some complications. What if you never respond? Or, how do I correlate a specific email message in my inbox with a specific email request that I sent out earlier?

Often, a correlation identifier is added to the message to allow the requestor to correlate replies. But this generally has to be implemented by the participants, not automatically by the system. This is the mechanism that Google Mail uses to associate requests with replies.

If you choose the simpler synchronous model, these complications are handled for you by the messaging system. If you choose an asynchronous approach, you must address them yourself.

In some scenarios, you send a message to a service but don't expect any response. For example, a Radio Frequency Identification (RFID) reader might send a message to an inventory service every time an RFID is read. In this case, you can send what is called a one-way message. The use of a one-way message is often associated with a guaranteed delivery messaging infrastructure.

Events

An alternative to request/reply messaging is an event-based approach. A common approach is a publish/subscribe style, as illustrated in Figure 6-7. Event-driven architectures rely on an intermediary, or an "event broker" to receive notification from event sources (publish) and inform (invoke) all interested parties (subscribers). The event paradigm is not only evident at the technology or messaging level. It must also be present in the design of business processes and interactions. Refer to Chapter 8 for a description of the publish/subscribe style for services composition.

Figure 6-7 Event-based invocation style

In this style, the service is a subscriber to specific events, such as "Mortgage application received." The mortgage application–processing service is invoked by the event broker to process the new application. The new application could have come from a single channel or perhaps from a variety of different channels. The "publish" paradigm allows for a loosely coupled many-to-one relationship between sources of mortgage applications and the service responsible for processing them. When the processing is complete, the service publishes a new event, such as "Application Processed." The event broker then passes the event on to any processes that have expressed interest (subscribed) to the event. It might be the submitter of the application. Or, it might also be an auditing service, and a compliance service. Again, the subscribe paradigm allows for a loosely coupled one-to-many relationship.

Although there are many excellent examples of event-driven architectures, the current crop of BPM tools are not well-suited to building business processes supported by event-based services. Although the same set of principles and practices that we describe in the book still applies to these services, we have focused our examples on the more common request/response style.

Mixed Style

Some scenarios are best served by a combination of invocation styles. The most common of these is a data provider service, as illustrated in Figure 6-8. In this scenario, the data provider publishes data change events. Processes that are concerned about data changes subscribe to these events. However, most processes are concerned with only a subset of all the data changes and ignore most events. When the event is about data they are concerned with, the requestor (subscriber) then makes a request/response invocation to the data provider to get the specific data that they care about, and that was changed.

Any of the invocation styles (request/response, event, or mixed) can apply to any of the different service styles (business, domain, utility, or integration).

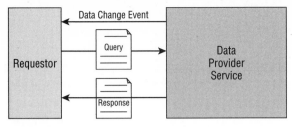

Figure 6-8 Mixed invocation style

Design Guidelines

Now that you have reviewed some important characteristics of services, it is time to address the primary design principles for services.

Isolating Responsibilities

One of the keys to achieving SOA success is creating a collection of services that can be composed to support a variety of different business processes and scenarios. We often talk about having "loosely coupled" services, but how does that help achieve these goals? Loose coupling is important in reducing dependencies between services so that they can be used in different scenarios or to isolate the effects of changes. Two types of coupling are especially important in service interface design: data and functional dependencies.

Let's take a look at a simple example to illustrate these dependencies. Say that you have an order-processing service. To process an order, the service must update information about the customer, determine the inventory status of the requested items, bill the customer, and so on, as illustrated in Figure 6-9.

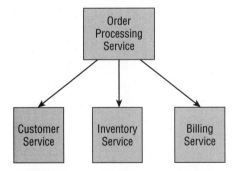

Figure 6-9 Order-processing example

The order-processing service coordinates all of these activities and then uses other services to help accomplish the order processing. So, obviously, the order-processing service is dependent on (coupled to) the customer service, inventory service, and billing service. This is normal. So, why don't you just implement all of these capabilities directly in the order services and be done with it? For two reasons: The first is that you want to be able to reuse the underlying capabilities in other high-level processes or services. The second is that order processing is not responsible for managing the customer, or for billing, or for inventory.

The customer service is used to manage access to customer information. It has the sole responsibility for providing, maintaining, and updating that information. You do this so that you can reuse the customer service in every place that needs to access customer data. But more important than the reuse of code is the isolation/centralization of access to customer information. Because there is only one way to access the data, the data is always consistent. So, although there are many services (order processing, billing, etc.) that need (are dependent on) the customer service, you understand and manage this kind of dependency through the use of patterns.

The same is true for the inventory service and the billing service. You isolate these functions in their own services because you want to be able to use the inventory or billing from more than just order processing. Again, it is not just the reuse of the services that you're interested in. Good service design also provides consistency. By creating services to perform the inventory and billing functions, you can perform those functions consistently wherever they are needed. (Nothing is more annoying to customers than inconsistent results.)

The next logical question is how do you decide what the services are? You use a combination of functional decomposition and information isolation. Back to the example: A functional decomposition of order processing led you to identify the inventory and billing steps. Information isolation led you to identify a customer as shared information across the order-processing activities.

Of course, order processing is just one of dozens or hundreds of processes that need to be performed to run the business. So, the problem of service design within an SOA spans many (or all) of these processes. In particular, you want to:

- Avoid overlaps in functions between services.
- Avoid gaps in functions between services.
- Avoid duplication of data.
- Coordinate access to data.
- Have a single, consistent way to perform a given function.

A key to achieving these goals is to keep the following questions in mind during the design of a service:

- Who is responsible for a given function? Where is that function used?
- Who is responsible for management of specific data?
- Who is responsible for defining and implementing specific rules?
- What step in the process owns the specific knowledge needed to perform a given task?

The answer to these questions helps to identify what the service should do and is responsible for. Just as importantly, it identifies what the service should not do, but rather what it should depend on other services for.

Understanding Overall Context

To achieve these goals within the intended scope of the SOA you must understand more than a single process, scenario, or use case. You must understand the overall context to which the SOA applies. The overall set of services within this context is referred to as the *service inventory*. This is where the business and domain model come into play.

The SOA business model asks and answers the following questions:

- What business are you in (e.g., what is the domain model)?
- What are the goals and objectives of this particular business?
- What outcomes are needed to achieve those goals?
- How will they be measured?
- What capabilities and information are needed to achieve those outcomes?
- What processes, services, entities, and rules are needed to implement those capabilities?
- What existing applications provide basic capabilities and information that can support these?

The first four questions describe the businesses requirements, while the rest describe the overall SOA context and provide the requirements for the service inventory. In other words, the service inventory describes the overall set of services necessary to support SOA within a context. In doing so, the inventory must identify:

- The overall scope
- Areas of service responsibilities
- Groupings of related services

- Entity (information management) services
- Functional and rule services

The service inventory supports two major design-time goals:

- It provides a mechanism for understanding the overall service context to aid in the selection of services for reuse. Specifically, what responsibilities does the service implement and how is it related to other services?

- It provides a mechanism for identifying the boundaries of responsibility of a particular service as a guideline for implementation of the service. This is critical to avoiding duplication of data and function across services.

Figure 6-10 shows a sample template for a service inventory. This sample shows how services might be organized according to service type. However, there are many different ways to organize the inventory, as discussed in Chapter 4. For example, it could also be organized by organizational structure, business domain, or line-of-business. Of course, the template is just one way of visually presenting the information contained in the inventory. The same inventory could be presented in more than one view. Figure 6-17 gives another example of an inventory related to the design example later in this chapter.

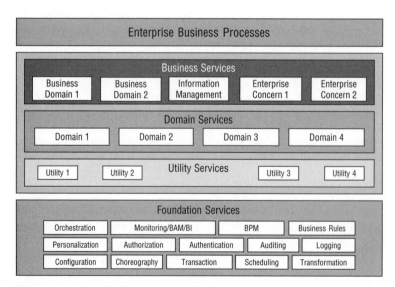

Figure 6-10 Service inventory template

Identifying Granularity

During design, as you narrow down the responsibilities of a service, you need to decide on the granularity of the service operations. In other words, how much of that responsibility is performed in a single interaction with the service? Should it be broken into smaller units to promote reuse, consistency, and loose coupling?

Let's review the basic premise of service granularity. A service operation should match the functional modularity of the expected service consumer. In other words, for each service interface, you need to answer the following questions:

- What is the intended usage of the service?
- What is the general (not business) functional responsibility of the service?
- What is the intended scope of the service?

With the answers to these questions, you can then use Table 6-2 to get guidance on the appropriate service granularity. For example, assume that you want to design a service that is intended to support the construction of processes that span lines-of-business across the enterprise. The service should expose a specific business function that is provided by that line of business and be publicly available to any process that needs (and is authorized to use) it. Summarizing, the scope of the service is enterprise or LOB, the visibility is public, the responsibility is to implement a specific business function. Table 6-2 demonstrates that this is most likely to be a business service, and this should support a fairly large granularity of operation. Some typical combinations of service types, interface styles, and granularity are shown in Table 6-2.

Table 6-2 Typical interface combinations

TYPE	STYLE	SCOPE	GRANULARITY
Business Service	Document Passing	Enterprise	Medium to Large
Domain Service	Document or Parameter Passing	LOB, Domain	Small to Medium
Utility Service	Parameter Passing	Enterprise	Small to Medium
Integration Service	Document or Parameter Passing	Solution	Small to Large

Stateless Interfaces

An important characteristic of service interfaces is to be as stateless as possible. This means that a service does not maintain state on behalf of its consumer between requests. Any given request can act on the state of particular information, but a subsequent request does not rely on the service maintaining the state from a previous request.

EXECUTION STATE VERSUS INVOCATION STATE

There is a profound difference between the notions of execution and invocation state: *Execution state* represents the state of the service during its execution. It always exists and includes internal variables created during service execution. It is used for keeping track of which part of the service execution has been completed, storing the results of partial service execution, and passing parameters between multiple components of a service implementation. This state is typically encapsulated in the service implementation and is invisible to the service consumers.

Invocation state is a shared context between the service consumer and service provider in a particular conversation. In this case, a consumer invokes different operations of the same service, assuming that the information that was passed to the service during an earlier operation invocation is available to the service during all consecutive invocations.

A service may participate in multiple conversations with different consumers and must keep track of each conversation separately. The notion of invocation state is used, for example in the session variables, or stateful session beans in J2EE. A better term describing this type of state is "conversation state."

Throughout this book when we talk about stateful versus stateless invocation of services, we are referring only to the invocation state.

Why is this important? Stateless interactions are important in terms of scalability, reliability, failover, and so on. For example, consider the following two pseudo-code segments below for checking the balance of your savings account:

```
myAccount = account_service.getAccount (myD);
myBalance = myAccount.getBalance ();
myTransactionHistory = myAccount.getTransactionHistory ();
myBalance = account_service.getAccountBalance (myID);
myTransactionHistory = account_service.getTransactionHistory (myID);
```

The first example is the classical object-oriented approach to the problem. Create an account object and then perform operations on the account. What this means is that the account service creates an instance of myAccount, and each subsequent call to the account object must go to the exact same instance of the account service. In other words, the first call to get an account creates the account instance. The second and third calls (to the account object) get information about the account, namely the balance and transaction history. Because the account object is maintained by the first service, it does not have to be created for each call.

The second example is the stateless service approach. The first call gets the balance. The second call gets the transaction history. Each time the account service is called, it needs to retrieve the requested information, which may require some duplicated access to the database. However, there is no dependency between the caller and any particular service instance. The first request can go to server 1 while the second request could go to server 19. The tradeoff is one of flexibility and reliability versus processing overhead.

But what happens in the first scenario if the server fails for some reason between retrieving the balance and the history? The server state is lost, and the client needs to find a new server, recreate the account instance, and then request the transaction history. This is a much more complicated failover scenario than the stateless case. In that case, because no state is being maintained by the server, the history request can be sent to any available server. Hence, nothing different is required to handle the failover.

What happens when the processing of account information becomes a bottleneck? In the stateless example, you can simply add more servers and requests automatically get routed to them. But in the stateful example, even though you add new servers, all existing requests are still restricted to the already overloaded servers because that is where the state is being maintained. Only new accounts' conversations are routed to the new servers.

There are many other scenarios where stateless services provide better nonfunctional characteristics. However, not all service interactions lend themselves to stateless interfaces. Sometimes, the added complexity of making something stateless is not worth the effort. For example, if accessing the information is very complex, you might want to do it once and get on with other things. Consider that getting the account balance might require accessing five or more different systems to collect information, which then has to be aggregated. In that case, the added flexibility of stateless services might well be outweighed by the overhead of accessing multiple systems to assemble the account information.

From another perspective, it's not so much that the service's interactions are stateless as it is how that state is handled. For example, a service could be implemented by saving all its state in a persistent data source between consumer invocations and reconstruct the state on the next service request; or the service could hand all the state information back to the consumer in message data and expect the consumer to return it on the next invocation. These are stateless services from the standpoint of the implementation of the service provider, but the service's interactions are stateful.

Ultimately, it is a design choice that needs to be made by weighing the various tradeoffs. However, the overwhelming preference should be for the creation of stateless service interfaces.

Exceptions

Unfortunately, not everything always goes right (oh darn). This is undoubtedly true with computers, and even more so with service-oriented solutions. In his classic text on distributed computing, Professor Andrew Tannenbaum said something like "a distributed system is one where a problem that occurs on a computer you didn't even know existed can cause your computer to fail." *Computer Networks* (1985).

Exceptions are an integral part of service interface design. We'll discuss three key aspects of exception design here. First, all exceptions have to be defined at the interface level. Second, like data, common exceptions should be defined the same across all services. And third, exceptions need to report correlation information.

To explain these first two points, we need to mention the two main types of exceptions: application exceptions, and system exceptions. *Application exceptions* are application-specific errors that occur, such as "insufficient funds" when a customer tries to withdraw more money than they have in their account. Each operation has a set of application errors. The interface needs to collect and declare the complete set of possible application exceptions for all operations.

System exceptions are those that occur because of system issues such as "access denied", "system unavailable", or a communications error. In general, these errors are common across most services and operations. They should be defined once in a common format. Then, every service should use the same exception definition for the same event. Usually there is a central system exception file that is used by all services.

When an exception occurs, it is reported to two important stakeholders. Obviously, the consumer of a service needs to have exception information about their request reported to them so that they can act appropriately. In addition, exception information needs to be logged for future analysis, either to address a specific problem or to analyze trends. Typically, in addition to the application or system error information, this includes information identifying the server where the exception occurred and a value that identifies the end-to-end transaction that is involved. Chapter 9 describes a logging architecture for collecting these errors in a central location.

Designing Documents

Chapter 5 described the development of a semantic information model. To summarize, the information model answers the following questions:

- What information is shared between services?
- What information must be passed into and out of each service?
- What information needs to be common across services?

Recall that a service separates the interface from implementation. In terms of data, this means that the interface describes the data that must be input to and output from the service. This is the information that is represented in the information model. It does not define the details of the domain data model needed by the service implementation.

One goal of the information model is to identify information that must be common and shared among services. It follows then that the information passed through the service interface should conform to the information model. So, how is this accomplished? The concept is actually fairly simple. If you use the document-passing style interface (which is what you generally use for business and domain services), that implies that a document contains the shared information that is passed between services, and that the definition of that document is described in a document schema. You impose a strict relationship between the information model and the document schema. The schema must be based on the shared information model (in fact, it is a subset of the model). Every element of the schema must exist in the information model. Figure 6-11 illustrates these relationships.

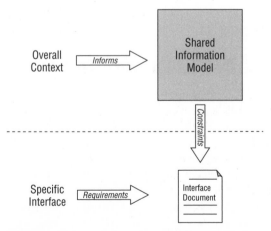

Figure 6-11 Documents are derived from the shared information model

The overall context of the SOA environment identifies the information that must be shared and common between services. This information informs the creation of the shared information model. The input and output of a specific service provide the requirements for the contents of the interface document, as described by the schema. The requirement for consistency between the information model and the document constrains the schema to contain only the elements that exist in the shared information model.

In fact, the same relationships and constraints should apply to data passed in operation parameters for the parameter-passing interface style. The primary requirement is that the data that is passed through the service interface is semantic data, or data defined by the semantic information model.

This requirement introduces a corollary requirement for the service design process. As you work through the design process, you inevitably discover more and more data that is required. How do you evolve the interface document to support this discovery, while also meeting the previous requirement? The answer is that you don't modify the document; you evolve the information model first and then redraw the schema and document based on the new information model. Later in this chapter, Figure 6-23 illustrates how to derive a schema from the information model.

Interface Design Illustrated

In this section, we describe the interface design process by using an example of an automobile insurance–quoting process. First, you'll look at the overall process and the models that can be created, as illustrated in Figure 6-12. You divide the overall process into two distinct parts: the problem model, which describes the problem in detail in business terms, independent of the potential IT systems, and the solution model, which describes the design of the solution in terms of SOA concepts. Each model consists of a set of related drawings, with traceability between the business model and the solution model.

IT'S OUR PROCESS . . . WHICH IS OURS . . .

There's more than one way to skin a cat, and more than one way to design services. The method that we present here is the way we have found to be the most effective with our clients. It's not the only way. What is important is to get the fundamental service design concepts from our approach so that you can apply whatever makes the most sense in your own environment. So chill . . . this example illustrates our approach. We hope you find it useful and adopt and adapt it to fit your needs. In any case, please look past any methodology specifics that you disagree with and get to the heart of the design decisions. Or, adopt it all. It works great for us.

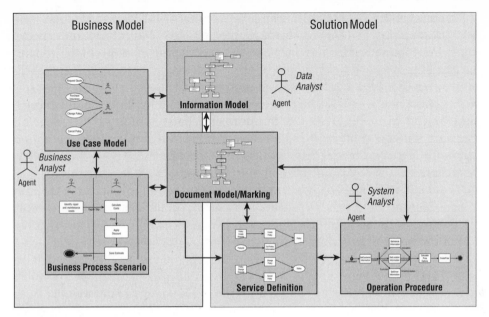

Figure 6-12 SOA design model relationships

Overview of Models and Diagrams

Before the analysis and design process, you should first have collected and understood the business requirements and created a business model, as described in Chapter 4. Now, you're ready to get into the analysis and design of the services to support those business requirements.

The first step in analysis is to identify the scope and features of the project. This is done by identifying the use cases that make up the project and defining scenarios (or processes) for each use case. Once this is done, there are two common approaches to system design: process-centric and data-centric. In the process-centric approach processes are described first, and the required data is derived from them. In the data-centric approach, the first thing to be defined is the data, and the processing is driven from that. Neither approach is right or wrong or better or worse; they are just different, and mostly correspond to the background and experience of the designer. Obviously, it is impossible to accurately define one without the other. For example, when defining the data, you must understand the functional dependencies needed to define the associations and normalize the data schema. Remember that services are a combination of both data and process. Arriving at the right interfaces that address both is what's important. Arguing over the right approach (can you say religious debate?) is not.

So, describing the business model can start with either the business process scenario or the information model (or both). The business process scenarios describe the activities that constitute the use cases and the information flow within scenarios in terms of business documents. The information model describes the main information that is part of the business problem domain space. In the example, later in the chapter, we take a process-centric approach, using scenarios to dig out the information requirements.

Together, the use case diagrams, scenario diagrams, information model, and document model make up the problem space model. As you develop the solution and continue to identify more detail, this detail will be added to the information model and document markings; thus, these two models span both the problem and solution models of your SOA design process.

The solution model follows from the problem model. Again, the solution model can start from either a process or data perspective, with either the information model or the definition of services. In one approach, you perform a functional decomposition of the processes and then identify the information needed to support the functions. In the other approach, you identify the information needs and then assign services to process the information. Neither approach is necessarily better than the other, and in reality, you generally identify both the information and functions together in an iterative fashion. One difference might be that a process-(or behavior-) centered approach is more goal-oriented, providing a better link to the business requirements and processes. Again, in the example later in the chapter, we take the process (functional) approach.

Each activity that is identified in a use case scenario is a candidate for a service operation. Each service is described by an interface and an implementation. The interface is described in the service definition diagram, which shows the collection of service operations and their inputs and outputs in terms of documents and parameters.

Finally, the implementation of each service operation is described in an operation procedure diagram (discussed in Chapter 7),which defines the internal steps of the operation, the data flow, and the data transformation of each step. Each step in the procedure may in turn invoke another service to implement that step. The overall procedure must match the input and output defined in the service definition.

Now, let's look at developing these models based on an example from the insurance industry, using the fictitious "ACME Insurance Company," which has recently acquired another company in order to add automobile insurance to their existing lines-of-business, such as property and casualty, life, and their unique line of roadrunner-confounding products.

ACME Insurance Example

Introduction — ACME Insurance Company sells multiple types of insurance to individuals and businesses (e.g. auto, homeowners, life, etc.). Like many companies, its internal IT landscape is a hodge-podge of existing applications and systems, many of which provide redundant or overlapping functions and that don't integrate with each other effectively. To stay competitive, ACME must upgrade its systems. A driving factor is to provide a single customer view across multiple lines of business. In order to achieve its immediate and longer term business goals, ACME is looking to Service-Oriented Architecture (SOA) to provide the agility, flexibility, and speed that it needs.

Business problem — Implement new insurance-quoting and -issuing processes that improve the customer experience. A customer's initial contact with ACME is through its own or independent insurance agents. Both web-based interactive sessions with the agents and automated Single Entry Multiple Carrier Interface (SEMCI) quote requests must be supported. After a policy has been issued, a customer can interact directly with ACME via self-service web applications to make policy changes and pay bills.

Enterprise context — This is the first of many initiatives that can be aimed at modernizing ACME so that it becomes a service-oriented enterprise. The development process must consider the overall enterprise context, which, of course, is just emerging. An initial version of the application architecture describes the high-level concepts for building an SOA, and the technical architecture describes the platform details on which it will be implemented. Together, these answer many of the typical "system requirement" questions.

Project context — For this project, we create services to support four use cases: Create a Quote (BU01), Purchase Insurance (BU02), Change Policy (BU03), and Cancel Policy (BU04).

PROCESS DOCUMENTATION STRUCTURE

Each step in the process is described in detail and then followed with a summary of the process that includes:

> **Goals** — The goals of this stage of the process and associated set of activities
>
> **Concerns** — The enterprise concerns that are introduced at this stage of the process
>
> **Concepts** — The SOA concepts that are used to express the analysis or design during this stage

In addition, occasional "Notes" provide tips and techniques for carrying out the step.

Conceptual Architecture

Often, the first step in a project is to create a *conceptual architecture*. This is an informal architecture overview with the purpose of conveying the overall project concept, goals, and approach to a nontechnical audience.

The conceptual architecture is intended to communicate the main concepts of the project, its scope, and its interactions. It is often structured in three parts, as shown in Figure 6-13. On the left are the "channels" or front ends that the new system has to interact with. On the right are the back ends, the internal, legacy, and external systems that the new system must also interact with. Together, these frame the scope of the interactions of the new system. In the center of the conceptual architecture is the high-level structure of the new system.

The ACME system is structured in terms of four major areas:

- **Enterprise business processes** — These high-level business processes interact directly with the channels and correspond to the high-level business use cases (quote insurance, process application) as well as future processes (portfolio management, risk management) that serve to show the future direction and potential of the approach.

- **Common services** — These are service groups that serve multiple lines of business. For example, to have a common customer across the many different insurance products requires a central "customer" service. Each service group has some representative higher-level business services and some lower-level domain services.

- **Line-of-business services** — These are service groups specific to a line of business. Notice that we have specifically called out a differentiation between centralized services and those owned by the lines of business to correspond to the organizational realities of the enterprise.

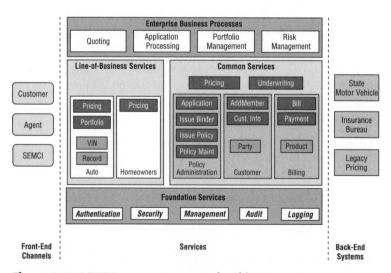

Figure 6-13 ACME Insurance conceptual architecture

- **Foundation services** — These services support the overall construction of the system (but do not implement business functionality). Because this type of service has been common in enterprise systems for a long time, we include the foundation services in the conceptual architecture to differentiate them from the business related services.

  - **Goal** — Convey the overall concept, structure, and direction of the project to sponsors and nontechnical viewers.

  - **Concerns** — Scope of the project, internal, and external interactions, and the structure of the system.

  - **Concepts** — Channels, external systems, processes, service groups, and services.

Problem Space Model

With the overall concepts laid out, it is time to start describing the problem in business terms to verify that all the requirements are understood and framed in the appropriate context.

Use Case Diagrams

The problem model is derived from the use cases and knowledge about the problem domain. For this example, we are using four business use cases: request a quote for insurance (BU01), purchase an insurance policy (BU02), change the coverage on a policy (BU03), and cancel insurance (BU04). The detailed use cases are included in Appendix A. Figure 6-14 shows the use cases and primary actors.

Each business use case becomes a use case in our use case diagram. In addition, we include the actors that have been identified from the business use cases. Often, we find that use cases are overdone and can result in analysis paralysis. We try to use the use case diagram as a "table of contents" of the overall set of use cases, and to help identify any relationships between them. But, we try not to make then too complicated and tend to avoid using <<extends>> and <<includes>> relationships. Instead, we prefer to specify the use case details in scenario diagrams or business process models.

Goals — Provide a table of contents of the major functions and users of the system.

Concerns — Interaction of business use cases with each other and external users and systems.

Concepts — Use cases, actors.

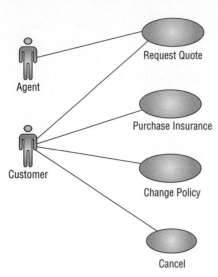

Figure 6-14 ACME Insurance use cases

Actors

Actors represent the system's interaction/interface with users and/or other systems and are involved in the value exchange that happens in the use case. But, you will identify two types of actors in the problem model. Actors also identify roles or areas of responsibility that are carried out in the use case. This second category of actors, which represents business workers, does not necessarily appear in the use case diagram, but will appear in the scenario diagrams.

External actors — The actors in the use case diagram represent the external interface to the system functionality.

Business workers — Primary business workers are the internal systems that are responsible for performing a function within a use case. A business worker collaborates with other business workers and manipulates business entities to perform its responsibilities. The primary business workers are often identified as secondary actors in the use cases. In our example, Underwriting, Pricing, and Billing were identified in BU01, BU02, and BU03. We also identified a primary business worker as responsible for each use case, hence we have created three additional actors: Quoting, Purchasing, and Policy.

Secondary business workers are often identified as you iteratively develop the scenarios. In our example, we identify three additional actors as secondary business workers, Correspondence Manager, Customer Manager, and Policy Manager. These secondary business workers are often identified based on the enterprise service inventory or experience, and may relate to existing services or be obvious candidates for supporting services.

Initial Scenario Diagrams

Each use case has one or more scenarios, which are described in a scenario diagram. In UML terms, the scenario diagram is a partitioned activity diagram. Partitions are assigned to actors.

The scenario diagram is a visual representation of the use case processing details. It is derived from the use case documentation. The initial scenario should contain the actors identified in the use case as well as the primary business worker for that use case.

Note that Business Process Modeling Notation (BPMN) business process diagrams could also be used for the same purpose. We have chosen activities' diagrams because not all UML tools support BPMN, but most are moving in that direction.

Request Quote Scenario

Figure 6-15 shows the initial scenario for BU01, Request Quote. Notice that the first two partitions are associated with the primary actors of the use case, Customer and Agent. The next partition is assigned to the primary business worker for the use case, Quoting. This is an example of an actor appearing in the scenario but not the use case diagram. The last partition is assigned to a secondary actor of the use case, Underwriting.

NOTE We chose not to have a separate partition for Pricing for the purpose of illustrating the thought process.

The scenario follows the use case description. Referring to the use case document, Step one of the basic workflow is for the Agent to collect information

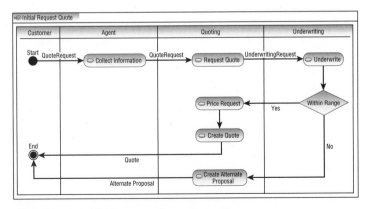

Figure 6-15 Initial Request Quote scenario

from the Customer about the requested insurance. Notice that this step will probably not become automated. But, at this level of design, you must specify the scenario independently of technology concerns. Obviously, later on in the process you need to be able to distinguish between automated and non-automated steps. Step 2 in the business use case is to underwrite the quote. From experience, you know that requests need to be validated for correction, so you insert that as the next step of the scenario, performed by the Quoting business worker even though it is not explicitly called out in the document. Next, the quote is underwritten. Because of its simplicity, we have chosen to incorporate the alternate flow into the initial scenario and indicate that a decision is made during the underwriting step to determine whether the quote is within acceptable risk limits. If so, the basic workflow continues, if not, the alternate workflow is followed, and an alternate proposal is made and presented to the Customer.

Back to the basic flow, Step 3 is to price the quote request, so we add a price request activity to the scenario. Step 4 of the business use case is to present the quote to the Customer. Obviously, you need to create it first, so you add an activity to create the quote and return the quote to the Customer for evaluation.

The last task in outlining the scenario is to identify the information flow between activities in the scenario. Each flow line can be adorned with one or more documents that facilitate the information flow. Some of the documents may have already been identified in the document model, but probably not all of them. For example, in Figure 6-15 we identified a QuoteRequest document that is passed to the agent, who collects additional information and sends the Quote Request on to the next step. An Underwriting Request document is used to pass the necessary information to Underwriting. This document was not identified in the use case, but you know you will need to pass something along, so you create the document definition as you're developing the scenario. Finally, either a quote or an alternate proposal is returned to the customer, as described in the use case document.

NOTE Remember that this is an iterative process. Don't worry about getting everything right the first time. You can go back to correct and improve the actors, scenarios, documents, and so on, several times during analysis as you work through other use cases. The important thing is to get the information down first. At this point, it's more important to be clear than it is to be correct. Reviewers will tell you if it's wrong, as long as they can understand it.

Purchase Insurance Scenario

Figure 6-16 shows the scenario diagram for the Purchase Insurance scenario based on business use case BU02. The process of creating this scenario is pretty much the same as for the Request Quote scenario, so we won't repeat all of the descriptions. However, we describe some aspects that are different.

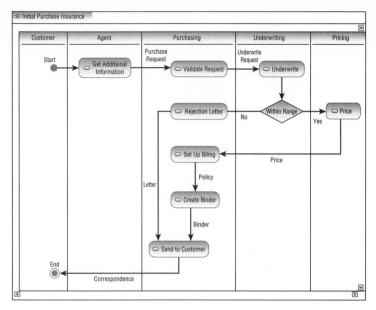

Figure 6-16 Initial Purchase Insurance scenario

Like before, you have included the primary business worker, Purchasing, as an actor in the scenario. Also, this time you have included Pricing in the scenario. As you begin to work through the scenario, you begin to recognize things that are common between the scenarios. This is the first step in identifying candidates for business services. Pricing is common to all three use cases and, therefore, is a likely candidate for a business service. If you have not already identified a business worker to be responsible for the behavior, you would add it now to the set of actors. Of course, Pricing was already identified as a secondary actor in the use case. This is also an indication that it is a good candidate for a business service.

ABOUT THE INITIAL SCENARIOS

We won't bore you with the scenario diagrams for Change Policy or Cancel Policy, which don't really introduce any new concepts. At this point in the process, you have created an initial scenario diagram for each use case identified in the use case diagram. For each use case, all actors identified in the business use case are present in the scenario, as well as the primary business worker for the use case. All steps identified in the business use case description are represented by activities in the scenario, and the responsibility for them has been assigned to one of the actors (by placing the activity into the partition). Simple alternative flows are included, as are other obvious activities (such as validation) that were left out of the use case description. Well-defined information flow for the scenario is represented by documents that are passed between the activities.

Goals — Formally describe the interactions, activities, and information for each use case as an activity diagram. Keep it simple enough to validate with the business users.

Concerns — Information flow, control flow, activities, and common activities.

Concepts — Actors, activities, control flow, and documents.

Enterprise Service Context and Inventory

Now that you have worked through the initial scenarios, you need to understand how they fit into the overall enterprise context. In an ideal world, you would have created such a context, which we call the *service inventory*, as part of the enterprise business architecture. Basically, the business goals and strategy lead you to a set of business processes needed to achieve those goals. Each business process is supported by a set of enterprise capabilities. These capabilities either already exist in current systems, or will in the future (perhaps identified in a roadmap). In the service-oriented approach, these capabilities are going to be implemented as business services. Alternately, if you don't have a service inventory to start with, you should create and populate it as you implement or use services on projects. You also have other sources to help us identify services, such as industry standard models. For example, the ACORD standards were used to help identify services that would be required for ACME.

The service inventory provides a way of organizing those services into sets of related services, called service groups.

Figure 6-17 illustrates a sample service inventory for ACME insurance. The inventory has the following attributes:

- **Enterprise process layer** — Identifies the enterprise processes that are enabled by the underlying set of services.

- **Business services layer** — The business services layer is where high-level business services are implemented. The business service layer is broken down into three layers of services: business, domain, and utility and further divided by line-of-business. For example, the Underwriting Service is an enterprise-wide business service, while the Billing Service is provided by the Billing line-of-business. Although we do not go into the details here, the organizational ownership of a service becomes an important consideration in its overall visibility and life cycle. This has a major organizational (not technical) impact on its reusability. As well, a consistent approach to service granularity across the enterprise enables reuse of services at different levels. Within each line-of-business, there are also lower-level domain services that provide common functionality

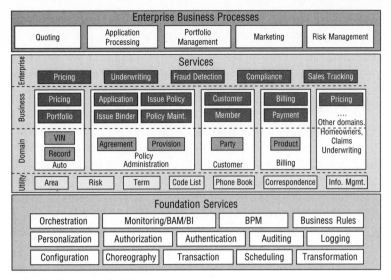

Figure 6-17 ACME Insurance service inventory

within the line-of-business. Finally, there are lower-level utility services that provide enterprise-wide common utility functions (i.e., used by all the different lines-of-business). For example, the "Area Service" provides geographically-based risk information that is useful to many different lines-of-business.

- **Foundation services** — These provide common capabilities that are used in the construction of business services, independent of any business domain. Examples are Security, Logging, and Orchestration.

The inventory has another important attribute. It is essentially a responsibility map of the service domain. The division of services into service groups and into individual services within a group is done based on specifying the roles and responsibilities of the services. The purpose of this is to minimize redundancy (overlap) and gaps between services. Before a new service is implemented, the service designer must consult the inventory to understand where that new service fits into the overall taxonomy. From this, the responsibility of the new service becomes clear; that is, what capabilities it is responsible for implementing, and, just as important, what capabilities it should not implement but instead get from other services. In other words, the inventory acts as a kind of roadmap that is used to create services over time.

Finally, the service inventory is used to help identify existing services for reuse.

Goals — Identify current and future services as a roadmap to enable the creation of services that meet enterprise goals, reduce service overlap, and encourage service reuse.

Concerns — Role, responsibilities, organization, scope, and visibility.

Concepts — Processes, business services, domain services, utility service, and foundation service.

Detailed Scenario Diagrams

Now that you have worked through the initial scenarios and put them into the overall enterprise SOA context, you want to go back and refine them with more detail. You will create a second, "detailed scenario" for each of the use cases. In the detailed scenarios, you factor in some additional information from the use cases and the service inventory. In addition, you apply common patterns, and assign responsibility for shared information and fundamental business entities identified in the information model.

Entity Managers

During the design process, you identify certain types of information in two ways. First, in the information model, you identify fundamental business entities, such as Customer or Policy. Second, you identify information that is shared across scenarios, or by multiple activities in a scenario, such as a Quote. The management of shared information needs to be coordinated, and you can create entity manager actors with that responsibility.

Request Quote Detailed Scenario

Figure 6-18 shows the detailed scenario for Request Quote. In the discussion, we compare the detailed scenario to the initial scenario in Figure 6-15. First, let's examine the actors. Because the customer had no participation in the scenario other than to initiate the request, we have omitted the customer actor from the detailed scenario. Next, we added pricing into the scenario because we earlier identified it as a shared responsibility. Also, we added the secondary business worker, Customer Manager, to the scenario.

The first few steps of the detailed scenario are the same as in the initial scenario, namely Collect Information and Validate Request. The next activity, Create Quote, is also taken from the initial scenario. However, as you define the service interface and implementation, you must take into account the more detailed scenario.

BU01 contains some important text. "ACME also offers a multi-policy discount of 5% for Customers already holding another policy with ACME, assuming the quoted policy would not replace an existing policy." This implies that you need to know if the requestor is an existing Customer or not. So, the next activity in the scenario is to ask the Customer Manager to return information about the Customer, including whether or not they already exist. Notice that the input to the Get Customer Info activities is a Customer

Information Document, and that the output is the same document. Here, you employ a common interface design pattern of passing partial information in and getting completed information back; recall the document-passing and state discussion from Chapter 5.

The next step is to request Underwriting. You have two options for how to model this. One option would be to go directly from the Retrieve Information activity of the Customer Manager to the Underwrite activity. Another option (the one you chose) is to have a new activity in the Quoting partition that makes the request. This choice is based on your questions about responsibility. Notice that the Customer Manager only has information about the Customer, not about the quote request, nor should the Customer Manager understand what information is required for Underwriting. Only the Quoting process understands why the Customer Manager is being called. As well, some additional information, and perhaps processing of the Customer Information may be required before Underwriting can be called. Since this is the responsibility of the Quoting process, you created the Request Underwriting activity to handle it. Another consideration is that you don't want to introduce an unnecessary dependency between the Customer Manager and Underwriting. These are examples of the questions you need to ask as you flesh out the detailed scenarios: How do you minimize dependencies? Who has responsibility for an action? Who has access to specific information?

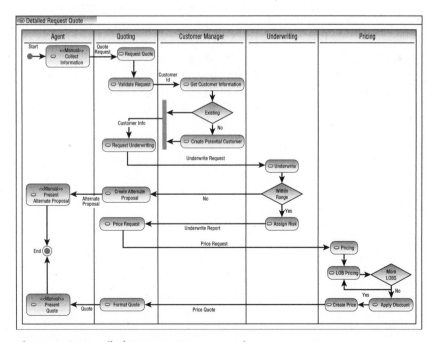

Figure 6-18 Detailed Request Quote scenario

The next activity is to price the quote. Again, rather than go directly from Underwriting to Pricing, you return to the quoting process for additional processing and information.

Now it is time to implement the pricing discount for multiple policies. To do so, you make use of the Enterprise Strategy pattern (see sidebar "Enterprise Strategy Pattern"). The Pricing activity calls all of the appropriate line-of-business (LOB) pricing mechanisms to get the base price, and then it applies the enterprise discount policy to get the final price. Notice how this assigns the responsibility for enterprise pricing to an enterprise pricing service, requires no change to existing pricing mechanisms or knowledge of discount policies at the LOBs, and isolates the pricing policy in a single location.

The last step is for the pricing information to be sent back to the quoting process when the actual quote is formatted and sent to the Agent to present to the Customer. But you are not done yet. You must also identify the information flow for the scenario. Although you were less strict in the initial scenario, all information that flows across partitions must be identified in the detailed scenario. Notice that this information is exactly the information that must be shared between services for them to be composed into the business process. Sound familiar? It is exactly the information that you need in the service interfaces, and that should be described in the semantic information model. In the process of identifying the information flow, you can discover numerous documents that were not identified in the original document model, and that need to be created and organized into the document model structure.

Finally, in this scenario, you have included some alternative path information. For example, if Underwriting does not approve a particular request, ACME has decided that rather than just reject the request, it should make an alternative proposal that would be within their risk boundaries (very nice of them). You include the Alternate Proposal activity in this scenario to show how it relates, but you need to create another scenario to define the complicated details of the alternate path.

We don't include the detailed scenarios for Purchase Insurance or Change Policy here, because again, there is not enough difference between the detailed scenarios to justify including all of them.

Goals — Describe each business use case as a detailed scenario. Identify commonalities between use cases. Identify data flows. Introduce managers for entities and other utilities.

Concerns — Information flow, control flow, activities, common activities, and entities.

Concepts — Actors, activities, control flow, and documents.

ENTERPRISE STRATEGY PATTERN

Name — Enterprise Strategy.

Intent — To provide an enterprise-wide solution that is based on both line-of-business policies and enterprise policies.

Problem — Policies need to be applied depending on scope. Only processes within a scope are aware of that scope's policies. In addition, processes are not aware of policies outside their own scope.

Forces:

- Enterprise policies are defined at the enterprise level, based on common (cross line-of-business) information and enterprise semantics.

- Enterprise polices require information from multiple lines-of-business.

- Individual line-of-business policies are defined within the lines of business.

- Different lines-of-business have different implementations, platforms, and data.

Solution — The enterprise strategy solution provides a mediator between the different lines of business. Each line of business is invoked to apply its own policy. Then, the enterprise policy is applied to the results.

Implementation —

1. Define the input and output, based on the common enterprise semantics.

2. Determine the context. This provides information on:

   - Which lines-of-business to call.

   - What enterprise policy to apply.

(continued)

ENTERPRISE STRATEGY PATTERN *(continued)*

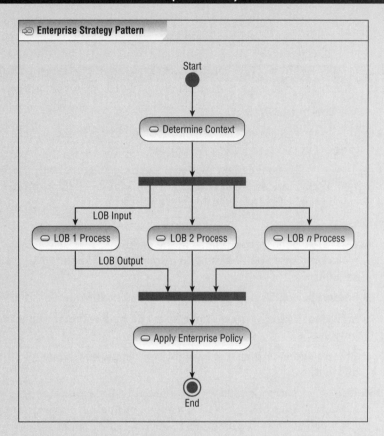

Enterprise Strategy pattern

3. **Define extraction/transformation of the data from the enterprise input into that for each line-of-business.**

4. **Determine the concrete lines of business. Determine if calls should be parallel or serial. Create <<call>> associations for each.**

5. **Define transformations from line-of-business to enterprise information as required.**

6. **Collect/combine information.**

7. **Define/apply enterprise policy.**

Variants — The line-of-business inputs/output may be defined to be the same as the enterprise input/output. In this case, the transformations take place within the line-of-business services.

Lines-of-business can be called serially or in parallel.

Information Model

Like the scenarios, the high-level information model is constructed from information provided in the use case descriptions and from basic information that you know about the business domain. From reading through the use cases, you identify several major business entities such as agency, customer, application, policy, binder, and quote. The very high-level information model in Figure 6-19 shows the entities and the relationships between them. You develop both the information model and the scenarios iteratively and make sure that all of the entities in the information model are represented as actors, documents, or subjects in the scenarios.

> **Goals** — Describe the fundamental business entities and the relationships between them.
>
> **Concerns** — Information, documents, entities, and actors.
>
> **Concepts** — Classes and relationships.

Service Specification

A service specification specifies everything that a consumer of the service needs to know to decide if they are interested in using the service, as well as exactly how to use it if they are. It also specifies everything a service provider needs to know to implement the service.

The service specification includes:

■ Service name

■ Provided and required interfaces

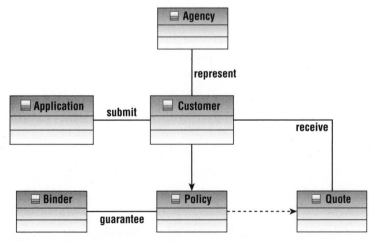

Figure 6-19 ACME high-level information model

- Protocol (rules for how the functions are used and in what order)
- Constraints that reflect what successful use of the service accomplishes
- Qualities that service consumers should expect such as cost, availability, performance, and the like
- Policies for using the service, such as security and transaction scopes

The Service specification of the Quoting Service is shown below:

Service Name — AutoQuoting.

Description — The AutoQuoting Service provides quotes for automobile insurance. It accepts a quote request as input. ACME underwriting and pricing rules are applied to determine the acceptability of risks and insurance premium options, and a variety of different quotes with different coverages and deductibles are returned. The service implements business use case BU01.

Provided interfaces — AutoQuoting provides the quoting interface with the following operations:

- `quote createQuote (quoteRequest);`
- `quote getQuote (quoteID);`
- `quote quotePolicyChange (quoteRequest);`
- `alternateQuoteProposal createAlternateProposal (riskAssessment);`

Required interfaces — AutoQuoting requires the use of the Pricing and CustomerManager interfaces.

Protocol — AutoQuoting follows a standard request/reply protocol. There are no callbacks.

Constraints — AutoQuoting must be called on behalf of an agency that is authorized to see insurance in the requested state.

Qualities of service — AutoQuoting has 99.9% availability, except between 02:00 and 03:00 EST when maintenance may be performed. A reply will be returned within 15 seconds 95% of the time. The service can handle up to 10 requests per second.

Policies — Requests for quotes can be submitted by company representatives or independent agents. For details see the run-time policy `UserIsAgent`.

NOTE This service specification provides textual information about the service. It's enough to help a potential consumer determine if the service is right for them but probably not enough for a developer to implement from. In Chapter 13, a formal UML service specification will be illustrated.

FORMAL VERSUS INFORMAL SPECIFICATIONS

To be or not to be formal? That is the question. Like many things in architecture, the answer is "that depends." There is a place for both informal specifications that are meant to communicate to a nontechnical audience, and formal specifications, which are intended to be complete and precise. Our position is that you need both to be effective architects.

One of the primary responsibilities of an architect is to communicate. If the communication medium is impenetrable, then it doesn't matter how correct it is, because some percentage of the audience won't touch it, and the architect has failed.

In this chapter, we present an informal software specification. In our case study example, we use a formal UML specification. You decide what you'd use with business process designers, and what you'd use with system analysts. We know what we'd do.

Solution Model

The solution model picks up where the problem model leaves off. It refines the business concepts (processes, activities, entities, and documents) into SOA technology concepts of services, interfaces, operations, documents, and information. Note however, that it does this in a way that is independent of the underlying platform (such as an ESB or .NET).

In this section, we look at the development of the service model that specifies the overall set of service, and for each service, the service interface definition, and how it relates to the enterprise context and semantics.

Service Model

The first part of the solution model is the *service model*. It contains a collection of related services, and shows the services and their relationships. Service models act as an organizing mechanism for grouping related services. In the problem model, we identified service candidates by looking for common behavior and shared information. The service inventory provided a roadmap for new and existing services and their responsibilities. Common behaviors were identified as scenario activities. We also identified some shared information and resources that are controlled by manager actors (and hence entity service). Now, we refine these into services.

The basic process is to work through each of the detailed business scenarios and evaluate every activity in the scenario as being implemented by a service. For each activity, there are three possible options:

- Define it as a manual task.

- Assign it to a service operation. This is done either by creating a new service for it, or assigning it to an existing service.

- Defer it as an internal task of another service. This often represents a lower-level service that is part of the composition of the business service.

For example, we address the Request Quote scenario as follows:

- **Collect Information:**   This is a manual process.
- **Validate Request:**   This is internal to another service.
- **Underwrite for Quote:**   For this, we create the Underwriting Service.
- **Price Request:**   For this, we create the Pricing Service.
- **Create Quote:**   For this, we create the Quoting Service.
- **Create Alternate Proposal:**   This is done by the Quoting Service.

WOULDN'T IT BE NICE . . .

Wouldn't it be nice if the information that the business provided to use is nice and uniform? Okay, pinch yourself and wake up to reality. This is rarely the case. More likely, you're happy to get any level of detail at all. And, when you do translate that business detail into something more IT-like, you need to verify that you did it accurately.

So, a scenario diagram has to accurately reflect the information provided by your business partners, and communicate to them that you have accurately accounted for all requirements. That's one of the most important aspects of a scenario diagram (especially the initial diagrams). So, the facts of life are that the details that are specified to you are at differing levels. Some are service operations; others are implementation details . . . hey, deal with it!

At this stage in the process, you need to deal with these different levels. Sorry if reality is messy. That's why they pay you the big bucks.

At the beginning of this task (assigning activities to services), you often need to create new services for the activities. Near the end of the task, many services have already been created, and you are adding new operations to them. As you create new services, you want to think about how to organize them into service groups (or packages) and make sure that those services align with the service taxonomy. You have chosen to group the Quoting and Pricing related services together into the Pricing group because of functional cohesion.

Another common principle is to group services by organizational unit or scope. For example, you might have groupings for each line-of-business or application group. The goal is to group cohesive services in the same service model so that it is easy to understand the responsibilities associated with those services.

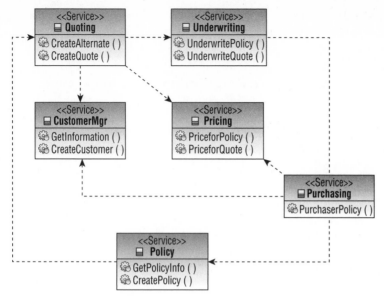

Figure 6-20 Quoting Services model

Figure 6-20 shows the diagram for the Quoting Services model. The white services are the ones that belong to this package. The gray services are related services in other packages. Another function of the service model is to illustrate the relationships between services. This helps in identifying cohesion, dependencies, and tight coupling and provides an opportunity to apply some dependency management patterns (e.g., Mediator) where appropriate.

Goals — Describe the services that are associated with a set of use cases, and their relationships. Identify coupling and dependency problems.

Concerns — Service relationships, coupling, and shared information.

Concepts — Service, relationships, and documents.

Service Definition Diagrams

Now that you have identified the services and their associated documents, it is time to define the specific service interfaces. The service definition diagram is a visual representation of the service's interface. Figure 6-21 contains five types of drawing elements represented as stereotypes on classes.

- Operations
- Documents
- Data types
- Exceptions
- Associations

The left-center column of classes are the service operations. The operations are the functions that the services perform. Each operation is defined as having a set of input (left), output parameters (right), and exceptions (far right). The parameters may either be documents or data types (depending on the interaction style chosen for the service). The associations connect the inputs and outputs with the operations.

A single service typically has several operations. We try to group operations according to the fundamental principles of cohesion and coupling. We want the operations to be cohesive, that is, have a similar business domain, similar information model, and so on. And, we want to minimize coupling between services and operations. There are no strict rules for how many operations a service should have. As an approximation, 4–7 seems to be a reasonable rule of thumb. If you have created much more than that, it is often an indication that the granularity of the service operations is too fine, or that the service is doing too many different things and should be refactored.

To identify the service operations, work through each of the detailed use case scenarios and evaluate each activity in the scenario, this time looking for those that are implemented by service operations.

As you include an activity in a service definition diagram, you should include the associated documents with it. Remember that the documents were identified on the flows between activities in the scenarios. Now, you need to assign them as inputs or outputs to the operations that implement those activities.

This provides an immediate visual clue to any incompleteness. All operations must have at least one input and output. When an operation is missing one or the other, you have to understand why, and perhaps go back and correct the scenario diagram if you forgot to identify an information flow in it.

Figure 6-21 is the service definition diagram for the Quoting Service. In the center left of the diagram is the Quote Request operation. Notice that it takes a Quote Request document as input and produces either a Quote or an Alternate Quote Proposal as the output. In addition, it can signal a "out of range" exception. In the detailed scenario, you identified that Create Alternate Proposal would be a separate operation, internal to the Quoting Service. Now, you need to include it in the service interface as well. So, at least for now, the service definition also contains an operation for it. Later, as you work out the alternate scenario for it, you will probably come back and revisit that decision. This is part of the normal, iterative design process.

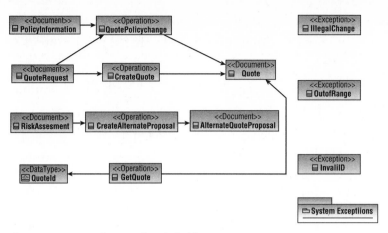

Figure 6-21 Quoting Service definition

In Figure 6-21, CreateQuote, is the QuotePolicyChange operation, which you defined in the Change Policy scenario. Finishing off the operations is Get Quote. Notice that the input to Get Quote is a type, not a document. There are some other important things to notice about the overall service definition.

Operations can have more than one input and output. Also notice that several different operations use the same document (QuoteRequest) as input. Also notice that several operation use the same document (Quote) as output. This is both normal and good. One of the fundamental principles of SOA is that services need to share common information, based on a common semantic information model. Documents are one representation of that semantic information that are used as input and output to operations. You want the same documents (representing the same information) to be shared across similar operations.

But alas, there is another mismatch between reality and what you'd like. For example, WSDL-based service definitions require single input, output, and/or fault messages. So, the implementation either requires the service to introduce coupled data items to package the inputs and outputs or to use WSDL-wrapped doc-literal parameter passing, which can do this automatically. At this stage in the process, the focus is on getting the right level of cohesion and coupling. You can deal with the implementation details later.

At the end of this task, you have worked through all of the scenarios and assigned all of the activities to services. Then, you will have made sure that all operations have inputs and outputs, and any similar or shared information is based on the common semantic information model and represented in related or the same documents. As with all aspects of an iterative development process, you may have to go back and update some of the scenario and document definitions with the new information you learned or discovered along the way.

Goals — Identify the service operations and their inputs and outputs.

Concerns — Service interaction and interface style, shared information, cohesion, and coupling.

Concepts — Services, operations, exceptions, types, and documents.

NOTE When a service definition is complete, all operations have inputs, outputs, and exceptions defined. Similar inputs should use similar or the same documents, based on the common information model.

Operations Procedures

Now that you have defined the service interfaces, the next step is to define the service implementations, or specifically, the procedures that implement the service operations. This is the subject of the next chapter.

More Information Model

You started to develop a high-level information model as part of the problem space analysis. The semantic information model is derived from a variety of sources as described in Chapter 5. First, from industry standards and domain and business knowledge of the business and data analysis. The result of this is the high-level business information model containing business entities and documents as shown in Figure 6-19. The second source is from the use cases. For ACME, the use cases specify a lot of the information that is used for insurance quoting. The third source is emerging requirements as the services and operations are designed.

DATA MODEL REUSE

An initial step that is always important is to take a look at relevant industry standards that can be utilized. Luckily for us, The Agency Company Organization for Research and Development (ACORD) develops standards for the insurance industry, and you should look there first. In this case, they define XML schemas for all of our use cases — requests and responses for quotes, as well as requests and responses for adding, updating, replacing, reissuing, reinstating, and canceling all different types of insurance policies. In this case, you can stand on the shoulders of this standards body and build directly to the spec. Usually, things aren't this easy — but this shows how reusing data standards makes a lot of sense!

However, in this example we do not use these documents because we want to illustrate the process of discovering the information requirements and representing them in documents.

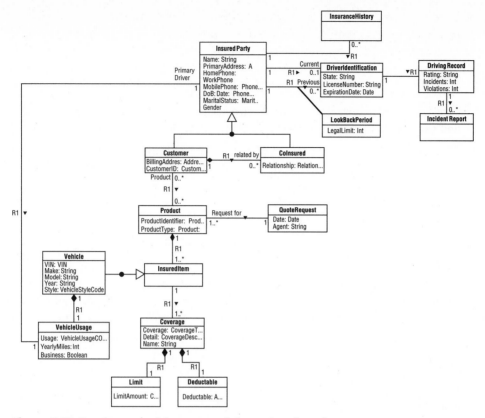

Figure 6-22 Quoting and pricing request information class diagram

Quoting and Pricing Request Information

Using the information from Steps 1 and 2 of use cases BU01, BU02, and BU03, you develop the information model shown in Figure 6-22. You represent the information model as a class model and identify attributes for each class and relationships between classes. On the associations, you specify multiplicities, and can add role names and end names where appropriate.

For the example, notice that an `InsuredParty` has two associations to `DriverIdentification`. One association is for the current information; the second is for previous information.

You must base the use case–specific information model on your high-level business or domain models. Here, notice that Customer, which is what is specified in the use case, is based on the industry domain object of Insured Party.

The use cases define the set of information that is required to request a quote, purchase insurance, or change the policy, but do not give much guidance on what information should be returned. This is something you have to figure out yourself as you walk through the scenarios and operations procedures. We have chosen to create a separate class model for the Reply Information as a way to organize the information into models, and for this example, to simplify the document markings.

> **Goals** — Define the details of the information that is required for input and output of all operations. Shared information should be described in the semantic information model.
>
> **Concerns** — Inputs, outputs, and shared information.
>
> **Concepts** — Classes, relationships, multiplicities.

Document Model

Now, you need to create documents based on the information model. Figure 6-23 shows the document marking for the `QuoteRequest` document. Notice that the underlying information model is the same as that in Figure 6-22 and that the documents are super-imposed on top of that. This is one of the ways to enforce the requirements for the common information model.

There are three important concepts in the document marking:

- Root Node
- Subelements
- References

Notice that the `QuoteRequest` class is surrounded by a double border. This is the indication that it is the root of the document. When constructing the document, you start here in the information model and then follow the arrows from there.

The solid arrows and solid outline classes represent subelements. So, starting from the root, the quote request will contain one or more products. Each product will have one or more insured items, and so on.

Coming out of `VehicleUsage` is a dashed arrow leading to `InsuredParty`. This is a reference marking, indicating that the document does not contain the entire information about a `VehicleUsage` customer, only a reference to the customer. In this case, it also contains a reference to the co-insured.

> **Goals** — Define the details of the documents based on the shared information model.
>
> **Concerns** — Enterprise shared information model.
>
> **Concepts** — Root, subelements, and references.

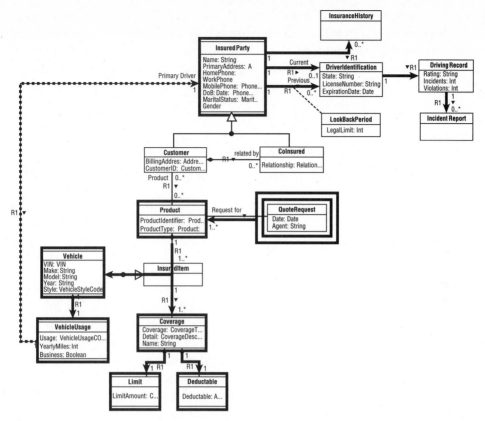

Figure 6-23 Quote request document marking

Summary

SOA solutions, like other IT solutions, deserve a systematic approach that aligns the implemented solution, with the initial business drivers and requirements. But, SOA introduces additional requirements. SOA solutions are not built in isolation. Rather, they are expected to be part of a larger, enterprise solution and to contribute to a growing catalog (inventory) of business-related services. This requires identification of shared behavior, coordination in the development of service interfaces, and a common information model at the service interface level. An SOA development methodology must address these requirements in addition to the other requirements of IT development.

In this chapter, we started by separating two primary concerns, that of the business requirements or problem space, and that of the IT solution. The business requirements are addressed in the Problem model and expressed in terms of business concepts, specifically those of: actors, business workers, scenarios, activities, documents, and information entities. Use cases are used to collect and organize requirements, and then to provide a high-level organization for the problem model itself.

The solution model addresses how the business requirements can be implemented in IT systems. It expresses the solution in terms of platform independent IT application concepts, specifically those of services, operations, procedures, interfaces, implementations, transformations, information, and documents.

Services are the fundamental concept in an SOA. A service is made up of its interface, which specifies the operations, inputs and outputs; and its implementation, which specifies how the operations are performed. A document is a fundamental concept in the specification of a service interface. It is a structured collection of information. In SOA, it is critical that the same information be used to represent the same concepts, across different services. The semantic information model is used to facilitate this, and the documents are constructed as collections of information from the semantic model.

The implementations of service operations are specified in terms of procedure definitions, which define a set of steps and transformations that together implement the operation. Services are often constructed, or composed, of other services, which may themselves be composed from other services, and so on. In other words, the procedures that implement a service operation invoke other services as part of the operation's implementation.

The design methodology is iterative and incremental. You do not complete one step for the entire model and then go on to the next step for the entire model, and so on. Rather, you divide the solution space into small increments, such as the definition and implementation of a specific service, and work through all of the steps for that service. Then, you incorporate what you learned back into the high-level design and start with another increment.

Within each increment, you work iteratively to do some information modeling, some interface design, some procedure specification, and so forth. In each step, you learn additional information that has to be folded back into the other areas of the design.

You start at a high-level, addressing the main steps outlined in the use cases and cover a set of related use cases. At this level, you are trying to identify behavior that is common across use cases and factor it out into shared behavior. These are the first candidates for business services. You also identify information that is shared across these use cases and include that in our information model. Fundamental business entities and other shared information may also be candidates for entity or resource manager services.

Next, you dig into the use cases in more detail, using what you've identified as common from the high-level scenario analysis along with additional details from the use cases themselves, your service inventory, and domain knowledge and experience. This identifies additional areas of responsibility and activities. You also specify the flow of information between the activities in terms of documents. Now, you have effectively represented the business requirements in terms of the Problem model.

The solution model translates these business concepts into SOA application concepts. One primary translation is from the activities in the business scenarios. Activities are either done manually, or, if automated, become operations on business services, or internal steps (composed services) within the implementation of an operation procedure. You work through the model, addressing each activity to determine its likely outcome and begin to define the services and their operations. The service model organizes services into cohesive collections of services. In addition to providing a table of contents for the services, the models illustrate the relationships between services. Here, you examine the relationships between services to reduce dependencies and coupling and to increase cohesion. This may result in a refactoring of some of the service definitions.

Next, you work out the details of the service interfaces. Initially, activities from the business scenarios can identify the service operations and data flows between those activities, and can define the documents that are used as inputs and output. As you elaborate on the operations, you identify additional internal operations that may become part of the service definition, as well as additional information that is needed in the interfaces.

For each operation, you define the procedure that implements the operation. Again, this is accomplished by iteratively working through the input and outputs, internal information requirements, and internal processing steps. As you work through these details, you also identify changes or additions to the service interfaces and information.

Whenever you identify additional information requirements at the interface level, you incorporate that new information into the semantic information model. As you create the detailed specifications of the documents, based on the information model, you will likely discover and implement more changes to the information model as well. Finally, when a service definition is complete, all operations will have inputs and outputs defined, and all document schema will be defined. Similar inputs should use similar, or the same, documents based on the common information model.

This chapter has focused on the design of the service interface. The next chapter goes into detail on the design of the service implementation.

CHAPTER 7

Designing Service Implementations

Out of intense complexities, intense simplicities emerge.
— **Winston Churchill**

In the last three chapters we focused on identifying business services (Chapter 4), defining the business data using information models (Chapter 5), and defining service interfaces (Chapter 6). Therefore, most of our focus has been *external* — how to define services based on high-level goals and requirements, and their interfaces based on semantically rich data resulting from information modeling. Information modeling is a key aspect, as it places service behavior in the context of the life cycles of enterprise information, providing a more complete view that is sometimes left out by simple functional analysis and decomposition alone. This is useful for the creation of all types of services (business services, domain services, utility services, and so on), and once you have gone through that process and have defined your interfaces and messaging, you have reduced complexity to the point where you can now focus on the *internals*, or the implementation design of your services. In this chapter, you learn how to define what is inside each service in order to create the service implementations. This is more than just a development or programming task, and it is more than just elaborating on a design. Good service implementation design ensures that the overall architecture is maintained by following the principles established in the enterprise architecture.

This chapter presents a strategy for constructing services that divides the problem into several key parts:

- Designing the implementation of a service interface
- Designing the implementation of the business logic (the logic of the domain itself)
- Designing the resource access layer of a service

The strategy presented in this chapter does not presume any particular implementation or platform technology. The approach is platform-independent, although a few examples are illustrated with particular technologies. The chapter presents the following information:

- Basic service architecture
- Using activity diagrams to describe operations
- Implementing the interface layer
- Implementing the business logic layer
- Implementing the resource access layer
- Example of implementation design

Basic Service Architecture

Before we get started with the service design, it is important to address some common misconceptions about the implementations of services. Although there is an abundance of "Hello World" example services in many programming languages, a service is *not* one simple class that implements a service interface. Certainly, a service *could* consist of one class (although this is typically a very bad design), but it is important to understand that a service should be looked at as an application with all the characteristics thereof. Therefore, it must include architectural focus for its implementation. Service design should use a layered architecture just like application design. The basic service architecture, presented in Figure 7-1, is composed of the following major layers: a service interface layer, a service business layer, and a resource access layer. This three-layered architecture is often referred to as a *service implementation model*.

The *service interface layer* implements the service contract (or interface) — the operations provided by the service (interaction patterns supported by these operations), the documents associated with each operation, and the data types composing these documents. The *service business layer* is responsible for implementing the business logic, rules, and state transitions. The *resource access layer* contains the logic necessary to access enterprise resources, which are utilized by the service's implementation. The resources used by the service may include data (databases used directly by a service), existing enterprise

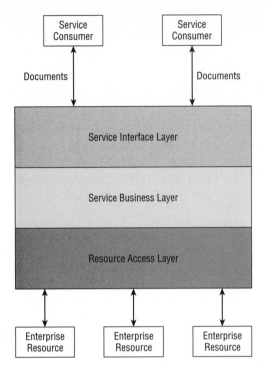

Figure 7-1 Basic service architecture — the service implementation model

applications (through integration services, more on this is in Chapter 10), and other business, domain, and utility services.

The service interface layer typically operates on data that is semantically tied to the enterprise (usually the messaging payload sent to the service, defined in accordance with the semantic information model). The interface layer's responsibility is to receive the input documents and make any necessary translations required to invoke business entities (business objects with business data) in the business layer in order to implement the functionality of the service's operation. Although it is technically possible to use the same semantic data types directly in the business layer, the more common case is to use business entities for the business layer implementation. As discussed in Chapter 5, semantic data types are often designed to optimize the information transport between services. Because of that, this type of data is not well suited for business processing, which often requires a different data model altogether.

The responsibility of the business layer is to do the business processing required to implement the service contract.

As stated earlier, no service is an island. Its implementation always leverages other existing enterprise resources, including databases, existing legacy applications, and other services. Interacting with these resources is a responsibility of the resource access layer. Business entities used by the business layer for business processing can be used here for accessing resources. However, this resource layer often introduces its own data model, called the resource access data model. In this case, the implementation of the resource layer first converts business entities into the resource data model, and then executes the actual accessing of resources.

Although a three-layered architecture for service implementations might appear complex, it provides the most flexible and maintainable service implementation. The separation of responsibilities and the separation of data support the architectural principle of separation of concerns and contribute to localization of potential changes. For example, changes to input data validation rules are completely encapsulated in the business layer. Therefore, they can be made without affecting the interface and resource layers.

Layer Responsibilities

Figure 7-2 illustrates an example of distribution of function and responsibility between layers for a typical operation. The interface layer receives the operation invocation and performs the syntactical validation of the input document. Then, any transformation between the semantic information model and the domain model is performed. Next, the business layer performs whatever

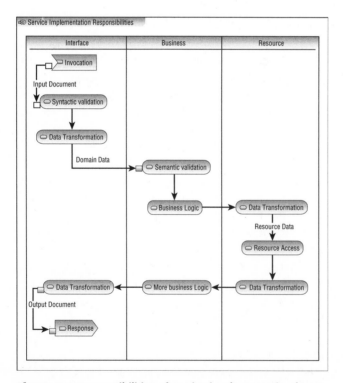

Figure 7-2 Responsibilities of service implementation layers

business logic or functions are required. This typically requires a call to the resource layer to access data, services, or other resources. The resource layer performs a required translation to and from the resource data model, before and after the resource access. Any additional business logic is carried out before the interface layer takes over again to transform the data back from the domain model to the semantic information model, format the document, and send the response.

The service implementation model presented here is gaining adoption in the industry. Many companies are using it as a foundation for designing and implementing services, and tooling is beginning to appear that enforces such a three-layered architecture. For example, the latest version of Microsoft's patterns & practices Web Service software factory is based exactly on this model and allows the generation of a solution layout ("solution" is a Microsoft's Visual Studio term, defining a set of interrelated projects that are developed and compiled together) adhering to the service implementation model outlined in Figure 7-1.

First, we discuss the general modeling techniques and diagrams used in implementation design. Then, we outline implementation approaches for these service layers.

Using Activity Diagrams for Modeling Operational Logic

Activity diagrams can be helpful in designing the implementation of services at all layers. Although they represent mostly execution in the business layer, they, nevertheless, outline responsibilities of both interface and resource layers, required for their implementation. Therefore, it is often helpful to diagram the logic of your services.

This section walks you through the process by looking at a simple example. (See Figure 7-3.) As discussed in the previous chapter, services provide their capabilities through the exposed operations in their interfaces. Operational logic can be stated in terms of code such as Java, C#, or BPEL (yes, operational logic can be purely a composition of other, lower-level services). However, in order to show the true technology-independent nature of these operations, it is helpful to illustrate the operational flow using UML activity diagrams, such as the one in Figure 7-3 where we have diagrammed the process of the creation of a simple purchase order. Not only do activity diagrams allow operations to be illustrated in a technology-independent manner, but each of the action bubbles can then be named and mapped to specific implementation concepts — a feature we use later in this chapter.

An activity diagram consists of *input and output parameters*, *actions*, and *datastores*. The input parameters to the operation are shown on the arrow out of the initial pseudostate (the black bubble labeled "Start"), and output parameters are shown on the arrow pointing to the final state (labeled "End").

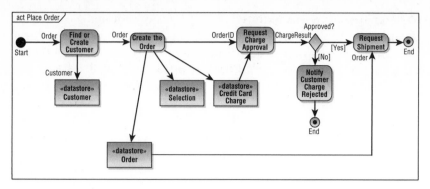

Figure 7-3 An activity diagram illustrating the creation of an order

These parameters may be simple types, complex types, or whole documents. Rounded rectangles represent *actions*, which can do calculations, access data (to and from datastores), and invoke other services. Finally, Squared-off rectangles with the ≪datastore≫ stereotype are datastores representing domain data. A datastore represents one class in the domain's information model, which encapsulates resource (database, additional services, or enterprise application) access. Arrows between datastores and actions may be labeled with the content that is written (with an arrow pointing to the datastore) or read (with an arrow pointing out of the datastore). Activity diagrams are helpful because they make it easy to visually understand the process of the operation. For example, the Place Order operation in Figure 7-3 does the following:

1. Receives an Order document.
2. Finds a Customer matching the Customer in the Order. If none exists, it creates a new Customer.
3. Creates the Order itself along with Selections and a Credit Card Charge.
4. Sends the credit card charge to the credit card company for approval.
5. If the charge is approved, notifies the customer and sends the order to be packed and shipped.

So why go through all the work to draw the activity diagram when text seems to be just as capable of expressing the operation? The value is not necessarily in the pictures; it is in the individual actions that make up the diagram. By dividing an operation into such basic actions, you can allocate these actions among existing services and define additional services that need to be built. Diagrams also introduce an additional rigor; omissions that might not be obvious in the textual representation are often immediately apparent by looking at the diagram.

Implementation Components

The activity diagram is used to illustrate the flow of an operation from input, through intermediate actions, to output. (Note that the flow traverses the different implementation layers of the service architecture, but this is not shown in the diagram.) Each activity in the diagram is implemented by some type of "implementation" component. Figure 7-4 shows the most common types of implementation components, organized by layers.

- **Interface** — The interface exposes the operations of the service to the rest of the SOA. The implementation of the interface must support the required protocols.

- **Transformation** — Transformation components change data from one format, schema, or semantic model to another. Transformations occur between the enterprise semantic information model used by the interface and the domain information model used in the business layer. Transformations also take place between the business and resource layers. The transformation may be hard-coded or make use of a platform-provided transformation service.

- **Logic implementation** — The business logic components implement the specific logical functions of the service operation.

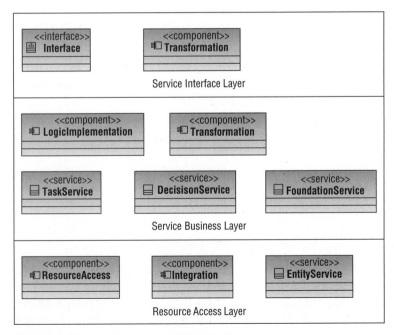

Figure 7-4 Implementation components by layer

- **Task Service** — Services may be composed of other services. Task services implement business or logical tasks, such as common domain functions or business utilities.

- **Decision Service** — Decision services implement (complex) business rules and provide an external mechanism for specifying and maintaining the rules.

- **Foundation Service** — Foundation services provide traditional platform distributed services such as authentication, logging, configuration, and the like.

- **Integration Component** — Integration components expose integration services and make their legacy functions and data available to the service operation.

- **Resource Access Component** — Resource access components encapsulate the access to resources, such as datastores.

- **Entity Service** — Entity services provide common service-based access to common business entities.

Implementing the Interface Layer

The service interface layer provides the interaction point between external service consumers and the capabilities provided by the service implementation. The main responsibilities of a service interface layer are to:

- **Implement the service contract** — This layer exposes the service operations to the outside world. In many cases, it is necessary to expose these operations via multiple transports (in order to provide different qualities of service or just support for many different consumer types), which means that one responsibility of the interface layer is to act as a listener on several required transports.

- **Support interactions with the business layer responsible for the execution of the service functionality** — The business layer often operates on domain entities, which are different from the semantic data objects passed into/out of the interface layer. The interface layer is also responsible for data transformation between these two information models.

- **Perform syntactic data validation** — It must perform this validation to ensure that the service input parameters are of the required type and conform to a set of legal values defined by the enterprise semantic information model. Some may argue that this function belongs in the business layer, but our take is that it does not complicate the implementation and is required anyway for data transformation in the interface layer. This is why we recommend keeping syntactic data validation here.

Implementation of the interface layer is typically based on a programmatic implementation of semantic data objects and documents.

Document Receipt

Implementation of a service interface starts with receiving an input document — the service request. The basic semantics of receiving a document are, "Make the contents of the objects (semantic data type implementations) match what's in the document." This means that the whole document and every subelement in the document needs a way to be identified so that in processing the document you can correctly populate appropriate semantic data types. With XML becoming a de facto standard of the "on-the-wire" representation of the document, this operation is typically carried out by XML parsers. In many cases, this operation is delegated to the underlying Web Service technologies, implementing both the actual document receipt and population of the semantic data types based on the WSDL definitions of the document. This works well when the structure of the documents is not very complex. As the complexity of the documents grows, especially if the document is using a lot of cross-references, leveraging these technologies becomes more problematic.

For example, the ACORD specification (defining very complex schemas for semantic messaging in insurance) does not rely on these technologies and passes XML documents as attachments, forcing users to process input documents programmatically. Newer XML implementations, for example, JAX-B, can be used for processing the input XML documents in these cases.

Syntactic Validation

Any operation that accepts input parameter data needs to be sure that the values are meaningful and correct for the operation. Such input validation is of two forms: *syntactic validation*, which determines whether the parameters are correctly formed, and *semantic validation*, which determines if the values themselves are correct and meaningful. Syntactic validation is the responsibility of the interface layer, whereas the responsibility for semantic validation falls on the business layer.

For simple parameters, syntactic validation generally answers the questions: Does the actual parameter meet the requirements of the type? Are numbers composed of numeric values, and do they fit within the ranges defined for the type? Do symbolic values fit the patterns defined for them? Do enumeration values fit the set of values for their type?

Document parameter validations need to look at the overall structure of the document as well as the individual attribute values. Is the document formed correctly? Do elements have the right attributes (required and optional)? Do elements have the right number and types of subelements? Are attribute values correct for their type?

Again, technologies such as Web Services make structural validations relatively straightforward to implement: The parameter structures can be specified directly in the schema files. The Web Service run times reject actual parameters that do not meet the structural requirements. Although this seems like a viable approach, many of the real-world implementations are trying to avoid it. The issue here (as with any distributed strongly typed implementation) is that validations are done by the run time before reaching implementation code. As a result, there is no place for the service implementation to execute any processing logic in the event of failures. The service consumer still receives an error reply, but this reply is produced by the run time, not the service itself. These exceptions can vary significantly from very explicit and easy to understand in some run times to very cumbersome in others. Our recommendation is to avoid run-time validation (easily done by passing all parameters as strings) and do syntactic validation in code. In this case, all validation errors can be collected and properly reported to a service consumer. As we have discussed, syntactic validations, depending on their complexity, can be implemented either in an interface layer or a business layer.

Transformations

Finally, it is the responsibility of the interface layer to transform semantic data types to business entities for use in the business layer. Typically, semantic data types and business entities are well aligned through design; these transformations are fairly straightforward and can be directly implemented using general-purpose programming languages. We recommend that you separate these transformations into specialized classes or components to improve the overall maintainability of the code.

In the case where transformation is more complex, the use of specialized transformation (foundation) services can be used. Typically, these are provided by the underlying SOA or Web Service platform. The transformation service consists of a design-time editor to define the transformation map between schemas, and a run-time component that executes the transformation on the specified input data.

Implementing the Business Layer

The business layer is the foundation of the service implementation, containing the implementation of the service's business logic and business entities that are used by the business logic. This can include the following:

- Semantic validation of incoming parameters.
- Sequence calls to other business logic, data access logic, other services or existing enterprise applications.
- Transaction initiation and control. All of the two-phase transactions are encapsulated in service implementations (see Chapters 8 and 10 for more information on transactions between services). The business layer is responsible for transaction demarcation.
- Conditional logic and business rule implementation.

Greatly simplified, the business implementation of an operation consists of three parts:

1. Semantic validation of the input parameters
2. Performing the business logic of the operation
3. Returning a result

This section covers each of these steps.

Semantic Input Validation

Operation logic needs to be sure that the input values are meaningful and correct. Semantic validation, the determination of correctness of specific input values (according to business rules) occurs here in the business logic layer.

Semantic validation differs from syntactic validation in that it requires information beyond just the type declaration. Generally, semantic validations require examining the data in the context of the service's overall environment, ensuring that all of the information for the service invocation is complete. For example, validation can ensure that the account used in the service invocation exists. In most development scenarios, semantic validations need to be coded, not just declared.

Table 7-1 Semantic validations on an Order

FIELD	TEST
`Order.OrderNumber`	Must be unique and must be a valid number for the store
`Order.Date`	Must be today or later
`Selection.Product.SKU`	Must identify an existing product
`Selection.SelectionTotal`	Must be a quantity greater than zero
`CreditCardAccount.AccountNumber`	Must be a properly formatted number according to the rules of the credit card company
`CreditCardAccount.ExpirationDate`	Must be later than today
`CreditCardAccount.CardValidationNumber`	Must be legal for the credit card type and account number

Table 7-1 shows a sample semantic validation for an Order. Each field in the order that requires validation is listed along with the rules that it must pass. All tests must pass for the Order to be processed.

Some semantic validations are simply constraints between parameter values and as such do not require any more information than just the parameter values themselves.

Some validation steps require calls to other services outside of the domain. For example, the credit card account number and card validation number in the Order example can only be checked by calling a service provided by the credit card company.

Other semantic validations require the domain's information model. Validations of this form include:

- Does an object already exist?
- Can a new object be created?
- Do references actually refer to existing objects?

Performing the Business Logic of the Operation

After semantic validation, the business layer must perform the logic of the operation itself. Often, the business logic required for a particular operation can be discovered by following the data flow through the operation's activities. Figure 7-5 illustrates this concept.

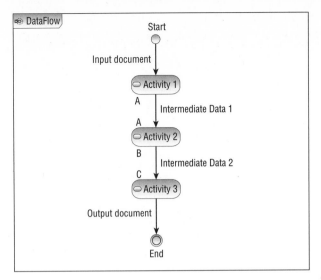

Figure 7-5 Discovering business logic by following the data

The start state of the activity diagram represents the initial request. You know what the data is at this point because it is exactly what's in the input document. If you know what the information required for Activity 1 is, then you can determine what, if any, data transformation is required between the start and Activity 1.

Likewise, if you know what information is required for Activity 2, you can design Activity 1 to return that data. Alternately, if it is already implemented as a component or service, then you can determine the required transformation. In the drawing, both the output of Activity 1 and the input of Activity 2 are in data format A, so nothing is required.

The case where an activity is implemented by a service provides an interesting opportunity. You know exactly what information is required and will be returned from a service (because it's defined in the interface). For example, assume that Activity 3 is implemented by a utility service. Referring to Figure 7-5 again, notice that the output of Activity 2 is in data format B, but the input to Activity 3 is in data format C. So, what can you do about this mismatch?

When implementing Activity 2, you can ask some simple questions:

1. Do you have all the information that you need to invoke the service (Activity 3)?

   ■ If yes, continue.

   ■ If no, then how do you get that information? Is there a service or data source that provides it? Do you have the information that you need to call that service? Or, do you have to change the operation's input document definition to get the required information?

2. Does the output of Activity 2 match the input of Activity 3? (Note that it doesn't have to match exactly, but all the information required for Activity 3 must be present.)

   ■ If yes, continue.

   ■ If no, then what transformation is required?

As you can see, you can follow the data flow from activity to activity in the diagram determining what, if any, additional information or transformations are required and implementing them through a combination of components, services, and transformations, until the final return document is completed. Alternatively, you can start with the output document and work backward through the service to the input determining the implementation design.

In following the data flow of your activity diagram, you may determine that you are actually building a composite service, where the logic of your service may be simply to combine services based on a logical business process. If this is the case, your business layer contains the process for orchestrating services. In this case, we refer you to Chapter 8, where we focus on various service composition strategies ranging from BPEL-based orchestration, and composition using such frameworks as Service Component Architecture (SCA).

Finally, as you prepare to build the implementation of the service, you must develop or adhere to a strategy for exception handling, typically established by your SOA governance policies (see Chapter 12). In Chapter 6, we discussed exceptions as part of the service interface definition, but the actual handling of these exceptions is typically implemented in the business layer, and their results are then propagated to the interface layer to report them to the service consumers. The typical implementation is based on the ability of application designers and developers to anticipate the possible exception conditions, appropriately instrument them in the code, and handle them at run time. From this point of view, exception handling in service implementations is no different from the exception handling in ordinary applications.

What makes exception handling different in SOA is the dynamic nature of services, which can be combined in a multitude of different ways (through choreography and service composition). It is necessary to propagate all of the exceptions to the interface layer to report the exceptions to the service consumer. This is usually done by executing all of the business logic in a single try/catch block defined in the interface layer. Such an approach allows the interface layer to catch, appropriately map, and report all of the service execution exceptions. Centralized error-handling techniques, as described in

Chapter 9, allow all of the service exceptions to be intercepted and delivered to the centralized location for complete system analysis.

Computing and Returning Results

Often the business logic requires the computation of specific results based on the input data. Computations can be implemented by custom code, components, or by invoking other existing services.

Depending on the type of computation, typically either task-oriented or decision services would be used to perform the calculation. When a service is constructed primarily from other services, service orchestration may be the appropriate implementation technique.

Returning results is almost the opposite of receiving the initial input document, except that no validation needs to occur. The activity involves collecting the data, calculations, and so on, from the business logic, doing any necessary translations, and formatting the return document.

As with the request document, with XML becoming a standard for documents, this activity is typically carried out by XML parsers or Web Service technologies.

Implementing the Resource Layer

The resource access layer is the layer between the business layer and a database, external services, or enterprise applications. The data access logic is responsible for persisting business entities to a database and retrieving individual business entities or sets of business entities on behalf of the business layer. The resource access layer may also contain invocation of other services (business, domain, utility, or integration) to retrieve resources, required for business logic implementation. This layer should encapsulate all the code that deals with external resources (such as databases or other services), without exposing any of these implementation details to higher layers. This includes transformation between business services and data required for resource invocation and the actual invocation of resources.

As mentioned in the previous section, many times, your service implementation may actually be a composite service, where business logic dictates the use of several other services combined with additional logical process to provide the functionality of your service. In this case, the business layer includes the definition of that process, and orchestrates the calling of the other services by invoking components in the resource layer. The business logic for orchestration occurs in the business layer, and the resource layer typically involves the utilization of frameworks such as SCA. We refer you to Chapter 8, which covers design techniques for composing services.

A typical implementation of resource access is through integration/resource components (see Chapter 10 for more details). Each component exposes an interface expressed in terms of business entities and is responsible for implementation of the access to a particular resource. From the point of view of the rest of service implementation, resource functionality is implemented by a resource component, hiding the details of integration and resource access. Invocation of these resource components is orchestrated by the business logic layer.

Implementation Design Illustrated

In this section of the chapter, we illustrate the implementation design process by continuing the automobile insurance–quoting example from Chapter 6. In that part of the example, the process of service interface design was illustrated. As a brief review, use cases to describe the problem space were identified along with detailed scenarios for the use cases and an information model to support them. The steps in the scenarios (specifically, the actions in activity diagrams used to specify them) were assigned to operations on business services and were organized into service interfaces based on cohesion and coupling principles. The information passing into and out of service interfaces was defined in terms of documents, which were based on the semantic information model. Now, it is time to define the specific service operations. This part of the example focuses on the implementation business layer.

Business Layer

With so many service operations, where should you start? We like to start with the "primary use cases operations" first. For example, for the Create Quote Scenario, the Create Quote operation corresponds to the primary use case.

The reason to start with the primary use case operations is to finish working through all the use case scenario actions. You can now make your final pass through the scenarios. Recall that for each scenario action, you have three possible assignments: Define it as a manual task, assign it to a service, or include it as an internal step of a service operation (possibly implemented by a lower-level service).

You should have completed the first two already. The remaining scenario activities (those still unassigned) should become internal steps within an operation procedure. We start with the primary use case because very often, the primary use case operation is part of a composite operation of a business service. In other words, the operation is composed of calls to other services as part of the procedure. These services come from a variety of sources. Some are defined and implemented as part of the current project, some come from packages imported from the same enterprise (from the service inventory), and some come from external providers.

Create Quote Operation (Quoting Service – Request Quote Scenario)

To develop the Create Quote operation procedure, refer to the Detailed Request Quote Scenario (see Figure 6-18) and specifically the partition for Quoting. Remember the meaning of a partition in an activity diagram. The actions within that partition are the responsibility of that actor. In this case, the actor is the "Quoting Business Worker," whose responsibilities are being implemented by the Quoting Service. More specifically, the responsibilities for this scenario are being implemented by the Create Quote operation.

In the partition, there are six activities: create quote, validate request, request underwriting, create alternate proposal, price request, and format quote. In an earlier step when the interface operations were being assigned, the create quote action was assigned to this operation. In other words, it is the external entry into the operation. The rest of the actions in the partition are still unaccounted for and are internal to the operation. Figure 7-6 shows an activity diagram detailing the operation's procedure.

Because the QuoteRequest document is defined as the input to the operation in the interface, it is automatically the first data flow. So, the first step that is performed is to validate the request. The output of this step is a validated QuoteRequest document. The next action in the partition is to request Underwriting. However, there is a problem. From the complete scenario, you can see that customer information is required for the underwriting, but that you haven't gotten it yet. So, a GetCustomer step is inserted in the procedure before the underwriting action. Next, the outcome of the underwriting has to be determined based on the status returned. If the underwriting is rejected, an alternate proposal is created. Otherwise, a price is requested, and the quote is formatted and returned. A decision action is used for this.

Once the control flow of the procedure is designed, the information flow between each action is defined, and then each action is associated with the component that implements it.

Price for Quote Operation (Automobile LOB Pricing)

Now, let's look at the Automobile LOB Pricing Service and the PriceforQuote operation procedure, as shown in Figure 7-7. The operation is initiated with a `PriceRequest` document. After validating the request, you need to get information about the vehicles and drivers that will be insured. There are two sources for this information. One is provided by the state based on `getVehicleInfo` and `getDriverRecord` operations. These are external services, whose definitions (contracts) have previously been imported into the model. The second source of information is from the Insurance Bureau, which has historical information about the vehicle's and driver's past insurance activities. Finally, location information is also needed. All of the actions to get this information can be performed in parallel, so a fork/join pattern is used to perform all five data collection operations in parallel.

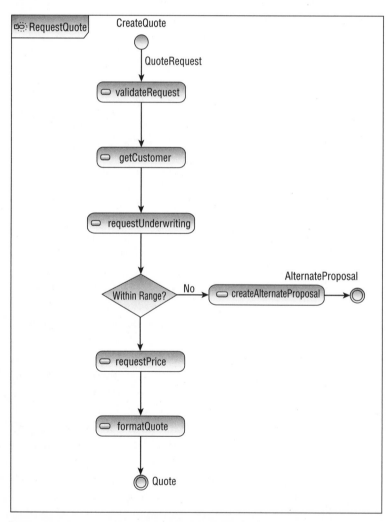

Figure 7-6 Create Quote operation diagram

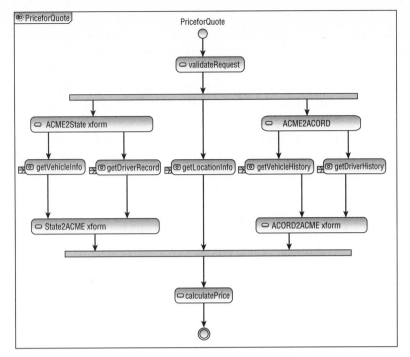

Figure 7-7 Automobile LOB Price for Quote procedure

But look at the information requirements of the external services. The information provided in the `PriceRequest` is not the same format as that required by either the state provided, or Insurance Bureau provided services. So, transformations that are needed for each source of information are inserted before and after the actions that call to the services. The `ACME2State` and `State2ACME` transformations convert the vehicle and driver information to/from ACME's format and the state's format. Similarly, the `ACME2ACORD` and `ACORD2ACME` transformations convert insurance history from ACME's format to/from ACORD's format.

It is common for there to be two transformations for each kind of information in a process flow corresponding to each direction of transformation. Notice that some transformations can apply to more than one specific piece of information. For example, the same `ACME2ACORD` transformation can convert all of the data types between the two formats. Also notice that if ACME had used the industry standard definitions to define its own domains, no conversions would be necessary.

Once all of the data is returned, it is collated for the calculation of pricing. In this case, pricing is done on the existing mainframe application, and an integration component has been implemented that will be invoked to make the call into the existing application.

All of the data collection actions are performed by other services, so we have modeled them as "call actions" in the activity diagram. But notice that we have purposely kept the activity diagram simple for illustration purposes of the example. We could have included the data flow and other details in the model (and in a real model we would have), but that would start to make things busy and difficult to illustrate. There are tradeoffs in everything, and this is not a book on UML, so we have chosen to keep the models more illustrative and less complete in order to get the design principles across.

- **Goals** — Define the control and data flow of implementation details for each service operation.

- **Concerns** — Inputs, outputs, control flow, and data flow.

- **Concepts** — Documents, procedures, actions, transformations, and other services.

Summary

This chapter has continued with the design issues of services, specifically the design of the service implementation. A basic service architecture was introduced that separates the responsibilities of a service implementation into three layers.

The interface layer is responsible for receiving the service requests. The interface layer operates at the enterprise semantic level (regarding data), so it is responsible for transformation between the input documents that conform to the semantic information model and the internal domain objects.

The business layer is responsible for the logic that provides the service capabilities. This may be custom code, reusable business components, or calls to existing services.

When resources are required, the final layer, the resource access layer, is used to access the resources and insulate the business logic from the vagaries of data access.

The use of activity diagrams as a way to illustrate the control and data flow in operation was introduced as well as a technique for discovering the logic requirements by following the data through the actions of the activity.

Composing Services

One LEGO block by itself is no fun at all.
— **Jason Bloomberg**

The return on investment (ROI) of SOA is achieved by providing business *value* and solving real-world problems, and you can solve these problems only if your *business processes* drive the technology — not the other way around. As discussed in Chapter 4, BPM provides the business process workflow that drives how you define business-level services and how you can compose existing services to form new applications and services. Services are reusable components and are meant to be combined to meet business needs for enterprise applications. Service composition is the practice of how this objective is achieved.

Good service composition is an art form, building on sound architectural principles and successful design patterns. Certain strategies are successful, other strategies are flawed from the beginning, and the success of many strategies depends on specific use cases and a number of different factors. This chapter provides a practical guide for composing services, applying concepts addressed in previous chapters. Earlier in this book, in Chapter 2, we introduced you to SOA fundamentals, and in Chapter 4, we provided an in-depth discussion on Business Process Management (BPM). This chapter builds on those two chapters, and it focuses on the following:

- Service layer interaction, orchestration, choreography, the role of business rules, and business processes in composition

- Business composition and transactions, human activities, and orchestration languages, including the Business Process Execution Language (BPEL)

- Strategies in service composition, providing the pros and cons of each strategy

- A case study that you can use as a reference guide

Understanding Service Composition

A funny quote heard at a recent technology conference was "the most loosely coupled service is one that doesn't communicate with anything." This is an interesting statement — obviously, a service that doesn't talk to anything else doesn't provide any business value, but the statement is a good one in that it identifies that when services begin to interact, there can certainly be collaboration dependencies between them. Conversation rules between services, semantics, and business-processing rules regarding how these services are used can certainly affect coupling. It is our goal to minimize such dependencies.

In keeping with the LEGO analogy of SOA from Chapter 2, when you start combining LEGO pieces to form other things, the toys begin to take on different properties and become, quite literally, tightly coupled to the new creation. Tight coupling in SOA composition is not the goal, but unfortunately it could certainly happen if service composition is not done correctly. Service composition builds on the use of loosely coupled services, but it also involves a focus on having loosely coupled *interaction processes* between services. You do this initially by separating services into a service hierarchy based on functionality, by abstracting the layers, and by defining business processes that can be separated from the makeup of the services themselves.

In service composition, the result of combining services is referred to as a *composite service*. When you use services together to achieve new functionality in a business process, the composition process itself that dictates that the order and interactions between the lower-level services is exposed as this composite service. This section discusses service composition, focusing on some of the fundamental prerequisites that are best practices — separation of services into layers and separating the business processes from the services. It also defines and discusses orchestration and choreography, two different approaches to service composition.

IS THIS CHAPTER ABOUT "MASHUPS"?

A Web 2.0 buzzword that is prevalent in software industry literature today is the "mashup," which refers to combining sources of various data into one application. From that high-level definition, you could certainly say that this chapter is all about *service-based* mashups.

Usually, when the term is used, however, a mashup is a more user-facing and user-directed process, where an end user directs an application to combine and aggregate data from various sources (RSS feeds, Atom feeds, web pages, etc.) and combines the data with a presentation to provide a comprehensive view of the aggregation. Such a mashup provides great value to the end user — however, it is a little different from what we call service composition because it typically combines presentation and content. Because the web mashup combines presentation and content, the mashup itself is hard to reuse in another application.

SOA compositions, on the other hand, are not user-facing. Like user-facing mashups, they aggregate other components. They combine lower-level services with business processes to provide a higher level of functionality, and the compositions themselves are exposed as services that can be called and reused with other higher-level services. So in that sense, they could be called service "mashups." User-facing mashups could certainly call these composite services in order to aggregate content for the end user, but we prefer the term "SOA composition" to the term "mashup," because mashup is not really a well-defined term.

Separation into Service Layers

In Chapter 2, we defined a service hierarchy that shows how enterprise business processes can make use of underlying services in SOA. This hierarchy is again shown in Figure 8-1. The higher-level services make use of the underlying services to perform business functionality in the enterprise. As a review, *business services* abstract high-level business functionality that are driven by *enterprise business processes*. This gives the benefits of SOA (decoupling, separation of concerns, dependency and complexity management, etc.) to the business as well as the service domains. It allows a single architectural style to be used at all levels of abstraction as well as across domains. *Domain services* provide mid-level business functionality specific to a certain domain, *utility services* provide low-level business functionality across the enterprise, *integration services* abstract existing applications with a service layer, *external services* are services provided by third-party providers, and *foundational services* provide infrastructure-type functionality for the entire enterprise. Each higher-level service aggregates lower-level services, according to the business process. As Chapter 2 defines this hierarchy and service types in depth, we will refer you to that chapter, as we will be referencing this hierarchy with the types of services throughout this chapter.

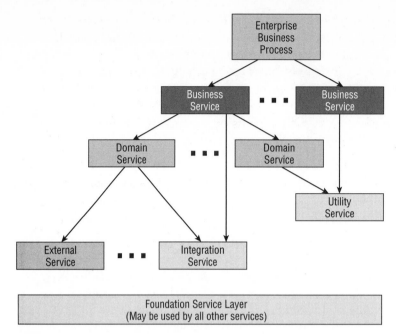

Figure 8-1 Service hierarchy

The key point here is that it is important to purposefully create such a service hierarchy, because it is important for service composition. This is not a new concept, and should be a no-brainer: Adopting a multilayered service architecture is helpful for decomposing functionality into reusable components, and having such components at various levels allows for flexibility as processes change and as new requirements come about. When you have an architecture in place where these layers are defined, new processes can use lower-level services together to achieve new functionality.

Orchestration and Choreography

Rules for service interactions in service composition can be defined in two different ways: orchestration and choreography. The differences between the two are:

- *Orchestration* describes the *workflow* of how services interact, including the business logic and order of interactions. The point of reference for orchestration is a single controller. Web Services Business Process Execution Language (WS-BPEL) is an orchestration language that is used to compose Web Services. Languages for orchestration can be used to build "orchestration scripts" that can be executed at run time by an orchestration controller (or an orchestration engine) based on rules and sequences.

- *Choreography* describes the *sequence of messages* between services, focusing on the public exchange of messages and conversational state. Unlike orchestration, which is shown from the perspective of a main coordinator, choreography focuses on the exchange of messages from the perspective of a third party observer. Intended for multi-party collaborations, each service involved in the choreography must be aware of the business process, when to execute its operations, and how to interact. Web service choreography languages, such as Web Services Choreography Language (WS-CDL) describe such peer-to-peer collaborations.

A pictorial view of the difference between orchestration and choreography is shown in Figure 8-2. The big difference is that orchestration is based on an executable business process from the perspective of one controller, and choreography is based on the messaging interactions, from the perspective of a third party, and is meant for multi-party collaboration. In practice, orchestration takes place with a central engine controlling an execution flow, whereas choreography allows for multiple parties, permitting a more peer-to-peer approach.

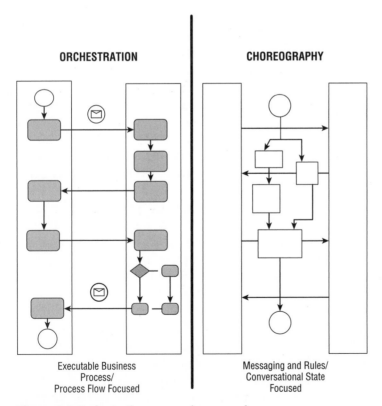

ORCHESTRATION

Executable Business
Process/
Process Flow Focused

CHOREOGRAPHY

Messaging and Rules/
Conversational State
Focused

Figure 8-2 Orchestration versus choreography

As you can see, orchestration and choreography approach two different methodologies of service composition. There are passionate debates between these two camps, and there are many strong opinions on both sides. It seems that at this point, the orchestration community has the most traction in the standards bodies and in technology adoption. WS-BPEL is a unifying orchestration standard from OASIS; it was adopted in 2007 and has been in the standards process since 2003. WS-BPEL evolved from the BPEL4WS specification (2003), which had roots in Microsoft's XLang (2000) and IBM's WSFL (2001). WS-CDL, a choreography language, has been a W3C working draft since 2004. Because WS-BPEL is a standard with widespread adoption, we focus primarily on that orchestration standard later in this chapter.

The Relationship between BPM and Composition

Business processes and good service design come together in composition. Business services are process-oriented, orchestrating lower-level services *according to business processes*. Because business processes change often, it is important when creating a composite service to separate the business processes and rules for combining them from the implementation of the service. Many frameworks for building composite services (for example, orchestration servers and service composition with SCA) provide the means to have configurable compositions that can change as the business processes change. This is an important aspect of composing services. If you hard-code rules and business process logic into the logic of services that aggregate other services, changes in requirements involve code changes. Real business processes are seldom simple, so separating them from your service logic allows you to end up with a simpler implementation of services.

One common area of confusion with service composition revolves around BPM. Obviously, business goals drive all aspects of a Service-Oriented Architecture, and one way of composing business services is based on the modeled business processes. Chapter 4 discussed how businesses can use a BPM-focused approach to take a more service-oriented approach to business analysis, and one typical way to express modeled business processes is by using Business Process Modeling Notation (BPMN). Obviously, modeling business processes is different from the actual service composition. The confusion lies in composition software tools, which commonly use *BPMN-like* graphical user interfaces for composing services, creating new services directly based on the business processes.

Certainly, the modeling done by business analysts can lead to the logic that is used in the composition phase for developing business-oriented composite services. Software developers and integrators can use the models created in that modeling phase in creating the composite services. We feel that it is important, however, to distinguish the difference between modeling and business process-oriented composition. Typically, those with the functional business knowledge, who create the models, are not the same people who develop and integrate composite services. This certainly is the vision presented to us by the tool vendors, but it is not quite reality! The important thing to understand here is that modeling of the business processes occurs earlier in the life cycle than composition does. Much as implementation always follows analysis and design in the waterfall model of software development, composition can be based on the business process model, but it occurs later and requires another skill set.

NOTE Composition can be based on BPM, but composition is not BPM.

Architectural Models in Service Composition

This section provides an overview of a few common architectural models used for service composition. Later in the chapter, we refer to these approaches as they are implemented in SOA.

Hierarchical and Conversational Composition

Figure 8-3 shows a diagram illustrating two common approaches to building a service composition that abstracts the details from lower-level services. The two most common design approaches are called *hierarchical* and *conversational composition*. In the case of hierarchical composition, the implementation of the composition is completely hidden from its consumer. Thus, it is sometimes called "black box" composition. A consumer who invokes this type of solution waits until its execution is completed and uses the results (either directly or in the form of side effects) of its execution.

Although the hierarchical composition approach is a very powerful way of dealing with the complexities, sometimes a consumer needs to control the execution of the solution based on the intermediate results of its execution. Such implementations are supported by conversational composition, as shown in Figure 8-3. In this case, the implementation of the composite service is also completely hidden from the service consumer, but selected intermediate execution results are exposed. Thus, conversational composition is sometimes called "gray box" composition.

The hierarchical composition approach is a natural fit for implementing solutions that do not require human or any other interaction from the solution invoker. Such an example might be a Truck Engine Manufacturing Service. If the service receives a message that says "Build me a Chevrolet 350 V8 Engine," no further communication with the requester is usually necessary. The Truck

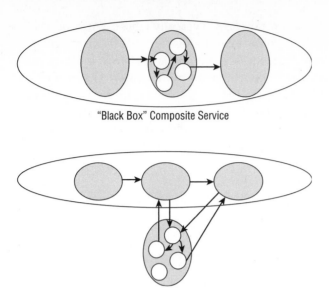

"Black Box" Composite Service

Conversational Composite Service

Figure 8-3 Hierarchical and conversational composite services

Engine Manufacturing Service is composed of low-level atomic services, such as creation services for pistons, crankshafts, camshafts, and timing chains. The service would also contain a utility service for various other aspects of engine assembly once all the parts are created, as well as the logic for combining all the parts to form the engine.

A *conversational composition* approach is typically used when an appropriate path of composition execution cannot be determined without an additional input from a service consumer, based on intermediate execution results. Such an example might be a Car Purchasing Service. This is a more complex example than the Truck Engine Manufacturing Service, because there is usually much negotiation (or haggling) involved in car purchasing. The Car Purchasing Service is a business service, most likely composed of domain services, such as a Car Loan Application Service, a Price Negotiation Service, and a Vehicle Finder Service. Any communication with the Car Purchasing Service would involve further interactions with some of these contained services. When someone goes to purchase a car, a series of interactions takes place between the consumer and the service. Such a composition strategy is helpful in modeling real-world interactions.

Conductor-Based and Peer-to-Peer Composition

There are two basic types of composition implementation strategies: *conductor-based* and *peer-to-peer*. In a conductor-based approach, a specialized service, sometimes called a mediator, interacts with a consumer and controls the execution of the other component services participating in the solution. In the case of conductor-based hierarchical solutions, the conductor implements an orchestration-invocation sequence of component services to achieve a solution. Different approaches to conductor-based composition can include the user of orchestration language/engines, OWL-S compositions, and Petri nets. Conductor-based conversational solutions implement their states and states' transitions according to the consumer inputs, typically based on the transition systems or finite state machines.

In a *peer-to-peer* approach, each participating service is responsible for partial orchestration (invoking a next step in the orchestration sequence), based on its individual rules without a central coordinator. A solution, in this case, is defined as a messaging template, and component services can be plugged into it. The target behavior is specified as a family of permitted message exchange sequences, which should be realized by the system. Typically, this topology is used only for the implementation of the hierarchical solutions because of the lack of mechanisms required for support of the conversational state. Later in this chapter, we look at these strategies as they relate to orchestration server solutions.

Service Composition Implementation

There are many techniques used to compose services. This section focuses on some of the common ways used in service composition and discusses the pros and cons of each.

Programmatic Composition

At first glance, it would seem that the simplest way to implement a service composition is to use a general-purpose programming language (such as Java, or C#, for example) to write the orchestration logic for composing services, as shown in creating a mediator in Figure 8-4. In such a programmatic approach, the logic for combining services is statically written and compiled in a programming language. Although such an implementation is technically doable, there are dangers of using this strategy.

This approach suffers from multiple drawbacks. First of all, it creates a fairly rigid implementation by hard-coding the orchestration aspects of the solution. Any change to the solution requires explicit reprogramming, and this obviously reduces flexibility to your architecture, tightly coupling your services based on interaction and the business processing logic that will most likely change. A change in the process will lead to reprogramming of your composing services. Over time, hard-coding turns into spaghetti code, making the services a nightmare to maintain and difficult to understand.

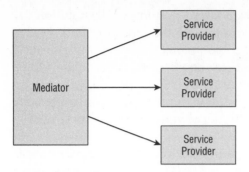

Figure 8-4 Programmatic implementation of mediator-based composite solution

It is important to understand that simple orchestrations may be easy to hard-code (although not always easy to maintain), but there are much more complex conversational composition scenarios with asynchronous services that require threading support. Programmatically, doing this in your service implementation can be problematic, especially when process engines are available. Synchronization of asynchronously invoked services and support for service contexts required for conversational solutions can make the implementation significantly more complex, and can require the creation of a specialized database and support of hydration/rehydration of the state data. Finally, the solution's implementation requires some form of transactional support to ensure correct behavior in the case of failures of participating services. To summarize, major drawbacks of the programmatic implementation of composition are:

- Hard-coding of composition logic, which makes it harder to modify and maintain
- Tight coupling with the services participating in composition, but directly accessing the services
- Potential introduction of a significant amount of infrastructure code into the service composition implementation

Having said this, programmatic composition is certainly doable. Well-designed code for orchestrations has been written before, with a certain amount of success. Because of the potential pitfalls, however, we feel that there are benefits to using some of the other techniques described in this section.

Service Component Architecture Composition

Some of the drawbacks of programmatic composition implementation, described in the previous section, can be alleviated through usage of a higher-level, executable programming model such as Service Component

Architecture (SCA). SCA is a language-neutral, technology-neutral set of specifications aimed at simplifying the composition of services by hiding (and implementing internally) many of the infrastructure elements of the service invocation. SCA is in the standardization process in OASIS in the Open Composite Services Architecture (OpenCSA), which is bringing together vendors and users, to unify the building of language-neutral components, in six technical committees (SCA-Assembly, SCA-Bindings, SCA-Policy, SCA-J, SCA-C–C++, and SCA-BPEL).

SCA specifies how to create components, combine them, and expose the component assembly as a service. Based on the SCA-defined programming models, components can be built with Java or another programming language (such as C++, Java, BPEL, or PHP) or they can be built using other technologies (for example, the Spring Framework). With SCA, communication itself is actually technology-neutral; a composite can consist of services using SOAP, Java Message Service (JMS), Representational State Transfer (REST), or other communication mechanisms. Each component has configurable properties (using deployment descriptors), and services in the same composite share a common context for many settings (such as logging and security). Whatever component technology is used, SCA defines a common assembly mechanism to specify how components are combined and exposed as a set of enterprise services.

SCA defines a component as an instance of an implementation that has been appropriately configured. (See Figure 8-5.) What makes such an implementation a SCA component is its reliance on a common set of abstractions, including services, references, properties, and bindings, to specify its interactions with the world outside itself.

Each SCA component contains fundamental parts, shown in Figure 8-5. Each component implements some business logic, exposed as one or more *services*. (In SCA, "services" are effectively interfaces, exposed by the component, which can be used by other components to access the component's functionality. They are very different from "services" defined earlier in the book.) An SCA service provides one or more operations that can be accessed by the component's client. How services are described depends on the

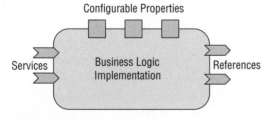

Figure 8-5 SCA component

technology that's used to implement the component and the way that consumers are planning to access it. A local component (used for the implementation of the service), implemented in Java, for example, might describe its services using ordinary Java or EJB interfaces, while an interface exposing a functionality of a component's assembly (a set of cooperating components, collectively providing service implementation) would likely describe its services using the Web Services Description Language (WSDL). Along with providing services to its own clients, a component might also rely on services provided by other components. To describe this, a component can indicate the services it relies on by using *references* (see the sidebar "Service Autonomy and SCA References"). Each reference defines an interface containing operations that this component needs to invoke. Finally, a component can also define one or more properties. Each property contains a value that can customize a component's behavior based on its usage requirements. The usage of properties is an effective mechanism for simplifying an SCA component's reuse.

SERVICE AUTONOMY AND SCA REFERENCES

Earlier in this book we defined service autonomy as being one of the fundamental characteristics of SOA. In light of this, SCA references might seem irrelevant. In reality, an explicit definition of references is extremely important:

♦ Components composing services are typically significantly more strongly coupled than the services themselves and typically have dependencies.

♦ Service composition is about the building of higher-level services from the lower-level ones. Consequently, composition always references participating services.

Explicitly defining references offers several advantages. Formally expressing dependencies can help make relationships clearer. This also directly supports the dependency injection pattern: A composition's implementation depends on interfaces of participating components (services), while their actual implementation can be inserted (dynamically) at run time. SCA allows you to simplify the implementation of this pattern: Instead of requiring a developer to write code that locates the service an implementation depends on, the SCA run time can locate that service, based on the dependency definition.

This simple model provides support for both assembling components into service implementations and assembling services themselves into enterprise solutions through composites (see Figure 8-6). Just as components expose services, a composite (business services) can also expose one or more services. These services are actually implemented by components within the composite.

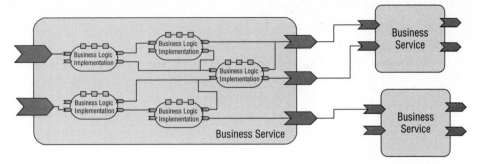

Figure 8-6 Building services from components and connecting services with SCA

Components within a composite and the composites themselves are connected to each other using *wires*. A wire is an abstract representation of the relationship between a reference and some service that meets the needs of that reference. Exactly what kind of communication a wire provides can vary depending on the bindings specified. Such a separation between the specification of each component's connections and the mechanism actually used for communication allows you to simplify deployments of components. Adjusting a wire's binding allows you to easily change a component's deployment model from a single process, to across processes on a single machine, or spread across processes on different machines.

SCA can be used for bottom-up composition — selecting a set of deployed components (services), configuring them, connecting them, and deploying the resulting composite service. SCA can also be used for top-down composition — creating a composite service from scratch and performing functional decomposition to break the composite into lower-level services.

SCA has much promise. A programming language and communications-neutral executable programming model, it provides a common composition methodology that can be used to build flexible and configurable SOA-based compositions.

Event-Based Composition

Another possible approach to the implementation of composition for SOA-based solutions is founded on event-based service interactions. In this model, service consumers publish events to a publish/subscribe intermediary, which delivers them to the actual service providers, as can be seen in Figure 8-7. Using a Publish/Subscribe ("Pub/Sub") engine as an intermediary provides, in this case, a decoupling layer between service consumers and the service provider. This allows for an extremely flexible implementation of composite solutions.

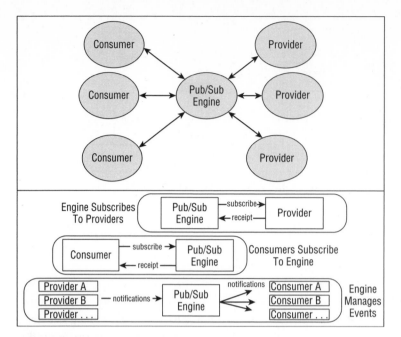

Figure 8-7 Publish and Subscribe composite service

In this approach, the consumer sends the initiating event that is delivered (through the pub/sub engine) to a set of services subscribing to this event. Every service can, in turn, send another message that will invoke (through the same pub/sub engine) yet another set of services. This sequence of events effectively creates a composite solution. By changing a set of services subscribed to a particular topic, it is possible to completely change an implementation. Alternatively, the same thing can be achieved by changing the topic to which a consumer sends an original event. However, a negative of this approach is that it does not provide the notion of the composite solution instance, which makes it very difficult to coordinate events. It also makes it very difficult to implement any form of transactional support to ensure corrective behavior if participating services fail. Further improvement of a composite solution's implementation can be achieved by using an orchestration engine, discussed in the next section.

Orchestration Engine–Based Composition

A common approach that can be successful is to use an *orchestration engine* (sometimes called a "BPM engine") to control the execution flow of a process expressed in an orchestration language, such as WS-BPEL. An orchestration engine, as shown in Figure 8-8, can be used to centralize process implementation and execution, and consequently it improves process maintainability.

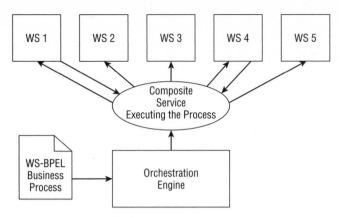

Figure 8-8 Executable business process orchestration

Using an orchestration engine approach, "orchestration scripts" can be executed, combining services based on the business requirements of a system, expressed in an orchestration language. The benefit of this strategy is that the executable process itself specifies the details and rules of the business process, abstracting the details from the services involved. Indeed, the services don't even "need to know" that they are being involved in an orchestration process. This model is extremely effective, because the business processes and workflow needed for service interactions are completely independent of the services involved. Such solutions are centralized processes and can accommodate many of the types of composition described so far (hierarchical, conversational, and event-based).

The emergence of the orchestration language resembles the adoption of database management systems, which started in the 1960s, or that of application servers in the 1990s. Those specialized platforms encapsulate data or web application management, introducing abstractions that free the developers from dealing with many low-level issues. (For example, developers of systems that employ application servers are not concerned with decoding and dispatching HTTP requests, thread management, or the implementation of a two-phase commit.) These specialized platforms allow developers to focus on their business problems rather than on commoditized infrastructure level functionality. Similarly, orchestration engines encapsulate concerns orthogonal to service orchestration, such as:

- Asynchronous service invocation and the use of correlation tokens for matching between messages
- Management of concurrent execution of process instances, including the routing of messages to the appropriate process instance

- Management of the execution context containing the information that determines the state of the business process: what activities have completed and what activity is currently executing

- Management of the data flow, including data flowing into services (i.e., invocation arguments), as well as out of services (i.e., return values)

- Management of the long-running actions, transactions, and semantic compensation

- Support for manual activities

- Collection and processing of business events and key performance indicators (KPIs), defining both the health of the engine itself and that of the processes it executes

- Support for achieving critical enterprise architecture goals such as scalability and availability

In engine-based orchestration, a business process server engine processes an orchestration script, and generates a composite service for executing interactions between the Web Services involved in the business process, as shown in Figure 8-6. Orchestration engines provide *recursive aggregation*, meaning that a composite service can be created to compose a new process involving interactions with services, and the resulting composite service can itself be used by other processes to create new composite services. Composite services can even instantiate and call themselves.

Further simplification of the use of orchestration engines is achieved through the use of orchestration languages — domain-specific languages (DSLs) — specialized for expressing and supporting concepts required for implementation of service compositions (see the sidebar "About Domain-Specific Languages"). Using such a language, supported by an orchestration engine (instead of using a general programming language) improves and simplifies an orchestration's implementation. It allows you to program and maintain composition logic using visual editors, allowing you to define all the major aspects of orchestration graphically.

ABOUT DOMAIN-SPECIFIC LANGUAGES

A common strategy for building executable processes for orchestrations involves the use of domain-specific languages (DSLs). DSLs are specialized for expressing and supporting domain-specific concepts. A DSL precisely captures a domain's semantics — a vertical DSL is industry-specific, whereas a horizontal DSL is meant for a specific problem domain. DSLs are helpful for building scripts that run in orchestration engines.

DSLs are highly declarative and describe what needs to happen, rather then the specifics of how the functionality is done. Because of this, DSLs are considered specifications (executable) and not programming languages. The key advantages of specific DSLs are that they are domain-specific abstractions and notations, and have more expressive power, focused on the specific domain involved. Orchestration languages, such as WS-BPEL, Microsoft's ODX (Orchestration Designer XML), and XLang are DSLs, languages focused on the specific domain of orchestration.

There are several reasons that DSLs are more attractive than general-purpose languages (GPLs) for some classes of applications:

◆ **Easier programming** — Abstractions and notations aligned with the particular domain and coupled with declarative formulations make a DSL program more concise and readable than its GPL counterpart. It allows closer interactions between developers and domain experts, that can understand, validate, modify, and often develop DSL programs. They also allow shortened development and improved maintenance of a DSL-based implementation.

◆ **Systematic reuse** — By capturing domain expertise, a DSL program promotes reuse either implicitly by hiding common program patterns in the DSL implementation, or explicitly by exposing appropriate parameterization to the DSL programmer.

◆ **Easier verification** — With advances in software engineering, formal code verification is playing an important role in successful development. In the case of GPLs, such verification only ensures that the code will execute. However, in the case of DSLs, because of their compactness and domain alignment, validation can often ensure that the code will produce correct results.

◆ **Increased cooperation** — The use of the same business-related semantics across the organization facilitates the sharing of information and reduces the risk of a mismatch between the actual implementation of the business logic and the business users' expectations.

Orchestration languages are DSLs because they apply to the problem set (domain) of business orchestration. At the same time, DSLs that apply to specific business domains can also be used for generating orchestration scripts written in orchestration languages. (For example, a higher-level tax-domain process language could be used to generate the BPEL that is interpreted by the orchestration engine.) Regardless, DSLs provide a level of abstraction that makes building composite services simple.

In addition to simplifying the composition process, the use of an orchestration language also allows you to leverage the inherent benefits of the orchestration engines, which provide built-in functionality that includes capabilities such as asynchronous invocations, state management, and compensation support. The use of orchestration engines for composite solution implementation provides the following advantages:

- Orchestration languages directly support the majority of orchestration concepts, which usually simplifies composite service implementation.

- Additional programming can be simplified through use of a visual editor.

- The orchestration engine natively supports orchestration instances and contexts that are required for implementing of SOA-based solutions.

- Compensation support, implemented in the orchestration languages, makes transactional support implementation significantly simpler.

Orchestration languages, such as WS-BPEL, are portable from any programming language platform, and they can be run on an orchestration server regardless of whether it is J2EE-based, .NET-based, or any other implementation. This is important because different business partners use different platforms. WS-BPEL separates interaction and business process functionality from the services themselves, and orchestration servers process the executable processes. This separation makes the implementation of your business services very straightforward.

Centralized and Decentralized Orchestration Approaches

Using an orchestration engine has a major advantage over creating hard-coded business routing decisions at design time or even routing decisions at compile time. It provides abstraction between services and the way that services are used. This increases the reusability of your services and the agility of your architecture. Later in this chapter, we discuss WS-BPEL, the executable process language used to describe Web Service compositions in these engines.

The most common approach to an orchestration server is to use a centralized server (sometimes called a "BPM server") for an enterprise or a business unit. This approach is effective because it is simple for management and event auditing, and it is sometimes easier to store your business processes in one place. In practice, however, centralized composition can scale only so far, because there is a danger of creating a processing bottleneck, leading to issues with performance and availability, and a potential for a single point of failure.

Distributed strategies (such as using multiple orchestration servers) promise scalability. Because of scalability concerns related to centralized orchestration, many organizations are investigating a deployment architecture in which an initial orchestration engine breaks up tasks into other composite service partitions and passes these on to other orchestration engines to process. (For more on this see Weihai Yu, "Peer to Peer Execution of BPEL Processes" [June 2007].) Implementations are usually home-grown, and developers integrate mini-coordination engines within each node, providing them with the capability to do orchestration and break up composition tasks. This methodology is the most scalable, but it is also the most complex. In order to build such a system, you may need to roll your own implementation.

Because of the potential scalability issues with a centralized approach, a hybrid model commonly uses multiple centralized coordinators, where tasks are, in advanced, planned to be distributed across orchestration servers, as seen in Figure 8-9. This is not a very dynamic solution — instead, based on the usage and the number of services that you are deploying, engineers decide how to split up services between orchestration services in a deployment.

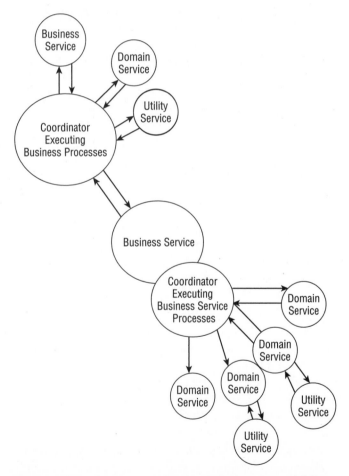

Figure 8-9 Combining centralized coordinators for scalability

As an architect, it is important that you treat a centralized orchestration solution like you would any central server — make certain that you understand the load and performance requirements, and investigate replication and duplication solutions that meet the demands of your enterprise. BPM servers that offer central orchestration based on executable processes all approach scalability differently, so if you are considering using them, you will want to ask the vendor how they approach enterprise scalability.

Service Composition and Business Rules

As mentioned throughout this chapter, service composition is driven by business rules, defining an invocation sequence of particular services participating in a process. This leads many practitioners to consider business rules as part of the broader BPM picture and consider business rules and business processes together. As a result, many consider business rules engines and business process engines as two competing technologies for business processes/business rules implementation. This is based on the following popular misconceptions:

- Business rules and business processes share the same design and implementation model.
- Business rules and business processes deliver the same artifacts and can be used the same way.

In reality, business rules and business processes are quite different. According to Wikipedia, "Business rules describe the operations, definitions and constraints that apply to an organization in achieving its goals. These rules are used to help the organization to better achieve goals, communicate among principals and agents, communicate between the organization and interested third parties, demonstrate fulfillment of legal obligations, operate more efficiently, automate operations, perform analysis on current practices, etc." Business rules can be viewed as a collection of business practices, *defining the actual implementations or business logic*. The implementation of such logic can often be simplified through the use of specialized tools — business rule languages and business rule engines. Declarative programming (i.e., prescribing the what) represents the paradigm of choice for rules: Something is triggered (i.e., an action) based on whether a rule evaluates to true or false. The control flow (i.e., the sequencing of these invocations) is implicit and emerges as the rules fire.

A business process definition, on the other hand, can be viewed as a *recipe for achieving a specific goal*. Imperative programming (i.e., prescribing the how) represents the paradigm of choice for business processes implementation:

Something is invoked after something else because the business process definition prescribes their sequence. The control flow is explicit.

Determining the right technology becomes critical when it comes to best supporting business requirements and achieving the optimal architectural qualities. At the end of the day, assuming that the appropriate DSL and engine are used, the implementation choice between business rules and business process paradigms depends on the two major factors: the capabilities of the engine and decomposition of the overall system.

When it comes to the capabilities of the rules versus business process engines, the following should be considered:

- **Synchronicity** — Rule evaluation is synchronous, and rules engines are designed to evaluate business rules as quickly as possible. Processes, on another hand, are typically long running and asynchronous in nature. The strength of a process engine is the ability to support long-running processes, where actions can take a long time to complete. As a result, they provide the mechanism required to deal with asynchronous invocations, such as request/response correlation, compensations, and so on.

- **Statefulness** — Rules engines are stateless — when a rule fires, an engine typically pulls its inputs either from the input parameters or the knowledge base. It evaluates it, and then it either updates the knowledge base or propagates results to output. Business process engines are specifically designed to hold the state of each active process instance, hydrate and store it between activities invocations, and rehydrate it for the execution of the next activity.

- **Determinism** — The rules engine fires rules whose conditions evaluate simultaneously. However, their ordering is nondeterministic. Business processes are, for the most part, deterministic (with the exception of parallel activities), and people typically add checks and balances to ensure determinism.

- **Granularity** — Although the business rules themselves can be used at the company level, they are usually considered to be components. As such, they provide a smaller granularity and offer a higher level of flexibility from maintenance and deployment perspectives. Business processes, on the other hand, can be viewed more as stable assets that are less likely to go through drastic changes over time.

Based on the previous comparison of business processes/business rules engines' capabilities and SOA decomposition (described in Chapters 2, 3, and 4), the following recommendations can be made for choosing a technology that supports business rules:

- **Service orchestration** — Service orchestration typically deals with long-running and asynchronous invocation of external activities/services.

Today's business rules engines do not support these capabilities. Business process language/engines, designed specifically to define and execute long-running coordinations with asynchronous invocations are the most appropriate paradigm for the service orchestration.

■ **Business service implementations** — Business service implementations are typically short-lived transactional implementations with only synchronous interactions. In this case, the line between business rules and business processes becomes blurry. Often the same problem can be defined, and consequently solved, with either technology. As a result, based on the design-time paradigm, one might consider using either a rule set or a business process approach for solving the same problem.

■ The advantage of using a business process approach, in this case, is simplified support for invocation of external activities (services).

■ The advantages of using a business rules approach, in this case, are the ability to change rules without recompiling and redeploying the business rule components, and the ability to reuse the implemented business logic at the component level (as opposed to the service level when dealing with business processes).

■ **Implementation of business rules controlling business process execution** — When rules define the execution of the business process itself, it is necessary to consider their complexity and change frequency. Modern business process engines usually provide capabilities for evaluating simple rules, either built into the business process language or available by invocation of general-purpose languages. Thus, it is entirely feasible to implement "simple" business rules in the business process engine. In this case, however, any change in the rules requires a full testing and deployment of the business process. As for complex business rules, they typically need to be extracted from the process and implemented as a separate service, using a rules engine.

Rules engines fit in at the service layer in the implementation of *decision services*, while business process (BPM) engines are better for the larger process implementations of service orchestration capabilities. Figure 8-10 shows this typical usage of business process and rules engines in the SOA implementation. In cases where rules control activities whose coordination is very complex (or that change much faster the process itself so that they require usage of the rules engines), these rules are usually externalized as a special rules service, invoked by the business process engine. Because this type of service invocation can be potentially expensive (network calls), some of the business process engines, for example, Biztalk from Microsoft, WebSphere Process Server from IBM, Smart BPM Suite from PegaSystems, and others, incorporate both a business process engine and a rules engine in a single application.

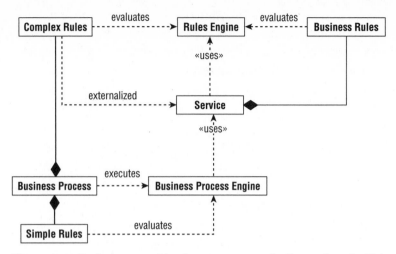

Figure 8-10 Typical usage of business process and rules engines in SOA

Service Composition and Transactions

The design and implementation of fault handling in software applications is as important as the implementation of the normal processing, and often requires an equal amount of care, time, and effort to build robust and reliable applications. Transactionality, in particular the atomicity, consistency, isolation, and durability (ACID) properties represent a prevalent approach for solving these types of problems. Financial applications employ this approach for funds transfers, e-commerce systems use it for payment processing, manufacturing applications use it for inventory control, telecommunications billing systems use it for call rating, and so on.

In these systems, a transactional boundary identifies a group of operations that execute as single units of work, that is, they all succeed or fail as a group (atomicity), and the partial results of the execution are not visible outside of the unit of work until it finishes (isolation). If any operation within the transactional boundary fails, the whole unit of work is rolled back, and the system is returned to the state it was in prior to starting the transaction (consistency). If all of the operations succeed, the new state becomes available to the rest of the system (durability).

Traditionally, systems that require atomic multi-party transactions employ the Two-Phase Commit (2PC) protocol. 2PC requires transactional support in all participants as well as a transaction coordinator that controls their execution. These requirements conflict with the loose coupling characteristics of service-oriented computing. In addition, isolation — which usually is implemented through resource locking (where after responding to the preparation phase each participant returning a commit response remains locked until it receives the coordinator's commit) — is particularly problematic with long-running business processes. In general, the traditional transactional architectures are not a good fit for long-running processes coordinating autonomous services for the following reasons:

- The requirements of the 2PC protocol conflict with the loosely coupled nature services. First, the participating services do not always support transactional behavior. Second, the introduction of a single transactional coordinator supporting transactional semantics of service execution is not always feasible, especially when service location crosses organizational boundaries. Finally, the locking nature of isolation makes it a poor choice for long-running processes.

- Silent rollback implemented by 2PC is not always applicable to SOA implementations, especially in the cases of economic transactions, where both commit and rollback imply agreement. In these situations, both transaction commitment and transaction aborting have to be explicitly confirmed by all participating parties.

- Well-designed services provide large-grained functionality, implemented as a business process or as collaboration between applications and/or business components. A single undo action (as in the Command pattern) is likely too fined-grained to cancel the effects of service invocation.

- Undo actions often depend not only on the results of the last service invocation but also on the overall state of the (process) execution. Loosely coupled services do not share state, which means that they are not always capable of "undoing" each other's actions.

An alternative to a true 2PC, supported by the majority of BPM engines, is *compensation* — invocation of business logic that can be called in case of a failure. Service compensation uses a set of compensating activities (i.e., service invocations) that, when executed, cancel out the effects of the "forward" execution. Although compensation does not provide the ACID properties of the 2PC protocol, it suffices in many practical situations.

The use of compensation instead of the true 2PC removes the requirements that make 2PC unsuitable for SOA — most notably temporal coupling through a transaction coordinator and resource locking for isolation. In addition, service compensation works well with both transactional and nontransactional service implementations. In both cases, the results of the "forward" invocation(s) can be rolled back through an additional invocation(s) that reverses their effects. Since there is no waiting for commit or rollback commands, no resource locking is required in this case. The tradeoff of this approach is an absence of isolation.

In effect, compensation extends the process definition. Defining an orchestration goes beyond composing the services participating in the business process ("happy path"). It must incorporate additional elements, namely the definitions of the compensation scopes (i.e., fault detection boundaries), the mechanisms for signaling faults, and definitions of the compensating actions.

Using orchestrations/processes as a mechanism for both invoking and implementing compensations has an additional advantage. Service compensation (unlike normal transactions) may depend on the state of the process and be stateful by itself. Because the orchestration engine implements service compensation as part of the orchestration, any state information required for compensation is available from the execution context, supported by an BPM server.

Incorporating Human Activities into Service Composition

In many cases business processes implemented through a service orchestration involve human activities. This typically happens when particular activities of the process are too expensive (not cost-effective) or too complex to automate.

Dealing with human activities poses the following problems:

- Humans interact with computers through interfaces very different than the ones of software systems. Their implementation requires dealing with presentation, a typical aspect of human-computer interaction.

- Besides working exclusively in an asynchronous manner, human workers also have slow response times, low throughput, and poor availability. Many organizations deal with the low availability by defining roles (rather than a specific individual) for each activity and defining several workers for each role. Roles address the low availability issues through delaying the binding of human workers to the activity until run time. However, they introduce an additional problem that doesn't exist in the context of automated activities — definition and synchronization of credentials.

Orchestration execution environments are well equipped to handle asynchronous interactions and long-running activities. However, the other characteristics of human interactions, including long response times, poor availability, and specialized interaction mechanisms make their execution radically different from automated process activities.

A typical approach to support human activities is the introduction of a specialized component human activities manager, collaborating with the orchestration engine to support human interactions, as shown in Figure 8-11.

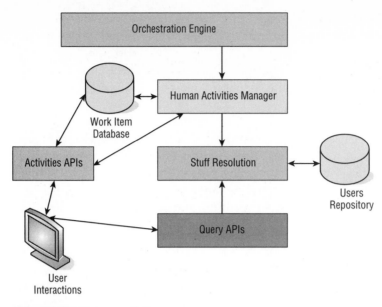

Figure 8-11 Human activity manager

Upon encountering a manual activity, the orchestration engine passes the relevant information to the human interaction manager. This creates the corresponding work item. The manager must ensure that the newly created work item is available until a human worker picks it up. To deal with the slow response times, the human interaction manager stores the work item into a dedicated database.

Staff resolution determines the workers that should be assigned to the task, based on roles and other criteria. The criteria are context-specific and typically translate into a query placed against a directory that holds information about the capabilities and qualifications of the human workers. In effect, staff resolution binds human workers to orchestration instances rather than orchestration.

Once the subset of potential workers is assembled, the work assignment policies determine how the work item is assigned. The manager could use the "push" model, selecting the target worker among the eligible ones based on factors such as current work load (thus, in effect, load balancing among the human workers). Alternatively, it could employ the "pull" model, where the work item is available to all eligible workers until one of them claims it.

A set of specialized interfaces supports the human interaction manager's interactions with human workers. Because the presentation details are context-dependent, graphical interfaces are usually supplemented with programmatic interfaces. Typically, these APIs provide queries that retrieve information from the work item database.

Orchestration with BPEL

BPEL stands for Business Process Execution Language and is the common term used to denote the WS-BPEL business process execution language that has evolved over the last seven years under different names. As mentioned earlier, the latest OASIS standard released in 2007 is WS-BPEL 2.0, an XML-based grammar used to describe logic to orchestrate the interaction between Web Services in a business process. WS-BPEL 2.0 evolved from BPEL4WS 1.0, which was a 2003 specification from OASIS that converged WSFL and XLANG. Although WS-BPEL is the standard, people still call it BPEL (and many people even pronounce it differently). Whether you pronounce it "Bipple" or "Bee-pell," architects agree, it is an important standard for use in an SOA. Because it provides a very expressive grammar for defining real-world business processes, and because it is a standard that has matured over the course of many years, and because there is so much vendor acceptance and support, it is a language that every service-oriented enterprise should consider using. It is also a very detailed standard. For this reason, this section provides only a bird's-eye view, not focusing on syntax, but on the big picture.

WHAT ABOUT A WS-BPEL REFERENCE GUIDE?

As mentioned at the beginning of this book, we want to make sure that you, as an architect, understand how to apply technologies, but we are not going to provide a primer on every standard we discuss. This is not that type of book, and frankly, such a book would be too heavy for you to carry around (it's heavy enough as it is!). We do, however, give you a big picture of what WS-BPEL provides, and we give you an overview of how architects use design tools that write WS-BPEL for use on orchestration engines and servers. Later, we provide a case study that applies these concepts.

There are many books that act as reference guides on all aspects of WS-BPEL and its earlier variant, BPEL4WS. At the point of writing, we noticed that many of these books were out of date already! We recommend, therefore, that you go to the web page for the OASIS WSBPEL Technical Committee (`oasis-open.org/committees/wsbpel`). This page provides the latest versions of the standard and links to reference guides and detailed examples.

BPEL grew out of the need to model and execute complex interactions between Web Services. WSDL-defined Web Services have a stateless interaction model, but real-world processes are usually very complex and require a robust interaction model. BPEL provides the means for expressing stateful, long-running interactions between services. As we have described in the last section, processes written in WS-BPEL allow you to separate business process interaction from the services themselves, providing independence and flexibility.

BPEL revolves around the definitions of two types of processes:

- An executable process, which contains internal process business logic that can be executed as a composite service on an orchestration server

- An abstract process, which is used to describe observable message exchange behavior between services, but cannot be executed as a composite service

Executable business processes are simple to understand, as we covered in the previous section. The concept of an abstract process is new and, therefore, requires more explanation. Abstract processes are useful for a number of reasons:

- First of all, they can provide a "public" view of an internal business process. This is helpful for interaction with business partners who don't need to know (and shouldn't know) internal decision-making processes but still need to know how to interact (semantically and syntactically). Abstract profiles specify constraints on message exchange, specifying the order in which messages need to be consumed and produced.

- Second, abstract processes allow you the freedom to change internal decision-making processes (in executable processes) without affecting observable behavior.

- Finally, an abstract process is useful because it can define a process template for domain-specific best practices. They can serve as a guide for creating the detailed executable processes. Common activities, data structure, and high-level control flow can be done at the beginning of the project, as a guide.

WS-BPEL is layered on top of and extends WSDL. WSDL defines the operations allowed, and WS-BPEL defines how WSDL operations are orchestrated in order to satisfy a business process. WS-BPEL also extends WSDL to support long-running asynchronous business processes. As a business process language, it is a very expressive and rich XML-based language, with constructs very similar to those of high-level programming languages. For executable processes you can declare and modify variables, define fault handlers and throw exceptions, invoke services, and use `case` statements, `while` statements, and loops. XPath and XSLT provide support for data manipulation in BPEL. You can specify actions to occur in a synchronous sequence or in an asynchronous parallel flow. The result is that this language can express almost any business process, the process can be executed on a server to compose services, and the executable process itself becomes a composite service that can be called and reused by other services. Finally, because it is a standard XML-based language, it is portable and can be run in any orchestration server.

In practice, constructing processes is done visually with various design tools, and many are free, including the BPEL Visual Designer for Eclipse, and the BPEL plug-in for NetBeans. There are also commercial BPEL designer tools from companies such as Oracle, IBM, Active Endpoints, and BEA. These tools allow you to create visual flows and generate BPEL that can be executed on an orchestration server. Most tools have their own look and feel, and are "BPMN-like" in their visual notations, but they all export to BPEL. Once a design tool exports the model to BPEL, an orchestration engine is able to execute the process.

BPEL-based solutions, like those of other orchestration languages, follow what Martin Fowler, in his book *Patterns of Enterprise Application Architecture*, (2002), calls "the transaction script" pattern. Solutions using this pattern organize business logic into procedural "transaction scripts." Much like other implementations of the transaction script pattern, BPEL solutions are powerful and are easy to use. However, it should be mentioned that they are not a "silver bullet" for composition — they have the potential to suffer certain drawbacks related to code complexity, sometimes leading to "procedural code spaghetti," which affects maintainability. However, as many tools progress to the point of allowing the designer to work purely with the user interface that generates BPEL, there is certainly the promise of the user interface providing that buffer between visual composition and the generated code, making maintainability easier. In the next section, we walk you through a composition example, and through the construction of a simple BPEL process.

Composition Example — Case Study

This section illustrates a simple example of composing services based on a company's business processes, applying the techniques of this chapter. Here, we are focused on identification of services and interactions for a business process. Based on modeling the process, we can create executable composite services.

The Problem

The scenario revolves around an auto body shop with a technology headache. This body shop often needs to order parts from suppliers. They work with many suppliers of vehicle parts, and for the longest time, all of their orders for automobile parts were done by negotiating over the phone with many vendors. The industry recently moved to a Web Service environment, and all purchasing can now be done electronically between businesses. For each type of vehicle, there is a different business process, where the body shop requests quotes for parts from a variety of different partners, chooses the cheapest quote, and orders the part. There are four separate business processes for cars, trucks, buses, and construction vehicles. Each process is different enough to be separated, but each process has many things in common; they request price quotes from partners, and they choose the lowest price.

The company made a bad decision. They hired a summer intern who was not a software architect or a seasoned developer, and the intern built a stand-alone application to manage all of these processes, with all of this process logic hard-coded in a single application. This worked great for a while (while the intern was employed during the summer). When the processes changed, nobody could understand the spaghetti code in the program. The application was full of complex, nested `if-then-else` statements corresponding to the logic of all of the processes. Now, the company has abandoned the stand-alone application, reverting to the old business style, using the telephone. Unfortunately, the company is having a hard time doing business now. They can't get the parts vendors on the phone, because most of the transactions for those vendors are done electronically (with little phone support!).

This auto shop company badly needs help. They need a solution that meets today's requirements and business processes, but more importantly, they need a solution that is flexible enough to accommodate changing business processes.

High-Level Design Decisions

You know from the problem statement that there are complex and different processes for ordering different types of vehicle parts. By applying the concepts from earlier in this chapter, you can look at those processes involved (car parts buying, truck parts buying, bus parts buying, and construction parts buying) as composite services that could be used together to build the main system process for ordering vehicle parts.

Following that logic, you would break up the task into a hierarchy of services. You can define a high-level business process for auto parts purchasing that uses domain-level services that correspond to the different processes involved in purchasing parts for different vehicle types. The solution shown here defines the business processes for Truck Parts Ordering, Car Parts Ordering, Bus Parts Ordering, and Construction Vehicle Parts Ordering, and those are executable composite services that the main process can use.

You want to create domain-level services that abstract the purchasing processes for each type of vehicle, and the higher-level business service can abstract these. An overview of the composition, shown in Figure 8-12, uses black box composition. Based on the type of vehicle, The Vehicle Parts Ordering Process simply propagates the request to the lower-level processes, and returns the purchase response to its consumer. The front-end application's interaction with the system will be simple. It must simply call the Vehicle Parts Ordering Service; all process logic is abstracted from the application (which is very different from before). The business service, the Vehicle Parts Ordering Service, does not have to manage the complex business processes associated with each lower-level service. It works as a mediator, simply propagates the request to the right service, depending on the vehicle type. You need to make the purchase request descriptive enough that the Vehicle Parts Ordering Service understands the vehicle type, and that request (defined in an XML schema) can be propagated directly to the lower-level services so that they understand it.

We model this high-level process in the next section, but first let's explore the processes of some of the lower-level services. (See Figure 8-12.)

Process Modeling

Now you must think about modeling the lower-level processes, of which there are four: ordering processes for car parts, truck parts, bus parts, and construction vehicle parts. As we mentioned before, a good modeling strategy is often to build a process for one aspect, and to try to reuse much of it as an abstract process. So to tackle the Truck Ordering Process, you can model it using a BPEL designer. Once you do that, model the very simple higher-level process that was discussed in the previous section.

Because BPEL designs can get pretty large, and large diagrams are often difficult to see when shrunk down to "book size," we make the truck parts ordering process pretty simple for the purpose of this example. In this case, there are only two competing vendors, "Redneck Ken's Truck Parts" and "Computer Mom's Trucks." Looking externally from the service consumer's perspective, you want to create a composite service that accepts a purchase request for a truck part and returns a response that shows the status of the transaction (whether the part was ordered, and if so, the specifics of the order).

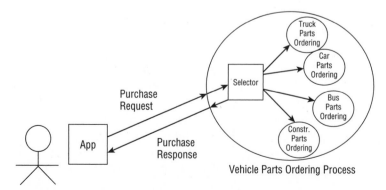

Figure 8-12 Managing complexity with black box composition

The internal flow of the simple process is as follows:

1. You must get information about the purchaser before you make the request.

2. You request a price quote from both vendors (Redneck Ken's Truck Parts and Computer Mom's Trucks) for a certain part.

3. You purchase the part from the vendor with the lowest price.

This Truck Parts Purchasing Process that is being created is shown in the BPEL diagram in Figure 8-13, and we now walk you through building this process. We are choosing not to walk you step-by-step through building this example in a specific BPEL designer tool because tools change, and each tool is different. The diagrams the tools create, however, look more or less the same, and the most important thing is that those tools output WS-BPEL that can be executed on a BPEL processing engine, creating a composite process.

As you look at the diagram in Figure 8-13, the main process for Truck Parts Purchasing is in the middle of the diagram, with the flow working from top to bottom. The sides of the figure include "partner links," which denote communication with partners in a BPEL process. The arrows between the process and its partners specify the detailed interaction and reference components of the WSDL for those services. For example, looking at the Customer Account Service on the right, the partner link specifies WSDL information (`CustomerAcctPT` port type and the `customerInfo` operation) of the specific service, and identifies the messages with which the main process must interact (`customerRecordRequest` and `customerRecordResponse`).

Starting at the beginning, you respond to the Purchaser's request, which initiates this process. Next, you make a synchronous invocation to the Customer Account service, where you get important information about the purchaser that can be used in the transaction. After that is done, in an asynchronous flow, you make two parallel calls to the quote services of Redneck Ken's Truck Parts and Computer Mom's Truck Parts, sending requests for quotes for a certain truck part. You then wait to receive a callback operation. (You could have made synchronous calls here. However, it is important to know that, in a more complex example, you may want a process to call 100 different vendors, and you may want certain timeout restrictions, so it is important for you know that calls can be made in parallel.)

Once you receive responses from each service, you are ready to make a calculation. You determine which price is cheaper. In the XML of the WS-BPEL, this is usually done in a conditional case statement, but chances are, you won't have to even look at the XML — whatever BPEL design tool you use will have a good graphical representation of a conditional statement,

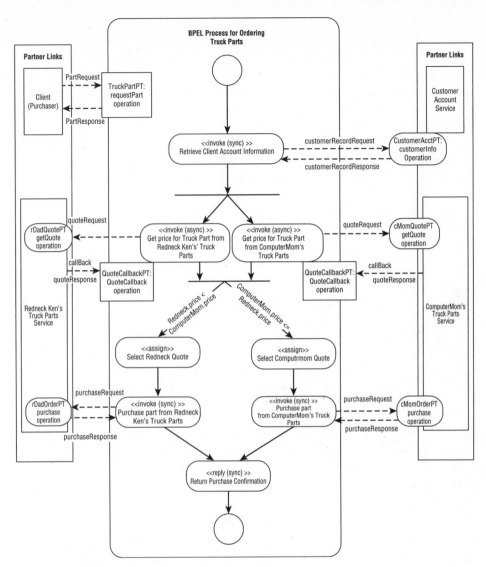

Figure 8-13 BPEL process for Truck Parts Purchasing

and it will write the WS-BPEL out for you. Based on the result of the conditional selection, you invoke the order service from either Redneck Ken's company or Computer Mom's company, and return the response to the purchaser.

Finally, you are ready to use this process as a template for the other processes. As we mentioned before, executable processes can be turned into abstract processes by hiding some internal process logic. Before this is done, however, it is important to look at the external interfaces and interactions of this process to make sure that it is indeed reusable. Conversational compositions can get more complex, but this one is more straightforward because you used black box composition — the external view of the process from the consumer is really the initial call to the service, focused on the interfaces and message types for request and response. Originally, when authoring this process, we used incoming and outgoing messages such as `TruckPartRequest` and `TruckPartResponse` between the purchaser and the truck parts service. Once we saw that we could use this as a template, where executable purchasing processes for other parts types could be created, we made sure to modify the message types to be more generic, using the messages `PartRequest` and `PartResponse` that could be used by other similar parts ordering services. In doing so, the payload of those messages would be more descriptive, defining the vehicle type. Using such a strategy makes it easier to define abstract processes that can be reusable by other services (for example, "car parts ordering," "bus parts ordering," and so on). By doing that, the interfaces to the services for all parts ordering can be the same, but the payload is more descriptive, allowing each implementation to process the incoming message differently.

We skip the modeling of the domain-level services, however, and instead we model the higher-level process that uses them all together. Figure 8-14 is a good example of how composite services can be used in new compositions. In this example, we used the abstract process we created as a template for the other vehicle purchasing services. In this case, this translates to all of the services in this example using the same incoming and outgoing messages. We used the `PartRequest` and `PartResponse` messages coming into each service, including the higher-level Vehicle Parts Ordering Service.

As you can see, the logic of the higher-level service was pretty simple. The process must inspect the payload of the `PartRequest` message, and depending on the vehicle type, simply passes the request through to the correct ordering service. The higher-level business service is a BPEL-based composite service, as are the domain-level services for ordering from vendors from the vehicle taxonomy.

Obviously, this was a high-level example that didn't actually expose any WS-BPEL or WSDL, but the point is this: BPEL design tools allow you to focus on the processes, not the technology. As an architect, it is important to be able to define these processes, where you focus on the interactions between partners and services in order to create an executable process.

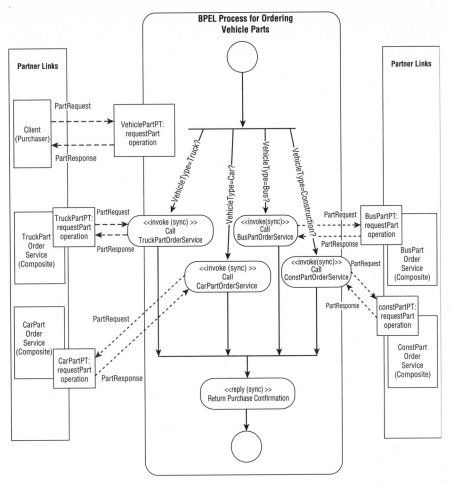

Figure 8-14 Using the BPEL process as a composite service in another process

Dos and Don'ts in Service Composition

This section brings together key factors in service composition, placing them into actionable items for you to use on your software architecture and design teams.

Avoid Static, Programmatic Orchestration

Since you have read this far in the chapter, it should be no surprise when we tell you that a pitfall for service composition is hard-coded, programmatic composition, where you use a programming language like Java, Perl, or C# to statically write your orchestration logic. As we mentioned earlier in this chapter, your orchestration logic will probably change over time. Using a configurable framework (such as SCA) or by using an orchestration engine that uses an orchestration language, you can provide more flexibility.

Use a Layered Service Approach

As we have already discussed at length in this book, services should be separated into layers that run the gamut from high-level, coarse-grained business processes to low-level fine-grained atomic services. This is not a new idea that came with Web Services. The "Gang of Four" Mediator design pattern and the Session Façade J2EE design pattern are two design solutions used to allow higher-level business services to centralize, control, and coordinate complex interactions with lower-level services.

You can also organize your team of designers and developers according to this layered approach. We recommend this, because sometimes teams simply focus on end-to-end functionality, with team members duplicating efforts. Once you establish your service hierarchy, you can assign designers and developers to services at each layer. The services they design and develop may be fine-grained utility services or higher-level business services. Business process engineers and architects can do process modeling and the designing of high-level business services and domain services during the service definition stage of the project in a "top-down" approach. Developers who focus more on discrete functionality can focus on building utility services.

When Using BPEL, Use Abstract Processes

In the last section, we gave reasons for BPEL-based abstract processes — they provide the "interaction process contract" to partners without giving them too much information, and they are useful to use as templates for other services in your enterprise. Abstract processes may also be useful for describing protocols for services that involve more than one operation; callbacks are a simple example, but there are many more. You can use abstract processes in either a top-down approach, where you first build the abstract process before you refine the executable process; or in a bottom-up approach, where you create the executable process first. Much like designing interfaces in object-oriented design, make sure that the abstract process is final and won't be changed before you give it to a partner.

In the example in this chapter, we created the executable process (for Truck Parts Purchasing) before we created the abstract process that was used for building the other processes. That approach has advantages, because it forces us to work through a concrete scenario before thinking about how the process would be used in related scenarios — this allows the architect to refine the process before he distributes the template. Fred Brooks in the *Mythical Man-Month* (1995) mentioned that a good software construction technique is "build one to throw away," because when you work through the process of designing and then developing a piece of software, you are most likely to understand the problem better after you have finished. In the case of business process modeling, building a process and changing it is remarkably easy. Once you work your way through building an executable process and think about how it may be used as a template, throwing it away or even "massively refining it" isn't difficult — the good thing is that you don't have to change and compile code. Instead, you use a BPEL designer, you press a button, and you create a new executable process.

Summary

Service composition is one of the great benefits of using SOA. This chapter focused on service composition, providing a detailed look at different approaches, fundamental issues, and best practices. We provided a case study and a simple example of composing services using a BPEL designer. Finally, we provided a list of best practices in service composition.

Using Services to Build Enterprise Solutions

While it's easy to grasp the theory of SOA, implementing well-designed, practical SOA systems can be a difficult challenge.

— Arnon Rotem-Gal-Oz

So far in this book, we have been concentrating on the approaches to designing and building individual services. Although each individual service is important, its functionality is limited to supporting a very specific capability. Building enterprise solutions typically requires leveraging existing enterprise applications for service implementations and combining multiple existing services into enterprise solutions.

This chapter discusses practical approaches to building enterprise solutions using existing enterprise business services (leveraging existing enterprise applications for building business services are covered in the next chapter). We start by defining the overall architecture of the service-based enterprise solutions and a discussion of its constituent parts. We then describe approaches to resolving issues arising during building service-based solutions, including locating and versioning services, and service security, monitoring, and management. We end this chapter with the description of the enterprise service bus — an SOA infrastructure pattern — simplifying the implementation of solutions to the previously mentioned concerns.

This chapter covers the following topic:

- Differences between typical applications and SOA-based enterprise solutions
- Overall high-level architecture for service-based enterprise solutions

- Integrating the layered SOA architecture with an *n*-tiered Applications architecture
- Implementing late binding using the service registry
- Implementing service versioning
- Architecting security in SOA-based solutions
- Architecting exception handling in SOA-based solutions
- Monitoring and managing SOA-based solutions
- Using an Enterprise Service Bus as a unified infrastructure for building SOA solutions

Enterprise Solutions versus Applications

Today's Enterprise IT Architecture is often viewed as a collection of applications. Design, development, enhancements, and maintenance of software systems revolve around applications. It comes as no surprise that many practitioners keep talking (and writing) about using SOA to build applications.

In our mind, SOA (especially Enterprise SOA) and applications are very different. Each application is traditionally built for a single purpose (e.g., loan origination, claim management, etc.), with its own datastore(s) and for a single set of users. A particular application implements only a subset of the enterprise functionality, using and producing only a subset of the enterprise data, typically without concerns about other processing within the enterprise. As a result, in our opinion, applications are a root cause of today's siloed nature of enterprise IT. The use of SOA for applications does not improve the situation. It provides a better approach for building applications, preserving all of the drawbacks of today's application-centric culture.

Table 9-1 Applications versus SOA Enterprise solutions

CHARACTERISTIC	APPLICATION-CENTRIC ARCHITECTURE	SOA ENTERPRISE SOLUTIONS
Design and implementation	Function-oriented Built to static requirements Long development cycles	Coordination-oriented Built to change Built and deployed incrementally
Resulting system	Application silos Tightly coupled Object-oriented interactions	Enterprise solutions Loosely coupled Semantic message-oriented interactions

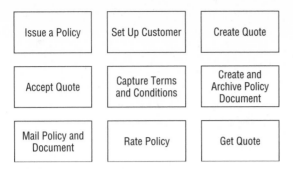

Figure 9-1 ACME's enterprise services

Instead this book (and this chapter in particular) concentrates on enterprise solutions. These solutions are dynamic (easily modifiable) compositions of enterprise services, which can be built, just in time, to adhere to changing enterprise requirements. Table 9-1 summarizes the key differences between applications and Enterprise SOA-based solutions.

Let's take a look at such a solution. Throughout this chapter we use a simple SOA-based example to illustrate the main concepts. ACME insurance company already has a set of enterprise services in place and now needs to assemble them into an enterprise solution for issuing insurance policies. (See Figure 9-1.) We frequently refer back to this set of services as we address the different aspects of enterprise solutions.

Service-Based Enterprise Solutions

At the core of SOA is the ability to compose and recompose existing services to quickly and cost-effectively build enterprise solutions, based on new or changing business requirements.

The basic architecture for building enterprise solutions using existing enterprise services is an adaptation of the Model-View-Controller (MVC) pattern presented in Figure 9-2.

The foundation of this architecture is an interaction controller (request router) that processes service requests submitted by multiple consumers. These consumers can be human users utilizing portals or external consumers utilizing B2B interactions. The interaction controller itself can be implemented in several ways, ranging from a pure logical concept, based on the enterprise registry, to routing to an intermediary (mediator), to a specialized controller service. The following issues should be considered when deciding on the specific interaction controller implementation:

- The controller can be used as a centralized enforcement point for enterprise security policies, enterprise semantic data, and so on. In the case

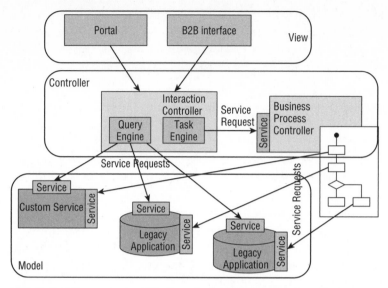

Figure 9-2 Conceptual architecture for building enterprise solutions

of B2B interaction, the controller is implemented as a specialized service that allows for centralization of these functions.

■ The controller can be used as a decoupling layer between the view and service layers. In this case it is implemented either as a mediator, or as a specialized service.

■ In some scenarios, especially ones involving human interactions, service invocation performance is often an important consideration. In these cases, both mediator and true service-based implementations of the controller can require additional network hops, marshaling/unmarshaling of request/response data, and so on. This inevitably leads to performance degradation of the service invocations. As a result, implementation of a controller as a pure logical construct may be a more appropriate approach.

NOTE The performance degradation can be significantly reduced by using network appliances (for example, IBM's DataPower) as an intermediary. There will still be performance degradation but it is typically negligible.

The interaction controller supports invocation of two major types of services:

■ **Entity services** — This type of service provides access to the enterprise data, which can be useful to both human users and business-to-business (B2B) interactions. This information can be used for better decision making. In addition, query services often include support for visibility into operations of the enterprise — for example, results of business activity monitoring, service usage statistics, and the like. In the ACME case, an example of a data service is the Get Quote Service. A customer can use this service to get the content of the current quote to decide whether he wants to accept it.

- **Task services** — This type of service allows you to start business processes (service compositions) and interact with those processes (human activity tasks). In the case of ACME insurance, Capture Terms and Conditions and Accept Quote are examples of such services. Capture Terms and Conditions allows customers to (re)enter insurance information, which causes regeneration of the quote, whereas Accept Quote signals the solution implementation to issue the policy.

NOTE As defined in Chapter 2, there are other types of services, but these two are the ones used by the interaction controller. Other service types are typically used for implementation of entity and task services.

Another core component of this architecture is a business process controller (typically a process engine), that orchestrates the execution of services participating in a given solution. This solution effectively brings together two of today's mainstream technologies — SOA and Business Process Management (BPM). Business services and business processes provide an ideal combination for implementing flexible enterprise solutions:

- Business services provide a foundation for the creation of business processes by supporting stable business artifacts, which incorporate business capabilities and rules that change relatively infrequently.
- Business processes support a quick time to market for enterprise solutions through easy implementation of fairly fluid business processing and rules, which can change every few months or even weeks.

NOTE For approaches to business process composition, refer to Chapter 8.

Finally, portals and B2B interfaces support the use of these solutions inside and outside the enterprise by human users and automated systems.

Human interaction with the SOA solutions is typically based on portals, providing "on-the-glass" integration of data from many disparate sources (services in this case). Using portals in SOA implementations allows for simultaneous execution of multiple enterprise solutions (and/or multiple services from the given solution). For example, a portal allows for simultaneous viewing of the process state, contents of the human task, and additional solution-specific data provided through data services. Combining all of this information in one place can significantly simplify enterprise decision making and leads to the improved quality of enterprise operations.

Modern portals provide these capabilities through componentization of the presentation using cooperating portlets (pluggable user interface components that are managed and displayed in a web portal) based on industry standards like Java Specification Request (JSR) 167, which define the implementation and integration of portlets and Web Services Remote Portlets (WSRP). These portlets can be either custom built (using Java Server Faces and Web Services) or can support web clipping to aggregate existing user interfaces from other applications (for example, the presentation of human activities provided by a process server).

Interactions between multiple enterprise solutions (whether inside the enterprise or across enterprise boundaries) is typically done through business processes; the business process implementing one solution invokes the business process of another solution. In the case of B2B interactions, it is typically a public cross-enterprise process, invoking one or more enterprise-internal solutions as private processes. (For further discussion on public and private processes, see Boris Lublinsky, "Approaches to Implementation of Business-to-Business Integration (B2Bi).")

In order to support the proposed enterprise solution architecture (see Figure 9-2), the following layered SOA architecture (see Figure 9-3) has to be in place. This architecture contains the following layers:

- The access layer (top) implements both human and machine access to business processes and individual services. Typically, only a subset of enterprise services is exposed to this layer.

- The process layer (middle) supports the implementation of enterprise business processes (enterprise solutions).

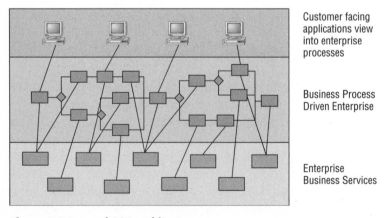

Customer facing applications view into enterprise processes

Business Process Driven Enterprise

Enterprise Business Services

Figure 9-3 Layered SOA architecture

- The enterprise business services layer (bottom) provides high-level business capability throughout the enterprise. Business services represent logical groupings of enterprise-wide functionality.

NOTE Notice that Figure 9-3 presents only a subset of the SOA layers defined in Chapter 2. Here, we are showing only the layers that are relevant to this chapter. Further elaboration of these layers is presented in the next chapter, where we talk about integration in SOA.

Layered SOA Architecture and Multitiered Application Architecture

The layered SOA architecture, presented in Figure 9-3, looks similar to the classic layered application architecture familiar to every application architect. But to underscore the difference, let's look more closely at the classic 3-tiered application architecture, shown in Figure 9-4.

The 3-tiered architecture applies the important architectural concept of separation of concerns, specifically separating presentation from logic, and logic from data. In this architecture, the presentation tier does not access databases directly. Access occurs only through the business tier, which is responsible for the execution of business logic. The 3-tiered architecture introduced many improvements into application design, including:

- Improved application flexibility through a better separation between presentation and business logic. With this architecture, the presentation

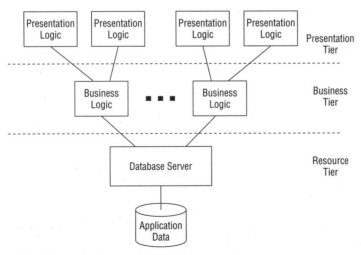

Figure 9-4 The 3-tiered application architecture

can change without impacting the existing application logic. Additionally, the same business logic can be (re)used by multiple applications (presentations).

- Through the introduction of a separate business tier, this architecture simplifies the incorporation of multiple databases into an application.

- It introduced additional application deployment and scalability options.

The 3-tiered architecture was the predominant style for early web applications, but it quickly ran into problems with the need for better scalability and support of multiple devices. The problem was that the architecture did not separate the logic used by a single user during his or her interactive session from the shared logic used to implement business functions and manage resources. Today, the more advanced architectural style for web-based applications is the *n*-tiered architecture, shown in Figure 9-5.

Tiers have the general responsibility for mediating the flow of data into and out of the system and the components that make it up. However, each tier has a specific set of roles and responsibilities, and the boundaries between the tiers are carefully constructed to achieve the architectural goals. The responsibilities of these tiers are:

- The user tier is where the system interacts with a single use of the system through a specific presentation. The user tier is responsible for device-specific presentation such as that needed for a web browser. The boundary between the user and workspace tier provides device independence, allowing the application to support multiple devices, such as a Web

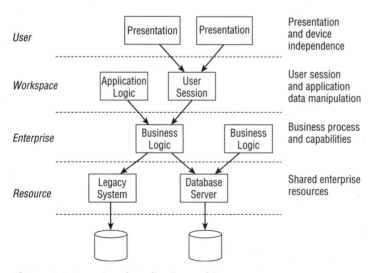

Figure 9-5 An *n*-tiered application architecture

browser and a mobile telephone, each of which would have its own user tier. The user tier:

- Manages user interface details for a single presentation.

- The workspace tier is where the system supports multiple interactions with a single user. It is responsible for coordinating and maintaining a user session, for manipulating the user data associated with that session, and for interactions with the enterprise tier. The workspace tier:

  - Coordinates and maintains the integrity of multiple, concurrent activities for the same user.

  - Maintains the user session.

  - Executes processes that do not require access to enterprise resources.

  - Puts and gets data to and from the enterprise.

The boundary between the user tier and workspace tier provides another advantage. It allows the same processing to be used with multiple different devices. In other words, by moving device specifics into a separate tier, you can achieve both reuse of processes and, just as important, consistency of operation across multiple devices.

Together, the user and workspace tiers support all interaction between the system and a single user (or other external partner). There is one instance of the user tier and the workspace tier for each user of the system. In contrast, the enterprise and resource tiers together provide resources and services to all users of the system. There is only one instance of the enterprise and resource tiers, which is shared by all users:

- The enterprise tier is responsible for implementing business processes and entities, and for making their functions available via service-oriented interfaces. The enterprise tier:

  - Maintains the integrity of enterprise resources.

  - Enforces system-level business rules.

  - Provides the scope and control for two-phase commit transactions.

  - Provides enterprise services to requestors.

The boundary between the workspace and enterprise tier provides a clear separation between the resources of the enterprise and the resources required to support a single user. This break allows enterprise resources to be better managed and protected. It also provides a clear access point for all enterprise services, so that they can be shared and reused by multiple applications and users.

- The resource tier is responsible for the management and access of shared enterprise resources. The resource tier:

- Provides access to shared resources of the enterprise.
- Provides access to enterprise data and databases.
- Provides access to legacy systems.

The boundary between the resource and enterprise tier provides a separation between the technology specifics of the resources and the enterprise's use (as well as the service's representation) of them. This allows changes in the resource or enterprise tiers to occur independently, without disruption to the other.

Services can be present in most of the tiers of the *n*-tier architecture (other than presentation). However, a common mistake is to misunderstand the relationship between service type and the roles and responsibilities of the tiers; the result is much like the 3-tier architecture that did not separate the responsibilities of different types of logic. Figure 9-6 illustrates how the different types of services line up with the tiers of an *n*-tiered architecture.

Let's look at each tier, its responsibility, and the types of services that are used to implement them. Starting at the top, the presentation tier is not implemented with services. Next is the workspace tier. This tier is responsible for coordinating and maintaining all activities for a single user, and being the intermediary between the presentation channel and the enterprise. In other words, the tier is responsible for coordinating and presenting business capabilities though a delivery channel. It fulfills a user request in the most effective manner based on presentation device, user role, user context, and user preferences. This requires a variety of different functions, many of which can be implemented as services. Some typical services at this tier are profile,

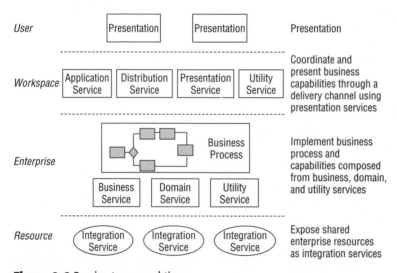

Figure 9-6 Service types and tiers

presentation, navigation, session state management, and so on. The tier is also responsible for the user specific "application" logic. So, you often see application services and utility services used in this tier.

The enterprise tier is where you traditionally think of SOA capabilities. It is responsible for the implementation of enterprise capabilities and processes, and for the enforcement of enterprise rules and policy. This is where the business processes are executed, and where the services that compose them are located. So here, you see business, domain, and utility services supporting the task, entity, and decision service types.

Finally, the resource tier is responsible for the shared resources, and for presenting those resources to the enterprise tier. In SOA, you want those resources presented as services, so this is where integration services are generally implemented.

Enterprise solutions span from the user or partner presentation through all the intermediate functions to the enterprise resources. When designing an enterprise service–oriented solution, it is important to understand both the architecture of enterprise solutions and the architecture of SOA. In this section, we have shown the intersection of enterprise tiers and services types. Now we move on to architectural considerations for using those services.

Locating Services

Typical enterprise SOA solutions rely on a variety of services. Invoking these services requires knowledge of their location (i.e., the service endpoint address). In the simplest case, it is possible to hard-code endpoint addresses in the solution's implementations. This approach, shown in Figure 9-7,

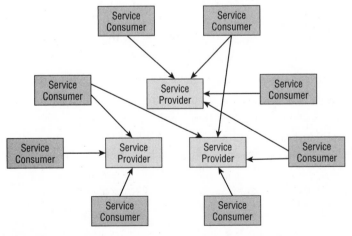

Figure 9-7 Direct invocation of services by consumers

introduces tight coupling between the solution's implementations and the service's location (location coupling).

NOTE Both Java and .NET tooling generate Web Service consumers with endpoint addresses encoded directly in the implementation. As a result, it comes as no surprise that many current systems resemble Figure 9-7.

Accommodating service endpoint address changes in the implementation requires modifications to the solution's implementations. This process is prone to error and scales poorly as the number of services and solutions grows. Accounting for multiple deployment environments (e.g., development, testing, quality assurance, production) only compounds the problem.

Externalizing the endpoint addresses into configuration files offers a potential improvement. This approach is more flexible because it removes endpoint addresses from the solution's code and externalizes them in configuration files. This allows the solution to accommodate address changes without any code modifications. However, this option also runs into scalability problems as the numbers of consumers and services (and consequently of configuration files) grow.

Using an intermediary that dynamically resolves service queries into endpoint addresses and invocation policies — a service registry — provides the most flexible and maintainable solution for this problem. The service registry contains all the information about service deployments, their locations, and the policies associated with invocation at each location.

ROLE OF THE SERVICE REGISTRY

Steve Vinoski, in his article "The social side of services," (January 2006), points out that the usefulness of the service registry increases with the number of services:

"The technical line of reasoning for reaching and managing this critical mass typically goes like this:

1. For services to operate as a collective, they have to know about each other.

2. For services to know about each other, they must either be hardwired together or be able to dynamically find one another.

3. Hardwiring would be bad, as it implies high coupling and potential difficulties in replacing one service implementation with another somewhere down the line.

4. To facilitate dynamic discovery, then, services need a place that they can advertise themselves and meet other services.

5. Of course, a registry!"

The notion of the service registry was initially introduced by the Web Services architecture group; which defined the Universal Description, Discovery and Integration (UDDI) registry as a "matchmaker" (broker) between services, consumers, and providers. The responsibility of UDDI was viewed as providing a dynamic choice of service producer based on the functionality required by the consumer. Its role is similar to that of the Yellow Pages. But, despite support from multiple vendors and standards bodies, UDDI use as the service matchmaker never took off. The majority of today's UDDI usage is limited to storage of the service WSDL files, which are used by a service consumer at design time.

A more practical use of the service registry is for run-time lookup of the service endpoint based on the service name and policies. Typical examples of such policies can be quality of service requirements, security requirements, preferred communication protocol, service version (see the next section), and so on. In this case, service definitions (interfaces) are available to consumers at development time through other means, and registry use is limited to the run-time resolution of the services endpoint addresses and dynamic binding. (See Figure 9-8.)

The late binding of the service endpoint address lessens location coupling by eliminating hard-coding service endpoint addresses. The registry allows for the centralized management of the service endpoint addresses and associated invocation policies.

Typical service registry implementations support one of two possible endpoint address resolution and routing models.

■ **Direct routing** — In this model the information required to query the registry resides in the consumer. This information includes the set of supported and required policies. Once the registry finds the matching services the consumer decides which service to use and routes the requests directly to it. (See Figure 9-9.).

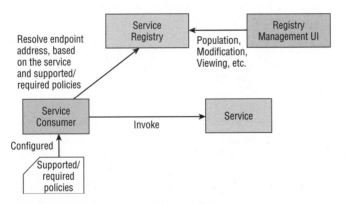

Figure 9-8 Basic service registry architecture

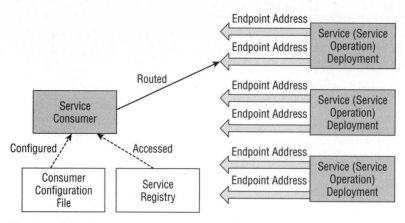

Figure 9-9 Direct routing using a service registry

∎ **Intermediary-based routing** — An alternative model relies on an intermediary to handle the routing. In this model, the service consumer doesn't have direct interaction with the service. Instead, all service requests are directed to an intermediary that queries the registry (with consumer-specific information), decides which service to use, invokes the service, and routes the reply to the consumer. (See Figure 9-10.)

Table 9-2 compares these two approaches.

The service registry is an important component in an enterprise solution because it decouples the service consumers from the actual service endpoint address. It is a foundation for late binding, providing the flexibility to change the address of the service provider without changing the service consumer. This provides a more dynamic, reconfigurable SOA-based solution.

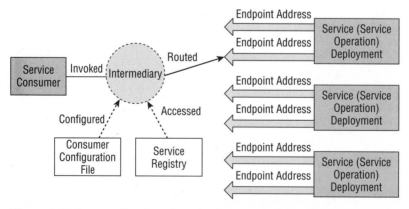

Figure 9-10 Intermediary-based routing using a service registry

Table 9-2 Comparison of routing approaches

	DIRECT ROUTING	INTERMEDIARY-BASED ROUTING
Advantages	Provides the best invocation performance. Provides minimal infrastructure overhead, especially in the case where Message Oriented Middleware (MOM) is used as a transport.	Provides a centralized point for deciding how to select between potential services, thus relieving the service consumer from storing and processing invocation information.
Disadvantages	Depending on the consumer implementation, changing the consumer policy file may require restarting/rebuilding the consumer.	Where different SLAs are required for different consumers/services, the intermediary has to be able to support the strictest SLA. Overall, invocation performance can suffer because of the additional network hop. The intermediary represents an additional (sometimes single) point of failure. Introduction of an intermediary usually requires additional infrastructure.

Example: Implementing Service Access for Policy Issuance

The example policy issuance solution at ACME employs only a handful of services and consequently could use a simplistic hardwiring of service locations. On the other hand, some of the services used in this solution (for example, archiving or mailing) can be used for far more than policy issuance. They can have multiple consumers, and, as a result, changes in their endpoint addresses can require a massive amount of changes in existing clients. Therefore, ACME decided to implement a full-fledged service registry as a foundation of a robust SOA infrastructure. Based on their comparison of different options for the overall registry implementation and topology (as shown in Table 9-2) and the fact that performance is the main requirement for them, they have chosen a direct routing topology for registry implementation. (Refer to Figure 9-9.)

Versioning: Dealing with Service Changes

A lot of internal and external factors lead to service changes. For example, at ACME:

- New insurance products are introduced with new terms and conditions.
- New rating rules are introduced.
- The format of the policy document has changed.

In typical SOA implementations (refer to Figure 9-3), every service is used simultaneously in multiple enterprise solutions. As a result, a change in an enterprise service (for example, creating and archiving a document) can have a significant impact on many existing solutions and, consequently, could require changes in each one of them. In the case of ACME, for example, the service is used in policy issuance (the creation and archiving of a policy document) and claims processing (the creation and archiving of a damage appraisal).

The implementation of these changes is not only extremely expensive (requiring a lot of coordination between development and testing, ensuring that none of the multiple enterprise solutions are impacted) but also goes against one of the fundamental SOA tenets, service autonomy.

Autonomy (see Chapter 2) is the fundamental concept behind service orientation that requires that services can be deployed, modified, and maintained independent of each other and the solutions that use them.

One of the most popular ways of coping with changes is *versioning*. Versioning assumes the simultaneous existence of multiple (different) implementations of the same thing, with every implementation distinguishable and individually addressable. In the case of SOA, service versioning equates to the coexistence of multiple versions of the same service, which allows each consumer to use the version that it is designed and tested for. (See Figure 9-11.)

A new version of a service is created based on the requirements of one or more consumers, who can start using this new version immediately. The other consumers of the service do not need to switch to the latest version immediately, but can continue to use the versions of the service they were

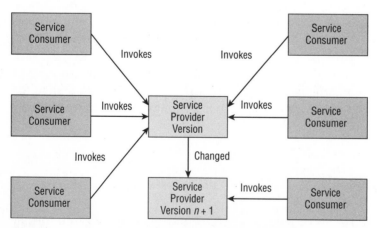

Figure 9-11 The coexistence of multiple service versions

designed for and tested with. They can switch to the latest version of the service when the need arises based on their own development and testing schedule. The introduction of multiple coexisting versions of the same service in the system allows for an independent life cycle of service providers and their consumers and minimizes the overall impact of changes. Although the necessity of a versioning mechanism is fairly obvious to anyone who has ever dealt with services, this topic still has not made it into the mainstream of SOA publications and implementations.

NOTE During several SOA conferences, which we attended, the absence of a well-defined and well-understood service versioning approach was quoted as one of the major obstacles to successful SOA adoption.

Although the basic idea of service versioning (refer to Figure 9-11) is fairly simple and straightforward, its implementation requires defining the following:

- Units of versioning
- Service changes, constituting a new version
- Service version life-cycle considerations
- Version deployment and access approaches

Here, we discuss only version deployment approaches. For more information on the other service versioning considerations, see Boris Lublinsky's article "Versioning in SOA."

Version Deployment and Access Approaches

There are two common approaches to the deployment of service versions: covenant or version parameter, and multiple endpoint addresses.

A covenant is an `if-then-else` agreement ("if you do this then I will do that"). In this case, there is a single endpoint address for all versions of the service. (See Figure 9-12.)

The covenant effectively implements context-based routing (the foundation of routing in EAI Message Brokers), taking an incoming message and routing it (based on a version parameter embedded in the invocation message) to the appropriate service version. The benefit of this approach is that it simplifies service addressing from the consumer's point of view. The consumer uses a single endpoint address to access all versions of a given service and encodes the required version in the invocation message. An endpoint address implements routing support, invoking the required version of the service implementation.

Although the covenant approach minimizes the impact of new versions on the service consumers, it introduces the complexity of packaging multiple

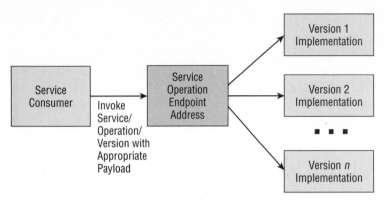

Figure 9-12 Implementation of versioning using a covenant

versions of a service together. This can lead to class name collisions, database name collisions, and so on.

> **NOTE** This approach effectively requires a versioning strategy not only for services themselves but also for the components used to implement the services. Considering the tighter coupling between components, this problem can be even more complex than service versioning.

Further improvement can be achieved by replacing the local router dispatching between the service versions with an external broker (mediator). In this case, all versions can be deployed independently, and it is the responsibility of a mediator to dynamically resolve the endpoint address of the desired service version and dispatch all messages accordingly.

> **NOTE** Although intermediaries (mediations) are often touted by ESB-related publications as a cure for most routing/transformation problems encountered in SOA, there are costs associated with them. Typically, they lower performance. They must also support the most stringent SLA of all the services accessed through it, which could be a very strong and expensive requirement.

The other approach to version deployment is to use multiple endpoint addresses. Every version of a given service is deployed at its own endpoint address(es) that is directly exposed to a service consumer. (See Figure 9-13.)

Multiple endpoint addresses assume that a service consumer can resolve endpoint addresses (typically using the service registry) for a required version, based on the service/version information. The advantage of this scheme is a complete separation of multiple service version deployments. The drawback

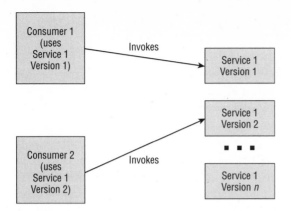

Figure 9-13 Implementing versions using directly exposed endpoint addresses

is a more complex addressing paradigm, requiring service registry support to resolve endpoint addresses, based on the service version.

The multiple endpoint address approach typically provides better scalability (one less network hop) and lowers the coupling between multiple versions of the same service.

Correct implementation of service versioning leads to the creation of much more loosely coupled enterprise solutions. The introduction of simultaneously deployed service versions allows both service consumers (enterprise solutions) and providers to evolve independently, with their own development and deployment schedules. As services evolve (not necessarily in an upward compatible fashion), old versions remain available for the consumers that are not ready to update.

Example: Coping with Changes in Policy Issuance Solutions

Considering the tight insurance market, which requires rapid implementation changes in order to stay competitive, ACME architects are designing policy issuance solutions to be as adaptable to changes as possible. A big factor in this future adaptability and the solution's overall agility is the ability of ACME to introduce new implementations of enterprise services without breaking currently deployed solutions. This requires architecting the overall SOA infrastructure to support policy issuance with service versioning in mind. After evaluating service versioning approaches and considering that performance is their main requirement, ACME decided to implement versioning support by exposing service versions' endpoint addresses directly to the service consumers (refer to Figure 9-13).

Architecting Security for Service-Based Solutions

Organizations have existing security infrastructures in place. These infrastructures protect enterprise resources on diverse platforms and often implement different security solutions for different applications.

The service invocation chain, typical for service-oriented solutions, accesses services that wrap different systems and applications. This model breaks not only the application boundaries but also the application-centric security model. The service implementation bridges multiple disparate applications into one service environment (more on this in Chapter 10). This shift requires a new security approach, above and beyond the existing application security.

In addition, outsourcing services makes security even more challenging. The ability to mix and match services from different providers, some of which reside outside the traditional trust boundaries (e.g., enterprise firewall) adds new security threats. Dealing with these new challenges requires extending the security model to support external services in addition to the internal ones.

The key goal of a security implementation is enabling the existing security infrastructures (both inside and outside of the enterprise) to interoperate. The foundation of the solution is the introduction of a security layer spanning existing security infrastructures.

NOTE This chapter outlines only architectural approaches to security in SOA solutions. For details on service security, refer to Chapter 11.

The responsibilities of this layer are:

- Accommodation of heterogeneity (i.e., multiple application platforms)
- Provide security management and identity propagation/management across multiple security domains (internal, external, business unit silos)
- Support multiple security credentials (Kerberos, SAML, various Token Profiles, Pass Tickets)
- Support multiple transport protocols (HTTP/S, JMS, MQ)
- Maintain the "thread of identity" across the service boundaries

There are two broad architectural options for implementing security in the context of SOA-based enterprise solutions: the security gateway and the interceptor.

Using a Security Gateway

A security gateway (sometimes called XML firewall or XML proxy) is a software package or hardware appliance that filters service traffic upstream of a service and blocks unauthorized traffic before it can reach a protected service (see Figure 9-14).

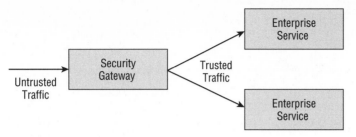

Figure 9-14 Security gateway

The security gateway enforces access control rules by processing security tokens contained within incoming messages, and by ensuring that the XML format and content are appropriate for the target service/solution. It may use a variety of techniques ranging from user/password to specialized tokens to SAML (see Chapter 11 for more details on the identity propagation techniques) to authentication of an end user or a particular company.

Security gateways strive to reuse the existing security infrastructure, including preconfigured users, groups, and roles, otherwise, the overhead of rekeying rules and user profiles into a security gateway would be cost prohibitive. To do so, they typically contain security adapters to existing security technologies such as LDAP directories, traditional firewalls, and PKI infrastructures.

The drawback of this architecture is that it leaves the actual service endpoint addresses unprotected (i.e., the "last mile" problem). If the incoming traffic bypasses the gateway and gets directly to the service endpoint, it also bypasses the security implemented by the gateway. Some of the approaches of dealing with this issue are:

▪ Restricting access to the service endpoint to a limited number of physical nodes

▪ Mutual authentication between the gateway and the service endpoint

In practice, a security gateway is typically used as a perimeter defense mechanism, preventing unauthorized access to the enterprise solutions from B2B consumers or other enterprise solutions, and as such it is not directly applicable to the implementation of ACME's policy issuance solution. It can be used, however, to protect the solution if it is directly exposed outside the enterprise, for example, to insurance brokers.

The prevalent architecture for securing individual services participating in enterprise solutions are interceptors.

Using an Interceptor in Security Implementations

The interceptor brings the security implementation directly to the service endpoint through the use of platform-specific hooks such as Internet Server Application Programming Interface (ISAPI) filters, Java API for XML-Based

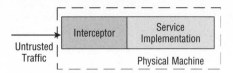

Figure 9-15 Security interceptor

RPC (JAX-RPC) handlers, Java API for XML-Based Web Services (JAX-WS) handlers, MQ exits, and the like. When a request arrives at the service endpoint, it is first processed by the interceptor (sometimes called an "agent"), which evaluates the security rules before passing the request to the service (see Figure 9-15).

Policy-aware environments such as Microsoft's Web Services Extensions (WSE) (2.0 and above), Window's Communications Foundation (WCF), or IBM's WebSphere Application server (WAS) (5.1 or above) provide implementations of an interceptor that can be configured using either WS-Policy files (WSE, WCF) or custom configurations (WAS) built directly into the run-time environment.

Although this architecture solves the "last mile" problem, it requires security configurations for every interceptor (i.e., service endpoint). This requirement can cause significant management overhead when the security policy changes. A modified interceptor architecture that alleviates this problem by combining an interceptor with a centralized security service is presented in Figure 9-16.

In this architecture, the interceptor still processes all incoming service requests, but it uses a specialized security service, which performs the actual processing of security rules. It effectively combines the advantages of the interceptor with the security gateway by centralizing security processing.

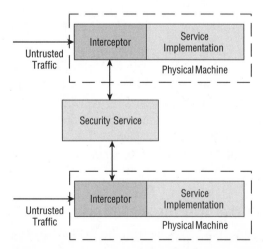

Figure 9-16 Security interceptor with centralized security service

Centralization allows the computationally intensive functions such as cryptography to be implemented in dedicated hosts (appliances). This minimizes the impact on invocation performance and provides a central point of management and reporting for service security processing.

Example: Architecting Security for Policy Issuance Solutions

Services participating in a policy issuance solution exchange a significant amount of sensitive information. As a result, a proper security implementation is paramount for this solution.

Using an interceptor is the most appropriate approach for the security implementation of the policy issuance solution. Every participating service (refer to Figure 9-1) should contain an interceptor supporting (and enforcing) the service's security policy. For more on policy enforcement, see Chapters 11 and 12.

For ACME's services implemented in Java, this interceptor can be implemented as a JAX-WS handler, invoked as part of the service invocation. For services implemented using WCF, programmatic WCF security can be used as a security interceptor.

Exception Handling and Logging in Enterprise Solutions

In the ideal world nothing ever fails, service invocations always complete successfully and return the required results. Unfortunately, in reality, services and solutions built using services may and do fail.

Let's consider a rate policy service, for example. A wide variety of problems can cause the execution of this service to fail, including failures of the service itself; for example, because of the validation of the incoming parameters, or just an implementation bug, or a communication problem, where the service cannot be reached, or the implementation cannot reach an underlying database.

A widely adopted mechanism for dealing with failures is exception handling, encompassing capturing and logging errors and choosing an alternative execution path in case of failures. It has become a standard mechanism in application development, where it is typically based on the ability of application designers and developers to anticipate the possible exception conditions and appropriately instrument code to handle them at run time.

NOTE The implementation of exceptions is usually based on `try`/`catch` blocks (supported by the majority of today's programming languages, for example, Java or C#), allowing you to determine the exception and use logging mechanisms to store exceptions for follow-up analysis.

This approach relies on the following assumptions:

- The application is designed as a whole in all of its completeness, including all of the possible exception situations. This means that all of the execution paths of applications can be fully defined and, as a result, completely tested by an application team.

- The application is executed on a single machine (limited set of machines) and reports all of the exceptions in the local log files using standardized exceptions reporting schemas.

- Changes in the application are administered centrally, thus providing a single application development team with complete control over all changes.

Implementing these exception-handling approaches becomes significantly more complex in the case of distributed systems due to the following:

- Exceptions can be caused not only by the application code itself but also by the infrastructure malfunctioning, which makes it harder to analyze all possible exception scenarios.

- Exception logs are spread between multiple physical machines, which make their reconciliation significantly more complex.

In the context of SOA, characteristics like loose coupling (both organizational and technological), autonomy, and reliance on existing applications for the implementation of the business capabilities complicate exception handling even more.

Every service is designed, implemented, and maintained by itself and can be used in multiple enterprise solutions, which might not be known at the time of the service design. As a result, the exception-handling implementation for a given service usually revolves around processing and logging exceptions that are local to the service implementation and, when they cannot be resolved locally, reporting them to the service consumer. If special measures are not taken, this results in "islands of exception handling" (see Figure 9-17).

As defined in Sean Fitts's September 2005 article "When exceptions are the rule: Achieving reliable and traceable service oriented architectures," exception processing in SOA introduces the following unique challenges:

- The distributed and heterogeneous nature of SOA makes it particularly prone to failures, causing exceptions at multiple levels. System-level exceptions result from the messaging, communications, and other infrastructure failures. Application-level exceptions result from incorrect message semantics or logical errors within the application. Business-level exceptions result in violation of best practices, compliance laws, regulations, or business policies mandated by business managers.

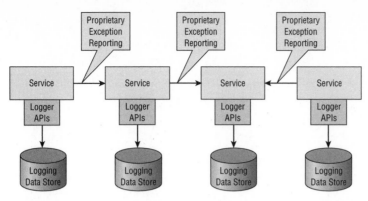

Figure 9-17 Islands of exception handling

- Exceptional conditions that are related to a particular enterprise solution spanning one or more services across different business processes cannot always be detected by exception handling localized within one of the participating services. Exception processing, in this case, has to be done on the solution level, which might require aggregation of the exception information from multiple participants. On the other hand, the same services can be used in multiple solutions requiring segregation of the service's exception information from solutions using this service. Additional requirements for this type of segregation can be reinforced by privacy, HIPAA, and other compliance requirements.

- Individual services provide no visibility into the entire solution, which makes it hard to make appropriate corrective actions in the case of error.

- Loosely coupled, heterogeneous services often discover and process exceptions differently. Some may use specialized components such as log4j, log4net, and so on. Others employ proprietary solutions. Additionally, wrapping the functionality of existing applications currently represents the prevalent approach to service implementation. These legacy applications can detect, log, and communicate exceptions in different ways.

An elegant solution to exception handling in SOA is to apply SOA principles to an exception-handling implementation — "servicizing" all of the major elements of exception management (i.e., logging, exception resolution, and notifications). Figure 9-18 shows the overall architecture for exception logging, resolution, and notifications.

NOTE Also see Chapter 12 on the role of centralized exception handling and logging in SOA governance.

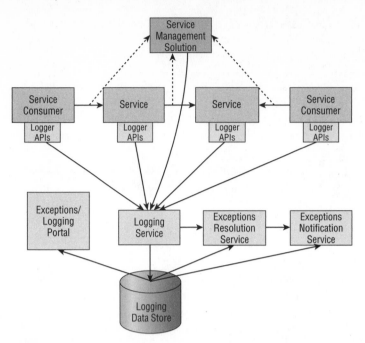

Figure 9-18 Unified architecture for exceptions logging, resolution, and notifications

Instrumentation code within the service implementation detects and logs system- and application-level exceptions. Logging takes place through common-purpose APIs exposed by standard logging components such as log4j, log4net, and so on. The implementation of logging within the service translates invocation requests into service calls to the exception-logging service. To lower the performance impact of exception logging, asynchronous invocations are typically used for the service invocation. Although this implementation revolves around the logging service, exception handling relies on several additional elements:

- The Logging Service accepts all logging requests, stores them in the logging database, and forwards them to the Exception Resolution Service.

- The Exceptions Resolution Service processes each log message using exception resolution rules. These rules specify whether the message should be ignored (e.g., information messages), resolved automatically, or whether human intervention is required.

- The Notification Service receives notification requests and uses a set of rules to dispatch the notification (e.g., email gateway, pager gateway, enterprise management solution).

- The Exceptions/Logging Portal allows people to view and browse the logged exception information.

- Service Management monitors service traffic to determine business-level exceptions and reports them to the logging service, which treats them the same way as any other exceptions in the system.

This partitioning of responsibility ensures that exception logging and resolution take place in a consistent fashion. This allows you to formalize enterprise best practices ("common knowledge") and improves auditing, monitoring, and the control of exceptions. This represents a big step toward regulatory compliance.

The centralized exception resolution service allows for faster implementation of changes in the handling of specific exception types. The most common approaches to exception resolution are:

- Automatic resolution that resolves the problem without the need for human intervention

- Semi-automatic resolution that evaluates a rule set and suggests possible resolutions

- Fallback to humans for manual resolution

The solution presented in Figure 9-18 has the following prerequisites:

- All logging and messages, including information, warning, exceptions, and so on must follow a standard format, for example, Common Base Events (see `www.ibm.com/developerworks/autonomic/books/fpy0mst .htm#HDRAPPA` for more information).

- All participants (i.e., service consumers and providers, logging, exceptions resolution, and notification services) should be able to interpret the exceptions/logging information, which should conform to the enterprise semantic model (refer to service exceptions definitions in Chapter 6).

- Analyzing and understanding failure entails linking log messages across service boundaries. This requires a unique correlation ID, spanning the scope of business transactions.

The logging and exception-handling architecture described here applies SOA principles to provide the foundation for the effective management of exceptions. It promotes the use of specialized infrastructure services to build flexible, extensible exception-handling solutions, which are easily integratable into SOA-based enterprise solutions.

Monitoring and Managing Enterprise Solutions

To compete in today's economic climate, it is not sufficient to automate a solution itself. Business intelligence, especially when it is actionable, provides the foundation of business competitiveness. Tuning the enterprise operation requires knowledge about customers, products, processes, sales, expenses, and so on. For example, in the case of policy issuance, it is important to know the following:

■ **The number of setup customers, rated quotes, and issued policies** — This measures the attractiveness of ACME's offerings and the effectiveness of their advertising campaigns.

■ **The ratio of rated quotes and issued policies, most common terms and conditions used by customers and premium amounts** — This additionally quantifies the effectiveness of the current offerings, providing insight into their improvement.

■ **The average and peak processing times for policy issuance** — In addition to indicating the turnaround time of the process, these metrics can also drive increasing capacity of the IT systems.

While many SOA practitioners are trying to rush SOA solutions to the market, considering solutions monitoring and management as nice to have, in our opinion it is an integral part of the solution itself. There are two major aspects to monitoring and management of enterprise solutions — business activity monitoring and technical service monitoring. Although both of them are about monitoring, they cater to two very different audiences:

■ Business activity monitoring supports evaluation of the business impact of the enterprise solution by business people and consequently is concerned with collecting and calculating the solution's key performance indicators (KPI), business measures, including historical trends, and so on.

■ Technical monitoring of SOA solutions aids IT personnel in day-to-day support of SOA-based solutions, including service utilization statistics, service level agreement (SLA) evaluation, resource and capacity planning, problem resolutions, and so on.

The rest of this section covers details of both business activity and technical monitoring of service-based enterprise solutions and outlines the main considerations of their implementation.

Business Activity Monitoring

An ideal BAM solution intercepts any significant business events in the enterprise, examines the content of the event's information, and decides how this information has to be interpreted and ultimately processed. The outcome of the BAM solution can range from simple reporting to personnel notification to real-time changes to the solution execution.

John Medicke, Feng-Wei Chen, and Margie Mago, in their article "Creating an intelligent and flexible solution with BPM, Business Rules, and Business Intelligence," (October 2003), define BAM in terms of the "Five Rs" of business activity monitoring and decision making:

- Recognition of particular situations
- Response to particular situations
- Resolution of a particular situation
- Review of the resolution actions
- Delivering return on investment (ROI)

At the foundation of BAM are several key business improvement concepts, which are becoming increasingly important to business executives. Incidentally, these concepts are in close alignment with the principles of the SOA-based solutions architecture (refer to Figure 9-2).

- Putting business process management at the core of business solutions. The explicit implementation of business processes provides the ability to quickly adapt to changes in the business environment. The introduction of the business process controller as one of the key components of enterprise solutions fully supports this concept.

- Driving business processes by actionable intelligence and improving them through analysis of key performance indicators captured during their execution. The use of semantic messaging models in SOA-based solutions simplifies the acquisition of business intelligence.

- Replacing thousands of pages of business intelligence reports with a smaller number of KPIs that reveal the critical characteristics of operational success. The introduction of specialized services dedicated to calculations of KPI promotes centralized, flexible KPI calculations.

- Driving business process execution by real-time actionable business events representing the current state of the enterprise. This requires business events to be produced and evaluated not after the completion of the business process but rather during its execution. The usage of services aligned with real business activities makes SOA-based solutions ideally suited for such implementations.

From the solution design point of view, at least the following need to be determined:

- What business measures and KPIs are applicable for a given solution? Typically, those are derived from the enterprise's business vision, goals, and objectives (see Chapter 4 for more details). For example, the number of policy ratings and issuances, the ratio of ratings to issuances, and the average and overall premium amounts, in the ACME example.

- How can these measures and KPI be calculated, based on the data contained in the solution? For example, the amounts of ratings and issuances can be measured through direct capturing of corresponding events; a ratio of ratings to issuances can be calculated by dividing two values; premiums amounts can be calculated based on the issuance information and so on.

- Which parts of the solution (including the solution's business process, participating services, UI, etc.) should be instrumented with business events, emitting the data required for business measures and KPI calculations? For example, the BAM implementation for the issuance example requires instrumentation of the issuance process with the events reflecting current terms and quote calculation, rating, and issuance. These events should contain enough information for the calculation of business measures.

- How should these business events be correlated (for example, solution-wise, solution-instance-wise, etc.) to provide a full picture of solution execution? For example, correlation in the case of issuance should be performed on the issuance process instance level.

Additional considerations can include such topics as alarming, in cases when KPIs are going out of the predefined range, alarm notifications, and so on.

Technical Monitoring and Management of SOA Solutions

BAM provides enough information to business personnel for the management and monitoring enterprise solutions. However, its information typically does not address requirements of the IT support personnel who use enterprise-monitoring tools that report on the health of hardware, operating systems, applications servers, and applications. These tools also do not solve the problem, because they provide information about the underlying applications, not services using these applications' capabilities. The proper functioning of all of the participating applications does not ensure support for required SLAs by the services utilizing these applications (for example, a problem in the integration service would not be noticed by monitoring the underlying application). Additionally, due to the potential sharing of application capabilities by multiple services, a single faulty application can impact several services simultaneously.

In the policy issuance example, different stakeholders within ACME are interested in various pieces of information about service execution. SOA governance and portfolio architects need to know which services are in place and how they are utilized, so they can improve the accuracy of the information about the enterprise services' asset repository and adjust service functionality and sizing, based on usage scenarios. Infrastructure support staff wants access to information about resource utilization so that they can optimize deployment topologies, scope additional hardware requirements, and find the best time for scheduled upgrades and patches. Finally, the IT support group requires information about any abnormalities in the service execution so that they can proactively manage IT functioning and more quickly determine and correct operational problems.

As a result, the implementation of SOA-based solutions typically requires creation of an additional layer of service monitoring and management on top of the existing application monitoring and management. This service-monitoring and management layer is not a substitute for traditional application monitoring and management solutions but rather supplements them by adding additional monitoring and management points and data. In our experience, the design of these points and associated data is an essential part of the business governance capabilities, which should often be designed and modeled as part of the business processes and services.

Responsibilities of this layer include capturing execution characteristics of a service as a whole (in the context of a specific business solution), including its performance, throughput, utilization, and so on. It does not, however, monitor and manage either execution of the JVMs, containers, and the like, which are hosting the service implementations, or of underlying applications used by the service implementation. Existing enterprise management systems are used for these purposes. In effect, service monitoring provides the big picture of the enterprise processes and their execution, which is supplemented by the information provided by application monitoring and management, allowing for drilling down into applications in order to perform root cause analysis of abnormal behavior.

A typical service management and monitoring solution architecture (see Figure 9-19) includes the following components:

- **Service management agents** — These agents collect information about service traffic and control service access, based on the service state (active, in which case all messages are delivered to the service, or suspended, in which case service traffic is not delivered) defined in the agent.

- **Service manager application** — The service manager collects information from service management agents and stores it in the service monitoring and management database. Additional service manager functionality usually includes:

  - Historical trends calculation.

  - Alerting functionality, evaluating SLAs, and sending alerts if they are not met. Alerting implementations can range significantly, from visual (color-coded) alerts in a service management console to storing alerts

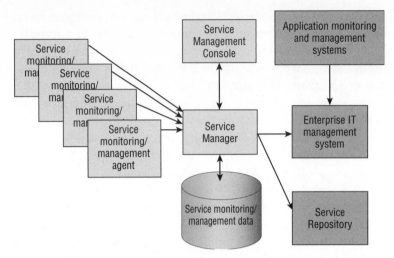

Figure 9-19 Typical service monitoring and management architecture

in the database to email notifications to integration with enterprise monitoring systems. The ability to provide real-time alerts allows you to use monitoring and management systems to alert support personal, not only in the case of service failures, but also, more importantly, when services are just starting to expose abnormal behavior. This often allows you to mitigate issues before they lead to catastrophic service failures.

- Providing data to more powerful business-management systems to assess the impact of service execution on the overall business (see BAM, above, for more details).

- Integration with a service repository to capture information about service utilization.

- **Service management database** — Stores information collected by service monitoring and management agents and current system settings, including service state (active/suspended), service objectives, and so on.

- **Service management console** — A presentation for managed service information and for providing information used by the system, including the desired service state, service objectives, and so on.

The implementation of enterprise solutions requires appropriate monitoring and management tools. Understanding the SOA service monitoring and management architecture (refer to Figure 9-19) is critical to the proper use of these monitoring tools. This includes the following:

- Choice and placement of monitoring agents. The three most popular options for monitoring agents are:

- **Proxy agent** — An agent, injected in the service traffic. The service consumer, talks to the agent, which passes the request to the service implementation. This is the least invasive approach to monitoring and management, requiring no changes to the existing service consumer and provider. On the other hand, this type of agent can lead to significant performance degradation, especially in the case of large messages and the use of SSL.

- **Interceptor agent** — An agent is deployed in the same process space as either the service consumer or provider (HTTP handler or JAX-RPC handler are the prevalent deployment options in this case). This option alleviates some of the problems of a proxy agent — for example, performance degradation. On the other hand, this option usually requires a significantly larger number of agents (one for every service provider and often for every consumer), which makes the overall solution implementation more expensive.

- **Callable agent** — An agent is outside of the service traffic, with access from the service consumer and provider. This architecture requires modification to both service consumer and provider. An advantage of this type of agent is a fixed size of communications between service consumer and provider, which eliminates performance degradation in the case of large service requests.

- Design of the service SLAs (objectives). The choices for the SLA definitions supported by different monitoring solutions vary significantly ranging from predefined SLA options to sophisticated SLA design toolkits.

- Design and implementation of integration and alerting options.

Implementation of service monitoring and management provides visibility into service traffic and consequently service deployment and utilization. It is a required element of an SOA implementation, allowing for proactive management of service resources.

Enterprise Service Bus-Unified Infrastructure for Enterprise Solutions

As we have shown in the previous sections of this chapter, there is a large and ever-growing number of techniques for delivering flexibility and agility to SOA-based solutions in a realistic and incrementally realizable manner. The majority of these techniques are based on intercepting service communications traffic and inserting additional processing of the service messages transparently to the service consumers and providers (compare this to the service communications layer, defined in Chapter 2). A common approach to supporting such architectures is an Enterprise Service Bus (ESB). In this section, we explain what an ESB is, and describe an overall ESB architecture and considerations for choosing an appropriate ESB for a given implementation.

Defining ESB

With so many conflicting definitions (see the sidebar "ESB Definitions") many practitioners consider an ESB to be a product. And in reality, there are more and more products labeled ESB on the market. Starting with an early implementation by Sonic Software (the company that actually coined the name), the number of ESB products has constantly grown. There are already open source ESB implementations (for example, MULE and Tuscany), and some companies have several ESB products (for example, IBM has three); it is not just Java anymore (Microsoft recently announced its own ESB).

ESB DEFINITIONS

Adding to the confusion around the Enterprise Service Bus is the multiplicity of definitions:

◆ "A Web-services-capable infrastructure that supports intelligently directed communication and mediated relationships among loosely coupled and decoupled biz components." — Gartner Group

◆ "The ESB label simply implies that a product is some type of integration middleware product that supports both MOM and Web services protocols." — Burton Group

◆ "A standards-based integration backbone, combining messaging, Web services, transformation, and intelligent routing." — Sonic Software

◆ "An enterprise platform that implements standardized interfaces for communication, connectivity, transformation, and security." — Fiorano Software

◆ "To put it bluntly: If you have WebSphere MQ and other WebSphere brokers and integration servers, you have an ESB." — Bob Sutor, IBM

◆ "The Enterprise Service Bus is a uniform service integration architecture of infrastructure services that provides consistent support to business services across a defined ecosystem. The ESB is implemented as a service oriented architecture using Web Service interfaces." — CBDI

◆ "ESB is an open standards–based distributed synchronous or asynchronous messaging middleware that provides secure interoperability between enterprise applications via XML, Web services interfaces and standardized rules-based routing of documents." — Webopedia

> ◆ "An ESB refers to a software architecture construct, implemented by technologies found in a category of middleware infrastructure products usually based on standards, that provides foundational services for more complex architectures via an event-driven and standards-based messaging engine (the bus)." — Wikipedia

Other practitioners consider ESB to be an architectural pattern and existing products to be implementations of this pattern. We belong to this latter camp. In our mind, an ESB is an enterprise-wide extendable middleware infrastructure providing virtualization and management of service interactions, including support for the communication, mediation, transformation, and integration technologies required by services. The foundation of the ESB pattern is a universal intermediary. (This intermediary does not have to be remote. We consider any abstraction layer, whether local or remote, used as an intermediary to be a service bus.) Rather than interacting directly, participants in a service interaction communicate through a bus, which can be implemented using a variety of middleware technologies and programming models.

VIRTUALIZATION

Virtualization is a commonly used approach for simplification of the IT infrastructure through unification of access to resources and the management of those resources. According to Wikipedia:

Virtualization is the process of presenting a logical grouping or subset of computing resources so that they can be accessed in ways that give benefits over the original configuration. This new virtual view of the resources is not restricted by the implementation, geographic location or the physical configuration of underlying resources.

Resource virtualization enables hiding many proprietary infrastructure components that are required for the proper functioning of particular resources, and minimizes the impact of IT infrastructure changes on the resource consumers.

A service implementation is a type of virtualization of IT resources hidden behind the service interface. An ESB adds an additional level of virtualization to the service through vitalizing the service infrastructure (access). In effect, SOA with ESB is virtualization squared.

The roots of the ESB can be traced to a common approach used in application integration architectures — hub and spoke (Message Broker), which support virtualization and decoupling in EAI implementations. In this architecture, invocations and routing rules are separated from implementations. The drawback of this architecture is the fact that a central hub becomes both a single point of failure and a potential bottleneck for communications.

In order to avoid these drawbacks, hubs can be joined together to form what is logically a single entity — bus — that provides a single point of control but is implemented as a collection of physically distributed components. A bus lowers coupling between service consumers and providers by serving as a communication intermediary supporting mediation between required and provided capabilities. This provides a clean separation between the business aspects of the solution supported by the service consumers and providers, and the technical aspects (for example, security, or dynamic routing) supported by the bus. Furthermore, in a bus architecture, the implementation of this technical aspect can change transparently to the service consumers and providers. For example, the introduction of a new security approach could be limited to changes in the bus mediation.

The ability of a bus to support communications between consumers and providers is based on the explicit declaration of capabilities and requirements of interactions — metadata describing domain models (set of services) and a set of policies governing access to these services. This metadata allows the bus to validate the request, map it to the location of the actual service implementation (supporting the required invocation policies), and invoke services on behalf of consumers.

ESB Architecture

The basic architecture of an ESB is presented in Figure 9-20 and usually contains the following:

- Distributed ESB engine, (run-time engine) responsible for communications between service consumers and providers. This engine is usually multi-transport and supports message delivery and service invocation, along with quality of service support for these operations. It often supports events and the publish/subscribe paradigm.
- Distributed ESB infrastructure services, including:
  - **Service location/routing directory** — Service registry containing service endpoint addresses and policies governing access to the endpoints.
  - **Transactional support** — An ESB usually implements multiple transactional models — business transactions, required for business service interactions and variations of two-phase commit transactions for integration services.

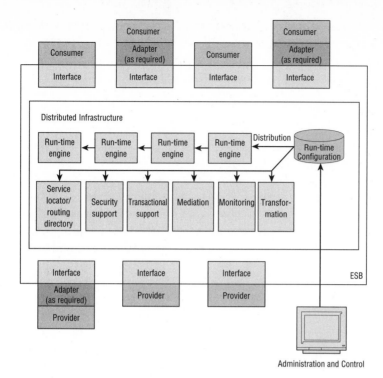

Figure 9-20 Basic ESB architecture

- **Mediation** — Framework, allowing for the injection of intermediate processing to "in-flight" messages.

- **Specialized engines** — For example, rules and orchestration engines.

- **Monitoring** — Including infrastructure monitoring of the ESB components, service traffic monitoring, and business level monitoring — BAM.

- **Service security support** — Including authentication, authorization, confidentiality, non-repudiation, and so on.

- Additional ESB services can include exception processing, logging, and so on.

- Run-time configuration — ESB metadata defining the configuration and distribution of ESB components (engines and services). This functionality allows you to add additional nodes to the ESB, and configure the location of the service registry, security policies, and so on.

- Centralized administration and control — Interface for viewing and modifying the ESB metadata. It also allows for viewing the service monitoring results and creating alarms in the case of missing service SLAs (for example, performance characteristics).

Service providers and consumers connect to the ESB either directly (through the ESB interfaces) or by using custom adapters.

There are three popular approaches to an ESB implementation:

- Stand-alone ESB
- ESB as a service container
- ESB as a framework

Stand-alone ESB

The stand-alone ESB architecture (see Figure 9-21), which was implemented by the majority of the initial ESB implementations, resembles a classical hub-and-spoke architecture. In this case, all of the service consumers and providers are communicating with the bus, which is responsible for mediating service traffic.

The important characteristic of this ESB architecture is its minimal impact on service consumers and providers. This is both a strength and weakness of this approach. On one hand, it minimizes vendor "lock-in" through the ability to change bus implementation (as long as the capabilities of the bus do not change). On the other hand, it limits the capabilities provided by the bus for things like service creation, deployment, and so on.

ESB as a Service Container

A new option for an ESB implementation, introduced by application server vendors, is the ESB as a container. This implementation (shown in Figure 9-22) is an extension of the application server, which hosts the service implementation and provides intermediary support and communications at the container level.

The advantage of this approach is the very rich container support for service design and implementation that comes from the existing application servers,

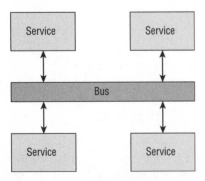

Figure 9-21 Stand-alone ESB

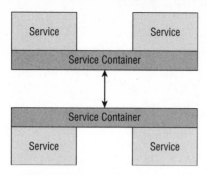

Figure 9-22 ESB as a service container

including tooling, container services, and so on. On the other hand, because of vendor's lock-in, which is significantly more pervasive in this case, changes to the ESB can require modifications to the service consumers and providers.

ESB as a Framework

The ESB as a framework approach (shown in Figure 9-23) is typically a "home-grown" implementation created by companies that have decided not to buy an ESB product, but rather to "wrap" their existing middleware capabilities (including existing application servers and EAI solutions) in a way that provides an ESB pattern.

The main strength of this approach is its complete vendor independence. Once designed and implemented, the framework can run transparently on any middleware platform providing a unified programming model and capability support. It also isolates service providers and consumers from middleware changes, version compatibility issues, and so on. On the other hand, such an implementation requires a potentially large investment in time and a vast amount of code to be implemented and supported by companies.

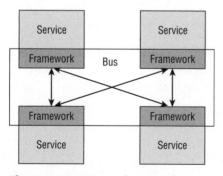

Figure 9-23 ESB as a framework

Choosing an ESB

With all the vendors' hype and different ESB architectures, choosing an appropriate ESB for a solution becomes a complex decision, which includes the following considerations:

- Support for most of the required functionality
- Extensibility of the product for additional functionality
- Adherence to a standards-based approach versus a proprietary implementation
- Vendor versus in-house support

The most important ESB capabilities can be defined as follows:

- Communications, including support for message routing; addressing schemas; supported middleware, protocols, and standards (for example, JMS, HTTP, and HTTPS); message encoding, (for example, SOAP; supported interaction styles request/response, fire-and-forget, asynchronous messaging, events, and publish/subscribe); and so on
- Service definitions, including support for service interface definition (for example, WSDL), service versioning support, support for service discovery (for example, service registry), and so on
- Integration, including support for accessing databases, legacy and packaged application adapters, connectivity to EAI middleware protocol transformation language interfaces for service invocation (for example, Java, C, C++, and C#), and so on
- Quality of service, including support for transactions (for example, atomic transactions, compensation, WS-Transaction) and assured message delivery paradigms (for example, WS-ReliableMessaging or support for persistent queuing), and so on
- Security, including support for authentication, authorization, non-repudiation, confidentiality, security standards support (for example, Kerberos and WS-Security), and so on
- Service level agreements, including capabilities for message delivery as performance, throughput, availability, other continuous measures that might form the basis of contracts or agreements, and so on
- Message processing, including support for encoded logic, content-based logic, message and data transformation, message validation, data enrichment, and so on
- Management, including support for service provisioning and registration; logging, metering, and monitoring; integration with systems

management and administration tooling; self-monitoring and self-management; alerting; and so on

- Modeling, including support for common business objects models, data format libraries, development and deployment tooling; and so on

- Infrastructure intelligence, including support for business rules; policy-driven behavior, particularly for service level, security, and quality of service capabilities (for example, WS-Policy); service orchestration; pattern recognition; and so on

NOTE For a full list of ESB capabilities, refer to the series of articles by Rick Robinson, "Understand enterprise service bus scenarios and solutions in service-oriented architecture, Part 1–3," (June 2004).

Although some of these capabilities are quite basic, others, such as intelligent routing capabilities, are quite advanced. It is important to recognize that a particular SOA implementation requires only a subset of the capabilities within a subset of these categories.

An ESB provides a unified service support infrastructure, supporting both business-focused and integration services (refer to Figure 9-3). This infrastructure supports service invocations over multiple transports with different QoS, usually governed by policies. An ESB also provides built-in support for the majority of the service's run-time patterns, including the service registry, service management and monitoring, and facilities for the centralized management of deployed services.

Although many practitioners, especially software vendors, would like you to believe that the use of an ESB product is a prerequisite for a successful SOA implementation, this is not true. We have seen and successfully implemented SOA solutions without them. On the other hand, an ESB (at least on the pattern level) is very powerful middleware, which often simplifies SOA-based implementations.

Summary

This chapter has defined a layered architecture for SOA-based enterprise solutions. It then discussed some of the key components that have to be taken into consideration when building solutions including:

- **Service locations** — Defining the ways to make endpoint addresses of services available throughout the enterprise, based on the service registry, which can be used as a universal service locator

- **Service versioning** — Defining the ways to evolve services and service-based solutions independently with minimal or no impact on each other

- **Service security** — Defining architectural approaches to securing service-based enterprise solutions

- **Exception handling and logging in the SOA world** — Defining the role of basic exception and logging architecture, which can be easily incorporated in any SOA-based implementation

- **Service monitoring and management** — Defining the role, place, and two important types of monitoring and management: BAM and technical management

Finally, we introduced the Enterprise Service Bus pattern, which provides virtualization of service communications and serves as a foundation for the implementation of the majority of the architectural components described in this chapter.

Designing and Using Integration in SOA Solutions

Existing software assets are essential to your business. Application systems contain a reservoir of business rules vital to operational continuity, yet remain undocumented outside the source code. These software assets and the accompanying business data are difficult to decipher and almost impossible to replicate using "green-field" approaches.

–William Ulrich

With all the advances in SOA that provide the best hope for efficient, flexible, and cost-effective implementations, the bulk of the business processing today is still carried out by legacy systems and packaged applications, like Enterprise Resource Planning (ERP), Customer Relationship Management (CRM), and so on. If there is a big bang conversion from existing applications to new systems, architecture will not work. Instead, IT organizations should bridge the gap via a carefully planned transition and migration process. This means that SOA solutions cannot be built in a vacuum — the only cost-effective approach is to base new solutions on the existing application portfolio and leverage integration as a mechanism for accessing the existing capabilities. But, it is not as simple as just Web- Service-enabling existing applications and data. Instead, the existing functions and data need to be transformed into new capabilities and information that can move the enterprise forward toward its current goals and strategies, and not keep it tied to the 20-year-old strategies associated with the 20-year-old systems.

This chapter discusses the role that integration plays in SOA and introduces more specific definitions of integration services and their implementation challenges.

The chapter covers the following topics:

- The role of integration and what makes its implementation complex
- The history of attempts to bridge SOA and integration
- Choosing integration implementation approaches
- Cross-cutting concerns for implementing integration, including data mapping, security, transactional support, versioning and support for large messages
- Supporting data access in SOA
- The Enterprise Data Bus as a pattern for virtualization of data access to services throughout the enterprise

Challenges of Integration in SOA

Integration is not new. It has been around for at least 10-15 years and is well understood and widely adopted. In today's reality, integration projects consume a lion's share of the IT budget, often impeding new developments. The need for integration is caused by the siloed nature of existing enterprise applications, which manifest themselves as islands of data, automation, and security.

Characteristics of Islands of Data

Each island of data has its own *meaning and/or definition* of enterprise objects. For example, in one application "insured party" defines an insured individual; in another application, the same term might refer to a company. Even if an object, for example, "address" has the same meaning in two applications, one application can define it as a set of address lines, while another might treat it as street address, city, state, zip, and country. Both cases create semantic dissonance between applications.

Each island of data has *information that overlaps* with the contents of another island. For example, applications dealing with the management of health and dental claims also store the demographics information for the insured. At the same time the CRM application contains both insured addresses and demographics. This duplication creates integrity issues.

No one can *provide a complete picture* of the enterprise data. For example, a personal auto Policy and Product Administration application doesn't contain information about the insured policies from other lines of business. Creating a unified view of the enterprise data requires integrating information from multiple sources.

Characteristics of Islands of Automation

Each island of automation focuses on a *limited set of activities* within the enterprise. For example, a health claim management application deals only with the processing of health claims without considering the role and place of these activities in the overall enterprise business process. This requires users to engage in "application hopping" to perform their work, thus affecting their productivity.

There is a *duplication of functionality* between multiple applications. For example, multiple applications that process insurance applications for different lines of business all implement address cleansing functionality. As a result, when changing address cleansing rules, these changes have to be coordinated between all applications.

There is *duplication of business processes* contained within different islands. For example, as a result of a merger or acquisition an insurance company can have several claim-processing systems. This requires synchronization of changes among multiple applications, ensuring consistency of the processes and business rules that support these processes.

Characteristics of Islands of Security

Different enterprise applications often use *different authentication mechanisms*. This makes it difficult to propagate user identity among multiple applications. For example, existing solutions such as Single Sign-On (SSO) cater to web-facing applications and employ browser sessions and cookies associated with them. Therefore, they are usually not applicable to application integration. Various applications also use application-specific identities, not tied into the global enterprise, which creates further integration difficulties. Additionally, different authorization mechanisms (roles versus security attributes versus individual authorization) employed by different applications often rely on incompatible representations for user identity. Complicating the matter further, individual enterprise applications may use application-specific authorization credentials and tightly coupled, deeply embedded security logic, making security integration very difficult.

Requirements for the *implementation of invocation privacy* can vary significantly between enterprise applications. Popular choices include implementing privacy at the transport level (e.g., HTTPS or SSL) or at the message level (e.g., S/MIME, WS-Security).

Different applications can provide radically *different mechanisms and locations for security audit trails*. Bringing together and correlating these trails for multiple integration activities can be a difficult task. In addition, the heterogeneity of storage mechanisms and formats often makes them virtually unusable. The necessity to create maintainable and manageable IT infrastructure positioned to better respond to the business needs requires a massive amount of integration work, aimed at bridging these islands.

Despite the fact that integration has been around for many years, a large portion of integration projects fail. The major reasons for these failures are:

▪ Although many integration vendors try to convince you otherwise, the complexity and cost of integration is not due to the complexity and cost of a particular tool but rather due to the complexity and cost of architecting interactions between heterogeneous applications that often were not designed to work together.

▪ In many of today's enterprises, each business unit is autonomous and has its own set of technologies, applications, and budgets. Cross-unit integration requires both technical (infrastructure and applications) and financial (sharing integration costs) cooperation between business units, which typically requires centralized IT governance.

▪ Defining the overall integration approach and implementation architecture is still as much art (based on the experience of the integration teams) as science. There is no well-established methodology for topics such as how to analyze overall data and process flow, when to choose simple data synchronization versus service-oriented architecture, and how to determine data and service interfaces. Standardized architectures should be in place when defining applicable EAI topologies, including the choice of the integration transports, definitions of routing rules, placement of the data transformation, security, failover, and load balancing. Considerations for each are important.

▪ Integration spans multiple existing applications and usually involves comparatively little development work but a lot of research and design activity. This requires teams, project management, and implementation approaches that differ significantly from those of traditional application development.

▪ As the size of the integration grows, so does the complexity. Unfortunately, unlike traditional applications, this growth is not linear, but rather exponential.

▪ Integration is considered by many companies to be a technical, rather than a business undertaking. This leads to the business impact of integration being ignored until deployment to production, at which time it is already too late.

▪ Data model mismatches between applications severely complicate integration. (This topic is covered in more detail later in the "Data Mapping in Integration" section of this chapter.)

Implementing integration as part of SOA makes integration even more complex. First, SOA is often an enterprise-wide undertaking, which makes the requirement for business unit cooperation and centralized governance even more stringent. Second, there is an architectural design mismatch between SOA and existing enterprise applications. SOA design defines business services based on the decomposition of the enterprise business model with the interfaces defined according to the enterprise semantic model. In contrast, existing enterprise applications have been created and/or acquired over time in order to fulfill specific tasks. The differences between these two approaches make it challenging to use existing applications to implement business services. In SOA, the role of integration is not only to bridge the islands described previously, but also to deal with the following:

- **Information fidelity** — The redundancy of business data between applications creates an inaccurate representation of enterprise data, even when periodic synchronization occurs. The representations themselves are difficult to reconcile, or at worst contradictory. As the individual applications evolve independently, the complexity of the problem increases. The role of integration in SOA is to rationalize data from multiple existing applications in order to provide accurate information to the business services. Furthermore, it requires data updates, executed on the business service level to be correctly propagated to all participating enterprise applications.

- **Business processes fragmentation** — Individual applications provide a limited, often duplicated, piece of enterprise functionality. The role of integration in SOA is not only to pick the most appropriate implementation of the existing functionality but also to ensure that it won't break existing applications.

- **Security fragmentation** — Different enterprise applications rely on users' identity/group membership for programmatic/declarative authorization implementation. These applications often use different authentication approaches, which can be based on different users' representations located in different users' identity stores. Therefore, integration in SOA is required to correctly convert a user's identity representation in order to satisfy each of the enterprise applications used.

All of the previous points require careful architecture and implementation of integration in SOA environments. In the rest of this chapter, we discuss different integration approaches and show how these problems can be solved. Also refer to Chapter 14 for a case study of building an integration solution for a fictitious insurance company.

Integration in SOA Defined

The first attempt to extend SOA to standardize integration implementation — Service-Oriented Integration (SOI) — was suggested by several authors in the early 2000s. SOI is defined by Anna Liu and Ian Gorton in their paper, "Process and Criteria for Evaluating Services-Based Integration Technologies," (July 2005):

> *The services-based approach to doing integration is about integrating computing entities using service interactions. The services-based approach to integration addresses problems with integrating legacy and inflexible heterogeneous systems by enabling IT organizations to offer the functionality locked in existing applications as reusable services.*
>
> *In contrast to traditional enterprise application, integration (EAI), the significant characteristics of the services-based approach to integration are:*
>
> - *Well-defined, standardized interfaces — Consumers are provided with easily understood and consistent access to the underlying service.*
>
> - *Opaqueness — The technology and location of the application providing the functionality are hidden behind the service interface. In fact, there is no need for a fixed services provider.*
>
> - *Flexibility — Both the providers of services and consumers of services can change — the service description is the only constant. As long as both the provider and consumer continue to adhere to the service description, the applications will continue to work.*

The original SOI approach was to simply replace any proprietary middleware with SOAP over HTTP as a ubiquitous middleware platform guaranteeing interoperability between service consumers and providers (see the sidebar "Service-Oriented Integration," which follows the approach described in "Integration Patterns" by David Trowbridge, et al. [June 2004]).

SERVICE-ORIENTED INTEGRATION

It is necessary to integrate information systems that were not originally designed to work together. These systems are built using different technologies, languages, and architecture.

Problem

How do you integrate applications at the business logic layer?

Forces

Integrating systems at the business logic layer involves balancing the following forces:

Explicit Machine Boundaries

Attempt to minimize coupling to improve interoperability.

Solution

Integrate applications at the business logic layer, through the use of Web Services Description Language (WSDL) contracts to describe the interfaces to these systems. Ensure interoperability by making the implementation compliant with the Web Services family of specifications (including Web Services Interoperability [WS-I]).

   Note: The term *service* is used in many different ways in the context of software engineering. In this pattern, the term *service* is used to mean XML Web Services.

Resolving the Forces

Basing service invocation (messages) on XML and XML Schema Definition language (XSD) results in a highly portable type system that dramatically reduces type-system coupling, which is a major impediment to cross-platform integration.

Benefits

The key benefit of using *Service-Oriented Integration* is interoperability between disparate technical architectures, which helps to decouple an enterprise's business architecture from its information technology. This decoupling gives an enterprise a great deal of flexibility in terms of how it implements specific business capabilities.

Liabilities

The key liability of using *Service-Oriented Integration* is the use of XML for marshaling data. Not only can marshaling/unmarshaling be very expensive, but it also leads to increased message size, which increases network traffic.

Although, using SOI provides for bringing SOA and integration together, it is a simplistic and not very practical approach because it treats integration the same way as business services. As a result, business services created using the SOI approach are aligned not with the enterprise business model, but rather with the existing functionality of a particular application, with all of the drawbacks of that approach:

- This approach goes against one of the most important SOA principles — services are the rationalization layer, hiding existing application portfolios and supporting the ideal enterprise business model.

  - Services built using the SOI approach expose existing application functionality rather than the functionality defined by the enterprise model, and this might complicate reuse later on.

  - The SOI approach creates a tight coupling between the existing application portfolio and the service interfaces. If one or more enterprise applications change, an undesirable ripple effect may be created in the existing service model.

- Services in SOI expose the underlying application's data model, rather than the enterprise semantic information model (detailed in Chapter 5), and this typically complicates interoperability.

- The granularity of a service is aligned with the existing application, resulting in a potential increase in network traffic.

Integration Services

This book takes a different approach. We treat integration as a specialized type of service — an integration service. The role of integration services is to provide access to the existing enterprise applications and data, so that they can be utilized by business and utility. Scott Simmons in his article "Introducing the WebSphere Integration Reference Architecture," (August 2005), defines integration services as "the bridging capabilities between legacy applications, pre-packaged applications, enterprise data stores (including relational, hierarchical, and nontraditional, unstructured sources, such as XML, text and content management systems), and the business services implementation."

With such integration services in place, a typical implementation of a business/utility service is an assembly of business components, the majority of which are implemented as wrappers using integration access to the existing legacy applications. See Figure 10-1. An *integration service*, as defined in Chapter 2, is represented here as a combination of integration access (a mechanism used to expose existing legacy functionality and business components) and an abstraction layer hiding details of the interaction with the integration access.

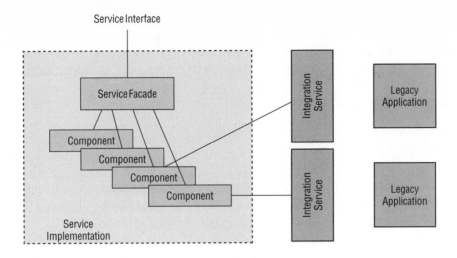

Figure 10-1 Business service implementation

Such an implementation has the following advantages:

■ Full utilization of the functionality of existing enterprise applications

■ The ability to extend the legacy system's functionality, through additional components, without extending or modifying existing legacy systems

■ Increased granularity of business services through combining the functionality of multiple legacy systems (or multiple interfaces of the same legacy system accessed using business components) and implementing additional functionality to rationalize this data and functionality

■ Rationalization of legacy applications and data and their alignment with the enterprise business and data models

The implementation presented in Figure 10-1 introduces an additional element to the overall business service implementation — a business component. Business components are not only building blocks for the business service but also a layer of abstractions for integration access. Integration access is not exposed as a service, but rather as business components encapsulating the access.

Regardless of the interface exposed by the existing legacy application, business components always support the interface that is aligned with the requirements of the business/domain/utility service. This means that business component interfaces are always designed on the basis of enterprise semantic (domain) data. Such a design simplifies the use of business components by business service implementers (we refer to "business services" throughout the chapter, but it could be any of the business-oriented services of our hierarchy, business, domain, or utility). Consequently, data exposed by existing applications has to be transformed (mapped) to the domain data representation. We discuss implementation and placement of the data transformation later in this chapter in the "Data Mapping in Integration" section.

The business components layer provides a simple, consistent programming model for the business service implementation, which hides idiosyncrasies (see "Integration Access Implementations" later in this chapter) of the integration access. For example, a single synchronous call to a business component can result in conversational invocation of the integration access. Furthermore, if an integration access does not expose an invocable interface directly (for example, it is implemented as a message exchange with an existing application), a business component can implement such an interface on its behalf.

In the majority of cases, one business component is created for every integration access. A notable exception to this rule is when integration access supports conversational interactions that require multiple interactions with more than one access to achieve the required result. For example, rating an insurance policy might require two invocations. One to send policy information, which returns a handle, and the other one that accepts the handle and returns the amount. These two integration access points represent a functional split within the legacy implementation, which is irrelevant to the business service implementation. A typical implementation of a business component combines these two integrations.

This approach is well aligned with the latest SOA programming model — Service Component Architecture (SCA). (Refer to Chapter 8 and Appendix C for more information.)

Introduction of the business components also has an impact on the integration reuse policy. In this case, reuse is at the level of the business component, which encapsulates the knowledge of the invocation of the integration access.

This separation between integration, business services, and business components leads to the following extension of the layered enterprise architectures for SOA presented in Chapter 9. (See Figure 10-2.)

Figure 10-2 presents a simplified, high-level view of the layered SOA architecture. In reality, integration exists within the existing IT applications layer as well, because the transition to SOA happens over time. As a result, the use of existing applications will have to coexist with the use of the new SOA implementation. This means that integration that has been put into place (for example, for propagating updates from one application to another) needs to be preserved during the transition to SOA. After the transition is completed, such integration can be moved to the business components layer. Additional layers introduced in Figure 10-2 are:

■ **Enterprise Resources and Operational Systems** — This layer consists of existing applications, legacy and COTS systems, including CRM and

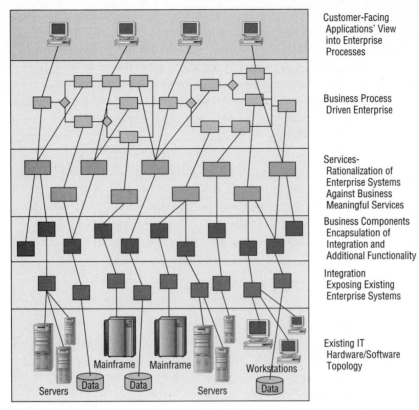

Customer-Facing
Applications' View
into Enterprise
Processes

Business Process
Driven Enterprise

Services-
Rationalization of
Enterprise Systems
Against Business
Meaningful Services

Business Components
Encapsulation of
Integration and
Additional Functionality

Integration
Exposing Existing
Enterprise Systems

Existing IT
Hardware/Software
Topology

Mainframe   Mainframe   Workstations

Servers   Data   Data   Servers   Data

Figure 10-2 Layered Enterprise Architecture for service implementation

ERP packaged applications, and older object-oriented implementations.
These applications provide business operation: transactions that represent single logical units of work in the enterprise's operational systems.
Execution of an operation typically causes one or more persistent data
records to be read, written, or modified in a System of Record (SOR).
Operations have a specific, structured interface, and return structured
responses.

■ **Integration Access** — Integration access provides access to an existing application's functionality. This separation between the business
services and integration is critical to maintaining a flexible enterprise
environment. Although integration directly exposes the functionality
of existing applications and is tightly coupled with the existing application, business services expose functionality that is aligned with the
enterprise business model and, therefore, is completely decoupled from
the existing application's portfolio.

■ **Business components** — Business components are deployable units
of software that provide the (integration) functionality required by the

business services. Components can either be implemented directly or wrap existing operational systems using integration services. Component implementations usually use container-based technologies such as application servers to provide workload management, availability, and load balancing. The components, acting as integration service consumers, provide a single point of access to the integration services. This prevents a proliferation of hard-to-manage cut-and-paste code for accessing the integration services.

This layering promotes architectural differences between integration services and business services:

- Unlike business services, integration services don't have to be coarse-grained. The granularity of the integration is defined by the granularity of the existing functionality, exposed by the application. It is generally advantageous to increase this granularity when possible.

- Synchronous invocations are a prevalent invocation pattern for integration services (with some exceptions for the data integration).

- ACID transactions are often a required property of the integration services, especially when their functionality is to update application data.

- Legacy integration often requires conversational interactions; consequently, integration services often have to be implemented as conversational.

Defining integration services as an implementation technique for business services is also well aligned with the service design approach described in Chapter 3.

Integration Access Implementations

Given the broad definition of integration access as a way to expose existing legacy functionality and data to business services, a wide variety of integration access implementations are possible. Specific implementation approaches depend on the following major factors:

- **Enterprise maturity in the EAI/integration space** — If a company already has either a robust EAI implementation (Message Broker) or a widely used messaging infrastructure that supports integration of the major enterprise applications, existing middleware can be leveraged for implementing integration services.

- **Composition of the existing application portfolio** — If the majority of the existing application portfolio is composed of packaged applications from major software vendors, and these applications are kept relatively current, there is a high probability that these applications expose their functionality by using Web Services. In this case, the implementation of integration services should leverage the Web Services supported by the packaged applications.

■ **Business service implementation platform** — If the majority of business services are implementated using J2EE applications servers, which provide prepackaged adapters (based on JCA/J2C) to the majority of existing application platforms, these adapters can be used as a basis for implementing access within integration services. An additional advantage of this approach is the ability to support two-phase commit (2PC) transactions if integrated applications also support them.

■ **Integrated application implementation** — If the integrated application is component-based with well-documented component functionality and interfaces, and the implementation platform supports the easy generation of Web Service wrappers, generated Web Services should be used as a basis for implementing integration services.

■ **Type of integration** — If integration is for the most part data integration and the majority of data is available in relational databases, database-specific middleware, for example JDBC, should be used for implementing integration services.

In this section, we discuss the architecture and implementation details for each of these approaches.

Using Messaging Infrastructure to Implement Integration Access

When the majority of enterprise applications are connected to a messaging infrastructure (for example WebSphere MQ, Tibco Rendezvous, etc.), this middleware can be used as a basis for implementing integration access.

In this case, the business component sends a request message to the request queue — a queue that the existing enterprise application is listening on. Once an application is done executing the request, it sends the reply to the reply queue that the business component is listening on. (See Figure 10-3.)

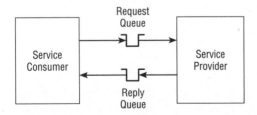

Figure 10-3 Implementing integration using MOM

The following should be considered when using MOM (Message Oriented Middleware) to implement integration access.

- Both the business component and enterprise application have to be able to connect to the messaging system. This typically requires some MOM client software to be installed with the business component and enterprise application.

- MOM is an asynchronous middleware, which means that it supports only one way messaging. Therefore, sending a request results in an immediate return of execution control to the business component, allowing for parallel execution of both business component and enterprise application. When synchronous communications with the enterprise applications are required, the business component should explicitly wait for the reply message to arrive.

- Existing MOM-based integration can use a wide variety of message formats, ranging from proprietary XML representations to position-oriented strings; for example, COBOL copybooks. The business component implementation has to be able to support the format used by the existing application. In doing so, it might be required to do EBS-DIC/ASCII conversions, data transformation, and so on.

- The majority of MOM implementations are transactional; a message is not delivered to the request queue until a transaction-initiated message send is committed. This might pose a problem in the case of synchronous communications using MOM. If an attempt is made to receive a reply message in the same transaction in which the request message is sent, a deadlock occurs. As a result, synchronous invocation of integration over MOM should be done outside of the business component's transaction.

- Typical MOM implementations provide both persistent and nonpersistent messaging. Persistent messaging is slower (messages are written to a hard drive or database) but provides guaranteed message delivery. In the case of asynchronous invocations, when guaranteed messaging is a main requirement, it is necessary to use persistent messaging. In the case of synchronous invocations, when performance is the main requirement, nonpersistent messaging is a better fit.

- Many of the modern MOM implementations support security. This security only controls access to MOM, not access to the enterprise application. The only way to implement security for the enterprise application, in this case, is to add the consumer's credential to the message content. Security is discussed later in this chapter in the section titled, "Security Support for Integration."

When the majority of existing enterprise applications are MOM-enabled (support request and reply messages sent to and from these applications), implementing integration using existing messaging middleware is usually straightforward.

Using a Message Broker to Implement Integration

A Message Broker introduces an additional layer on top of traditional messaging systems — sometimes called a messaging hub. In this architecture, all messages are routed between consumers and providers indirectly through the hub, providing a centralized processing layer for control of the message flows. This allows integration architects or developers to reformat and route information moving from one system to another programmatically. Centralized processing capabilities reduce the impact of changes on both source and target systems, thus reducing the coupling between them and the cost of integration.

Message brokers are a robust and well-established integration technology, providing the following features:

- Message (message format) transformation using sophisticated mapping tools, including support for industry standards, for example Electronic Data Interchange (EDI), Financial Information Exchange (FIXML), and so on

- Context-based message routing

- Data enrichment through additional integration points

- Management of complex application interactions

- Monitoring and auditing of transactions and/or data flows

- A wide range of adapters for connecting applications to the broker, for example databases, flat files, SAP, and the like

CONTEXT-BASED ROUTING AND BUSINESS RULES

Context-based routing is a very powerful approach for routing messages based on their context. It is applicable to solving infrastructure issues, for example, versioning (see Chapter 9), quality of service support, and the like.

Unfortunately, many practitioners overuse it and tend to use it for the implementation of business logic (rules). Although this might seem like an easy-to-implement solution initially, maintenance often turns out to be very costly. The business logic implementation is scattered among multiple routing rules and becomes hard to understand and follow. As a result, the overall implementation becomes very fragile.

We strongly recommend that you separate solutions for infrastructure concerns, using context-based routing, from the implementation of business logic by using business rules and specialized decision services (see Chapter 8).

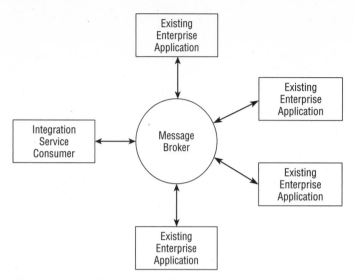

Figure 10-4 Implementing an integration service using a message broker

Implementation of integration access based on existing, message-broker-based integration, as shown in Figure 10-4, is fairly straightforward. The business component connects to the broker, allowing the reuse of integration access that is already in place.

The following should be considered when using Message Brokers to implement integration:

- All of the Message Brokers support some form of MOM connection to the broker, allowing for a MOM-based implementation of the business component. See the considerations for such an implementation in the previous section. In addition, many Message Broker implementations (for example, WebSphere Message Broker) provide Web Service support, which can also be leveraged to access existing integration. The choice of the particular access mechanism depends on the implementation platform and integration requirements. Although Web Service access typically does not require any additional software to implement connectivity, it lacks support for guaranteed delivery and asynchronous invocations. MOM-based access, on the other hand, requires additional software on the client side, but provides richer communication options.

- Because the Message Broker comes with built-in support for format and data transformation, its facilities should be used for transforming data between the formats used by the business component and the existing applications. A canonical data format, widely adopted by Message Broker implementations, is a good starting point for such transformations.

See more on data transformation later in this chapter in the section titled "Data Mapping in Integration."

■ Existing EAI implementations are created for reuse and often provide granularity that is too low for SOA. Integration designers should consider combining (where possible) several existing related integration services as a basis for a business component, leveraging it as an orchestrator or an additional mediator for existing integration services.

If a message-broker-based implementation is already in place, it is typically a good starting point for implementating integration services.

Using Existing Web Services to Implement Integration

With the growing popularity of Web Services, the majority of application vendors are starting to expose their functionality as Web Services. These Web Services can be used as a foundation for implementing integration. Web Service support today is pervasive. They are supported by virtually all execution platforms. There are also plenty of tools on the market that provide generation of a service consumer skeleton based on the service provider's WSDL file, which makes implementation of the service consumer even simpler.

Implementing integrations based on Web Services that are exposed by existing applications is fairly straightforward. (See Figure 10-5.) The business component simply invokes a Web Service provided by the existing enterprise applications.

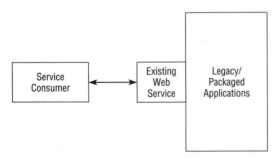

Figure 10-5 Implementing an integration service using existing Web Service

The following should be considered when using existing Web Services to implement integration:

■ There are a vast number of Web Service standards today. On one hand, this simplifies the use of Web Services — these standards provide a lot of capabilities. But it also makes implementation more complex because it requires a user to understand these standards and causes compatibility issues between different Web Service implementations, especially in the areas of attachments, security, and transactions.

■ Many vendors rushed into Web Service support purely because of its popularity, resulting in numerous implementations that are not integration-friendly. In some cases, object-oriented interfaces were directly exposed as Web Services, resulting in hundreds of inappropriate Web Services, each with tens of methods. In many cases, the granularity of the service operations is so low that it is not even applicable for integration, and it is necessary to combine several exposed Web Services in the business component implementation. Often these Web Services are modeled after UI interactions and require passing around "session ID" in the form of a proprietary SOAP header. Another approach (illustrated by the sidebar example of the useless WSDL file) is to use name/value pairs wrapped in a WSDL file for passing interaction parameters to and from the exposed Web Services. In this case, in addition to a WSDL file, a deep knowledge of the parameters and structure of invocation is required. Yet another approach (in response to the limitations of WSDL2Java support for complex XML schemas) is passing complex XML payloads as attachments. In this case, the WSDL file describes only "commands," although the payloads themselves are passed around as attachments that contain XML documents. In these cases, custom XML processing is required to implement integration services.

THE USELESS WSDL FILE

An example of "useless" WSDL is presented in the following listing (this is a real example encountered by the authors). In this WSDL file both input and output are defined as sequences of parameters, where every parameter is defined as a name/value pair. Although it is possible to generate the service consumer based on this WSDL file, it is impossible to use this consumer without complete knowledge of the service functionality, breaking the principles of loose coupling.

```
<?xml version="1.0" encoding="UTF-8"?>
<wsdl:definitions xmlns:wsdl="http://schemas.xmlsoap.org/wsdl/"
      xmlns:soap="http://schemas.xmlsoap.org/wsdl/soap/"
      xmlns:tns="http://www.example.org/useless/"
      xmlns:xsd="http://www.w3.org/2001/XMLSchema" name="useless"
      targetNamespace="http://www.example.org/useless/">
  <wsdl:types>
    <xsd:schema targetNamespace=http://www.example.org/useless/
          xmlns:xsd="http://www.w3.org/2001/XMLSchema">
        <xsd:complexType name="parameter">
        <xsd:element name="name" type="xsd:string"/>
        <xsd:element name="value" type="xsd:string"/>
      </xsd:complexType>
      <xsd:element name="OperationRequest">
```

```
            <xsd:complexType>
              <xsd:sequence>
                <xsd:element name="parameter" type="tns:parameter"/>
              </xsd:sequence>
            </xsd:complexType>
          </xsd:element>
          <xsd:element name="OperationResponse">
            <xsd:complexType>
              <xsd:sequence>
                <xsd:element name="parameter" type="tns:parameter"/>
              </xsd:sequence>
            </xsd:complexType>
          </xsd:element>
        </xsd:schema>
      </wsdl:types>
      <wsdl:message name="OperationRequest">
        <wsdl:part element="tns:OperationRequest" name="parameters"/>
      </wsdl:message>
      <wsdl:message name="OperationResponse">
        <wsdl:part element="tns:OperationResponse" name="parameters"/>
      </wsdl:message>
      <wsdl:portType name="useless">
        <wsdl:operation name="Operation">
          <wsdl:input message="tns:OperationRequest"/>
          <wsdl:output message="tns:OperationResponse"/>
        </wsdl:operation>
      </wsdl:portType>
      <wsdl:binding name="uselessSOAP" type="tns:useless">
        <soap:binding style="document"
                   transport="http://schemas.xmlsoap.org/soap/http"/>
        <wsdl:operation name="Operation">
          <soap:operation
                   soapAction="http://www.example.org/useless/
                   Operation"/>
          <wsdl:input>
            <soap:body use="literal"/>
          </wsdl:input>
          <wsdl:output>
            <soap:body use="literal"/>
          </wsdl:output>
        </wsdl:operation>
      </wsdl:binding>
      <wsdl:service name="useless">
        <wsdl:port binding="tns:uselessSOAP" name="uselessSOAP">
          <soap:address location="http://www.example.org/"/>
        </wsdl:port>
      </wsdl:service>
    </wsdl:definitions>
```

Using JCA/J2C Adapters to Implement Integration

J2EE Connector Architecture (J2C), formally Java Connector Architecture (JCA), is a standardized Java-based solution for integration. (For more information see "J2EE Connector Architecture" at `http://java.sun.com/j2ee/connector`.) The J2C specification defines three key functions: the Common Client Interface (CCI), which provides a uniform client API across multiple enterprise information systems; the Service Provider Interface (SPI), which defines system-level contracts for connection management, transaction management, and security between an application server and the adapter for a specific enterprise application; and a deployment and packaging protocol. The advantages of J2C are:

- It provides a uniform client programming model for accessing any application supported by the adapter.

- It tightly integrates with the application server in terms of security, transaction management, and connection pooling. The J2C SPI standardizes the following:

  - Connection management, standardizing the way that application servers establish and manage connections to an enterprise system, including support for connection pooling

  - Transaction management, specifying the way the application server's transaction manager can manage transactions across applications through connected applications

  - Security management allowing, J2C adapters to either propagate the current user, or impersonate another one for the application invocation

- It increases the number of adapters on the market and lowers their price by standardizing on implementations.

Enterprise systems for which J2C adapters are available today include Enterprise Resource Planning Systems (PeopleSoft, Baan, JD Edwards, and SAP), Transactions Monitors (CICS), Database Management Systems (Oracle, DB2, SQL server), and messaging systems (WebSphere MQ, Tibco Rendezvous).

Because a majority of J2EE application servers support J2C, it appears to be a very powerful mechanism for implementing integration when the business service implementation is based on a J2EE application server. In Figure 10-6, an adapter implements access to a legacy application, messaging middleware, or database. The business component is implemented as a set of the adapter API calls.

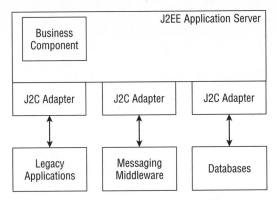

Figure 10-6 Implementing an integration service using J2C adapters

The following should be considered when using J2C adapters for implementing integration:

- Business components are limited to the J2EE platform. If the same integration is required from other platforms, J2C might be the wrong approach.

- Many adapters provide low-level APIs with granularity that is too small. A typical business component must use multiple adapter API calls in its implementation. For example, J2C adapters are often used to invoke CICS transactions on a mainframe. In this case, the size of the invocation/reply data is limited to 32k bytes (the CICS limitation). A typical J2C-based implementation includes data "chunking" and multiple adapter invocations.

- Many legacy applications support several different APIs, providing different access to their functionality. For example, with SAP R/3, there is the widely used high-level business API (BAPI), a lower-level (and no longer strategic) Remote Function Call (RFC) interface, as well as the intermediate document (IDoc) scheme for EDI-oriented interactions. When evaluating a J2C adapter for integration, it is necessary to make sure that it supports the required APIs.

- J2C adapters support only synchronous invocations. Although the use of bidirectional adapters allows for emulation of asynchronous invocations, in general, J2C adapters are not appropriate technology in these cases.

J2C adapters are a very powerful approach for implementing integration, allowing you to expose functionality and data from legacy applications in a "standard" programming model. The fact that there are widely available adapters for many applications makes this option even more attractive.

Using Web Service Wrappers to Implement Integration

Although this approach seems similar to using existing Web Services, there is a profound difference between the two. This one requires slightly more work because the actual Web Service has to be built, based on the existing implementations. However, this process provides significantly more flexibility; because you are building Web Services yourself, you can build them to suit your needs. This approach assumes that existing legacy applications are built using platforms that provide easy Web Service support; for example, J2EE application servers, the .NET environment, CICS v3.1, and so on, and the implementation is well componentized (for example, EJB-based, COM/.NET classes–based, or CICS transactions-based).

The overall implementation of integration is fairly straightforward. Components that need to be exposed are wrapped in the Web Service interface (usually using generation tools provided by a given platform). Business components can then be built based on the generated WSDL files. Figure 10-7 shows an example.

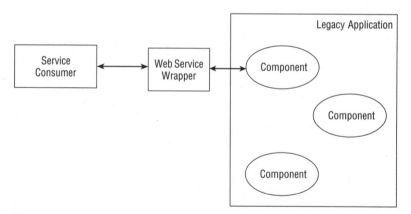

Figure 10-7 Implementing an integration service using Web Service wrappers

The following should be considered when using Web Service wrappers to implement integration:

- Existing component interfaces can be built using language classes with fairly complex structures; using collections makes them even more complex. When these classes are used for direct Web Service generation, this can lead to very complex WSDL files. Always try to simplify interface classes even if this requires some additional data mappings in the Web Service implementation

▪ Although WSDL supports multiple data types that can be used to support strongly typed interfaces, conversion between stringified representation of these parameters (XML representation) and typed representation is done in generated code, before the service implementation is invoked. As a result, such implementations are typically more fragile (e.g., service implementation code has no access to the data conversion errors and can't implement custom validation). One of the common practices to avoid this situation is to define the service interface (WSDL file) in terms of string variables and move type conversion to the service implementation.

▪ The fact that every component of the legacy application exposes its own interface does not necessarily mean that a method of a component can be invoked by itself. In a majority of cases, exposing the legacy application's components as Web Services requires the implementation of custom classes (within legacy application), to coordinate the invocation of the legacy components and expose the class as a stateless Web Service. An additional advantage of these custom classes is the ability to align the required granularity of the integration with the granularity of existing components.

The pervasive nature of Web Services today and the constant advances in their implementation makes this approach to integrations a very attractive option.

Using Direct Database Access to Implement Integration

In a lot of cases, the major purpose of integration services is to provide business services with data from the existing enterprise applications. In these cases, the simplest way to build an integration service is to read this data directly from the application's databases. With standardization of database access programming, for example using JDBC, this implementation becomes even simpler. (See "Java Database Connectivity" at `http://java.sun.com/javase/technologies/database` for more information.)

The implementation of integration in Figure 10-8 is similar to the J2C case. (JDBC implementations today are typically built on J2C.) Database access middleware provides access to the database to submit an appropriate query and returns results. Business components can orchestrate multiple database requests to achieve the required functionality.

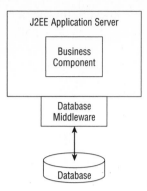

Figure 10-8 Implementing an integration service using direct database access

The following should be considered when using direct database access for integration implementations:

- Using stored procedures for database access is not recommended because of its poor portability. However, in the case of integration services, it might be a valuable option for reducing the number of database calls and improving database querying performance. Additionally, the use of stored procedures minimizes the impact of database changes on the business component.

- A variation of this implementation is to access multiple disparate databases from a single business component. This can be very useful for aggregating data among multiple legacy applications. This is one of the exceptions from the one-to-one correlation rule between business components and integration services.

- If business components that use direct database connectivity are widely used to implement business service, this could cause saturation of the database connections. A common solution to this problem is to combine this integration approach with the Web Service wrapping approach described previously. In this combined approach, database access is implemented inside a specialized integration service, which is exposed by using Web Services.

Using direct database access is a very powerful approach to implementing integration services when legacy applications expose mostly data, which is available in existing relational databases.

Using an Enterprise Service Bus to Implement Integration

In the typical large organization, there is always a mixture of the previously described approaches to integration. They require support for the different middleware platforms utilized for the different implementation approaches.

Fortunately, the ESB products described in Chapter 9 support the majority of the communication mechanisms discussed here, in a single product. This makes ESBs a very attractive platform for implementing integration.

A typical ESB implementation, as shown in Figure 10-9, supports multiple middleware options to connect to the bus, including popular MOM systems, J2C adapters, database connectivity, Web Services, and so on.

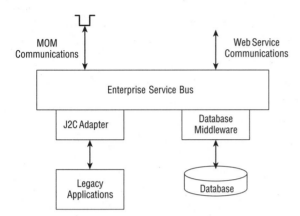

MOM
Communications

Web Service
Communications

Enterprise Service Bus

J2C Adapter

Database
Middleware

Legacy
Applications

Database

Figure 10-9 Using ESBs to connect to integration services

This approach combines the benefits of the standards introduced by Web Services with the features of traditional EAI products, while often avoiding their proprietary nature, implementation complexity, inflexibility, and vendor lock-in. ESBs are popular because:

- Their open architecture is based on the current and emerging standards (mostly Web Services) and technology.

- They are lightweight compared to Message Brokers or hubs.

- They support an incremental approach to integration rather than "big bang" investment in proprietary products.

- They support independent deployment of "services" based on the need of the particular solution.

- They provide built-in transformation capabilities.

Special Considerations for Implementing of Integration

According to Peter Cousins and Ivan Casanova, implementation of integration services requires the following special considerations (for more information see "Service-Oriented Integration: A Strategy Brief" [January 2004]):

- Data mapping
- Security

- Transactional support
- Versioning
- Large messages

We discuss these concerns and their typical implementation architectures here. Keep in mind that these concerns are common to all of the integration implementation approaches described in this chapter. Although solutions might be slightly different, depending on the implementation, these approaches have enough in common to describe them together.

Data Mapping in Integration

Because of the data fidelity issues in existing enterprise applications, data mapping was traditionally one of the main concerns of EAI implementations. This problem is still relevant for implementations of integration in SOA. Although enterprise business services are based on the enterprise semantic model (see Chapter 6 for more details), each legacy system is based on its own data model, which is typically different from the enterprise data model and from other data models. At some point, these proprietary data models have to be mapped to the enterprise data model.

Picking the appropriate place for this transformation is one of the main issues during integration service design and implementation. Based on the architecture of the business service implementation (refer to Figure 10-1), the following solutions are possible:

- **Implementing data mapping as part of the integration access implementation** — This solution works well when the Message Broker is used to implement the integration access. The Message Broker's data-mapping capabilities typically provide good support for these implementations. It also might be an option when using Web Service wrappers or direct database access (when it is implemented using stored procedures). In other integration access approaches, such a solution requires changes to the existing legacy implementation, which is never a desirable option.

- **Implementing data mapping as part of the message delivery** — This solution is possible for all of the integration service implementation approaches except J2C and direct database access (there is no message delivery per se in this case). A variation of this solution, especially in the case of an Enterprise Service Bus, is to use mediation for the data transformation, as shown in Figure 10-10.

- **Implementing data mapping as part of a business component that wraps the integration service invocation** — This is the most generic solution, applicable for any implementation of integration services.

Figure 10-10 Using mediations for service invocation

Regardless of exactly where you implement data mapping, there is the issue of how you implement the data mapping itself. Today, approaches to data transformation range from numerous visual mapping editors (included with many ESB implementations) to general-purpose programming languages (Java, C#, ESQL, etc.) supplementing these editors in the case of complex structural transformations.

Regardless of the actual implementation approach, transformations are typically coded by developers. There are multiple issues with this approach:

- The knowledge of the data, both enterprise semantic models and application data models, usually resides with business analysts, not developers. As a result, it is necessary for business analysts to somehow convey transformation definitions (requirements) to developers. This is traditionally done using Excel spreadsheets, which are far from ideal for requirements specification. As a result every company introduces their own, Excel-compatible notation for this purpose.

- Ambiguity in Excel notation often leads to the misinterpretation of transformation rules, resulting in prolonged development and testing cycles for transformation implementations.

- Because Excel-based definitions are not directly translated into code, but rather are interpreted by a person, it is extremely difficult to keep the two in synch. As a result, any transformation defect requires potentially lengthy investigation to determine whether it is a definition error, interpretation error (misunderstanding on the developer's part), or a code defect.

- It becomes extremely difficult to make changes in the transformation. Because transformation definitions are owned by the business analysts, they tend to make changes in the original spreadsheets, which go back to developers. Depending on the organization of the transformation code, the most "seemingly trivial" transformation changes can require significant modifications in the implementation code.

All of the above issues make implementation of data transformations (complex by themselves) even more difficult.

A better approach for implementing data transformation is to use a specialized tool that provides a clear separation between transformation design (that can be done directly by business analysts) and run-time execution (that is implemented as a standard library, available on the majority of execution platforms). In this case, the majority of data transformation/mapping changes can be made (and tested) directly in the transformation tool with minimal or no impact on the execution code. Additionally, such an approach provides maximum deployment flexibility. The integration architect can pick an appropriate place to run the transformation based on the overall architectural requirements.

Security Support for Integration

One of the characteristics of current enterprise application portfolios in the majority of enterprises is islands of security. The key goal of security for integration is to enable existing security infrastructures to interoperate. The solution to this problem lies in introducing a security layer that spans existing security infrastructures. Not surprisingly, this resembles the introduction of services as a rationalization layer on top of existing applications, to create a "standardized" enterprise business model. To achieve this goal, the enterprise needs a single identity management (federated identity management) and security policy infrastructure that governs the access to all participating enterprise applications. This means that security support for integration services should include the following:

NOTE This chapter covers only a thin slice of services security. For an overall approach to SOA security refer to Chapter 11.

- Accommodate heterogeneity (i.e., multiple application platforms)
- Provide security management and identity propagation/management across multiple security domains (internal, external, and business unit silos)
- Support multiple security credentials that can identify subjects (and optionally, their authorization credentials [for example, Kerberos, SAML, etc.])
- Support multiple transport protocols (HTTP/S, JMS, MQ)
- Provide a mechanism for maintaining the "thread of identity" across the integration services invocations

Implementation of security support for integration typically consists of two main parts:

- Propagating the user identity as a part of the invocation of integration services

- Converting the user identity (or its representation) into a form required by a specific legacy application

The implementation of identity propagation depends on the integration access and can vary significantly. For example, J2C adapters provide direct support for the user identity in the form of either configuration or direct API calls. In the case of direct database connections, on the other hand, specific user identity is rarely used (in order to enable connection pooling), and security has to be applied at the business component layer. Finally, in the case of MOM and Web Services–based implementations, user identity propagation is typically implemented on the message level (using, for example WS-Security and its various token profiles to extend the SOAP header of Web Service messages). There are several strategies for identity propagation for messaging security discussed in Chapter 11.

Conversion of user identity requires a centralized infrastructure for managing user identity (including identity conversion support) across the enterprise; for example, Tivoli Federated Identity Manager (TFIM). In Figure 10-11, the overall implementation of integration includes converting the current user's identity into a format required by the target enterprise application and passing this information as part of the invocation request. When user identity can't be directly propagated through the integration access (for example, a direct database connection), the business component can validate that the user is entitled to access a specific system/resource.

User identity (representation) conversion requests are usually done using "standard" Web Service requests (based on WS-Trust standard) and consequently can be implemented on virtually any platform.

Transactional Support in Integration

Transaction processing is a cornerstone of today's software technology, which makes distributed computing reliable and manageable. A transaction is

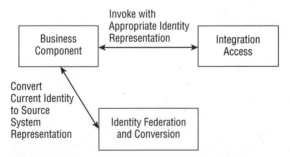

Figure 10-11 Centralized identity management

a consistent change of application(s) state that is governed by ACID (atomic, consistent, isolated, and durable) properties:

- **Atomic** — The transaction executes completely or not at all. Atomicity of transaction ensures that either all of the updates are performed or none is performed. Atomicity also ensures that underlying data returns to a known valid state following the failure, thus reducing the requirements for manual intervention during failures and restarts.

- **Consistent** — The transaction preserves the internal consistency of underlying data. This means that if a transaction is executed by itself on the underlying resources, which are initially consistent, at the end of the transaction these resources will be consistent again.

- **Isolated** — The transaction executes as if it were running alone, with no other transactions. An execution is isolated if its effect is the same as running transactions serially, one after another, with no overlap of execution of any of them.

- **Durable** — The transaction results are not lost in the case of software or hardware failures. So once a transaction is committed, its results are durably stored and can be used for automatic system recovery.

ACID transactions are usually implemented using transaction monitors (for example, Tuxedo, CICS, or Encina) or component platforms (for example, a J2EE application server or MTS). This means that support for ACID transactions requires coupling through the transactional environment, thus limiting interoperability and flexibility. In addition, some of the legacy applications do not support transactions at all. Finally, a requirement for ACID transaction implementations is resource locking for the duration of the transaction, which requires a guaranteed short execution time of services. Longer transaction times usually lead to worsening overall throughput of transactional resources.

ACID transactions, although perfectly appropriate for objects and components, are usually too restrictive for services.

In an attempt to overcome the limitations of the traditional two-phase commit protocol, several standards defining business transactions have been proposed and implemented.

Unfortunately, business transactions are supported only for Web Services and require SOAP enveloping, which is not always possible for integration and often requires specific support from the existing enterprise applications (which is also not a simple sell).

The most generic approach to the implementation of transactional support for integration is to use compensations, also called compensating transactions. This means creating appropriate "undo" methods as part of integration

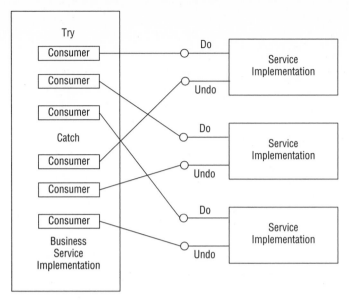

Figure 10-12 Implementing compensation for integration services

access and using `try/catch` blocks around individual or related groups of integration invocations. (See Figure 10-12.)

In this implementation, during normal functioning (try block), "do methods" on integration access are invoked to implement the desired functionality or access the desired data. If an error occurs (whether in the business component implementation or invocation of an integration access), control is transferred to the `catch` block to invoke the undo method, compensating for actions that have been executed so far.

The compensations described here do not really provide ACID properties (in particular isolation) but are easy to implement and are often "good enough" to solve specific business problems.

Versioning Integration

Versioning has always been an Achilles' heel of distributed systems, and services are no exception. A possible solution for service versioning, discussed in Chapter 9, is not applicable in the case of integration. The issue here is that integration relies on the existing enterprise applications that do not adhere to the versioning policies and practices. It is rarely possible to have more than one version of the existing application running simultaneously. The typical approach is to replace the older version of the application with a newer one. As a result, it is rarely possible to have multiple versions of an integration deployed simultaneously.

Because the implementation of a business service never uses the integration access directly, but rather does so through the business component, this business component is a natural unit of versioning. If the integration access changes, these changes can be encapsulated within the implementation of the business component, assuming that its interface and characteristics do not change.

Dealing with Large Messages

When integration is based on Web Services or MOM middleware, the size of the invocation payload can have a significant impact on both invocation performance and the scalability of the business service implementation. The issue here is twofold:

> **NOTE** When we say large we mean several megabytes. For example, we have seen an integration service retrieve an insurance policy from the legacy system, which can return up to 20 megabytes of data.

- Large size messages create additional strain on the network and underlying middleware. For example, in the case of MQ, the limit of the supported message size must be increased explicitly, which increases the toll on the resources used by the MQ infrastructure. In the case of HTTP transport, middleware splits messages into 4 Kb "chunks" for delivery, with the "Ack" message, accompanying every "chunk." As a result, there is severe (nonlinear) degradation in the message delivery performance as the message size grows. Message encryption can worsen the situation by adding additional CPU load and performance degradation due to encryption/decryption operations.

- Large message size is also one of the reasons for peak memory utilization on the service consumer. There are typically several representations of the same payload, for example, XML string, OO representation, and so on, which have to be present in memory simultaneously. As the size of the message grows, the load on the garbage collector (Java and/or C#) and memory paging increases, thus slowing down the implementations.

One of the possible solutions to this problem is "chunking" of the service payload, replacing, for example, a single inquiry method that returns the whole insurance policy with the multiple partial inquiry methods each returning parts of the policy. Although this solution seems like a good one, it does not always work. It can contradict the way the enterprise system that provides this functionality works.

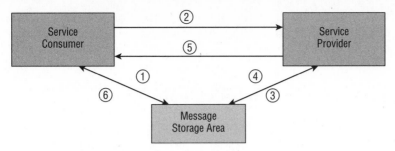

Figure 10-13 Store-and-forward pattern for large messages

A different approach to solving this problem is a variation of a store-and-forward pattern shown in Figure 10-13.

This pattern introduces an intermediate storage area for passing around large payloads. It allows the message sender (consumer and/or provider) to control whether to send corresponding data as part of the message, or through the storage, or a combination of both. A request/response interaction between a consumer and a provider looks as follows:

1. (Optional) The consumer stores a complete or partial data payload in the message storage area.

2. The consumer sends a request to the service provider, including a complete, partial, or no data payload. In these two cases, the consumer provides a reference to the message storage area location, where actual data exists.

3. (Optional) If the request contains a reference to the message storage area, the service provider picks up all of the required data from the message storage area.

4. (Optional) The provider stores a complete or partial data payload in the message storage area.

5. The provider sends a reply to the service consumer, including a complete, partial, or no data payload. In these two cases, the consumer provides a reference to the message storage area location, where actual data exists.

6. (Optional) If the reply contains a reference to the message storage area, the service consumer picks up all of the required data from the message storage area.

This pattern effectively combines a Web Service or MOM-based integration with the power and flexibility of the direct data access approach. Its use allows for piecemeal processing of both request and response data (in the message storage area), combined with the existing services' granularity, and typically requires significantly fewer changes in the existing legacy applications compared to chunking.

Data Virtualization and Enterprise Data Bus

In typical SOA implementations, a large portion of the integration supports access to existing enterprise data. Aligning this data integration with the business services is often a challenge for large-scale SOA implementations.

Although typical SOA implementations hide enterprise data behind service interfaces, the following data access issues must still be resolved:

- **Consolidation of data among multiple applications** — Today's enterprise data is typically scattered across multiple siloed applications. This means that enterprise data access from business services requires the invocation of multiple data integration services, and then the correct alignment and consolidation of data from them. It is also necessary to ensure the propagation of data changes to all applications that rely on this data.

- **Ownership of enterprise data by services** — The foundation of the modern service definition technique — functional decomposition — is not easily mapped to enterprise data. For example, the notion of the customer (and corresponding data) is usually shared between multiple functional services. The problem is that functional and data decompositions are driven by completely different rules. Functional decomposition is defined based on enterprise business processes, whereas data decomposition is defined based on the enterprise domain data taxonomy. As a result, aligning the enterprise data with enterprise services becomes a daunting task.

- **Business service interface definitions** — Because business service invocations are always remote, their design strives toward large-granularity interfaces, aiming at minimizing the amount of network traffic. Data access, on the other side, can require both high and fine granularity of interfaces, depending on the data access requirements. Finally, data access typically implements pure CRUD (create, read, update, delete), whereas enterprise services implement meaningful business interfaces, such as rate policy, and so on.

> **NOTE** Although this is true in general, there are plenty of exceptions. There are situations where CRUD-type business services are well aligned with the business functionality; for example, `GetPoliciesForACustomer`(customer), is an example of a business meaningful CRUD service.

A possible solution to this problem is a complete separation of data access from service access through a logical Enterprise Data Bus.

Similarly to the way that the Enterprise Service Bus "virtualizes" access to business services, *the Enterprise Data Bus allows for virtualization of access to enterprise data* (refer to Chapter 2 for a discussion of data access virtualization). The role of the Enterprise Data Bus is to provide direct access from any service to any piece of enterprise data (see Figure 10-14.)

The origins of the Enterprise Data Bus can be traced back to federated database technology — virtualization of access to disparate databases in the enterprise. Unfortunately, this technology is rarely applicable to SOA implementations. The issue here is that existing applications effectively control enterprise data access through the implementation of their data access and validation logic. Bypassing these applications and going directly to databases requires reimplementation of this logic, which is typically not cost-effective. As a result, data virtualization is typically implemented using an integration layer. (Refer to Figure 10-2.)

Effective implementation of the Enterprise Data Bus requires separation between integration that provides enterprise data access and integration that provides enterprise functional capabilities. Considering that both data and functional integration get and return enterprise data, the most straightforward approach is to consider all of the integrations as data access integration. For example, integration to the legacy rate policy implementation provides a typical case of functional integration. On the other hand, it can be viewed as a consumer of policy information and a producer of rate information.

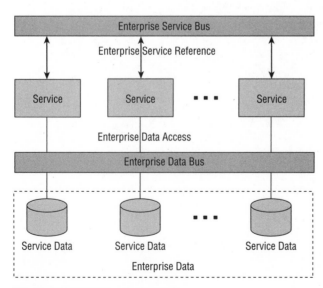

Figure 10-14 Enterprise Data Bus

NOTE Additional rationale for this approach is that regardless of the type of integration, data or functional, both input and output data needs to be transformed between the domain data model and the legacy data representation. Treating any integration as a data access allows for consolidation of this transformation, in addition to the consolidation of the data access.

This leads to extension of the layered enterprise architecture for SOA presented at Figure 10-2 with an additional layer added, as shown in Figure 10-15.

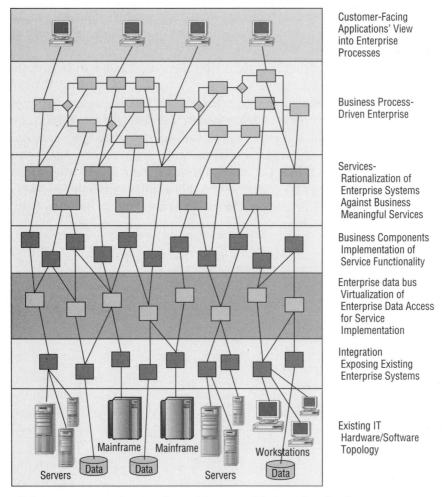

Customer-Facing Applications' View into Enterprise Processes

Business Process-Driven Enterprise

Services-Rationalization of Enterprise Systems Against Business Meaningful Services

Business Components Implementation of Service Functionality

Enterprise data bus Virtualization of Enterprise Data Access for Service Implementation

Integration Exposing Existing Enterprise Systems

Existing IT Hardware/Software Topology

Mainframe   Mainframe   Workstations

Servers   Data   Data   Servers   Data

Figure 10-15 Layered Enterprise Architecture with data virtualization

The additional layer — data virtualization — provides access to the enterprise data contained in either enterprise applications or their subordinated databases. It also modifies implementation of the business component layer; in this implementation, it no longer contains "wrapper" components. Business components are composed only of the components that implement service functionality based on existing application functionality, and data that is accessible through the Enterprise Data Bus. The advantages of such an architecture are:

- Explicit separation of concerns between implementation of the business service functionality (business logic) and enterprise data support logic effectively creates an abstraction layer, shielding the business functionality from details of enterprise data/functionality access.

- By encapsulating all of the access to enterprise data/functionality, the Enterprise Data Bus provides a single place for all of the transformations between the domain data model and the data models of enterprise applications.

- Because any service implementation can have access to any of the enterprise data it requires, you can significantly reduce coupling between services — service invocations contain only data references (key), which change extremely rarely, while the actual data access is implemented by the service itself. This means that if the service implementation requires additional data for its processing, it can access it directly without affecting its consumers.

Two possible approaches to the Enterprise Data Bus implementations are:

- Specialized servers, for example, the IBM Information Server
- Providing support for both direct database access and integration, and distributed data caching, for example IBM's Object Grid

Summary

This chapter defined integration as a foundation of successful SOA implementation. It described general integration challenges and showed different approaches for bringing integration and SOA together.

It then introduced a precise definition of integration, the relationship to business services, and the role in business service implementation, including different approaches to implementing integration, among them: MOM,

Message Broker, J2C, data access, and two different Web Service solutions. It also discussed the main implementation considerations for each approach. It highlighted the role of the ESB as a universal connectivity middleware solution, which simplifies the implementation of integration.

Next, it discussed major architectural concerns for implementing integration services, including data mapping, security, transactional support, versioning, and large message impact, and presented possible solutions for each problem.

Finally, it introduced the concept of the Enterprise Data Bus, to unify and encapsulate different approaches to implementing integration.

11

SOA Security

If you think technology can solve your security problems, then you don't understand the problems, and you don't understand the technology.
— **Bruce Schneier**

In the very brief history of SOA architecture and design, security is one aspect that is sometimes overlooked. A vital piece of the SOA puzzle, security consists of a series of requirements that demands a well-thought-out plan, design, and implementation. No specific technology is a silver bullet — a successful SOA security solution can only be accomplished by understanding the foundational principles of information security and mastering SOA architecture and design. Anyone who has such knowledge can understand that it is essential to adopt a security strategy for SOA and a security architecture roadmap early on. A smart SOA security strategy allows business applications to meet the needs of organizations and their business partners by incorporating the classic security goals of authentication, authorization, integrity, confidentiality, non-repudiation, auditing, and availability.

The security challenges in SOA are complicated by the state of today's business practices. This is the age of dynamic business partners, whereby organizations share information on a short- and long-term basis with other enterprises, and as a result, networks have become porous, blurring the lines of the definition between "internal" and "external" networks. Gone are the days of monolithic applications protected only by corporate firewalls. Instead, organizations are moving toward a policy-centric SOA model enforced at the application and service levels, providing security between clients and services in a multi-domain environment. As a result, an organization must adopt an agile SOA security strategy that fits this model, and architectures must be adaptable enough to change as policies and relationships change.

This chapter is aimed at the SOA architect and designer; it provides a focus on security fundamentals and key standards, and offers practical strategies and blueprints for securing the components of an enterprise SOA. It is divided into five sections, and each section builds on the foundation of the preceding ones to provide a clear understanding of SOA security principles, standards, and practical tips:

- Key security terminology, common security goals found in SOA-based projects, and the security challenges related to achieving these goals

- Major standards that can help you achieve SOA security goals

- Guidance for using standards and different security methodologies in various SOA security scenarios

- A case study providing an example of how to use the concepts in this book

- A roadmap and common-sense practical advice for achieving success in SOA-based projects

SOA Security Goals and Fundamentals

To plan a sound SOA security strategy, SOA architects must have an understanding of information security fundamentals and how they can be applied to build SOA solutions. Many security goals require some explanation, and understanding SOA security standards and best practices is dependent on understanding security terminology. This section defines an information security vocabulary, giving examples, scenarios, and challenges from real-world SOA deployments. Because there are entire books dedicated to these concepts, this section is simply meant to be a "bird's-eye view" introduction, focusing on the scope of what the SOA architect needs to know. The terms defined in this section are important for the discussions of SOA security in the subsequent sections of this chapter.

Authentication

Authentication means validating the identity of a subject. A subject can be a user, a Web Service, a computer, or an application. Authentication is the first step in access control. To enforce an access control policy, a system needs to initially identify the subject with some level of assurance. Mutual authentication is two-way authentication, and proves the identity of both parties involved in communication, providing both sides with identity assurance.

Several mechanisms are used for authentication: Some common ones are username/password login, digital certificate authentication, and the use of a biometric device. User-facing solutions commonly use cryptographic protocols, such as SSL/TLS with its built-in authentication mechanisms (digital certificate authentication or username/password), and REST-based point-to-point SOA security solutions also build on that model. SSL is a fine protocol, but it is not the silver bullet for every problem. From an SOA perspective, it is important to realize that the authentication capabilities of SSL/TLS can be used for mutual or one-way authentication between two points only, but they do nothing to provide assurance of identities beyond two points. Figure 11-1 illustrates this point.

In Figure 11-1, a user authenticates him- or herself to a portal via digital certificate authentication over SSL and then clicks on a portal application. Based on the user's request, the portal then authenticates itself to a Web Service, using digital certificate authentication over SSL, and sends a request for a resource. Each point in the solution has strong assurance of the identity of each party with which it communicates. However, these strong authentication mechanisms between each point provide no assurance of the identity of the initial user to the final Web Service in Figure 11-1. This is a simple example with only three points, and the point we are making may seem subtle. An important concept to understand is that there are commonly many intermediary services between a user's front-end application and the final service in the life cycle of a message request, and in such requests it is often important to provide some level of assurance of the end user's identity. Point-to-point security protocols such as SSL may be a piece of a security solution for SOA, but such protocols must be complemented by other security mechanisms for end-to-end solutions.

The last example makes an important point: in end-to-end SOA-based messaging solutions, it is important to realize that there are multiple parties

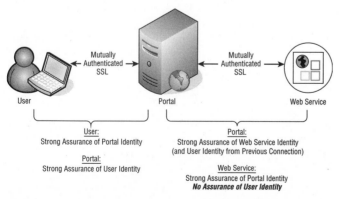

Figure 11-1 Identity establishment in point-to-point security

that may need to be authenticated in message requests. For every message that is sent, there are usually two parties involved with the request: the *message sender* and the *ultimate end user*. The message sender (the service consumer) works on behalf of the ultimate end user, sending requests to services. It is important to understand that in most situations, services may need a high level of assurance of the identities of both of these parties. To enforce its access control policy, the service may need a level of trust for the sender of the message (trusting the sender not to manipulate the data in the request, for example), and the service needs a high level of assurance of who the ultimate end user is. We demonstrate this concept by walking you through an example in Figure 11-2.

Figure 11-2, shows a very simple example of a user "Alice" authenticating herself to a portal that sends a request to a service. In this situation, a "sender-vouches" approach is used, meaning that the portal "vouches for" the identity of the end user that it authenticates in its requests to services. This is one method of *identity propagation* used in some of the WS-Security token profiles, where the identity of a subject is propagated to services and applications in the enterprise to achieve Single Sign-On (SSO). For the service to trust the identity of that vouched-for end user in Figure 11-2, it must have a high degree of trust in the portal that vouches for the end user. Therefore, the service must not only be able to authenticate the portal in this situation, but it must trust the portal to accurately vouch for its end users. These two types of trust (trust of message sender identity and trust of message sender to vouch) should be treated differently and separately. Obviously, this is a simple example of identity propagation, and it demonstrates the importance of understanding that in some scenarios both the message sender and the ultimate end user may need to be authenticated. As you might imagine, identity propagation can get even more challenging as more intermediaries are added between the end user's application and the final service in the

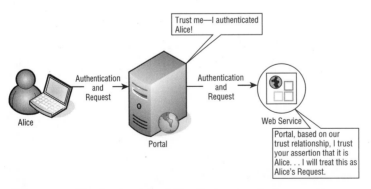

Figure 11-2 Simple example of identity propagation

message chain. Other approaches and challenges in identity propagation are discussed in detail in the "SOA Security Blueprints" section of this chapter.

Providing a solution for authentication in your SOA typically means providing or integrating with identity management infrastructure that supports authentication, and utilizing a messaging solution that adequately provides proof of identity. Authentication is one of the most important aspects of providing security — the mechanisms you choose dictate how flexible your SOA is. It is important that you stay away from proprietary implementations and adopt accepted and broadly used standards that allow you to integrate with the systems and products that your organization has now — and the ones they will have in the future.

Authorization and Access Control

Authorization means determining what a subject has permission to do, and this is the second step in access control. After the subject's identity is validated (which was covered in the previous section), systems must determine the subject's authorization credentials and must compare them with expressed authorization policy for enterprise resources. Because authorization is the foundation of access control, and as there are so many authorization strategies and mechanisms that can be used in SOA solutions, this section covers much ground.

Architectural flexibility for authorization in a Service-Oriented Architecture is usually achieved by logically separating duties into Policy Decision Points (PDPs) and Policy Enforcement Points (PEPs). A PDP is the point at which access control decisions are made, based on an expressed access control policy and a subject's authorization credentials. The enforcement of the decision is delegated to a PEP, as shown in Figure 11-3. Some standards, such as the eXtensible Access Control Markup Language (XACML), discussed later in this chapter, decompose the policy model further into Policy Administration Points (PAPs) that create policy and the Policy Information Points (PIPs) that query attributes for subjects requesting access to resources. There are many

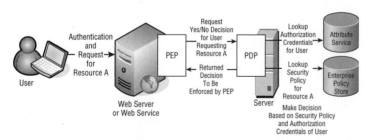

Figure 11-3 Example of PDP/PEP interaction for access control

architectural strategies for how PDPs and PEPs can work together, which are covered in the "SOA Security Blueprints" section of this chapter.

Two Types of Access Control—DAC and MAC

Authorization can be separated into two types of access control: Discretionary Access Control (DAC) and Mandatory Access Control (MAC). *Discretionary Access Control* restricts access based on permissions, roles, attributes, and groups to which subjects belong. This type of access control is common in commercial-based SOA systems. *Mandatory Access Control* is more commonly found in government-based systems and is an access control mechanism that restricts access based on the security clearances and formal accesses of subjects and the security labels on the resources. To enforce MAC, the data itself must be labeled with security markings containing security labels and dissemination controls, and the enforcement points must be able to determine the clearances and formal access controls of the subjects requesting the resources.

In SOA solutions that enforce DAC, system resource policies are expressed referencing global enterprise authorization credentials, and PDPs determine the authorization credentials of subjects when they request access to resources. Figure 11-3 showed one simple example, where a central PDP looked up the authorization credentials of a subject and the policy of the requested resource, returning the decision to a PEP, which enforced the discretionary access control policy.

In SOA-based systems that enforce MAC, standard XML markup in the payload of SOAP messages is used to express the security label of the data. Figure 11-4 shows a simple example: A request is sent to a service that queries data that is labeled with a security classification and dissemination controls. Inspecting the response, the service's PDP determines the user's formal access

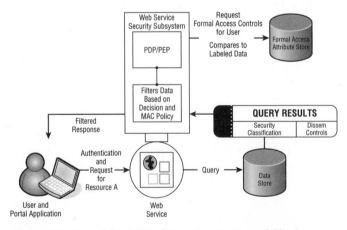

Figure 11-4 Example of Mandatory Access Control filtering

authorization credentials, compares it to data's security label, and the PDP then makes an authorization decision, resulting in the PEP filtering the results into data that only the end user has permission to see.

Role-Based Access Control (RBAC) is a common credentialing strategy used in DAC enforcement. Using RBAC, security roles are defined and assigned to subjects, resource access control policies are expressed using security roles, and PDPs make decisions based on the roles of subjects and the policies of resources.

Attribute-Based Access Control (ABAC) is a strategy similar to RBAC, but it utilizes security attributes rather than security roles. Many systems have moved to the ABAC model because of the desire to separate a user's duties (roles) from other types of credentials that could be used in access control systems. An ABAC credentialing strategy enables both Mandatory and Discretionary Access Control in SOA. In such a solution, a trusted enterprise attribute service may store and expose subject authorization credentials such as role, group, security clearance, and citizenship as attributes. In many ABAC-based SOA systems, RBAC roles are included as authorization attributes.

Predetermined Authorization Decision-Based Access Control (PADBAC) is an access control strategy defined in this book where access control policy (either DAC or MAC) is used in making an authorization decision for a subject accessing a resource, and where those digitally signed authorization decisions are distributed to the subjects as "tickets" for future access. For example, a laundry service may issue an authorization decision to a user when the user drops off his or her laundry; for instance, "Parker Cullinan is authorized to pick up his laundry (bin #228)." Later, that signed authorization decision would be presented by Parker Cullinan to the laundry service in order to pick up his laundry. PADBAC can be used to model such real-world situations and is discussed later in this chapter (in "SOA Security Blueprints").

Many service security standards revolve around authorization — Security Assertion Markup Language (SAML), XACML, and WS-Trust are just a few examples of standards that provide many of the fundamentals of authorization in an SOA. Both standards and authorization strategies are discussed at length throughout this chapter.

Federated Identity and Cross-Enterprise Access

Federated identity is a security goal where a policy arrangement is made among multiple security domains that allows users to use the same identification data to access resources in partner security domains. The collection of partner enterprises is called a *federation*, and this security goal provides users of this federation the capability of SSO to applications throughout the federation. In an effective federated identity solution, partners share an explicit mutual trust pertaining to the way the identity of users is validated and how authorization of resources occur. A key point is that in such solutions, a resource provider in a partner enterprise relies on an externally managed identity, rather than creating another locally managed identity for the subject requesting access. This reliance relieves the burden of cost and management complexity.

The success of federated identity is dependent upon the ability to share a rich and commonly understood set of claims between an *identity provider* (the organization vouching for the identity) and a *relying party* (the organization providing access to resources). The notion of identity federation is broad and evolving, and as a result, there are certain situations where information besides identity is federated. In practice, access control in a federation can occur in multiple ways: Partners can grant certain accesses to users from one enterprise, based on their identity in their host organization (true identity federation); partners can assign everyone from a host organization certain authorization credentials (enterprise-based policy and not really federated identity); or access can be granted based on authorization credentials of the user, and the federation arrangement can include a translation of mappings of authorization credentials between the two organizations (federated authorization). In practice, there are protocols for both *browser-based SSO*, where browser clients and web applications use standard HTTP extensions and redirections for identity federation, and *service-based SSO*, intended for identity federation between services.

One important concept for the SOA architect to understand is the dynamic nature of relationships in a federation. Although it is common for federated identity partnerships to be long-lived, it is important to realize that the new age of dynamic business partners requires a more fluid model. The way organizations do business is complex, and if you are going to be able to share information successfully, your architecture must adapt to these business processes. In sharing information in these partnerships, it is vital that each organization protects its information assets. A flexible SOA, therefore, can utilize federated identity technology to allow *dynamic communities of interest* to share data. Figure 11-5 shows such a model, where enterprises may join multiple federations at any given time. To meet the authentication and authorization needs of partners in this dynamic environment, organizations must adapt cross-enterprise access policies, and they must adopt a policy-centric model for enforcing access control, utilizing open standards that maximize interoperability.

Standards related to federated identity have been evolving. There are currently two specifications in OASIS revolving around federated identity. In 2005, OASIS finalized the SAML 2.0 standard, which unified previous specifications of identity federation, such as Shibboleth and the Liberty Alliance Identity Federation Framework (ID-FF). The Liberty Alliance also released the Identity Web Services Framework (ID-WSF), which relies heavily on

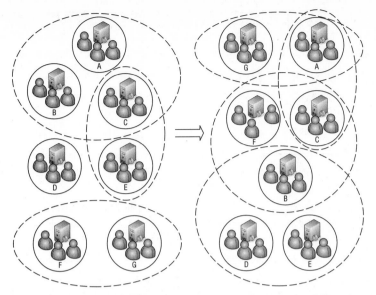

Figure 11-5 Identity federation between dynamic communities of interest

SAML 2.0 for Web Services-based SSO. In 2007, OASIS created a committee to drive the direction of WS-Federation, a proposed standard that relies on other WS-* standards, such as WS-Policy and WS-Trust. Although WS-Federation and SAML had different design goals, there are some overlaps, and it remains to be seen how the two federation standards merge or interact. For now, many vendors have adopted both models in their products. These standards are discussed later in this chapter.

SECURITY TERMINOLOGY AT A GLANCE

This section covers a lot of ground, focusing on the fundamental goals of information security, applying them to the SOA enterprise. Each of the subsections (Authentication, Authorization and Access Control, Federated Identity and Cross-Enterprise Access, Confidentiality, Integrity, and Non-Repudiation) not only define these terms in depth, but also provide the context for how these goals are achieved in SOA. For convenience, we have decided to also list some of the key terms and acronyms defined in this section, with abbreviated, simple-to-read definitions for your reference.

◆ **ABAC** — Attribute-Based Access Control

◆ **Access Control** — Providing control to a resource, based on a subject's proven identity, the subject's authorization credentials, and the resource's access policy

(continued)

SECURITY TERMINOLOGY AT A GLANCE *(continued)*

◆ **Authentication** — Validating the identity of a subject

◆ **Authorization** — Determining if a subject has permission to do something

◆ **Confidentiality** — The security goal aimed at hiding sensitive information, done with encryption

◆ **DAC** — Discretionary Access Control

◆ **Federated identity** — A security goal where a policy arrangement is made among multiple security domains that allows users to use the same identification data to access resources in partner security domains.

◆ **Integrity** — The assurance that data has not been altered in transit or at rest, usually achieved by message digests, hash codes, or as a side effect of a digital signature.

◆ **MAC** — Mandatory Access Control

◆ **Non-repudiation** — Strong assurance that a subject signed a message (legal proof that can be validated by a third party) achieved through a digital signature.

◆ **PADBAC** — Predetermined Authorization Decision-Based Access Control

◆ **RBAC** — Role-Based Access Control

Confidentiality

When sensitive information is transmitted between authorized parties, it is important that this information not be seen in transit by eavesdroppers. *Confidentiality* is the security goal aimed at hiding sensitive information, and this is done with encryption. In the encryption process, a plaintext message is scrambled with a cryptographic algorithm to produce a ciphertext message. Using a key (or shared secret), the intended recipient can decrypt the data. There are many different cryptographic algorithms, symmetric (secret key) and asymmetric (public key) algorithms that can be used to provide different levels of protection for data.

In an enterprise SOA solution, there may be certain elements of messages that are confidential and require a level of encryption. Many higher-level protocols, such as SSL/TLS, provide bulk encryption (and data integrity) between two points. If bulk encryption satisfies your security requirements, this may be sufficient. However, there are scenarios in SOA solutions where bulk encryption protocols do not offer the correct solution, as shown in Figure 11-6.

In Figure 11-6, the bulk encryption protocol provides confidentiality between every point in the solution. However, if there is one element of the original

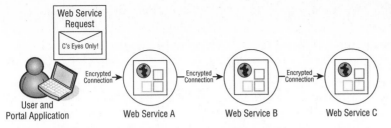

Figure 11-6 When end-to-end confidentiality is needed

message that is only intended for Web Service C in this example, the bulk encryption protocol does nothing to satisfy this security requirement. It certainly ensures that only Web Service A, B, and C can see the message, but it does not cryptographically prevent Web Services A and B from inspecting the part of the message only intended for Web Service C. Luckily, the W3C XML Encryption standard can be used in XML-based messaging for achieving this level of confidentiality, and it can be used with both WS-Security SOAP messaging and REST-based Web Services.

In creating a solution to satisfy confidentiality requirements, there are many other things to consider: key management for distributing keys, ciphers to use, cryptographic protocols that provide these services, and the amount of encryption necessary to achieve enterprise security requirements. A major challenge involves the establishment of secret keys used for encrypted exchanges. Because public key cryptography is slow and computationally expensive, it is often used for key negotiation (the establishment of secret keys used for data encryption), rather than for the data encryption itself. Standards such as SSL provide this functionality by establishing session keys for long-lived HTTPS sessions, where many message exchanges may use the session key for the confidentiality of the conversation between two parties. Standards such as WS-Security SOAP messaging, however, have no concept of "sessions," and this is problematic when there is a requirement for long-lived exchanges between parties, because slow secret key negotiation with public key encryption typically has to occur for each message (for example, between a portal and an enterprise service that are constantly communicating). As a result, many implementers can achieve success by combining WS-Security SOAP messaging with SSL between two points. WS-SecureConversation, an OASIS standard in 2007, is also used to establish keys for long-lived sessions using the WS-Trust model.

Integrity

It is sometimes important to make sure that data (especially for service transactions) has not been tampered with in transit or at rest. Validating a message's *integrity* means using techniques that prove that the message has not been altered. Because it is possible that message injection, IP spoofing, and packet tampering can occur on TCP/IP networks, many applications may require the use of digital signatures, Message Authentication Codes, or hash algorithms to validate the integrity of the data.

In SOA enterprises, there may be integrity concerns between every service consumer and provider. The recipient of every message should have a high level of assurance that the message has not been altered by a malicious third party. In addition, the recipient of each message needs to have assurance that a valid message with integrity is not being *replayed* by a malicious third party. In a replay attack, an attacker captures valid messages between two parties, and resends these messages to the recipient at a later time, pretending to be the message sender. A message requesting "Please withdraw $100 out of my bank account" may be digitally signed by the owner of the bank account, providing integrity (and non-repudiation), but unless there are mechanisms that prevent it from being replayed, an attacker could replay that message until the user's bank account is empty! For this reason, successful secure messaging protocols use integrity mechanisms to combine messages with a time stamp and message identifier, guaranteeing the integrity of the date and time the message was sent, the message ID, and the message itself. If an integrity check of the time stamp or message ID fails, if the time stamp has expired, if a message with the same message identifier has already been received, or if the message itself has been altered, the message is rejected by the recipient. The mechanisms in the WS-Security SOAP messaging specification provide integrity mechanisms, in addition to preventing replay attacks.

The SSL/TLS protocol can provide the necessary message integrity between any two points in your enterprise, as it combines integrity mechanisms with confidentiality and authentication. This may satisfy security requirements between two points in your SOA, but there may be some scenarios where this is not sufficient. As discussed in the "Authentication" section of this chapter, SSL is a point-to-point security solution; it does not provide assurance beyond two points. This is an issue regarding authentication, but it is also a very important issue to understand regarding data integrity. Figure 11-7 shows the dilemma, where SSL protects the integrity (and confidentiality) of the data between each point, but does not ensure that the intermediary services do not manipulate the data before passing it on.

Figure 11-7 shows a business scenario where there is a company's business transaction service that brokers transactions to the correct services, such as accounting, contracts, and human resources. In the case of payroll transactions, the company's business transaction service routes requests to an accounting service that updates records, and that then forwards requests to a payroll service. In this case, Bob from Accounting issues a request via a web

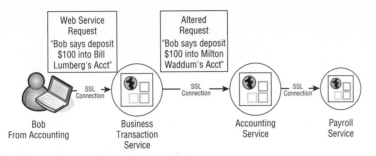

Figure 11-7 When end-to-end integrity is needed

portal to deposit $100 into the account of an employee, Bill Lumberg. Between the user's client application and the business transaction service is a mutually authenticated SSL connection, ensuring confidentiality, data integrity, and identification of the identities of each party. In fact, between every point in Figure 11-7 there are mutually authenticated SSL connections, ensuring this level of security between each point. As you can see from Figure 11-7, however, the security provided by SSL doesn't prevent one of the Web Services from altering the user's original request — even though SSL protects data from being altered in transit, it does not prevent one of the nodes in the solution from modifying the request before propagating the request on to the next service. Indeed, Figure 11-7 shows that the compromised business transaction service alters the user's original request, resulting in the wrong employee getting a payroll deposit.

The W3C XML Signature standard can be used as part of the data integrity solution for solving the problem demonstrated in Figure 11-7, because a by-product of a digital signature is a hash code used to validate integrity. If the user's original request is digitally signed, and that signed request is propagated to all of the nodes in the solution, this ensures the integrity of the original request. If any Web Service attempts to alter the message, it fails an integrity check. At the same time, mechanisms must also be used with XML Signature to prevent the replay of the request, and there are some potential pitfalls with signatures that are covered in the next section. XML Signature can be used in XML-based messaging, and can therefore be used with both WS-Security SOAP messaging and REST-based Web Services.

Much about providing integrity is straightforward, but some of the cases addressed in this section (related to message replay and integrity in end-to-end solutions) are more subtle. It is important, therefore, for architects to look at SOA usage scenarios and security requirements ahead of time in order to prevent these attacks.

Integrity is usually a key requirement in business, commercial, and government SOA initiatives, and is therefore very important to understand.

Non-Repudiation

Non-repudiation is the side effect of digitally signing a message, and it is legal proof that a subject signed a message. A digital signature cryptographically ties the identity of the signer to the contents of the data being signed, which is an important concept in SOA-based messaging. Because digital signatures are based on public key cryptography, the sender of the signed message can not successfully deny the fact that he signed the message. Using public key cryptography, the signature can be mathematically proven to be done by the signer of the message, because of the nature of the cryptographic operation performed with the sender's private key. Because of the size of the keys involved, digital signature validation produces a very high level of assurance that a message signer indeed signed the message.

The W3C XML Signature standard is a W3C standard used for providing integrity and non-repudiation, and it is used to sign XML documents and elements of XML documents. It can be used in REST-based Web Services as well as WS-Security SOAP Messaging. Often, digital signatures are used in establishing trust in challenge-response scenarios for authenticating service consumers for Web Service requests. A message sender may send a digitally signed message to a service, providing strong assurance of the sender's identity, strong assurance that the data was not altered in transit (data integrity), and cryptographically tying the sender to the data.

Due to the strong level of assurance provided by digital signatures, it is important that anyone implementing SOA messaging solutions realize the potential dangers in the way that signatures can be applied and used. If an XML element is signed without stating its conditions of use or without being bound to a specific request, this could be very dangerous. For example, a voting authority could sign an assertion that says "This is Joey Bush" for a user named Joey Bush to use for voting purposes in the 2008 election. If, however, the authority doesn't include an expiration date on that assertion (2008) and an explicit condition of use (voting), anyone could use that signed assertion in a way for which it was not intended. Without specific constraints, the assertion in this example meant to be used in a voting application could be used to empty Joey's bank account or run up Joey's credit card purchases. For this reason, it is common practice in SOA messaging to explicitly state constraints and conditions of use in signed data, and when identity assertions are involved, the constrained assertion should be cryptographically bound with the request by a digital signature, making sure that the assertion is not used for another purpose. It is important, therefore, to use digital signatures wisely.

There are many other subtleties and potential pitfalls related to the use of digital signatures in SOA environments. SOAP-based messaging standards, such as WS-Security SOAP Messaging, SAML, and others, document these risk areas well and provide a framework for avoiding such issues, but it is often easy for the errant software developer to introduce something potentially harmful. Obviously, developers creating XML messaging solutions for REST-based services need to be extremely careful with digital signatures, and should carefully look at warnings and trouble areas documented in SOAP-based messaging protocols such as the OASIS WS-Security SOAP Messaging standard.

Web Service Security Standards and Specifications

There are a large number of Web Service security standards, and we have chosen to focus on the major standards that we feel are most important for the SOA architect to understand. Most of the specifications in this section are accepted and well-established standards that are used throughout industry. A few other specifications were included because they are well on their way to standardization and are already being adopted by major SOA vendors. This section is intended to provide enough background to prepare SOA architects for the "SOA Security Blueprints" section of this chapter; thus, we do not spend this section regurgitating the specs. Instead, this chapter briefly describes what the standards are, why they are important, where the full specifications are, and a little about the architecture(s) involved, if applicable. Although many of these standards are based on SOAP messaging, many of these (specifically SAML, XML Signature, XML Encryption, and XACML) can also apply to REST-based security solutions.

WS-Security SOAP Messaging

WS-Security SOAP messaging is a widely used and accepted OASIS standard, and it provides the capability to supply integrity, non-repudiation, confidentiality, and token passing in Web Service–focused SOA environments. WS-Security provides much flexibility, marrying SOAP messaging with multiple security standards and technologies: The standard extends the SOAP Header to provide security information for secure messaging, it leverages lower-level standards such as XML Signature and XML Encryption, it is extensible to support multiple token formats for identity and authorization, and it supports multiple trust models for sharing security contexts. By itself, WS-Security does not provide a complete security solution for SOAP-based Web Services. It is a building block for secure messaging, accommodating many technologies and messaging models, and it can be used with higher-level complementary standards and other protocols to build a solid SOA security solution.

Many standards build on the foundation of WS-Security SOAP messaging. WS-Trust and WS-SecureConversation, discussed later in this chapter, can be used together to create security contexts used in WS-Security SOAP messaging. There are other related standards, such as the WS-Security SOAP with Attachments Specification, and there are notable higher-level OASIS standards for passing tokens for identity, authorization, and rights using WS-Security SOAP messaging:

- The WS-Security Security Assertion Markup Language (SAML) Token Profile specifies how SAML tokens can be used in WS-Security SOAP messaging for identifying subjects, identifying authorization credentials of subjects, propagating identity and attributes in end-to-end solutions, and expressing authorization decisions.

- The WS-Security X.509 Certificate Token Profile specifies how X.509 Certificates representing a subject's identity can be passed in WS-Security SOAP messaging.

- The WS-Security Kerberos Token Profile utilizes Kerberos tickets with WS-Security SOAP Messaging, accommodating enterprises that use Kerberos for authentication and trust.

- The WS-Security Username Token Profile shows how usernames, and, optionally, passwords, can be passed in WS-Security SOAP Messaging.

- WS-Security REL (Rights Expression Language) Token Profile specifies how the Rights Expression Language can be used to achieve authorization in an SOA by using attribute licenses and authorization tokens.

Every one of the WS-Security token profile standards comes with different strategies, guidance, and scenarios for their use in SOA environments. The use of some of these token profiles are referenced in the "SOA Security Blueprints" section of this chapter.

WS-Security is the standard to use in any SOAP-based SOA, and most products support it. Because it is independent of security infrastructure, and because it can be used with so many other standards and token formats, it provides a flexible mechanism for secure messaging in any SOA solution. The OASIS WS-Security SOAP Messaging family of standards is available at OASIS at `http://oasis-open.org/committees/wss`.

WS-Trust

The OASIS WS-Trust standard, a part of the WS-Security family of specifications, defines a Security Token Service (STS), and a protocol for requesting and issuing security tokens used by WS-Security SOAP Messaging for establishing trust. Figure 11-8 illustrates the WS-Trust STS model. In the figure, the STS is a trusted identity provider, providing claims about requestors of services. Providers of resources rely on tokens issued by the STS for

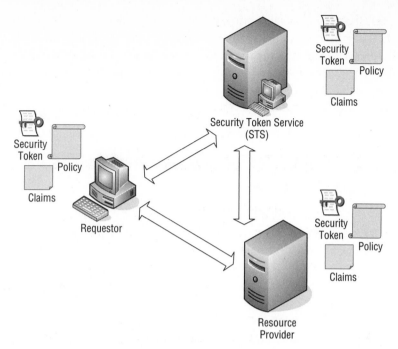

Figure 11-8 The STS model defined by WS-Trust

determining the trust of all requests. In SOA enterprises that utilize WS-Trust, each service provider and service consumer in the model has its own policies, which combine to determine security tokens and associated claims required to communicate.

In Figure 11-8, a requestor wanting to make a connection with a resource provider queries the resource provider for its policies to determine its security requirements, usually defined in a WS-SecurityPolicy expression. This policy lists the tokens needed for communication with the service, and optionally lists the appropriate STS that can issues the necessary tokens it trusts. If the requestor does not have an appropriate token, it can request one from the STS, which authenticates the requestor and issues a token identifying the requestor (and possibly asserting claims about the requestor, such as the requestor's authorization credentials). Finally, the requestor connects to the resource provider with the token from the STS, and the resource provider provides access based on the contents of the token. The resource provider may, if necessary, use the STS to validate tokens presented to it.

The WS-Trust model is flexible to accommodate standard token formats, including SAML, and its protocol processing is designed to be agnostic of the type of token being transmitted. What is positive about WS-Trust is that it allows services to rely on trusted identity providers for explicit trust (instead of having to determine out of-band trust for every message sender). This provides a model that scales well for identity federation, as an STS identity provider may act on behalf of a partner organization in a federation. WS-Trust is used with the WS-Federation specification for identity federation, and it is used with WS-SecureConversation for the purpose of establishing security contexts in WS-Security SOAP Messaging. The WS-Trust standard is governed by the Web Services Secure Exchange (WS-SX) Technical Committee, and can be found at `http://oasis-open.org/committees/ws-sx`.

SECURITY STANDARDS AT A GLANCE

This section covers many standards — as a result, we felt that it would be helpful to list them here and briefly define them, and the subsections.

◆ **WS-Security** — A family of Web Services (WS-*) security specifications from OASIS, "WS-Security" usually refers to Web Services Security (WSS) SOAP Messaging, a unifying standard for securing SOAP messaging security.

◆ **WS-Trust** — An OASIS standard that defines an STS, and a protocol for requesting and issuing security tokens used by WS-Security SOAP Messaging for establishing trust.

◆ **WS-Federation** — An OASIS specification that extends the WS-Trust STS model and protocol for federating identity across organizational boundaries.

◆ **WS-SecureConversation** — An OASIS standard that specifies mechanisms for establishing and sharing security contexts and deriving session keys from those contexts; it can be used to exchange multiple messages for long-lived relationships ("conversations") beyond a typical one message request/response.

◆ **WS-Policy** — An OASIS standard, WS-Policy is an assertion framework and a model for expressing policies that refer to capabilities and requirements for Web Services. Other languages, such as WS-SecurityPolicy.

◆ **WS-SecurityPolicy** — A WS-Policy language, this OASIS standard is used to convey policy assertions for use by WSS: SOAP Messaging Security, WS-Trust, and WS-SecureConversation, the security messaging requirements of a Web Service.

◆ **SAML** — The Security Assertion Markup Language is a standard from OASIS, and it is an XML-based framework that is used for communicating user authentication, entitlement, and attribute information as assertions. It defines an XML format and a protocol for specifying and exchanging assertions between parties.

◆ **XACML** — The eXtensible Access Control Markup Language is an expressive and flexible XML-based language for conveying access control policies for resources. An OASIS standard, XACML not only provides an XML format for conveying access control policy but includes a request/response protocol for querying for policy decisions to be made.

♦ **XML Signature** — A W3C Standard, it is used for digitally signing elements of XML documents. It is a lower-level standard used in both SOAP and REST implementations for providing non-repudiation and message integrity for XML-based messaging.

♦ **XML Encryption** — A W3C Standard, it is used for encrypting elements of XML documents. It is a lower-level standard used in both SOAP and REST implementations to provide confidentiality and information hiding in XML-based messaging.

WS-Federation

WS-Federation, a specification introduced into OASIS in 2007, is in the WS-Security family of specifications, and utilizes and extends the WS-Trust STS model and protocol for federating identity across organizational boundaries. By defining a variety of federation services, including authentication, authorization, attribute, and pseudonym services, for the purpose of federating access across multiple domains, and by providing a federation metadata model describing such services, participants in a federation can discover how to access and use services for the purpose of cross-domain Web Service communication.

WS-Federation offers the capability of a new STS called an authorization service which provides decision brokering services (PDP/PEPs) for participants in a federation. WS-Federation also defines a model for parties to access attribute services based upon the security token service concept and reliant on the token issuance protocol defined in WS-Trust. Pseudonym services are provided in that a Resource Provider can describe the set of attributes required to access a resource, and an Identity Provider (an STS) can assert that a particular subject possesses those attributes, without divulging the actual identity of the subject. WS-Federation also includes extensions to the Security Token Request protocol of WS-Trust to allow a requestor to list privacy requirements, ensuring that sensitive and confidential data is not conveyed in token transmission.

WS-Federation can be used in both browser-based and Web Service–based identity federation, and as such, there is some overlap between SAML 2.0 browser HTTP federation capabilities and the capabilities of WS-Federation. As WS-Federation is now moving to standardization in OASIS, hopefully WS-Federation and SAML 2.0 can complement (and not compete with) each other. The WS-Federation documentation is at the OASIS Web Services

Federation Technical Committee at the following URL: `oasis-open.org/committees/wsfed`.

WS-SecureConversation

WS-SecureConversation is built on top of WS-Security to provide secure communication between services. An OASIS standard that specifies mechanisms for establishing and sharing security contexts and deriving session keys from those contexts, WS-SecureConversation can be used to exchange multiple messages for long-lived relationships ("conversations") beyond a typical one message request/response. In situations where constant communication between services is expected (between a portal and an enterprise Web Service, for example), this is helpful in that performance greatly increases by utilizing derived session keys for encryption communications, instead of having to do slow key negotiation with each message.

The WS-SecureConversation standard complements WS-Security SOAP messaging. WS-SecureConversation defines a new WS-Security token type that is a security context obtained by using a binding of WS-Trust. This security context can be used to derive a "shared secret" for encrypted communications. In the WS-SecureConversation standard, a security context token may be created by an STS, it may be created by one of the communicating parties and propagated with a message, or it may be created by negotiation between parties. WS-Security alone has no capability of deriving this context, so WS-SecureConversation provides needed functionality for WS-Security SOAP Messaging.

An OASIS standard since 2007, WS-SecureConversation is beginning to be adopted by many vendors and toolkits. For more information, visit the OASIS Web Services Secure Exchange (WS-SX) Technical Committee at `http://oasis-open.org/committees/ws-sx`.

WS-SecurityPolicy and the WS-Policy Framework

WS-Policy (or Web Services Policy Framework) is an XML language that is used to represent the capabilities, constraints, and requirements of Web Services, and these capabilities and requirements are expressed as policy assertions. Because the Web Service Definition Language (WSDL) is not expressive enough to define Web Service capabilities and requirements such as quality of service (QoS) and messaging security, WS-Policy complements WSDL, and is used for many aspects of SOA governance that are discussed in Chapter 12. WS-SecurityPolicy is a subset of WS-Policy, and provides a set of WS-Policy security policy assertions describing the messaging security policy requirements involved in communicating with Web Services, and these are used with WS-Security SOAP Messaging, WS-Trust, and WS-SecureConversation.

The WS-Policy Framework has been a W3C recommendation since September 2007, and WS-SecurityPolicy is an OASIS committee standard, which has seen acceptance and is being used by major SOA vendors. Used for expressing messaging security requirements, WS-SecurityPolicy describes the granular details required for secure messaging for SOAP messages. For example, if a Web Service requires a WS-Security Header containing a signed BinarySecurityToken (WS-Security X.509 Certificate Token Profile), WS-SecurityPolicy would be used to express that policy. If certain elements in a Web Service operation are required to be signed or encrypted, WS-SecurityPolicy is used to express this policy. WS-SecurityPolicy supports a wide variety of token types used to provide authentication and authorization information, and is very helpful in a dynamic SOA environment, where interactions and security policies of business partners are dynamic, and where a complement to WSDL is needed to achieve this security collaboration.

The use of WS-SecurityPolicy is discussed more in the Blueprints section of this chapter and is also discussed in Chapter 12. The WS-Policy proposed recommendation is found at the W3C at `w3.org/TR/ws-policy`, and the OASIS WS-SecurityPolicy specification is found at `http://docs.oasis-open.org/ws-sx/ws-securitypolicy`.

SAML

The Security Assertion Markup Language (SAML) is an XML-based framework that is used for communicating subject authentication, entitlement, and attribute information. There are many uses of SAML, and it is commonly used with many other standards and specifications, including WS-Security SOAP Messaging, WS-Trust, WS-Federation, XACML, and the Liberty Identity Web Services Framework (ID-WSF). An OASIS standard since 2002, SAML revolves around the concept of an *assertion*, which is simply a declaration about a subject. An assertion may be a declaration about a subject's authentication (and therefore its identity), a list of a subject's authorization credentials, or an expression of an authorization decision granting a subject to access a resource. The trust of a SAML assertion is based upon the trust of the entity issuing an assertion, usually referred to as an Asserting Party or a SAML authority. Since the specification was adopted in 2002, it has gained significant momentum and its 2.0 version includes federated identity capabilities, in addition to its use as an XML-based token and a protocol for exchanging assertions.

Figure 11-9 provides a snapshot of a few of the many capabilities of SAML. The figure provides a high-level view of the format of a SAML assertion. The figure shows an example of SAML being used as a request/response protocol for requesting assertions for access control decisions; it shows the use of SAML tokens in WS-Security and shows a conceptual use case of SAML assertions being utilized in browser-based SSO.

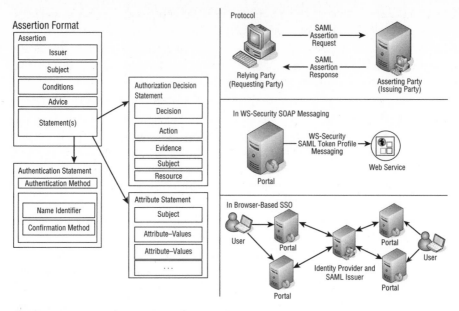

Figure 11-9 Uses of SAML in SOA enterprises

There are three types of statements in assertions: An authentication statement conveying a subject's authentication information (how the subject authenticated, when the subject authenticated, and by whom the subject was authenticated), an attribute statement that lists attributes associated with a subject, and an authorization decision statement, which is used to assert a subject's right to access a particular resource. SAML tokens, by themselves, can be used in token based messaging in SOA enterprises, and they are commonly used with WS-Security and other messaging protocols. The OASIS WS-Security SAML Token Profile standard specifies ways in which SAML tokens can be used to assert information about subjects in WS-Security SOAP Messaging, and a WS-Trust STS can be used to issue SAML tokens in this model.

SAML also defines a request/response protocol for requesting assertions from an SAML Issuing Authority, and this protocol is commonly used in SOA authorization scenarios. SAML protocols allow providers to request assertions from a SAML authority about certain subjects. For example, the following can be requests: "Return an authorization decision about User X accessing Resource Y" and "Give me the security attributes of User X." The SAML protocol can also be used to request that an identity provider authenticate a subject and return an assertion. The SAML protocol is sometimes used to request a logout of a collection of sessions (single logout), and it is also used to carry XACML policies, policy queries, policy responses, authorization decision queries and responses.

SAML 2.0 provides support for SSO. Some of the types of SSO supported are: Identity SSO, where the user identity is registered in both security domains, and Attribute SSO, where access control to resources in a domain is controlled by authorization attributes. Anonymous SSO can be accomplished by only passing SAML attribute statements, and SAML also has the capability for using pseudonym-based SSO for privacy concerns. The SAML Web browser SSO profile specifies how SAML authentication assertions are communicated between an identity provider and a service provider to enable SSO for a browser user, and this is significant because this model brokers trust relationships between the user's browser and services in the enterprise.

SAML is used as one of the "building blocks" for federated identity. The SAML profiles lend themselves to federation beyond the host organization. The Liberty Alliance, a consortium focused on federated identity and SSO, was instrumental in adding federation capabilities (from ID-FF) into SAML 2.0 for browser-based SSO, and now utilizes SAML 2.0 in the ID-WSF (the Identity Web Services Framework), a framework focused on Web Service SSO.

As there is some overlap between SAML and WS-Federation in the federated identity arena, it remains to be seen how the identity federation capabilities of SAML and WS-Federation play together in the future. As noted earlier, WS-Federation is able to use SAML tokens in its architecture, but uses the WS-Trust STS architecture and protocols for exchanging information.

SAML has been widely adopted as a token format for conveying authentication and authorization information, and many products (such as policy servers and federated identity management systems) have adopted the SAML protocol and federation capabilities of SAML. Documents on SAML are at the OASIS Security Services Technical Committee online at `http://oasis-open.org/committees/security`.

XACML

The eXtensible Access Control Markup Language (XACML) is an expressive and flexible XML-based language for conveying access control policies for resources. An OASIS standard since 2003, XACML provides not only an XML format for conveying access control policy, but includes a request/response protocol for querying for policy decisions to be made. XACML as an XML policy language is used to describe general access control requirements, and is extensible in that you can define new functions, data types, and combing logic. The request/response language allows components to form a query to ask whether or not a given action should be allowed, and interprets the result.

A data flow diagram view of the XACML architecture is shown in Figure 11-10.

In the XACML data flow shown in Figure 11-10, a PAP creates XACML policies for resources and makes them available to a PDP. When a subject requests access to a resource, a PEP sends the access request to a context handler, which propagates that request to a PDP. The PDP then requests access to attributes (about the subject, resource, and environment) in order to make an access control decision. The attribute requests are sent to a PIP, which returns the requested attributes, and when the PDP receives this information, it returns an authorization decision, which is returned through a context handler to the PEP, which makes the decisions, based on obligations returned from an obligation service.

Although XACML does provide a request/response protocol for many of the interactions in Figure 11-10, much of the information passed in the data flows could be SAML tokens, and many of the exchanges could use the SAML protocol. Although SAML addresses provide a mechanism for transferring attribute statements, authorization statements, and authorization decisions between cooperating entities, XACML focuses on the mechanism for arriving at those authorization decisions. Many SOA-based systems use XACML policies for access control, while utilizing the SAML request/response protocol or using SAML tokens for identifying subject information. The SAML profile of the XACML standard defines a profile for the use of SAML to carry

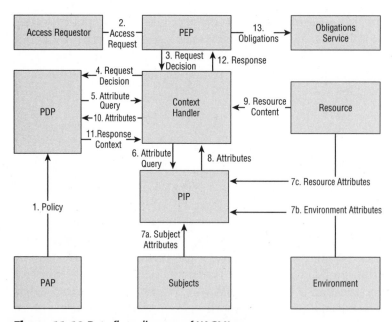

Figure 11-10 Data flow diagram of XACML use

XACML policies, policy queries and responses, and authorization decisions and responses.

In practice, XACML is used primarily for its expression language, and policy servers use XACML for the expression and storage of policies in the enterprise. The future of the success of the XACML protocol remains to be seen.

XACML is a platform-independent policy language and continues to be refined in the OASIS XACML Technical Committee. Documents, news, and current progress can be found at `http://oasis-open.org/committees/xacml`.

XML Signature

XML Signature is a W3C standard that is a way to provide message integrity and non-repudiation of XML documents and elements of XML documents. XML Signature, sometimes called XML-SIG or XML-DSIG, relies on public key technology in which the hash (or message digest) of an element or a set of XML elements is signed by the signer's private key and, therefore, can be validated by third parties by performing a cryptographic operation on the hash of the data with the sender's public key.

A message may have elements that are digitally signed by many different parties, and a signature of a message may cryptographically tie elements together. For example, identity, authorization, and time information from the WS-Security header and the SOAP request in the SOAP body are often cryptographically bound together by the digital signature, preventing an attacker from reusing security information with other requests, providing proof that the message was not altered in transit, and providing proof that the signer sent the message. XML Signature is heavily utilized by WS-Security SOAP messaging for providing integrity and non-repudiation, but it can be used in any XML messaging solution where those security goals need to be met. The XML Signature standard can be found online at `http://w3.org/TR/xmldsig-core`.

XML Encryption

XML encryption is a W3C standard that provides confidentiality of XML documents and elements of XML documents. XML encryption is used with various encryption ciphers to encrypt data to different parties. As discussed in an earlier section on confidentiality in this chapter, XML encryption can be used at the element level, providing confidentiality of sensitive XML elements intended for only certain parties, safely protecting encrypted data through intermediary Web Services, until the intended recipient is able to decrypt the element. Like the XML Signature standard, XML encryption is heavily utilized by WS-Security SOAP Messaging, as well as other XML-based messaging protocols. The XML encryption standard can be found online at `http://w3.org/TR/xmlenc-core`.

SOA Security Blueprints

This section of the chapter builds on the first two. Now that you have an understanding of the classical information security goals, and a high-level understanding of some of the most important SOA security standards, this section provides practical advice, tips, and methodologies to use in different scenarios used to satisfy security requirements in your SOA.

As you read this section, please note that the Web Service security landscape (relating to standards) is continuing to mature and evolve. For this reason, we focus more on architectural principles than on the usage of the key standards in the last section. Where applicable and where it is deemed necessary, we refer to the standards, but most of the concepts and strategies discussed in this section for achieving your security goals can be implementation- and standard-agnostic. It is our goal in this section to have these blueprints be in use as standards evolve and change, regardless of the technologies used.

Separation of Security into Components and Services

Some of the fundamental architectural principles, as we have discussed in Chapter 2 and throughout this book, revolve around abstraction and accommodation of change. To accommodate change, it is important for your architecture to be loosely coupled. For this reason, it is important to separate security from the business logic of your service consumers and providers As architectures moved to client/server in the 1990s, many adopted a more loosely coupled model with the Model-View-Controller (MVC) design pattern, separating presentation, business logic, and data into three components. In SOA, we separate functionality even further, and one of the ways that we do this for security is by abstracting enterprise security into a service layer and into local security components for service consumers and producers. Such an abstraction is necessary because it is otherwise easy for the presentation, data, and business logic to be tightly coupled to security, which provides performance and management problems — in the case study section of this chapter, we show you such an example.

It is important that you realize that creating a security service layer is not tantamount to creating a set of "central" security processing services that act as performance bottlenecks and single point of failures in your enterprise. As we address later in the "Access Control Blueprints" section, there are many strategies for using enterprise services for access control, addressed by the type of services used and the amount of security delegation/federation to local security components used. Figure 11-11 shows the separation of security into a security layer of enterprise security services and local security components. In practice, security components, sometimes called "security interceptors" (with various implementations discussed in Chapter 9), are often implemented in security handlers or security plug-ins to application servers — these separate much of the security processing and the interaction with security services from the business logic of the services.

Figure 11-11 shows a high-level diagram of abstracting security from a user-facing service consumer and a service provider. Both the service consumer and service producer have a local security component that performs security functionality and integrates with enterprise security services. These local security components abstract security from the other components of the services and perform functionality such as message validation, policy enforcement, and various levels of access control. In Figure 11-11, because the service consumer is a user-facing client application with presentation, its local security component may perform PKI authentication with the user and then call enterprise security services to validate the revocation status of the user's certificate and to request the user's security roles. Based on the security roles of the user, the application's presentation component can provide a filtered view of the data at the presentation layer. The local security component for the service consumer may also be responsible for constructing messaging security for a request to the service provider, propagating the identity and attributes of the authenticated user, and validating the security of the response of the message from the service provider. The service provider, on the other hand,

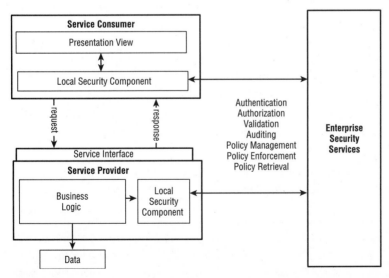

Figure 11-11 Abstraction of security into services and security integration components

has a local security component that may validate the security of the incoming message, and may act as a PEP, calling enterprise security services to make access control decisions.

To accommodate flexibility in your security architecture, it is important to establish an array of security services that meet the current and future security needs of your enterprise. Many common services are the following:

- **Identification and Authentication Services** — These types of services are used for identification of subjects in the enterprise. Depending on the type of authentication used, a specific "authentication service" may not be needed, but other services, such as certificate validation and certificate revocation status verification services, would certainly fall under this category.

- **Attribute Service** — This service is typically used for retrieving attribute credentials (security roles and other credentials used for authorization) for subjects in the enterprise.

- **Access Control Policy Management Service** — This service is typically used for storing the access control policy for resources in the enterprise.

- **Policy Retrieval Service** — This service is used for retrieving the stored policy for resources in the enterprise, for the purpose of making access control decisions.

- **Authorization Decision Service** — This service is usually used to make authorization decisions about a subject's request for a resource, acting as a PDP based on access control policy and attributes about subjects.

- **Identity Transformation Services** — Although such services would not exist in a "perfect world" network, where each subject has one identity credential, it is sometimes helpful to provide services that aid in trans-formation of identities between multiple enterprise applications and support different authentication credentials for the same user. Such a service can be helpful with identity propagation.

- **Security Token Service (STS)** — This service is used for issuing trusted assertions of identity, security attributes, and authorization decisions in the enterprise.

- **Auditing Services** — These types of services are used for providing a centralized view of logs and alerts in the enterprise.

Providing all of these services allows options and flexibility for security, especially for access control. Later on in this section, you can see several blueprints for various mechanisms of access control that use a combination of these enterprise security services and local security components in the enterprise.

SELECTING PRODUCTS FOR ENTERPRISE SECURITY SERVICES

It is sometimes a temptation to pick a vendor's commercial off-the-shelf (COTS) product that supplies all of your security services and components, thinking that this can solve all of the problems for your enterprise. The key to selecting products revolves around *standards compliance*. Look for supported standards that we discussed in the "Web Service Security Standards and Specifications" section of this chapter. Make sure to do your research. If you hear or read phrases like *"Our supported messaging is based on WS-Security,"* or *"Our security tokens are SAML-like,"* this should throw up a few red flags. Either products are standards-compliant or they are not.

In the same way, be warned that many vendors attempt to lock you in to their product by both supporting standard security mechanisms and supporting very easy-to-use proprietary mechanisms for security. (For example, some application servers support JAX-WS or JAX-RPC security handlers but urge you to only use their proprietary plug-ins for security.) It is easy for the well-intentioned developer to go down the proprietary road, because the proprietary road usually offers very easy integration. As the security architect, make certain that you warn your developers not to do this.

If you use a product and make sure to only use services that use standard protocols and standard security components, you can reduce your dependence on that vendor. This way, if the product becomes unsupported in the future or becomes unreliable or unusable, you can have a much easier time replacing it with another product!

Separating security functionality into enterprise security services and local security components is essential. The next few sections of blueprints show various options that the SOA architect has when using these enterprise security components. Later in this chapter, we provide a simple case study, where enterprise security services and local security components are used in an example enterprise.

Authentication and Identity Blueprints

This section contains blueprints and best practices related to authentication and identity. As we discussed in the first section of this chapter, there is usually a requirement to identify both the *message sender* and the *identity of the end user* in each service request. Initially, the message sender and the end user are the same when the user authenticates to a front-end application. Beyond that, the architect has options related to identifying users. Every SOA security architect should understand the issues related to SSO, trust propagation, and authentication in an SOA, and this section focuses on these issues and offers practical solutions based on security policy and infrastructure.

Identity Propagation for SSO Solutions

There are usually two models of trust of user authentication: *direct trust*, where the service provider has first-hand knowledge of the user's authentication, or *transitive trust*, where the service provider must trust the identity of the user based on an assertion of another party. Figure 11-12 shows examples of direct and transitive trust, and the next sections show successful blueprints for achieving different mechanisms of trust.

The transitive trust model exists because of the desire for SSO in SOA. Instead of forcing a user to authenticate to every service, there are mechanisms of propagating a user's credentials through multiple nodes, and this is known in some circles as *deep authentication*. Transitive trust is based on a strong trust of every Web Service client and every Web Service in a request chain. The bottom two examples in Figure 11-12 show transitive trust, where a portal vouches for the end user it authenticates. If the next Web Service authenticates the portal and trusts the portal to make an assertion about the end user; then this level of assurance may be adequate, depending on the security requirements — the important issue is the chain of trust. Transitive trust can be acceptable when there are only a few entities trusted to assert identity in the Web Service pipeline.

Tokens provide the ability for trust propagation in Web Service messaging, and token profiles, such as the WS-Security SAML Token Profile, are used

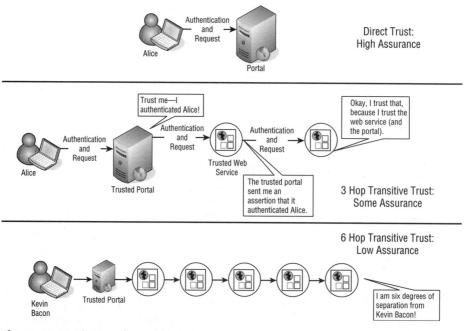

Figure 11-12 Direct and transitive trust

in WS-Security SOAP messaging. Because WS-Security SAML Token Profile is common in deployed SOAs, we use this standard as an example in this section. It has one option called a "sender-vouches" confirmation method that provides a formal method of propagating identity, where the sender vouches for the identity of a user in an assertion. The standard mandates that the message sender (or attesting entity) must cryptographically bind the assertion with the body of the message so that the assertion (or the main message) cannot be altered, and that the receiving entity must have an existing trust relationship with the sender. WS-Security SAML Token Profile is not alone in offering this option; there are many other standards that use identity propagation mechanisms.

Where transitive trust usually goes wrong is when every node in a particular SOA enterprise is trusted to assert identity, or when there are large numbers of services in between the end user's authenticating client and the final Web Service. Using the transitive trust model, trust of the end user's identity goes down as the distance to the user increases. The final example of transitive trust in Figure 11-12 (six hop transitive trust) provides little assurance of the identity of the user, regardless of the trust between each node in the chain. When the distance between the user and the final Web Service is so large, trust degrades.

To have a higher degree of assurance of the identity of a propagated user, you can either trust fewer nodes to propagate identity or minimize the amount of transitive trust hops. This section uses these strategies to provide a few blueprints for propagating identity with a high-level of assurance.

Identity Propagation within an Application Server or ESB

One blueprint that can be effective in certain situations is to use an application server or Enterprise Service Bus (ESB) product to share security information among all services within, collapsing the number of hops for identity propagation. Because all of the services on an application server can have access to security information about the end user, every Web Service hosted on that server in the message chain has access to the user's authentication credentials. In practice, if all of the Web Services share a container, no special messaging security is needed between the services in the message pipeline, and usually calls are in-memory object invocations. In addition to limiting the hops of transitive trust, this has a positive performance impact.

Figure 11-13 shows two usage examples where a portal and an ESB share the same container. In one scenario, User A authenticates directly to the portal, and this authentication information is shared by all of the services hosted in the ESB, reducing the number of trust hops to one (between the user and the portal/ESB container), and maximizing the assurance of the user's identity. The second scenario in Figure 11-13 is where User B authenticates to a trusted application, and that trusted application authenticates to the first service in

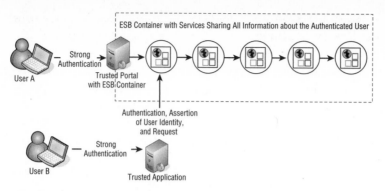

Figure 11-13 Using an ESB to share trust between services

the ESB, and sends a token vouching for the end user. Based on the ESBs trust of the trusted application, the propagated identity information is trusted and shared with the rest of the services in the container. The assurance of the identity of User A is higher in the first scenario, because the container has direct trust of the user's identity, and the assurance of the identity of User B is dependent on the ESBs trust of the trusted application. In both examples, we have limited the number of trust hops.

A word of warning on this blueprint — such a strategy can *only* be used in situations where services are co-located, and it is, most likely, only a short-term solution for identity propagation. Chances are, all of your services are not deployed on the same container, and in some cases, load-balancing mechanisms may separate co-located services between servers, and this requires another strategy. However, it can be effective in the right situations. If you deploy services on the same container that must communicate with each other, it makes sense to make internal invocations between them instead of the services sending cryptographically protected on-the-wire network messages to each other, bringing performance to a crawl.

Such a strategy may also not be an end-to-end solution — instead, it can be a performance-enhancing complement to another identity propagation solution we discuss in this section. For an SOA enterprise, it makes sense to choose a secure messaging "on-the-wire" mechanism for identity propagation, but when the services are deployed, it may be wise to factor in service co-location using this strategy.

Assigning Attesting Trust to a Limited Number of Entities

If you have a situation where there are only a few authenticating applications in your enterprise, and only a few services that do service composition and orchestration, you may be able to get by with setting up a small number of trust relationships between the enterprise and the applications and services that are trusted to attest to the identity. An example is shown in the "3-Hop

Transitive Trust" scenario in Figure 11-12, where there is one trusted portal and one trusted Web Service doing orchestration. It should be pointed out, however, that trust of any assertion of identity is based on the trust of the attester, so if there is a large number of entities trusted to attest identities (for example, the "Kevin Bacon Game" chain situation shown at the bottom of Figure 11-12), this strategy is not very successful.

This strategy can be a successful solution, but it must be closely managed. In many cases, the solution may be a short-term solution. Because services are reusable components, there may be other services and applications that can build orchestration solutions, and this may require adding more and more entities to the "trust list." The longer the message chains get in this solution, and the more entities allowed to attest identity, the lower the assurance of this model. However, if you are absolutely certain that the number of trusted entities can be limited, this can be a successful strategy.

Using a Trusted Token Service

A more promising trust strategy used in identity propagation involves a situation where there is one trusted token service that vouches for the identities of end users. This model is commonly used in both Browser-Based SSO and Web-Service-based SSO. Both models rely on the assurance of a single identity provider that may act as a token issuer. This identity provider has the responsibility of authenticating end users and issuing short-lived signed assertions that can be used in transactions. Figure 11-14 shows a conceptual diagram, based on a few of the SSO standards in use today. (This is conceptually similar to the WS-Federation/WS-Trust model, as well as a combination of the

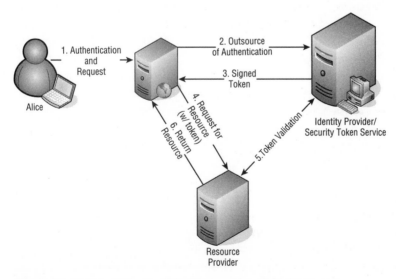

Figure 11-14 Using a trusted identity provider and token issuer

SAML Browser SSO Profile and the Liberty ID-WSF model.) In the example, a user authenticates to a portal, which has a strong trust relationship with an identity provider. The portal "outsources" or redirects authentication to the identity provider, so that it directly authenticates the user. Based on a user's valid authentication, the identity provider returns a signed SAML assertion, which is returned to the user's browser for subsequent portal interactions, but this can also be used by the portal to propagate identity to other Web Services in the enterprise.

The trust of the identity of the user in this model is based on the trust of the identity provider issuing the token, with a bit of trust placed on the portal that is integrated with the identity provider/token service. This limits the amount of trusted entities (eliminating the "Kevin Bacon Game" problem), providing a high degree of assurance.

Identity Propagation with REST Using Browser SSO

The introduction of the SAML Browser SSO Profile in 2005 makes identity propagation for Representational State Transfer (REST) possible. Because REST does not differentiate between a service call and a click from the user's browser, distance is minimized between the user's browser and the Web Services using browser-specific profiles, such as the SAML Browser SSO Profile, and we anticipate that when WS-Federation is standardized, its Browser SSO capabilities can bring similar success to REST-based services.

Figure 11-15 shows a high-level sequence diagram of the Browser SSO model provided by the Profiles for OASIS SAML Standard. Each service provider redirects authentication to an identity provider that issues tokens (similar to the browser-portal interaction in the last section). For an initial browser-based request, HTTP redirections or other mechanisms initiate a login sequence with an identity provider, and the identity provider's response (in the form of a SAML token) is returned to the user's browser, which is delivered to the service provider, which then grants access based on the token and the trust of the identity provider. If the service provider makes a call to another service provider on behalf of the user, the same sequence can be used.

The beauty of this approach compared to the previous one is that one standard is used, instead of multiple standards. Because the user's browser is able to have token information, standard HTTP redirects allow direct connection between the user's browser and each service. Because each service trusts one identity provider that issues assertions to the user's browser, there is trust of one entity, not several. It not only works in an organizational SSO model, but it is used in federation scenarios as well.

Because this model embraces HTTP and open standards, implementers using REST-based services should consider using this standard when organizational SSO or service federation to multiple enterprises is needed.

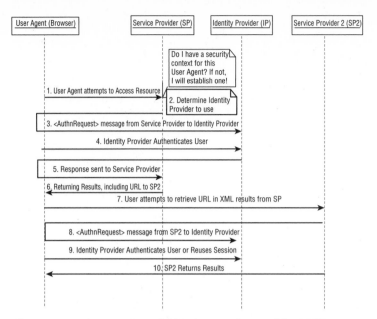

Figure 11-15 Browser-Based SSO that can be used for REST

Decision Diagram for Propagation and Trust — How Do You Decide?

This section has covered many potential solutions related to identity propagation — we provided a blueprint for successful identity propagation in an ESB, we discussed techniques for limiting trust to specific services in the enterprise, we discussed the STS approach, and we discussed a Browser-Based SSO model for REST-based services. Figure 11-16 provides a decision flow diagram for choosing the type of propagation trust model used. There are five end states and potential solutions in this decision flow diagram, based on the content of this section, and each end state (labeled solutions A–F) references a figure and a section in this chapter.

Point-to-Point Authentication

Throughout the beginning of this book, we repeatedly made the point that SSL does not solve many of the security requirements needed in end-to-end messaging solutions. It is, however, a wonderful standard that can be used for authentication and mutual authentication between any two points in your SOA. Because SSL provides authentication, confidentiality and integrity, it is a complement for many scenarios, especially when you need to provide mutual authentication between a user and a front-end application. Another scenario where SSL is useful is when you may need to provide mutual authentication and a long-lived security session between two points in your SOA that constantly communicate. Allowing a long-lived SSL connection between two

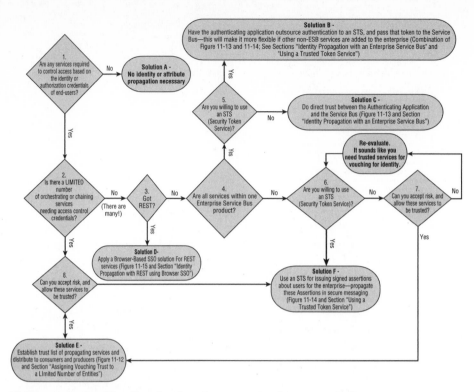

Figure 11-16 Decision flow for choosing a propagation trust solution

points provides a large performance advantage over repeated key agreement and encryption for every request. SSL can even be coupled with many identity propagation scenarios discussed in the previous section, but it depends on your project's security requirements.

There are other mechanisms for point-to-point authentication that provide additional benefits. For example, a digitally signed message (with a reference to the sender's X.509 certificate) combines sender authentication with non-repudiation, in addition to integrity of the data, and this mechanism can be accomplished with WS-Security using XML Signature. Based on the trust of the issuer of the certificate, and based on the validation of the signature of the message with the sender's public key included in the certificate, the receiver has strong assurance of the sender's identity. One benefit of having requests digitally signed is that these messages can be saved and a third party can validate them later, whereas SSL session statistics are typically lost and records do not show the non-repudiation. Certain WS-Security token profiles, such as WS-Security X.509 Certificate Profile, allow a message sender to sign a message with its own X.509 Certificate in the header, providing that level of proof. REST-based messaging can simply use XML Signature to provide this mechanism.

Access Control Blueprints

Building on the authentication-based blueprints of the last section, this section focuses on practical solutions for access control. Once a user is identified, it is important to determine what that user can do (authorization). Access control can be done by expressing and enforcing access control policy based on the identity of the user and the user's authorization credentials. This section focuses on key aspects of access control in SOA-based solutions, providing approaches and best practices.

Controlling Access to Data, Not Just Services

One important thing to remember when providing access control to service resources is that, although you can provide authorization at the service level for incoming requests, you can also secure access to the data itself by labeling the data itself with access control policy information and allowing your PDP/PEP to enforce authorization policy based on the label of your data. This is often used in both commercial and government systems where data may be labeled with sensitivity levels, such as "FOR INTERNAL USE ONLY." A security classification example dealing with Mandatory Access Control was shown in Figure 11-4.

In providing access control to data, security handlers or security components are most likely to constrain requests based on the data labels, or they can filter service results before they are returned to the user (sometimes called "response filtering" or "response pipeline filtering"). For those enterprises that need this level of security, security metadata tagging on messages is quite important for controlling access to the data. Some approaches involved security metadata tagging at the message level, where each message is labeled with security metadata — this is helpful, because the label of the entire message can be placed in the SOAP header with other security information. Other approaches involve tagging at the XML element level directly (right along with the data). The positive aspect of that particular approach is that, in the message response pipeline, the response message would actually be *filtered* on the way back from the service, whereas providing response security using the message-level labeling alternative simply would either accept or drop the response. The benefit of labeling at the element level is that potentially more information would be returned to the user. On the other hand, the benefit of labeling at the message level is that the security data (in the header) can be separated from the business data (in the body).

Certainly, there are other database-centric solutions that do not necessarily use security tagging. In such approaches, a service queries a database with constraints of access (for example, "give me these search results, except for records labeled 'FOR INTERNAL USE ONLY'"), and the database does the access control filtering. Where the database-centric approach can get somewhat complex is in orchestration solutions, where results of many services, and thus data with many sensitivity levels, are combined. It is, therefore, helpful to combine a database-filtering approach with a message tagging approach.

The next section discusses many approaches for controlling access to services and data.

Access Control Policy Enforcement Approaches

There are many different models for managing and enforcing access control information in SOA. The conceptual model of XACML (shown earlier in Figure 11-10) uses widely accepted security terminology that can be applied to any architecture, regardless of whether or not XACML itself is used. For this reason, we discuss access control architecture in terms of a PEP and a PDP. We do, however, attempt to stay technology neutral.

Because there are so many options for propagation of assertions (identity, attribute, and authorization decision assertions), the SOA architect has many options for where these access control policy points should exist in the enterprise. This section provides strategies that can be used based on different goals and security requirements, and for each strategy, we offer pros, cons, and implementation tips. For each strategy, we illustrate the concept, and it should be noted that for the purpose of simplicity, we have combined the user and his/her front-end application (for example, the user's portal) — in all interactions, the front-end application, not the user, is doing the communicating with the back-end Web Services.

The Purely Centralized PDP Model with Global Policy

The first approach to policy enforcement, shown in Figure 11-17, is a purely centralized approach. Common to many SOAs, a centralized policy server is called to make a yes or no decision for a subject request for resource. In this model, all policy is globally managed, and services in the SOA request authorization decisions from the policy server. The policy server acts as a PDP, retrieving security attributes about subjects requesting resources, and making decisions based on a subject's credentials and enterprise policy for the

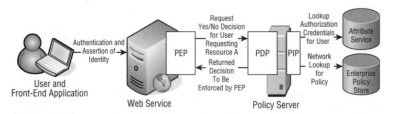

Figure 11-17 Centralized policy management and enforcement

requested resource. In this model, the policy server PDP returns a "yes" or "no" authorization decision and enforces the decision.

A positive aspect of the solution shown in Figure 11-17 is information hiding. None of the services that request authorization decisions know exactly *why* decisions are made, and at no point in the life cycle of the message are user authorization credentials revealed. This can be positive from an information security standpoint. Because applications and services may not have a need to know about authorization credentials of the user or the specific policy of a resource, this model protects that information in cases where this information may be sensitive or confidential.

Potential negatives about this model, however, relate to performance and availability. If all services in your SOA enterprise need to connect to a central authorization server for every request, it is a no-brainer that the server must always be available. If the authorization server ever goes down, you have two grim choices that you want to avoid at all costs: Allow all access for all subjects or deny all access to all subjects. Complicating the issue is that calls to such a service are usually cryptographically protected in order to have high assurance of the integrity and identity of the policy server. That cryptography, combined with network latency of each request, slows down the response time of all services and applications that are forced to call the policy server. Using such a centralized model has the potential of bringing the performance of your network to a crawl.

Regardless of the negatives, a centralized policy server can still be effective, and some of the risks can be mitigated. Centralization can be a "virtual" concept, meaning that various mechanisms for load-balancing and failover for many authorization servers can be used when using the centralized policy management and enforcement model. Because of the performance and availability concerns, it may be prudent for service PEPs to cache policy decisions for a certain period of time for repeated requests to resources by the same subjects. To reduce the overhead of cryptography, PEPs should consider establishing long-lived sessions with the policy server using SSL or WS-SecureConversation, and the use of hardware cryptography acceleration technology should be investigated for further accelerating cryptography performance.

The Purely Decentralized PDP/PEP Model with Attribute Propagation

The second approach, shown in Figure 11-18, is another common model used in SOA access control systems. In this approach, the authenticating application retrieves attribute credentials from a Security Token Service and propagates that trusted assertion about the user to a Web Service, which has a local PDP and PEP. The Web Service PDP refers to locally expressed policy, and therefore, its PDP can inspect the policy, combined with the attributes propagated in, in order to make an access control decision.

Figure 11-18 Decentralized model with attribute propagation

This model is effective and alleviates the performance concerns of the purely central model. Because all authorization credentials are propagated in a trusted assertion, the Web Service does not have to use a network call to look up the user's security attributes. Because the policy is locally expressed, the Web Service does not have to cryptographically call a PDP over the network — instead, all of the policy is local, and all policy decisions are local, based on global attribute credentials. Because all of the policy is declared locally, there is no longer concern about the availability of a central policy server.

There are two potential concerns with this model, however. One concern is that there is no information hiding in this model. Because a user's security attributes are propagated in to the Web Service, the Web Service has full read access to the security credentials of the user, which may be sensitive. The second concern revolves around policy management. In situations where an organization may want to have control over policy, this purely decentralized model does not allow it, as it gives Web Services full control over policy and policy enforcement. Regardless, this model, combined with a good propagation strategy, is effective and works.

Decentralized PDP/PEP with Identity Propagation

This model of access control, shown in Figure 11-19, is similar to the last model, but it alleviates one information-hiding concern of attribute propagation. The knowledge of the user's security attributes is removed from the authenticating application and is placed on the Web Service. This is a common model used in

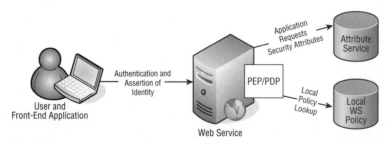

Figure 11-19 Decentralized model with identity propagation

approaches to access control management, when the service container assumes responsibility of all back-end security processing. In practice, it may be wise for the logic of the security component of the service to cache user security attributes for a certain period of time so that subsequent calls from the same subject do not result in repeated queries to an attribute service.

Combining Local and Global Enterprise Policy

There are two common methods that provide a "happy medium" between local control of policy (where services express all policy) and central control of policy (where a central policy server expresses all policy). These methods are shown in Figure 11-20, and occur regardless of where attributes are queried in the solution. In these models, each Web Service expresses local policy but combines this with global organizational policy in order to make decisions. This alleviates policy control concerns related to the purely decentralized model.

In these approaches, a Web Service's PDP must get access to global policy and combine it with its locally expressed policy in order to make a decision. It is usually important that a conflict-resolution mechanism be in place (for example, where global policy trumps local policy). Two SOA approaches that use this strategy are the method where the Web Service's PDP retrieves global policy from a central policy server (*a policy retrieval method*) and caches it for a period of time for access control decisions, and an approach where the policy server syndicates global policy to the Web Service PDP (*a policy push method*). Both are illustrated in Figure 11-20.

Similar to the purely centralized model, there may be performance and availability issues related to all services using the policy retrieval method. However, the difference is that the global policy is only downloaded on a periodic basis (on container instantiation) as opposed to the strategy of doing so for every request, which makes this approach better from a performance perspective. A potential issue arises related to the frequency of global policy changes: There may be a time window between the time that policy changes are made and the retrieval of the policy by the Web Services.

The policy push method alleviates performance and availability concerns, as the policy is pushed immediately to the Web Service PDPs as the policy

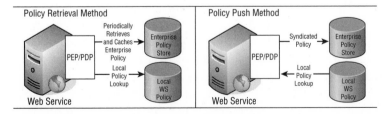

Figure 11-20 Combining local and global enterprise policies

changes are created. This alleviates the time window concern, because as the policy is changed, it is immediately sent to the Web Service PDPs. The security of syndication in this model does need to be addressed. The security model needs to protect against entities "spoofing" the syndication server, replaying syndication policy update messages, tampering with messages in transit, and denial of service attacks that would prevent syndicated policy messages from being received by all PDPs.

Both methods discussed in this section are effective for access control in an SOA. Which you choose depends on your security and performance requirements.

Predetermined Decision-Based Models

One unique approach to access control is a methodology that we call PADBAC (Predetermined Authorization Decision-Based Access Control). Such a model of access control revolves around services issuing authorization decisions for resource access in advance, before these resources are requested. In this model, the services issue authorization decisions to the appropriate subjects, who later use them to gain authorized access to resources. These decisions are digitally signed by the service and tied to the identity of the subject who can later request access. When it is time for the subject to request access, the subject signs a request for the resource, including the previously issued assertion in the message.

Such solutions model real-world, day-to-day scenarios. When you drop your clothes off at a dry cleaner, the clerk typically gives you a receipt with a number, listing the day that you can pick them up. Later, you bring that receipt back and the cleaner finds your dry-cleaned clothes and gives them back to you. This process is simple; you don't have to pull out your ID card, or show the cleaner any authorization credentials in order to get your dry cleaning. In the same way, a PADBAC-based approach requires no identity or attribute propagation in the service transaction. Once a subject gets a signed authorization decision to do something, the subject simply signs the request to do it, attaching the signed authorization decision along with the request.

A service-based example of using the PADBAC model can be demonstrated in an example implementation of an airline ticket service, illustrated in Figure 11-21. An airline ticket booking Web Service needs to provide access control to allow only the ticket-booking agents of the airline to book tickets for airline flights. Instead of using one of the access control policy models we have discussed before, the SOA architect has chosen to use a model that utilizes pre-issued authorization decisions for access control. In the example, Gwen, Emma, and Isabella are agents who book flights for customers, so the airline ticket booking service issues signed authorization decision assertions to Gwen, Emma, and Isabella, expressing the purpose of the privilege (booking seats on flights) and a timeframe of validity. When one of the agents needs to later book

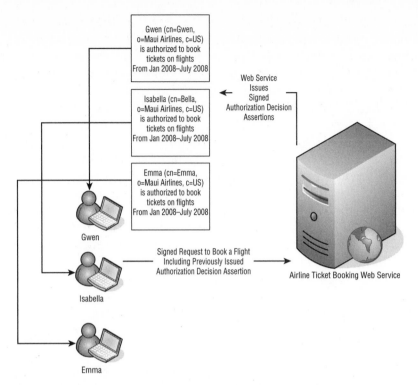

Figure 11-21 Example of using pre-issued authorization decisions

a customer's seat on a flight, the agent must send this request to the airline ticket booking service in a secure message, digitally signing the request and including with it the original signed authorization decision that granted her access. Because the Web Service receiving the assertion is the one that issued it, there is no question of the trustworthiness of the assertion. As long as the sender is proven to be the signer of the message and the subject of the original assertion, as long as the original assertion is valid for this purpose, and as long as the sender's certificate has not been revoked, this model works well and effectively. In order for this model to work, a PKI needs to be in place, and all services need to make sure to check Certificate Revocation Lists (CRLs).

One variant of PADBAC involves delegated assertions. For example, the airline ticket booking service may issue the assertion only to the flight-booking manager, who would have permission to delegate that decision to others. In order for this to be accomplished, the flight booking manager would create a new assertion that delegates the permission to use the original assertion to his or her subordinates. The subordinate, in turn, would digitally sign a request, attaching the two signed assertions (the assertion issued by the airline ticket booking service, and the assertion made by the booking manager that gives the subordinate permission to use the original assertion). By allowing this type of delegation, message chaining can be achieved in SOAs, where each service link in the chain can delegate authority, until the final service in the chain is reached. In such a delegation scenario, a chain of signed authorization decisions is visible for service requests at each point, providing end-to-end non-repudiation and integrity.

Another variant of PADBAC is similar to the "beer ticket" system used at concert events. For those of you who are not familiar, people must wait in one line to buy tickets for alcoholic beverages, and then wait in another line to exchange the ticket for the actual beverage. The beer ticket counter enforces authentication, authorization, and minimum drink policies, and the tent that sells beer simply ensures the integrity of the ticket — making the actual beer transaction simple and quick. In the same way, in the SOA world, there can be a trusted authorization decision issuer that enterprise services trust, and in order to communicate with services, the users of the services must apply for such a "ticket," or these tickets may be issued to the users in advance.

Such a model can be successful because it does not focus on propagating identity and run-time decision making in the service transaction. Instead, it focuses on decision making in advance, validating those decisions at run time. From a performance perspective, this means that services do not have to do lookups (to a central server or locally), and from a messaging perspective, it means that no identity (or attribute) propagation has to happen at all in the business transaction, simplifying messaging. It is important to know that this model is not appropriate for every use case. It only works when requests are anticipated and where authorization decisions can be made before the actual authorization request.

Decision Flow Chart for Access Control — How Do You Decide?

Obviously, this section has many options for access control. For this reason, we have included a decision flow chart, shown in Figure 11-22. The end state of the decision flow chart contains six potential solutions for not only the access control model, but also provides what type of propagation (identity, attribute, or authorization decision) you should use between the service consumer and the Web Service. Each solution references a section and a figure in this chapter referencing the chosen implementation.

Certainly, any type of standards-based messaging security can be used between service consumers and service providers to propagate identity, attribute, or authorization decisions, but we do have some recommendations:

■ Where identity or attribute propagation is utilized (Solutions A, B, D, E, and F), we recommend using the WS-Security SAML Token Profile (either using the sender-vouches confirmation method, or by using a signed token from an STS).

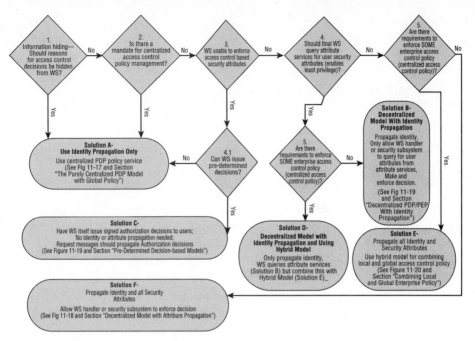

Figure 11-22 Decision flow for access control

▪ In the one instance where propagation is not used (Solution C), we recommend having the Web Service issue signed SAML assertions containing a SAML `AuthorizationStatement` that can be used for a certain period of time by the recipient in WS-Security SAML Token Profile messaging, where the issued assertion is sent to the Web Service. Each SAML assertion states conditions of use and period of validity. When a request to that Web Service is sent, the signer of the WS-Security message is the one to whom the SAML assertion was issued. Thus, the Web Service is easily able to validate that the service consumer has authorized access.

Auditing and Troubleshooting

Enterprise management is one subject that we have not addressed in this chapter, but there are some aspects that relate to information security in an SOA. As discussed in Chapter 9, many SOA architects make the mistake of not focusing on enterprise management requirements, and when auditing and logging is involved, write logs only at the local file system level. Because of the dynamic nature of SOA and the possibility of orchestration and message chaining where the life cycle of a service request may go through many "hops," it is often difficult to troubleshoot security incidents and errors if every service logs information to its local machine. It is prudent, therefore, to use either a centralized logging capability or an SOA enterprise management COTS package, which integrates with your Web Service consumers and producers, providing not only "the big picture" of your SOA but also the big security picture. Chapter 9, the section "Exception Handling and Logging in Enterprise Solutions" provides detailed strategies for auditing and logging that apply to both security and enterprise management.

Flexibility with Dynamic WS-SecurityPolicy Adaptation

The introduction of WS-SecurityPolicy allows SOA security solutions to use dynamic run-time mechanisms for discovering and adhering to security policy. Similar to the way that applications can download WSDL and dynamically create stubs to access services, Web Service consumers and producers can now dynamically discover messaging security requirements and adapt at run time.

The following is a good example: Suppose that a Web Service that once required a token of a user's authentication (an Authentication Assertion) in WS-Security SOAP messaging now requires a token of the user's attributes (an Attribute Assertion). If that Web Service modifies its expressed WS-Security-Policy, which can be referred to in the service's WSDL, the calling application initially calls the Web Service. When it receives an error notification that the security policy is changed, it can download the new policy, discover that changes have been made, and adapt by retrieving a new type of assertion from an Asserting Provider or an STS in its enterprise. It can then call the service correctly.

Expressing the security messaging requirements in a discoverable way using WS-SecurityPolicy gives service consumers the capability to be more loosely coupled to the security messaging of services. If the security messaging is hard-coded in your service's clients, any change in security messaging would break the client's interactions with the service. Dynamic policy adaption, therefore, provides a very flexible model. Although developers can write software to accomplish this in security interceptors and security handlers, it should be mentioned that many COTS vendors are building these dynamic policy adaptation capabilities (sometimes called "Policy Application Points") into their products, supporting many messaging formats and token formats in order to support SOA security flexibility in enterprise deployments. This approach is also used beyond WS-SecurityPolicy to adapt to other WS-Policy requirements of services in the enterprise.

NOTE This strategy is discussed in more depth in Chapter 12, in a section called "Run-Time Policy Enforcement and Adaptation." There we discuss how a service client's "Policy Application Point" can be used to adapt to adhere to many types of governance policies (including security) at run time. Chapter 9 also focuses on adaptation and the role of the registry in SOA.

Complete Architecture Analysis

Now that we near the end of this section, you can see that as an SOA security architect, you have many options related to achieving security goals. It is important, therefore, to make certain that your chosen solution is reviewed by a security authority early on in your project. Security authorities are able to identify risks and vulnerabilities of your proposed security architecture and allow you to mitigate them before your project begins.

Applying Concepts from This Chapter — A Simple Case Study

Throughout this chapter, we have tried to give examples of various techniques and examples that can be used to achieve certain security objectives. In this section, we provide a case study, utilizing the techniques discussed in this chapter.

Our case study revolves around a fictional travel agency. This agency has been in business for over 50 years, and over the years, it has acquired many companies and legacy systems. Travel agents have accounts on 20 legacy systems, which allow them to book hotels, airfare, and ground transportation. A few years ago, a fly-by-night (excuse the pun) dot-com company sold the travel agency on a solution overhaul of all of their systems that would fix their problems. Unfortunately, the result of "project overhaul" is that the travel agency now has the same old problems exhibited by new technology. Figure 11-23 shows the current state of the travel agency enterprise, with three of the twenty systems being used.

Because travel agents have to keep track of 20 front-end applications and username/password combinations, they are constantly having trouble. Travel agents have the database administrators of 20 different systems on speed dial because of forgotten passwords and access control privilege updates. When a travel agent is promoted to a higher level of access, all 20 databases must be updated. The users of the system are fed up, and so are the database administrators.

After a little study of the current design and historical documentation, you see that the engineering that was done a few years ago was not completely bad. The developers rewrote 20 monolithic applications to make them client/server based, separating the presentation from the business logic using the Model-View-Controller design pattern. The designers of the Web Services

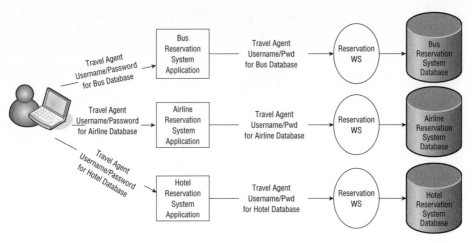

Figure 11-23 Three of the twenty systems in current travel agency enterprise

also created a well-designed schema for reservations that could be used for all of the applications, independent of the type of reservation used. Each back-end database is fronted by the same Reservation Web Service interface, and each implementation abstracts the details of each database.

Unfortunately, the attempted overhaul was not complete. The designers had originally intended to create a portal-based user interface that allowed the travel agents to do all of their reservations from one application. Because the designers of this system did not account for security until the end of the project, they were unable to tie the systems together because they ran out of time and made poor decisions about username/password propagation between every tier in the system. For each system, the front-end application passes on the user's security credentials to the Web Service, which passes them on to the database. As a result, every travel agent must log in separately for each system, and the original developers finally abandoned the idea of one front-end interface. You recognize this pattern as something that you have seen often: This was a case of thinking about security requirements too late in the game. Any design improvements that were made during the project overhaul are unseen, because the system is still difficult to use and manage.

Because you are well into this book, you understand the design problem that is the root of the travel agency's woes. The problem is tight coupling: Security in the travel agency enterprise is tied specifically to each of the 20 individual databases. This not only tightly couples the database data to access control security policy, but its effect is that each front-end application continues to be coupled to its back-end database because of the separate authentication credentials. This is frustrating to the users because of the lack of SSO and frustrating to the database administrators as well.

Applying the concepts of this chapter, you realize that two major enhancements must be made. First of all, the project is in need of enterprise security services containing global user credentials for travel agents using the system. This removes the burden of security logic from each individual database and enables SSO in the enterprise. Second, some sort of identity propagation must be used because of the multiple "hops" between the tiers in this solution; the current system propagates specific usernames and passwords based on the application. This certainly can be done here, but this type of messaging would be dependent on the *type* of authentication. It would be a much more flexible solution if some sort of identity token were used for identity propagation. This can be used, regardless of the authentication type. If the system ever needed to support digital certificate (or even biometric) authentication, a token-based solution would never need to be changed.

After considerable thought, you provide a high-level sketch of a new architecture that provides desired functionality for the travel agency enterprise. This is mainly achieved by placing core enterprise security services in the enterprise for enabling SSO. You can do this by creating a portal-based front end that can host multiple portlets for back-end reservation systems and by creating a reservation aggregator service that performs all reservation transactions for a travel agent in one request. A token representing the travel agent's identity is propagated through each tier. A high-level diagram of this functionality is shown in Figure 11-24.

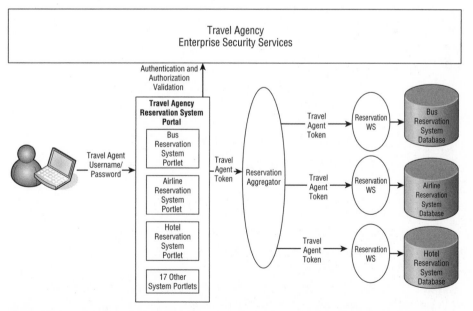

Figure 11-24 High-level view of desired functionality in the travel agency enterprise

Figure 11-24 shows that a travel agent logs in to the portal, and each portal has portlets associated with each back-end system. Once the travel agent enters all travel requirements and reservation information for the customer, the portal system sends a bulk request, along with the user's token. The enterprise reuses the well-designed abstract Reservation Web Service interfaces that abstract the details of each system.

Establishing Enterprise Security Services

At this point in the case study, more decisions need to be made. Specifically, it is important to define the enterprise security services. After having read the concepts and security solution blueprints in this chapter, you know that there are many options for access control, depending on the security services available. Architectural flexibility is provided when you provide the security services needed for all of the alternatives for access control policy enforcement. This allows different future applications with different requirements the ability to use multiple options. For this reason, you create the following:

- An Authentication Service, which identifies the user (and/or applications in the enterprise).

- An Attribute Service, which exposes authorization credentials of users in the enterprise. In the travel agency, the current security roles are `reservation_approver`, `travel_reserver`, and `purchasing_approver`. Such an attribute service accommodates those roles and also accommodates growth and flexibility.

- A Policy Management Service, which is used by policy administrators to create, update, and manage security policy.

- A Policy Retrieval Service, which exposes the policies of resources in the enterprise. Policies can be expressed in XACML for resources in the enterprise, regardless of the resource. In the travel agency enterprise, policy logic can be taken out of each individual database and instead be expressed by these policies.

- An Authorization Decision Service, which acts as the service that makes access control decisions based on enterprise policy for a subject's access to a resource. In order for the Authorization Decision Service to make a decision, it must know the identity of the subject requesting the resource (via an identity token), the authorization credentials of the user (via the Attribute Service), and the policy of the resource and the enterprise policy (via the Policy Retrieval Service).

- An STS, which issues tokens related to the identity and security attributes of users, as well as authorization decisions. This token service identifies users, and in doing so, communicates with the other services.

In creating an identity token, the STS would communicate with the Authentication Service in order to authenticate the user. In creating a token containing identity AND attributes, the STS would communicate with both the Authentication Service and the Attribute Service. In creating an Authorization Decision token, the STS may need to talk to all services.

These services accommodate the blueprints referenced in Figure 11-22, where we provided a decision flow chart for access control, with six potential methods of enforcing enterprise access control. By separating security functionality into these services, you provide a great deal of architectural flexibility, with many options for the enterprise, which accommodates changes in security requirements over time. In many cases, a centralized policy decision-making service (with the Central PDP) may be required. In other cases, the final tier may be able to make "local" decisions based on a token issued from the STS, and various combinations to calls to other services (see all the options in Figure 11-22).

Defining Identity Propagation and Access Control

You decided earlier to use token-based propagation for the travel agency, because this alleviates a dependence on any particular authentication type. At this point, it is important to look at the decision flows for both identity propagation (see Figure 11-16) and access control (see Figure 11-22) to make decisions for propagation, because the type of access control dictates what type of token to propagate (identity, attribute, or both). Because you have decided to establish an STS, and because the only intermediate service between the portal and the reservation Web Services is a trusted aggregation service, you decide to adopt the STS approach in identity propagation (Solution F in Figure 11-16). Because of the security requirements in the enterprise, it is important that access control be managed centrally but remotely enforced, combining a local and central policy (Solution D in Figure 11-22). For this reason, you propagate identity tokens in the solution and have the security handler for each Web Service retrieve the central policy and look up the local policy and the user's security attributes to make access control decisions.

Figure 11-25 shows a picture of the security architecture, based on the decisions made. Looking at the services that you have defined, the user's front-end application (the portal) can authenticate the user, initiating communication with the STS, which retrieves a token that asserts the user's identity. Because SAML is a standard and has much support in various products, you decide to use SAML tokens in the STS, and WS-Security SAML Token Profile for secure messaging. Based on a user's successful authentication, and based on authorization credentials and the access control policy, which can be retrieved from

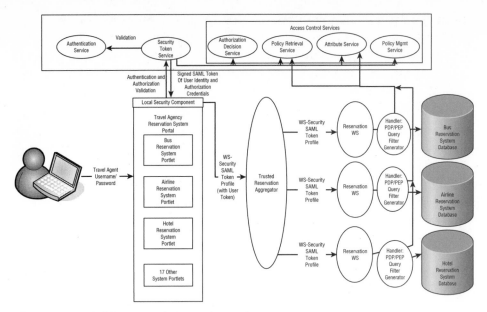

Figure 11-25 Architecture using security services

enterprise security services, each Web Service can perform filtered queries across each database.

Figure 11-25 shows how security functionality is further abstracted from each implementation of the Reservation Web Service for each back-end database. Security logic is separated into a local security component, which in this case is labeled PDP/PEP Query Filter Generator. This component may be a plug-in or security handler that inspects and validates the SAML token that is propagated into the Web Service, queries global enterprise policy from the Policy Retrieval Service, queries the Attribute Service for the user's credentials, and based on that information, creates a filtered transaction on the database. For performance reasons, the query for global enterprise policy can occur on an infrequent basis, and user attributes can be cached for a certain amount of time.

Finally, security requirements dictate other aspects of messaging in the solution. If non-repudiation of the results of each transaction is needed, each Web Service security component would also have the responsibility of digitally signing the Web Service response, providing a receipt of the transaction with high assurance. If confidentiality in transit is also needed, XML Encryption could be used to encrypt the response of the transaction to the Travel Agency Reservation System portal application.

This use case provides one example of how to use some of the strategies discussed in this chapter. The next section provides a common sense guide to security, with practical steps that an architect can take in any project.

The Security Game Plan for the SOA Architect

If you are new to information security principles or to some of the standards discussed in this chapter, you may be overwhelmed at this point. The learning curve related to understanding the security fundamentals alone is quite steep, and there is quite an "alphabet soup" of security standards that overlap or compete with each other in many areas. Because each of the security standards has multiple options, it is easy to see that there is not one clear usage scenario — there are many! It is also important to note that there is never "one answer" for every SOA security solution. Every SOA is unique and, therefore, has its own individual security requirements. Providing all of this security background information necessitated going "into the weeds" in some areas of this chapter. Now, however, we would like you to sit back and focus on the "big picture." This section provides a high-level game plan for providing SOA security solutions in your projects.

Plan from the Beginning, Focusing on Requirements

The big picture is that focusing on security from the beginning is essential, and the plan needs to be based on the requirements of the organization(s) involved. When SOA architects wait until the last minute to plan for security, disaster awaits. In too many projects, the initial emphasis is solely on developing the core functionality of services, and adding security is postponed until the end of projects. As you can imagine, adding the security capabilities discussed earlier in this chapter not only requires a steep learning curve, but also retrofitting security at the last minute leads to a brittle architecture and probably leads to burned-out developers! For this reason, security architecture planning needs to be at the beginning of your roadmap.

In order to plan for security, however, it is important to understand your security requirements. Regardless of the technologies used, you cannot achieve your goals if you do not understand what your goals are. A requirements analysis phase is critical for this understanding. Because most customers are focused on functionality, they may not think about security until right before deployment when their security officer mandates certain requirements. When asked, most stakeholders say "Yes, I would like you to make everything secure. Thanks!" At the beginning of each project, you need to determine what requirements exist for authentication, authorization, confidentiality, integrity, non-repudiation, auditing, and availability. Find out who is levying security requirements, ask them specific questions, and determine the true requirements together. Once you discover the true requirements of your SOA, you can then begin planning and you can determine the approaches that you can take in order to satisfy your security goals.

In doing requirements analysis, it is also important that you understand the current enterprise architecture with which your SOA needs to interoperate. Your SOA may need to integrate with LDAP directories, policy servers, Attribute Services, and a PKI. It is important that your planning includes this infrastructure so that you don't architect in a vacuum.

Crawl and Walk before Running

It is certainly a temptation at the beginning of SOA-based projects to attempt to achieve too much and "boil the ocean" in an unrealistic period of time. To satisfy security requirements, it is paramount that methods of achieving security goals be rigorously tested against your requirements and against potential threats and vulnerabilities. If the security requirements for your SOA require much to be achieved, it is preferable to create a phased approach to separate complexity and to make certain that each individual goal is successfully achieved. Moving from an SOA with no security to an SOA with high-levels of access control and dynamic, federated access to partners can be done over time, but stampeding toward this goal too quickly causes disappointment and could cause disaster. A phased, incremental approach, where additional security requirements can be rigorously tested in each phase, is more likely to succeed.

Use Accepted Standards (in a Standard Way)

The second part of this chapter focused on accepted standards and specifications used in SOA security solutions. They were chosen to be included in this chapter because they are produced by standards bodies, and they are accepted and used by major vendors. It is certainly possible to use proprietary technologies to achieve your security goals, but doing so flies in the face of interoperability, one of the main reasons for using SOA in the first place. Trust us, tying yourself to a proprietary solution is painful in the long run, and may necessitate a total rewrite or redesign in order to be interoperable with other systems, tools, and technologies. It is therefore important to use standards.

It is also important to use standards in a *standard way*. In the early days of SOA, when standards such as WS-Security and SAML were in their infancy, security architects had to create XML-based messaging security themselves, acting as "amateur cryptographers." Even when WS-Security SOAP Messaging became a higher-level standard that combined lower-level standards such as XML, SOAP, XML Encryption, and XML Signature, it alone did not specify how it would be used with security tokens such as SAML, X.509 Certificates, or Kerberos Tickets. Security architects had to meet security requirements by determining how to use the standards together in a secure way. The results during this period of time introduced security vulnerabilities, as SOA architects aren't expected to be cryptographers. Just as important, the results were standards-based but proprietary, non-interoperable messaging solutions that used standards in a nonstandard way.

Thankfully, over the years, the standards have evolved, and higher-level standards specify how to use standards together (such as the various WS-Security Token Profiles). As a result, there is no reason to create new messaging protocols! Instead, it is important to choose those standards that achieve your requirements, looking to standards that are accepted and adopted by many commercial vendors, so that your SOA is interoperable with other systems as your enterprise evolves in the future.

Understand the Details of the Standards

Unfortunately, understanding the standards at a high level are not enough when you are creating security solutions for your SOA enterprise. These standards provide many options and each option can be used in different ways in order to achieve different security requirements. The standards therefore need to be fully understood by the security architects involved in your SOA projects, which means you need to read the specifications involved.

Each standard lists security considerations related to their use in operational SOA deployments, and they need to be fully understood. For many of the standards, advice is given related to the threat of message replay, denial of service attacks, and other attacks and countermeasures. In each standard, there may be options that provide different security capabilities that are important to understand. For example, WS-Security SAML Token Profile has multiple confirmation methods — holder of key and sender-vouches; understanding the requirements and security goals of each method could have an impact on the trust models (and the infrastructure) of your SOA. This is just one example, but the key point here is that the security architect needs to understand the ramifications of the use of all options in your standards.

Finally, it is important (and probably fairly obvious at this point) that most standards in SOA security do not stand alone. Many have dependencies and other interactions with standards and infrastructure provided by other standards. For example, WS-SecureConversation and WS-Federation rely on the specifications and infrastructure (the STS) of WS-Trust. WS-Security and various token profiles are used together, and these interactions are documented in the various WS-Security Token Profile standards. SAML and XACML can be used together, and as a result, there is a standard called "The SAML 2.0 Profile of the XACML 2.0 Standard." The list goes on. In most cases, the interactions and dependencies of standards are documented in each standard but refer to other standards.

Vendor toolkits and containers sometimes provide default capabilities for using specific standards, but these default capabilities may not be sufficient.

In order to satisfy your security requirements, you need to understand the details of the security mechanisms of your SOA. The bottom line? Spend some time reading the standards! If you don't understand them, you should hire an SOA security architect on your project who does.

Understand the Impact of Security on Performance

When developing the security architecture for your SOA, remember that security always has an impact on the performance of service consumers and providers in your enterprise. Network calls made to authenticate subjects, retrieve authorization credentials, and obtain policy information have an effect on bandwidth as well as performance. The file I/O and bandwidth associated with auditing to local and remote file systems can have an impact on system performance. When cryptography is used in secure messaging, there is always an impact on performance, because cryptography uses computationally expensive operations.

Cryptography is a "double-edged sword," meaning that cryptography can certainly be used to achieve security goals, but it always has a negative impact on performance. It is important for the SOA architect to realize that more cryptography does not mean more security. It is indeed possible to create a very slow solution that does not achieve your security goals. For this reason, it is important to understand the security requirements for SOA. If encryption is not needed, then don't use it! If there is no requirement for integrity or non-repudiation, don't use digital signatures! Be intentional in your use of cryptography and understand its potential performance impact.

From a performance perspective, it is important to look at technology solutions and architectural solutions focused on maximizing performance and availability, and some strategies related to access control were discussed in the "SOA Security Blueprints" section of this chapter. Finally, depending on your performance requirements, it may be wise to investigate XML and security appliances that offload XML processing and cryptographic operations to hardware. If you do this, determine the impact at the beginning of your projects, just in case a large amount of integration needs to be written.

Try to Keep It Simple

The most elegant and secure solutions are usually the most simple. The more complex a solution is, the greater the possibility of introducing bugs and vulnerabilities. Therefore, try not to over-engineer your solution, and try to use standard practices and blueprints for securing your SOA. Try to apply security mechanisms to all of your clients and services in the same way, reusing security components. Treat services as "black boxes," and make sure that all inputs, outputs, and side effects of calling them are documented, intuitive, and well understood. Finally, try to anticipate use cases in your SOA, and always expect and plan for message-chaining scenarios and Web Service orchestration in your security design.

Summary

This chapter has provided a brief but in-depth look at SOA security. Building on a security vocabulary and discussing SOA security goals in the first section, we provided a look at the major standards in Web Services that are accepted and are being adopted by industry in the second section. In the third section of this chapter, we focused on SOA Security "blueprints" that can be used for you to make practical decisions about your security architecture. In the fourth section, we provided an example case study putting the blueprints and concepts of this chapter into action. Finally, in the last section, we have provided some common-sense guidance and a game plan for achieving your SOA security goals. Use this guidance and blueprints to achieve success in your SOA-based projects.

CHAPTER 12

SOA Governance

With the widespread adoption of SOA, the challenges associated with SOA projects are emerging. SOA governance isn't optional — it's imperative. Without it, return on investment will be low and every SOA project out of the pilot phase will be at risk.
–Paolo Malinverno

SOA governance is essential to a successful SOA. Without it, well-intended SOA pilot projects spiral into chaos when they go operational. We have seen it before — an organization spends a lot of money developing services, it declares success when everything works well in the lab, but because they didn't plan ahead for every aspect of the project for real-time operations, there is constant pain at all levels of the organization when the project goes "live." In cases like these, where governance is largely ignored, the isolated technology benefits of SOA adoption are outweighed by the hassle of managing chaos. Managers, architects, and developers get burnt out as they make necessary massive "Band-Aid" solutions to real-time deployed systems. There are many people (like us) who have the battle scars from the early days of SOA, and by reading this chapter, you can benefit from the lessons we have learned. This chapter provides an introduction to SOA governance. It defines and describes the SOA governance life cycle, and it provides a practical guide for implementing it in your organization.

Specifically, this chapter covers the following topics:

- Important terminology, principles, and goals related to SOA governance

- The case for SOA governance, where we explain why every organization needs to focus on these processes

- The SOA governance life cycle as it applies to the life cycle of services, with each process and the roles of stakeholders explained at every step

- Practical actionable steps and key processes that can be used in setting up SOA governance in your organization

SOA Management and Governance Defined

The terms *SOA management* and *SOA governance* are terms whose definitions intersect with each other. For this reason, we feel that it is important to formally define them in this section.

SOA governance is the creation, communication, enforcement, and adaptation of *policies* used to direct and control the creation and implementation of the life cycle of services. It is a run-time and design-time administrative capability that no organization should be without. Jean Jacques Dubray, in his October 2007 InfoQ article "Establishing a Service Governance Organization," provides a well-written objective of service governance:

> *The main objective of Service governance is to achieve the benefits of a Service Oriented Architecture by fostering the creation of reusable, enterprise class services. As a cross functional organization, service governance ensures the timely resolution of issues and conflicts due to the necessary tradeoffs that are made when shared requirements are defined.*

An organization's governance process is policy-centric, and these policies involve enterprise standards, capabilities, and constraints for use of specific services in run-time service policies and best practices. Simply put, governance sets policies in place, and provides the mechanism to enforce them. Governance itself is not a process that is unique to SOA — it can be applied to any business domain used to accomplish business objectives. SOA governance does have some unique characteristics, different from those of general governance, as it applies to the service life cycle, and this chapter focuses on these characteristics. *SOA management* establishes control of the Service-Oriented Enterprise (SOE) — first, by creating a holistic view of the entire enterprise, and then by providing the capabilities to control, monitor, and measure information about services and other enterprise components. By having access to a "big picture" view of your SOA, you are able to understand real-time requirements by comprehending how the services are being used, and you are able to make changes in order to accommodate those requirements. Sometimes called Enterprise Service Management (ESM), SOA management involves the real-time control and collection of data about services in the enterprise.

While SOA management provides the big picture, its definition collides with governance when it involves measuring and monitoring the adherence to SOA governance policies. Information collected in the SOA management process may directly affect governance. For example, response time guarantees for service level agreements (SLAs) may be refined over time, based on the metrics collected as the services are used. The SOA governance life cycle is commonly referred to in four different phases — design time, deploy time, run time, and change time:

- Design-Time Governance refers to the defining and controlling of enterprise services to be created in the enterprise, and the creation of policies used to direct and control the implementation of the enterprise service life cycle. Key aspects of design-time governance are the *creation of enterprise policies* used to direct and control the implementation of the life cycle of enterprise services, and the *creation of run-time service policies* that specify constraints and capabilities for specific enterprise services. In this phase, an SOA architect is responsible for defining and authoring policies for standards compliance, privacy requirements, access control, reliability, performance, messaging, and developing SLAs.

- Deploy-Time Governance involves the process of *testing and controlling compliance* to enterprise policies in order for services to be deployed in an SOA. It involves deployment options and topologies, and adherence to policy should dictate whether or not a service can be deployed on a network.

- Run-Time Governance refers to the process of *enforcing the adherence to run-time service policies at run time*. In addition to policy enforcement, this term is often used to include aspects of SOA management as it relates to these policies and to include real-time policy compliance monitoring, auditing, and measuring and collecting result statistics.

- Change-Time Governance involves *managing services through the cycle of change*. In a service life cycle, interfaces, service policies, and agreements may be modified many times. Change-time governance focuses on such issues as service versioning, deprecation, and run-time policy adaptation. Governance tools can be used to achieve such strategies as adding service intermediaries to intercept messages and route them to the appropriate previous versions of services.

As you can see, governance revolves around policy. Policies are created, edited, and refined throughout the life cycle of a project. The following are common types of policies used in SOA governance:

- **Messaging Security** — What are the policies related to confidentiality, integrity, and non-repudiation for each service? What kind of authentication is used? Are tokens, such as Kerberos, username/password, or SAML used to convey the identity of the end user? What standards to support these mechanisms are used?

- **Access Control Policy** — What are the access control policies used for the services?

- **Conformance to Enterprise Vocabulary and Schema** — What schemas need to be supported for a service to deploy? Is there a common enterprise vocabulary that needs to be used? Is there a reference data model?

- **Conformance to Technical Standards (WS-I, WSDL, WS-Security, WS-ReliableMessaging)** — What are the standards to which a service must conform in order to deploy?

- **Deployment Process** — What is the process for deploying new services? Related to standards conformance, are there run-time tests that enable a service to be deployed on the network?

- **Versioning Policies** — What are the policies related to service versioning and deprecation of existing services?

- **Discovery Policy** — What is the process of discovering a service and determining its access policies?

- **Privacy Regulations** — What privacy regulations must be enforced, and how can they be enforced?

- **Quality of Service (QoS)** — Are there guaranteed response times for each service? Are there levels of service responsiveness and priorities for each classification of user? (For example, employees, customers, and partners may each get a different guarantee of responsiveness and be put in a priority queue for the same service implementation.) Are there service levels (for example, gold, silver, bronze) for each type of customer, or are they individualized? Can service levels be negotiated at run time according to the requestor's requirements?

- **Reliability** — Are there policies related to in-order delivery, at least once delivery, and at most once delivery?

- **Auditing and Reporting Requirements** — What type of auditing and reporting needs to be supported by each service?

- **Service Level Agreements (SLAs)** — Are there formal agreements between service consumers and providers related to QoS response times, business units of work, and action guarantees based on met conditions? Are there service load conditions related to guarantees?

Certainly, this is not an exhaustive list. These examples of governance policies involve standards conformance for service deployment, changing service interfaces, agreements between parties, domain-specific requirements and regulations, and enterprise best practices. SOA governance policies for standards compliance can usually be run in automated service testing scripts, determining whether or not a service can be deployed. SOA governance policies used at run time should be easily discoverable and be written in a declarative, configurable, and machine-understandable language (such as WS-Policy), allowing services and clients to adapt to changing policies at run time.

All of the types of policies mentioned in this section do not apply to every SOA; each enterprise may have different requirements. It is also important to know that SOA governance policies do not have to be exhaustive and overwhelming — a little bit of policy and guidance often goes a long way. The key thing to understand is that there needs to be some level of governance; enterprise requirements dictate exactly how much.

SOA governance is necessary for providing guidance and keeping things in order, increasing the chance of success. Policies developed for services govern how services and their consumers interoperate, providing a contract more expressive and descriptive than interface bindings. In many cases, SOA governance solutions are legally necessary; there are costly penalties for not conforming to laws such as Sarbanes-Oxley (SOX), HIPAA (Health Insurance Portability and Accountability Act), and other domain-specific regulations which include the management, control, monitoring, and auditing of events. Finally, adopting a successful SOA governance strategy means that your enterprise architecture can evolve by design, not by accident!

The Case for SOA Governance

Many engineers new to SOA (or those who have not had to be involved in an operational SOA) question the need for governance. They design, develop, and deploy their services, and they feel that this is enough. In this section, we demonstrate to you why SOA governance is indeed important.

The Reality of Change in Real-World Deployments

The stories of ill-fated SOA pilot projects are not always the same. Certainly, in many cases, projects fail because of a poor architecture or poor service designs, when architects and designers ignore much of what we've talked about in this book. Sadly, however, the most unfortunate projects are those with good architectures and elegant designs that fail because of a lack of planning for change and what goes on in real-world operations.

The stories of these cases are often the same. The designs were initially solid, everything went well in the development lab, and services were rigorously tested. There may have been some inherent governance involved related to the architectural process. When they were initially deployed in operations, everything went okay *until something needed to be changed*. Because there was no process for service versioning and deprecation, changes temporarily broke the connections between clients and services, requiring changes in client applications. And that was only the beginning.

In this true story, lack of governance had a downward spiral effect on the project. Security changes broke connections, requiring client upgrades. When services needed to support specific functionality for different classifications of users, service code got larger. As requirements changed, overworked developers quickly modified the service interfaces to support the requirements. The larger the enterprise and customer base, the more intense the chaos. To keep up with the constant change and the deadlines, enterprise schemas were abandoned or hastily changed without thinking. Over time, the Band-Aid fixes evolved into spaghetti code and spaghetti WSDL written by overworked developers trying to keep up with constant change. With every change, there were irate customers who needed to understand and rebind to the new service interface. Sadly, such a project with initially nicely designed and adequately developed services became an operations and maintenance nightmare. Finally, because it took too much time, money, and effort for the system to adapt to the changing requirements, the project was abandoned, or the scope of the project was reduced to the point where it was effectively "dead."

If that story is familiar to you, we feel your pain. Change is inevitable. If you have an organization focused on governance that defines processes in your service life cycle, you are ready for change. Service governance mechanisms allow you to plan for change, putting run-time service policies in place, and allowing you to adapt to these policies at design time and run time. Certain enterprise policies, as simple as service versioning and service deprecation, can happen at design time (or policy authoring time). Policies related to SLAs and messaging security should not have to change the service interfaces. If the run-time service policies are written in a declarative, software-readable format (WS-Policy, for example), client applications can dynamically adjust to such agreements at run time. The result of good service governance is a project and an organization that is prepared for change, increasing its chances for success.

The Need for an Enterprise Big Picture

An enterprise has many moving parts. One of the greatest benefits of Service-Oriented Architecture is that services are reusable components that are combined with other services to build enterprise applications. As a result, there are many permutations of the ways services can be used together. There are lots of things that can go wrong, and there is a need to have a centralized, big picture view of your SOA. Based on this operational big picture, you can detect and fix problems, and adapt aspects of your services to meet the needs of what goes on in real-time operations.

As we also discussed in Chapter 9, a simple example of this need involves troubleshooting errors. When a service throws an exception, the error message may not be descriptive or intuitive enough for troubleshooters to understand the problem, and looking at detailed logging may be necessary in order to understand the problem. Figure 12-1 shows a scenario that demonstrates this example. A client sends a SOAP request to Service A, and the resulting service transactions involve message routing all the way to Service F, which throws a SOAP fault (or exception) because Service E created the request incorrectly. In this example, each service returns the SOAP fault to its caller. In such an environment, where there is no centralized view of your SOA, determining what went wrong is only accomplished by inspecting the logs of the services in the life cycle of the request. If each service logs information locally, troubleshooting sometimes involves the painful process of calling the systems' administrators who manage each service — one at a time.

> **NOTE** Chapter 9 focuses in depth on solutions used for solving these types of problems. You can refer to such solutions as blueprints and recommendations when developing enterprise governance policies for your organization.

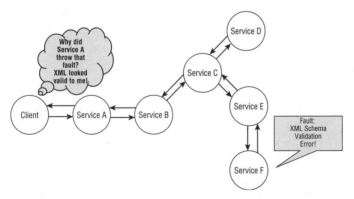

Figure 12-1 Example scenario showing the need for a central SOA view

Certainly, such an example underscores the need for SOA governance. In design-time governance, architects provide enterprise policy guidance related to detailed messaging and error handling. This example also demonstrates the need for SOA management, where software tools can provide monitoring, a centralized view of audit logs, and the mechanisms necessary to have the big picture of the enterprise. Based on analysis of statistics gathered in service monitoring, governance policies may be edited and refined over time, and decisions related to availability and performance may be made. Having a high-level, operational view of how clients and services interact increases the probability of success in real-time operations.

The Need for Explicit Run-Time Service Policies

Ever since the advent of Web Services, books and magazine articles have shown a picture similar to Figure 12-2. This famous "publish-find-bind" triangle has been used in literature to show how Web Services can dynamically work with UDDI and other service registries. In practice, the service provider usually registers its WSDL with a service broker, who stores the service provider's information in a registry. A service consumer registers with the broker to discover the Web Service, and finally, the service consumer downloads the service's WSDL and dynamically binds to the Web Service. As we discussed in Chapter 2 (see sidebar "Dynamic Discovery and Binding"), the "publish WSDL, find, and bind" model is a fallacy because it is woefully incomplete in practice.

Conceptually, this abstract publish-find-bind model is solid. The typical WSDL use case, however, is sufficient for your operational SOA only if you are still living in the Garden of Eden. In the real world, there is a lot more to connecting with a service than just knowing the syntax of its interface. In an operational environment, you are more than likely to have different policies for security, transport, authorization, and service level guarantees based on different customers, partners, suppliers, and employees that interact with your

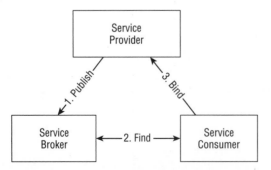

Figure 12-2 The famous publish-find-bind triangle

services. Service clients (or agents or intermediaries who work on behalf of the clients) have to understand these policies, and they also have to understand the semantics of what is in the payload of the services. The service providers have to enforce these policies at run time. Due to certain legal requirements (for example, SOX, HIPAA, and other similar policies), service providers have to monitor and audit interactions, policy enforcement, and compliance at run time.

What does this all mean? First, it means that in order for services to operate in the real world, there must be policies in place that account for all of these requirements (capabilities and constraints) beyond interface binding. Services have to enforce these policies, and both service consumers and service providers have to adapt to policy change. Second, it means that projects without design-time governance evolve into chaotic systems that never scale. Third, it means that projects without run-time and change-time governance are never able to adapt to the rigors of policy compliance and change. Finally, our experience is that a huge percentage of pilot projects that did not begin with SOA governance ended up failing.

Applying design-time governance with discoverable run-time service policies that express the constraints and capabilities of services can help realize the vision of the conceptual publish-find-bind triangle. In a policy-driven enterprise, expressed and exposed policies provide more information in discovery of services for how clients can connect. We talk about this later in this chapter.

The Need to Separate Policy Logic from Business Logic

Some who are new to SOA agree with governance in principle. They believe that certain policies need to be in place (design-time governance), but they argue that run-time and change-time governance can be accomplished by hard-coding compliance logic in the business logic of the services involved. This assumption is another example of theory versus practice. It sounds doable in theory but becomes quite complicated and unmanageable in practice.

First of all, policies change over time, and although changing service code to adapt to the policy changes is theoretically doable, it introduces very tight coupling. It is laborious for anyone to change the code of their services for every policy change, and every service change may require changes to service clients. Complicating the matter is the fact that real-world services undoubtedly have different policies in place for every partner. Figure 12-3 shows an example of how a simple service may have different policies, depending on the types of consumers using the service. In the figure, a book store has a service called the Book Ordering Service, which allows customers, business partners, and employees to order books.

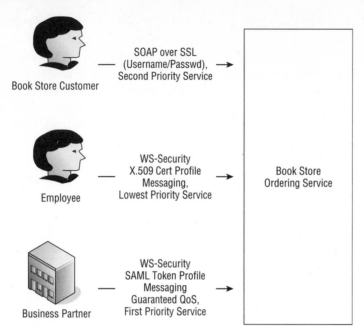

Figure 12-3 Different policies for different consumers

In Figure 12-3, each consumer of the service has different messaging security requirements and receives a different service priority. Business partners of the book store have guaranteed quality of service, they have first priority over all active requests, and they use WS-Security SAML Token Profile messaging for authentication. Customers, however, simply use SOAP with username/password-based SSL, and have secondary priority. Employees of the book store use WS-Security X.509 Certificate Profile messaging over SSL and have the lowest priority. Each has separate auditing requirements. When receiving a queue of requests, a service must answer requests based on priority, and the service (or the service container or handler) has to enforce the security requirements for each case. This is an extremely simple and common case; a service may have to enforce many other different types of policies based on who the consumer is.

Although this is a simple example, hopefully you can see that hard-coding such policy logic in the business logic of this service for these three consumers is more complex than if the policy logic was separate. Without even mentioning the code for the actual functionality of the service, there would need to be consumer identification, code for three different styles of messaging security, and service queuing based on the consumer's priority. The problem with embedding policy with a service's business logic is tight coupling. In doing so, no matter how your service is otherwise designed, you are tightly coupling your services based on policy, and in this case, you are tightly coupling your service's business logic to your service consumers. More importantly, your service client has to understand this policy and may have to write different code for the different messaging mechanisms required. If any of these policies ever change, you have to rewrite your service (or the code in your interceptor or handler if you componentize this policy logic), and changing this messaging implementation breaks the interactions with your clients. Your clients, in turn, have to rewrite the interaction with the service if the messaging security implementation changes. In practice, adapting to policy changes without run-time governance involves pandemonium, weeping, and gnashing of teeth. Unfortunately, this a common problem.

An effective way to avoid this predicament is by explicitly declaring your policies in a discoverable and software-readable format, by using *run-time governance* mechanisms to enforce the policies on the service side, and by discovering and adhering to the policies on the client side. In the "Practical SOA Governance" section later in this chapter, we explore how this can be achieved.

SOA Governance and the Service Life Cycle

The SOA governance life cycle, as we define it, is shown in Figure 12-4. We have overlaid it with the Service Life Cycle from Chapter 3 in order to provide context, since the governance drives all aspects of the service life cycle, from cradle to grave. This section walks you through every phase of the service life cycle, focusing on the processes that occur in each phase, as well as the stakeholders involved.

An organization's SOA governance team dictates the processes that occur throughout the service life cycle, as well as the roles and responsibilities of the stakeholders. Therefore, processes and stakeholders may be different from organization to organization. However, this section defines typical successful processes, as well as stakeholders and their roles and responsibilities. SOA governance affects the entire organization, and one person often fills multiple roles. Throughout the following sections, we refer to the following stakeholder roles:

- **Solution Lead** — A business architect tasked with solving a particular business problem. This stakeholder's responsibilities mostly revolve around the translation of business requirements into a service proposal.

- **Functional Architect** — An architect who maintains and enhances an enterprise functional model. He or she maintains a messaging dictionary (semantic messaging) that ensures interoperability between enterprise services, and he or she ensures service alignment with the functional model.

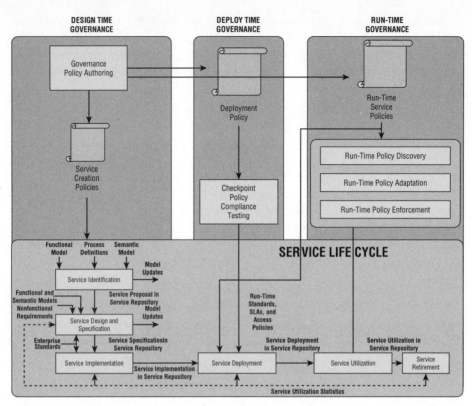

Figure 12-4 SOA governance in the service life cycle

- **Portfolio Architect** — An architect managing an application portfolio that includes services, this stakeholder ensures that services are aligned with the directions for a particular portfolio. He or she also maintains the business relationships with business units, as well as other portfolios. Finally, he or she serves as a Subject Matter Expert on the existing functionality of the applications within the portfolio.

- **Enterprise Architect** — This stakeholder plays a pivotal role in service identification and design. He or she is responsible for making sure that each service fits into the overall enterprise context. In addition, the architect is responsible for the integration approaches and adapter designs. The architect chooses appropriate implementation platforms for services and is responsible for nonfunctional requirements for services and their implementation.

- **Business Process Architect** — An architect managing enterprise business processes and their evolution, he or she works closely with the functional architect, ensuring the alignment of services with the current and future business processes.

- **Services Librarian** — A person responsible for maintenance of the service registry, a backbone of service governance. This stakeholder works to ensure that all of the service information is in a standardized form, accurate, up-to-date, and properly classified.

- **SOA Run-Time Architect** — An architect responsible for maintenance of and enhancements to the service run time, including standardization of service APIs, and service run-time support — registry, monitoring, and so on.

- **Application Developer** — This stakeholder is a developer building and maintaining business functionality for base services.

- **Service Assembler** — The developer building and maintaining business functionality for composite service (business processes).

- **Service Tester** — A quality assurance (QA) representative responsible for testing of the services.

- **Service Infrastructure Specialist** — An infrastructure engineer responsible for the creation of the service deployment diagrams and topologies, and maintenance of the service registry and service management solution. He or she also monitors service usage and SLA adherence.

SOA governance directly affects people from different parts of organization. The policies, processes, and procedures that are developed in SOA governance need to be comprehensive, and must cover all of these stages of the service life cycle. The next sections of this chapter provide an overview of each aspect of governance, focusing on design time, deploy time, and run time. Each section refers to the life cycle in Figure 12-4. Although we don't specifically call out "change-time governance" as an explicit phase, accommodation of change is built-in based on service utilization statistics and metrics collected in run-time governance and, therefore, is addressed in that section. This section focuses on all phases of governance and walks you through the service life cycle.

NOTE Remember as you go through the next few sections that the SOA governance activities throughout the service life cycle can vary from organization to organization, and they depend on many things, including the makeup and culture of your organization. It is important to know that this section covers the "whole nine yards" of SOA governance, and its elements are representative of the processes, roles, and stakeholders of a very mature organization. If your organization is new to SOA (or new to governance processes), you probably want to start small, evolving to the mature process that we discuss (see the "Governance from Day 3" sidebar later in this chapter). Finally, the mature processes and activities that we define serve as a model that should be tailored to fit your organization.

Design-Time Governance

Design-time governance involves legislation (policy creation) that affects processes throughout the service life cycle. Initial policies are typically enterprise-wide policies focused on technical standards compliance, adherence to an enterprise vocabulary, and service creation policies. In an organization with a mature process, such policies already exist, and new projects usually inherit or customize the policies, according to their requirements.

It is important that clear ownership of SOA issues be established, providing efficient resolution of SOA-specific issues, defining SOA funding approaches, enabling maturity tracking, aligning the organization's SOA strategy with other enterprise strategies, ensuring infrastructure readiness, creating policies and processes, and ensuring adherence to them. This is typically done by establishing a team responsible for SOA governance in an organization. At the beginning of SOA projects, service creation policies dictate the service proposal, design, and implementation processes. Adherence to compliance policies is regulated by the SOA governance group, and this group determines whether or not the services can be deployed (deploy-time governance).

Run-time service policies defining capabilities and constraints of specific services are also defined during the design-time governance phase in the service life cycle. Unlike enterprise-wide policies, these policies are related to the services themselves and are based on business requirements, domain-specific rules, and specific regulations. These run-time policies revolve around constraints and capabilities (security, reliability, and quality of service), and are policies that act as contracts between the service and the service consumer.

SLAs are typically part of the run-time service policy. An SLA relates to guarantees of benchmarks related to performance and availability, and includes acceptable performance parameters, the duration of the agreement, procedures for monitoring the service levels, exceptions to the agreement, and problem resolution procedures. Metrics such as messages per hour, service response time, uptime, throughput, number of errors, units of business work completed, different roles for the parties involved, and other factors are used when creating SLAs. Classes of customers may have different SLAs for the same service — a "Gold" customer may be promised a better priority of service than a "Silver" or "Bronze" customer, and each may have different connection requirements.

Run-time policies are authored in the design-time phase and are typically defined by a declarative language such as WS-Policy. Typically, run-time service policies are refined over time, based on the collection of metrics and use cases in the operational environment.

DIFFERENTIATING SERVICE POLICIES AND BUSINESS PROCESSES

A point of confusion for some relates to the difference between Business Process Management (BPM) rules and run-time service policies for services. Policies that affect run-time decisions are usually discoverable through a registry. Some vendors offer both BPM and Governance using the same framework. A service's policy contract can also be seen as "rules." So what is the difference between BPM rules and service policies?

Most business processes are based on business rules and workflow (see Chapters 4 and 5), where most run-time governance policies for services are sets of constraints and capabilities that describe how a service and a client interact. For this reason, we refer to such policies in this book as "run-time service policies," because the term "policy" is an overloaded term. The following may be rules for a fictional service; some of these rules involve BPM, and some involve the service policy:

1. The Book Store Order Service requires WS-Security X.509 Certificate Profile Messaging, and only recognizes certificates issued by "`Trumantruck.com`."

2. Users with "Gold Status" get 10% off all orders.

3. The Book Store Order Service accepts requests for its last two deprecated versions until December 5, 2008.

4. The Book Store Order Service has equal to or better than a 5 second response time.

5. Once the Book Store receives an order, orders must be checked and approved by the corporate VISA and MasterCard representative.

6. If a book is not available, the customer's request is routed to a partner business service, and the Book Store Order Service facilitates this communication.

   The rules (1), (3), and (4) relate to governance, because they relate to how clients interact with the service. Rules (2), (5), and (6) relate to the internal business process logic of the service itself. You would declare your governance policies for the service (1, 3, and 4) in a standard language that is discoverable through a registry. The other rules are internal to the service, and they are best delegated to a business rules engine or workflow solution for the implementation of that service.

Design-time governance processes impact every area of the service life cycle. In this section, we focus on the three parts of the service life cycle that occur during the design-time governance phase for a project: service identification, service design and specification, and service implementation.

The Service Identification Process

The first step in the service life cycle, shown earlier in Figure 12-4, is *service identification*. This process is dictated by the SOA governance group, and it is driven off of the functional (business) model, process definition, and semantic information model, resulting in a proposal for a new service. These artifacts are usually located in a service repository (we discuss the role of the service repository in detail later in this chapter). The service identification process should include multiple activities, as shown in Figure 12-5.

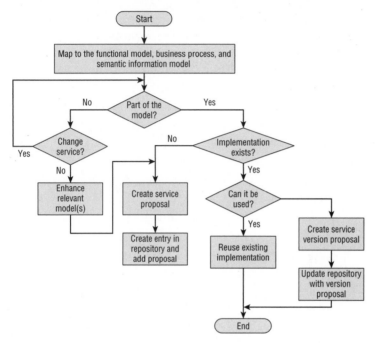

Figure 12-5 The Service Identification Process

Since the resulting proposal relies on the functional and semantic information models, step changes can be introduced to those models to ensure that they always reflect the current state of the enterprise. Stakeholders during this phase include the Enterprise Architect, the Solutions Lead, the Portfolio Architect, Functional Architect, Business Process Architect, and Services Librarian, and the duties that they perform are shown in Figure 12-6.

As a result of this process, a service proposal is created, and it is typically a free-form document (depending on the organization's policy on service proposals), containing the following:

- Description of the service functionality
- The mapping of the proposed service to the functional architecture model

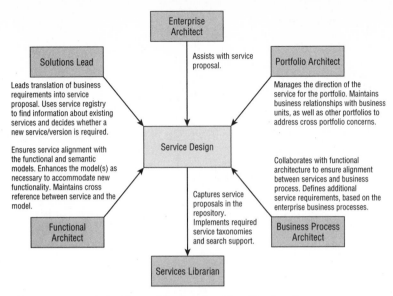

Figure 12-6 Stakeholders of the Service Identification Process

- The mapping of the proposed service to the semantic information model
- The mapping of the proposed service to the relevant processes that may use it as an activity
- The service interface, outlining business entities used as a service input and output
- A statement conforming to the plan to adhere to relevant enterprise policies established by the SOA governance group

This service proposal is then stored in the service repository. Storing it in the service repository before the actual design and implementation allows for a better tracking of services and improving the service reuse.

The Service Design and Specification Process

After the service proposal phase, the *service design and specification process* is the next step in the service life cycle. Enterprise service creation policies developed by the SOA governance group dictate the service design process and the way that stakeholders work together in order to achieve the goals of the process. A typical design process is shown in Figure 12-7. Similar to the service proposal process, a key aspect of the design process involves the use of the service repository, reviewing and updating the semantic information model and functional model, and placing the resulting design in the repository. The design itself includes the interface as well as run-time service policies.

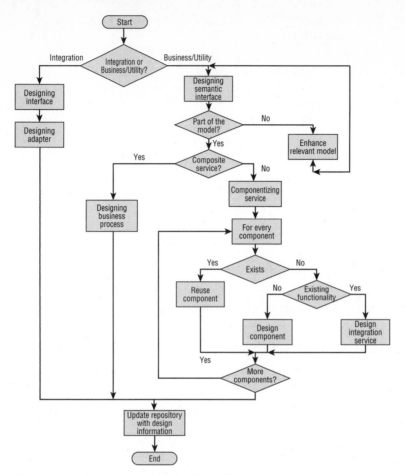

Figure 12-7 The service design and specification process

This process typically involves the Enterprise Architect, Solutions Lead, Portfolio Architect, Functional Architect, Business Process Architect, and Services librarian. These stakeholders, and their roles associated with service design, are shown in Figure 12-8.

Service design artifacts created in this process include:

- Service invocation pre- and postconditions
- Interface design
- Informal run-time policies for service invocation that can be refined in the implementation process
- A list of components and their interactions for service implementation
- Design of lower-level components that comprise the service

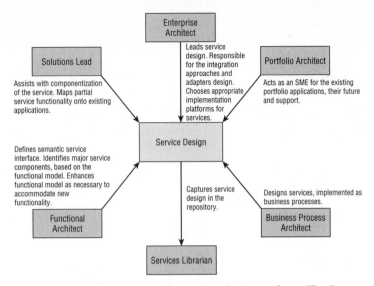

Figure 12-8 Stakeholders of the service design and specification

- Interface design
- Updates of the relevant model(s)

All of the service design artifacts are added to the service's proposals in the repository, thus ensuring that it is always current with the service's development.

The Service Implementation Process

After design is the *service implementation* phase. Service implementation process guidance is defined by the SOA governance team, with a typical process shown in Figure 12-9. Certainly, each service implementation differs, depending on what type of service it is. An enterprise's policies and procedures, established by the governance team, provide such a process, including standards, guidance, blueprints, and best practices for implementing services. Much like the other processes in design-time governance, all of the service implementation artifacts are captured and maintained in the service repository.

Stakeholders in the implementation process involve the Application Developer, the Services Assembler, the Enterprise Architect, the Service Tester, the SOA Run-Time Architect, and the Services Librarian, as shown in Figure 12-10. The role of the Enterprise Architect typically focuses on the governance issues adherence to enterprise policies and procedures, and refining informal service run-time policy from the design phase into formal service run-time policy used to express constraints, usage, and the capabilities of the service.

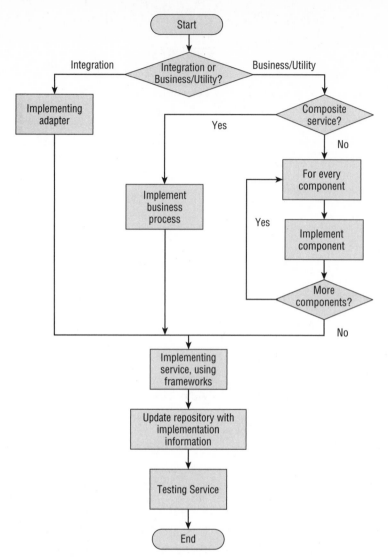

Figure 12-9 Typical Service Implementation process

As a result of this process, service implementation artifacts are created. They include:

- Detailed design
- Actual implementation code
- Formal run-time service policy (usually expressed in WS-Policy)
- Build scripts
- Test scripts

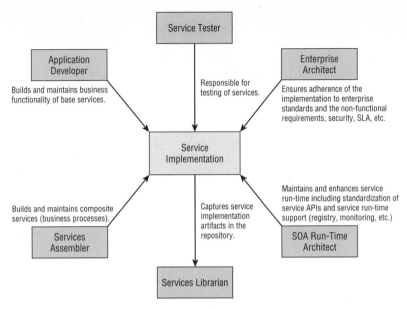

Figure 12-10 Stakeholders of the service implementation process

All of the service implementation artifacts are added to the service's information in the repository, thus ensuring that it is always current with the service's development.

Deploy-Time Governance

Deploy-time policies are defined during the design-time governance phase, and they establish the process for deploying services in the enterprise. Based on these policies, tests can be created that test adherence to the enterprise-wide policies and specific service policies, and compliance testing happens in the deploy-time governance phase.

The *service deployment process* of the service life cycle, defined by the SOA governance team, includes multiple activities, with a typical process shown in Figure 12-11. Service deployment includes the configuration of the deployment of the individual service instance and the topology for multiple instance design, where multiple instances of services are deployed simultaneously to support multiple run-time service policies. The service deployment process also includes definitions of service access transports (e.g., MQ versus HTTP) and interaction styles supported by different deployment instances. This information is used for updating the service registry and the service monitoring solution with the information about a new service and its deployment. Finally, prior to deployment, compliance checking is done to ensure that the service adheres to the enterprise service policy.

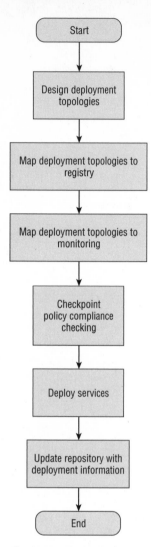

Figure 12-11 Typical service deployment process

This process involves the stakeholders shown in Figure 12-12, which shows the roles of the Enterprise Architect, the SOA Run-Time Architect, the Service Infrastructure Specialist, and the Services Librarian.

As a result of this process, service deployment artifacts are created and are added to the service's information in the service repository. They typically include:

- Logical and physical deployment diagram for the service
- Physical topology for service deployment, including all endpoint addresses and their mappings to service policies and interaction styles

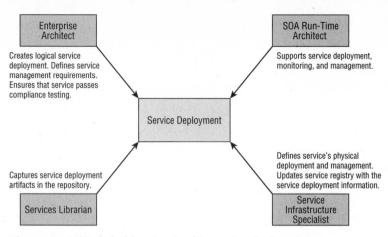

Figure 12-12 Stakeholders involved in service deployment

- Mapping of this topology to service registry and update of the registry with the service's deployment information
- Service monitoring and management points
- Mapping of the points to the monitoring solution and configuring solution to support monitoring and management

The deploy-time governance phase establishes this service deployment process, as we have defined in this section. Policy compliance is tested prior to the deployment, ensuring that services meet the enterprise policy requirements.

Run-Time Governance

During the run-time governance phase, explicit run-time service policies are discovered by service clients. Run-time service policies, as we have discussed earlier in the chapter, express the constraints, capabilities, and requirements for using a service, and such a policy acts as a formal contract between a service and its consumer. Based on the run-time policy and connection requirements discovered at run time, clients adhere to those policies, which are then enforced by Policy Enforcement Points (PEPs) for the services. SOA governance processes involve mechanisms for service policy discovery, adaptation, and enforcement (we cover these mechanisms later in this chapter).

In addition to run-time service policy enforcement, the other main governance activities in this phase relate to monitoring and management, as shown in the *service utilization process* of the service life cycle in Figure 12-13. All services are monitored and statistics are gathered so that results can be analyzed

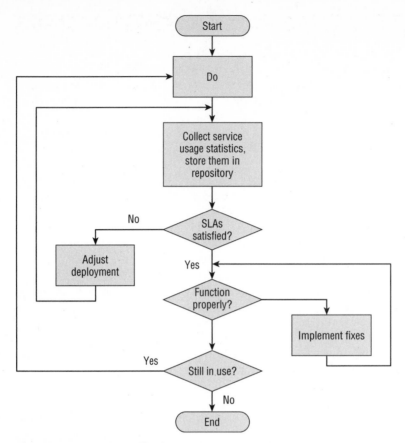

Figure 12-13 Service utilization process

for troubleshooting, policy enhancement, and other potential enhancements and changes. In this aspect, the run-time governance phase applies to what is referred to as change-time governance. In many cases, run-time governance engines provide "run-time scorecards" related to reliability, response time, and policy adherence. During this phase, all activity, exceptions, and errors are logged in such a way that the enterprise managers can have a big picture view of the SOA for real-time network tracking and alerts. For discovered problems related to service deployment or run-time service policies, services can be taken offline and put back into the deployment process of the life cycle. For more serious issues revolving around software bugs, design errors, or implementation issues, the service should be sent back to the design or implementation process.

MONITORING YOUR SOA

SOA management tools (also called *run-time governance tools*), provide capabilities that allow you to monitor, measure, and analyze service interactions. Based on understanding the way that enterprise services are used, you are able to refine aspects of service design and run-time service policies, as we discuss in this section.

Most SOA governance products offer the automatic discovery of services in the enterprise, an analysis of how these services interact with other service consumers and providers in the enterprise, and visibility into the end-to-end service messaging flows. Such tools collect customized metrics at run time. Based on these metrics, they provide a centralized view of service performance, audit logging, actions, errors and error root-cause analysis, business transaction monitoring (providing business-level visibility in message content), run-time analysis of enterprise bottlenecks, latency, and unauthorized access. All of these are important for traceability, auditing requirements, and refining policy — specifically related to refining quality of service in SLAs.

Many management tools provide the capability to specify automated actions, usually related to adapting services for failover (message routing and service instantiation for continuous availability). If a particular metric is not being met, alarms can be raised and real-time alerts can be sent to administrators. This information provides a much needed big picture of your SOA in order to support decision making related to refining policy, design changes, and planning for availability.

The activities in the service utilization process involve the stakeholders shown in Figure 12-14. This figure shows these organization roles and their responsibilities during the run-time governance phase. Artifacts during this phase include:

- Utilization of statistics of a service as a whole and the deployment end-point address(es) if instantiated multiple times
- Information about consumers using the service
- Information about service SLA support, run-time policy enforcement, and adherence

All of the service usage artifacts are added to the service repository, to allow analyzing service utilization.

Finally, the last phase of the service life cycle as it relates to run-time governance is *service retirement*, which includes activities as shown in Figure 12-15.

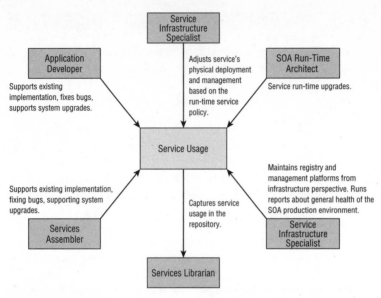

Figure 12-14 Stakeholders in the service utilization process

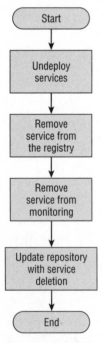

Figure 12-15 Service retirement process

Main activities during service retirement include undeployment of the service, which encompasses not only the undeployment of the service run-time instance, but also removal of the service information from the registry (thus ensuring that it is never invoked). It also includes removal of the service information from the service's monitoring and management solution.

Finally, these activities typically involve two stakeholders — the service infrastructure specialist, who removes the service, and the SOA librarian, who captures the service deletion in the service repository. These stakeholders are shown in Figure 12-16.

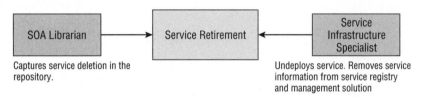

Figure 12-16 Stakeholders in the service retirement process

This section has walked you through governance in the service life cycle. In the next section, we provide a practical guide for addressing SOA governance in your organization.

Practical SOA Governance

This section provides a practical guide for setting up a model for SOA governance in your organization, following the SOA Governance Life Cycle in the last section. Throughout this section, we provide practical tips as "anti-patterns" that you should watch out for.

Structuring Your Organization for Governance

SOA governance needs to establish chains of responsibilities, decision-making rights, authority, and communication, which usually requires the creation of the SOA governance group. Responsibilities of such a governance group are as follows:

■ Position SOA as a critical element of IT tool set and align it with the Enterprise Business strategy. Define business opportunities for SOA adoption and implementation.

- Create clear ownership, supervision, and escalation of SOA specific issues, thus providing quick and efficient resolution of SOA-related issues.

- Define SOA funding approaches, including reuse charge backs, and so on.

- Enable SOA maturity tracking and its controlled evolution based on the metrics for SOA adoption benefits, services reuse, and so on.

- Align SOA strategy with other enterprise strategies, including security, presentation, portfolio management, and so on.

- Ensure adherence to service definition and implementation policies and processes.

- Ensure infrastructure readiness for SOA (see Chapter 10 for an expanded discussion of this).

- Maintain and advertise major SOA artifacts — services, business processes, and so on.

Out of all these tasks, establishing processes and procedures is the most important functions of the SOA group. These policies, processes and procedures have to be comprehensive and need to cover all of the stages of the service life cycle, as we discussed in the last section.

There are a few different ways to establish authority for adherence to policy. One of the best ways is to establish a team-based policy authoring model, where the team is led by an energetic and persuasive leader, and where everyone feels that they have a "say" in the process. In such a collaborative approach, the team feels ownership in the process, leaders step up, and it increases the likelihood of success. It is important that governance has management support — adherence to policy needs to be mandated from the top. For this reason, a centralized SOA group reporting to the CTO, CIO, or chief architect of the organization with "built-in" management support is usually the best option. Because SOA impacts business as much as IT, this group must also have representation from the business staff as well as the technology staff. Although it is theoretically possible to create a decentralized SOA group comprised of the representatives from multiple departments, in reality it rarely works. It is important that the group govern effectively without being too heavy-handed. A few anti-patterns in governance discipline are illustrated in the "The Powerless Committee and the Ivory Tower Dictator" sidebar.

THE POWERLESS COMMITTEE AND THE IVORY TOWER DICTATOR

There are two extremes of the SOA governance discipline that are common but are also ineffective. The first extreme is the establishment of a *powerless committee*, where a committee is appointed to develop policies for the SOA project, but it is set up to have no control because management does not mandate the control. The second extreme is an anti-pattern we call the *ivory tower dictator*. The ivory tower dictator is the architect who has the power, authors all the policies from on high, and shoves it in the designers' and developers' faces without their input. The ivory tower dictator rules with an iron fist and is despised. As a result, the rest of the team can find ways around the policies or can rebel and try to sabotage the process. Both of these models are well intentioned but wrong. Neither the powerless committee nor the ivory tower dictator is ever successful. One model has no power to discipline, and the other has all the power but the dictator lords it over the project. The effective alternative is a collaborative, team-based approach, led by a persuasive leader who has management support.

As you can see from the SOA stakeholders and their roles in the last section, SOA governance brings together people from different parts of the organization. It does not mean, however, that all of the participants have to be administratively in the SOA group that establishes the policies for the organization. The SOA governance group usually employs:

- The group leader (the SOA group "champion")
- A Services Librarian
- An SOA Run-Time Architect and development group
- A Functional Architect (optional)
- A Service Infrastructure Specialist (optional)

This group also maintains the service repository and best practices for different steps in the SOA process. It facilitates conversations during different steps of the SOA process and ensures quality of deliverables on every step. The rest of the participants supplement the SOA group during specific projects.

Developing Enterprise Policy

After the SOA governance group is formed for an organization, the first step in governance involves the establishment of enterprise-wide policies for building services. Policies developed in this stage revolve around compliance with technical standards, the use of common vocabularies, service versioning policies, common namespaces for services, and guidance for best practices and reuse. Such enterprise policies affect the entire organization, applying to all services and their consumers.

In our experience, it is best to start small, borrowing experiences from other projects. Although too little governance is an unacceptable extreme, going overboard, and setting up too many rules, checklists, and policies from the beginning can be overwhelming. Enterprise policies should be sufficient to provide order but should not be stifling. The following are some basic guidelines that are usually effective in most projects but obviously should be tailored to your organization:

- **Standards compliance** — It is important to use accepted standards in order to ensure both current and future interoperability. Organizations that create their own standards for SOA, instead of using accepted standards, are essentially creating "SOA stove pipes" that lead to inflexibility and integration difficulties. At the bare minimum, common best practices for messaging for SOAP-based services involve compliance related to WS-I and WS-Security. Every organization is different and may support other standards.

- **Common vocabulary** — As we have discussed throughout this book (specifically, in Chapters 2, 3, and 6), it is a best practice for your services to adopt a common vocabulary. Policies for using a common vocabulary involve the reuse of existing organizational schemas, a data reference model, or referencing an organizational ontology. The reuse of common vocabularies is key to semantic interoperability.

- **Naming conventions** — Certain fundamental standards, such as defining the organizational namespaces, are determined at this stage.

- **Error handling and auditing** — Much of this involves your choice of auditing tools, but common best practices involve the standardization of SOAP fault message descriptions to include the IP address and the Service Name where the fault occurred, as well as streaming audit logs to a centralized location. Many times, the implementation of this policy involves the integration of run-time governance software. For more information, see the "Exception handling and logging in enterprise solutions" section in Chapter 9.

- **Run-time service policy authoring** — A typical best practice involves the establishment of how a service policy is described (usually in WS-Policy) and stored in a central registry. If a project has chosen a policy authoring tool, this is stated at this point.

- **General best practices and blueprints** — It is good at this stage to establish a repository of best practices for the SOA project. They should include coding guidelines, design patterns, and typical use cases for achieving repeatable solutions.

■ **Service versioning** — Enterprise policy should be written that dictates how the versioning and deprecation process works, and the communication plan associated with changing versions. The implementation of this policy should be addressed and may depend on the run-time governance and management software tools that are available for managing this process. A simple policy for service versioning may be: "After deployment of a new version of a service, the earlier version of the service can be supported and available for six months, and users of the original service are notified. The corporate registry is updated with the new version of the service." For an in-depth look at service versioning, see the "Dealing with service changes" section in Chapter 9.

For most development organizations, many of these policies (especially related to standards and best practices) were already in place before anyone started using the word *governance*. Governance brings a little more formality to the mix, because it involves making sure that all services are compliant. It is important that adherence to these policies is checked before deploying new services on the network (deploy-time governance). Many SOA governance tools have automated compliance testing software that allows you to test adherence to these policies.

One potential pitfall that you can run into during this process is "analysis paralysis" on authoring specific policies. For example, Data Architects could (and *will* if you let them) spend three years building a huge data model that would be used in the common vocabulary of all services. As admirable as that is, it is better to start small and build for "evolveability." Remember that the SOA governance life cycle is a continuing spiral, where policies can be refined over time. Start small and simple so that projects can get started quickly with some policies and guidance in place. Build for today, while planning for incremental change tomorrow.

GOVERNANCE FROM DAY 3

We've seen many articles that espouse "Governance from Day 1." Depending on your organization, this may or may not be the right step for you. It all depends on the maturity of the organization and the type of project that you're doing.

If you have an established architecture or SOA program, and you don't have governance, that's a big problem. Many times, however, the scenario with SOA is that you're trying to introduce architecture to an organization. This may involve a change to processes, techniques, tools, technologies, or organizational structure. To have a fighting chance, you need to remove every

(continued)

GOVERNANCE FROM DAY 3 *(continued)*

unnecessary obstacle from the path of the transition. At this phase of the game, architecture needs to demonstrate value, not add additional steps.

Let's look at an SOA introduction as an example. First, you need to introduce the concepts of service orientation and demonstrate where they are useful. This is often done by implementing a single service as a proof point. But, at the same time, you want to make sure that the service follows architectural principles, patterns, standards, and so on. The problem is that you don't have those well articulated yet, nor have you really figured out what processes and tools work for implementing services in the organization. One approach to this dilemma is to assemble an initial service team, staffed from the architecture group, to assist the project in implementing and deploying the service. The team has several goals. First and foremost is to implement a service that meets the requirements of the project and provides value to the business. The second goal is to demonstrate how the architectural approach provided a better service than you would have gotten if you had just followed the same old process. And the third goal is to figure out what process, patterns, techniques, and standards can work in this particular organization for implementing SOA within the context of the architecture.

The next step of the initiative is to take what was learned on the first project and expand that to a few more projects. The original service team can be broken up and each member assigned to lead an additional project team, so instead of a single service being implemented, four or five services can be developed in the second round. Again, the primary goal is to implement services that meet project requirements and provide value to the business. The second goal is to implement services that can work together to start to demonstrate the power of service composition, and also to find a project that can reuse the initial service. This allows the team to learn how to accomplish the important requirements of reuse and versioning. The third goal is to refine the process and architecture so that it is well articulated and mature enough to be rolled out to teams throughout the organization.

By this point, the SOA initiative should have delivered value by helping projects to create services that meet their need and at the same time, demonstrated some of the values of an SOA approach. It should have, a fairly well defined architecture and process, and a good understanding of what can and won't work in this organization (every organization is different). There should also be a small handful of services. Now is the time to flesh out governance. If you think about it, you really don't need much governance yet, especially development governance, when you only have a few services, and it's too early to introduce it before you really understand the processes, organization, and architecture.

It's true that you might have to go back and update some of the initial services once you get the governance model in place, but that's okay. That's what versioning is all about. But at least architecture will have gotten a foothold and gained momentum before governance can be perceived to slow it down. Remember that architecture is a delicate balance. It must specify enough context and process to achieve important enterprise goals. If it specifies too little, then the goals cannot be achieved. If it specifies too much, it will just be ignored (and the goals won't be achieved either). Getting it just right is a constant challenge for architecture.

One point to remember: Do not confuse "Governance from Day 3" with the procrastination slogan "Governance Tomorrow," where you never end up adding governance, and it only becomes important when you experience things going wrong in an operational SOA. This is not what we are advocating — once things go wrong, it is probably too late! Going operational without any governance is just stupid. By the time you are operational, the cost of having to retrofit governance once things go wrong is so much higher than if you started from the beginning.

But, if you're in a situation where you need to introduce architecture to the organization, the Day 3 approach often works. Introduce architectural ideas and apply them to a small selection of projects on Day 1. On Day 2, refine what works, prove value, and expand your scope. If you are successful, you actually get the chance to get to Day 3, where you can finally add governance. This can be a successful model for new adopters of SOA.

Using the Service Repository

Implementation of the processes and procedures established by SOA governance is based on a service repository providing a foundation for collaboration between people involved in service design and implementation. Such a service repository integrates all of the sources of service related information, including design artifacts, run-time topologies, information collected by your service monitoring and management solution, and more. It provides a unified representation of all of this information allowing all of the SOA stakeholders to centrally access it, based on their job functions, as shown in Figure 12-17.

A service repository provides information required to support the complete service life cycle starting from its inception, through design, implementation, deployment, usage, and maintenance.

During service identification, business analysts identify the requirements for new services. These requirements are evaluated against the functionality

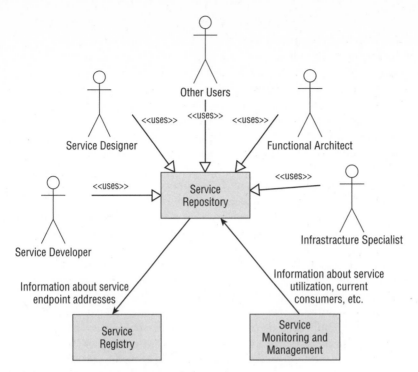

Figure 12-17 Basic service repository architecture

of the existing ones and the new services are inserted in the repository. As these services get approved, appropriate run-time service policies are created and stored in the repository as well. At this point, the service moves into implementation. The development team becomes responsible for the creation and maintenance of service implementation artifacts and storing them in the repository. Once the implementation is completed and tested to adhere to deploy-time governance rules, the service is deployed in production, and the repository information is enhanced with the deployment information.

During normal service usage, a service's utilization metrics, including information about service consumers and their location is periodically imported into the repository from service management and monitoring systems. Over time, service usage defects and additional requirements are created and captured in the repository. After appropriate approval, they are translated into service enhancements or new service versions that are captured in the repository as well.

Essential capabilities of the service repository include service cataloging and discovery, validation, dependency management, service evolution and versioning, artifact publishing governance, and support for multiple artifact types. The next sections address these capabilities.

Cataloging and Discovery

The main purpose of the service repository is to provide the ability to find artifacts, based on the artifact-specific metadata. This metadata is typically contained in the artifacts themselves. Consequently, the service repository should automatically extract this metadata (based on the cataloging policies) whenever new artifacts are published to the repository. An example of such a policy can be the automatic generation of the following information during service definition cataloging:

- Links to the auxiliary documents imported by the service definition document, such as XML schema documents, messaging semantics definitions, and so on
- The XML namespaces used by the service contract documents
- The name and description of the interfaces, and the XML types used by the service contract
- Links to the policies governing service invocation and execution

The implementation of cataloging requires defining the metadata for every artifact placed in the repository. The metadata must be rich and flexible enough to support different types of service artifacts stored in the repository, as well as their evolution.

The collection of the metadata stored in the service repository encompasses the information that business analysts and service designers can use to discover existing services and decide on their applicability for a given solution. Thus, the repository should provide discovery capabilities that are extensible and can accommodate a wide range of domain-specific discovery queries. This requirement typically translates into the repository's ability to support multiple business-related taxonomies.

Validation

Finding artifacts that are not valid does not do the enterprise any good. As the point of access to service-related information, the service repository should enforce organizational and domain-specific business rules, ensuring conformance of these artifacts to the enterprise policies and standards. This ability to enforce validation rules makes the repository a focal part of Service-Oriented Architecture governance.

Dependency Management

Service-related information typically includes multiple interrelated artifacts, such as service interfaces, message schemas, implementation code, usage profiles, and so on. Because the services themselves can be reused by other services or business processes, understanding the relationships and dependencies between services is quite important. As the number of services grows, tracking all these dependencies and evaluating the impacts of changes becomes a difficult task.

The service repository can simplify this task by supporting the management of relationships between service artifacts. The repository should provide standard relationship types. It should also allow the organization to extend these types with additional ones based on their additional requirements.

Service Evolution and Versioning

Once created, services typically evolve over time. This evolution can be caused by changes in the service functionality, semantic messaging, implementation, and so on. Many of these changes require creation and deployment of a new version of the service. In order to track all of this versioning information, the service repository should provide versioning capabilities for all service artifacts, regardless of their type.

Additionally, the service repository should provide change/versioning notification capabilities, allowing interested parties to be notified about upcoming and current changes. This allows you to provide change information to all interested parties such as the service consumer's development teams. Such a subscription mechanism should allow specifying the types of events that are of interest, thus preventing the flooding of the subscriber with notifications.

Artifacts Publishing Governance

As the service repository becomes a centralized collection of all of the information about service-related assets, it requires the same governance as any other enterprise assets repository. This type of governance typically includes permissions for publishing service-related artifacts and an artifacts-publishing approval process.

Support for Multiple Artifact Types

One of the main challenges in the creation of a service repository is the great diversity of service-related artifacts, which run the gamut of XML documents, service interfaces, messaging schemas, implementation code, UML diagrams, and text documents. The use of a generic representation for the different asset types can significantly simplify the repository implementation (see the "Reusable Asset Specification" sidebar.)

REUSABLE ASSET SPECIFICATION

OMG's Reusable Assets Specification (RAS) covers the generalized representation of different asset types. RAS defines an asset as a collection of related artifacts that provide a solution to a problem.

An asset may represent a complete solution, including requirements, use cases, design models, component specifications, components, test cases, test drivers, and test data, or it may be just a set of use cases and their models and the rules for extending the use cases.

A good asset has the following characteristics:

◆ It should be easy to use, customize, and apply to another context.

◆ It should possess the characteristics of good software engineering: tight cohesion, loose coupling, and sufficient capabilities.

◆ Its purpose and intent should be easy to understand.

◆ It should be easy to conduct fit analysis on, to determine the asset's match to a particular context.

To achieve these goals, an asset needs to be more than just a collection of run-time artifacts (e.g., code and components). It should also include artifacts that explain goals, purpose, motivation, and assumptions. In many cases, these are best captured as subsets of the original requirements and the vision-related artifacts used in the creation of the asset's run-time elements.

RAS describes assets using metadata captured in a form of XML manifest provided as part of the asset's packaging, as shown in the following RAS Metadata Format figure. The manifest contains at least the asset specification, including attributes such as name, version, and description. An asset specification can be extended through classifications expressed as a set of simple name and value descriptors and through the declaration of contexts such as a specific development or deployment context. The asset's payload is composed of a collection of artifacts addressing a particular problem. The usage section provides guidance on applying and customizing the asset. Finally, the related assets' section defines the asset's relationships to other assets and helps to create collections or families of assets to form larger-grained solutions.

(continued)

REUSABLE ASSET SPECIFICATION *(continued)*

```
Asset: Name, Description, State,
          Version, Profile

    Classification
Descriptors:   Name/Value Pairs
Domain:        Development, Test,
               Productions, etc.

       Solution
Artifacts:   Documents, Diagrams, Test
             Scripts, Code, etc.

         Usage

     Usage Instructions

      Related Assets

Associations, Aggregations, Dependency
```

RAS Metadata Format

There are many types of assets, each represented by a different RAS profile. The asset's types are extensible to support customization for particular needs. The asset customization is accomplished through profiles which preserve the core structure of RAS but specify profile specific extensions.

Search engines and repositories can use the manifest file to discover the contents of an asset, its classification, its related assets, and so on.

Developing and Registering Run-Time Policies

Whereas many enterprise policies are general policies that affect the design process of services, *run-time service policies* always affect the run-time interaction between the client and the service. Such policies are contracts for service interaction that are exposed for discovery by service consumers, and include rules for access, messaging security, and SLAs that are in place.

There are a few different languages that are used by SOA governance tools, but the most well-supported standard is the Web Services Policy Framework (WS-Policy), discussed in Chapter 11. Initially drafted in 2002, it has been a W3C recommendation since September 2007. WS-Policy was discussed in the last chapter in the context of security (as WS-SecurityPolicy is a child specification that uses WS-Policy). WS-Policy is an assertion framework and a model for expressing policies that refer to constraints, capabilities, and requirements for Web Services. WS-Policy is extensible and is currently heavily used for expressing messaging security policies (WS-SecurityPolicy) and expressing policies for reliable messaging (WS-ReliableMessagingPolicy).

The following code from the W3C WS-Policy Primer, shows an example contract for a Web Service, utilizing WS-SecurityPolicy. The plain English translation of this policy says "you need to either sign or encrypt the message body for this service." This is a simple example of a policy that complements WSDL. Based on policies like these, a service client knows what is necessary for interacting with the service.

```
<wsp:Policy
    xmlns:sp="http://docs.oasis-open.org/ws-sx/ws-securitypolicy/200702"
    xmlns:wsp="http://www.w3.org/ns/ws-policy" >
  <wsp:ExactlyOne>
    <wsp:All>
    <sp:SignedParts>
        <sp:Body/>
    </sp:SignedParts>
  </wsp:All>
    <wsp:All>
    <sp:EncryptedParts>
        <sp:Body/>
    </sp:EncryptedParts>
  </wsp:All>
  </wsp:ExactlyOne>
</wsp:Policy>
```

Many tools in the SOA governance market support WS-Policy, but some products use their own proprietary languages or extensions to WS-Policy to bridge the current gap in WS-Policy support; this is usually the case for SLAs. SLAs are typically authored by architects using SOA governance tools, and the process is usually software vendor-specific. A best practice for developing SLAs involves a "spiral model," where requirements are refined over time after run-time metrics are analyzed. Typically, SLAs are not finalized at the beginning of a project. Instead, an SOA management tool is used at the beginning to collect and analyze performance statistics. Based on these metrics collected at run-time, policies for SLAs can be refined over time, based on understanding the use of services in real-time operations.

Finally, run-time service policies are published in a registry. In the SOA design-time life cycle, the registry points to services and their supporting artifacts (WSDL, run-time service policies) for consumption. Run-time service policies defining capabilities and constraints of services need to be discoverable to be used. A centralized view of policy is necessary for actualizing the publish-find-bind vision of services.

Run-Time Policy Enforcement and Adaptation

Once run-time service policies are authored and published, software needs to be in place to enforce the service policy. This is done with a service's Policy Enforcement Point (PEP). In Chapter 11, we talked at length about PEPs in the context of security and access control. In this chapter, we take a much broader view of policy enforcement, which includes enforcing all of the connection constraints used between service consumers and providers. Much of the discussion of PEPs in Chapter 11 certainly does apply, as these policies typically do involve security constraints, but it is also important to understand that run-time service policies extend beyond security and include reliability constraints and different options for connecting. There are a number of governance software tools and hardware appliances providing the capability of policy enforcement, and of course it is also technically possible to write your own.

Figure 12-18 shows a revised publish-find-bind triangle discussed earlier, where the service's container registers its artifacts with a corporate registry. The service client searches for a service and retrieves all artifacts about the service necessary for connecting. At this point, the client must understand the bindings (WSDL) and must also understand the connection policies and messaging security before binding. As a policy can be quite sophisticated, a *policy application point*, working on behalf of the client, interprets the service's policy, dynamically conforms to policy, and works on behalf of the client application to bind to the service. In practice, such an adaptation point can be created in a few different ways: Some software vendors provide this functionality as an agent or local component that works on behalf of the client, some run-time governance tools use intermediary services to apply the policy between clients and services, and some organizations choose to author their own as client handlers which do policy lookups and dynamic adaptation.

> **NOTE** The term "policy application point" has been used in Web Services literature since 2004, first introduced in an article authored by Toufic Boubez, Scott Morrison, and MaryAnn Hondo, "Policy — It's More than Just Security — from Just-In-Time Integration to Web Services," and is also used in many white papers from Layer7 technologies focusing on dynamic policy adaptation. It is important to understand that this "policy application point" is not to be confused with XACML's *Policy Administration Point (PAP)* discussed in Chapter 11. We have therefore tried to be careful to not refer to the "policy application point" as an acronym in this section.

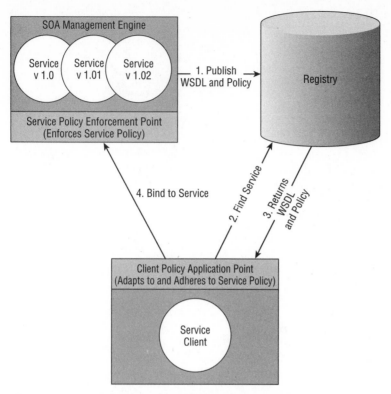

Figure 12-18 Policy-enhanced publish-find-bind triangle

The concept of client-based dynamic policy adaptation is an innovative concept that allows client applications to dynamically react and adapt to policy changes without modifying code, and we briefly talked about this concept in the "blueprints" section of Chapter 11. Take the simple example of a messaging security change. If a popular service on your network changes its requirements from WS-Security X.509 Certificate Profile messaging (WS-Security passing X.509 tokens for identity) to WS-Security SAML token profile, there is no reason that your client cannot dynamically adapt to that policy change. Although many disagree on the nomenclature (some call it a Client PEP, and some call it a Policy Application Point), the concept of having policy negotiation and compliance handled by a local component is powerful. Such a component realizes the vision of loose coupling, where such a simple change no longer breaks the interaction between clients and services.

Figure 12-19 shows an example of dynamic policy adaptation using this model. In the figure, a new policy of a service is registered, and a client, conforming to the old policy, sends a message. The service's PEP inspects the message and returns a message to the client describing the noncompliance. The next steps happen one of two ways: The service itself may return the

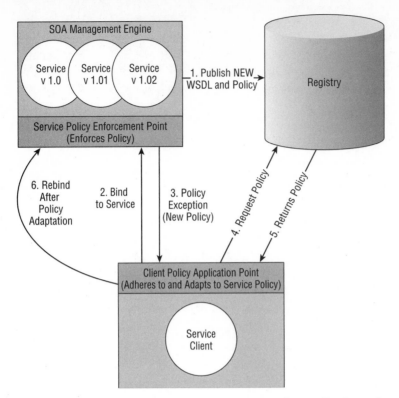

Figure 12-19 Dynamic policy adaptation using a policy application point

signed new policy in the response, or the client's policy application point can query the registry for the new policy, dynamically adapt to the new policy, and resend the message. Because policy is meant to be descriptive enough, clients can adapt to changing policies.

Utilizing a process that allows you to dynamically adapt to run-time service policies provides the great benefit of flexibility. Most of the pain associated with deployments revolves around change. If your policies and the enforcement of your policy logic can be decoupled from your services and consumers, and if you utilize a flexible architecture where run-time policies can be discovered and dynamically adhered to, this makes SOA change management easier as run-time policies inevitably change.

Summary

This chapter has provided an introduction to SOA governance, and it has provided a comprehensive and practical guide for setting up these processes in your organization and managing your SOA. Specifically, this chapter has provided insight into structuring your organization for governance; establishing enterprise policies and procedures; defining the process for the phases in a service life cycle; and using solutions that express, dynamically adapt to, and enforce run-time service policies. Following the processes and examples in this chapter as a model can provide you with a methodology that you can use to effectively govern your enterprise.

Part

III

Case Studies

In This Part

CHAPTER

13

Case Study — Travel Insurance

A journey of a thousand miles begins with a single step.
— Loa Tzu

In the previous chapters, we presented the general architecture of SOA and an overall process for approaching SOA projects. We then presented a chapter for each major step of the process, including business/domain analysis, information modeling, service interface design, service implementation design, service composition, security, and solution design. In this chapter, we provide a case study that incorporates all of these aspects.

In the example, we cover:

- Case study scenario
- Conceptual architecture
- Solution architecture
- Security design
- Business concerns
- Analysis and design review
- Business analysis
- Process and service models
- Use cases
- Information model
- Service interface design
- Document design
- Service implementation design

Travel Insurance

This chapter presents a fictitious scenario related to selling travel insurance as part of an overall, travel-related, customer interaction. Although the scenario is based on real-world travel industry practices, the services provided and company names have been invented for the book.

The Scenario

Hollis, Inc. is a travel information and reservation provider, sometimes generically known in the travel business as a Global Distribution Service (GDS). Hollis has relationships with major airlines, hotels, and the like on the supplier (vendor) side, and with travel agencies, web sites and consolidators on the sell (customer) side. Hollis wants to upgrade their systems to support selling travel insurance and other trip add-ons in a uniform and consistent manner. Travel insurance is an emerging and lucrative product. Hollis want to facilitate the sale of add-on travel insurance as a natural part of the travel shopping experience, and to get their cut of the transaction in the process. To maximize profitability, Hollis wants to create the best volume and wholesale relationships with the insurance companies and the most flexible retail relationship with the agencies and travel web sites.

Hollis, and other GDSs, are essentially brokers between the buyer and seller of travel products. However, the relationship is not so simple. The ultimate end user, for example you or me, does not deal directly with Hollis but instead goes through an intermediary agency or web site. There are two primary types of end users, business travelers and leisure travelers. Figure 13-1 illustrates the different relationships in the scenario.

Each intermediary channel (agency, web site, etc.) and each vendor can have specific contractual relationships with Hollis. These relationships can specify the type of insurance products that are offered, the insurance vendors, and the pricing, commission, and markup. In the past, dedicated and inconsistent solutions were implemented for selling insurance, depending on the relationship

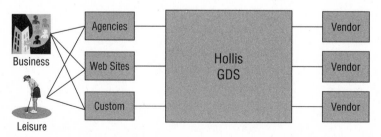

Figure 13-1 Hollis GDS insurance relationships

between the buyer and seller and Hollis. The goal of the project is to replace all the different one-off solutions with a unified and extensible solution.

The solution has to support the evolving SOA efforts and plans going on at Hollis, utilize and augment the existing services, and fit into the overall business architecture.

Conceptual Architecture

The first things to understand are the scope of the project and its interactions. Figure 13-2 illustrates the high-level conceptual architecture for the project. On the left of the figure are the different channels through which insurance might be sold. These include:

- **Hollis.com** — Hollis has its own travel web site.
- **Agencies** — Travel agencies.
- **Web sites** — Third-party web sites, such as Expedia, including confirmation emails.
- **Branded GUIs** — Private-branded GUIs provided by Hollis for specific clients.

On the right side of the figure are a variety of insurance vendors. The middle of the drawing shows the set of services that are needed to provide an end-to-end transaction that includes insurance. The services are divided into two main categories: Insurance Services and Common Services. The common services show only the service groups that are needed. They are out of the scope of this project. The insurance services show the insurance-specific functions as

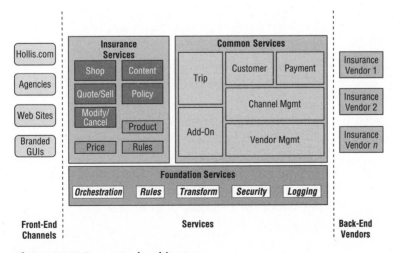

Figure 13-2 Conceptual architecture

either business or domain services. This set of services comprises the scope of the project.

Insurance services include:

- **Shop** — Supports shopping for different insurance products and options
- **Quote and Sell** — Supports validating a request and providing a price quote; also supports purchasing insurance based on the quote
- **Modify** — Supports changing an insurance policy or trip, including cancellation
- **Content** — Supports vendors providing insurance products and other content
- **Policy** — Supports insurance policy creation and modification with vendors

Common services include:

- **Trip** — The set of services associated with the creation and maintenance of a trip; a trip is the primary entity in travel that all other transactions interact with.
- **Add-on** — Suggest and sell trip add-ons such as ground transportation, tickets, events, and so on.
- **Customer** — Manage customers and partners, including itineraries, histories, and preferences.
- **Payment** — Manage payments to and from channels and vendors, including commission and markups.
- **Channel Management** — Manage the relationship and rules for the different channels.
- **Vendor Management** — Manage the relationships, rules, and contracts for the different insurance vendors.

Business Concerns

Now that you have the high-level service-oriented vision, it is time to take a look at the business issues. It is always a goal, and a challenge for IT organizations, to build systems that "align with the business." You've heard this refrain so often that it is hard to consider it more than a cliché. But at the same time, it is an important aspect of an SOA project. If the services don't align with the business, they don't stand much of a chance of being usable across a variety of applications.

More often than not, the business hasn't really thought about how the business is structured, what is important, or what the goals and strategy are.

The bad news is that it makes it more difficult to align with. But the good news is that it provides an opportunity for IT to engage the business in the development of some business architecture.

Business Value Chain

One way to get started with the business is to create a business value chain as described in Chapter 4. Figure 13-3 illustrates a sample extended value chain for Hollis.

The value chain is divided into two main sets of activities. The activities on the bottom are called "supporting activities." These are things like Human Resources and Finance that must be in place to keep the company operating, but that do not add value to the products or services.

The top part of the diagram describes the "primary activities." The main business that Hollis is in is trip planning and reservations. This is composed of five main value-adding activities: Shopping and Content; Inventory Management; Add-On Marketing and Sales; Pricing and Yield Optimization; and Reservations. This is the primary activity of Hollis, as identified by the arrow that connects the steps and ties them to the goals.

Channels, Vendors, and Customers need to be interacted with, managed, and maintained across all of these steps in the value chain, so you list them as primary activities as well. However, they are not part of the primary value chain but rather are primary activities that span all of the individual activities of the chain.

In addition, the primary activities consist of management functions, such as process and project management, monitoring and business intelligence, billing

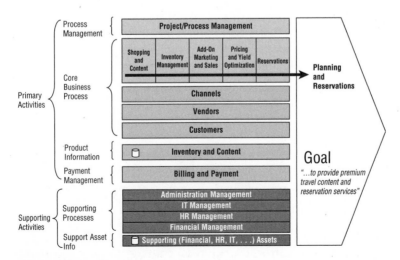

Figure 13-3 Hollis extended value chain

and payments, and information management. These are all necessary to keep the primary value chain going.

The value chain is useful for identifying the different functional areas of the company and focusing attention on the most important. It is a good mechanism for bringing out the goals and objectives. As well, it starts to identify areas of services. For example, each different step or primary activity is likely to have one or more service groups associated with it. This provides a first step in creating a service inventory.

The primary business goal of Hollis is "to provide premium travel content and reservation services." Some secondary goals are shown in the following list:

- Be the primary travel content provider in the industry.

- Provide integration with all types of travel content.

- Support a customer-centric approach to travel reservations (to optimize customer experience) and product marketing and sales, across multiple channels where possible.

- Provide the best price and inventory optimization and management on behalf of partner providers.

Business Motivation

So, if the objective is to align your SOA solution with the business goals, how do you go about doing that? First, you need to ask the right questions. For SOA, you must answer the following questions:

- What business are you in?

- What are the goals and objectives of this particular business?

- What outcomes are needed to achieve those goals?

- What is the strategy for achieving them?

- How will they be measured?

- What capabilities and information are needed to achieve those outcomes?

- What processes, services, entities, and rules are needed to implement those capabilities?

- What existing applications provide basic capabilities and information?

- How are the applications, processes, and so on aligned with the business strategies and goals?

Business architecture helps you understand and answer these questions, but how do you describe all the different concepts? And how do you tie the operational concepts (processes, services, etc.) back to the business goals and establish traceability?

Let's not forgot that although it is focused on the business, BA is still architecture. It should not be any less precise or formal just because it is about business concepts. Architecture needs to have two complementary views, a conceptual (informal) view, usually as a Visio diagram, designed to communicate concepts to a particular audience (such as those in Figures 13-2 and 13-3); and a formal view, usually as a formal model, designed to be a precise specification of the architecture that can be implemented and validated. You use the Business Motivation Model (BMM) for this.

A key expectation of business architecture is that it helps to align IT with the business. The BMM provides a formal way to trace the tactics back to goals and objectives and tie IT systems to the tactics that they implement. For example, in an SOA, business processes and services are the IT constructs that should implement tactics. So, you can create formal traceability between the services (IT) and the business by modeling a formal relationship between the service and the tactic it is intended to implement. Let's apply these concepts of business motivation and traceability to Hollis. Figure 13-4 shows an extract of the Business Motivation Model that addresses this business scenario.

Figure 13-4 expresses the main concepts of the BMM, specifically:

- **Vision** — Be the travel (and associated) content provider of choice for agents and end users.

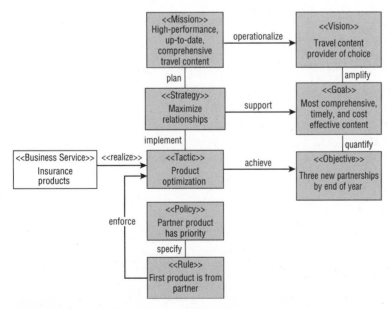

Figure 13-4 Hollis Business Motivation Model

- **Goals** — Provide the best, most comprehensive, timely, and cost-effective travel content (including insurance) in the industry. Remember that goals are long term and more broadly defined.

- **Objectives** — Create three new partnerships with insurance providers by end of year. Objectives are specific, actionable, measurable, and time-bound.

- **Mission** — Provide high-performance, up-to-date, and comprehensive travel related content to travel consumers.

- **Strategy** — Maximize relationships with travel insurance providers. Remember that strategy is broad and typically supports goals.

- **Tactics** — Provide product optimization capabilities to partnered insurance providers. Tactics are the more specific realization of strategy, directed at achieving specific objectives.

- **Policies** — Partnered insurance is given priority over other products. Policies provide a set of directives.

- **Rules** — The first product offered in any given request comes from a partnered provider. Rules specify actions to achieve policies in support of enforcing tactics.

The vision of being the travel content provider of choice for agents and end users is operationalized by the mission, which is to provide high-performance, up-to-date, and comprehensive content. The vision is amplified by the goal of providing the best and most comprehensive insurance content, and the goal is quantified by the objective of signing three new insurance partners this year. The goal is supported by the strategy of maximizing relationships with travel insurance providers. The objective is achieved by the tactic of providing product optimization capabilities for partners as an enticement to get new partners to sign. The strategy and tactics are governed by the policy of providing priority to partners' insurance products, which are enforced by the rule of offering the partners' products first.

Finally, the business service `InsProduct` realizes the tactic, providing traceability from the service to the tactic that it implements and to the objective that the tactic achieves.

Brief Review

Before you dive into the case study any further, let's review the analysis and design steps (from Chapter 4) that are followed in the example. These are:

- Identify business goals, objectives and requirements.
- Understand business context and interactions.

- Understand use cases and scenarios.
- Put them into an overall context.
- Design or align the information model.
- Identify service interfaces.
- Define documents.
- Define service implementation.

Figure 13-5 provides a high-level overview of the process.

The left side of Figure 13-5 shows the business architecture aspects. Here, you start with business strategy and goals as input to the business motivation model and business value chain.

The BMM helps you formalize the business concepts and provides traceability and alignment. The value chain helps you to identify the major areas of business activities, and to prioritize them in terms of importance and value creation. For each of these major areas, you need to specify the next level of details.

You use the business context model (described next) to identify the major parties and areas of business capability and the interactions between them. The context model leads directly to identification of the information model and specific business process models.

The steps are fairly straightforward. (The numbers in the following list correspond to the numbers in Figure 13-5.) First, you establish the overall context.

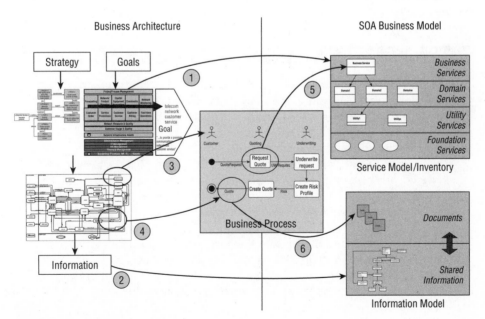

Figure 13-5 Analysis and design process

1. The overall set of processes, as identified by the value chain and the set of all context models provides the enterprise SOA with a context that can be represented in the service inventory.

2. The enterprise information model describes the superset of information that is needed to be shared between services. This becomes the basis for the more detailed service information model.

Next, you refine context models into process models or scenarios.

3. Parties or functional areas in the context model become actors in the business process models.

4. Messages in the context model become data that are passed into and out of the business processes.

Finally, you focus on the specific business processes.

5. Activities in the business processes become operations on services. The services fit within an overall service hierarchy, but at this level you are primarily identifying business services.

6. Inputs and outputs of the business processes become documents that are passed through service interfaces. The documents are derived from the information model.

Figure 13-5 shows the relationship between the business and SOA in terms of models and transformations. Figure 13-6 provides a more detailed view of the service design and implementation aspects.

EVERYTHING IS CONNECTED

In an SOA solution, you are not designing an application or process from scratch. Instead, you are starting with an existing context, based on your business and information architectures, and building on top of it. You are extending and reusing, adding value to what exists, not duplicating responsibilities and adding inconsistencies.

But to make this actually work, you need to make sure that the architecture and design processes support each other. The artifacts that you produce with business architecture have to directly support the design of processes and services. The mechanisms for business processes need to produce artifacts that directly lead to the development of appropriate services. Any time that the output of one step is not the input to the next step, you introduce an opportunity for errors and disconnect. More importantly, however, an additional step in the process encourages developers to ignore the outputs of the previous step, creating extra work rather than providing value.

Tying all of this together is traceability. Because all aspects share a common root and are part of a continuous development process, you can follow one to the other. Starting from your strategic outcomes, you can trace down to the processes required to implement them, and then to the capabilities necessary for those processes, and then to the services that implement those capabilities, and all along to the business entities and information involved. Or, if you're going to make changes to a service, you can trace back up to see what processes might be affected and what impact that may have on business outcomes.

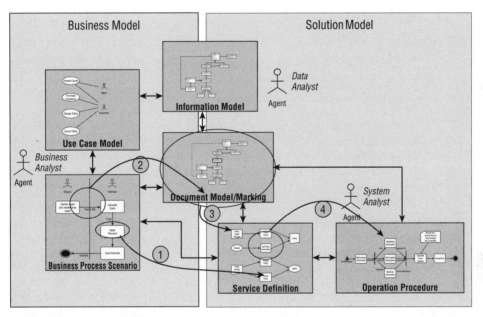

Figure 13-6 Service design process

In the service design model, you often start with use cases. There should be a direct relationship between the use cases and the business strategy, goals, and objectives. In fact, the use cases should describe the tactics used to meet those objectives. Use cases are a well established and understood mechanism for collecting and stating requirements and seem to be a good place to start. One major goal of the use case diagrams is to provide a table of contents for the project. Because you are specifically expecting to discover common behavior and information across the use cases, it is important to have a view of the total set. (Note that shared behavior and information translate directly to services.)

Next, you use scenario (activity) diagrams to specify the details of the use cases in terms of activities, information flow, and control flow. The scenario diagrams serve the same purpose as the Business Process Models. The main difference is that they are the type of model supported by UML tools, which is what you use for the design process.

The information model is derived from the overall enterprise model and additional details from the use case models. Once the scenarios and use cases are in place, you're ready to start with service interface design. Again, the numbers in the following list correspond to the numbers in Figure 13-6.

1. Activities in a scenario diagram become operations on a service interface. You include the operations in a service interface diagram.

2. The information passed into and out of operations become documents. The documents are defined by deriving the specific information for each operation from the overall information model.

3. You also include the documents in the service diagram. This gives you an overall view of the service from which you can evaluate the cohesion, coupling, and complexity.

4. The implementation of each operation is described in procedure diagrams, including activity and class models.

Of course, this is an iterative process. You constantly discover new operations and new information as you work through the details of the service design. In addition, you constantly need to refactor the models to accommodate shared behavior, shared information, and variability. This may require you to go back and update use case scenarios, information models, service inventory, and so on. It is best to keep things up-to-date as you go.

At the same time, you don't want to get bogged down in analysis paralysis. An agile approach to development is often best. You first want to get a big picture view in place; for example, an overall service inventory or an overall understanding of the service interface. But this should not take too long and does not require a complete model. Then, you can completely implement and test one operation at a time and one service at a time. As you build the services, you continue to evolve the models and to refactor them based on what you learned and new or changed requirements.

Now, let's get back to the business analysis of the case study.

Business Analysis

The first step in the business analysis is to understand the overall business interactions that take place regarding insurance. The conceptual architecture has identified the main parties in this interaction, namely the channels, the insurance and common services, and the vendors. Now, you want to understand exactly what interactions these parties have and what information they need to exchange. For this, you use a business context diagram, as illustrated in

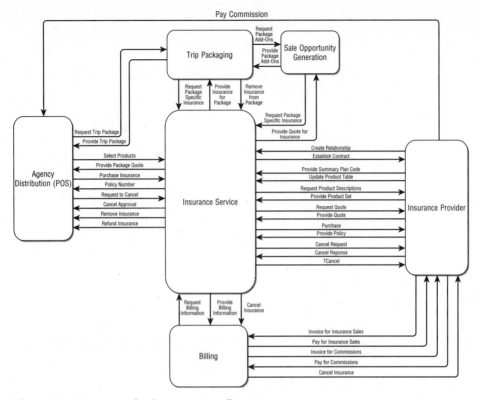

Figure 13-7 Insurance business context diagram

Figure 13-7. The context diagram includes the major parties, represented by the rounded rectangles, and the messages that they exchange, represented by the arrows. You create the context diagram by talking with the business analysts and walking through all of the different interactions (use cases) required for end-to-end insurance capabilities.

Central to this context diagram is insurance (the large rounded rectangle in the middle). It interacts with the channels (on the left) and the vendors (on the right). Initially it addresses only the agency channel. Other channels can be added in the next iteration of the model. To complete the interaction, you also need the trip creation systems, add-on sale opportunity functions, and billing and payment systems.

The interactions between the channel and insurance support: shopping for an insurance product, getting a quote for the trip insurance, purchasing insurance and getting a policy, and modifying and canceling the policy. Typically, each interaction involves a request and response message.

The interactions between the vendors and insurance support setting up a relationship, providing prepackaged insurance products, providing dynamic insurance products, purchasing a policy, and modifying the policy.

In addition, there are interactions between the channels, insurance service, vendors, and payments to support billing, payments, and settlements.

Remember what a context model, such as the one in Figure 13-7, provides:

- **Overall interaction** — The context model represents the overall interaction of all aspects of the system related to insurance. It is purposely kept at a high level and includes only business concepts, no technology. It is a combination of all the different use cases. Any single use case represents one path through the overall diagram (a subset of functional areas and messages). The context diagram is the first place that you can start to identify commonality between use cases.

- **Shared information** — The messages describe the information that must be shared and exchanged between parties to complete the different insurance-related transactions. It does not describe the details of any information within the different functional areas, only the information exchanged — that is, shared. Remember that this is exactly the information that you need for your semantic information model and to design your service interfaces.

THE FIRST RULES OF MODELING . . .

1. **The first model is always wrong!**

   Modeling is an iterative activity. You constantly learn more about the problem as you progress. New details emerge and cause you to rethink and change what you've done before, until you've iterated through the model and reached a point of completeness and correctness.

2. **It's more important to be clear, than correct!**

   Because you know that the first few models won't be complete or correct, you need to facilitate the steps of getting them there. In order to do that, you need to get feedback and input on the model. The most important thing (initially) is that the model is easy to understand. That allows the experts to tell you what about it is wrong.

3. **Good enough is good enough!**

   You could easily iterate the model 10 or 20 times trying to get it perfect and complete. In general, assume that the model can never be 100% complete. It needs to be good enough for your purposes. If the purpose is to understand the problem and identify requirements, you should usually be able to get there in 3–5 iterations. The remaining details emerge during detailed design. The one exception to this rule is if the model is intended to be executable. In that case, being good enough for your purposes requires it to be complete.

Business Process Model

Now that you have an overall understanding of the interactions involved in travel insurance, let's start to look at the processes involved. For this, you use a Business Process Model. Figure 13-8 illustrates a very high-level process for insurance. The process involves two actors, the agency that is selling the trip and the insurance services that provide the insurance capabilities.

At this level, the process is fairly straightforward.

- The travel agent, working with their customer, creates a trip.

- The agent shops for insurance products that are available for this trip. A set of products and prices is returned.

- The agent or customer picks the product he or she wants and sends a request to purchase the insurance. The first step is to get a price quote. The quote implies that the insurance request has been validated and that the price is correct. The agent or customer then asks to purchase the insurance.

- The insurance is sold, and a policy number is returned.

- This is added to the overall trip, and the sale is completed.

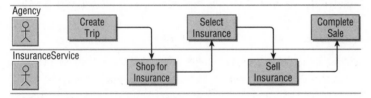

Figure 13-8 High-level insurance process

Of course, it's not really that simple. Each step of the process at this level can be broken down into another level of detail. Let's look at the activities involved in shopping for an insurance product, as illustrated in Figure 13-9. Note that this is not a "subprocess," which is really no more than a notational convenience supported by some tools. Often, a subprocess has no formal interface and can't be effectively reused. It is better to use separate processes so that they can be reused and it is clear who is responsible for them.

Shopping for insurance involves the following activities:

- **Shop** — The initial invocation of the insurance service. This is responsible for orchestrating the rest of the activities.

- **Get Channel Preferences** — Determine if the channel has a preferred vendor or preferred product type and any other contractual requirements for selling insurance through this channel.

- **Calculate Trip Value** — Determine the overall value of the trip, which will influence the type of insurance available and the cost.

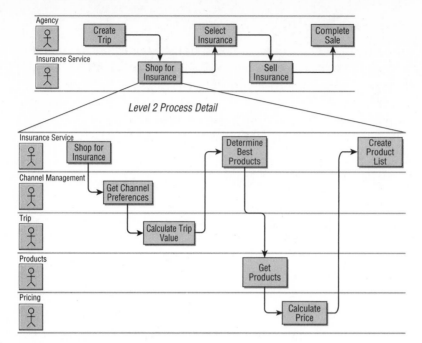

Figure 13-9 Insurance shopping process

- **Determine Best Product** — Compare preferences and determine the best fit vendor or product if any.

- **Get Products** — Get a product set and vendor price quotes. The products may be preconfigured, or dynamic depending on the capabilities of the vendor.

- **Calculate Price** — Create the quoted price of insurance by calculating discounts, markups, commissions, and so on.

- **Create a List of Products** — Format and return a list of the available insurance products.

This is just one of many different use cases. You need to model the complete set of business processes, at both the high level and the detail level for all of the different scenarios involving insurance to identify all the opportunities for shared function and information (services).

Service Conceptual Architecture

To further illustrate the service concepts, you can represent the insurance service group somewhat differently. Figure 13-10 shows the insurance service group at the top center. The services that support the channel are listed on the left (next to the channels) and the services that support the vendors are shown

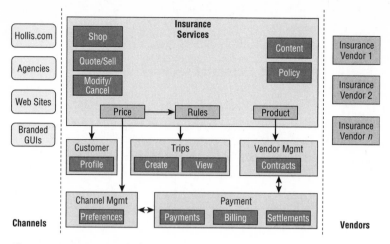

Figure 13-10 Conceptual view of service interactions

on the right (near the vendors). The common services that are used in the process are shown below insurance. To keep things simple for the example, we have not shown all the different services or possible interactions.

Finally, to complete the illustration, you map the process view to the service view. Figure 13-11 shows how the quoting process is implemented by the different services:

- **Shop** — This is the insurance service that we are demonstrating.

- **Get Channel Preferences** — Uses the ChannelManagement Profile Service.

- **Calculate Trip Value** — Uses the Trip Value Service.

- **Determine Best Product** — Uses the internal Rules Service (Domain Service).

- **Get Products** — Uses the internal Product Service (Domain Service).

- **Calculate Price of Products** — Uses the internal Pricing Service (Domain Service).

- **Create Product List** — Done within the Shop Service itself.

The service decomposition can be continued. For example, each of the previous services can be broken down into their internal steps and the services that they call to perform them. We do not go into this level of detail now.

But you might ask, why bother with these drawings in the first place? When doing an SOA project, there are several things that you potentially need to accomplish. First, you need to collect and understand the business requirements. The business context model is one tool that you use for that. Next, you need to communicate what you're doing to the business and to

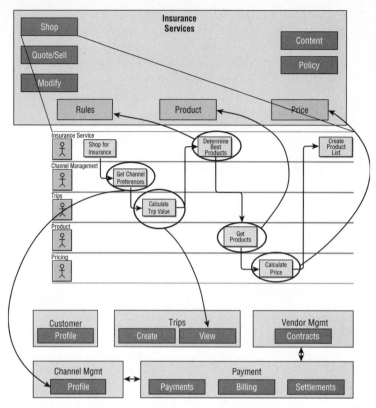

Figure 13-11 Service composition of shopping process

IT. In many cases, these groups are not familiar with SOA concepts and may have difficulty understanding or imagining the solution. We find that these conceptual diagrams are very effective in helping to communicate the concepts and to get everyone on board and on the same page. Finally, you need to design the services themselves. For that, you need a more formal approach.

Use Cases

You start the formal definition of your problem with use cases. Figure 13-12 shows the use cases involved in selecting and purchasing travel insurance. Figure 13-13 shows the use cases associated with the insurance vendor. For brevity we have not included all of the use cases associated with establishing the different channels.

The use cases of interest for this example are:

- **Shop** — Shop for insurance. This can either be associated with an entire trip or specific insurance associated with the details of a trip.
- **Sell** — Sell the insurance and return a policy number.

- **View** — View the policy, quote, payment, or trip.
- **Modify** — Modify the policy, including canceling it, which may involve some refund.

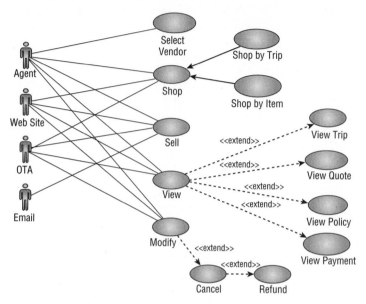

Figure 13-12 Travel insurance use cases

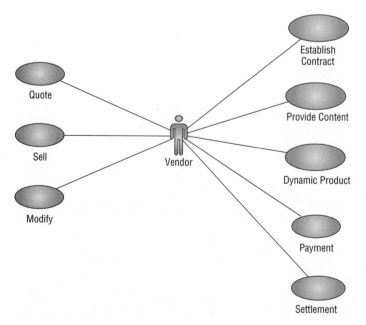

Figure 13-13 Vendor use cases

Following the method described in Chapter 6, you create a detailed scenario diagram for each use case. Figure 13-14 shows the initial scenario diagram for the Shop by Trip use case. The scenario works as follows:

1. The customer or agent is purchasing a trip. They combine the set of products, such as airfare, hotel, and auto into an overall trip. Each item that is selected is added into the trip by calling the Trip Service.

2. After the trip has been created, the customer or agent wants to get insurance for the trip. They call the ShopByTrip operation of the Insurance Service. (See Figure 13-14.)

3. ShopByTrip sells what is called "price banded" insurance. In other words, the cost of the insurance is based on the total cost of the trip. So, the insurance service must determine the cost. Although it is not immediately obvious, this is much more complicated than you might imagine. The Insurance Service does not want to have to understand all the

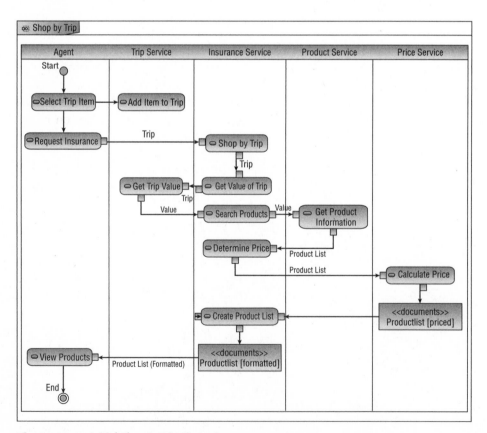

Figure 13-14 Initial ShopByTrip Scenario

complexities of trip pricing. The knowledge lies with the Trip Service. So, you design the interaction for insurance to call the trip service to determine the price of the trip.

4. Now, you need to find insurance products that support that price range. The price banded products are preconfigured. The Insurance Service calls the Product Service to find acceptable products.

5. Almost done. You still have to determine the final price of each potential product. This is done based on relationships with the vendor and the channel. Again, the main insurance service does not want to be responsible for knowing these things. Instead, it calls the Pricing Service whose purpose is to isolate this responsibility.

6. Finally, a list of potential products and their price is returned to the agent requesting it.

The initial scenario diagram should walk through the use case descriptions and describe the sequence of events that take place. First you create an initial scenario for all of the related use cases (shop, sell, view, and modify). Then, you look for commonality between them, factor that out, and add an additional level of detail that emerges as you work through the use cases.

Working through the initial scenarios, reveals that some important information is missing. You don't know enough about the channel to calculate the price. You also don't know anything about the customer, missing the opportunity to meet the business goal of improving customer experience. You address these new found requirements in the detailed scenario diagram.

Note that Figure 13-14 uses object flows between actions to model the exchange of documents between the processing steps. Furthermore, in the case of the ProductList, a datastore node is introduced in order to indicate that the state of the document has been changed by the action. These are the requirements for proper UML2 design; however, they do add a bit of complexity to the diagram. Figure 13-15 shows the detailed ShopByItem scenario where we have taken some liberties with UML and labeled the control flow with the information that is exchanged, for illustration purposes only, to reduce clutter of an already busy diagram. The ShopByItem scenario works as follows:

1. The scenario starts at the call to ShopByItem. We have removed the customer actor from the diagram because it did not add anything.

2. The first step in the process is to determine the preferences (if any) of the customer and to determine the preferences and requirements of the channel. These activities can be performed either sequentially or in parallel as we have illustrated them.

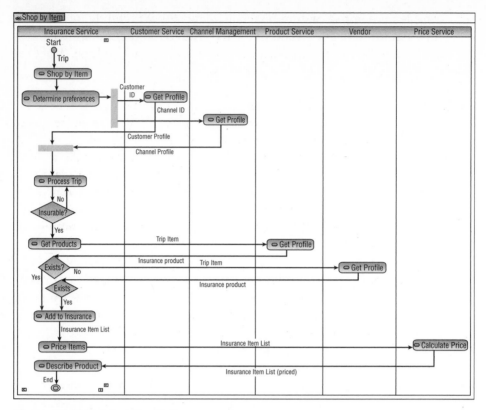

Figure 13-15 Detailed ShopByItem scenario

3. Now, the insurance service processes the trip. A trip is a collection of related trip items. For each item, such as airfare, hotel, and so on, the service determines whether the item is subject to additional insurance. If not, you move on to the next item in the trip. If it is, you go to the next step.

> **NOTE** There is an important design decision made in Step 3. We allowed the insurance service to understand the format of a trip object and to be able to divide it into individual items. Because a trip is a fundamental entity of the business, we decided to allow this. The other alternative would have been to call the trip service and have it return a list of items.

4. For each insurable item, you first go to the insurance product service to see if there are any preconfigured products that support it. If not, you go to the next step.

5. If there are no preconfigured items, you make a call directly to the insurance vendors and see if they want to offer insurance for a particular item. For example, to a traveler who is going to Florida in June, they may choose to offer special "Hurricane Insurance."

NOTE The insurance service is responsible for deciding if an item is insurable. This is a tradeoff between performance and flexibility. Calling out to an insurance vendor for every item in a trip has performance implications. We reduced the number of calls by filtering out items that we know can't be insured, such as rental cars (which have a different kind of insurance) or theatre tickets. The tradeoff is that when a new kind of insurance is added (or deleted), the insurance service must be updated by the vendor. In an ideal world, only the insurance vendors would know what products they offer at any given time, and the insurance service would call them to get the latest product information. The vendors could add or remove products at any time. But the cost of this flexibility is performance, which is a critical requirement for the travel industry. Because insurance products don't change very often, we chose a less dynamic method that has less overhead.

6. If a product exists, you add it to your list of potential insurance items.

7. If a product exists, you need to apply the pricing policy to it. Again, you call the Pricing Service to do this.

NOTE Here is another design decision. You could call the Pricing Service after each product is discovered, and then add the priced items to the list. Instead, we built the list of unpriced items and passed the entire list to the Pricing Service in a single method call. This is a common pattern for reducing service invocation overhead.

8. Finally, a list of potential products and their price is returned to the agent or customer. They can select from the list of items and purchase those that they are interested in.

Enterprise Context

Before you get much further in the design, you need to understand the enterprise context that the SOA architecture fits into. This context influences the design of your solution, services, and documents. First, you need to look at the overall solution in order to define service policies. Then, you need to look at the context in terms of service responsibilities and the information that is passed through service interfaces.

Solutions Architecture

The insurance services are intended to support overall enterprise solutions. Those solutions should conform to an application architecture style, such as the *n*-tier style described in Chapter 9. Figure 13-16 illustrates how the insurance services fit into the *n*-tier architecture.

The scope of Hollis is delineated by the solid lines in the figure. The boundary between tiers is delineated by the dashed lines. So immediately, it is clear that Hollis does not provide any of the user-tier presentations.

In the workspace tier, Hollis provides a variety of services to support interaction with the channels. Application services are used to manage channel preferences and provide user/channel specific logic such as document preprocessing. Distribution services are used to manage session state, perform authentication and authorization, and so on. Utility services provide common discrete business functions, such as airport code lookup. The user and workspace tiers are not the focus of this example.

On the right of the figure are the external insurance vendors. Connectivity to these vendors is achieved through the use of integration services in the resource tier. Again, these are not the focus of this example.

The common services and insurance services described in the conceptual architectures (see Figures 13-2 and 13-10) and that are the focus of this example reside in the enterprise tier. Recall that the enterprise tier is responsible

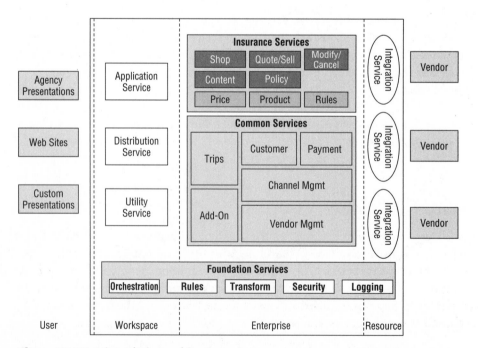

Figure 13-16 *n*-tier solution architecture

for maintaining the integrity of enterprise resources, enforcing system level business rules, and providing enterprise services to requestors. So far, the example has addressed the business requirements for those services and shown how they fit into an overall solution architecture. Part of that architecture is the responsibility for enterprise integrity, so now let's look at the design of security for this example.

In Chapter 11, we discussed many of the security goals that may need to be addressed in an SOA implementation — authentication, authorization, confidentiality, integrity, and non-repudiation. The requirements of each security goal dictate a solution or set of solutions that can be used and that affect the overall SOA design for this case study.

Authentication

In looking at authentication, you need to look at those parties who interact with the services in the scenario. For each, you need to ask whether or not you need assurance of identity, and if so, you need to determine how to do this. It is helpful to write out all of the parties of the scenario that may need to be authenticated. In this case, you need to identify the *agent* using the services, the *channel* used to connect to the services, the *insurance companies* with which the services communicate, and the *services* themselves. Specifically:

- The *agent* using the system needs to be identified by the channel to determine if the agent has permission to use the services, and it must be identified to the travel services (Hollis) for auditing purposes. Since the agent uses a particular channel (web site or application) that communicates with Hollis, the agent must authenticate him- or herself with the channel.

- The *channel* used to communicate with Hollis does the authentication of the agent, and since it needs to vouch for the identity of the agent, it needs to have a trust relationship with Hollis. In this relationship, the channel needs to provide a strong assurance of its own identity.

- The *insurance companies* with which Hollis interacts need to prove their identity in order for Hollis to trust the transactions.

- The *services* themselves (Hollis) need to prove their identity, in order to be trusted by the channel (and therefore the agent) and insurance companies with which they communicate.

Figure 13-17 shows a very high-level overview of this process. Keep in mind that there may be many different channels and many different insurance companies in this process. In drawing this diagram, you see that an agent needs to authenticate to a channel, which must vouch for the agent's identity over a mutually authenticated connection to Hollis. At the same time, transactions

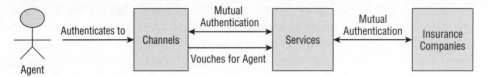

Figure 13-17 Authentication scenarios

that take place between Hollis and the insurance companies must occur over a mutually authenticated connection.

In summary, there are several points of authentication:

- **Between the agent and the channel** — The agent must authenticate to the channel in order to use Hollis's travel services. For many business domains, there may be common authentication and authorization services that can be used by all applications involved in the interactions (for example, a PKI, a central LDAP directory, and/or a Security Token Service (STS) trusted to issue tokens that vouch for identities). Here, it is assumed that this may be the case sometime in the future for these services. In the current situation, however, there is no such environment, and each channel's authentication process is specific to its capabilities and individual security requirements. Therefore, Hollis does not have control over the authentication process between the agent and the channel, so how this is implemented is up to the particular channel. Hollis however, must trust the channel to authenticate its users, and as the channel maintains ownership of its authentication process, it is responsible for any security violations. In such a scenario, the owner of the services should dictate minimum authentication requirements for its channels. In this case, Hollis requires that the minimum security requirements are username/password over SSL.

- **Between the channels and Hollis** — The channel must authenticate itself to Hollis and vouch for the identity of its agents. Because a "global identity" of the agent is not used by the travel industry, the channel-specific identity of the agent is sufficient. The services, therefore, must trust the channel to correctly vouch for the agent's identity, so a trust relationship must be in place. The agent's identity needs to be known by Hollis for auditing purposes. The authentication mechanism also depends on performance requirements. In looking at the requirements, there is heavy traffic between the channels and Hollis's services. Therefore, it is advisable to establish long-lived SSL connections between the two points, allowing session key reuse for performance reasons. There is also money in the budget for using cryptographic accelerators, and this also helps with performance. Therefore, Hollis specifies the following security requirements:

■ **Mutual authentication** — All transactions must occur over a mutually authenticated SSL connection. This means that the channel's digital certificate must be trusted by the services, and vice versa. In order for a new channel to use the services, that channel must obtain a digital certificate and enter a process to put a trust relationship in place with the services.

■ **Vouching for agent identity** — Because Hollis does not have control over the method of authentication performed by the channel, a standard such as the Security Assertion Markup Language (SAML) can be used, as it is authentication technology "agnostic." Hollis, therefore, specifies that all messaging between the channel and the services must be WS-Security SAML Token Profile Messaging (with the sender-vouches confirmation method), since the services have explicit trust of the channels involved. The SAML token propagated conveys authentication and identity information about the user. Although you may think that using this style of messaging (for mere auditing purposes in the services) is overkill, such a strategy can better accommodate change when the insurance industry eventually provides global authentication and authorization services. At that time, the channels will use those services to identify agents, and Hollis's services will perform authorization checks on the agent.

■ **Between Hollis and the insurance companies** — Hollis must prove its own identity to the companies, and vice versa. In this case, you can use the same methodology that is used between the channels and Hollis: mutually authenticated SSL. All transactions must occur over a mutually authenticated SSL connection. This means that the insurance company's digital certificate must be trusted by Hollis, and vice versa. In order for a new insurance company partner to participate in this process, it must obtain a digital certificate and enter a process to put a trust relationship in place with Hollis.

Authorization

For authorization, you follow similar steps to flesh out the requirements. For example, you may need to know if the parties in the scenario have authorization requirements. Specifically, do agents, channels, or insurance companies have special privileges or security roles that allow them to do certain things? In such a scenario, if this were the case, Hollis would typically have an entitlement service containing attributes of subjects, or a policy server or database conveying access control policies.

Some state governments require agents to be licensed to sell insurance, so only certain agents are permitted to do so. Agencies typically have supervisors who can see everything, whereas individual agents are limited to their own sets of transactions or customers. It may be possible, in the next generation of services, to create a security infrastructure for both authentication and authorization, providing security services that allow the travel industry (channels and service providers) to have a common methodology for authentication and authorization, checking global identity, and licenses. In the current scenario, however, this is the responsibility of the channel authenticating the agents. Because each channel controls its own authentication methodology, it also must validate the licenses of agents, according to the state's laws.

Confidentiality

Because sensitive information is transferred between all points in the scenario, it is important that some of the information be encrypted. In looking at the requirements, you can see that the travel business is very data- and transaction-intensive, with requirements for high transaction rates. For this reason, the solution needs to be very performance conscious, so whatever would be adequate for security with minimal impact on performance is the best choice.

Since you are using mutually authenticated SSL between all of the points in this solution, this covers confidentiality, but it is important to note that there is a performance impact. As mentioned in the authentication section, you can establish long-lived SSL connections between the nodes in the solution, eliminating the need for repeated computationally expensive public key cryptography for session key negotiation each time. In addition, the budget allows you to invest in cryptographic accelerators that offload the performance burden.

Integrity and Non-Repudiation

It is important that there be assurance of integrity (that data has not been altered in transit). Luckily, this is accomplished by the SSL connections between the channels, Hollis, and the insurance companies. In addition, it is important that you have a high level of assurance of the transactions, binding the message senders to the transaction requests and responses. As discussed in Chapter 11, non-repudiation, using digital signatures, accomplishes this goal of providing legal proof of such a binding.

In this case, receipts of purchase requests need to be long-lived and digitally signed, providing legal proof that can be validated by a third party. This means that the insurance companies must digitally sign the responses to requests, providing such a proof. These signed documents may be stored for archive by Hollis, providing legal proof, and can be returned in the responses of messages to the channels. In doing so, WS-Security SOAP Messaging is used between Hollis and insurance companies, with the insurance companies using XML Signature to digitally sign purchase receipts (signed using an enveloped signature, where the purchase request, complete with its signature, can be returned to the channel). WS-Security SOAP Messaging is used between the channels and the services, so the passing of these receipts is supported.

The Big Security Picture

Figure 13-18 shows the overall security design:

- Agents authenticate themselves to channels, using an authentication method determined by the individual channel, and the channel confirms that the agent is authorized to perform a transaction with the travel services.

- Each channel must establish a trust relationship with Hollis in order to participate in transactions — Hollis must explicitly trust the digital certificate of each channel, and each channel must explicitly trust the digital certificate of Hollis. The channel initiates a request over a mutually authenticated SSL connection, propagating the identity of the travel agent in WS-Security SAML Token Profile messaging. Responses from Hollis to the channel also use WS-Security SOAP Messaging.

- Hollis audits the channel-specific agent identities that were propagated in requests.

- Each insurance company must establish a trust relationship with Hollis in order to participate in transactions — Hollis must explicitly trust the digital certificate of each company, and each company must explicitly trust the digital certificate of Hollis. Hollis initiates a request over a mutually authenticated SSL connection, participating in messaging with

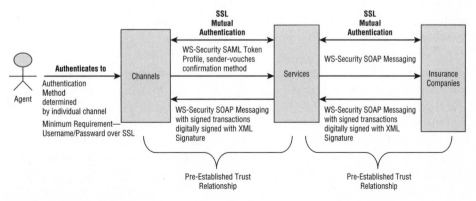

Figure 13-18 Security design

the insurance companies. When request confirmation receipts are created by the companies, they are digitally signed using XML Signature in the WS-Security payload.

- Digitally signed receipts are stored by Hollis and copies are sent back, through the channels, to individual agents.

- SSL connections between each point are configured to be long-lived connections, to support SSL session key reuse for performance reasons, and all cryptography is offloaded onto hardware appliances.

This security design meets the current requirements, but more importantly, it accommodates future enhancements. With the success of this system, it is anticipated that a formal authentication and authorization infrastructure will be established for partner channels, providing authentication services for clients and allowing Hollis to provide specific authorization at the transaction level. The messaging security accommodates such a change by utilizing WS-Security SOAP Messaging and by propagating identity using the WS-Security SAML Token Profile. Any changes to such an infrastructure does not change the messaging security, but instead may require modifications to Hollis's interceptors providing the access control.

The next part of the enterprise context that needs to be considered is the overall set of services.

Service Inventory

The service inventory lays out the overall set of services and their relationships to each other and the overall enterprise goals. You can think of the service inventory as a "responsibility map" of service interfaces. It should clearly describe the overall set of services and what responsibilities the different service groups perform and don't perform. Figure 13-19 shows a partial service inventory for the travel insurance project.

The inventory helps you make decisions about what capabilities to include within your service implementations and what capabilities you should expect to be performed by another service. For example, the Trip service group shows that it is the responsibility of the trip service to add items to a trip. So, although you have allowed the users of trip information to understand some details of a trip (such as what the individual items are as discussed previously), you do not allow them to modify the trip. If you want to add items to a trip, you must call the trip service to perform that task.

Figure 13-19 expands on the services initially identified in the conceptual architecture and includes additional utility and foundation services. However, it is not a complete list of all the services or service groups. For example, it does not include sales tracking, marketing, compliance, or similar services. Also remember that it is just a visualization of much more detailed information

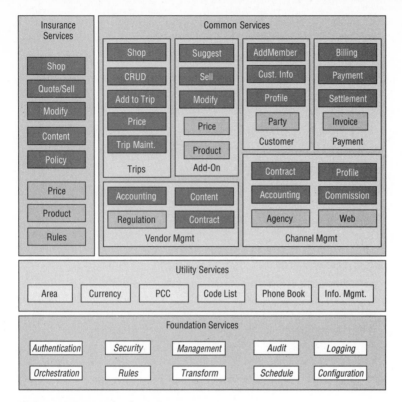

Figure 13-19 Service inventory

about each service, as contained in the service specification and stored in the repository.

Entity Diagram

The other important part of enterprise context is the information that is shared between services. Here, you describe the main entities involved in the business domain and their relationships. The model keeps things at a high level and generally does not describe the details of each individual entity. The model is constructed through a combination of internal domain knowledge, reverse engineering of existing systems, and industry standards. For example, standards from the Open Travel Alliance (OTA) define specific schema for information exchange between travel-related companies. Entities identified in those schema are factored into the information model. Figure 13-20 shows a segment of the information model for Hollis.

Primarily, the model shows the relationship between the Trip, Traveler, and Insurance Policy. For example, you can see that an `InsurancePolicy` is related

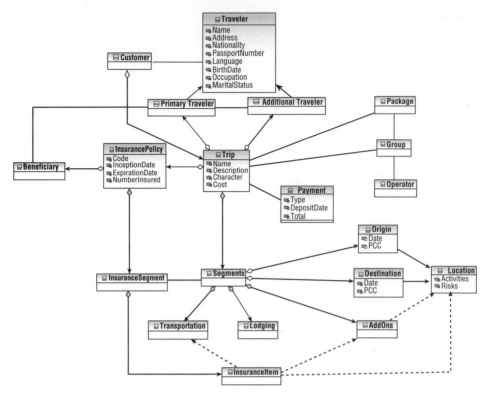

Figure 13-20 Entity model

to a Trip in that a Trip can have an Insurance Policy. It is not possible (at least in this model) to have a Policy without a Trip.

The diagram shows that a Trip is composed of Trip Segments (or Items), and that each segment can be insured with an associated Insurance Segment. Segments contain Transportation, Lodging, and other Add-Ons (theatre, golf, etc.). Each segment has an Origin, including the origin Date, and a Destination, including the Destination Date. It is important that these dates correspond to the Inception and Expiration Dates of the insurance segment.

A Trip has a Primary Traveler and zero or more Additional Travelers. Each traveler is related to the Customer, who "owns" the trip but may or may not be the same. The Insurance Policy has a Beneficiary who has a "beneficiary" relationship to the Primary Traveler. Again, the Beneficiary may be the same person, or someone (or entity) completely different. Although it is not shown in this model, Travelers, Customers, and Beneficiaries are all different types of "Parties," based on an industry standard Party model for describing individuals, companies, and roles.

Information Model

The semantic information model provides the next level of detail after the entity model. In a sense, it is a refinement of the entity model. The model can often be broken up into many different diagrams designed to focus on a specific aspect of the information, as described in Chapter 5. It is mainly a matter of style, but we like to keep the diagrams to about one or two pages. When they get much larger that that, it is difficult to comprehend all the different aspects (much less display or print it).

MODEL, DIAGRAM, METADATA

What is the difference between a model, a diagram, and metadata?

- ◆ **Model** — A model is a representation of a system. There are many different kinds of models, for example Business Models, Business Process Models, and Service Design Models. Each model describes some specific aspect or set of aspects about a system or subsystem.

  - ■ A **Conceptual Model** is an informal visualization intended to communicate concepts. It is often rendered as a Visio diagram. It is important as a means of communication to a variety of audiences, but it is not meant to (nor is it detailed or precise enough) specify an architecture, design, or implementation. Figure 13-2 (Conceptual architecture) is such a model.

  - ■ A **Specification Model** is a formal model that is intended to precisely define the system to the point that it can unambiguously be implemented. A formal model is based on precise semantics, such as BPMN or UML. A formal model is created in a modeling tool, such as Rational Software Modeler. Figures 13-12 through 13-15, and 13-20 through 13-29 are examples of formal models.

- ◆ **Diagram** — A diagram is a specific visualization of some aspect of a model. A model usually contains many diagrams. For example, all the formal diagrams shown in this chapter are part of the same model. The model for the insurance project contains about 50 different diagrams. One thing you may notice is that the same model elements (such as Trip) often occur in more than one diagram. This does not mean that the model element occurs multiple times in the model. Instead, it points out the important distinction between model diagrams and model metadata.

- ◆ **Metadata** — The model is a combination of its metadata and its diagrams. Metadata describes the general modeling concepts, rules, and relationships but not the specific contents of a particular model. Metadata is an external description of a resource. Common usages for metadata include providing the context of a data resource, managing its life cycle, and extending it to new uses.

(continued)

> **MODEL, DIAGRAM, METADATA** *(continued)*
>
> The specific details about every model element are stored in a repository according to the specification of the modeling language. For example, Trip is stored as a UML Class and all the information that is associated with it. The diagrams are structured visualizations of the model elements and their metadata. The same model elements can appear in many different diagrams. For example, the same service often appears in a class diagram, a collaboration diagram, and a sequence diagram. This is because the modeling language has established certain relationships between these types of diagrams and maintains those relationships (and traceability) for us.
>
> People often refer to conceptual drawings, formal diagrams, and formal models all as "models." Perhaps trying to correct this would be an exercise in frustration. But it is important to know the difference and be able to distinguish among them when it really matters.

You create the information model from several sources.

- **Domain information** — Detailed information from industry domain sources (such as OTA).

- **Use case descriptions** — Often the use cases describe specific details about information that is collected, passed, or displayed.

- **Use cases scenarios** — As you create the use case scenarios, you specify the information that is passed into and out of the service interfaces. All data that is passed in a scenario needs to be contained in the information model.

- **Service design** — Finally, as you work out the details of the service interfaces, and especially the implementations, you discover many details about the information that is needed. You follow an iterative process in development, adding detail to the information model as you discover it.

Figure 13-21 is an example from the information model showing the details of the insurance policy. Remember that at this level you are still describing the information that is passed between services and described in the service interfaces, that is, the semantic information model. You are not yet identifying the details of the internal implementation information.

In this diagram, you can see that an InsurancePolicy has Benefits, Exclusions, and a Premium. The Premium is associated with a Payment, which also includes Tax and Commission and can be paid by CreditCard or Voucher. The policy is associated with a ProductPlan (remember that it is an instance of a type of Product). The policy is offered by a specific Vendor. The Vendor might

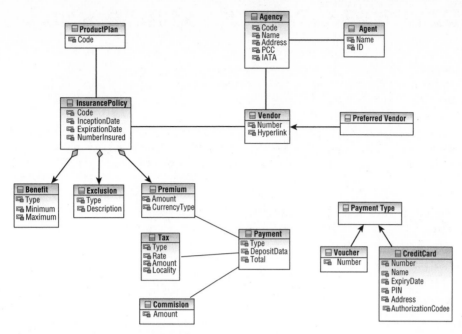

Figure 13-21 Insurance Policy Information model

be a `PreferredVendor`. The `Vendor` has an association with specific `Agencies`, and the specific `Policy` was sold by a specific `Agent`.

Document Model

Because you need to establish and maintain a link between the information model and the documents (which are based on it), it is sometimes useful to create a diagram that lists all of the different documents. Although this is an optional diagram, we find it useful for a number of reasons:

- It helps you keep track of all the documents that you need to specify.
- By looking at the overall set of documents, you can identify potentially redundant documents that perhaps can be merged or simplified.

Figure 13-22 is an early document model for the travel insurance. Essentially, as you work through the use case scenarios and identify information flow and documents, you add those documents to the model. The left and center columns are the documents identified in the two scenario diagrams (see Figures 13-14 and 13-15).

The right column lists an additional set of documents. These are documents designed by the OTA industry standards organization. These essentially represent constraints on the design of the interfaces because you are required to use them for interaction with the insurance vendors and channels.

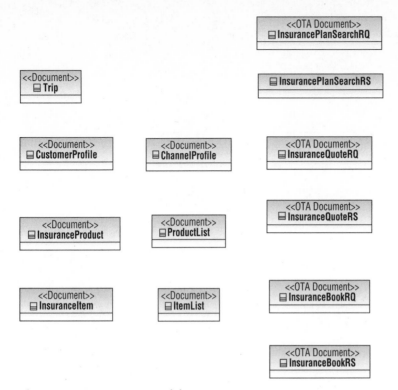

Figure 13-22 Document model

Service Interface Design

You now need to define the service interface by assigning the actions within use case scenarios to service operations. You do this by walking through all of the scenarios. Each action in a scenario either becomes a manual activity, an operation on a business service, or an internal step within an operation implementation (which can most likely be delegated to a domain, utility, or integration service).

This results in two different diagrams. The first is a diagram of the insurance service group, as shown in Figure 13-23. Again, this is a convenience diagram (optional) that provides an overall view (table of contents) of the set of insurance services. Notice that the services are using the naming convention of *Group-nameService-name*. We keep the names simple and do not bother to call them services because the stereotype already identifies them as that, and the context that they are used in doesn't require it.

Then, for each service in the group, you need to define the service interface, specifically the operations that make up the interface, the parameters (documents) passed through them, and the exceptions that are returned. You do this with a service interface diagram (Class diagram), as shown in Figure 13-24.

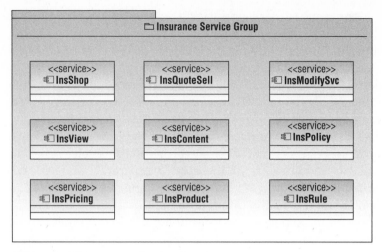

Figure 13-23 Insurance Service Group

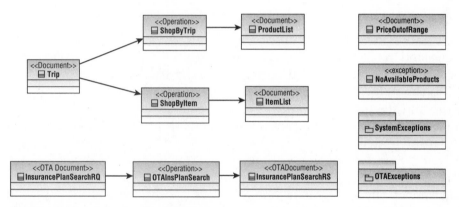

Figure 13-24 Service interface diagram

The figure is basically a graphical representation of the service interface, with inputs on the left, operations in the center left, outputs in the center right, and exceptions on the right. It identifies three operations on the Shopping Service as required by your use case scenarios earlier: the first two, ShopByTrip and ShopByItem both take a Trip as the input document and return either a ProductList or an ItemList. In addition, one of the use cases is the support of an OTA-based channel. In this case, you need to support the standard OTA interface for insurance shopping (even though it does not support much of the new functionality yet). So, the diagram includes a third operation for OTAInsurancePlanSearch, with its associated documents.

The service interface diagram gives you a graphical way to evaluate the complexity of the service operation, and the cohesion. For example, it is normal to see multiple operations that support the same input and/or outputs.

Notice that in this example, all of the inputs and outputs are documents. You first define the documents in the document model (refer to Figure 13-22) and then include them in the interface definition model. If you discover an interface that doesn't have a document defined for it, you don't add the document to the interface diagram. Instead, you add it to the document model, and then include it in the interface diagram. This keeps your model organized and prevents you from duplicating or forgetting about documents.

In the design of the service interface, we made a few design decisions. Should there be one service that contains all of the Shop, Quote, Sell, and Modify operations, or should each of these be a separate interface? We decided on separate interfaces for a few reasons. First, the interface started to get crowded when we added all the different variations of these operations to it. We find between four and seven is a pretty good rule of thumb for the number of operations on a service interface. Second, we wanted to align the service capabilities with the OTA request and reply messages.

Service Interactions

There is one more thing to check about your service design. You need to understand the dependencies (coupling) between this and other services. For this, you use a service interaction diagram, as shown in Figure 13-25.

This shows the different services, both those within the Insurance Service Group and the common services that are required to implement the Shop, Quote, Sell, and Modify scenarios. We look at these scenarios together because they are all related.

What you're looking for is complexity. You want to keep the service interaction simple and certain kinds of services, particularly entity services, independent. The services in Figure 13-25 have a fairly low level of complexity and a minimum of unnecessary dependencies, so we are happy with the interface design and can now move on to the document design.

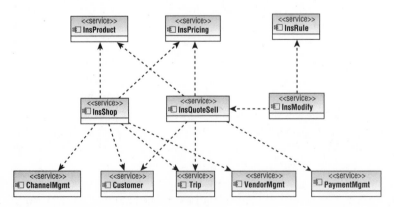

Figure 13-25 Service interaction diagram

Document Design

It is critical that the documents be defined based on the semantic information model. The best way to do this is to derive the documents definitions directly from the semantic information model. Keep in mind that the information exchanged between consumers and providers should be limited to the minimum required. This keeps the interchanges short and avoids exposing information that is not needed or should not be known.

You use a marking technique to illustrate how this is done. Figure 13-26 shows a simplified subset of the insurance policy information model that is part of the `InsurancePolicy` document.

In this case, the `InsurancePolicy` is the root of the document (identified by the double box surrounding it), and it contains three elements: `Benefits`, `Exclusions`, and `Premiums`. It also contains a reference to another major entity, the `Vendor`. During the layout of the document schema, a design decision was made. You could have passed the vendor information either completely (by value), or as an identifier (by reference). We choose to pass by reference to both reduce the amount of data that needs to be passed, and to reduce the coupling needed around vendor information. Note that this is not the same as passing an object reference in object-oriented systems. In this case, the ID can be used by the recipient to retrieve information about the vendor from

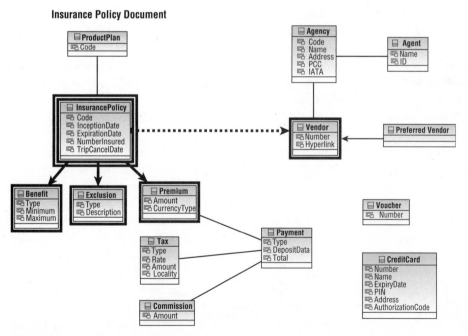

Figure 13-26 Insurance policy document

a vendor management service. There are no operations supported by the ID, nor is there a transient state maintained by the system in association with it.

Service Implementation Design

Finally, you are ready to design the service implementation. The implementation design describes the details of each service operation. The implementation should follow the layered architecture defined in Chapter 7. Often, as is the case here, the implementation of a service operation requires the use of other services. This should be described in the service specification created during interface design.

Service Specification

The service specification may consist of a text document, such as the example illustrated in Chapter 6 (but not shown here), which is generally intended for the service consumer, and a formal model, as shown in Figure 13-27, which is intended for the service implementer. The service specification is described in terms of a UML collaboration for each service operation.

The model contains two parts. The main top box (labeled ShopByTrip) is the collaboration. It indicates that the InsShop service implements the InsShop interface (top-left component). In addition, it uses the Trip, InsProduct, and InsPrice interfaces. These two different types of interfaces are known as provided interfaces and required interfaces. In other words, the InsShop service *provides* the InsShop interface and ShopByTrip operation, and *requires* (uses) the Trip, InsProduct, and InsPrice interfaces. You may not know how those interfaces are implemented (nor should you care), so they are illustrated as components that realize the required interface roles.

Of course, there is more to it than that. There is a specific protocol associated with the interaction of these interfaces within the collaboration. The protocol is specified by an activity diagram (the bottom half of Figure 13-27). The diagram illustrates the sequence of the interactions, the operations that InsShop calls on each of the other services, and the input and output provided by each (note that the output names have been suppressed, but they are part of the model data). The activity diagram is associated with the collaboration. This is indicated by the circle with the + inside of it on the bottom of the collaboration box, and the line that attaches the collaboration to the activity diagram. This notation indicates that the activity is an "owned behavior" of the collaboration.

Note also that we have simplified the collaboration and implementation design to be able to fit it onto a reasonable sized drawing. The customer profile and channel management services have been excluded for illustration purposes.

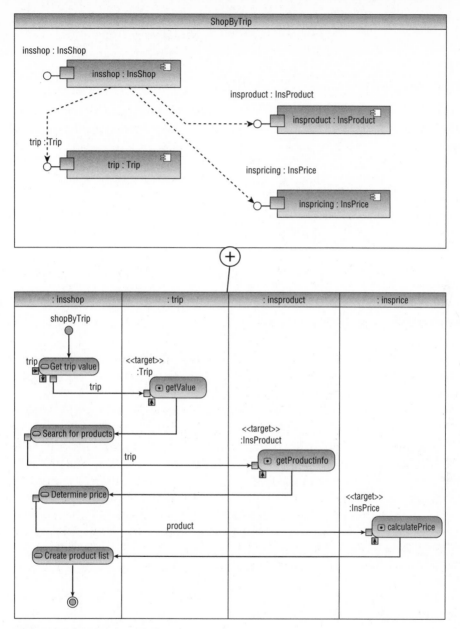

Figure 13-27 Service specification

Implementation Layers

The implementation design should follow the layered approach containing the interface layer, business logic layer, and resource access layer. Within each layer, components are used as the basic unit of software construction.

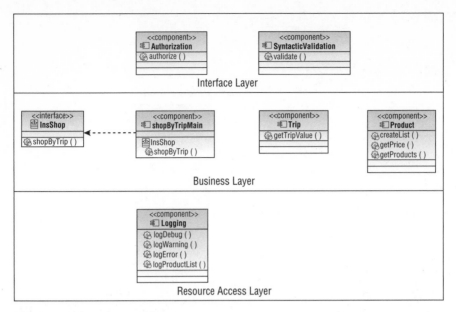

Figure 13-28 Implementation components

Figure 13-28 shows a diagram that lays out all of the implementation components for the ShopByTrip operation. We have superimposed the implementation architecture layers on top of the UML.

The interface layer contains components for authorization and syntactic validation. The business layer contains the main ShopByTrip component as well as components that encapsulate the interaction with other services. The Trip component is used to make a call to the Trip service. The Product component is used to make calls to the InsProduct service to get the product list, and the InsPrice service to calculate the price. It also performs the internal function of formatting the priced productList for return. Finally, the resource layer contains the logging component that is used to log error information and to log a record of productLists that are returned by the service. No data resources are used directly by this service operation.

Operation Procedure

The final step (for this operation at least) is to define the control and data flow of the operation implementation. Again, an activity diagram is used for this purpose, as shown in Figure 13-29. The diagram is broken into three partitions to illustrate the layered architecture approach. These are for illustration purposes and do not represent collaboration roles.

The operation starts in the interface layer when the ShopByTrip call is accepted. The first step is to verify that the user is authorized to perform this

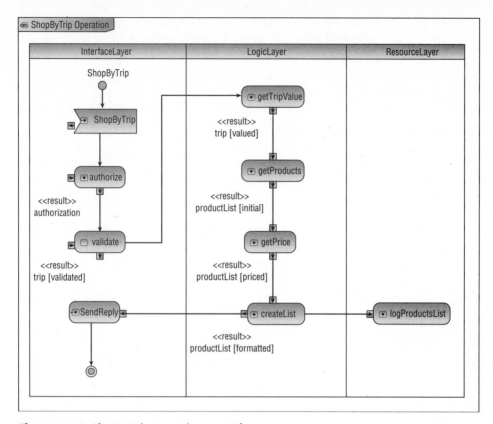

Figure 13-29 ShopByTrip operation procedure

operation according to the run-time service policy as specified in the security design and service specification. Notice that the authorization component encapsulates the security logic to allow for future (expected) changes. If authorized, then syntactic validation is made to ensure that the request is well formed and that all parameters conform to schema definitions. The result of this operation is a validated `Trip` document, which is then passed as the input to the `getTripValue` action in the logic layer. Notice that the names of the action steps in the activity diagram conform exactly to the names of the operations of the implementation components. This is not an accident. The actions steps are created from the components, not independently of them, and the actions are implemented by the operations of the components.

The output of this action is a valued `Trip` document which is them passed (via an object flow) to the input of the next action `getProducts`, which corresponds to the `getProducts` operation of the `Product` implementation component. The flow continues through the `getPrice` action and on to the `createList` action, which is the last step in the logic layer. Here, two steps are performed in parallel. The formatted `productList` is passed to the interface layer for return to the requestor (via the `SendReply` reply action). At the same time, the `productList` is passed on to the logging component in the resource layer for auditing purposes.

What remains is to define the operations' procedures for the rest of the `InsShop` service interface, and then to define the interface, documents, and implementation for the rest of the insurance services. We leave that for another day.

Summary

In this chapter, you looked at an actual service scenario from the travel industry to illustrate the design concepts of the book. First, you start with the business. In this case, we used several different business architecture artifacts, including a value chain, a context diagram, and a business motivation model.

Next, you refine the business model into business process scenarios. You looked at several related scenarios to maximize the opportunity for shared behavior and information, which are first-class candidates for services.

But, services don't exist in isolation. They are part of an overall solution and must be seen within the larger enterprise context of all services. You use an established architectural style, such as *n*-tier, to describe the overall solution and to position the insurance services where they belong in the enterprise tier. Then, you analyze the interaction between the parties to determine the security implementation and policies for the application. Next, you use the service inventory as a way to map responsibilities of services and service groups and get an overall picture of all the enterprise services and their relationships. You also use the common semantic information model as a way to formally define the common information shared across these services.

Then you are ready to define individual service interfaces. Here, you rely on use cases to express the requirements, and elaborate the use cases in scenarios. First, for each use case, you create a high-level scenario, and in the process of looking at all the use cases together, you identify additional requirements, and common behavior and information. You factor this new information into a more detailed set of scenarios.

Each of the actions in the detailed scenarios is implemented as an operation on a service. The information flowing into and out of the actions is implemented as documents. You set about organizing the operations and documents. You combine operations into interfaces in accordance with cohesion and coupling principles. Documents are the parameters passed into or out of those interfaces.

Finally, you provide the design for the implementation of each service operation in a technology-independent fashion that conforms to a three-layered implementation architecture. The specification is created in terms of a collaboration showing provided and required interfaces and protocols, a diagram showing the main implementation components, and activity diagrams describing the control and data flow of each operation. This should be clear, complete, and specific enough to be the software specification given to the development organization that is responsible for implementing the service. Now that's another book in itself.

CHAPTER 14

Case Study — Service-Based Integration in Insurance

Start where you are. Use what you have. Do what you can.
— **Arthur Ashe**

SOA has defined a new approach to the design and implementation of enterprise IT systems. But using SOA does not, by any stretch of the imagination, mean that you should abandon the existing applications that are the backbone of today's enterprises or the best integration approaches developed over the last 15–20 years. Furthermore, SOA does not mean automatically and blindly turning everything into a service. It means defining and implementing enterprise business services to support the primary enterprise capabilities. When it comes to implementing these services using existing enterprise applications, integration approaches can vary widely. There is no hard and fast rule that all integration has to be implemented as services. On the contrary, each specific integration scenario has to be analyzed carefully and an appropriate implementation chosen, based on the requirements of the higher-level business services.

This chapter provides an example that demonstrates the implementation of service-based integration in the insurance industry. It illustrates the approaches defined in Chapter 10 as applied to a fictitious insurance company — ACME Insurance — and its current IT applications. Then, it illustrates the implementation of enterprise services, focusing on the integration architecture aspects of the implementation. Although the example in this chapter is fictitious, it is based on real projects done by the authors.

The chapter and example are structured as follows:

- An overview of ACME's existing IT systems
- A description of the new enterprise business service interfaces
- For each interface, an examination of design approaches for mapping existing capabilities to new interface operations
- A summary of the different integration approaches required to support these mappings
- For each integration approach we provide:
  - Analysis of the integration approach and discussion of pros and cons
  - Details of how ACME implemented the particular approach
  - Additional enterprise concerns of location and the registry, security, exception handling, and monitoring

ACME Insurance

ACME Insurance is an insurance company specializing in two lines-of-business: commercial auto and commercial property. ACME deals with all the issues associated with the full insurance life cycle, including rating, underwriting, and servicing insurance policies. All of these capabilities currently work fine and are implemented on existing but separate systems. Unfortunately, it is difficult to share the capabilities across products, to add new products, or to take advantage of marketing and sales opportunities across lines-of-business. In order to improve flexibility and stay competitive, ACME must improve the integration of and synergy between these legacy applications and enable new, cross-line-of-business, and cross-product business processes. To accomplish this, an SOA approach has been chosen. The strategy is to expose existing business capabilities from the legacy systems as new business services that can then be used in the business processes.

ACME's architects and business analysts have been hard at work defining the company's goals, objectives, and outcomes and then designing business processes to meet them. This has been taken to the next level of detail, the specification of new business services (based on the enterprise analysis and decomposition) that can support the requirements of the current and future business processes. Now comes the tricky part: how to map the new enterprise business service interfaces to the capabilities of the existing systems and how to provide the technical connections to those systems. Answering these questions is where we begin our case study.

To keep the complexity under control in the example, we are limiting the scope and focus of the solution to a handful of enterprise underwriting services designed by ACME personnel and the existing applications relevant for those service implementations. We also leave out details that, while necessary from the insurance company's perspective, would not add value to our discussion.

ACME's existing applications and databases relevant to our example are shown in Figure 14-1.

The implementation and functionality of these applications and databases are described here:

- Commercial Auto Policy and Products Administration is a mainframe application built by ACME insurance in-house. This application supports all the functionality required for the development of new commercial auto insurance products and the policy administration for these products, including customer and policy information gathering, policy rating integration, and so on. This application was originally created as a "green screen" application but was later modified to provide Customer Information Control System (CICS) transaction interfaces to the majority of its functions.

- Commercial Property Policy and Products Administration is also a mainframe application acquired from a vendor and modified by ACME Insurance personnel. Its functionality is similar to the functionality of the Commercial Auto Policy and Products Administration application, but it is used for a different aspect of the business. This application also exposes its functionality in the form of CICS transactions.

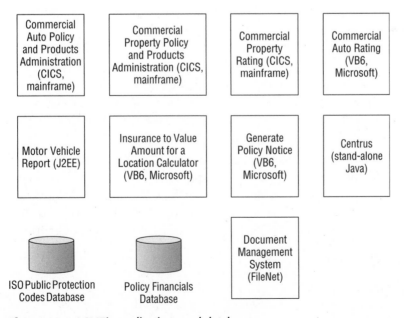

Figure 14-1 ACME's applications and databases

- Commercial Property Rating and Commercial Auto Rating are two core ACME applications, both developed in-house. They allow employees to determine the risk associated with issuing an insurance policy. They are based on the rules and risk factors associated with the particular line-of-business and defined for a specific insurance product. The commercial property rating engine is a mainframe application, exposed as a CICS transaction; whereas Commercial Auto rating is a VB6 application, componentized using Microsoft's COM.

- The Motor Vehicle Report is a B2B J2EE application that communicates with the state's Motor Vehicle facilities over a VPN and stores current information about drivers in the local Oracle database. This application exposes its functionality over a web interface, allowing a user to submit a list of drivers and get back a report for each driver. The reply comes back to the user only if the requested driver's information already exists and is current in the local application's database. Otherwise, a request is sent to the relevant state's Motor Vehicle facility and the user is advised to use the application at a later time. To avoid making multiple requests to a Motor Vehicle facility, a local database keeps track of sent requests and does not send a new request if there is an outstanding one.

- The Insurance to Value Amount for a Location Calculator is a vendor's application that calculates insurance to value amount for a property in a given location. It is a batch VB6 application, retrieving input from a local file and returning the results of the execution to a different file. It can be invoked from a command string with two parameters: input and output filenames, or as a COM component.

- Generate Policy Notice is another vendor application, which generates policy documentation. This is a VB6, UI-based application that allows users to interactively create and query policy information. Information access is based on the details stored in the user's session information. Recently the vendor has added a Web Service interface that mimics the UI functionality (screen scraping using Web Services).

- Centrus is a vendor application that supports functions such as address cleansing (converting addresses to the standard representation); geocoding (assigning geographic designations, such as latitude and longitude, to an address); catastrophe data for location, including terrorism, waterway, floodZone, earthquakeZone, and windTier information. Centrus is a stand-alone application, deployed by ACME on an AIX machine. The vendor provides Java APIs, which can be used for accessing the application.

- The Document Management System is an IBM/FileNet content management system used by the company. All content management functionality is exposed either via Web Service interfaces or Java APIs, which are internally based on Web Services.

- The ISO Public Protection Codes Database is a database that contains public protection class and occupancy codes for a given property location.

- The Policy Financials Database is a database that contains the financial history for a given policy, including pricing data and claims payoffs.

As a result of business analysis and service-oriented decomposition, ACME defined enterprise services to support the majority of the company's business capabilities. A subset of these service interfaces (supporting underwriting) is shown in Figures 14-2 through 14-5.

NOTE We are not showing complete services here, just the operations that are relevant to our example.

This service contains the following operations:

- `EstablishPolicySubmission` — This operation creates an account in a policy administration system for a new customer and returns a policy ID.

- `UpdateInsurancePolicy` — This operation updates policy information in the system of record (policy administration system) and returns a unique ID (key) for the policy.

- `CancelInsurancePolicy` — This operation updates the state of the policy in the system of records (policy administration system) based on the cancellation date, policy ID, and cancellation reason.

- `ReinstateInsurancePolicy` — This operation updates the state of the policy in the system of record (policy administration system) based on the policy ID, reinstatement reasons, and, optionally, a new amount due.

- `RetrieveInsurancePolicy` — This operation retrieves complete policy information based on a policy ID.

- `RateInsurancePolicy` — This operation rates a policy based on the policy ID and generates the required forms, based on the policy information. It returns premium, rates, and associated forms.

- `GeneratePolicyNoticeDocuments` — This operation creates legal documents for a given policy (pending cancellation, rescission, cancellation).

- `RetrievePolicyComplianceInformation` — This operation retrieves the termination effective date for a policy.

- `CalculatePolicyFinancials` — This operation calculates policy and claim financial summary information. (See Figure 14-2.)

Figure 14-2 Policy Management Service

For this service, we discuss only one operation:

- `GetDriversInformation` — This operation retrieves driver information in the form of the standard state Motor Vehicle Report for commercial auto insurance policies. (See Figure 14-3.)

«interface»
PartyManagement
+getDriversInformation (in DiverLicenseNumber : string) : MotorVehicleReport

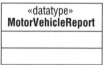

Figure 14-3 Party Management Service

«interface»
LocationManagement
+assessInsuredLocation (in locationAddress : PostalAddress) : LocationInformation

LocationInformation
-LocationScore : string
-GeoCode : string
-OcupancyCode : string
-InsuranceToValueRatio : double
-CatastrophicCode : string

Figure 14-4 Location Management Service

For this service, we also discuss a single operation, as shown in Figure 14-4:

- `AssessInsuredLocation` — This operation calculates categorized location information, including GeoCode, Occupancy codes, the Insurance to Value Ratio, catastrophic data, and so on.

This service provides support for document management capabilities, including creating, retrieving, updating, and searching documents, as shown in Figure 14-5.

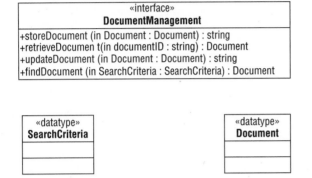

Figure 14-5 Document Management Service

High-Level Integration Design

After performing a functional analysis, comparing the existing application capabilities (see Figure 14-1) and the business service requirements (as expressed by the interfaces in Figures 14-2 through 14-5), ACME architects have defined the mapping and high-level integration architecture illustrated in Figure 14-6. In the rest of this chapter, we explore the details of the business component and integration access layers. But first, let's review the overall architecture.

The integration architecture is based on mapping requirements of the newly defined enterprise business services to the capabilities of the existing enterprise applications and deciding how they can be leveraged in the implementation of those business services, based on the layered architecture defined in Chapter 10.

The bottom layer of the architecture consists of the existing systems whose capabilities we leverage. The next layer up is the integration access layer. This layer uses a variety of techniques and access methods to connect to the existing systems and expose their functionality and data. The implementation of this layer is the topic of the second part of the chapter.

Above the integration access is a layer of business components. These components encapsulate the details of the integration layer and provide the

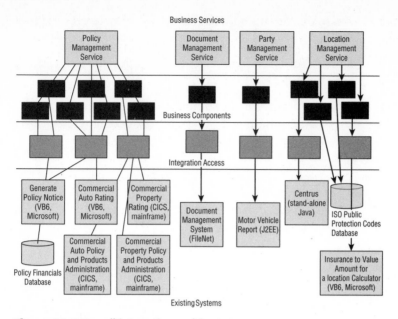

Figure 14-6 Overall integration architecture

building blocks for the implementation of the business services in the top layer. The design of the mapping and components is the topic of the next section of this chapter.

SOA implementation is very different from traditional object-oriented or components-based development in the sense that a service is a logical (not physical) grouping of participating operations (see Boris Lublinsky's article, "Defining SOA as an architectural style" [January 2007]). As a result of the logical grouping, in the majority of cases each operation can be designed and implemented separately. In this chapter, we follow this approach. In this section, we describe the design of the different integration services and their operations. Because many of the operations require a similar technical implementation, we cover the technical implementation aspects together in the next section.

Establishing Policy Submission

This functionality already exists and is supported by policy administration applications for auto and commercial property. Several additional assumptions are made about this business method implementation:

- ACME wants to continue using the existing mainframe GUI for establishing policy submissions in the existing policy administration applications. As a result, they want to use the existing account tables as a "golden copy" of information about existing policy accounts.

- Policy administration applications are using unique IDs that are meaningless (in addition to the account numbers) to distinguish accounts. These IDs are specific to each policy administration application and, thus, should not be visible outside of them. Account numbers, on the other hand, are made of information that is meaningful to the business and should be used as a key for accessing accounts. To ensure the uniqueness of the account numbers among multiple lines-of-business (uniqueness for the same line-of-business is ensured by the application itself) and to simplify the business operation implementation, a letter, designating a specific line-of-business is added to the corresponding account number. This does not require changes to the application itself and can be handled (added/removed) by an integration access implementation.

- Operation execution returns a result code, denoting the success or failure to establish a policy submission.

Two integrations need to be designed in this case:

- Policy submission for a commercial auto policy needs to utilize the existing CICS transactions exposed by the Commercial Auto Policy and Products Administration application.

- Policy submission for a commercial property policy needs to utilize existing CICS transactions exposed by the Commercial Property Policy and Products Administration application.

Additionally business components that wrap integration capabilities, including access to the integration and, potentially, data mapping should be implemented to simplify integration usage.

The overall implementation of this business operation is illustrated in Figure 14-7.

From the point of view of the business service implementer, he is using two local components, which implement the required capabilities, and is unaware of the integration details performed by the components. This design approach allows the component to completely encapsulate access to the existing legacy applications and simplifies maintenance of the resulting system. If a decision is made later on to reimplement all (or part of) the existing enterprise capability (contained in the legacy application), the impact on the business service implementation is minimal.

This means that the design of the business component's interface should be aligned with the requirements of the business service, not of the integration. More specifically, the business component's interface has to be designed based on the domain model used by the business service (not the legacy data model). The actual data mapping is then done either by the integration access piece or the component itself.

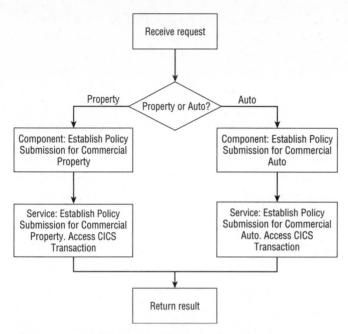

Figure 14-7 EstablishPolicySubmission operation

Both integrations for this operation are implemented through the access to the CICS transactions on the mainframe. The technical implementation of the integration is covered later in this chapter.

A similar design applies to several other operations that were identified as part of ACME's business analysis and service decomposition. These operations are:

- UpdateInsurancePolicy can be implemented based on two integrations utilizing existing CICS transactions — update commercial auto policy and update commercial property services. ACME has made a decision to use existing policy administration applications as a "golden copy" of the policy data. As a result this operation requires the complete insurance policy, along with the policy identification information — policy number and effective data — as its input. To ensure uniqueness of policy numbers between lines-of-business and to simplify request routing, a letter specifying a line-of-business is appended to the policy number. The overall business operation implementation is similar to that depicted in Figure 14-7. This operation returns back an ID for an updated policy.

- CancelInsurancePolicy can be implemented based on two integrations utilizing existing CICS transactions — cancel commercial auto policy and cancel commercial property services. Cancellation is done using policy identification information as its input. The overall business service implementation is similar to the one, depicted in Figure 14-7. The status returned by the operation defines the success or failure of execution.

- `ReinstateInsurancePolicy` can be implemented based on two integrations utilizing existing CICS transactions — reinstate commercial auto policy and reinstate commercial property services. Reinstatement uses policy identification information as its input. The overall business service implementation is similar to the one, depicted in Figure 14-7. The status returned by the operation defines the success or failure of service execution.

- `RetrieveInsurancePolicy` can be implemented based on two integrations utilizing existing CICS transactions — retrieve commercial auto policy and retrieve commercial property services. The policy is retrieved based on the service identification information. The overall business service implementation is similar to the one depicted in Figure 14-7. The operation returns a complete insurance policy.

Rate Insurance Policy

The capability for this operation already exists in two applications — commercial property rating and commercial auto rating. This operation is purely a calculation; it executes a set of rules (that are different for different lines-of-business and are contained in existing applications). The rules are used for calculating premiums, rates, and forms. `RateInsurancePolicy` takes an insurance policy, including the account information, terms and conditions, as input and returns calculated premiums.

Two integrations have to be designed to support this operation:

- The `RateCommercialProperty` integration can utilize existing CICS transactions exposed by the Commercial property rating application.

- The `RateAutoPolicy` integration can utilize existing COM components exposed by the Auto policy rating application.

Business components that wrap the integration access further simplify the business operation implementation. The overall implementation of this business operation is presented in Figure 14-8.

We describe the technical implementation of integration with CICS transactions and COM components later in this chapter.

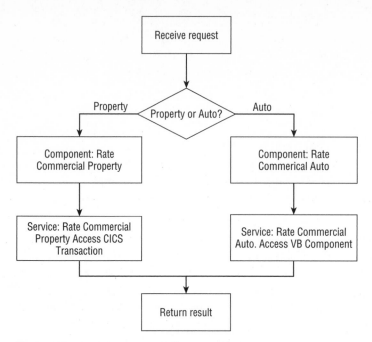

Figure 14-8 Rate Insurance Policy operation

Assess Insured Location

The AssessInsuredLocation operation is also based on the existing capability of the existing ACME applications and databases, including the ISO Public Protection Codes database, the Insurance to Value Calculator, and Centrus. Based on the location of the property, this service collects a set of data required for calculation of the insurance premiums for a commercial property at a given location.

Implementation of this operation requires the design and implementation of the following integrations:

- GetPublicProtectionCode can utilize the existing ISO Public Protection Codes Database.

- GetInsurancetoValue can utilize the existing Insurance to Value amount for a location calculator exposed as a COM component.

- GetGeoCoding and GetCatastrophicInformation can utilize the existing Centrus application exposed through vendor-provided Java APIs.

Unlike the previous implementations, this one does not choose which integration to invoke. Instead, it invokes all supporting integrations to collect the required information. In this implementation, the GetInsurancetoValue

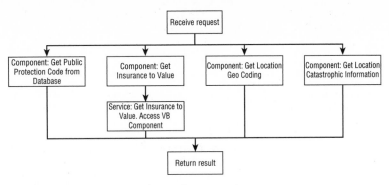

Figure 14-9 Assess Insured Location operation

integration is wrapped by business components, simplifying its usage. The rest of the integrations are implemented directly in business components.

The overall implementation of this business operation is shown in Figure 14-9.

We discuss the technical implementation of integration with COM components, existing databases, and exposed Java APIs later in this chapter.

Get Driver's Information

This functionality already exists in the Motor Vehicle Report application. Based on the list of drivers (driver license numbers), this operation allows collection of data about recent violations, required for the calculation of the auto insurance premiums for a given set of drivers.

At first glance, it might seem that it is not necessary to explicitly create a `GetDriversInformation` operation; simply exposing the functionality of an existing application seems to satisfy requirements. We do not recommend this approach for the following reasons:

- The application can change over time, while an enterprise service is aligned to the overall Enterprise Architecture, specifically, the interface capabilities and semantics of the enterprise service. Wrapping an application's capabilities in an operation of the enterprise service provides a decoupling layer, shielding potential service consumers from application changes.

- Additional functionality might be required from the operation over time. Introducing the enterprise service as a separate entity enhances the application's functionality directly in the operation's implementation without modifying the existing application.

- Implementation of the enterprise service's operation provides a logical place for transforming data between the enterprise-wide semantic information and the application (Motor Vehicle report, in this case) data models.

Implementation of this operation requires design and implementation of integration access for `GetDriversInformation`, which can utilize the existing J2EE Motor Vehicle Report application and a business component, wrapping the integration and simplifying its usage. The overall implementation of this business operation is shown in Figure 14-10.

We discuss the technical implementation of integration with existing J2EE applications later in this chapter.

Generate Policy Notice Documents

The purpose of this operation is to generate a set of policy notice documents, based on the full information of the insurance policy. This functionality already exists in the Generate Policy Notice operation. In this case, as in the `GetDriversInformation` operation, there is a one-to-one correspondence between the operation's functionality and the existing application. Following the same line of reasoning, ACME's architects decided to explicitly implement this operation based on the vendor provided Web Services. Unfortunately, none of the vendor's Web Services expose the exact functionality required by ACME. Several Web Services have to be invoked to support business

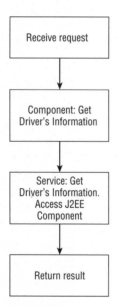

Figure 14-10 Get Driver's Information operation

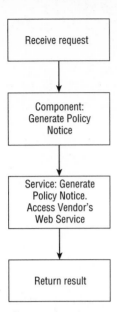

Figure 14-11 Generate Policy Notice Document operation

requirements. These multiple invocations can be encapsulated in a business component implementing the logic of sequential invocations of vendor's Web Services. A BPEL orchestration solution was examined, but it was considered too heavyweight for this simple integration problem. The overall implementation of this business operation is shown in Figure 14-11.

We discuss the technical implementation of building integration services based on the vendor's exposed Web Services later in this chapter.

Collect Policy Financials

This operation calculates the policy and claim financial summary information, based on the data that already exists in the Policy Financial database. Based on the policy ID, this operation calculates a set of financial characteristics of the policy. As recommended in Chapter 10, integration can be implemented through direct database access and consequently requires only a business component that encapsulates access to the existing database. (See Figure 14-12.)

Although technically it is possible to expose the database access directly to the business service, the introduction of a specialized business component to encapsulate this access reduces coupling between business, the service implementation, and the existing enterprise database.

We discuss the technical implementation of integration based on the existing databases later in this chapter.

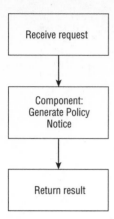

Figure 14-12 Collect Policy Financials' operation

Work with Documents

This functionality already exists in the company and is provided by an existing FileNet application. The FileNet application provides a set of Web Services, which can be directly used by the business services implementation. Although this approach is technically feasible, it is not the optimal one. The FileNet Web Services expose a set of (too) low-granularity services, allowing for fine-grained operations on the documents. Using these services requires the business service implementation to be aware of a lot of FileNet's inner workings, thus creating a tight coupling between the business services implementation and FileNet. This would make switching to a different document management system very difficult.

The implementation architecture, as shown in Figure 14-13, allows you to hide these details through the introduction of specialized business components, exposing only a set of business-level document operations and orchestrating FileNet Web Services for these operations' fulfillment.

We discuss the technical implementation of integrations based on the vendor's exposed Web Services later in this chapter.

Integration Requirements for the ACME Implementation

Based on the integration service designs in the previous section, the following integrations are required to implement the integration services for ACME:

- **Integration with the existing CICS transactions** — This type of integration is required to implement `EstablishPolicySubmission`, `UpdateInsurancePolicy`, `CancelInsurancePolicy`, `ReinstateInsurancePolicy`, and `RetrieveInsurancePolicy` for both commercial auto and property policies. In addition, it is needed for `RateCommercialProperty` policy operations.

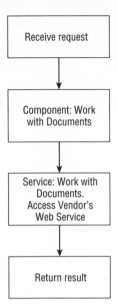

Figure 14-13 Work with Documents operation

- **Integration with the existing COM components** — This type of integration is required to implement the `RateCommercialAutoPolicy` and `GetInsuranceToValue` operations.

- **Integration based on the existing Java APIs** — This type of integration is required to implement the `GetGeoCoding` and `GetCatastrophicInformation` operations.

- **Integration with the existing J2EE applications** — This type of integration is required to implement the `GetDriversInformation` operation.

- **Integration with the existing databases** — This type of integration is required to implement `GetPublicProtectionCode` and `GetPolicyFinancials` business components.

- **Integration based on the vendor's Web Services** — This type of integration is required to implement the `GeneratePolicyNotice` and `RetrievePolicyComplianceInformation` operations and the `WorkWithDocuments` service.

Integration with Existing CICS Transactions

Despite many promises made in the last 10–15 years, the mainframe, in general, and CICS, in particular, is still very much alive and is often the workhorse of existing enterprise IT systems. As a result, not surprisingly, many vendors are offering approaches for exposing existing CICS transactions to use throughout the enterprise.

Integration Approaches

The most popular approaches use a software/middleware abstraction layer, "standard" messaging middleware (for example, WebSphere MQ), and standard-based Web Services, available in CICS 3.1 and higher.

Examples of software/middleware abstraction layers are JCA adapters in Java or Host Integration servers in .NET. An abstraction layer simplifies the integration's implementation by providing a native API (for the environment it supports) for accessing CICS transactions. In most cases, this layer comes with tools, allowing the direct generation of a set of APIs, mapping one-to-one to the set of CICS transactions that need to be invoked. The tool set also generates data objects (in native languages) based on the copybooks used by CICS transactions and provides marshaling support for conversion between these objects and copybooks. This makes this approach a fairly simple integration implementation option. The overall implementation of integration, in this case, includes the following (see Figure 14-14):

- An integration component encapsulating the mapping from the enterprise semantic information model to a set of objects that represent the copybooks used by CICS transactions, and invoking of one or more APIs representing existing CICS transactions

- An abstraction layer that converts data objects into copybooks, and API calls into CICS transactions invocations

- A CICS region that executes transactions

It is rare that an existing CICS transaction directly corresponds to the capability required of the integration, and typically it is necessary to combine multiple existing CICS transactions to support the required functionality. There are two places where these transactions can be orchestrated:

- A new CICS transaction that is directly exposed to consumers can be created on the mainframe to orchestrate multiple existing CICS transactions together. This transaction, implementing orchestration (and any additional processing required for the orchestration), has to be developed

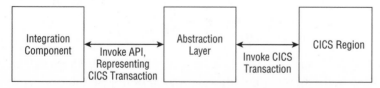

Figure 14-14 CICS integration using an abstraction layer

on the mainframe, which, depending on the makeup of the enterprise developers, is not always the preferred solution.

- An integration component can orchestrate the invocation of multiple existing CICS transactions, including all intermediate processing required. Because an integration component is typically implemented on the enterprise's preferred platform, this is typically a better solution.

Usually, when abstraction software is used, orchestration is implemented in the integration component. Although it typically leads to some performance degradation (which is not significant for a small to medium number of CICS transactions), it provides a solution that is easier to implement and maintain than the creation of new CICS transactions.

The advantages of this integration approach are:

- The provided tools typically do all the heavy lifting, providing user-friendly APIs to the existing CICS transactions.

- Most existing middleware products support the inclusion of CICS transactions in the transactions that govern business service execution. This is especially important when the business service updates multiple databases, including mainframe databases that are updated using CICS transactions.

- Most existing middleware products support security integration between service consumers and CICS-based service implementations.

The disadvantages of this approach are:

- Limitations on the size of the input/output message (32KB size of the CICS region). Some of the services (for example, those that retrieve or rate insurance policies) require sending and receiving a full insurance policy, which is significantly larger than 32KB. (We have seen policies of the size of several MB.) In these cases, it is necessary to design a set of cooperating CICS transactions that have to be invoked in a specific sequence and require use of a mainframe database to keep an invocation state. Such a design is error prone, especially in the case of multiple consumers.

- Load balancing and failover are problematic with this approach. Typically, a middleware implementation is a single point of failure in the overall system. All invocations from all consumers to all CICS transactions are routed through a single middleware instance.

WebSphere MQ has been used for integration of mainframe systems for a long time. The overall architecture for such integration is presented in Figure 14-15.

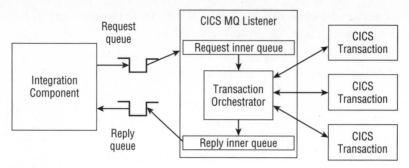

Figure 14-15 CICS integration using MQ

CICS transactions are invoked by putting a request message on the MQ queue that the mainframe is listening on. When the message is received, a listener examines its content and based on it, invokes an appropriate CICS transaction(s). The size of the MQ message is limited not by the size of the CICS region but rather by the limitations of MQ infrastructure. A typical listener reads the whole message into a mainframe input pipe and then processes it piecemeal, using existing transactions. Transaction execution results are stored to the output pipe. When all transactions are complete, the listener sends the content of the output pipe to the output queue.

In this case, the contents of MQ messages are typically copybooks used by CICS transactions, and it is the responsibility of the integration consumer to implement the conversion between these copybooks and any objects used by the integration consumer. There is no support for generation tooling (with the exception of IBM's copybook library), and this conversion should be done "manually." Using the WebSphere Message Broker with built-in support for XML/copybook conversion can simplify this transformation.

In the case of MQ integration, the orchestration of existing CICS transactions are typically done on the CICS side, requiring additional coding on CICS.

The advantages of using MQ for mainframe integration are:

- **Support for both synchronous and asynchronous communications** — This can be extremely important in the case of long-running mainframe transactions, or when the integration transaction execution has to coexist with online processing on the mainframe. In this latter case, it is possible to receive integration requests as they are posted but process them based on the mainframe resource's availability.

- **Support for a virtually unlimited size of input and output messages** — Using CICS internal queues on the mainframe allows the chunking of input and output messages directly on the mainframe, which significantly simplifies large message processing.

■ **Improved scalability and failover** — This can be achieved with this integration approach because of the scalability and failover of the underlying MQ middleware.

Disadvantages of this integration approach are:

■ Implementation is complex because of the requirements to programmatically build, process a CICS request, and reply to copybook messages.

■ The lack of transactional integration between the service consumer and the CICS transaction. A consumer's transaction can include sending the MQ message to the CICS transactions, but sending and receiving MQ messages requires two different transactions. This can make consumer implementation more complex, especially in the case of updates on the mainframe.

■ There is no standard security support for this integration approach. It is possible to secure access to MQ from both service consumer and CICS but not propagate security credentials from the service consumer to the CICS transaction.

Web Services have become a popular integration solution. IBM has added Web Service support in CICS v2.1, and has significantly improved their implementation in CICS v3.1. This latest version provides support for the following: generation of WSDL files based on the CICS transaction interface, SOAP over HTTP and SOAP over MQ, unlimited message size through dynamically expanding pipelines, and WS-Security and WS-Transactions. Additionally, this version of CICS introduced the Service Flow Runtime and Service Flow Designer, allowing you to convert existing "green screen" applications to CICS transactions and to orchestrate the execution of these transactions. The overall architecture for Web Service integration is shown in Figure 14-16.

As illustrated, the integration component invokes a Web Service over either HTTP or Java Messaging Service (JMS). A request is delivered to

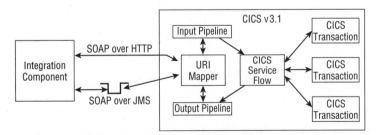

Figure 14-16 CICS integration using Web Services

the URI mapper, which decides what type of transformation needs to be applied to the incoming message (XML to copybook). The URI mapper transforms the message and stores the incoming request in the input pipeline. It then invokes an appropriate transaction — CICS Service Flow in this case. Service Flow is responsible for invoking a set of existing CICS transactions, required for a given integration implementation and passing to them chunks of the invocation message (from the input pipeline). It is also responsible for assembling the execution results (in the output pipeline) and combining results of all participating CICS transactions. When execution is completed, control is returned to the mapper, which converts the copybooks to XML and sends replies back to the service consumer.

Advantages of using Web Services for mainframe integration are:

- Generation support allows you to represent existing copybook-based CICS transactions in a form of standard WSDL. The generation tools that exist on most application development platforms, including J2EE and .NET, allow the generation of native interfaces based on this WSDL.

- Virtually unlimited input and output message sizes because the new CICS pipelines automatically adjust to the size of the messages.

- Support for the service flow, simplifying transaction composition and consequently the implementation of composite transactions that are aligned with the business requirements for the mainframe.

- Security and transaction support through implementation of Web Service standards, including WS-Security and WS-Transactions.

NOTE When considering WS-Transactions implementation with MQ as a Web Service transport, keep in mind the transactional limitations of messaging.

A disadvantage of using Web Services on the mainframe is the requirement that you upgrade to CICS v3.1, which might be problematic for some companies. Fortunately such an implementation does not require upgrading all CICS code to version 3.1. An additional gateway region(s) running CICS v3.1 can be introduced to provide access to existing transactions with lower versions of CICS.

Comparison of CICS integration approaches is summarized in Table 14-1 (see Régis Coqueret and Marc Fiammante, "Choosing among JCA, JMS, and Web Services for EAI," [March 2003]).

ACME's Implementation of a CICS-Based Integration

ACME decided to use CICS 3.1-based Web Services for their implementation of CICS integrations.

Table 14-1 Comparison of CICS Integration Approaches

INTEGRATION CHARACTERISTIC	SPECIALIZED MIDDLEWARE	MQ	WEB SERVICES
Interface coupling (abstract service definition)	Yes, generation based	No	Yes, using WSDL
Technical coupling (protocol stack)	Yes	Yes	No, different SOAP run times can be used
Portability	No, middleware dependent	Yes, assuming MQ support exists	Yes
Reliability	No	Yes	Yes, using WS-Reliable or MQ
Load balancing and failover	No	Yes	Yes
Transactional Support	Yes, XA	Only to the queue entry point	Yes, through WS-Transactions
Security	Yes	Do it yourself	Yes, through WS-Security
Invocation styles	Synchronous	Asynchronous, synchronous can be implemented through code	Synchronous and asynchronous

For their implementation they have allocated two new CICS 3.1 integration regions, supporting Web Service access to the existing mainframe functionality. These regions are load balanced for HTTP transport (using BIG-IP load balancer from F5 Networks) and MQ transport (using an MQ cluster). In their implementation, ACME uses two transports: HTTP for the short running services, the results of which must be immediately available to the user (for example, account setup and policy manipulation); and MQ for long-running services (policy rating). ACME has also discovered that policy information varies significantly and can be fairly large (up to tens of megabytes) for larger accounts. During preliminary testing, ACME discovered that these sizes can impact the performance and scalability of the solution. To solve this problem ACME's architects decided to use an intermediate DB2 database on the mainframe to store large (over 1MB) messages (see Chapter 10, dealing with large messages for details) on both the integration consumer and the provider sides.

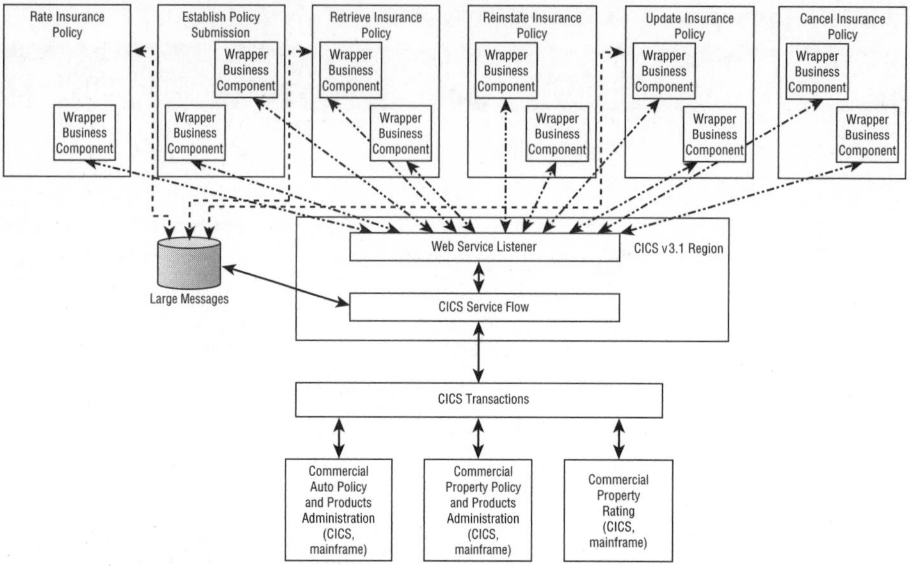

Figure 14-17 Overview of CICS integrations

The overall implementation of ACME's business services utilizing existing mainframe transactions is illustrated in Figure 14-17.

Figure 14-17 shows only the basic topology of the integration. In addition to the components shown there, ACME leverages the service registry, allowing Web Service consumers to bind to the Web Service listener dynamically. This allows ACME to relocate the listener to another IP address or MQ queue without disrupting their systems. Although the addition of the registry allows for deployment flexibility, ACME architects wanted to ensure that CICS-based services are never accessed directly, only through the predefined Web Service Listener, shown in Figure 14-17. They have achieved this by partitioning their service registry into two areas, a business service registry available to all service consumers throughout the enterprise, and an integration service registry, accessible only by integration components wrapping these services.

This partitioning was done using registry access permissions. Access to the integration service partition is allowed only to consumers with integration component credentials. The current mainframe applications contain signifi-cant amounts of sensitive data, which means that security is an important consideration of the overall integration solution. One of the challenges is that user credentials used by the service implementation are based on the corporate LDAP, which is different from the mainframe user credentials which are stored in a mainframe RACF system. This means that the security architecture for this integration needs to support both securing messages used for exchanging data with the mainframe, and user identity conversion between LDAP-based identity and mainframe-based identity.

Based on the SOA security techniques, described in Chapter 11, ACME architects decided to use WS-Security support (provided by IBM's Web Service implementation for CICS) to do both message encryption and identity token propagation. They also used Tivoli Federated Identity Manager (TFIM) to implement identity conversion between Kerberos tokens (standardized by ACME as an identity token) and the Passtickets used by the mainframe.

One of the biggest challenges for any integration implementation is error handling and logging. In order to implement an overall exception-logging architecture, described in Chapter 9, ACME architects did the following:

- Designed integration service interfaces in a way that allowed them to return any exception information to the Web Service consumers.

- Designed and implemented a daemon (for the mainframe environment) that periodically scans existing mainframe logs and submits their information (appropriately converted) to a centralized logging service. Such an approach allows them to keep the existing logging mechanism in CICS transactions (minimize required changes), while centralizing their processing through a centralized service.

Typically, integration services do not participate in the overall BAM solutions, and the mainframe integrations designed by ACME are no exception. Technical monitoring, on the other hand, is required for all services. Following the overall architecture, described in Chapter 9, the decision was made to instrument integration components with service monitoring/management agents.

Integration with the Existing COM Components

The most popular approach for integration with COM components today is to use a Web Service façade for the legacy applications. The basic design guidelines and implementation considerations for this approach are outlined in "Web Service Facade for Legacy Applications," Microsoft Patterns and Practice, June 2003.

The overall architecture for this integration type (which is shown in Figure 14-18) relies heavily on two technologies from Microsoft. The .NET/COM bridge, allowing automatic wrapper creation for existing COM components (which results in the ability to treat them like an ordinary .NET class, for example C# class), and Visual Studio with its ability to easily expose the language (for example C#) class as a Web Service.

When implementing this type of integration, it is important to correctly map existing COM components to the integration Web Services. Considering that COM interfaces are local and create very little communications latency, while

Web Service invocations can be fairly expensive from the performance point of view, you should design these integrations based on Web Service requirements. This minimizes the total number of the Web Service communications and consequently improves overall system performance. Once the integration Web Services are designed, a local C# controller (adapter) is typically implemented, mapping Web Service interfaces to the existing COM components. Additionally, this adapter is responsible for mapping data between the Web Service interface and the existing legacy data model.

Because this type of integration requires an adapter supporting Web Service implementations, it is often desirable to use the semantic information model in the implementation of the integration services (Web Service interface). This simplifies the implementation of the business component responsible for the invocation of the integration services.

Additionally standards such as WS-Security, WS-Transactions, WS-Reliability, and the like can be used to provide secure, reliable, transactional access to these services.

An alternative approach to integration of COM components is using Java Native Interface (JNI) or a specialized Java-COM bridge to expose existing COM components as Java classes (similar to exposing them as C# classes) and then using either Java Remote Method Invocation (RMI) or Java-based Web Services for integration. This integration method was widely used about 5–10 years ago, but with the advances of Web Service support and COM bridge

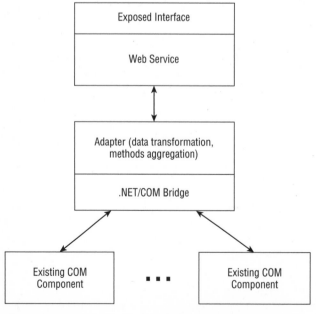

Figure 14-18 Web Service facade for COM components

implementation in .NET "native," this integration approach has become the prevalent integration implementation for COM components.

ACME's Implementation of Integration with COM Components

ACME's architects decided to use .NET-based Web Services for their implementation of integration services.

All existing COM-based applications (e.g., Commercial Auto Rating and Insurance to Value amount for a location calculator) and the integration Web Services exposed by these applications are deployed on two servers ensuring load balancing and failover for the implementation. (The number of servers can be increased in the future to support higher throughput/performance requirements.) The actual load-balancing and failover implementation is based on BIG-IP load-balancer from F5 Networks.

The overall implementation of ACME's business services utilizing existing COM components is presented in Figure 14-19.

To simplify the maintenance of COM integration services, ACME architects decided to use the same integration registry here that is used for mainframe integration. Web Service consumers are using late binding to connect to Web Services, exposing integration.

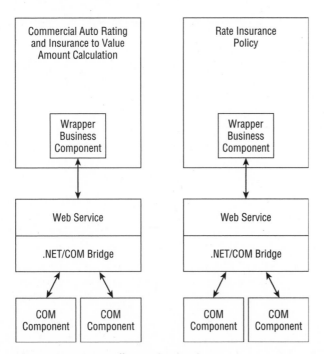

Figure 14-19 Overall COM integrations

Implementation of security in this case is fairly straightforward. As we mentioned above (see the mainframe integration implementation section), ACME is using Kerberos tokens for identity propagation. These tokens can be "natively" processed by Windows-based Web Services, thus simplifying identity propagation to COM components. Additionally, the support for WS-Security baked into .NET Web Service implementation allows for the simple implementation of sensitive data encryption.

Implementation of exception handling, in this case, is similar to the case of mainframe integration. Existing exception logs are left in place and a specialized daemon is created to send the content of these logs to the centralized logging service.

Technical monitoring implementation in this case is done through instrumenting of integration components with the service monitoring/management agents, similar to mainframe integration implementation.

Integration Based on the Existing Java APIs

Some of the application vendors provide their own remoting APIs. These APIs can be implemented using the vendor's communications mechanism of choice — Web Services, Java RMI, straight TCP/IP, and so on. The advantage of this approach, from the vendor's point of view, is the ability to control (and evolve) the distribution mechanism transparently to its users by encapsulating it behind APIs they provide.

From the user's point of view, remote APIs simplify integration. Users have to implement only local invocations, while the vendor takes care of remoting the invocations. On the other hand, integration implementers are limited to the integration functionality and quality of service (security, transactionality, etc.) provided by the vendor's APIs. This means that any additions to the integration capabilities have to be coordinated with the vendor and its release schedule. Additionally, this approach to integration limits the choice of the platforms for other service implementations; only platforms certified and supported by the vendor can be used.

As a result, despite its simplicity, this integration approach is not always the best fit for integration service implementation. Because existing Java APIs provide all the required remoting capabilities, integration is usually implemented as local business components that encapsulate invocations and coordinate existing APIs. The overall integration architecture for this approach is presented in Figure 14-20.

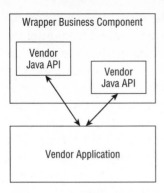

Figure 14-20 Building integration services using Java APIs

ACME's Implementation of Integration Based on Java APIs

The Centrus vendor provides remote Java APIs, which ACME has chosen to use to access the application's functionality. They have used these APIs to build a business component that exposes the required Centrus functionality. (See Figure 14-21.) This component can be used to implement `AssessInsuredLocation` and/or any other services requiring geocoding or catastrophic data information.

Security for this implementation requires both authentication and authorization for invoking operations on the vendor's Java components. Authentication

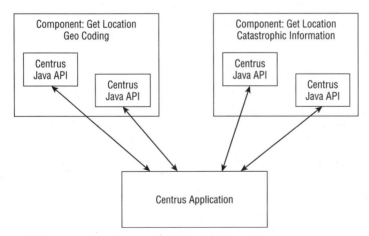

Figure 14-21 Overall integrations using Java APIs

requires mapping the enterprise user's identity to the identity understood by the application (typically username and password), much like the mainframe integration approach. ACME architects decided to use TFIM to support this security goal. Authorization is achieved by implementing authorization at the boundary of an integration component, allowing only users with specific roles to execute certain components. This authorization can be easily implemented using the standard Java security model, where you configure Role-Based Access Control (RBAC) security on operations of Java components, and as such, this functionality does not require any approaches specific to Web Services.

Exception handling is typically limited to the exception handling of remote Java APIs. Although implementation of a specialized daemon pushing the application's log to the centralized logging service is possible, it's rarely done because of changes that can be introduced by the vendor in newer versions.

Technical monitoring for this implementation is done through instrumenting the integration components with service monitoring/management agents, similar to approaches described earlier.

Integration with the Existing J2EE Applications

The majority of J2EE application servers provide three basic mechanisms for exposing server-based applications: JMS, Java RMI and Web Services. Theoretically, all three mechanisms can be used for building integration services that expose the capabilities of existing J2EE-based applications.

When building integration services, RMI seems like the most straightforward approach due to its simplicity and other advantages. Java objects can be exposed over RMI, and a different quality of services (transactionality, security, etc.) is supported. However, it suffers from the following drawbacks:

- RMI-based implementations are applicable only if the business component that wraps the integration is implemented in Java. Access to RMI-based services from non-Java implementations is possible but very complex.

- Although RMI is highly standardized, numerous interoperability issues arise with RMI when the consumer and provider use Java virtual machines (JVM) from different vendors or even different versions of a JVM from the same vendor.

- An RMI service exposes Java-based interfaces, which makes it very sensitive to changes, thus increasing the coupling between service consumers and providers.

JMS seems like a good integration option because of its support for asynchronous invocations, guaranteed delivery, and so on. But, it also suffers from the following drawbacks:

■ Although JMS APIs are standardized, the on-the-wire format is not. This means, that achieving interoperability between JMS implementations from different vendors requires software bridges between these implementations. Unless a messaging provider is standardized throughout the enterprise, JMS does not appear to be a viable integration option.

■ Use of a messaging provider as an integration transport typically requires the installation of a messaging client on every machine that utilizes messaging. This can require massive amounts of updates throughout the enterprise to accommodate newer versions of a product. Additionally, it is necessary to ensure that messaging software is supported on all hardware and software platforms throughout the enterprise.

■ Effective use of JMS on the enterprise level requires standardization of the messaging payload formats. The most widely accepted format is XML with SOAP enveloping. This effectively means a Web Service over JMS. We consider this a flavor of Web Services, rather than JMS implementation.

Based on these issues, Web Services (using different transport, including HTTP, messaging, etc.) are the most appropriate approach for building integration that expose existing J2EE applications.

The overall implementation of Web Services–based integration (as shown in Figure 14-22) is similar to the implementation for COM components. (Refer to Figure 14-19.)

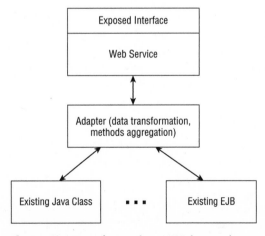

Figure 14-22 Implementing J2EE integration services

Access to existing functionality is implemented by the service adapter, which can use a variety of mechanisms, including local Java class invocations, Enterprise Java Beans (EJB), and so on to implement access. In addition to accessing existing functionality, an adapter is responsible for coordinating the access and for exposing the integration interface.

ACME's Implementation of Integration for J2EE-Based Applications

The Motor Vehicle Report application used by ACME is a J2EE application that is implemented utilizing IBM's WebSphere 6.1 application server, which provides advanced support for Web Service implementations. As a result, ACME has chosen Web Services as an integration mechanism for this application.

Traditionally, Web Services, especially those using HTTP as a transport, are synchronous. This is because HTTP communications are synchronous in nature. However, this invocation style does not match well with the nature of the Motor Vehicle Report application. Depending on whether the driver's information already exists locally (in the application's database) or a request has to be made to the Motor Vehicle facility of a given state, the duration of this service execution can vary from milliseconds to several days. Asynchronous invocations are a more appropriate implementation approach for these potentially long-running service executions.

The asynchronous invocations can be implemented by using two synchronous request/replies and Web Services addressing (WS-Addressing), to provide an address for a second request (asynchronous reply). This is illustrated in Figure 14-23.

In this implementation, the service consumer sends a request to a service provider along with the address for the asynchronous reply (in case a request can't be fulfilled immediately). The service provider checks whether it can provide a reply immediately, and if it can, it does so. When the response is not readily available, the address of the reply is stored in the database and a reply is returned to the service consumer stating that the actual reply will be delivered later. When the execution is complete, the address of the reply is retrieved from the database and is used for delivering the reply.

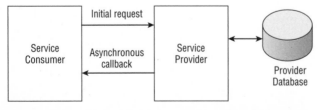

Figure 14-23 Asynchronous invocation using Web Services

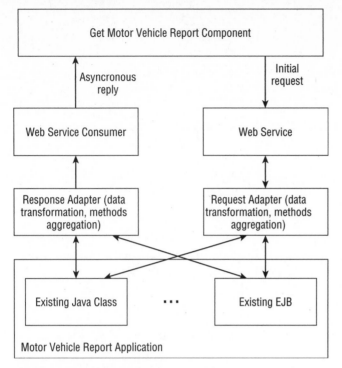

Figure 14-24 Overall J2EE integrations

This approach is also used for the overall implementation of integration with J2EE-based applications (Motor Vehicle Report application), presented in Figure 14-24. Here, the integration component implements both Web Service invocations and the reply sink. This component is inherently multithreaded (the asynchronous reply is delivered on a separate thread) and requires a callback class as its parameter.

Implementation of this J2EE integration uses the same set of technologies and approaches as the mainframe and COM component integration described earlier. As a result, the same approaches can be used for locating, securing, monitoring, and exception handling.

Integration with Existing Databases

Databases provide their own remoting mechanisms such as database client, Java APIs, JDBC, and so on (compare these to the Java APIs for integration section earlier in this chapter). These remoting mechanisms can be used for accessing data in the remote databases. (See Figure 14-25.)

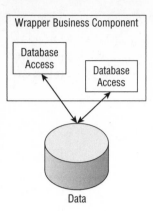

Figure 14-25 Implementing database integration services

Although database-based integrations are very simple to implement, these implementations often suffer from the following problems:

- They often create tight coupling between service consumers and providers. This coupling is location and implementation coupling. *Location coupling* means that moving the database can break the service consumer. This coupling can be overcome using multiple techniques, the most common of which is externalization of the database location. For example, if the wrapper business component is implemented inside an application server, the database connection pooling supports the externalization of the database location in a pool property, thus making the implementation location–independent. *Implementation coupling* means that the business component's implementation is directly dependent on the database layout and, consequently, any changes in the database schema need to be reflected in the business component's implementation. The way to deal with this type of coupling is to use stored procedures, allowing you to hide the actual database layout behind a stored procedure interface (a layout can change, without changing the interface).

- Having numerous business components pointing to the same database can have a negative impact on database performance. Having numerous components requires many database connections, which are expensive and require a lot of resources on the database server. This situation is similar to the issues that people were experiencing with two-tier systems. The traditional approach to minimizing the number of database connections is connection pooling, which is done in the middle tier (typically in the application server). Similar approaches can be applied to integration with existing databases: Business components, implementing database integration, can be factored out into a specialized integration service available, for example, over Web Services. Although such an approach decreases the load on the existing database, it increases integration execution duration and creates more points of failure in the overall system. As a result, such an approach is justified only in the case of very large numbers (thousands) of required database connections.

ACME's Implementation of Database Integrations

For integration with their existing databases — ISO Public Protection Codes and Policy Financials — ACME has implemented two business components to provide the integration and expose the required data. These components can be used for the implementation of AssessInsuredLocation, CollectPolicyFinancials, and/or any other services requiring this data. (See Figure 14-26.)

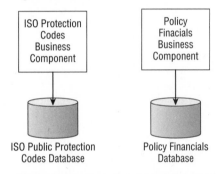

Figure 14-26 Overall database integrations

Because database integration is done through local components, rather then services, usage of the service registry is not applicable. Increased deployment flexibility for database integration is achieved through externalization of the database connection information (compare to the configurations files for service location in Chapter 9).

Although all the existing databases provide built-in security mechanisms, these mechanisms are rarely used for integration. The majority of database access mechanisms are based on connection pooling, which requires a standard user name and password. As a result, authorization in this implementation is done at the component boundary, similar to the Java APIs example.

NOTE Newer application servers allow you to utilize database security on top of database connection pooling. This enables you to start utilizing database security for integration.

Because integration component runs within business service implementations, exception handling is done using the exception handling of the business services. Any database errors are intercepted in the form of JDBC exceptions and can be reported to a central logging service.

Technical monitoring is done through instrumenting the integration components with service monitoring/management agents, similar to other implementations.

Integration Based on the Vendor's Web Services

In the last several years, many vendors that used to provide different proprietary integration mechanisms (for example, Java APIs, COM interfaces, MQ interfaces, and so on) have switched to supporting Web Services for accessing their functionality. This switch, on one hand, provides more flexible integration capabilities because these Web Services can be accessed from virtually any execution platform. On the other hand, this solution often suffers from the same drawbacks, described in the "Integration Based on the Existing Java APIs" section. The drawbacks are reiterated here:

- Integration is limited to the functionality and quality of service (security, transactionality, etc.) provided by the vendor's APIs. This means that any additions to the integration capabilities have to be coordinated with the vendor and its release schedule.

- Data models exposed by these Web Services are aligned with the vendor's data model, which typically is different from the semantic information model use in the interface and implementation of the business services.

- The granularity of these services is typically designed to provide maximal flexibility of integration and as a result is usually much lower than the granularity of business service operations defined based on the enterprise model.

- In many cases, these vendor-supplied Web Services are defined in a way that requires an intimate knowledge of the application's internals. This includes (but is not limited to) requirements to invoke the Web Services in a particular order, invoke different services based on intermediate execution results, and so on.

The majority of these shortcomings can be mitigated by implementing a local business component to encapsulating integration invocations and coordination. This local business component serves as a rationalization layer between the functionality provided by a vendor and the requirements defined during design of the business services. The overall integration architecture for this approach is presented in Figure 14-27.

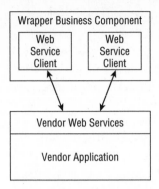

Figure 14-27 Integration using vendor's Web Services

ACME's Implementation of Integration Using the Vendor's Web Services

For integration with the IBM/FileNet document management system, which provides Web Service interfaces, ACME has implemented a business component that provides the required integration and exposes the required FileNet functionality. (See Figure 14-28.) This component can be used for implementation of Document Management and/or any other services that require access to and manipulation of existing documents.

Security for this example requires both authentication and authorization for invoking operations on the Web Services. This requires that the WS-Security Policy for identity propagation be configured in the Web Service container, specifying WS-Security Kerberos Token Profile messaging. This is done in order for the service consumer to know how to adapt to policy (see the policy adaptation information in Chapters 11 and 12) and for the container

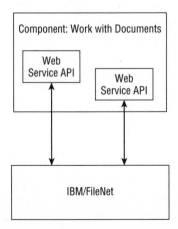

Figure 14-28 Overall integrations using vendor's Web Services

(and thus the Web Service) to identify the user. At the same time, authorization is achieved by configuring the access control policy (using XACML or a container-specific methodology) at the boundary of an integration component, expressing the policy to the services' Policy Enforcement Points (PEPs). The PEPs enforce the policy, allowing only users with certain authorization credentials to execute certain components.

Exception handling is limited to exception handling of the Web Service invocations. Although implementing a specialized daemon for pushing the application's log to the centralized logging service is possible, it is not done because of changes that can be introduced by the vendor in newer versions.

Technical monitoring is done by instrumenting the integration components with service monitoring/management agents, similar to the approaches described earlier.

Summary

This case study demonstrates the design and decision processes for the creation of integration services that support an enterprise business service. We have presented an example from an insurance company that illustrates the variety and complexity of integration solutions that need to be implemented in an enterprise. First, we described the functional requirements and how the new enterprise business service interfaces are mapped to existing capabilities. Next, we provided an analysis of the different integration scenarios and outlined a thought process for picking an appropriate integration approach. As a result of this analysis, some integration was implemented through integration access mechanisms, while in other situations "local" integration components with no special integration access turned out to be a better solution. We provided the detailed integration solution for each scenario, and then described additional enterprise aspects such as a registry, security, and exception handling.

Although your implementation will probably be different, we strongly encourage SOA architects to go through a similar decision process every time they need to incorporate existing functionality in their SOA implementation.

Business Use Cases

This appendix contains the business use cases for the examples described in Chapters 6 and 7 on service interface design and service implementation design.

Business Use Case BU01 — Quote Insurance

This section provides an overview of the use case, goals, and actors.

Description — This is the process by which a quote for insurance is produced and presented to a Customer in response to a Customer request. ACME's underwriting and pricing rules are applied to determine the acceptability of risks and insurance premium options.

Actors —

- **Primary Actors** — Customer, Agency
- **Secondary Actors** — Underwriting, Pricing

Business goal — To obtain new business by providing competitive insurance offerings

Triggers — Customer requests an insurance quote

Basic Workflow

1. **Gather information for quote** — The Agency gets information from the Customer about the insurance desired:

   - Customer information
   - Customer contact information: phone, address, and email address
   - Whether this is a new Customer
   - Auto insurance
     - Auto information
       - Make, model, year, and body type
       - VIN
       - General condition
     - Customer information
       - Driving record
       - Age
       - Gender
       - Information on other drivers (same as above)
     - Auto usage
       - Expected yearly commuter miles and total miles
       - Whether the auto is used for business purposes
     - Coverage desired
       - Liability
       - Collision
       - Comprehensive
       - Towing
       - Auto glass
   - Homeowner's insurance
     - Property information
       - Location (physical address)
       - Year built
       - Dwelling type (single family, duplex, condo, etc.)
       - Type of construction (stick frame, balloon frame, stone, brick, etc.)
       - Whether located in a flood plain

- Whether smoke alarms are present
- The value of the property
- Occupancy (owner-occupied, rental, or unoccupied)
- Coverage desired
  - Liability
  - Replacement value versus actual value
- Personal property
  - Property item information
    - Type
    - Value
    - Serial number (if applicable)
  - Whether the item is used for business
  - Coverage desired
    - Replacement versus actual value
    - Damage

2. **Underwrite the quote** — Underwriting examines the information on the quote to determine which risks can be accepted and which cannot, based on the company's underwriting guidelines. A risk factor score between 1 and 100 is assigned for each coverage on each covered item. Covered items include:

- Auto insurance
  - Liability
  - Physical damage to the auto from collisions
  - Physical damage to the auto that is not the result of collisions
  - Physical damage to other autos from a collision
  - Physical damage to other property from a collision
  - Injuries, from collisions, sustained by covered persons
  - Injuries, from collisions, sustained by other persons
  - Towing services
  - Auto glass replacement
- Homeowner's insurance
- Personal property

3. **Price the quote** — For each quoted coverage, the Agency creates a set of options to present to the Customer. Each option includes a coverage

limit, a deductible, and a premium. The premium is based on ACME's pricing rules, and is based on the coverage limit, deductible, and risk factor.

ACME also offers a multipolicy discount of 5% for Customers already holding another policy with ACME, assuming the quoted policy does not replace an existing policy. ACME also offers a 7% employee discount for all policies.

4. **Present quote** — The Agency presents the quote to the Customer.

Alternative Workflow: Unacceptable Risk

If in Step 2 above, Underwriting determines that the coverage requested by the Customer falls outside of ACME's underwriting guidelines, one of the following actions may be taken:

■ The Agency suggests to the Customer alternative coverage options, which are then quoted.

■ The Customer decides not to pursue further quoting.

Performance Goals

Quick quote turnaround — ACME has determined that a quick response to a request for a quote plays a significant role in a Customer's decision as to whether to purchase insurance. For this reason, ACME has a goal of producing quotes in 1 hour's time, with an ultimate goal of producing quotes during an actual Customer interaction.

Business Use Case BU02 — Process Application

Overview — This section provides an overview of the use case, goals, and actors.

Description — This is the process by which a Customer obtains insurance coverage. Based on a preexisting quote, the Customer submits an application for insurance. The insurance is underwritten and priced to take into account additional coverage details and information about the Customer and/or covered items that were not included in the quoting process. Billing is set up, and the Customer receives an insurance binder.

Actors —

■ **Primary Actors** — Customer, Agency

■ **Secondary Actors** — Underwriting, Pricing

Business goal — Agency goal: to book new business
Triggers — Customer asks to apply for insurance

Basic Workflow

1. **Complete application** — The Agency works with the Customer to fill out an insurance application, based upon the Customer's selection of coverage options presented on a preexisting quote. The Agency works with the Customer to obtain additional required information and/or to update any information that may be different from what was on the original quote. Additional information includes:

   - Driver's license number, state, and expiration date for all drivers.

   - Similar information for prior driver's licenses held within the "look-back" period allowed by state regulations for the state in which the Customer resides. The look-back period is the number of years back that a person's driving record may be considered when underwriting insurance.

2. **Gather additional information for policy processing** — The Agency obtains additional information required for completing and underwriting the application. Some of this information is immediately available, such as VIN verification, police reports, insurance history, and so on. Some information takes longer to obtain, such as that derived from an on-site dwelling inspection. The intent is that the information be as complete as possible, while still processing the application within the stated performance goal guidelines (see below under "Performance Goals").

   - Auto insurance
     - Auto information
       - **From Kelley Blue Book** — Verification that the VIN number matches the vehicle; incident history
       - **From local and state police** — Verification that the vehicle is not stolen
       - **From local and state police** — Police reports involving the vehicle
     - Customer information
       - **From state driver's license bureaus** — driving record(s) from state(s) of previous residence (all drivers)
     - Insurance information
       - **From insurance industry consortium** — Claim history
       - **From insurance industry consortium** — History of denied or canceled auto insurance
   - Homeowner's insurance

- Property information

  - **From on-site inspection** — Condition of the property, existence of smoke alarms

  - **From appraisal** — Value of the property

  - **From state department of natural resources** — Verification of flood plain status

- Personal property insurance

  - Property item information

    - **From appraisals or purchase receipts supplied by the Customer** — Item value

    - **From local and state police** — For items that have a serial number and a stated value of over $5000, verification that the item wasn't stolen

- **All insurance lines** — Fraud detection

  - **From internal ACME information** — Was the Customer a claimant as an uninsured person on multiple claims against insurance policies underwritten by ACME?

3. **Underwrite the policy** — Based on information on the application, underwriting performs the same process of evaluating and scoring risks as is done in BU01 Quote Insurance.

4. **Price the policy** — The Agency sets the premium for each coverage, with its Customer-selected limit(s) and deductible, in the policy. As in BU01 Quote Insurance, each coverage premium is based on ACME pricing rules and is based on the coverage limit, deductible, and risk factor.

   Also, as in BU01 Quote Insurance, multipolicy and employee discounts apply.

5. **Set up billing and payment method** — Billing is notified of the new policy application.

6. **Send insurance binder** — The Agency creates an insurance binder, which is effective when the Agency receives the completed application. Continued coverage is contingent upon the Customer making an initial payment within 5 business days of acceptance of the application. The Agency also mails the Customer a hard copy of the insurance binder.

Alternative Workflow: Unacceptable Risk

If in Step 2 above, Underwriting determines that the coverage requested by the Customer falls outside of ACME's underwriting guidelines, the application is declined.

Performance Goals

Quick application processing — As part of its overall customer service strategy, ACME has a goal of completing underwriting and final pricing within 10 business days of receipt of an insurance application. However, ACME has a corporate policy of maintaining an open underwriting period of 20 business days after receipt of an insurance application. This means that a policy may be canceled because of underwriting activities even after the insurance binder or the policy itself is sent out.

Business Use Case BU03 — Change Policy

Overview — This section provides an overview of the use case, goals, and actors.

Description — This is the process by which an existing insurance policy is changed per the Customer's request. The changes are underwritten, priced, and quoted. The policy is updated accordingly, necessary changes are made to billing, and the Customer is sent an updated copy of the policy.

Actors —

- **Primary Actors** — Customer, Agency
- **Secondary Actors** — Underwriting, Pricing, Billing

Business goals — To meet the Customer's needs by modifying an existing policy, thereby retaining the Customer's business

Triggers — Customer requests that the agency make one or more changes to an existing policy

Basic Workflow

1. **Gather information regarding requested changes** — The Agency obtains information from the Customer about the changes that the Customer wishes to make to the policy. Changes may include:

- Auto insurance
  - Auto information
    - Add or drop an auto

- Add or drop coverage
- Change deductible
- ▪ Customer information
  - Contact information change (other than address)
  - Address change
  - Add or drop a driver
- ▪ Homeowner's insurance
  - ▪ Property information
    - Add or drop coverage
    - Change deductible
    - Value of property changes
- ▪ Personal property insurance
  - ▪ Property item information
    - Add or drop an item
    - Value of an item changes
    - Change deductible
    - Add or drop coverage

2. **Gather additional information for processing policy changes** — As applicable, the Agency obtains additional information required for processing and underwriting the policy changes. Some of this information is immediately available, such as VIN verification, police reports, insurance history, and so on. Some information takes longer to obtain, such as that derived from an on-site dwelling inspection. The intent is that the information be as complete as possible, while still processing the application within the stated performance goal guidelines (see below under "Performance Goals").

- ▪ Auto insurance
  - ▪ Auto information (for autos added)
    - **From Kelley Blue Book** — Verification that the VIN number matches the vehicle; incident history
    - **From local and state police** — Verification that the vehicle is not stolen
    - **From local and state police** — Police reports involving the vehicle
  - ▪ Customer information (for drivers added)

- **From state driver's license bureaus** — Driving record(s) from state(s) of previous residence (all drivers)
  - Insurance information (for drivers added)
    - **From insurance industry consortium** — Claims history
    - **From insurance industry consortium** — History of denied or cancelled auto insurance
  - Homeowner's insurance
    - Property information (for property value change)
      - **From appraisal** — Value of the property
  - Personal property insurance
    - Property item information (for added items or for items whose value has changed)
      - **From appraisals or purchase receipts supplied by the Customer** — Item value
      - **From local and state police** — For items that have a serial number and a stated value of over $5000, verification of whether the item was stolen

3. **Underwrite the policy** — The policy changes are underwritten using the same process of evaluating and scoring risks as in BU01 Quote Insurance.

4. **Price the policy** — The Agency reprices the policy based on the requested changes, generates a new quote, and presents it to the Customer, as in BU01 Quote Insurance.

5. **Update billing** — The Agency notifies Billing of any premium changes.

6. **Update policy package** — Document Processing makes necessary changes to the hard-copy policy package.

7. **Send copy of policy package to the Customer** — Document Processing sends a copy of the updated policy package to the Customer via surface mail.

Alternative Workflow: Unacceptable Risk

In Step 2 above, if Underwriting determines that the requested policy change(s) presents an unacceptable risk, the changes are denied and one of the following may happen:

- The Customer modifies the requested changes, and the Agency requotes the policy.

- The Customer retains the policy as is.
- The Customer cancels the policy.

Extension Points

This section describes any extension points.

Billing change — Step 4 above may activate BU05 Adjust Premium.

Customer cancellation — Alternative Flow Underwriting Required may activate BU04 Cancel Policy.

Evaluating SOA Services

This book discusses the fundamentals of Service-Oriented Architecture, including the design and technical concerns of building SOA services. As stated in Chapter 2, simply having services is not enough; you need the right kind of services, and you need well-designed and properly built services. How do you know if you have the right kind of services or if the services will satisfy the current or future requirements? Is there an objective way to assess services and their alignment with business needs?

This appendix contains an evaluation matrix for assessing the design of SOA services. It consists of four categories: *Alignment Characteristics*, *Design Characteristics*, *Technical Characteristics*, and *Housekeeping Characteristics*. Within each category, there are several characteristics pertaining to the category and questions to ask about how well the service satisfies that characteristic. The collected answers to the questions in the matrix indicate how well a service fits into an SOA solution.

- Categories group together service characteristics that address specific architectural principles and practices.

- Characteristics are the service dimensions that you evaluate. The goal of the evaluation is to determine how well the service follows the SOA principle or practices. Each characteristic has a brief description and is followed by a list of the outcomes of the evaluation.

- Questions help you evaluate each characteristic. The matrix provides a set of questions to use while assessing the service. For example, how well the service aligns with the business drivers or the composability of the service. Each question is followed by a list of possible answers.

We have tried to keep the table brief and manageable. Following the table is a detailed explanation of each characteristic, the meanings of the associated outcomes, motivation and elaboration of each question, and the meanings of the associated answers.

You use the evaluation matrix throughout the process of service design and implementation. The evaluation criteria allow you to rate the service in an objective manner. The results provide insight into how well the service satisfies the key requirements, such as reusability or alignment with business goals and needs.

Throughout the design and implementation process, each perspective (role) checks the services against the evaluation criteria that fit within their concern. For example, there is no need for the business analyst to evaluate the Autonomy characteristic or the interface style. In general:

- The Business Perspective is concerned with the Alignment Characteristics.

- The Design Perspective is concerned with Alignment and Service Characteristics, along with a selection of Technical and Housekeeping Characteristics.

- The Implementation Perspective is concerned with Alignment, Service, Technical, and Housekeeping Characteristics — basically, the entire matrix.

How Do I Assess Services?

The service evaluation matrix asks questions designed to help you evaluate services both qualitatively and quantitatively. You use the matrix throughout the service design and implementation process. Depending on your perspective within the process — *Business, Design,* or *Implementation* — you ask the questions in the categories that are appropriate for your concerns. Once your answers are collected, you identify gaps in the service's design or implementation.

For the first three categories in the matrix, the assessments ask multiple-choice questions. The list starts with the most desirable answers and ends with the less desirable answers.

The fourth category of the matrix — Housekeeping Characteristics — is different from the rest. Instead of assessing the quality of the service, it focuses on the quantitative aspects of the services in your enterprise. The

Housekeeping Characteristics describe the service's attributes or dimensions. The information listed in this category provides a basis for the monitoring, measuring, and analysis of your service repository.

The following table contains the evaluation matrix.

Table B-1 SOA Service Evaluation Matrix

	CHARACTERISTIC	QUESTIONS
A L I G N M E N T C H A R A C T E R I S T I C S	**Business Alignment** Assess whether the service aligns with and supports the enterprise's business needs. * Aligned * Partially aligned * Misaligned * Not aligned	Is there a clear link between one or more business requirements and the service? *Yes | No
		Can you trace the service back to a business outcome, objective, or goal? * Yes | No | Don't know
		If the service provides rules or decisions, are they associated with specific business rules or policies? * Yes | No | Don't know
		Do the service operations perform a specific business process activity? * Yes | Partially | No
	Specification Determine if the specification tells both business users and technical users what the service does. * Good * Adequate * Poor	Does the service have a specification? * Yes | No
		How well does the specification describe what the service does from the business perspective? Is it sufficient for a business analyst to decide whether a service can be used in a solution? * Good | Adequate | Poor
		How well does the specification describe what the service does from the technical perspective? * Good | Adequate | Poor
		Are the expected kinds of consumers of this service clearly defined? * Yes | No
		Does the service conform to enterprise standards for the type of service? * Yes | No
		Is the interaction style of the service appropriate for this type of service? * Yes | No

(continued)

Table B-1 (*continued*)

CHARACTERISTIC	QUESTIONS
Fit for Purpose Assess how well the service fits its intended use. * Good * Adequate * Poor	Does this service provide a single, consistent way to access data or perform a business function? * Yes | No
	Is the usage type of this service appropriate for the purpose? * Yes | No
	Is the scope, granularity, and interface style of the service appropriate for its purpose? * Yes | No
Security Measure the extent with which the service aligns with the enterprise security goals and requirements. * Aligned * Partially aligned * Misaligned * Not aligned	Does this service adhere to the security requirements of the enterprise? * Yes | No
	Does the security of the service adhere to the security standards established by SOA governance in your project? * Yes | No
Semantic Alignment Measure the extent to which the service aligns with the enterprise and other shared semantics. * Semantic alignment * Duplicate information * Misaligned * Not aligned	Does the service share common information definitions with other services or processes? If so, does the Semantic Information Model define the shared information? * Yes | No
	Does the service interface adhere to the Semantic Information Model? * Yes | Partially | No
	Does the service interface redefine common information or duplicate information separate from the Semantic Information Model? * Yes | No
D E S I G N	**Isolation of Responsibilities** Assess the degree to which the service isolates discrete responsibilities into one place. * Yes * No	Is each service operation responsible for a discrete task? * Yes | No
		Is this service the sole provider of these tasks or resources? * Yes | No

	CHARACTERISTIC	QUESTIONS
C H A R A C T E R I S T I C S	**Abstraction** Determine if the service interface represents essential concepts and hides private behavior and information. * Full * Partial * Low	Does the service express the essential concepts and information? * Yes | Partially | No
		Does the interface hide the details of the implementation? Is there a strict separation of what the service does from how the service does it? Are only the necessary details available to the consumer? * Yes | No
		Is the level of abstraction appropriate for the intended use? * Yes | No
	Coupling Measure the dependencies between a service consumer and provider. * Independent * Minimal coupling * Tight coupling	Does this service limit what the consumers must know in order to invoke it to what is described in the service specification? * Yes | No
		Does the service avoid making assumptions about the purpose or business characteristics of the consumer? * Yes | No
		Does this service have minimal, but well-known, dependencies on the services it invokes? * Yes | No
		Is run-time policy logic expressed and implemented separately from the business logic? Is the policy logic configurable? * Yes | No
		Is the security logic separate from the business logic of the service? Is the security logic configurable? * Yes | No
		Does the service separate the public view of the data from the private view? * Yes | No
	Granularity Determine if the size and complexity of the service, in terms of the business function, are appropriate.	Does the service use other services and components in order to achieve the functionality? * Yes | No

(continued)

Table B-1 (*continued*)

CHARACTERISTIC	QUESTIONS
* Good * Adequate * Poor	Is the amount of functionality provided by this service well understood? * Yes | No
	Is the service's granularity appropriate for its intended use? * Yes | No
Stateless Assess whether the information or the other state is retained between requests. * Stateless * Retains State	Does the service avoid keeping state information between method calls? * Yes | No
	Can additional instances of the service be created to support scale? * Yes | No
	Can subsequent client requests go to different service instances? * Yes | No
Composable Determine the ease of including the service in a composition with other services. * Good * Adequate * Poor	Do you expect other services to use this service? * Yes | No
	Is the service granularity appropriate for composition within the intended context? * Yes | No
	Is the combination of the service's usage type and output conducive to composition? * Yes | No
Governance Measure adherence to policies throughout the service life cycle. * Good * Adequate * Poor	Does the service have a responsible owner? * Yes | No
	How well does the service adhere to the design-time governance policies? * Good | Adequate | Poor
	How well does the service adhere to the deploy-time governance policies? * Good | Adequate | Poor
	How well does the service adhere to the run-time governance policies? * Good | Adequate | Poor
	How well does the service adhere to the change-time governance policies? * Good | Adequate | Poor

	CHARACTERISTIC	QUESTIONS
T E C H N I C A L C H A R A C T E R I S T I C S	**Service Specification** How complete is the service specification? How good is the service specification? * Good * Adequate * Poor	Does the service specification completely describe the interface? * Yes | No
		Does the specification clearly describe the behavior and interaction style of each of the operations? * Yes | No
		Does the specification contain all constraints and pre- and postconditions for the operations described? * Yes | No
		Does the service specification describe all exceptions? * Yes | No
		Does the service specification include one or more independent run-time service policies? * Yes | No
		Do the run-time policies specify the run-time constraints, messaging format related to security, reliability/QoS, interaction styles, and SLAs? * Yes | No
	Service Level Agreement How complete is the service level agreement (SLA) for this service? * Completely specified * Partially specified * Poorly specified	Does the service have at least one SLA, as specified in the run-time policies? * Yes | No
		Is each SLA formally specified? * Yes | No
		Does the SLA provide a description of the service's technical performance, such as availability, reliability, throughput, and response time? * Yes | No
		Does it include business characteristics, such as business units of work? * Yes | No
	Extensibility Extensibility measures the ability of the service design	Is the service designed to support the implementation of future requirements? * Yes | No

(continued)

Table B-1 (*continued*)

CHARACTERISTIC	QUESTIONS
and implementation to support enhancements. * High * Medium * Low	Have the appropriate patterns or abstractions been used to facilitate future enhancements? * Yes | No
Variability and Configurability These characteristics measure the ability of the service to support multiple users. * Variable * Partially variable * Not sufficiently variable	Does the service support necessary variability mechanism? * Yes | No
	Does the service use standard enterprise mechanisms for configuration? * Yes | No
	Does the service use common data for configuration? * Yes | No
Autonomy Autonomy is the characteristic that allows services to be deployed, modified, and maintained independently from each other and the solutions that use them. * Autonomous * Not autonomous	Is this service loosely coupled, and are its responsibilities well isolated? * Yes | No
	Is this service's life cycle independent of that of other services? * Yes | No
	Can the service be deployed independently from other services? * Yes | No
H O U S E K E E P I N G	
Scope	The intended range of users of a service * Enterprise | Line of Business (LOB) | Domain | Solution
Visibility	The range of users that are allowed to see the existence of a service, and subsequently to use it * Public | Private
Ownership	Organizational unit responsible for the support of a service * Organization name
Granularity	The size of a service in terms of the amount of business function performed in a single request/response exchange of messages * Large | Medium | Small

	CHARACTERISTIC	QUESTIONS
C H A R A C T E R I S T I C S	**Type**	Derived from scope, visibility, granularity, and responsibility * Enterprise business | Business Service (LOB) | Business Service (Common) | Domain | Utility | Integration | External | Foundation
	Interaction style	Pattern of the service's operation signatures, specifically how information is passed into and out of the service * Parameter passing | Document passing | Data Passing | Request/Reply | Event | Mixed
	Usage type	Indication of the primary purpose of the service * Task | Entity | Decision
	Composition	Whether the service uses other services and components in order to achieve the functionality * Atomic | Composite
	Run-Time Service Policy	Run-time constraints and capabilities of a service * List run-time policy artifacts
	Service Level Agreement (SLA)	Formal agreement specifying QoS response times, business units of work, and action guarantees * List SLAs artifacts
	Specification	Description of service functionality, how to use it, and how to implement it * List specification artifacts
	Construction	How the service was implemented * Buy | Build | Integrate
	Reuse	Count of the uses of this service. * Count of how many different solutions use this service
	Versions	Versions under development, test, and deployed * List of versions: Development, Test, Deployed

Alignment Characteristics

One of the key principles of SOA is that services are aligned with the business goals, strategies, and operations of an enterprise. The Alignment Characteristics allow you to assess how well the service will facilitate your enterprise's business operations and future strategy. The questions in this portion of the evaluation matrix help you determine the degree to which your services are aligned with the enterprise's needs.

Business Alignment

A good service aligns with the business's needs and strategy. The effort to design and implement a service, regardless of type, should only be expended if the service satisfies one or more specific business requirements.

This collection of questions helps you to assess how well the service aligns with the enterprise's activities and objectives and supports its business needs. The business alignment of all services should be evaluated. Be aware that, because of their general or technical infrastructure focus, you may find it more difficult to trace utility and foundation services back to business requirements.

The overall assessment of this characteristic is one of the following:

- **Aligned** — This is what you are aiming for. The service is aligned with the business strategy and goals.

- **Partially aligned** — The service partially addresses a requirement, or the requirement is ambiguous enough that there is potential for not satisfying the business goal. The gap between the requirements, service design, and service implementation should be evaluated to resolve the differences.

- **Misaligned** — The service performs functions that are contrary to the business objectives.

- **Not aligned** — The service does not meet any requirements. The enterprise has no need for this service. Evaluate if and why it is being developed.

Business Alignment Questions

- Is there a clear link between one or more business requirements and the service? Services must be designed and developed in response to specific business requirements. The resulting service implements specific enterprise business functions and accesses its data and resources. (Chapters 2, 3, 4, 12)

  - **Yes** — The service satisfies one or more business requirements.

  - **No** — The service is not related to a business requirement.

- **Can you trace the service back to a business outcome, objective, or goal?** — The same forces that drive the business, drive SOA; these forces include strategy, competition, market forces, regulatory forces, and so on. They all combine to drive the business's strategy and the resulting business architecture (model). Because services are created in response to business needs, you should be able to trace the purpose of the service back to a specific business driver. (Chapters 2, 3, 4)

- **Yes** — One or more business outcomes, objectives, or goals is satisfied.
- **No** — The service is not related to a business need.
- **Don't know** — It is not clear if the service is related to a business need.

- **If the service provides rules or decisions, are they associated with specific business rules or policies?** — Services must support specific business rules and decisions. Their behavior must be consistent with the business operations. (Chapters 2, 3, 12)

  - **Yes** — The service is associated with a specific business policy or rule.
  - **No** — The service is not associated with any business policy or rule.
  - **Don't know** — It is not clear whether the service is associated with a specific business policy or rule.

- **Do the service operations perform a specific business process activity?** — Now you are looking in more detail at the service. Specifically, you want to determine if the service's operations address activities of a specific business process. The operations of business and domain services should be traceable back to specific business activities. (Chapters 2, 4, 6, 12)

  - **Yes** — All of the operations within a service are associated with a specific business activity.
  - **Partially** — Some of the operations execute specific business activities.
  - **No** — None of the operations is associated with a specific business activity.

Specification

These questions help you ensure that the stakeholders, such as business users and technical users, have an unambiguous description of the service, its behavior and information, how to interact with it, usage constraints, and so on. As stated in Chapter 3, business analysts need to decide whether a particular service can be used in the solution that they are designing, and technical users, or developers, need to know how to invoke the service.

This section has a different focus than the "Specification" section under "Technical Characteristics." Here, we are assessing how well the specification conveys the necessary information to its audiences. The "Technical Characteristics" section focuses on the technical aspects of the specification contents.

The overall assessment of how well a service's specification communicates with its intended audience is one of the following:

- **Good** — The specification clearly describes what the service does and how to use it.

- **Adequate** — The specification describes the service, but there may be slight ambiguities or minor missing information.

- **Poor** — The specification is nonexistent or insufficient to understand what the service does and how to interact with it.

Specification Questions

- **Does the service have a specification?** — A specification is required for others to assess whether to use the service and how to use it. (Chapter 3, 12)

  - **Yes** — A specification exists.

  - **No** — A specification does not exist.

- **How well does the specification clearly describe what the service does from the business perspective?** — Is it sufficient for a business analyst to decide whether a service can be used in a solution? Does it include a description of what the service accomplishes, appropriate use, limitations of use, quality of service (QoS), and requirements for use? Is there a detailed description of how the service is used? Is there at least one service level agreement (SLA)? (Chapter 3)

  - **Good** — The service's behavior is clearly described in business terms.

  - **Adequate** — The service's behavior is described in business terms but could use improvement.

  - **Poor** — The description of the service's behavior is not sufficient to communicate with the business analyst.

- **How well does the specification clearly describe what the service does from the technical perspective?** — Is it sufficient for an architect to do adequate resource planning? Can the developer implement the service? Does the specification describe how to use the service (invocation, protocols, etc.), invocation policies, and quality of service guarantees? (Chapter 3)

  - **Good** — The service's behavior is clearly described in technical terms.

  - **Adequate** — The service's behavior is described in technical terms, but could use improvement.

  - **Poor** — The description of the service's behavior is not sufficient to communicate to the technical audience.

▪ **Are the expected kinds of consumers of this service clear?** Just as with any other customer relationship, the service must know what kinds of consumers it is serving. Even though loose coupling dictates that services be designed with little or no assumptions or knowledge of any particular service consumer, the design must take into consideration what types of consumers will use it. This is because the consumers' expectations influence granularity and interaction style. A consumer could be a business process, enterprise, line-of-business, other service, and so on. (Chapter 2, 3)

  ▪ **Yes** — It is clear what kinds of consumer would use this service.

  ▪ **No** — It is not clear what kinds of consumer would use this service.

▪ **Does the service conform to enterprise standards for the type of service?** — In any complex system or environment, you would expect to see a range of service types. Given the common service patterns, does this service meet the enterprise standards? If the service varies from the standards, determine if the exception is acceptable. (Chapter 6)

  ▪ **Yes** — The service is in conformance.

  ▪ **Partially** — The service varies in some aspect from the standards.

  ▪ **No** — The service does not conform to the standards.

▪ **Is the interaction style of the service appropriate for this type of service?** — An important concern in the design of service interfaces is the style of interaction between the service consumer and provider. Chapter 6 provides guidance on the typical kinds of interaction styles for different service types and their appropriate use. See "Housekeeping Characteristics" for a list of valid interaction types. (Chapters 2, 3, 6)

  ▪ **Yes** — Each operation's interaction is appropriate for this type of service.

  ▪ **No** — The interaction style is not appropriate.

Fit for Purpose

As stated in Chapter 2, the business principle behind SOA is to build up a collection of independent services that can be quickly and easily combined in a variety of ways into different, higher-level business services and business processes. Because each service provides a discrete unit of business functionality, you want to be sure that the functionality is appropriate for its intended purpose, according to its service type (Business, Domain, Utility, etc.) and its usage style (task, entity, etc.).

The overall assessment of how well a service fits its purpose is one of the following:

- **Good** — The service clearly fits its purpose without extraneous functions.

- **Adequate** — The service does a good job of accessing information or performing a business function, but there is room for improvement.

- **Poor** — The service is a poor fit for its intended purpose.

Fit for Purpose Questions

- **Does this service provide a single, consistent way to access data or perform a business function?** — When a service provides a single, consistent way to access information or perform a business function, it is clear what its responsibilities are. When the responsibilities are clear, business analysts and technical users can easily combine the service with others. (Chapters 2, 6)

  - **Yes** — There is a single, consistent way to access information or perform tasks.

  - **No** — There are multiple ways to access information or perform tasks.

- **Is the usage type of this service appropriate for the purpose?** — This may seem like an obvious question, but you want to be sure that the service focuses on its primary purpose and that a little extra processing has not crept in at some point. For example, a decision service does not do a task based on the results of the decision. The usage type indicates, in a broad sense, the primary purpose of the service. See "Housekeeping Characteristics" for the list of usage types. (Chapter 2, 4)

  - **Yes** — The usage type is appropriate.

  - **No** — The usage type is not appropriate.

- **Is the scope, granularity, and interface style of the service appropriate for its purpose?** — Does this service do too much or do too little for the service layer? The combination of scope, granularity, and interface style indicate the enterprise context in which the service interface is expected to operate. See "Housekeeping Characteristics" for valid measures of scope and granularity. (Chapters 2, 6)

  - **Yes** — The scope, granularity, and interface are appropriate.

  - **No** — The scope, granularity, and the interface do not match the service's purpose.

Security

As we discussed in Chapter 11, a service's security is dictated by the enterprise's security goals and requirements. From a business alignment perspective, it is important that a service satisfies these goals and requirements; otherwise, they are not achieving what is required. It is important that the security requirements' analysis at the beginning of a project determine such requirements. In addition, security standards and practices established in SOA governance also drive the mechanisms of service security.

This section of the evaluation matrix focuses on how a service adheres to these requirements and standards. The overall assessment of this characteristic is one of the following:

- **Aligned** — This is what you are aiming for. The service is aligned with the enterprise security requirements and goals.

- **Partially aligned** — The service partially addresses the enterprise security requirements and goals. The gap between the security requirements and the service's security capabilities should be evaluated to resolve the differences.

- **Misaligned** — The service's security capabilities are contrary to the enterprise's goals and strategy.

- **Not aligned** — The service does not meet any security requirements.

Security Questions

- **Does this service adhere to the security requirements of the enterprise?** — Specifically, you want to know if the service aligns with security goals such as authentication, authorization, confidentiality, integrity, and non-repudiation. (Chapter 11)

  - **Yes** — The service does adhere to the security requirements.

  - **No** — The service does not adhere to the security requirements.

- **Does the security of your service adhere to the security standards established by SOA governance in your project?** — Does the service provide security using the standard mechanisms? If not, is the variance acceptable? (Chapter 11)

  - **Yes** — The service does adhere to the security governance standards.

  - **No** — The service does not adhere to the security governance standards.

Semantic Alignment

The Semantic Alignment characteristic is concerned with the extent to which the service aligns with the Semantic Information Model. The information model contains the common understanding of business entities and information shared between services, and provides the definitive source for the messages exchanged by services.

The overall assessment of this alignment is one of the following:

- **Semantic Alignment** — The service relies solely on the Semantic Information Model to define the information exchanged between it and other services.

- **Duplicate Information** — The service duplicates information from the Semantic Information Model, which may lead to ambiguity or differing sets of information passed between services.

- **Partial alignment** — The service relies on the Semantic Information Model but defines some information on its own.

- **No Alignment** — There is no alignment between the service and the Semantic Information Model. The service does its own thing about information.

Semantic Information Model Questions

- **Does the service share common information definitions with other services or processes?** If so, does the Semantic Information Model define the shared information? The Semantic Information Model provides the definitive source for the messages exchanged by services. Therefore, all shared information should be contained in the model. If the information is in the model, then the service must use it. If it is not in the model, then it should be added. If the service does not share information with other services, then it may not be a candidate for being a service. (Chapter 2)

  - **Yes** — The service shares information and its information is in the Semantic Information Model.

  - **No** — The service does not share information or its information is not in the Semantic Information Model.

- **Does the service interface adhere to the Semantic Information Model?** — Using the Semantic Information Model to define business service interfaces leads to the creation of semantically interoperable services. If a service interface varies from the semantic model, interoperability and composability may be at risk. (Chapter 3, 4, 5, 6)

  - **Yes** — The service adheres to the Semantic Information Model.

  - **Partially** — The service partially adheres to the Semantic Information Model.

  - **No** — The service departs altogether from the Semantic Information Model.

- **Does the service interface redefine common information or duplicate information separate from the Semantic Information Model?** — Best practices for SOA state that the service interface uses the Semantic

Information Model as the source for shared information. The service should not define a one-off variation or duplicate the information. (Chapters 2, 3, 4, 5, 6)

■ **Yes** — The service interface has redefined or duplicated information from the Semantic Information Model.

■ **No** — The service interface does not redefine or duplicate information from the Semantic Information Model.

Design Characteristics

One of the keys to achieving SOA success is creating a collection of services that support a variety of different business processes and scenarios. The characteristics and questions in this section of the evaluation matrix help you to understand how well services adhere to the key design principles of SOA.

Isolation of Responsibilities

A key characteristic of service design is ensuring that the responsibility for discrete tasks or the management of specific resources is the responsibility of a single service. When responsibilities are isolated, there is one, and only one, place for each function, providing consistency and reducing redundancy.

This collection of questions help you assess how well the service provides consistency and reduces redundancy by isolating responsibilities.

The overall assessment of this characteristic is one of the following:

■ **Yes** — This service is the sole source of its responsibilities.

■ **No** — This service is not the sole source of its responsibilities.

Isolation of Responsibilities Questions

■ **Is each service operation within this service responsible for a discrete task?** — Although a well-designed service is responsible for a cohesive set of operations relating to the same resource, each operation within that service performs a discrete task to manage the resource. If an operation provides functions for more than one discrete task or resource, the operations may need to be separated into additional services. (Chapters 2, 6)

  ■ **Yes** — Each service operation is responsible for a discrete task.

  ■ **No** — One or more service operations does too much.

■ **Is this service the sole provider of these tasks or resources?** — If more than one service provides functions for specific tasks or resources, then you have duplication and the potential for divergent behavior or information. (Chapters 2, 6)

- **Yes** — This service is the sole provider for these tasks or resources.
- **No** — Duplication of responsibility exists.

Abstraction

When designing and building services, good abstraction reduces coupling, accommodates change, and facilitates separation of concerns. The abstraction characteristic measures the extent to which the service interface and information represent essential concepts and information separate from the internal behavior and information.

The overall assessment of this characteristic is one of the following:

- **Full** — The service is fully abstracted. It cleanly hides private implementation and information.
- **Partial** — The service is partially abstracted. It could do a better job of hiding private implementation and information.
- **Low** — The service exposes its private implementation or information.

Abstraction Questions

- **Does the service express the essential functions and information?** — To determine whether the service expresses the essential functions and information, you evaluate the service interface. This is where you find what the service does and what information is involved. (Chapters 3, 6)
  - **Yes** — Only the necessary details are available to the consumers.
  - **Partially** — The service interface could do a better job of hiding the service's private implementation and information.
  - **No** — Internal implementation or information is made public.
- **Does the interface hide the details of the implementation?** — Is there a strict separation of what the service does from how the service does it? Are only the necessary details available to the consumer? Well-designed services keep their internal working opaque to the consumers. They exhibit a strict separation of the service interface from the service implementation. (Chapters 2, 4, 6)
  - **Yes** — The service interface cleanly hides the service's private implementation and information.
  - **No** — The private implementation or information is not hidden.
- **Is the level of abstraction appropriate for the intended use?** — Abstraction is the suppression of irrelevant detail. Each layer of the service hierarchy provides an abstraction and integration of the layer below, breaking the direct dependence between processes and existing

systems. Higher-level services hide all the complexity and details of the underlying implementation behind a consistent business focused interface that is appropriate for a business process. Lower-level services have less abstract interfaces that expose smaller modularity of capabilities and information. Therefore, the level of abstraction of a service should support the intended use as related to the service type. (Chapters 2, 6)

- **Yes** — The level of abstraction is appropriate for the service's intended use.

- **No** — The level of abstraction is inappropriate for the service's intended use.

Coupling

Coupling describes the amount of dependencies between a service consumer and service provider. The degree of coupling between services directly affects the flexibility and extensibility of a system. The looser the coupling, the more flexible the service. Loosely coupled services have few, but well-known and well-managed, dependencies. Tightly coupled services have many known, and more importantly unknown, dependencies. From the service's perspective, coupling is twofold. First, as a provider, the service is concerned with the degree of coupling it requires of its consumers. How much beyond the service interface should the consumer know to use the service? The less that the consumer must know, the looser the coupling. Second, the service is concerned with its dependencies on other required services (when it is a consumer of other services).

The assessment of a service's coupling with its consumers and providers is:

- **Independent** — The service has no dependencies.

- **Minimal coupling** — The service has a few, but well-known and well-managed, dependencies.

- **Tightly coupled** — The service's dependencies are onerous or unknown.

Coupling Questions

- **Does this service limit what the consumers must know in order to invoke it to what is described in the service specification?** — It is important to enable the independent evolution of both the service consumer and provider. This is done through a variety of techniques, technologies, and policies. A service increases the coupling when the consumer must know details of internal things such as communications protocols or location. (Chapter 2, 3, 9)

  - **Yes** — Nothing beyond the service interface is required of consumers.

- **No** — Consumers must know more than what is in the service interface.

- **Does the service avoid making assumptions about the purpose or business characteristics of the consumer?** — The service implementation should make no assumptions as to the purpose, technical, or business characteristics of the service consumer. (Chapter 2)

  - **Yes** — The service makes no assumptions, or only necessary assumptions are made, about its typical consumers.

  - **No** — The service makes unnecessary assumptions about the consumers.

- **Does this service have minimal, but well-known dependencies on the services it invokes?** — In this case, you are looking at the service as a consumer of other services. You need to determine how tightly coupled this service is to the services it invokes. (Chapter 2, 6)

  - **Yes** — The dependencies are few, well-known, and well-managed.

  - **No** — The dependencies are numerous or unknown. This directly impacts flexibility and extensibility.

- **Is run-time policy logic separately expressed and implemented from the business logic?** — Is the policy logic configurable? Separating the run-time policy logic from business logic makes your service more loosely coupled. When service policies are separated from business logic and are expressed in a discoverable way, the consumer can dynamically adapt to future service policy changes. (Chapters 9, 12)

  - **Yes** — The service has decoupled its policy logic and business logic, as well as its expression of run-time service policy.

  - **No** — The service's run-time policy logic is implemented directly in the service and/or run-time policies are not expressed.

- **Is the security logic separate from the business logic of the service?** — Is the security policy logic configurable? Best practices recommend loose coupling between the implementation of security logic and the implementation of business logic. Standard security interceptor mechanisms can be used, either embedded as functionality in your application server or written with security handlers. (Chapters 9, 12)

  - **Yes** — The service has decoupled its security logic and business logic.

  - **No** — The service's business layer implements security logic.

- **Does the service separate the public view of its data from its private view?** A service should never expose its internal data structures. Only the information described in the semantic model should be exposed through the interface. Even the smallest amount of internal information that is exposed outside the service will result in unnecessary dependencies. (Chapters 2, 3, 4, 6, 7)

- **Yes** — The only information exposed is from the Semantic Information Model.
- **No** — Private, internal data is exposed.

Granularity

In SOA, business processes are decomposed into modular "services" that are self-contained. Services themselves can be composed from other modular services, and can be mixed and matched as needed to create new composite services. Granularity is a quality of functional richness for a service — the more coarse-grained a service is, the richer the function offered by the service.

This characteristic measures whether the service's granularity is well understood. The possible assessments are:

- **Good** — The granularity of the service is appropriate for its type and purpose.
- **Adequate** — The granularity may need refinement.
- **Poor** — The granularity is inappropriate for its type and purpose.

Granularity Questions

- **Does the service use other services in order to achieve its functionality?** — A composite service's implementation invokes other services. The implementation of an atomic service does not require or use any other services. Atomic services are the lowest level of service composition. Whether a service is atomic or composite will affect its granularity. Coarse-grained services provide a greater level of functionality within a single service operation. Fine-grained service operations provide the exchange of smaller amounts of information to complete a specific discrete task. In general, the finest-grained services are more likely to be atomic and the coarser-grained services will be composite. (Chapter 2, 6)
  - **Yes** — The service is composite.
  - **No** — The service is atomic.
- **Is the amount of business functionality provided by this service well understood?** — Services may be course-grained (have lots of functionality), medium-grained, or fine-grained (have little functionality). There is not a single, correct size for all services. What is important is that the functionality provided be consistent, modular, and understandable. (Chapter 6)

- **Yes** — The amount of business functionality is well understood.

- **No** — It is not clear how much business functionality is provided.

- **Is the service's granularity appropriate for its intended use?** — A service's granularity should match the functional modularity of its typical consumer. For example, a business process expects to call services with granularity that corresponds to that of a process activity. (Chapter 6)

  - **Yes** — The service's granularity is appropriate for its use.

  - **No** — The service's granularity is not appropriate for its use.

Stateless

An important characteristic of a service is to be as stateless as possible. This means that services neither remember the last thing they were asked to do nor care what the next is. More specifically, the service does not maintain state on behalf of its consumer between requests. Any given request can act on the state of particular information, but a subsequent request does not rely on the service maintaining the state from a previous request. Stateless interactions are important in terms of scalability, reliability, failover, and so on.

Assessment outcomes:

- **Stateless** — The service is sufficiently stateless.

- **Retains state** — The service retains too much state.

Stateless Questions

- **Does the service avoid keeping state information between method calls?** — If the service maintains a session, context, or data across invocations, then it retains state. This affects the ability to scale, load balance, or fail over. (Chapters 2, 6)

  - **Yes** — State is not maintained between calls.

  - **No** — State is maintained between calls.

- **Can additional instances of the service be created to support scale?** — Adding services to improve performance or support scale is much easier when those services do not maintain state. Maintaining state ties a service instance to a particular datastore. (Chapters 2, 6)

  - **Yes** — Additional services may be added with predictable results.

  - **No** — State is maintained in a store tied directly to a service instance.

- **Can subsequent client requests go to different service instances?** — Relocating or duplicating services is much easier when those services do not maintain state. (Chapters 2, 6)

- **Yes** — Client requests are not tied to a specific instance of a service. They may be directed to different instances of the service.

- **No** — The client is limited to a specific server instance.

Composable

SOA promotes the concept of a business-aligned enterprise service as the fundamental unit for designing, building, and composing enterprise business solutions. This means that services can be composed from other services — and, in turn, they can be combined with other services to compose new services or business processes. Several of the characteristics found throughout the evaluation matrix, such as semantic alignment, isolation of responsibilities, and coupling, are essential for creating services that lend themselves to composability.

Assessment outcomes for composability are:

- **Good** — The service is a good candidate for composition.

- **Adequate** — The service is a candidate for composition, with limitations.

- **Poor** — The service is not a candidate for composition.

Composable Questions

- **Do you expect other services to use this service?** — Services are often constructed, or composed, of other services, which may themselves be composed from other services, and so on. If this service is expected to be used in the construction of another service, it must adhere to the Semantic Information Model, have loose coupling, and other characteristics that increase composability. (Chapters 2, 3, 6)

  - **Yes** — This service expects to be part of a composition.

  - **No** — This service does not expect to be part of a composition.

- **Is the service granularity appropriate for composition within the intended context?** — Service granularity describes the amount of business functionality performed by a single interaction with a service operation. It is important that the granularity of a service interface match the functional modularity of the expected service consumers. Otherwise, the consumers are limited in how they can use the service in a composition. (Chapters 2, 6)

  - **Yes** — The granularity is appropriate for using this service in a composition.

  - **No** — The granularity is inappropriate.

- **Is the combination of the service's usage type and output conducive to composition?** — The questions to ask here start with the usage type: If the service is an entity service, is the information it provides independent of other entities? If the service is a task service, does it provide discrete, reusable functions? If the service is a decision service, are the decisions and rules adaptable to different contexts? (Chapters 2, 6)

- **Yes** — The usage type and output are conducive to composition.
- **No** — There is a mismatch between the usage type, output, and intended use.

Governance

SOA governance is essential to a successful SOA. Governance enforces compliance with the architecture and common semantics, and facilitates managing the enterprise-wide development, use, and evolution of services. The questions in this section determine the extent to which a service conforms to governance policies and guidelines. They are not intended to evaluate the governance policies.

Assessment outcomes for governance are:

- **Good** — The service adheres well to governance policies.
- **Adequate** — The service adheres to governance policies with exceptions.
- **Poor** — The service does not sufficiently adhere to governance policies.

Governance Questions

- **Does the service have a responsible owner?** — An owner may be a group or an individual. Ownership defines which organizational unit is responsible for the support of a service. In an SOA, this extends well beyond simple maintenance and operations, to the overall life cycle of the service. (Chapter 2)
  - **Yes** — An organization is identified as the owner of the service.
  - **No** — The service has no responsible owner.
- **How well does the service adhere to the design-time governance policies?** — Governance at design-time consists of a set of policies and practices that developers use to ensure that the services are designed and implemented correctly. (Chapters 3, 12)
  - **Good** — The service adheres to design-time governance policies without exceptions.
  - **Adequate** — The service adheres to design-time governance policies with necessary exceptions.
  - **Poor** — There are many exceptions to policies or no adherence.

- **How well does the service adhere to the deploy-time governance policies?** — Deploy-time governance involves deployment options and topologies, and adherence to policy should dictate whether a service can be deployed on a network. (Chapter 12)

  - **Good** — The service adheres to deploy-time governance policies without exceptions.

  - **Adequate** — The service adheres to deploy-time governance policies with exceptions.

  - **Poor** — There are many exceptions to policies or no adherence.

- **How well does the service adhere to the run-time governance policies?** Run-time governance enforces adherence to run-time service policies. (Chapter 12)

  - **Good** — The service adheres to run-time governance policies without exceptions.

  - **Adequate** — The service adheres to run-time governance policies with exceptions.

  - **Poor** — There are many exceptions to policies or no adherence.

- **How well does the service adhere to the change-time governance policies?** Change-time governance involves managing services through the cycle of change. It focuses on such issues as service versioning, deprecation, and run-time policy adaptation. (Chapter 12)

  - **Good** — The service adheres to change-time governance policies without exceptions.

  - **Adequate** — The service adheres to change-time governance policies with exceptions.

  - **Poor** — There are many exceptions to policies or no adherence.

Technical Characteristics

The technical characteristics address the implementation concerns for a service.

Specification

The notion of the service specification is widely recognized as one of the prerequisites for successful service use. Usually, the problem is not whether a specification exists — it most likely does — but what it contains. A good service specification clearly describes everything that a consumer of the service needs to know to decide if they are interested in using the service, as well as exactly how to use it if they are. It also specifies everything a service provider needs to know to implement the service.

This section has a different focus from the "Specification" section under "Alignment Characteristics." Here, you are assessing the quality of the service specification itself, as opposed to how well the specification conveys the necessary information to its audience.

The overall assessment of the service specification is one of the following:

- **Good** — The specification clearly describes what the service does, how to use it, and who uses it.

- **Adequate** — The specification describes the service, but there may be slight ambiguities or minor missing information.

- **Poor** — The specification is nonexistent or insufficient to understand what the service does and how to interact with it.

Specification Questions

- **Does the service specification completely describe the interface?** — The service specification should include:

  - Service name

  - Provided and required interfaces

  - Exceptions

  - Protocol (rules for how the functions are used and in what order)

  - Pre- and postconditions

  - Constraints that reflect what successful use of the service accomplishes

  - Run-Time Service Policies for using the service (one or more) and that contain each of (one or more) SLAs, QoS, and run-time constraints

  Portions of Chapters 3, 6, and 12 describe the contents of a good service specification,

  - **Good** — The specification is complete and easily understandable.

  - **Adequate** — The specification is complete.

  - **Poor** — The specification is lacking in some manner.

- **Does the specification clearly describe the behavior and interaction style of each of the operations?** — The service interface specifies the service operations — that is, what the service does, the parameters that are passed into and out of the operation, and the protocols for how those capabilities are used and provided. A service typically contains several different, but related, operations. (Chapters 2, 6)

  - **Yes** — The interaction styles are clearly defined for each operation.

- **No** — The interaction style is either not defined or is unclear for one or more operations.
- **Does the specification contain all constraints and pre- and postconditions for the service operations?** Along with the inputs and outputs of the service operations, the service interface defines any preconditions, postconditions, and constraints of those operations. Service constraints describe rules, limitations, and facts about a service and its operations. (Chapters 2, 3, 6, 12)
  - **Yes** — All constraints and conditions are specified.
  - **No** — Some constraints or conditions are not specified.
- **Does the specification describe all exceptions?** Exceptions are an integral part of service interface design. All exceptions have to be defined in the interface. (Chapters 6, 9, 12)
  - **Yes** — All exceptions are described.
  - **No** — Some exceptions are not described or are poorly described.
- **Does the service specification include one or more independent run-time service policies?** — One important aspect of the service interface is the run-time service policy. A run-time service policy defines the characteristics, constraints, and capabilities of a service that consumers of the service can discover and use at run time. (Chapter 12)
  - **Yes** — Run-time service policies are included.
  - **No** — There are no run-time service policies in the service specification.
- **Does each of the run-time policies specify the run-time constraints, messaging format related to security, reliability/QoS, and SLAs?** A service policy contains one or more of the following: SLA, QoS statements, messaging formats, and run-time constraints. (Chapters 3, 12)
  - **Yes** — The run-time service policies contain the necessary information.
  - **No** — Information is missing from the run-time service policies.

Service Level Agreement

The service level agreement (SLA) specifies two important performance criteria about the service: the technical performance and the business performance in terms of business units of work. An SLA is a formal agreement between service consumers and service providers related to QoS response times, business units of work, and action guarantees.

The overall assessment of the SLA is one of the following:

- **Good** — The SLA clearly describes the technical and business performance.

- **Adequate** — The SLA describes the technical and business performance, but there may be slight ambiguities or minor missing information.

- **Poor** — The SLA is nonexistent or insufficient to measure or monitor the service performance.

Service Level Agreement Questions

- **Does the service have at least one SLA, as specified in the run-time policies?** — In an SOA, services are a managed, governed set of enterprise assets responsible for ensuring conformance to SLAs. Thus, a service is required to have at least one SLA. (Chapter 2, 12)

  - **Yes** — At least one SLA is provided.

  - **No** — There are no SLAs in the run-time service policy.

- **Is each SLA formally specified?** — An SLA is a formal agreement between service consumers and service providers related to QoS business units of work, and action guarantees. (Chapter 12)

  - **Yes** — The SLA is formally specified.

  - **No** — The SLA is informally specified or unspecified.

- **Does the SLA provide a description of the service's technical performance, such as availability, reliability, throughput, and response time?** — Technical users need to know what to expect from the service, including response time, throughput, availability, planned maintenance, and so on. (Chapter 2, 3, 12)

  - **Yes** — The technical performance is specified.

  - **No** — The technical performance is not specified or it is lacking key aspects.

- **Does the SLA include business characteristics, such as business units of work?** Business users need to understand what a service does in business terms, such as business units of work. (Chapter 2, 3)

  - **Yes** — The SLA contains business characteristics.

  - **No** — Business characteristics are not sufficiently specified.

Extensibility

Services will inevitably evolve to support broader user requirements and new business requirements. A well-designed service can handle these changes gracefully because extensibility is designed in from the beginning. "Flex points" in the design support likely areas of change.

The overall assessment of the extensibility is one of the following:

- **Good** — The service can easily be extended in the future.

- **Adequate** — The service can accept some changes for future requirements but not without a moderate amount of impact on its consumers.

- **Poor** — Future extensions to the service are expected to be painful affairs.

Extensibility Questions

- **Is the service designed to support the implementation of future requirements?** — Well-defined, business-aligned services are a critical ingredient of a flexible, extensible enterprise SOA implementation. The structure of services allows them to be independently developed and extended. Adhering to the principles of loose coupling, encapsulation, isolation of responsibilities, and autonomy, and following extensible design patterns allow for extensible services. (Chapters 2, 3)

    - **Yes** — The service design supports future enhancements.

    - **No** — The service design does not accommodate future enhancements.

- **Have the appropriate patterns or abstractions been used to facilitate future enhancements?** — Best practices provide patterns, techniques, and tools for service composition that help reduce dependencies, limit coupling, and maximize flexibility, all of which promote extensibility. Specific design patterns should be followed to keep services independent, extensible, and reusable.

    - **Yes** — Best practices for accommodating enhancements were used.

    - **No** — Best practices for accommodating enhancements were not used.

Variability and Configurability

Standard mechanisms for variation and configuring services should be defined as part of the SOA. These mechanisms facilitate the use of a common, technology-independent configuration service, and more importantly, common configuration data to be shared between services.

The overall assessment of the variability is one of the following:

- **Variable** — The service supports sufficient variability mechanisms and can easily be configured in a standard way when deployed.

- **Partially variable** — The service varies from the standard mechanisms in an acceptable way.

- **Not sufficiently variable** — The service cannot be configured or uses nonstandard mechanisms that do not scale, are location-specific, require tight coupling, or have similar drawbacks.

Variability and Configurability Questions

- **Does the service support a necessary variability mechanism?** In order to support a wide range of clients, services need the ability to vary certain aspects of their operations, such as rules, locations, datastores, QoS, and the like, at run time or deployment time. The specific type of variability mechanism used depends on the requirements for that service.

  - **Yes** — The service supports sufficient variability.

  - **No** — The service does not support sufficient variability.

- **Does the service adhere to enterprise standards for configuration?** — When services use common configuration capabilities, the configurability of the entire solution is greatly enhanced. It is important that the configuration standards and practices established in SOA governance drive the mechanisms of service configuration. If the service does vary from the standards, then is the variance acceptable? (Chapter 2)

  - **Yes** — The service uses the standard mechanisms.

  - **No** — The service does not use the standard mechanisms.

- **Does the service use common data for configuration?** — In addition to using standard configuration mechanisms, the service should leverage common configuration information. Externally modifiable configuration parameters support common configuration needs. (Chapter 2)

  - **Yes** — Common configuration information is used.

  - **No** — Private configuration information is used.

Autonomy

Autonomy relates to the entire service life cycle, including deployment, run time, and change time. An autonomous service's life cycle is independent of other services. It can be deployed, modified, and maintained independently from other services and the solutions that use it. Loose coupling and isolation of responsibilities help facilitate autonomy.

The overall assessment of the autonomy is one of the following:

- **Autonomous** — The service can easily be deployed, modified, and maintained independently.

- **Not Autonomous** — The service cannot be deployed, modified, and maintained independently.

Autonomy Questions

- **Is this service loosely coupled, and are its responsibilities well isolated?** — The tighter the coupling and the less isolated the responsibilities of a service, the weaker the autonomy. (Chapter 2, 12)

  - **Yes** — The service is loosely coupled and responsibilities are isolated.

  - **No** — The service's coupling is tight or responsibilities are not isolated.

- **Is this service's life cycle independent of other services?** — If this service is required to change because of a change in another service, or this service requires other services to be updated when it changes, then it is not autonomous. (Chapter 2, 12)

  - **Yes** — The service's life cycle is independent of other services.

  - **No** — Dependencies based on versions exist between services.

- **Can the service be deployed independently of other services?** — If deploying this service requires other services to be deployed at the same time, in the same configuration, then it is not autonomous. (Chapter 2, 12)

  - **Yes** — The service's deployment is independent of other services.

  - **No** — Deployment dependencies exist with services.

Housekeeping Characteristics

The Housekeeping Characteristics allow for the management and reporting of services and provide a place to collect additional information that may be useful in analysis. These characteristics are not meant to evaluate the quality of the service. Instead, they provide a baseline for certain management and metrics, such as the number of outsourced services or how many utility and foundation services you have.

Additional Reading

It is virtually impossible to cover all of the facets of designing and building SOA solutions in one book. We encourage additional reading on the topics we have covered. As a starting point, you can use the following list of references that we have found useful:

ACORD. `www.acord.org/home/home.aspx`.

Arsanjani, Ali. "Principles of Advanced Software Engineering: Variation Oriented Analysis, Design and Implementation." January 2000. `cs.mum.edu/cs525/Refs/VOD-12-27-99.PDF`.

_____. "Service-oriented modeling and architecture." IBM developer-Works, November 2004. `ibm.com/developerworks/library/ws-soa-design1`.

_____. "Towards a Pattern Language for Service-Oriented Architecture and Integration, Part 2: Service Composition." IBM developerWorks, December 2005. `www-128.ibm.com/developerworks/webservices/library/ws-soa-soi2`.

Arsanjani, Ali, Liang-Jie Zhang, Michael Ellis, Abdul Allam, and Kishore Channabasavaiah. "Design an SOA solution using a reference architecture." IBM developerWorks, March 2007. `www-128.ibm.com/developerworks/library/ar-archtemp/index.html`.

Baeyens, Tom. "Process Component Models: The Next Generation in Workflow?" InfoQ, February 2008. `infoq.com/articles/process-component-models`.

Balcer, Marc J. "BPM Implementation with SOA and MDA." OMG SOA, BPM, and MDA Workshop, Burlingame, CA, October 2006. `omg.org/news/meetings/workshops/soa-bpm-mda-2006/06-1_Balcer_Revised.pdf`.

Baresi, Luciano, Andrea Maurino, and Stefano Modafferi. "Towards Distributed BPEL Orchestrations." *Proceedings of the Third Workshop on Software Evolution through Transformations (SeTra)*. Rio Grande de Norte, Brazil, 2006.

Berners-Lee, Tim, James Hendler, and Ora Lassila. "The Semantic Web." *Scientific American*, May 2001. `www.sciam.com/article.cfm?id = the-semantic-web`.

Bloomberg, Jason. "The LEGO Model of SOA." ZapThink, December 11, 2006. `www.zapthink.com/report.html?id = zapflash-20061212`.

Booch, Gary. "SOA Best Practices." Software architecture, software engineering, and Renaissance Jazz blog, March 11, 2006. `www-03.ibm.com/developerworks/blogs/page/gradybooch?entry = soa_best_practices`.

Booch and Kruchten. *The Rational Unified Process — An Introduction.* Addison-Wesley, 1999.

Brooks, Jr., Fred P. *The Mythical Man-Month: Essays on Software Engineering, 20th Anniversary Edition.* Reading, MA: Addison-Wesley Professional, 1995.

Byrne, Brian, and Brian Yarow. "Building SOA solutions with Industry Models and the IBM Rational Software Development Platform." IBM developerWorks, July 2006. `www-128.ibm.com/developerworks/rational/library/jul06/byrne_yarow`.

Cousins, Peter, and Ivan Casanova, "Service-Oriented Integration: A Strategy Brief." IONA Technologies, January 2004. `http://microsites.cmp.com/documents/s=9077/int1077662028640`.

Daconta, Michael C. *Information as Product.* Outskirts Press, 2007.

Daconta, Michael C., Leo Obrst, and Kevin T. Smith. *The Semantic Web: A Guide to the Future of XML, Web Services, and Knowledge Management.* Hoboken, NJ: Wiley, 2003.

Dubray, Jean-Jacques. "Composite Software Construction — Understanding SOA in the Context of a Programming Model." C4Media, 2007. `infoq.com/minibooks/composite-software-construction`.

_____. "Establishing a Service Governance Organization." InfoQ, October 2007. `infoq.com/articles/soa-governance-organization`.

Duermeyer, Karin. "Bridging Business Value to SOA: SOA Best Practices." May 24, 2005. `websphere.org/docs/presentations/Duermeyer-SOA_Executive_Event_Muenchen.pdf`.

Eeles, Peter, and Oliver Sims. *Building Business Objects*. New York: Wiley, 1998.

Erl, Thomas. *SOA: Principles of Service Design*. Upper Saddle River, NJ: Prentice Hall, 2007.

Evdemon, John. "Principles of service design: Service patterns and anti-patterns." MSDN, August 2005. `http://msdn2.microsoft.com/en-us/library/ms954638.aspx`

_____. "The four tenets of service orientation." BPMInstitute, May 2005. `bpminstitute.org/articles/article/article/the-four-tenets-of-service-orientation.html`.

Fitts, Sean. "When exceptions are the rule: Achieving reliable and traceable service oriented architectures." *SOA/WebServices Journal*, September 2005. `http://webservices.sys-con.com/read/121945.htm`.

Fowler, Martin. *Patterns of Enterprise Architecture*. Reading, MA: Addison-Wesley, 2002.

Fuller, Tom. "A Foundation for the Pillars of Software Factories." *The Architecture Journal*, no. 9, 2006. `architecturejournal.net/2006/issue9/F4_Foundation`.

Hay, David C. *Data Model Patterns: Conventions of Thought*. New York: Dorset House, 1995.

Heffner, Randy. "A strategic SOA platform vision." *SOA World*, January 2006. `soa-world.com/FeatureRO.asp?Featureid=188`.

Helland, Pat. "Data on the Outside vs. Data on the Inside: An Examination of the Impact of Service Oriented Architectures on Data." 2008. `http://msdn.microsoft.com/library/default.asp?url=/library/en-us/dnbda/html/dataoutsideinside.asp`.

High, Jr., Rob, Stephen Kinder, and Steve Graham. "IBM's SOA Foundation: An Architectural Introduction and Overview." IBM developerWorks, November 2005. `http://download.boulder.ibm.com/ibmdl/pub/software/dw/webservices/ws-soa-whitepaper.pdf`.

Hofmeister, Christine, Robert Nord, and Dilip Soni. *Applied Software Architecture*. Reading, MA: Addison-Wesley, 2000.

Hohpe, Gregor, and Bobby Woolf. *Enterprise Integration Patterns: Designing, Building, and Deploying Messaging Solutions*. Boston: Addison-Wesley, 2004.

Hubert, Richard. *Convergent Architecture: Building Model Driven J2EE Systems with UML*. Hoboken, NJ: Wiley, 2001.

Hutchison, B., M.T. Schmidt, P. Lambros, and R. Phippen. "SOA programming model for implementing web services, Part 4: An introduction to the IBM enterprise service bus." IBM developerWorks, July 2005. www-128.ibm.com/developerworks/library/ws-soa-progmodel4.

Infravio. "The Definitive Guide to SOA Governance and Lifecycle Management." 2006. infravio.com

"Insurance Application Architecture." www-1.ibm.com/industries/financialservices/doc/content/solution/278918103.html.

"J2EE Connector Architecture." http://java.sun.com/j2ee/connector.

"Java Database Connectivity." http://java.sun.com/javase/technologies/database.

Keen, Martin, Oscar Adinolfi, Sarah Hemmings, Andrew Humphreys, Kanthi Hanumanth, and Alasdair Nottingham. "Patterns: Implementing an SOA using an Enterprise Service Bus in WebSphere Application Server V6." IBM Redbooks, 2005. redbooks.ibm.com/abstracts/sg246494.html?Open.

Krafzig, Dirk, Karl Ganke, and Dirk Slama. *Enterprise SOA: Service Oriented Best Practices*. Upper Saddle River, NJ: Prentice Hall, 2005.

Kruchten, Philippe. "The 4+1 View Model of Architecture." *IEEE Software*, vol. 12, no. 6:42–50, November 1995.

Lhotka, Rocky. "A SOA Version Covenant." April 2005. theserverside.net/articles/showarticle.tss?id=SOAVersioningCovenant.

Liu, Anna, and Ian Gorton. "Process and Criteria for Evaluating Services-Based Integration Technologies." *The Architecture Journal*, July 2005. http://msdn2.microsoft.com/en-us/arcjournal/aa480046.aspx.

Lublinsky, Boris."Achieving the Ultimate EAI Implementation." *EAI Journal*, 2001. eaijournal.com/Article.asp?ArticleID=303&DepartmentId=7.

_____. "Approaches to Implementation of Business-to-Business Integration (B2Bi)." *EAI Journal*, vol. 4, no. 2:38–47. eaijournal.com/PDF/B2BLublinsky.pdf.

_____. "Data transformation in SOA using WebSphere Transformation Extender (TX)." IBM developerWorks, August 2007. www.ibm.com/developerworks/library/ar-datatrans.

_____."Defining SOA as an architectural style." IBM developerWorks, January 2007. www-128.ibm.com/developerworks/architecture/library/ar-soastyle.

_____."Explore the role of service repositories and registries in Service-Oriented Architecture (SOA)." IBM developerWorks, May 2007. `www-128 .ibm.com/developerworks/architecture/library/ar-servrepos/ ?S_TACT=105AGX78&S_CMP=HP`.

_____."Implement WS_Notification in WebSphere Application Server V6.1." IBM developerWorks, December 2006. `www-128.ibm.com/ developerworks/architecture/library/ar-wasnot`.

_____. "Implementing Exceptions in SOA." InfoQ, May 2007. `infoq.com/ articles/lublinsky-soa-exception`.

_____. "Service Composition." InfoQ, July 2007. `infoq.com/articles/ lublinsky-soa-composition`.

_____. "SOA Design: Meet in the Middle." *JavaPro*, Fawcette Technical Press FTP site, August 2004. `ftponline.com/javapro/2004_10/ magazine/features/blublinsky/default.aspx?CP=true`

_____. "SOA Programming Models," InfoQ, October 2006. `infoq.com/ articles/SOA-programming-models`.

_____. "Supporting policies in Service-Oriented Architecture." IBM developerWorks, 2004. `www-128.ibm.com/developerworks/ webservices/library/ws-support-soa`.

_____. "Transactions and Web Services." *EAI Journal*, January 2003. `bijonline.com/PDF/TWSLublinsky.pdf`.

_____. "Unifying Data, Documents and Processes." *Enterprise Architect*, vol. 2, no. 2, 2004. `ftponline.com/ea/magazine/summer2004/features/ blublinsky`.

_____. "Versioning in SOA." *The Architecture Journal*, no. 11:36-41. `http://msdn2.microsoft.com/en-us/arcjournal/bb491124.aspx`.

Lublinsky, Boris and M. Farrell. "Top ten reasons why EAI implementations fail." *EAI Journal*, December 2002, 41–42. `bijonline.com/PDF/ LublinskyEAIFails.pdf`.

Lublinsky, Boris and Michael Rosen. "Enterprise Integration Architecture and Web Services." *Cutter Executive Report*, vol. 5, no. 11, November 2002. `cutter.com/architecture/abstracts.html#2002`.

Lublinsky, Boris and D. Tyomkyn. "SOA & BPM: Living Happily Ever After?" *Business Integration Journal*, March/April 2006, 22–24. `bijonline .com/index.cfm?section=article&aid=239`.

Maldonado, Martin F. "Virtualization in a nutshell: A pattern point of view." IBM developerWorks, June 2006. `www-128.ibm.com/ developerworks/grid/library/gr-virt`.

Malinverno, Paul. "Service-Oriented Architecture Craves Governance." Gartner, January 20, 2006. `http://www.gartner.com/ DisplayDocument?id=488180`.

McGovern, James, Oliver Sims, Ashish Jain, and Mark Little. *Enterprise Service Oriented Architectures: Concepts, Challenges, Recommendations.* Dordrecht, The Netherlands: Springer, 2006.

Medicke, John, Feng-Wei Chen, and Margie Mago. "Creating an intelligent and flexible solution with BPM, Business Rules, and Business Intelligence." IBM developerWorks, October 2003. `www-128.ibm .com/developerworks/db2/library/techarticle/0310medicke/ 0310medicke.html`.

Mellor, Stephen J. and Marc J. Balcer. *Executable UML: A Foundation for Model-Driven Architecture.* Boston: Addison-Wesley, 2002.

"Oasis SOA reference model." April 2006. `oasis-open.org/ committees/tc_home.php?wg_abbrev=soa-rm`.

Oasis SOA rm wiki: Architecture/governance. `http://wiki.oasis-open .org/soa-rm/TheArchitecture/Governance`.

O'Neill, Mark. "Architecting security for web services." *JavaPro*, August 2003. `ftponline.com/channels/security/javapro/2003_08/magazine/ features/moneill`.

Open Group, The. "Part IV: Resource Base: Developing Architecture Views." The Open Group Architecture Framework 8.1.1, August 2006. `www.opengroup .org/architecture/togaf8-doc/arch/chap31.html`.

Orr, Ken. "BPM Project Perspectives." *BPTrends*, April 2007. `bptrends .com/publicationfiles/04-07-COL-BPMandSOA-Rosen-final.pdf`.

_____. "Business Architecture — Linking Business, Data, and Technology." *Cutter Consortium Enterprise Architecture Executive Report*, vol. 10, no. 2, February 2007.

_____. "Business Process Modeling Fundamentals." *Cutter Consortium Business-IT Strategies Executive Report*, vol. 10, no. 7, 2007.

_____. "Business Reference Modeling — The New Rosetta Stone for Managers." *Cutter Consortium Enterprise Architecture Executive Report*, vol. 9, no. 12, December 2006.

_____. "Business Semantics." *Cutter Consortium Business Intelligence Executive Report*, vol. 5, no. 7, 2005.

_____. "Information Integration in the Real World." *Cutter Consortium Enterprise Architecture Executive Report*, vol. 6, no. 4, 2003.

Pereira, Jude. "Enterprise Application Integration: Approaches to Integration." MindTree white paper, 2006. `mindtree.com/white_paper/EAI-integration-approaches.pdf`.

Porter, Michael E. *Competitive Advantage: Creating and Sustaining Superior Performance.* New York: Free Press, 1985.

Ranganathan, Ramesh. "Managing exceptions in a SOA world." IT Toolbox: Emerging Technologies. September 2005. `http://hosteddocs.ittoolbox.com/RR091605.pdf`.

Robinson, Rick. "Understand enterprise service bus scenarios and solutions in service-oriented architecture, Part 1." IBM developerWorks, June 2004. `www-106.ibm.com/developerworks/webservices/library/ws-esbscen`.

_____. "Understand enterprise service bus scenarios and solutions in service-oriented architecture, Part 2." IBM developerWorks, June 2004. `www-106.ibm.com/developerworks/webservices/library/ws-esbscen2.html`.

_____. "Understand enterprise service bus scenarios and solutions in service-oriented architecture, Part 3." IBM developerWorks, June 2004. `ibm.com/developerworks/webservices/library/ws-esbscen3`.

Rosen, Michael. "5 Key Requirements for SOA." *BPTrends*, May 2006. `bptrends.com/publicationfiles/05-06COL-5KeyReqforSOA-Rosen.pdf`.

_____. "Adoption of Best Practices in SOA Development." *Cutter Benchmark Review*, vol. 6, no. 10, October 2006.

_____. "Business Architecture and SOA." SOAInstitute, August 2006. `soainstitute.org/articles/article/article/business-architecture-and-soa.html`.

_____. "Business Driven SOA." SOAInstitute, February 2007. `http://www.soainstitute.org/articles/article/article/business-driven-soa.html`.

_____. "Designing Service Oriented Applications — Part I: Architecture and Methodology." *Cutter Consortium Enterprise Architecture Executive Report*, vol. 9, no. 10, October 2006.

_____. "Designing Service Oriented Applications — Part II: Analysis and Design." *Cutter Consortium Enterprise Architecture Executive Report*, vol. 9, no. 11, November 2006.

_____. "Implementing an SOA with common technologies." *Cutter Enterprise Architecture Executive Report*, 7. The Cutter Consortium, July 2004. `cutter.com/content/architecture/fulltext/reports/2004/07/index.html`.

_____. "Key Components of SOA." SOAInstitute, July 2006.
`soainstitute.org/articles/article/article/`
`key-components-of-soa.html`.

_____."Making Sense of SOA Standards Activities." SOAInstitute,
December 2006. `soainstitute.org/articles/article/article/`
`making-sense-of-soa-standards-activities-part-i.html`
`.cutter.com/architecture/abstracts.html#2005`.

_____. "Service Usage Types." *BPTrends*, December 2007. `bptrends`
`.com/publicationfiles/12-07 SOA Service Usage Types-Rosen-final`
`.pdf`.

_____. "Services and Versioning." SOAInstitute, November 2007.
`soainstitute.org/articles/article/article/`
`services-and-versioning.html`.

_____. "SOA, EA, and Tools: Part I." *BPTrends*, November 2006.
`bptrends.com/publicationfiles/11-06-COL-SOAEATools-Rosen.pdf`.

_____. "SOA, EA, and Tools: Part II." *BPTrends*, January 2007.
`bptrends.com/publicationfiles/01-07-COL-BPM-SOA-Rosen-Final`
`.pdf`.

_____. "SOA Governance: Adoption and Best Practices." SOAInstitute,
January 2007. `soainstitute.org/articles/article/article/`
`soa-governance-adoption-and-best-practices.html`.

_____. "What Kind of Service Does a Business Process Need?" *BPTrends*.
July 2006. `bptrends.com/publicationfiles/`
`07-06COL-WhatServiceDoesABPNeed-Rosen.pdf`.

Rosen, Michael, and Boris Lublinsky. "Service-Oriented Integration:
Aligning SOA with enterprise integration." *Cutter Executive Report*,
vol. 8, no. 1, January 2005.

Rosenbloom, Scott. "An Introduction to Service-oriented Integration."
April 2003. `wrq.com/info/newsletters/03/april/soi_vision.html`.

Rummler, Geary A., and Alan P. Brache. *Improving Performance: How
to Manage the White Space in the Organization Chart*. San Francisco, CA:
Jossey-Bass Wiley, 1990.

Selvage, Mei, Dan Wolfson, Bob Zurek, and Ed Kahan. "Achieve semantic interoperability in a SOA." IBM developerWorks, June 2006. `www-128`
`.ibm.com/developerworks/webservices/library/`
`ws-soa-seminterop.html`.

Shlaer, Sally and Stephen J. Mellor. *Object Lifecycles: Modeling the World in
States*. Englewood Cliffs, NJ: Yourdon Press, 1992.

_____. *Object-Oriented Systems Analysis: Modeling the World in Data*. Englewood Cliffs, NJ: Yourdon Press, 1988.

Simmons, Scott. "Introducing the WebSphere Integration Reference Architecture." *IBM WebSphere Developer Technical Journal*, August 2005. `www-ibm.com/developerworks/websphere/techjournal/0508_simmons/0508_simmon`.

Smith, Kevin T. "Creating Secure Web Service Sessions." *SOA/Web Services Journal*, July 2006.

_____. "Six Basic Rules for Securing SOA-Based Projects: Common Sense SOA Security." *SOA/Web Services Journal*, October 2006.

_____. "SOA Access Control Policy Management — Approaches, Common Pitfalls, and Best Practices." *SOA/Web Services Journal*, September 2006.

Specifications: Service Component Architecture (SCA) and Service Data Objects (SDO). `www-128.ibm.com/developerworks/webservices/library/specification/ws-scasdosumm`.

Taylor, D. A. *Business Engineering with Object Technology*. New York: Wiley, 1995.

Tilkov, Stefan. "10 Principles of SOA." InfoQ, 2007. `infoq.com/articles/tilkov-10-soa-principles`.

Topinski, Jan, Bartosz Kiepuszewsky, and Borys Stokalski. "Service Oriented Integration: A Report from the Trenches." *Cutter Consortium Enterprise Architecture Executive Report*, vol. 9, no. 5, May 2006.

Trowbridge, David, Ulrich Roxburgh, Gregor Hohpe, Dragos Manolescu, and E. G. Nadhan. "Integration Patterns." Microsoft Corporation, June 2004. `http://msdn2.microsoft.com/en-us/library/ms978729.aspx`.

Ulrich, William. "Business Architecture: Aligning Strategy & Deployment." BPMInstitute, June 2, 2006. `www.bpminstitute.org/articles/article/article/business-architecture-moving.html`.

US Department of Agriculture (USDA). Working paper. USDA, 2003. `www.usda.gov/da/property/RealProp.pdf`.

Vinoski, Steve. "The social side of services." *IEEE Internet Computing*, January 2006. `iona.com/hyplan/vinoski/pdfs/IEEE-The_Social_Side_of_Services.pdf`.

"Web Service Façade for Legacy Applications." Microsoft patterns & practices Developer Center, June 2003. `http://msdn.microsoft.com/en-us/library/ms979218.aspx`.

"Web Services Architecture." W3C Working Group Note 11 February 2004. `w3.org/TR/ws-arch`.

"Web Services Composite Application Framework (WS-CAF)." August 2006. `oasis-open.org/committees/tc_home.php?wg_abbrev=ws-caf`.

Whittle, Ralph and Conrad B. Myrick. *Enterprise Business Architecture: The Formal Link Between Strategy and Results*. Boca Raton, FL: CRC Press, 2004.

Wikipedia. `http://en.wikipedia.org/wiki/Virtualization`.

XFire User Guide. "Versioning best practices." `http://docs.codehaus.org/display/XFIRE/Versioning`.

Yu, Weihai. "Peer to Peer Execution of BPEL Processes." *Proceedings of the CAiSE 2007 Forum at the 19th International Conference on Advanced Systems Engineering, Trondheim, Norway, 11-15 June 2007*.

Index